The Slavonic Book of Esther

HARVARD UKRAINIAN RESEARCH INSTITUTE
Harvard Series in Ukrainian Studies

Cambridge, Massachusetts

THE SLAVONIC BOOK OF ESTHER

Text, Lexicon, Linguistic Analysis,
Problems of Translation

Horace G. Lunt
Moshe Taube

Distributed by Harvard University Press
for the
Harvard Ukrainian Research Institute

Publication of this volume has been made possible by the
Paul Sawka Bequest to Harvard University

The Ukrainian Research Institute was established in 1973 as an integral part of Harvard University. It supports research associates and visiting scholars who are engaged in projects concerned with all aspects of Ukrainian studies. The Institute also works in close cooperation with the Committee on Ukrainian Studies, which supervises and coordinates the teaching of Ukrainian history, language, and literature at Harvard University.

ISBN 0-916458-80-6
LC no. 98-19993

Text typesetting: Gary Bisbee, Chiron, Inc.
Cover illustration: Miniature of the reading of the Megillah at Purim, late fourteenth century. From the Vatican, Biblioteca Apostolica, Cod Vat ebr 324, f. 180r.
Cover background typography: Initial lines of the Esther text from a c1490 manuscript, Warsaw, Biblioteka Narodowa, BOZ 105.
Printed on Acid-Free Paper by Transcontinental Printers, Inc., Canada.

For editorial correspondence or to receive a full list of the publications of the Harvard Ukrainian Research Institute, please contact:

HURI Publications Office
1583 Massachusetts Ave.
Cambridge, MA 02138 USA
tel. 617-495-3692 / *fax.* 617-495-8097
e-mail: huri@fas.harvard.edu / *website:* www.sabre.org/huri/publications/index.html

TABLE OF CONTENTS

PREFACE

The Old Testament Book of Esther in Slavonic translation is known from East Slavic manuscripts of the late fourteenth to late sixteenth centuries. The two oldest copies date from just before and after 1400, but the text surely existed somewhat earlier; there is no direct evidence as to just when it was translated—or where.

The shape of the text corresponds to that of the 167 verses of the standard Hebrew (the Masoretic text) but is quite different from either the longer or shorter of the known Greek versions. Textually, therefore, it is simpler to hypothesize that the book was translated directly from Hebrew. Such a theory has served as the cornerstone of a broader hypothesis that envisions an active group of translators—from Hebrew as well as from Greek—in early Rus′. In the absence of clear linguistic support for the thesis of direct Hebrew-to-Slavic translation and because of the tentative and tenuous arguments for the presence of highly cultured and productive writers and translators in Rus′ before the mid-twelfth century, it is plausible to suggest on cultural grounds that, like the entire Orthodox written culture of early Slavdom, Esther was translated from Greek. This entails a further conjecture, that a Greek Esther text of this particular shape existed, but was lost after it had been used by the Slavic translator.

It is the aim of this book to establish a solid groundwork for discussion of these questions by providing a full edition of the earliest retrievable form of the text. The edition is accompanied by a full word index, grammatical analysis, verse-by-verse commentary, and discussion of the vocabulary of selected semantic fields, not only in Esther but in comparable texts. The lexicon of Esther contains many unusual or unique words, along with unexpected meanings for some common items; we have tried to provide a wide linguistic and textological context for these special words. Attention is given to general problems of translating biblical texts and to typical factors that affect changes that can be observed in the transmission of a text, such as copyists' mistakes, subsequent efforts to correct the mistakes, minor emendations made from comparisons with the original language, and major editorial revisions of a type that may produce a text so different that it may be regarded as a new translation.

Scholarly literature on the Slavonic Esther has been skimpy and often has failed to separate fact from theory and speculation. Our principal goal has been to establish facts wherever possible; we try to operate with specific and overt methodological principles, and to label speculation clearly when we are speculating.

Comparative material is often lacking, for the study of the Slavonic version or versions of most Old Testament books is in its beginnings. The Psalter, which alone is attested in Old Church Slavonic form, has been analyzed fairly thoroughly. Genesis is well known through the excellent study by Vasilij Mixajlov and his edition of the text, although, unfortunately, both volumes are bibliographic rarities and remain unknown to many Slavists. Daniel was published in full by I. E. Evseev, whose study of Isaiah makes possible some factual observations as well as some theoretical conclusions. N. L. Tunickij's edition of Hosea, Joel, Amos, Obadiah and Jonah unfortunately remains incomplete. The short book of Ruth is well known. However, Exodus, Numbers, Leviticus, Joshua, Judges, and the four Kingdoms—the books with which Esther is associated in the Slavic tradition—remain untouched (Lebedev's book on Joshua being almost useless). Nevertheless, we have ventured to use materials from a late copy of Joshua, Judges, and the Tetrabasileion and/or the printed Ostrih Bible of 1581 as parallels for passages in Esther. It is to be hoped that full studies, and, in particular, editions of important manuscripts of these books will be undertaken to fill in serious gaps in our knowledge of these fundamental texts.

This book has been written primarily for Slavists. We are aware that most Slavists have little Greek and are not intimately acquainted with problems of biblical textual criticism. We assume that most of our readers will not know Hebrew. We have therefore tried to give explanations that will make our references to these languages as clear as possible. For typographical reasons, Hebrew is usually cited in Roman transliteration of the consonantal text.

Our book had its beginnings in 1984, when the two authors corresponded about the Altbauer-Taube paper that Lunt edited. At that time Lunt put the text of the oldest manuscript into the computer and generated a concordance; the result was a series of new questions. Long-distance collaboration has meant many delays. Taube spent the academic years 1986–87 and 1992–93 at Harvard, and made short visits in 1989, 1990, and 1996. Lunt visited Jerusalem briefly in 1991.

It is our pleasant duty to thank many colleagues for their help. Professor Moshé Altbauer of Jerusalem introduced us to the topic and furnished the vital photocopy of the oldest manuscript, thus making initial independent observations possible. Subsequently he provided photocopies of a later manuscript which proved to be a significant basis for comparison of variants. Dmitrij Bulanin, Natalia Kobiak, Andrej Pliguzov, Elena Švarc, and Viktor Zagrebin took time from their busy schedules to check manuscripts in Moscow and St. Petersburg to establish more precise dating and other codicological information. Professor Francis J. Thomson of the University of Antwerp offered helpful comments on major and minor matters too numerous to list; we are grateful for his significant contributions.

Philip Nikolayev and Vladimir Gitin graciously suppressed their high stylistic standards to produce a Russian translation of the Hebrew text in accord with our demand for a Procrustean literalism; we appreciate their cheerful cooperation.

Lunt's understanding of the Hebrew text owes much to the patient tuition of Agustinus Gianto Kentjanaputra, S. J., and to the lists of specific grammatical forms and constructions Gianto compiled. Professor Frank L. Cross, Jr., was a constant source of sound advice, and Professor James Kugel was always ready to answer the most trivial query about Hebrew grammar or to listen to shifting speculative guesses about translation problems or transmission theory with unfailing patience, good humor, and understanding.

Taube's work in Cambridge benefitted greatly from the hospitality of the Russian Research Center (now the Davis Center for Russian Studies) and the Ukrainian Research Institute of Harvard University.

The initial steps in compiling a concordance and creating Slavic fonts were made possible by the whole-hearted cooperation of Scott Bradner, then of the Computer Based Laboratory of Harvard, and a series of helpers who were always ready with practical support during the long period the book was being composed on the computer. Gary Bisbee and Joe Snowden deserve special thanks for their help.

Harvard University
The Hebrew University of Jerusalem

Abbreviations

For abbreviations of names of libraries and conventional labels for manuscripts of Esther, see E1, pp. 11–12 (and E7, p. 18).

A, Acc	accusative
adj	adjective
Akad	Academy copy of PVL
Arx	Archangel Gospel of 1092
Assem	Codex Assemanianus (OCS)
AT	Altbauer and Taube 1984 (see bibliography)
Bg	Bulgarian
BR	Belarusian
c	circa
CE	Common Era
ChSl	Church Slavonic
Chron	Chronicle(s)
ČOIDR	*Čtenija v Obščestve istorii i drevnostej rossijskix*
comm	commentary (pp. 81–140)
Compl	Complutensian Polyglot Bible, 1514–17
ComSl	Common Slavic
Cor	Corinthians
Čud	Čudov Psalter (see bibliography)
Cz	Czech
d, du	dual
D	dative
Dan	Daniel
Deut	Deuteronomy
E	English
EBg, ESl	East (Bulgarian, Slavic)
Efr. Korm	*Efremovskaja kormčaja*
ES	Trubačev's *Ètimologičeskij slovar'* (see bibliography)
Est	Esther
Euch	Euchologium sinaiticum (OCS)
Ex, Exod	Exodus
f	feminine
f.	folio
fn	footnote
FP	Full (Chronographic) Paleja
Fr	French
G	genitive
GC	Vaillant's *Grammaire Comparée* (see bibliography)
Gen	Genesis
Ger	German
Gk	Greek
Glag	Glagolitic
GorNev	Gorskij and Nevostruev (see bibliography)
H	Hebrew
Ham	Hamartolos (see bibliography)
Hyp	Hypatian Chronicle
IE	Indo-European
inf	infinitive
Inst	Instrumental
Is	Isaiah
Izb	Izbornik
J	Gospel of John
J	Jewish Chronograph, Warsaw ms cim. 83
Josh	Joshua
Judg	Judges
Ki	Book of Kingdoms
KJ	King James Bible
L	locative
Lu	Gospel of Luke
L	'Lucianic' or Alpha-text of Gk Esther
Lat	Latin
Lav	Laurentian Chronicle (1377)
lit.	literally
LT	Lunt and Taube 1988 (see bibliography)
LXX	Septuagint

M56a, M78a	Meščerskij 1956a, 1978a (see bibliography)
Mac	Macedonian
Mar	Codex Marianus (OCS)
MCoS	Middle Common Slavic
Mikl	Miklosich's *Lexicon* (see bibliography)
Mk	Gospel of Mark
Mod.	Modern
Mst	Mstislav Gospel of 1117
Mt	Gospel of Matthew
MT	(Hebrew) Masoretic Text
N	nominative
NEB	New English Bible
Neh	Nehemiah
Nik	Gospel of Nicodemus (Vaillant 1968)
NM	Nikita Meščerskij
NT	New Testament
O	Origen-based variants of LXX
OB	Ostrih Bible
O(Cz, Pol)	Old (Czech, Polish)
OCS	Old Church Slavonic
*OCS	to be attributed to OCS
OHG	Old High German
OLDP, OLDRP	Obščestvo ljubitelej drevne-russkoj pis′mennosti
Ost	Ostromir Gospel (1056)
OT	Old Testament
p, pl	plural
ppp	past passive participle
P, Pol	Polish
PSRL	*Polnoe sobranie russkix letopisej*
Ps	Psalms
PsSin	Psalterium Sinaiticum (OCS)
PVL	*Povest′ vremen i let,* Rus′ Primary Chronicle
R	Russian
Radz	Radziwill copy of PVL
RES	*Revue des Études Slaves*
Rev	Revelations
Rječ	Rječnik (see bibliography)
RM	Robert Mathiesen 1983a (see bibliography)
Ro	Roždestvenskij (see bibliography)
s, sing	singular
Sam	Samuel
Sav	Savvina kniga (OCS)
SC	Serbo-Croatian
SJS	*Slovník jazyka staroslověnského* (see bibliography)
Sl	Slavic
Slk	Slovak
Sln	Slovene
SoS	Song of Songs
Srez	Sreznevskij's *Materialy* (see bibliography)
SRJaXI	*Slovar′ russkogo jazyka XI–XVII vv.* (see bibliography)
SSl	South Slavic
SSUM	*Slovnyk staroukrajins′koji movy*
Su, Supr	Codex Suprasliensis (OCS)
Syn.	Synodal
TrChr	Trinity (Troickij) Chronograph
U, Ukr	Ukrainian
Usp. (sb.)	Uspenskij sbornik (see bibliography)
v	verso
v.	verse
Vil.	Codex Vilensis 262
VMČ	(see bibliography)
Voc	vocative
Vyg. (sb.)	Vygoleksa sbornik (see bibliography)
WdS	*Die Welt der Slaven*
WSl	West Slavic
Zo, Zogr	Codex Zographensis (OCS)

The Slavonic Book of Esther

Introduction

The background.

In1.1 Slavic written culture began as a direct result of the success of Christianity in incipient Slavic states, first in Morava and shortly afterward in the Bulgarian Empire. The major accomplishment of the "Moravan" Mission of Constantine-Cyril and Methodius, 863–885, was the establishment of a new written language, solidly anchored in translations of most of the New Testament, along with the Psalter and selections from other Old Testament books and extensive liturgical, homiletic, and hymnodic literature. Although the mission was abruptly curtailed and its accomplishments largely lost in Central Europe, its work survived to some extent in Croatia, and it was revived and continued in Bulgaria.

In1.2 It is the Bulgarian period of early Slavic Christianity, particularly the reign of Simeon, 890–927, that shaped the firm outlines of Slavic Christian literature of the earliest retrievable sources. Older translations were revised and a flood of new translations were produced in order to fill out the works required for the complex liturgy and the teaching needs of churches and monasteries.[1] There is reason to believe that the Moravan books might well have been strongly influenced by (if not indeed translated from) Latin sources in conformity with long-established usage in the bishoprics of Bavaria and Italy. In the classical Old Church Slavonic period, however, the models were strictly from Greek Orthodox traditions. Earlier western influences were almost completely wiped out. In effect, Slavic Orthodoxy was a translation from Greek.

In1.3 From a high level of cultural activity in the tenth century, the Slavic Christians were forced by successive triumphs of Byzantine armies, first in eastern Bulgaria and then in the Macedonian lands, to curtail and eventually abandon their independent work. We may assume that as late as 1010 in Macedonia disciples were being trained, copyists were reproducing needed books, and perhaps some independent translation and original work was still being accomplished. The brutal destruction of the Slavic armies by Basil II the Bulgar-Killer in 1018, however, must be seen as the beginning of a rapid decline, so that by 1100 cultural activity was reduced to a bare minimum.

In1.4 Once again, however, the major books were rescued, and Slavic Orthodox Christianity and its attendant culture were given new life in the newly Christian Land of Rus′. The official baptism of Volodimer in 988 cannot be shown to have been accompanied by an influx of Slavonic books and the institution of education in the Slavonic language, but under his son Jaroslav, Prince of Kiev, 1019–1054, the spread of the Slavonic rite and the official use of Slavonic writing surely became established. During the eleventh and twelfth centuries, Slavonic books were copied, perhaps some new translations were made to meet new cultural requirements, and surely the men of Rus′ began to write sermons and other works of their own. The South Slavs began to revive the almost stagnant culture toward the end of the twelfth century, and the late thirteenth and the fourteenth centuries witnessed a flowering of original works and new translations, much of which was soon available in Rus′.

[1] The choice of works to be translated was dominated by monastic requirements and tastes to a surprising extent.

In2 Where does the Old Testament book of Esther fit into this picture?

In2.1 We are now accustomed to think of the basic writings of Christianity as a large volume called the *Bible*, a specific collection of varied books traditionally organized into the Old Testament and the New Testament. Students of early Slavic culture must keep in mind that such a tome was not to be found in a Greek Orthodox church or even a monastery library; there was no call for it during services and individuals were not encouraged to read the Scriptures for personal edification. In view of the rarity of Greek codices containing essentially the full Bible, it is remarkable that Methodius, at the end of his life, set about completing the translation of all the books "except Maccabees" as we are told in the fifteenth chapter of his Life. Much of this translation (if we accept the hagiographical account) was lost, probably at once; six centuries later the Archbishop Gennadius of Novgorod, seeking to put together a full Bible, was forced to commission new translations of many books.

In2.2 Both for Methodius and for Gennadius, the book of Esther surely was one which would be needed for a complete Bible, although no part of the text was used in any service of either the Greek or the Roman rite. Its inclusion among the canonical works certified by Church authorities as divinely inspired had been questioned in early centuries, but it was on the lists of approved books circulating in the ninth century and later. Its name is to be found in two of the three lists given in the miscellany translated for Simeon, as witnessed by the Kievan Izbornik of 1073 (in three different spellings, ѥсѳєрь, ѥсѳир', иосѳир).

In2.3 In the Jewish tradition, Esther seems to have been considered canonical by Josephus Flavius, who uses it as a source for his *Jewish Antiquities* (Book XI, vi) in the 90s of the first century C. E. It is a familiar text, for the Scroll of Esther is read every year on the holiday of Purim, a joyous festival of great importance in Jewish custom.

In2.4 The traditional Hebrew shape of the book has come down to us in the authoritative Masoretic Text (hereafter, MT). No trace has been found in any of the fragments discovered among ancient manuscript relics anywhere in the Near East, nor do any of the translations into other languages provide information that significantly modifies any detail of the MT text.

In2.5 The old Greek translation of the Hebrew Bible was made by Jews in the third and second centuries before the Common Era, apparently for the use of Greek-speaking Jews in the large Jewish community in Alexandria and elsewhere in Egypt. In many Biblical books, the Greek text of the Septuagint (LXX) generally corresponds sentence by sentence to the traditional Hebrew wording of the MT. In Esther, the MT has a considerably shorter text than the LXX, and most authorities believe that the supplementary portions were originally composed in "Biblical Greek."[2] In the portions that do agree, however, the Greek is not the sort of literal rendering usual in other books, but a verse-by-verse paraphrase that tells the same story with considerable differences in wording. Moreover, there is a second Greek version which has the additions but has abridged much of the tale and made other changes.[3]

[2] The 167 verses of MT Esther are divided into 10 chapters. Conventions for identifying individual sentences of the "additions" vary. We follow Hanhart: A:1–17 procedes MT 1:1; B:1–7 goes between 3:13 and 14; C:1–30 and D:1–16 follow 4:17 and take the place of 5:1–2; E:1–24 goes between 8:12 and 13; F:1–11 follows the final verse of MT, 10:3.

[3] The shorter version is usually known as the *L-text,* since it is attested in manuscripts that in other books contain the special recension attributed traditionally to Lucian, although it has repeatedly been shown that Esther does not share the distinctive features of the other 'Lucianic' books, cf. Tov 1982 1–2. Most scholars now prefer

In2.6 The story of Esther is known, then, in three ancient shapes: the shorter Hebrew of the MT, the long Greek of the LXX, and the abridged Greek of the L-text.[4] The Slavonic book of Esther corresponds verse by verse to the MT; it differs significantly from either of the known Greek texts. The simplest explanation would be to assume that the translation was made directly from Hebrew. However, questions immediately arise: Why would Esther be needed for a Slavic-speaking community? Who might have the knowledge to translate the work? Where? When?

In2.7 There is no evidence: any answers to these questions *must* be speculative. Speculation must be kept within the bounds of plausible hypotheses that are based on known facts and generally accepted views.

In3.1 We must recall that Slavic written culture of the 9th–11th centuries in the southeast and east was almost wholly based on Greek Christian culture. Much earlier, the diffusion of Christianity itself was made possible precisely because Greek was a lingua franca. Not only works and ideas approved by official ecclesiastical authorities came through Greek, but also numerous utterly diverse elements from earlier religions and philosophies (especially variant movements within Judaism), along with continually new developments within various Christian communities. It was in Greek form that Christian orthodox and heretical works came to Egypt and Rome, where they were translated into Coptic and Latin. Even in Palestine the same ideas were expressed in Greek alongside Hebrew and Aramaic.[5] The language of the books of the Septuagint is not quite the "koine" of the New Testament, but they can be treated together as "Biblical Greek" and show strong influence of Semitic idiom and syntax.[6]

In3.2 Since all of this is well documented and uncontroversial, scholars, when faced with a text in Coptic or Latin which is not known in any Semitic or Greek manuscript, start with the working assumption that the translation was made—like those of the overwhelming majority of known texts—from Greek.[7] Assuming a lost Semitic text is the exceptional, marked case, and needs to be backed up with massive evidence if it is to be plausible. The pervasive problem is that the occurrence of Semitisms in a Latin or Coptic text is not in itself sufficient proof of translation directly from Semitic, precisely because Semitic elements frequently survive through Greek into texts in other languages. Moreover, Semitisms were subsequently introduced into texts originally composed in Greek because of their "Biblical" flavor for readers familiar with the LXX, New Testament, and other texts. Therefore it is unwise to assume that such "Semitisms" constitute evidence of a Hebrew original. On the contrary, it has been demonstrated that biblical and quasi-biblical works which exist in Cop-

---

the neutral term *A-text* (or alpha-text), as opposed to the standard *B-text* (beta-text), cf. Moore 1971 lxii–lxiii. In accordance with the older tradition best known in Slavic scholarship, we will use *L-text,* to indicate contrast to LXX.

4 When Jerome made his Latin translation, the Vulgate, in 391–405, he put the 167 MT verses first, and then added the materials he could find only in Greek (or the Old Latin translation that had been made from Greek). These "additions" are traditionally divided into verses starting with 10:4–13 and then chapters 11–16. This arrangement confuses the narrative sequence, compare note 2 above.

5 Numerous peculiarities of the MT Esther have inspired several variants of a theory that the book was composed in Aramaic, and not translated into Hebrew until c100 C.E. No fragments of this hypothetic Aramaic book are known, however.

6 Some works which were not fully accepted either in the Jewish or Christian mainstream traditions were composed by Greek-speaking Jews in even more deviant sorts of Greek that have been called "Jewish Greek."

7 Indeed, the assumption holds even if a Semitic but not a Greek text is known.

tic or Latin were translated from Greek; this is the normal course of cultural diffusion.[8] The study of many pseudepigraphical and other non-canonical works must start with a decision as to whether one assumes a normal situation—i.e., a lost Greek source—or an exceptional one, direct translation from a lost Semitic source.[9]

In3.3 We will look at some of the specific problems of judging the origin of translations later on (pp. 56–65). Here we will discuss more general questions involving cultural factors. First, what communities might desire either a new Greek or a Slavic version of Esther?

In3.41 The Septuagint was originally quite specifically a Jewish work, made because Hebrew was no longer widely spoken and not everyone could read it. Yet the LXX text was always less authoritative than the Hebrew wording, and the contrast became increasingly important after the new Christian sect began to rely on Scriptural citations from the Greek. For this reason Jews continually made modifications to the Septuagint in order to keep their understanding of the Hebrew text in line with current perceptions of Greek, or, indeed, to remove the possibility of Christian interpretations of key passages. It is to this specifically Jewish view that Aquila, Symmachus and Theodotion addressed their efforts for the Greek-speaking Jewish communities, as a parallel to translations of the Hebrew scriptures into the vernacular of the various Jewish diaspora communities. This insistence on the availability of translations that render the Hebrew intelligible to each group continued, giving rise to a long series of translations, many of which we know only by indirect information. Certainly Greek-speaking Jews in the 12th to early 15th century made new Greek translations of some books, an indication of the continuing rejection of the Septuagint.[10] It is plausible then, we submit, to hypothesize that at some time before 1300 a Greek version of Esther was made for the use of a Greek-speaking Jewish community. It might have been very early, by Jews who were dissatisfied with the efforts of Aquila, Symmachus, or Theodotion.

In4.1 The Babylonian Talmud (*Megilla* 17–18), in discussing the obligation of reciting the Scroll of Esther on Purim, raises the question of whether recitation in Greek fulfils the obligation. In view of the general awareness of the LXX's textual deviations from the MT (see the discussion in *b. Megilla* 9), we must conclude that a suitable Greek text—one more faithful to the MT than the Septuagint—was known to the 3rd-century rabbis. The propriety of reciting the Esther story in Greek in the synagogue on the second day of Purim was addressed by Rabbi Eliyahu Ben Ḥayim Mizraḥi (c1437–1526), an outstanding scholar and leader of the Jewish community in Constantinople (in his *responsa*, published in Venice in 1674 under the title *Mayim 'Amuqim*, question 79, fol. 137). This fits the evidence of the 1547 Constantinople Polyglot Pentateuch, which contains the Hebrew MT along with the Aramaic Targum and the Ladino and Judeo-Greek translations of the Pentateuch, all in Hebrew characters. The title page promises not only the five books of Moses, but also the Five Scrolls, a combination that is customary in printed Hebrew Pentateuchs. Unfortunately, we know of no copy of this 1547 volume that contains any of the scrolls.

[8] There is evidence, however, that Hebrew and Aramaic were known to some translators. Thus, while the Old Latin copies of the OT books were made from Greek originals, the Vulgate was translated by Jerome from Hebrew.

[9] For examples, see the introduction to the individual works in Charlesworth, especially F. I. Andersen's judicious summary of the problems posed by 2 Enoch (known only from Slavonic mss), p. 94. These principles apply also to Armenian and Ethiopian cultural traditions.

[10] The book of Jonah has survived in a Greek version in Hebrew letters, dating to the 12th or 13th century; see Hesseling for transcription and further literature. The *Graecus Venetus*, published by Gebhardt in 1875, contains the Pentateuch, Proverbs, Ruth, Song of Songs, Ecclesiastes, Lamentations, and Daniel. For a discussion of the use of Greek biblical texts by Byzantine Jews, see de Lange (1993).

In4.2 Yet some Christians also found fault with the Septuagint and looked to the Hebrew books for sure guidance. The *hebraica veritas*, the authority of the Hebrew books, was valued, for example, by Origen, a third-century Christian theologian. He undertook to compare them with Gk versions in his *Hexapla,* a monumental work that has mostly been lost. His text of Esther (as of most other books) is known only indirectly (see Hanhart). Origen's efforts to bring the LXX text closer to the Hebrew provide useful hints as to how specific phrases were rendered by a 3rd-century translator.[11]

In5 There is no question that the 167 verses of the Slavonic book of Esther have as their ultimate source the 167 verses of the MT or a Hebrew text nearly identical with the MT. It is our contention, however, that Esther, like the rest of the books known to the Slavs before c1400, was translated from the Greek. (We except, of course, the few items obviously translated from Latin and the prayers translated from Old High German.) Since no such text is known, we assume that it must have been lost after having been translated into Slavonic.

In5.1 The simpler hypothesis that our text represents a direct translation from Hebrew has two variants, Jewish and Christian.

In5.11 Esther is important for Jews. Jews are mentioned in 11th-century native East Slavic works such as the *Primary Chronicle* (Повесть времен и лет) and the Life of Theodosius of the Caves Monastery, and it is to be assumed that they lived in the same sort of organized and segregated communities we know from many other regions and eras.[12] Jews everywhere in the diaspora adopted the local tongue for everyday purposes. It is therefore safe to assume that Jewish communities in Kiev and other Rusian centers were Slavic-speaking.[13] Moreover, they would surely have ties with Jewish centers in the Khazar lands, where Hebrew is believed to have been widely in use.[14] In Jewish communities that

11 Jerome too revered the *hebraica veritas,* and the work of Origen formed the basis for his early work on revising Old Latin translations and his later complete translation of the whole Old Testament.

12 The fact that Hebrew books and Jewish scholars might be close by would not, *pace* Anatolij Alekseev 1993 47, constitute "conditions for translation of biblical and Talmudical works" for the simple reason that Christians met Jews only in specific situations, chiefly in the market-place, that were divorced from religion and books. The history of Byzantine and European Christianity for the ten centuries after Jerome's work with the Hebrew scriptures affirms that the chasm between Jewish and Christian intellectual life was unbridgeable.

Meščerskij (1956a 218) speaks of the Kievan monk Nikita who, through the work of the devil, became a prophet, famed for knowing the books of the OT by heart and scorning the NT. The wording of the Caves Monastery Paterikon, particularly in the older redaction (Abramovič 1930 126) makes it clear that "Jewish books" in this context means OT books (cf. Heppell 144 n. 452). No knowledge of Hebrew is implied. (Meščerskij fails to note that his interpretation of Nikita's role goes back to G. M. Barac 1924 [ch. 3, 4, and *passim*], who speculated that Nikita was a Jew converted to Christianity and was the author of the first redaction ["первоначальный свод"] of the PVL. Cf. also Lunt-Taube 1988 151 and note 34 for another unacknowledged debt of Meščerskij's to Barac.)

13 In the Life of Theodosius, the holy man comes into the princely court and finds musicians and dancers, some "ꙁамарьныꙗ пискъı гласѧщемъ"—perhaps "sounding forth with *zamar* squealing" (Usp 59d27, cf. Srez). The stem *zamar* is possibly from the H root *zmr* (*zamar* 'musician, singer'; *zimmer* 'sing, play (instrument)'; *zimrah* 'melody, music'), but Hendler 1993 shows that it it is also Arabic and widespread throughout Persian and Turkic dialects. As for the Kievan text, it is unclear whether the clause refers to a specific type of music or to a musical instrument. Perhaps this phrase shows that Jewish musicians were involved. If so, there may well have been the kind of social situation that obtained recently in the Balkans with Gypsy musicians; Gypsies were marginal to "normal" society, but no celebration, such as a wedding, was complete without Gypsy music. *Pace* Meščerskij (1956a 218), this isolated word in no way demonstrates the sort of intellectual Slavic-Hebrew contact required in translating religious or literary works.

14 See, e.g., Golb and Pritsak, Pritsak 1990.

Let us again emphasize that there is no *evidence* for the use of Slavic by Jews in the South and East Slavic areas of Orthodox Christianity before 1400. Hints much later come in such forms, for example, as a 17th-century *responsum* concerning the legal validity of a hybrid phrase, "Ja tebe estim mekadeš byl," roughly "I hereby thee

spoke Yiddish and Judeo-Spanish, translations were first made for women and for uneducated men who were unversed in the holy tongue. We may conjecture that similar conditions led to Slavic translations.[15] If we hypothesize a Slavic version of Esther made by and for Jews at some time and place in the South or East Slavic world after about 900, we must forge one more theoretical link in our chain of reasoning: how did this Jewish book make its way into the Christian milieu in which we find it at the end of the 14th century?[16]

In5.12 An alternate theoretical line of reasoning starts with the fact that Esther was a canonical book for Christians. It therefore would be needed by any new Christian establishment that wished to have the full set of books in the native language. If Methodius translated the whole Bible (except Maccabees), then he surely must have included Esther. Yet if such books as 1–2 Chronicles and the Wisdom of Solomon perished between 885 and the time Gennadius had to order a new translation in the 15th century, why should Esther survive? It had, after all, no place in the voluminous Orthodox liturgy, and is utterly disregarded by the Church Fathers. But whether Esther was needed to fill out the set of canonical books in 884 or 1100 or 1300—why was it not translated from the LXX or L-texts that were available?

In5.13 Perhaps an answer is provided by the fact that the authority of the *hebraica veritas* continued to be revered long after Origen and Jerome. In many times and places Christians, similarly concerned with purity of doctrine and convinced of the importance of detailed understanding of Scripture, undertook a study of Hebrew and even made new translations. Such views were held late in the 14th century in Central Europe (e.g., by Jan Hus), and they had spread to the East Slavic lands by the 1470s. Archbishop Gennadius of Novgorod worried about the influence of such thinking, and it was a major factor in his efforts in the 1490s to produce a full Slavonic Bible. In the 19th century, the scholars who first dealt with the Slavonic Esther quite understandably concluded that the translation was the work of "Judaizers" after 1470—an example of the kind of activity Gennadius was opposing. This specific hypothesis[17] was invalidated by the discovery of manuscripts dating from c1400, but there is no evidence to prevent us from imagining that earlier groups of this type existed. It is characteristic of unsuccessful deviant doctrines that we know little or nothing of their specific tenets because our only sources are the triumphant official Church authorities who have successfully repressed the heresies. This leaves us to speculate that Esther may have been produced by earlier Bible-oriented sectarians, but there are no serious candidates. An attractive possibility is 14th-century "Judaizers" in Bulgaria (recently exhumed by Alekseev

---

wed." This implies that the community spoke a form of Slavic as a rule, with Hebrew words for special religious or legal purposes.

15 Our analysis of Esther uncovers no evidence of direct translation from Hebrew. This means that we have no reason to believe that Slavic-speaking Jews in the East or South Slavic regions in fact made any translations.

16 A further difficulty is that translations made for Jews were always written in Hebrew characters; we must assume that someone had to transcribe the book into conventional Greek orthography.

17 References to "Judaizers" are usually negative and it is often hard to perceive the outlines of the group or the essence of their deviant and undesirable behavior. Words meaning "become Jewish" or "act like a Jew" often occur in extremely broad contexts. In the Church Fathers, ἰουδαΐζειν means (1) *embrace Judaism, be converted to the Jewish faith,* or (2) *behave like a Jew, imitate the Jews* (a) by observing the Sabbath, (b) by denying the divinity of Christ, or (c) by adhering strictly to the word of scripture, see Lampe. The infinitive, in sense 2a, was translated by жидовьскъı творити in the OCS nomokanon reflected in the 11th-century *Efremovskaja kormčaja.* The noun ἰουδαϊστής may be used correspondingly; with reference to Sabbatarians it was translated into *OCS as жидовьствоуѭще (Srez sub жидовьствовати), which renders ἰουδαΐζοντες in sense 2b in Gregory of Nazianz (GPB ms Q.п.I.16, fol. 152d, see SRJaXI sub нещадство). The words tend to occur in polemic contexts that deplore the action of "Judaizing" without specifying precisely what it is.

1993 55): we could imagine there both the requisite Jewish communities, who could furnish Hebrew texts and knowledge of the language, and the zealous Christians who would make, or commission, translations into their own language for their own edification. However, evidence for Bulgarian Judaizers (in any sense of the term) is extremely uncertain, and this theory too lacks substance.[18]

In5.14 In any of these variant hypotheses, someone with a knowledge of Hebrew is required. Since Biblical scholarship does have examples of converted Jews who served as teachers or even became distinguished as anti-Jewish polemicists, it is appropriate to assume that such a person was available at whatever time and place the other components of a thesis might require.[19]

In5.15 It is generally true that only someone intimately acquainted with a doctrine is in a position to refute it successfully. Archbishop Gennadius sought certain books precisely because the Jews and heretics (presumably including the "Judaizers") used them for argumentation. Moreover, he was concerned that his opponents often rejected standard LXX citations because they claimed that the translation was distorted and unreliable.[20] The 167-verse Esther is precisely the kind of model of *hebraica veritas* that an anti-Jewish polemicist might find a useful weapon. It is not, however, a book that is likely to come up in doctrinal disputations because of its marginal position in the Orthodox tradition. Yet it might be obtained by a polemicist from a source that offered it by chance along with other translated books that were of value to him. This at least suggests a mechanism whereby a 167-verse Greek Esther might become known to a Christian. Once available, this book could then be used by a historian who was not content with the summary available in the Slavonic Hamartolos—the popular *Chronicle of George the Monk.*

In5.16 Unfortunately, we really know none of the details of the transmission to the Bulgarian lands of texts produced by Cyril and Methodius, nor is there evidence of how these early works and the texts produced during the next two centuries found their way to Rus′ (cf. Thomson 1988). Esther will remain a conundrum within these larger enigmas.

*

In6 All this has led us to posit a 167-verse Greek version of Esther, made by a translator conversant with traditional Jewish views of the meaning of certain passages. At some time between 863 and about 1375, at some place in the Christian Orthodox Slavic world, this Greek Esther was translated into the written Slavic appropriate to the time and place. Evidence that allows more precise delineation of the circumstances and persons involved is not available. Whatever its history, the Slavic version of Esther survived only in seriously corrupt form, in a single faulty copy made most probably by a scribe in the western East Slavic lands in the mid-1300s.[21]

18 Sobolevskij mentions and dismisses the notion at the beginning of his discussion of the writings of the late 15th-century East Slavic жидовствующие (1903 396). It is based on obscure phrases in the *Life* of Patriarch Euthymius of Trnovo, examined at length by Syrku 1898 267–77. One fairly solid fact of interest is that Theodora, the second wife of the Bulgarian tsar Ivan-Alexander (1331–71), was of Jewish origin. Unfortunately, nothing specific is known about her background, i.e., how she came to the tsar's attention, or the dates of her baptism and marriage.

19 For example, one of Jerome's Hebrew teachers may have been a converted Jew.

20 See his 1489 letter to Ioasaf, former archbishop of Rostov, Kazakova and Lur′e 319, 320.

21 We reject the alternate hypothesis, apparently held by Alekseev, that the faults and misunderstandings that must be ascribed to the reconstructable hypothetical ancestor are in fact features of the original Slavonic text, in other words that the Slavic translator was ignorant, erratic, and careless. See below, p. 67, fn. 21 (and cf. Lunt-Taube 1988 169 n. 9).

In6.1 The text as we know it was copied repeatedly during the 15th century, and in the 1490s it was used by the compilers of the Gennadius Bible, with modifications we will discuss later. In the first half of the 16th century, Maksim Grek, as he became acquainted with this official Muscovite Bible, seems to have been dissatisfied with its Latin order of text and the deviations in the first nine chapters from the LXX wording. He made a new Slavonic translation, faithful to the LXX text both in the ordering of the additional elements (sections A-E in modern scholarly terms) and in the exact wording of each verse (cf. Taube-Olmsted). Maksim's translation, together with the older version from the Gennadius Bible, served as the basis for the first complete printed East Slavic Bible, published in Ostrih in 1581.[22] The Ostrih Esther was reproduced without significant modification in the 1663 printed Bible, which remained the authoritative text among the East Slavic Orthodox faithful until 1751.

Previous investigations of Esther

In7 The history of scholarly interest in the Slavonic book of Esther starts with a brief note by Aleksandr **Vostokov**, who declared in 1842 that Esther was translated from Hebrew in "Russia" at an early date.[23] Archimandrite Leonid (1883, kn. 4, p 2), in describing a 16th-century ms, #19 in our list, cites a marginal note (unfortunately without estimating its age): "на верху надпись: ни Вулгата, ни 70-ть а переводъ с еврейскаго преточный. странное дѣло!"

In7.1 Far more important are the three pages devoted to this text by A. **Gorskij** and K. **Nevostruev** in their 1855 description of the Gennadius Bible (1499 and two later copies) in the Synodal Library. These two assiduous scholars were observant and precise, and their remarkable erudition was admirably up to date. They recognize that the Gennadius version consists of the equivalent of the MT, 1:1 through 10:3, followed by the equivalent of the Greek additions—that is to say precisely the ordering Jerome used in translating the Vulgate. The first part, in the view of Gorskij and Nevostruev, was translated into Slavonic directly from Hebrew, probably in the mid-fifteenth century, by someone from "near Poland."

In7.11 The direct translation is demonstrated, they believe, *first* by the close textual correspondence between Hebrew and Slavonic, particularly when both deviate from the Greek and/or Latin; *second* by the fact that the transcription of proper names fits the Hebrew forms (e.g., Ахаӡверосъ for H '*Aḥašweroš,* rather than Greek Ἀρταξέρξης, Vulg. *Assuerus*), and *finally* by the literal rendering of many phrases.[24]

[22] Two essentially Belarusian versions stand outside this tradition. The first is one of 9 OT books translated from the Hebrew into vernacular Belarusian in the second half of the 15th century; they are found in Vilnius codex 10 (262) and Esther was published by Altbauer 1992 (with Ruth, the Song of Songs, Ecclesiastes and Lamentations; Job, the Psalter, Daniel, and Proverbs are in preparation). The second was part of the series of biblical books published by Francisk Skaryna, in a translation adapted from Czech, which in turn is based on the Vulgate. Esther appeared in 1519 in Prague.

[23] His comment (1842 35), prompted by his description of Rum 30, a contemporary copy of a 15th-century ms in St. Petersburg (#5 in our list, p. 11 below), sums up the effect Esther evoked in most readers: "Замечательно, что книга Есфирь переведена с Еврейского, и повидимому в России, однакоже в весьма давнее время. Здесь встречаются слова: *Тиѹнъ* и *староста*, вместо еѵнухъ. болярамъ земнымъ вм. земльнымъ сатрапомъ. *Росполонъ* вместо разграбление, *охвота* вместо веселіе, и проч."

[24] In fact their claim is too comprehensive: удержаны все обороты речи Еврейской и коренные значения слов, иногда вопреки связи речи (54). We will discuss their examples, from 1:13; 2:10, 12, 13; 6:9, and especially 9:26–28, under various headings below (referring to them as GorNev).

In7.12 The hypothesis that the translator was from близь Польши (55) is based on certain words and idioms "that approximate the Polish language," such as абы (чтобы), приклѧкаа (припадая), and ѡхота (веселие). The dating was deduced from the presence of a considerable number of words and expressions "from the folk dialect, rather than the Church Slavonic" (55–6), and a speculative connection with a translation of the "Psalter" made from Hebrew in the third quarter of the 15th century (55, fn.).[25]

In7.13 As for the second part of Esther, Gorskij and Nevostruev demonstrate that it was translated, not very skillfully, from Jerome's Latin. This new translation, and the redaction of the older Slavonic, was part of the work organized by Gennadius in Novgorod in the 1490s. A more detailed examination of the translation was included in an ambitious but inept study by Ivan **Roždestvenskij**, Книга Есѳирь в текстах: еврейском-масоретском, греческом, древнем латинском и славянском, published in St Petersburg in 1885. The author, apparently a student of theology, devotes but eleven pages (194–204) to the text of the manuscript *sborniki,* by which he means items 5, 6, 10, and 21 of the list in E1 below; he contrasts them to the Gennadius Bible. He agrees completely with the major points made by Gorskij and Nevostruev: Esther was translated directly from Hebrew by a Slav from somewhere near Poland in the 15th century. Even more categorically he attributes the translations to the Judaizers.

In7.2 Aleksej Ivanovič **Sobolevskij**, a prolific linguistic historian of great erudition (1856–1929), noted in 1897 that two codices of about 1400 (T and Q) contained Esther; this removes the post-1450 Judaizers from the list of possible translators. Moreover, Sobolevskij cited linguistic archaisms and items he considered Hellenisms. Following the logic of the general pattern of cultural borrowing from Byzantium to the Slavs, he boldly hypothesized a now lost Greek translation made from the MT. He took the general Mediterranean and Byzantinoslavic cultural pattern as the norm, thereby putting the burden of proof on anyone who might posit deviation from this norm. The theologian-philologist Ivan E. **Evseev** was outraged by this notion; any such proposal exceeds the limits of scholarship.[26] It must be emphasized that neither Sobolevskij nor Evseev bothered to demonstrate their beliefs with more than anecdotal evidence; both considered their conclusions so self-evident that detailed argument was unnecessary. Sobolevskij's 1903 sketch added nothing new.

In7.3 For half a century matters rested; in textbooks and summary articles Esther was occasionally mentioned as an example of early East Slavic translation activity that was attributed, without serious examination, to the 11th–12th centuries.[27] The high cultural level of Kievan Rus′ was axiomatic. Conjectural lists of alleged Rusian translations were combined in the 1930s and 1940s with the patriotic theses of an autochthonous literary language, different from the modified forms of OCS that have actually survived.

In7.31 It was in this atmosphere of heightened Russian nationalistic fervor that Nikita A. **Meščerskij** wrote a dissertation (in 1946) about translated texts in early Rus′. It is to Meščerskij's merit that he reopened the field of Slavic biblical philology for Soviet scholars

[25] The alleged Psalter has turned out to be selections from various traditional Jewish rituals, translated not from a written text, but from the imperfect memory of Feodor, a converted Jew; see Zuckerman 1987.

[26] "Выходило бы совершенно за пределы науки и погружалось бы в область неожиданностей" (1898 341).

[27] Istrin's dating of the translation of Esther to the mid-13th century (1912b 21) was overlooked, and Evseev's vaguer statement that the translation seemed to be a century or two prior to the oldest, 14th-century, mss (1912 1357) went unmentioned.

at a time when any attention, however indirect, to religious matters could still be interpreted as an anti-Soviet activity, and he dared—in the high season of Stalin's anti-Semitic measures—to suggest positive Jewish influence on Russian culture. Not until after Stalin's death in 1953 could his theses be published. A sort of belated *avtoreferat* (1956a) summarizes the work, concluding that Esther was translated directly from the Hebrew in Rus′ no later than 1190, and that it was but one of several works translated from Hebrew in this early period. A scant ten pages (207–216) deals with the text and language of Esther. The tone is utterly assured, and the major conclusions are repeated with varied wording. A casual reader may be disturbed by the rather disorganized argumentation, the anecdotal character of the data, the obvious misunderstandings and factual errors. Yet the constant implication of many "etceteras" and offhand references to a putative vast body of evidence allows one to grant that the conclusions are not implausible. In fact, this oft-cited article has become the basis of a Russian dogma that Esther (unquestionably) and some other works (probably) guarantee the existence of a school of translators in Rus′ in the 12th (and possibly 11th) century.[28]

In7.4 Not until 1978, when Meščerskij published the full text of Esther, was it possible for scholars without direct access to Soviet libraries to make independent analyses.[29] Two Israeli Slavists, Moshé **Altbauer** and Moshe **Taube**, prepared studies for the 1983 International Congress of Slavists in Kiev. Their papers were merged into an article that was edited by H. G. **Lunt** and published in 1984. The firm conclusion was that the Slavonic Esther was not translated directly from Hebrew, but from Greek; thus they agreed with Sobolevskij against Evseev and Meščerskij. Anatolij A. **Alekseev**, a pupil and devoted follower of Meščerskij's, responded by repeating the old theses (1987a), and Lunt and Taube offered more detailed analyses of Meščerskij's and Alekseev's assumptions and arguments (1988).[30] Lunt and Taube outlined the hypothesis of a lost Greek Esther for biblical scholars in 1994. Andrej **Arxipov** expresses dissatisfaction with this hypothesis in a sketchy essay (1994, republished under a different name in 1995) that seems to be based on Alekseev's presentation, although bibliographic references to our English-language 1984 and 1988 articles are included. Arxipov hesitantly posits a hypothetical translator who knew Hebrew and Greek, and who translated Esther from the MT into Slavonic, looking at the LXX from time to time. This desultory analysis of some fifty examples and eight names (from a text whose manuscript base he does not specify) fails, in our opinion, to validate Arxipov's assumptions.

[28] Soviet scholarship never discussed Meščerskij's work in detail precisely because it involved the dangerous mix of religious and Jewish controversies, and the conclusions were highly favorable to the approved thesis of Russian cultural superiority. Moreover, the article, published in Petrozavodsk, was scarcely accessible even for many Soviet scholars. In the appropriate sections of this book, usually in footnotes, we cite and analyze in detail every statement about Esther that Meščerskij makes in this hard-to-get but ubiquitously influential essay. [In 1995, this article was reprinted in a volume that reached us late in 1997; the faulty Roman transcriptions of Hebrew words and phrases have been replaced by Hebrew-alphabet equivalents that are not always correct. We regret that we could not adjust the paging in our references. Most of the items we mention fall between pp. 204–218 of 1956a, 278–296 of the reprint.] Hereafter, we usually cite this article as M56a.

[29] Hereafter, in references, we will usually cite this edition as M78a.

[30] Anatolij Alekseev's repeated assertions about putative early Rusian translations from several languages constitute a refusal to deal with scholarly argumentation. Instead of methodically demonstrating why he disagrees with certain theses and systematically adducing facts that support his view, he merely cites out-dated works and declares, without explanations, that long-standing puzzles are not puzzles at all (1996). His insistent declarations are not supported by reasoned discussion of the available evidence; they are ritual recitations of an article of faith.

EDITION

E1 The Slavonic book of Esther is known only from East Slavic manuscripts, and it is always in the context of other Old Testament books. We know of thirty-one mss written before 1600 that contain the complete book; they are listed in the accompanying table.[1] Chance fragments, apparently copied from two stray folia, are found on the last page of the Xlebnikov copy of the early southern Rusian chronicles (see below), and an even shorter bit is in another ms.[2] The usual position for Esther is after the Four Kingdoms (MT 1–2 Samuel, 1–2 Kings), which are reckoned as a unit, the Tetrabasileion. The East Slavic tradition, which is not attested before c1350, counts Esther as the tenth book and the Tetrabasileion as the ninth book, following the Pentateuch (Genesis, Exodus, Leviticus, Numbers, Deuteronomy) of Hebrew tradition, plus the three books that fill out the Octateuch of Greek tradition (Joshua, Judges, Ruth).[3]

1 Our major source is the efficient handlist of OT manuscripts in Mathiesen 1983a. In principle we follow Mathiesen and others who consider it improbable that manuscripts produced after 1600 will provide any significant evidence for the history of pre-Gennadian OT texts. Meščerskij 1956a knew of 18 mss; his numbers are noted in parentheses in column f of our table. We omit his #13, a 17th-century copy of his #10 (our 25).

2 Ms 41 of Mathiesen's list (GPB, Pogodin 84), has only Esther 3:7–16, cf. Tvorogov-Zagrebin 70.

3 Esther is not found in this position in Greek, Latin, or Hebrew usage.

Manuscript Sources

a: number of manuscript used in this book
b: M - Moscow, SP - St. Petersburg, B - Bucharest, V - Vilnius, W - Warsaw
c: BA - Academy Library, Bucarest; BAN - Library of the Russian Academy of Sciences; BN - National Library, Warsaw; GIM - Historical Museum; MCAB - Library of the Lithuanian Academy of Sciences, Vilnius; RGB - Russian State Library (formerly GBL - Lenin Library); RNB - Russian National Library (formerly GPB - St. Petersburg Public Library)
d: signature of manuscript
e: date of manuscript
f: number in Mathiesen's *Handlist*, 1983a (number in Meščerskij 1956a 203–4)
g: number in Šmidt 1966, *Predvar. sp.. . .XI–XIV v.,* if marked *.
number in Turilov 1986, *Predvar. sp.. . .XV v.,* if no mark.
h: siglum used in this book, see §**E7** below.

a	b	c	d	e	f	g	h
1	M	RGB	TSL 2 (2027)	end 14th–beg. 15th century	69 (1)	1302*	T
2	SP	RNB	Q.I.2	beg. 15th century	28 (2)	437	Q
3	M	GIM	Čud. 25[1]	last qtr. 15th century	98 (-)	1801	
4	SP	RNB	Sol. 3/75[2]	end 15th–beg. 16th century	45 (5)	2494	
5	SP	RNB	Kir.-Bel. 4/9	end 15th–beg. 16th century	32 (6)	2498[3]	E
6	SP	RNB	Kir.-Bel. 5/10	end 15th–beg. 16th century	33 (7)	2499[3]	
7	M	RGB	Volok. 12	16th century	88 (-)		
8	W	BN	BOZ 105	c1490	134 (-)		W

a	b	c	d	e	f	g	h
9	SP	BAN	Osn. Sobr. 17.13.12	16th century	14 (-)		
10	SP	RNB	Sof. 82	16th century	42 (4)		
11	M	GIM	Sinod. 462[1]	1530s	116 (-)		
12	V	MACB	52/224	16th century	132 (-)		V
13	SP	RNB	Pogod. 77	beg. 16th century	431		
14	M	GIM	Bars. 2[1]	1490s		2492	
15	SP	RNB	Q.I.838	c1500		449	S
16	M	RGB	Und. 1	c1483	79 (3)	1799	U
17	SP	RNB	NSRK 1918:F.27	15th–16th century	36 (-)	3190	
18	M	GIM	Uvar. 18/3 [1]	1470s	121 (16)	1800	
19	M	RGB	MDA 12	2nd hf. 15th century	51 (18)	1797	
20	SP	BAN	Osn. Sobr. 45.13.4	15th–16th century	18 (17)		A
21	SP	RNB	Kir.-Bel. 1/6	16th century	29 (9)		
22	M	RGB	Tixonr. 704	16th century			Tn
23	SP	RNB	Kir.-Bel. 7/1084[4]	c1470	34 (-)	3414	
24	SP	BAN	Osn. Sobr. 17.17.9	16th century	15 (8)		
25	M	GIM	Sinod. 915	1499 *G* [5] 119 (10)	336		G
26	M	GIM	Sinod. 21	1558 *G*	107 (11)		
27	M	GIM	Sinod. 30	16th century *G*	108 (12)		
28	M	GIM	Uvar. 1/652	16th century *G*	120 (14)		
29	SP	BAN	Osn. Sobr. 33.10.4	end 15th century	17 (-)	2495	
30	B	BA	Ms. slav. 86	16 c.	7 (-)		
31	M	RGB	Volok. 9	2nd hf. 15th century	85 (15)	1808	B

Note 1: For the dating of mss 3, 11, 14, and 18 we are indebted to Natalia Kobiak and Andrej Pliguzov.
Note 2: Ms 4 is labelled Sol 3/73 by Meščerskij, but 75/75 in Turilov 1986; we follow the reference in Mathiesen 1983a 22 that derives from Porfir′ev et al.
Note 3: Turilov indicates that 2498 and 2499 contain Prophets; in fact both have Joshua, Judges, Ruth, Tetrabasileion, and Esther.
Note 4: Descriptions of this ms do not mention Esther; we are indebted to Elena Švarc of the RNB manuscript division for informing us that Esther is in the ms.
Note 5: *G* indicates copies of the Gennadius Bible.

E2.1 The sequence Tetrabasileion-Esther is found in mss 2–21 of our list, and in ms 1 the scribe explicitly points out that he is jumping from Ruth, the eighth book, to Esther, the tenth. After the 'Amen' which ends the text of Ruth on folio 120r, the scribe writes:

> ѡкончавшє оубо ѡсмыꙗ книгы руфь. тачє по си^{х} начїнают сѧ девѧтыꙗ книгы цр̅^{с}ства. ꙗжє нарїцают сѧ тєтровасилиѡсъ. рекшє четырє цр̅^{с}тва. ꙗжє соуть индѣ писаны. по сих жє по плѣнєньи иер^{с}лмьли. и прєсєлєньи вавилоньстѣ^{м} начинаю^{т} сѧ дєсѧтыꙗ кнїгы гл̅емыа єсфїри. имжє є^{с} начало сицє.[4]

The full ten books of this Slavonic десятикнижие or Decateuch are found in seven

[4] Not having access to this note, Mathiesen 1983b 198 was led to remark that "there is even one manuscript in which [Esther] occurs after Ruth"; his statement is true, but must not be understood as proof that the ideal sequence is violated by this exception.

manuscripts (14, 16–21), and books six through ten (including Esther) in twelve (2–13).[5] In ms 15 the Tetrabasileion and Esther follow the *Bogoslovie* of John the Exarch;[6] the juxtaposition was not intentional, but came about when two defective manuscripts of different origins were bound together.[7]

E2.2 The codices containing one or more of these "historical" OT books often also have non-biblical items of varying length, usually concerning the history of Greece and Rome. Thus in ms 1 (TSL 2) Esther is followed by miscellaneous short pieces that are largely concerned with chronology and calendars.[8] Ms 16 contains more OT books and the Trinity Chronograph (which includes a special redaction of the *Aleksandrija)*; ms 17 is a copy of 16 (omitting certain items). Mss 18–20 contain the Academy Chronograph, 20 being a copy of 18.[9] Ms 21 has the chronicle known as Летописец Еллинский и Римский. Ms 22 has another chronograph, that incorporates a distinctively unusual form of Esther (see E4.3 below). Ms 23 is a "хронограф особого состава" that contains Joshua, Judges, Ruth, and Esther plus Hamartolos and excerpts from the *Chronographic Paleja*.[10] The compilers of the chronographs and various types of *Paleja* obviously regarded these OT books as historical sources, to be used in whole or in part to retell events of the past.[11]

E3 The Slavonic Bible compiled in the 1490s at the behest of Archbishop Gennadius of Novgorod is found in mss 25–28. Here Esther is removed from the more specifically historical context (Decateuch and/or chronographic texts) and placed between Judith and Job, in accord with Latin tradition. Mss 29–31 are miscellanies of OT books in the Gennadian redaction; Esther is between Judith and Job in 29, between Judith and Wisdom in 30 and 31.[12]

5 Tvorogov and Zagrebin (1988 66) imply that ms 13 (Pogodin 77) has an additional work, a *Life of Elijah* between 3 Ki and 4 Ki. This is surely a misunderstanding. The deeds of Elijah are recounted in 3 Ki, and just before 3Ki 17:1 mss G (and its copies, GorNev I 41) and S insert a heading, житьє Ильи пророка, while W has бытьє Ильи пророка and the standard LXX text continues. See Lebedev 36.

6 We use the traditional Slavonic title for the originally OCS translation of the Ἔκθεσις ἀκριβὴς τῆς ὀρθοδόξου πίστεως by John of Damascus, made by John the Exarch early in 10th-century Bulgaria. It has been published by Linda Sadnik. Ms 15 is not among the manuscripts she utilized for her edition.

7 The Exarch text starts in the fourth *Slovo,* corresponding to Sadnik 1.68 (34b6), and breaks off in the thirty-eighth *Slovo,* Sadnik 3.20a (267a3), with the end of folio 94. Folium 95 begins a new gathering with the last words of 1 Kingdoms 20:10 (ѡц҃ь твои злѣ). The Tetrabasileion continues to the end, but fol. 297 ends at the beginning of 4 Ki 25:29, и измѣ[ни ризы]; a single page must be missing, with only the few lines of verses 29 and 30. Esther begins with fol 298 and ends on 313; the final page, 313v, remains blank.

8 The 1878 description of Troice-Sergievskij mss identifies the additional materials as follows: 137–143, от книг Хронографа, 143; О Пророцѣх и о Пророчицах; 144, О именех глаголемых жидовьскым языком в книгах церковных сказаною, преложено на разум; 151 об., Св. Епифания от Панария (отрывок), от Анкюрота (исчисление народов от трех сынов Ноя); 156, Сказание в образ притчи о житьи человѣчьстѣ. The third item is a dictionary including explanations of Jewish names and definitions of Greek and occasionally Slavic terms, based on a translation from a Greek work. For the text see Kovtun 418–20.

9 Cf. Tvorogov 1975 17, fn. 37. (M56a 204 incorrectly labels ms 19 [his #18] as "TSL 1/12, 16th century"). A component of this chronograph is the Slavonic version of a portion of Josephus's *History of the Jewish War,* cf. Meščerskij 1958a 16. Note that we use *chronograph* as an equivalent of Russian хронограф, referring to specific written works.

10 Most details are from Popov, *Обзор хронографов,* I 215–17, cited in Tvorogov 1975 12, fn. 18; it remained for Elena Švarc to establish the presence of Esther in this ms.

11 Often books are abridged. The story of Esther in the 1512 Chronograph (PSRL 22/1 165–6) is drastically condensed, but though it still retains some oddities of the old translation (e.g., прутъ 'scepter'), it is not helpful for reconstructing the *pervospisok.*

12 Several books in ms 30 represent the Gennadian text-form (cf. Mathiesen 1983a 34); from the limited data provided in Meščerskij's notes (1978a), Esther appears to be among them.

E4 Our evidence comes chiefly from photocopies of mss 1, 2, 8, 12, 15, 16, 22, and 25, supplemented by notes Taube made on ms 7.[13] It appears that all texts derive from a single copy, very likely not much older than the middle of the 14th century.

E4.1 The copies we have studied belong to three types: conservative, innovating, and hybrid. The older copies 1 and 2 share characteristics that set them clearly apart from the common text of the younger ones 8 and 12. (The chronographic version in Tn stands apart: it is radically innovating, but preserves important passages that are missing elsewhere.) The Gennadius Bible of 1499 (ms 25, hereafter G) and ms 15 (hereafter S) contain hybrid texts that lie approximately midway between the other two types. Another kind of hybrid is found in two Esther fragments in the Xlebnikov Codex of early Rus′ chronicles, used by the editors of the Hypatian Chronicle (Полное собрание русских летописей, II, 1923) for variants.[14] See E4.3 below.

E4.11 The oldest ms is 1 (TSL 2, Russian State [formerly Lenin] Library: hereafter T), and has been available to us from the beginning of our studies of Esther in the form of photocopies of folia 120–136 of the codex. We should like to record here our indebtedness to Moshé Altbauer for providing these copies. The most detailed description of the whole ms we know is Lebedev 1890, 10–16, but he concentrated on the book of Joshua, and his point of view is extremely old-fashioned. He does provide the information that folios 1–56 (including Joshua) and 137–166 (non-biblical materials) were written by one scribe, while the books of Judges, Ruth, and Esther are in a different hand, apparently with a somewhat different orthographical system. The 1966 *Preliminary listing* (Šmidt) dates T "End 14th [?]–beg. 15th century" (no. 1302); the 1986 summary list (Turilov), dealing exclusively with the 15th century, does not include it: we conclude that the current consensus puts T—the only parchment ms in the list—in the 1390s. Manuscript 2 (St Petersburg Public Library Q.I.2: hereafter Q) can be dated by watermarks to the beginning of the 15th century.[15] Therefore these two are of about the same age.[16]

E4.12 The other manuscripts we have studied were all written some three generations later; apparently after about 1475 OT manuscripts were in demand and many copies were made. Mss 8 (hereafter W, for Warsaw) and 12 (hereafter V, for Vilnius) share both conservative

[13] In June, 1991, Taube examined ms 1 (TSL 2) to clear up some minor points that could not be decided on the basis of the photocopies. He also was able to note significant variants from ms 7 (Volokolamskij 12), which is not on Meščerskij's list, and to consult ms 16 (Undol′skij 1, a well-known codex referred to by Meščerskij for Esther and used by Mixajlov as the base for his editions of Genesis and Ruth). A photocopy of ms 16 was obtained by Taube in August 1997. Although it lacked one frame (with 9:12–24), it allowed us to affirm that, as Kloss concluded (1971), Und 1 is a copy of ms 1 (T), with corrections by a contemporary hand.

[14] Five of the 31 listed mss are copies of other listed items; we have direct information on nine mss of Esther and partial data from 6 more, leaving ten about whose text we know nothing. Roždestvenskij, Evseev, Sobolevskij, and Meščerskij agree that all copies that they looked at go back to a single *Vorlage* or *pervospisok*. Though it seems improbable that a really new text-type has gone unnoticed, one or more of these codices may, like Xleb and Tixonravov 704, contain significant new details about the *pervospisok*. We hope that each of them will be studied carefully.

[15] Dmitrij M. Bulanin kindly examined the codex for us. He reported that a single scribe wrote the entire text, except for the last page, which is a later replacement (containing Est 9:23–10:3). He found three watermarks: leopard, type Lixačev N 2448, 2449 (beginning 15th century); goose, type Briquet N 12104 (1399–1400); siren, type Mošin-Traljić N 7019 (1394). The last is particularly common at the beginning of the ms. We are grateful to Dr. Bulanin for his help.

[16] Meščerskij 1956a 205 puts mss 16 (see above, note 13), 21, and 23 with 1 and 2 as sharing the same type of text, but his criteria are inadequate and Roždestvenskij's rather vague citations of ms 21 do not support this view.

T (2) parchment, 1390s	: **W** (8) 1490s		
Q (1) watermarks of earliest 1400s	: **V** (12) 16th century		
U (16) 1480s?	: **G** (25) 1499	: **Tn** (22) Tixonravov 704: 16th century	
S (15) c1500	: **Vlk** (7) 16th century	: **X** c1575	

T and Q are textually almost identical (Q better), common ancestor ?*1370.
W and V share many innovations, diverge on others; often agree with QT.
U is a copy of T which then has been "corrected" from a text of the WV type.
S is a copy of the hybrid text that resulted from corrections to U.
G is the same sort of hybrid, but with a different distribution of WV-type readings.
Vlk is very similar to G but with individual innovations.
X is fragmentary, but preserves readings omitted in QTWV, along with WV innovations.
Tn has been idiosyncratically modified, but shares with X readings omitted in QTWV.

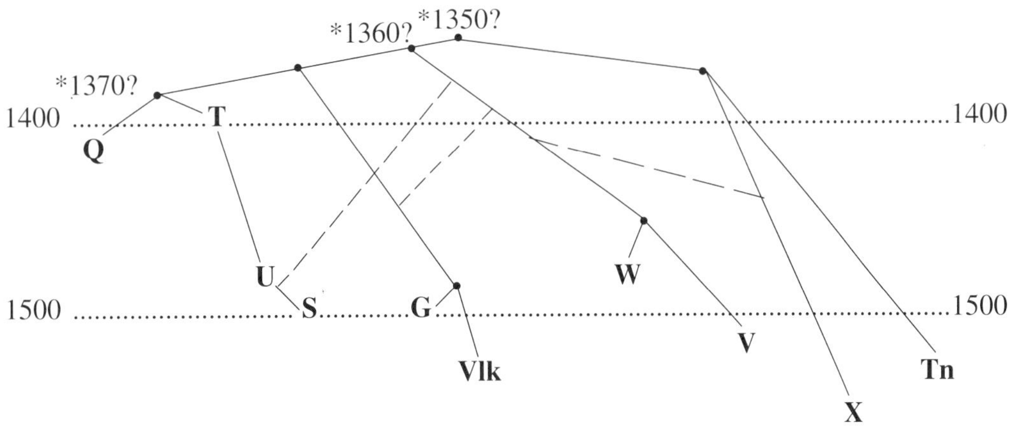

Stemma of witnesses of Esther in Slavonic

readings and innovations and serve to define a second type. Both the older QT text and the younger WV text appear to have arisen by successive copying with no conscious editorial intervention. Ms 15 and G, however, show different combinations of readings from the QT and WV types of text.[17] These surely resulted from scribes or correctors who had two or more manuscripts at hand and who undertook to choose just what words and phrases to include in the new copy. A model of this type is provided by ms 16 (hereafter U): it was copied in the 1480s from T, and thus is essentially identical with with the older TQ type of text. However, it was extensively corrected—according to Kloss 1971 by the Muscovite bookman Ivan Černyj (who died in 1490)—on the basis of the WV tradition. Surely his intention was to produce a text that would serve as a model for new copies; the text of such copies would be a blend. The texts of 15 and G represent two other blends of the QT and WV text-types. (See App. II.)

[17] Ms 15 (Q.I.838) is ascribed by Turilov 1986 to the *early* 15th century. V. M. Zagrebin kindly looked at the codex and dates it to the very *end* of the 15th century (fleur-de-lis watermark, Briquet 7233, 1485); we are grateful for his aid. Andrej Pliguzov, on paleographical grounds, dates the Esther text to the first decades of the 16th century.

E4.2 The filiation of Q and T and of W and V leads to two fairly certain fore-texts. The common readings of the two oldest copies that are opposed to variants in the two younger copies (QT versus WV) imply a common source we might term *1370. When all four agree, they point to the ancestor of all known copies of Esther except for Tn and the Xlebnikov fragments. We refer to this important hypothetical stage as *1360.

E4.3 Two very different witnesses furnish readings that, with *1360, establish a common source for all the surviving copies: the Tixonravov Chronicle and the Xlebnikov Chronicle.

The first, ms 22 (hereafter Tn), is a unique compilation that imbeds the book of Esther in accounts of the Persian and Jewish history involving in particular Daniel. Istrin showed (1912b) that the non-biblical texts in Tn have been independently edited to produce idiosyncratic versions. Esther has also undergone extensive rewriting, but the text obviously is directly descended from a copy ancestral to *1360. For our purposes the most important traits are the presence of clauses that are missing in both the QT and WV traditions as we know them (such as 3:4, 9:4, 9:16), and the absence of superfluous words (as in 3:14, 9:17).[18]

The Xlebnikov chronicle, containing the Повѣсть временъ и лѣтъ, the Kievan Chronicle, and the Galician-Volhynian Chronicle, was copied in about 1575. The last entry concerns the year 1291. Immediately, in mid-line, Esther 2:1 follows (with omission of the first words): (ста^л^ сѧ гнѣвъ Ахаѕъвероса), continuing into 2:21 въ д҃ни тыа Мордоухаи, jumping then into 9:2 ч҃лвкь нѣкыи^ж^. The text continues, with some minor confusions, into 9:17. After the words въ д҃і д҃нь it goes back to 2:1, in slightly different wording, и състави сѧ гнѣвь ц҃рѧ Ахаѕвероса, въспомѧнȣ Вастїи—this is the end of the manuscript.[19] It is obvious that the scribe copied two stray folia from an older manuscript; why he did so is unknown. The orthography has been updated and the wording of these verses is eclectic, usually corresponding to QT or to WV, with individual errors. The value of these fragments lies in their agreement with Tn on the wording of 9:4 and 9:16.

E4.4 The hypothetical *pervospisok* to which all evidence points will be called *1350.[20] It was a poor text, with serious corruptions in many verses, and numerous internal inconsistencies. The only available term of comparison is the standard Hebrew of the MT. In terms of expectations based on the MT, Q reflects *1350 most faithfully, but it has some singular deviations that can be corrected by T. Some of QT's common deviations from the sense of the Hebrew can be corrected by WV, but on the whole the later mss show further deterioration and corruption of the text.[21] The differences between W and V surely arose after c1400

18 Taube was able to look at the manuscript in 1991, but did not have time to study its idiosyncratic traits. Tn's text of Esther has many omissions and additions of its own, many blatant errors, and extensive (and often misguided) reshaping of numerous clauses; we regarded the notes Taube had made with reserve. In August 1997, when this book was already in the hands of the printers, Taube obtained a photocopy of Tn. (We should like to express our thanks to Angelica Sineva for her aid.) We have incorporated information from Tn into our Slavonic text of *1350, but our exploitation of Tn's individual variants in the commentary and in discussions of lexicon is spotty. More information on Tn is given in Appendix III.

19 The manuscript has been published in facsimile, *The Old Rus' Kievan and Galician-Volhynian Chronicles: The Ostroz'kyj (Xlebnikov) and Četvertyns'kyj (Pogodin) Codices* (Harvard Library of Early Ukrainian Literature, Texts: vol. VIII). The Esther passages are on pp. 391–93 of the edition, starting with ms p. 384, line 13.

20 We will use the term *pervospisok* in order to avoid the misunderstandings that might be associated with *original* or *archetype, protograph, Vorlage* or *model.*

21 Apart from orthographical differences, Q has about 22 singular variants, of which 9 are inferior to T's equivalent. T has over 50 singular readings, only two of which are superior to Q. WV deviate from QT in more than 180 instances; perhaps 15 of these are preferable to QT readings.

and do not concern us here.[22] Our aim is first to restore as far as possible the text of *1350 and then to speculate about the relation of that faulty text to hypothetical stages in its history.

E5.1 We estimate that the *pervospisok* was written in the middle or early 1300s by an East Slavic scribe. Its major characteristics, determined by comparison with the Hebrew text, are more than 20 omissions and at least a dozen additions that are of textual importance, along with the following faulty words or phrases (unless otherwise noted, QTWV agree).[23]

1:17 вниде: H 'went out'
1:18 рекоша: future tense required
1:19 аще: {ать}
1:19 пришла: future required
1:20 срамоту QT, драготу as replacement: H 'honor'
2:7 домаѵадицю сироту (WV сиру.то): H 'Hadassah'
2:9 пред нью Q, нею TWV] H has masculine, 'him' - н{имь}, or Acc н{ь}.
2:23 въображена: 'found'
3:4 ине = иже
3:9 стръю Q, строю TV, страю W: H 'stewards, officials'
3:15 всплака сѧ: H 'was perplexed'
4:1 сукно: H 'ashes'
4:3 сукна: H 'ashes'
4:6 вниде: H 'went out'
5:9 не подвигнуща сѧ ни приклѧнуща: H 'and did not stand up or tremble'
5:10 и въѕдъхнувъ: H 'and he contained himself'
6:12 повѣсивъ главу свою: H 'with his head covered'
7:1 къ: H съ 'with'
8:13 оумьсти сѧ: infinitive
8:14 внидоша: 'went out'
9:1 враѕи: вра{гы} 'by (their) enemies'
9:15 .д҃. QWV, .ід҃. with і added later, and in wrong place T: H '14th'

E5.2 The three text-types represented by QT, WV, and Tn surely arose by normal scribal activity, with no systematic editorial intervention. The book of Esther in the Gennadius Bible of 1499 is quite a different matter. Its text of the first 164 verses (ch. 1–9, excluding 10:1–3) agrees with QT in more than 90 readings and with WV in more than 70 that cannot be ascribed to the reconstructible *1350, along with close to 50 singular readings.[24] These

22 W and V differ in over 50 instances, whereby W usually has the better text. With regard to the *pervospisok*, W provides a single superior reading (2:9), where V omits the pronoun еи and QT have only е. V has the historically correct *č* in цр҃ѵинъ in 1:18, but this spelling does not necessarily go back to *1350.

23 Omissions and additions are signalled in the text, pp. 26–54 below, and discussed in the commentaries to individual verses, pp. 81–140.

24 Comparisons made by Taube show that in Joshua, Judges, the Kingdoms, and Ruth, mss W and G are extremely close; they surely share a common recent ancestor. In Esther, however, W differs significantly from G.

verses of Esther are the work of an earlier editor who consciously blended the wordings of at least two manuscripts, representing the older QT and the more contemporary WV traditions.[25] Then the "additions" of LXX were translated into Slavonic from the Vulgate and appended as 10:3 through ch. 16; and finally 10:1–3 were also translated from the Latin and substituted for the older Sl text.[26] The Gennadius redaction of the first nine chapters is markedly inferior to the already corrupt text of either the QT or the WV tradition, and the new parts are so literally rendered as to be incomprehensible in places. It is no wonder that Maksim Grek made a new translation from the LXX and that the editors of the Ostrih Bible accepted, on the whole, Maksim's wording (see Taube-Olmsted).

Editorial principles

E6 This edition is intended primarily to present the text of manuscript Q.I.2 in a form that will allow readers to reach their own conclusions about details. Inasmuch as there are corruptions and doubtful spots that mar or destroy the sense and even the continuity of the story, we have found it necessary occasionally to provide signals that mark omissions and additions and even to make a few outright emendations. We have tried to label all of our editorial interventions. The usual principles of dividing the text into words and traditional verses have been followed, with capitalization of proper nouns and initial words in sentences. Punctuation has been kept to a minimum.

E7 Supplementary evidence is given in the variants that accompany each verse. Sigla of the manuscripts we are able to cite for our edition are as follows (cf. the full list in the table in E1, above).

T : Russian State (formerly Lenin) Library ms. Troice-Sergievskij 2/2027, c1400 (1)
Q : St. Petersburg Public Library ms. Q.I.2, beg. 15th century (2)
A : Russian Academy Library, St. Petersburg, ms. 45.13.4, 15th–16th century (20)
B : Russian State (formerly Lenin) Library ms. Volokolamsk 9, late 15th century (31)
E : Evseev's edition (ch. 1) of St. Petersburg Pub. Lib. ms. Kirillo-Belozerskij 4/9, 15th–16th century (5)
U : Russian State (formerly Lenin) Library ms Undol′skij 1, 1480s (16)
G : The 1499 Gennadius Bible, Moscow Historical Museum, Sinod. 915 (25)
V : Lithuanian Academy Library ms. 52/224, 16th century, Altbauer 1988 (12)
S : St. Petersburg Public Library ms Q.I.838, (end 15th–)beg. 16th century (15)
Tn: Russian State (formerly Lenin) Library ms. Tixonravov 704, 16th century (22)
W : Warsaw National Library ms. BOZ 105, c1490 (8)
X : St. Petersburg Public Library ms. F IV 230, c1575 (see E4.3)

E7.1 Our work is based on photocopies of Q, T, S, U, G, V, W, and Tn. Variants from A and B are taken from Meščerskij's 1978 edition of Esther; they are to be regarded with caution.[27]

[25] The diagnostic readings noted by Taube for ms 7 (Volok. 12) show essentially the same blend of QT and WV variants that characterizes G.

[26] Ms 7 has ch. 10 in the wording of the old translation.

[27] Meščerskij's edition is unsatisfactory and unreliable. Our detailed assessment is given in Appendix I.

E7.2 Variants are intended largely to explain the emendations introduced into the text. Items cited before the bracket] belong to Q and T unless otherwise indicated. Thus for 2:6

ѡхониемь G] иѡхониемь SWV, ѡхонїею TnX

means that ѡхониемь occurs in Q, T, and G, while for 2:7

бѧше G] бѣша T, бѣѧше W, бѣаше SV

means that бѧше is only in Q and G, since another form is specified after the] for T.

Our major aim is to illuminate the oldest establishable form of the Slavonic text of Esther, the *pervospisok* from which all known copies are descended. Tn is mentioned chiefly when it provides a significant contrast to QT.[28] A secondary aim is to show the sources of the Gennadius Esther; to that purpose we provide variants that establish the main outlines of the WV branch of younger copies in contrast to the conservative QT state of affairs, plus the information from the hybrid or compromise text S.[29]

E7.3 Fuller discussion of each item is in the commentaries to individual verses (pp. 81–140). In citing parallels, we use H to refer to the Hebrew text, LXX for the ordinary Septuagint Greek, with L for the shorter alpha-text and O for the Origen-based variants; Greek sources are cited from Robert Hanhart's 1966 edition of Esther.

Russian translation

E8 Solving problems about the relations between the Slavonic text and the Hebrew (which is its ultimate source) requires judgments about the faithfulness of the Slavonic phraseology to the Hebrew—or the degree and nature of the deviations. We assume that most of our readers are Western-trained Slavists with little or no knowledge of Hebrew. Therefore, we provide a modern Russian translation—a maximally literal rendering—to serve as a term of comparison that is more useful than a text in English would be. Proper names have been transcribed in accord with Hebrew pronunciation.[30] In order to show distinctions not possible in modern Russian, we use the letter *fita* for 'weak ת' (e.g., Θаршиш 1:14). 'Strong תּ' is transcribed т (e.g. Вашти), except for the many instances of Есѳирь, where we retain the spelling established by a tradition going back to the different usage found in LXX and related texts. Since the Synodal text ordinarily transcribes Hebrew [h] with the letter "г" (e.g., Hadassah > Гадасса), we apply the rule rigorously, and Haman becomes Гаман rather than the traditional Аман. This defamiliarization allows a direct confrontation of Hebrew-based spellings of names with the attested forms in the Slavonic text, and helps to illustrate the systematic differences in the two approaches.

28 Thus for 2:6 we record that Tn has ѡхонїею (without specifying the orthographic variant охонїею for X) to indicate the possibility that *1350 had an a-stem desinence in this masculine name. For 2:7, the fact that Tn and X agree with QG is unimportant.

29 The details of the post-1400 proliferation of variants do not concern us and in any case we have solid (but limited) data only from one other manuscript, Volokolamsk 12 (ms 7). This material contributes nothing to establishing the readings of *1350 and therefore we do not include it in our variants. The fact that U is a copy of T that was corrected in the 1480s makes it an instructive sample of how some editors worked, and we offer a brief survey of examples in Appendix II.

30 Note that the version in modern Synodal editions has a number of reminiscences of the LXX text. In particular, the names show an uneasy compromise between traditional forms from Slavonic biblical texts (e.g., Артаксеркс, Астинь, instead of Ахашверош, Вашти), and new transcriptions based on Hebrew pronunciation.

E8.1 The Russian wording was constructed to reflect the Hebrew phrasing as accurately as possible within the constraints of Russian grammar. Style has been sacrificed to literalism; **this is not to be regarded as a work to be read independently**, but only as a device to help readers with no knowledge of Hebrew to understand the problems and our discussion. Two typographical devices provide additional information. *Italicized words* mark elements added in order to make acceptable Russian. Items in square brackets [] give more idiomatic equivalents of words chosen to reflect certain Hebrew lexemes.

Editorial conventions

E9.1 *Abbreviations* have normally been expanded without comment, and superscript letters have been brought down to the line without comment. In a number of cases we use superscript letters to denote items we have added to resolve abbreviations. Thus бы^{с} is printed быс^{ть}.

E9.2 *Emendations* and indications of *omissions or additions* have been kept to a minimum. Two theoretical terms of comparison are assumed: (1) the shape of the original Slavonic translation, which can be measured only by reference to the Hebrew text; and (2) the details of the *pervospisok*—the lost copy, probably made by an East Slavic scribe in the 14th century, from which all known copies apparently are descended. In principle, we do not emend passages which make reasonable sense, even if that sense does not correspond to expectations based on the meaning of the Hebrew text.

- The *degree sign* ° marks instances where, if we take the Hebrew wording as the standard, a word or phrase has been omitted (e.g., in 1:1 "that [particular] Ahašweroš," in 1:2 "all").
- *Parentheses* enclose the obvious glosses which give the names of the months (e.g., 2:16, 3:17).
- *Square brackets* [ ] enclose superfluous elements (e.g. [и], 1:11).
- *Curly brackets* { } mark editorial emendations. Most of them are reconstructions of the hypothetical 14th-century *pervospisok* and they are usually justified by manuscript evidence from mss W, V, S, Tn, G, and X (8, 12, 15, 22, 25) that is provided in the variant apparatus to the text (e.g., своєго in 1:2). A few, however, have been introduced to rectify sense-distorting deviations already present in the *pervospisok*, and they are based on the Hebrew text; this includes omissions (e.g., {бысть} 2:8), and, rarely, other modifications (e.g., врази, standing for Instrumental plural, is printed вра{гы}, 9:1; †пришла 1:19 is inappropriate grammatically). The problems they involve will be discussed individually in the commentary (suggesting, e.g., an original сатрапомъ for 1:3, a conditional or future for 1:19). A word or phrase enclosed by daggers (e.g. †ижє† 1:13, †ижє рєкоша† 1:17) involves more complex difficulties that are discussed in the commentary.

E10.1 Since in many cases the precise domain of obscurity or textual corruption is by no means certain, our choice of symbols is not fully consistent; many puzzles which are discussed in the commentaries are not marked in the text at all. Our aim has been to aid the reader without imposing our own views too intrusively. If one attempts to read the text as it stands, without insisting that it correspond closely to the known Hebrew text, it sometimes can easily be parsed, but sometimes the contradictions of sense become intolerable. The problem is that different readers have different degrees of tolerance, often proportionate to one's familiarity with the traditional text. We hope that each reader will examine the text independently so that future discussions can rest on a common basis of items that can be agreed on as certain and other items that doubtless will require further investigation and more detailed discussion.

E10.2 We will not discuss matters of paleography (such as variant shapes of letters and the use of ligatures) that have no textual significance.[31] Not infrequently we find it hard to discern whether a *titlo* or superscript letter is present in a manuscript, but rarely has this made it difficult to decide what the common text of the underlying *Vorlage* was; such cases are discussed in the commentaries. There are clear spellings with Аман- 'Haman,' and with Амон-; when one spelling has been changed to the other, as in 5:8 in T or 7:9 in Q.I.2, it is impossible to tell from the photocopy which is original, but the decision is of little importance.

Spelling conventions

E11 The orthographies of T and Q are unremarkable for the time, and can be regarded as variants of the systems followed by the two scribes of the Laurentian Chronicle of 1377.[32]

E11.1 The sequence оу is used regularly in *unblocked*, or syllable-initial, position, while у follows a consonant-letter (*blocked* position), e.g., тиоунъ but тивунъ, although there are exceptions. Q has оу in blocked position somewhat more often than T. The scribe of T added a small superscript "o," apparently intended to turn Хусъ into Хоусъ and the like. Neither T nor Q has the letter ѥ or the "е лежачее" that mark unblocked position in contemporary manuscripts. Both use an apostrophe to mark any vowel-letter in unblocked position. As for sequences, both scribes occasionally use ї, primarily before another vowel-letter, but also simply as a space-saving device; there is no systematic principle in either manuscript. The letter ы is used after к, г, х; apart from the foreign name Агаги, only аки violates the rule in both manuscripts.[33] We have noted a single possible archaism, but it may represent simply a stylistic mannerism of the scribes: иꙁдрѧднѣѥ (see A1.6).

E11.2 The scribes of T and Q used superscript letters and titla freely (see E11.6 below). Usually there is no difficulty in discerning their intention, but there are obscurities and errors, and in some cases we must conclude that words written in full are based on a misreading of an earlier abbreviated spelling at some point in the history of the text. Thus, for example, the єжє of 5:6, where we expect єсть, surely is based on an earlier є^{с} misread (and possibly then miswritten) as є^{ж}, copied subsequently as єжє. We have provided discussion in the commentaries of each case we felt to be at all doubtful, but otherwise bring

[31] T has obviously been marked up by modern investigators, who have underlined interesting words and made various marginal notes, most of which are illegible in our photos. Since Kloss 1971 remarks that Ivan Černyj made marginal comments and textual corrections in T, someone should examine the emendations in Esther to see whether they might be ascribed to him.

[32] This section deals only with the two oldest copies that form the basis of our edition. Characteristics of W, V, and G are treated in Appendix II, those of Tn in Appendix III.

[33] In T in fact we see ѧкѡ, 1:8, where аки has been corrected to ѧко. It might be tempting to call on the orthographical rule as a justification for seeing ꙗко as the original reading. Yet it is precisely this word аки that illustrates the sequence ки in 12th-century manuscripts, where кы remains the norm. The аки of Q.I.2 affirms the probability that this shared peculiarity is to be attributed to the common model from which the two texts were copied.

superscript letters down to the line and resolve most abbreviations under titlo without comment.

Choice of details from mss Q and T

E11.3 The text of T and Q is essentially identical. Differences include some omissions of words or syllables, but chiefly concern individual letters. Q generally has the superior reading. Thus it has и сътворити мысль мою in 5:8, цр҃євъ мадѣискыхъ in 10:2, своєго in 1:2, and бы in 2:3, all of which are missing from T. It supplies letters or syllables omitted in T, such as ѡграда for града 1:5, єи for є 2:9, or уими for уми 6:10; съсуду for суду 1:7, погыбну for побну 4:16, or любо бѧшє for the incomprehensible любѧшє 2:10. It lacks letters that are superfluous in T, such as людии, not людиєи, 3:6, бѧшє, not болѧшє, 7:9. It has correct letters or syllables where T has lapses, such as ф "500," not ѳ "9" 9:6, 12; прутъ, not пругъ, 4:11; повѣсѧт, not -сит, 5:14; его, not єꙗ, 2:7; жєньского, not -ому, 2:11; оупочиша, not оупооуч҄ыша, 9:17. Yet some of Q's mistakes can be corrected by T's reading, e.g., Q врачюющи 'healing' or perhaps 'working spells,' for 'returning,' T въꙁвращающи сѧ 2:14, Q цр҃и for Dsf, T цр҃ци 7:1.

All discrepancies of this kind will be noted in the variants.

E11.31 The mass of differences between T and Q lies in the spelling of *words which historically contained jers, and the graphic abbreviation of final syllables.* For example, T є^{г} but Q єго, or T гра^{д} but Q градѣ in 2:8, градъ in 8:15, and града in 4:1. Instances with final non-jer vowels are very limited, being particularly common with the reflexive particle сѧ, with жє, and in the adverb пачє and the aorist рєчє. Omission of final jer and superscription of the consonant is common, but since this was a mechanical spacing device that each scribe used at will, the two manuscripts frequently disagree. Thus T has своихъ in 1:17 and своих in 2:10, while Q has the opposite distribution.

In cases of this type we print the fuller form if it is in either manuscript—thus своихъ in both 1:17 and 2:10—with no mention in the apparatus.

E11.32 The spelling of words with old jers varies pervasively. On the whole, Q follows conservative habits. In old liquid diphthongs, T nearly always writes "є" and "o," while Q maintains "ь" and "ъ," e.g., T вєрвьми, Q вьрвьми 1:6, T пєрстєнь, Q пьрстьнь 8:2, T молчиши молчачи, Q мълчиши мълчачи 4:14. T is more likely to spell strong jers with "є" and "o" than Q. Thus in T the prepositions съ, въ, and къ may have "o": e.g., T во всѣх, but Q въ всѣх 2:3; T со мною, Q съ мною, 4:10; T ко оубою, Q къ оубою 4:11.

E11.4 In principle, we reproduce the spellings of Q, but in the case of historical jers or final syllables, we follow T if it is more archaic or more explicit. For example:

9:3 Q вєлможа, T вєльможа, edition = T
1:17 Q всѧ, T в'сѧ: ed. = T
1:19 Q лучши, T лучьши: ed. = T
1:19 Q иꙁидє^{т}, T иꙁидєть: ed. = T
1:19 Q прєда^{с}, T прєдасть: ed. = T
2:1 Q рѣ^{ч}хъ, T рѣчьхъ: ed. = T
4:16 Q сбєри, T събєри: ed. = T

1:12 Q старость, T старостъ: without context they are two different words; this context requires Gpm, so ed. старост{ъ}, with information about all six mss in the variants.
7:9 Q въꙁвышѣ: -шє is better, but no misunderstanding arises, so ed. = Q.[34]
1:6 Q ωстьꙗ, TWV оустьꙗ: the word is not clear, but we favor the majority reading and therefore the edition has {оу}стьꙗ. Variants are given on the facing page.
1:9 Q жьньскыи: ь is an obvious hypercorrection, but one that needlessly distracts attention from the text; we therefore print ж{є}ньскыи, and provide variants.
1:20 QT силна, therefore ed. силна.
4:8 QT да, with no superscript element visible: ed. да{сть}.

E11.5 The names *Mordecai* and *Haman* are spelled as in Q, with no note of the fluctuation in other mss: Мардохаи, Мардахаи, Мардъхаи (etc.) and Аман-, Амон- and, in the later copies, Аммон-.

Abbreviated stems

E11.61 The stem meaning 'king; rule' is strikingly frequent in Esther.[35] It occurs some 236 times, nearly always abbreviated in T and always in Q. Although we cannot always discern a superscript *c* and titlo, we assume that they were originally present. When written out, however, this root has the shape цар- in T; surely this was the normal 14th-century pronunciation. To "restore" the hymnological shape цесар- or either of the older shapes (цьсар- [surely normal East Slavic usage] or the classical цѣсар-) seemed unwise. Thus we have expanded цр̄ь, цр̄ва, цр̄ца, цр̄ство (and the like) to царь, царєва, царица, царство (and the like).

E11.62 Other commonly abbreviated stems are: глагол-, дѣв- (дв̄а, дв̄ца), душ-а, дьн-, милост-, мѣсѧц-, сын-, and чьст-. We have tacitly resolved the abbreviations unless there was a question, in which case we discuss the problem.

[34] The unexpected letter represents a desinence that might possibly have some variants in dialects; we do not believe this spelling is significant, but reproduce Q so that readers can judge for themselves.

[35] The Hebrew text is extraordinary because *mlk* 'king' is the most frequent word, constituting 6.5% of the running text, almost as much as the next two most common words (the accusative-marker '*t* and the relative '*šr*) combined. The derivatives *mlkwt* 'kingdom' and *mlkh* 'queen' bring the total to over 8%.

КНИГЫ {ЄСѲИРИ}

1:1 Бысть въ дн҃и Ахасъвєросовы ° иже царствоваше ѿ Ѡдоу даже и до Хусъ,
седмью и двѣма десѧтьма и 100-мь власти.

1:2 Въ дн҃и ты, єгда сѣде царь Ахасъверосъ на столѣ царства своєго иже въ
Сусанѣ градѣ,

1:3 въ лѣто ° царствиꙗ своєго [и] створи пиръ ° велможамъ своимъ и рабомъ
своимъ, силѣ Фарисѣистѣи и Мадѣистѣї, †странамъ и болѧромъ
ꙁемнымъ [и] иже ихъ ѡ немь,

1:4 єгдаже покаꙁа богатьство [и] чьсти царства своєго и чьсть красоты [и]
величьствиꙗ своєго дн҃ьми многыми, 80 и 100-мь дн҃ии.

1:5 Вънегда же испълн{иша сѧ} дн҃и ты, створи царь всѣмъ людьмъ єликоже
ихъ ѡбрѣте въ Соусанѣ градѣ ѿ велика дажь и до мала [бысть же] пиръ
по 7 дн҃овъ въ дворѣ ѡграда оутрьнего царева.

1:6 Бобрьмь и оутринъмъ и чьрвемь сниманънъ върввми шьлковыми, и
лептугъ на главахъ сребреныхъ, и стълпи мраморѧни, ложа ꙁлата и
сребрена, на блиску камениꙗ драгаго †стѣны и {оу}стыꙗ†.

1:7 И пьꙗху въ съсудѣхъ ꙁлатыхъ и съсоудъ съсоуду неоуподобленъ, но все
раꙁноличь, и вино царьское много ꙗкоже сила царева.

1:8 А питва аки вольна беꙁ нꙋжа, ибо бѧше такъ оуставъ царевъ на всѣхъ
старѣишинахъ до{му} своєго створити волю мужеви мужю.

Title: Книгы иесиѳли Q; Книгы десѧтыꙗ Єсфїрї TU (in margin), Книгы десѧтыꙗ Есфирь (in top margin) S; Книгы гл҃емыѧ Есѳерь WV(E), Книга гл҃емаа Есферь G; Книгы гл҃мыя Естерь Мудраѧ и цр҃ь 20, 24 (Kopanev 9); Книгы прѣимѣꙗ и ѡбъдръжително U, S.

1:2 своего QSGWVEA] om. T

1:3 въ лѣ҃ цр҃твиꙗ QTWV -ства SG] H ‘in the 3rd year’; superscript г҃ added by later hand in T || фарисѣистѣи QG, фарѣсѣистѣи T] фарсїистѣи S, фарисѣисьтѣи и перстѣи WV, прьстѣи A || мадѣистѣи WV] мидїистѣи S, медеистѣи G || болѧромъ SG] болѧрѧмъ W, болѧрамъ VE

1:4 красоты и S] om. и GWVE || ѡ.п.и.рмь Q, · ’ ·п·и·р·мь T, .п҃.й.р.мь S, , .п҃.р҃.мъ G, .п҃.й.р҃. W, п҃.й.р҃. V

1:5 въньгда же GWV] егда ж S || исполниша[с] Tn; испълнѧше Q, исполнѧше TSGWVE || бы[сть] же] om. Tn || по 7 дн҃овъ] по семь дн҃їи V, по седмь дн҃їи GA, по 7 днїи S || ѡграда] града TSGWV || цр҃ва QV, цр҃ева SGWE, ца|рства T

1:6 оутринъмь, -номь T, -омъ S] оудромъ W, оудрѡм V, оутромъ GE || сниманъ.нъ Q] сниманъ.но TGWV, сниманъ S || вьрвьми Q, вервьми TSG] верьми WV, вер’бми E || сребреныхъ SG] сребренахъ WV || на блиску S, -ӡкꙋ G] близу WVE || ѡстьꙗ Q, оустьꙗ TV, оустїа SG, оустиѧ W

1:7 съсоудъ съсоуду QSGWVE] съсоудъ суду T || Q possibly цр҃ское[с], цр҃ское SGWV] цр҃ско T

1:8 такъ QGWV] так[ов]ъ T, таковь S || домоу Tn; до QTSGWVE; || волю SG] волꙋ W, волѫ V

1:1 И было во дни Ахашвероша, — тот *самый* Ахашверош, что царствовал над ста двадцатью семью областями от Годду и до Куша,—

1:2 в дни эти, когда царь Ахашверош сел на престол царства своего, что в Шушане-городе:

1:3 в третий год царствования своего *он* устроил пир для всех князей своих и рабов своих, для *военной* силы персидской и мидийской, для первых сановников и князьей провинций *своих, собравшихся* перед ним,

1:4 показывая богатство славы царства своего и славный блеск величия своего много дней — сто восемьдесят дней.

1:5 И по окончании дней этих устроил царь для всего народа, находившегося в Шушане-городе, от большого и до малого, пир семидневный во дворе внутреннего сада царя.

1:6 Белые и лиловые бумажные *завесы были* прикрепленны льняными и пурпуровыми шнурами и серебряными кольцами *к* мраморным колоннам, золотые и серебряные ложа *стояли на мозаичном* помосте, *выложенном* порфиром, мрамором, перламутром и разноцветными камнями.

1:7 Напитки *подавались* в золотых сосудах, и сосуды *были* разнообразными, и вино царское *было* в обилии, *подобающем* руке царя.

1:8 Питье *шло* по закону, никто не принуждал, потому что так установил царь всем управляющим в доме его, чтобы делали по воле каждого.

1:9 И пакы Вастиꙗ царицꙗ створи пиръ ж{е}ньскыи в' домꙋ †царевѣ иже
царь Ахасъверосъ†.
1:10 Въ дн҃ь 7, вънегда сꙗ оудобрꙗше мысль царева въ винѣ, и рече
Емоуоумановi и Визъсаноу и Харву{н}анови и Вигъфаноу и Ваавахфану
и Зъвихфароу и Варкохасоу, седми старостъ иже служаху предъ царьмь
Ахасъверосъмъ,
1:11 привести Вастию царицю предъ царꙗ въ вѣнци царевѣ показати людьмъ
и велможамъ [и] красоту еꙗ †и еже† добрыи възоръ еꙗ.
1:12 И абие не въсхотѣ царица Васти прити по рѣчи царевѣ иже по рукахъ
старост{ъ}. И разгнѣва сꙗ царь велми зѣло, и гнѣвъ его ражьже сꙗ в
немь.
1:13 И рече царь мудрьцьмъ иже познаꙗху годины иже° рѣчь царева предъ
всѣми иже познаꙗху законъ и [съ]судъ,
1:14 а иже ближнии ему Карсона, Сефаръ, Адамафана, Т{арс}исъ, Мересъ,
Марсона, Мумуханъ, 7 болꙗръ Фарисѣискых и Мадѣискыхъ иже видꙗху
лице царево, иже сѣдꙗху наипьрвѣе въ царьствѣ,
1:15 ꙗко по закону что створити царици Васти иже не створи повелѣниꙗ
царева Ахасъвероса иже по рукахъ старостъ.
1:16 И рече Моумуханъ предъ царемь и болꙗры, не царю единомоу съкривила
Вастии царицꙗ, аще не на всꙗ боꙗры и на всꙗ ꙗзыкы иже въ всѣхъ
{властьхъ} царꙗ Ахасъвероса.
1:17 Ꙗко в{ы}ниде глаголъ царицинъ на в'сꙗ жены, ꙗко не оувредити мужь
своихъ [и не въ послухъ] пред ними, †иже рекоша† царь Ахасоверосъ рече
привести Вастию царицю предъ нь, ѡна же не рачи прити.
1:18 А въ дн҃ешнии дн҃ь рекоша болꙗрынѣ Фа{рс}ѣискыѣ и Мадѣискыѣ ꙗже
оуслышаша глаголъ царицинъ всѣм болꙗромъ царевъмъ. а довлѣеть
срамоты и гнѣва.
1:19 Аще цареви оулюбѣе †аще изидеть рѣчь царьскаꙗ ѿ него, и въпишеть въ
книгахъ Фарисѣискахъ и Мадѣискахъ а не преступи ꙗко не †пришла
Вастиꙗ царицꙗ предъ царь Ахасъверосъ, ꙗко да царьство еꙗ предасть°
подрузѣ еꙗ лучьши еꙗ.

1:9 жьньскыи Q, женьскыи TSWV
1:10 вънєгда, внє- SGWVE] въньгда T || сѧ] жє сѧ S; жє GWVE || Харвȣнанови Tn; Харвуванови Q, Нарнунанови T, Харнунанови S, Харнунановѣ GWVE || Ваавахфану SG] вавaавахȣ V, и вавахван [?] in marg. W, ваавахвану E
1:11 вѣнци V] вѣнцѣ TSGW || [и] om. GWVE
1:12 Васти] Вастии TS || рѣѵи GVEA], рѣѵѣ T, рєѵи W, роѵи V || старость QV, -стъ TSGW
1:13 съсудъ Q, судъ TSGWV
1:14 карсона] кар'рона SGWVE || сєфаръ S] софаръ GWVE || Тарсисъ Tn; Тирисъ QTSG-WVE
1:15 ахасвєроса] -вєросова SGWVE
1:16 царицѧ SG] ца|рѧ T; царици WVE || въ всѣхъ QTG; въ вєсѣхъ SWVE; H 'in all provinces' || властєⷯ Tn only
1:17 внидє QTSGWV; 'вынидє' H || цр̃цинъ на SG] црⷭинъ на T, цр̃ѵинъ но и на V, црцинъ но и на W, црици но на G, царици но и на E
1:18 Фарсѣиска Tn, фарисѣискыѣ Q, фариискыѣ T, фарсєискыѧ S, фарисѣскыѧ W, фарисѣскыѧ G, фарисиис'кыѧ V, пєрсьскыѧ фарѣсѣискыѧ E || цр̃цинъ QSGW] црⷭинъ T, цр̃ѵинъ V || а довлѣєть] и дов. GWVE, и довлѣть S
1:19 оулюбѣє] оулобѣє T, оулюбиє SGWVE

1:9 Также и Вашти царица устроила пир для женщин в царском доме, что *принадлежелал* царю Ахашверошу.
1:10 В день седьмой, когда развеселилось сердце царя от вина, он сказал Мегуману, Бизѳе, Харвоне, Бигѳе и Авагѳе, Зеѳару и Харкасу—семи евнухам, служившим пред лицом царя Ахашвероша,
1:11 привести царицу Вашти пред лицом царя в венце царском, чтобы показать народам и князьям красоту ее, потому что она *была* хороша видом.
1:12 И отказалась царица Вашти прийти по слову царя, *переданному* через евнухов. И разгневался царь очень, и ярость его загорелась в нем.
1:13 И сказал царь мудрецам, знающим времена (ибо таков *был* обычай царя—*говорить* перед всеми, знающими закон и суд:
1:14 ближними же его *были*: Каршена, Шеѳар, Адмаѳа, Ѳаршиш, Мерес, Марсена, Мемухан, семь князей персидских и мидийских, видящих лицо царя *и* сидящих первыми в царстве):
1:15 «По закону ,как поступить с царицею Вашти за то, что она не сделала по повелению царя Ахашвероша, *переданному* через евнухов?»
1:16 И сказал Мемухан пред лицом царя и князей: «Не перед царем одним провинилась царица Вашти, но перед всеми князьями и перед всеми народами, что по всем провинциям царя Ахашвероша,
1:17 потому что поступок царицы дойдет до всех жен, и они станут пренебрегать мужьями своими и говорить: «Царь Ахашверош велел привести царицу Вашти пред лицом своим, а она не пришла».
1:18 И в тот же день княгини персидские и мидийские, услышав о поступке царицы, станут *то же* говорить всем князьям царя, и будет довольно срама и гнева.
1:19 Если угодно царю, да изойдет повеление царя от него, и да впишется в законы персидские и мидийские, и да не отменится, чтобы Вашти не входила пред лицом царя Ахашвероша; а царское достоинство ее царь передаст другой, *которая* лучше ее.

1:20 И будєть послушан{а} рѣчь царєва ижє створи въ всємь царьстви єго, ижє †силна єсть и всѧ жєны възложать †срамоту на мужь свои ѿ вєлика дожє и до мала.

1:21 И добра быс^{ть} рѣчь прєдъ царємь и болѧры, и створи царь ꙗкожє рєчє Мумуханъ.

1:22 И посла книгы къ всѣмъ властємъ царѧ, къ власти и власти ꙗко писаниє ихъ, и къ людьмъ къждо ꙗкожє ꙗзыкъ єго оутвьрдити всѧкому мꙋжю власть в дому своємь и глаголъ ꙗкожє ꙗзыкъ людии къждо ихъ.

2:1 И по рѣчьхъ тѣхъ ꙗко оустави сѧ гнѣвъ царєвъ Ахасъвєросовъ, въспомѧноу Васти и створєниє єꙗ и єжє ѡсоуди на ню.

2:2 И рѣша ѡтроци царєви слоугы єго да поискали быхомъ царєви дѣвыхъ дѣвиць добровзорных,

2:3 да бы приставилъ царь приставникы въ всѣх властьхъ [своихъ и власти] царства своєго да быша събрали всѧкоу дѣвоую дѣвицю добровзорну къ Соусану граду в домъ жєньскыи по руцѣ Егаєвѣ, ижє бѣ тивоунъ царєвъ, хранитєль жєньскыи, даꙗ имъ пристрою ихъ.

2:4 И дѣв{а} южє оулюблѧшє царь и цар{є}вати начнєть въ Вастии мѣ{сто}. И оулюбѣ рѣчь царєви и створи тако.

2:5 Моужь Июдѣискыи бѧшє въ Соусанѣ градѣ, имѧ єму Мардахаи, сынъ Аировъ, сына Симаина, сына Кисова, моужь Вєниаминовъ,

2:6 єжє полонєнъ бѧшє изъ Ерусалима съ {полонъмь} ижє полон{єн}и съ Ѡхониємь царємь Июдинъмь, ижє полони Навходъносоръ царь Вавулоньскыи.

2:7 И бѧшє пѣстуꙗ †домачадицю сир{у, то} бѧшє† Есфирь дщи стръꙗ єго, єижє нє бѧшє ѡтьцѧ ни матєрє, дѣвица сущи добротварна и добровзорна, да єгда оумрє ѡц҃ь єи и мати єи и приꙗтъ ю Мардъхаи въ дщєрє мѣсто собѣ [Июдѣи].

2:8 И {бысть} въньгда оуслышанъ быс^{ть} глаголъ царєвъ и законъ єго и ꙗкожє събра дѣвица многы въ Соусанѣ градѣ по руцѣ Егаєвѣ и быс^{ть} поꙗта Есьфирь в домъ царєвъ на руцѣ Егаєвѣ, ижє бѧшє хранитєль жєньскыи.

1:20 послушание QTSG, послушаннаꙗ E, послушалнаꙗ ѥꙗ V, послушальнаꙗ W || царстви, -ствїи SG] -ствѣ WVE || срамоту SG] срамоту драготу E, драготу V, драготу marked by superscript dots, срамоту in marg., W, др8готоу Tn || мужь свои G] мужа своꙗ SV, мужжа своꙗ W, мужже своꙗ E || доже и] даже и TS, даже G
1:21 мумуханъ SVE; мумѧханъ W] муханъ T; ем8 м8ханъ G
1:22 властемъ] властелемъ SGWVEA
2:1 црѣвъ Ахасъверосовъ, Ахаꙁъверосовъ SG] црꙗ Ахаꙁвероса WV || створение QG, сътворение STn, со- WVX] створенее T
2:3 бы SGWV] om. T || своихъ и власти SGWV] om. Tn || дв҃оую Q, дв҃у и GT, дв҃у SWV || тивунъ SG] староста VTnX, староста, marked with dots, + тив8нъ in margin W
2:4 дв҃у QTSGW, дв҃ую V || оулюблꙗше SG] оулюбꙗше T || црствати Tn, црь ꙁвати QTSG, црити WVAX || оулюбѣ SG] оулобѣ T, юлюбѣ W, юлюби V || мѣ Q, мѣсто T
2:6 полоненъ GWV] плѣненъ S || съ полнѣмь Q, с полоном G, посломь ST, с плѣном WV || полонени TnX; полони QTG, плѣни WS (V) || ѡхониемь G] иѡхониемь SWV; ѡхонїею TnX
2:7 бꙗше QTG] бѣша T, бѣꙗше W, бѣаше SV || домаѵадицю Q, -ц8 V] домоѵадицю TWGS || сироту QTG, сиру. то WV, сироу . та X, сир8 . таꙗ Tn, сироту. та S || его SGWVA] ѥꙗ T || добротварна W] добротворна TSGV || еи (twice)] еꙗ SGWV || Июдѣи QTSGWV, om. TnX
2:8 И QTSG; И быс WVTnX || бы (twice) T || поꙗта QGWV, поета corrected later to поꙗта T; ꙗко поꙗста S

1:20 И будет услышано царское дело, что он сделал, по всему царству его, как бы оно ни было велико, и все жены будут воздавать честь мужьям своим, от большого и до малого».
1:21 И угодно было это слово в глазах царя и князей; и сделал царь по слову Мемухана.
1:22 И послал *он* письма во все провинции царя, *писанные* в каждую область письмом ее и всякому народу на языке его, *чтобы* быть каждому мужу господином в доме своем, и говорить на языке своего народа.
2:1 После этого, когда утих гнев царя Ахашвероша, он вспомнил о Вашти и о том, что она сделала, и о том, что было решено о ней.
2:2 И сказали отроки царя, слуги его: «Пускай изыскали бы для царя девиц девственных, хороших видом.
2:3 И пускай назначил бы царь чиновников во все провинции своего царства, и чтобы собрали всех молодых девиц, хороших видом, в Шушан-город, в дом женщин, под надзор Гегая, царского евнуха, стража женщин, и пускай дают им притирания.
2:4 И дева, которая понравится глазам царя, станет царицею вместо Вашти». И угодно было слово это в глазах царя; и он так и сделал.
2:5 Муж-иудей был в Шушане-городе, и имя его *было* Мардохай, сын Иаира, сына Шимея, сына Киша, мужа *из колена* яминова,
2:6 который был изгнан из Иерушалаима вместе с изгнанниками, что были изгнаны с Иехониею, царем иудейским, которого изгнал Невуходнеццар, царь бавельский.
2:7 И был он воспитателем Гадассы (она же Есѳирь), дочери дяди его, ибо не было у нее ни отца, ни матери. И девица *была* красива станом и хороша лицом. И после смерти отца ее и матери ее взял ее Мардохай к себе как дочь.
2:8 И было, когда услышано было слово царя и закон его и когда собрались многие девицы в город Шушан под надзор Гегая, *тогда* взята была Есѳирь в царский дом под надзор Гегая, стража женщин.

2:9 И оулюби дѣвицю [царь] ѡчима своима, и въꙁнесє милость прєдъ {нимь},
и оубърꙁи пристрою єи и дары єи даꙗти єи и 7 дѣвиць иже {достоꙗшє}
дати є{и} иꙁ дому царєва, и пр{ѣ}стро{и} ю {и} дѣвица єꙗ †оудобрѣло в
дому ж{є}ньстѣмь.

2:10 И нє {по}вѣда Есфирь людии своихъ ни роду своєго, любо бѧшє Мардохаи
ꙁаповѣдалъ єи абы нє повѣдала.

2:11 И на всѧкъ дн҃ь и {дн҃ь} Мардохаи въсхожашє противу двору дому
женьского оувѣдѣти миръ Есфири и что быша створили єи.

2:12 И ꙗкоже придѧшє ꙁнамєниє дѣв{ы}ꙗ дѣвы прити къ царю Ахасъвєросоу,
по нєм'же бы^{сть} єи ꙗкоже ꙁаконъ женьскыи въ 12 мѣсѧць нєбо{нъ} тако
напълнѧху сѧ дн҃ьє пристроꙗ єꙗ 6 мѣсѧць {въ маслѣ маститѣ и [въ] 6
мѣсѧць} въ кандилѣхъ и въ пристроꙗхъ женьскыхъ.

2:13 И в томь дѣваꙗ дѣва придѧшє къ царєви, и всє єжє ащє рєчашє дадѧшє
єи прити с нєю иꙁ дому женьского дажь и до дому царєва.

2:14 [И] на вєчєръ та бѣ приходѧщи, и ꙁаоутра бѣ {въꙁвращаюши} сѧ къ дому
женьскому другому по руцѣ Сааꙁъгаꙁовѣ тивуна царєва, хранитєль
{на}ложниц{ам}. И нє прихожашє лапь къ царєви нъ єгда будѧшє волѧ
царєва на нєи, и тъгда поꙁ{ва}шє ю имєнємъ.

2:15 И вънєгда доступи жрєбии Есфиринъ дщєрє Авихаиловы строꙗ
Мардохаєва, иже поꙗлъ ю бѧшє собѣ въ дщєрє мѣсто, прити къ царєви,
нє проси рѣчи, нъ ꙗкоже рєчашє Егаи тивȣнъ° , хранитєль женьскыи. И
быс^{ть} Есфирь ѡбнєсєна милостию прєдъ всѣми слугами своими.

2:16 И бы^{сть} поꙗта Есфирь къ царю Ахасъвєросоу в домъ царства своєго въ
мѣсѧць 10 глаголющии сѧ Тєвєфъ (по жидовьскому, а по грєчьску
Дєкѧбрь) въ лѣт^{о} 7 царства єго.

2:17 И ѡбълюби царь Есфирь пачє всѣхъ жєнъ, и ѡбнєсєна быс^{ть} милостью и
любовью прєдъ нимь пачє всѣхъ дѣвыхъ дѣвиць, и въꙁложи вѣнєць
царьскыи на главу єи и створи ю царицю въ {Вастии} мѣсто.

2:9 оулюби GVTnX] оулоби T, оулѫби (?) W. възлюби S || дв҃цю царь WTWV; царь дв҃цѹ SG] дв҃цю TnX || прѣд нью Q, нєю TSGWVTnX; H 'him' || пристрою єи ... єи G] п. єѧ ... єѧ SWV || V om. from даꙗти to из || дати є из QT] дати єи из SG, дати єи и из W, V om. || стоꙗху QTSG; достоꙗшє WVA || є QT; єи SGWV || пристрою QSG, пр҆|строю T; пристрои ю WVA || оудобрѣло G] оудобрил SWVA; оудобри ю Tn

2:10 вѣда QG, вѣдѧ, with later superscript по added, T; повѣда SWVTnX || роду G] рода SWVTnX || любо бѧшє SGWV] любѧшє T

2:11 жєньского, -аго SGWV] жєньскомѹ TS || Есфири G] -ринъ SWTnX, -рьнъ V || дн҃ь omit QTSGWV

2:12 ꙗкожє SG] акы WV || дв҃оуꙗ дв҃ы QTSG, дв҃оѣ дв҃ы WV || нєбо QGV; нєбо нє TSW, бо нє Tn || пристроꙗ єꙗ SG] п. єи WV || въ маслѣ маститѣ и (а S) въ 6 мц҃ь SWV; QTG om.

2:14 врачюющи QTnX; възвращающи TSGWV || тивуна SGV] тивуна marked with dots, + старосты in marg. W, старосты X, староста Tn || наложница[M] TnX, наложница W, -цѧ V; ложницѧ QTSG || и тъгда, и тогда SG] ти тогда WV || позвашє TSG; познавaашє WV, Q with -зн- corr. to -зв-

2:15 мардохаєва SG, мардахаєва WV] -хаива T || бѧшє собѣ (SG сєбѣ)] собѣ V, сєбѣ W || тивунъ SG] староста WVTnX

2:16 своєго S] єго WVTn; моєго G || тєвєфъ STn, тєвєѳь GX] тєвєтъ WV

2:17 ѡбълюби GX] възлюби SWV; полюби Tn || єи G] єѧ SWV || цр҃цю GTnX] цр҃цєю WV; цр҃ца S || Мастиѣ Q, Мастѣѣ T; вастїа S, вастїи G, Вастѣа W, Вастѣѧ V

2:9 И понравилась девица глазам его, и обрела у него благорасположение, и он поспешил дать ей притирания и *всю* долю ее и приставить к ней семь девиц, достойных быть при ней, из дома царя; и переместил ее и девиц ее в лучшую *часть* женского дома.

2:10 Не рассказывала Есѳирь ни о народе своем, ни о родстве своем, ибо Мардохай приказал ей, чтобы она не рассказывала.

2:11 И каждый день Мардохай проходил перед двором дома женщин, чтобы узнать о здоровье Есѳири и о том, что делается с нею.

2:12 И когда приходил черед каждой девице прийти к царю Ахашверошу после того, как за двенадцать месяцев *выполнено* было над нею все, определенное женщинам (ибо так исполнялись дни притирания их: шесть месяцев мирровым маслом и шесть месяцев благовониями и *другими* притираниями женскими),

2:13 и потом девица входила к царю, *и* все, что она просила, давалось ей принести с собой из дома женщин в дом царя.

2:14 Вечером она входила и утром возвращалась в другой дом женщин, на руки Шаашгаза, царского евнуха, стража наложниц. Более не входила к царю, разве если царь пожелал ее и она была позвана по имени.

2:15 И когда пришел черед Есѳири — дочери Авихаила, дяди Мардохая, которую *он* взял к себе как дочь,—войти к царю, она не просила ничего, кроме того, о чем сказал *ей* Гегай, евнух царский, страж женщин. И обрела Есѳирь милость в глазах всех, кто видел ее.

2:16 И взята была Есѳирь к царю Ахашверошу, в дом царства его, в десятый месяц, то есть *в* месяц Тевеѳ, в седьмой год царства его.

2:17 И полюбил царь Есѳирь более всех женщин, и она обрела его милость и благорасположение более всех девиц, *и он* возложил царский венец на голову ее и сделал ее царицею вместо Вашти.

2:18 И створи царь пиръ великъ всѣмъ вельможамъ своимъ и рабомъ своимъ,
и тъ пиръ [ꙁваше сѧ пиръ] Есфиринъ и створи оутѣху ꙁемлѧмъ и дасть
дары ꙗкоже бѣ сила царева.

2:19 И ꙗкоже събраше дѣв{ыꙗ} дѣвиц{ѧ} въ другыꙗ, Мардъхаи же сѣдаше въ
вратѣхъ царѧ.

2:20 И не бѧше Есфирь повѣдающи рода своего ни людии своихъ, ꙗкоже
ꙁаповѣдалъ еи бѧше Мардъхаи, и повелѣнье Мардахаево Есфирь
творѧше, ꙗкоже бѧше оутвердила сѧ с нимь.

2:21 Въ дн҃и ты и Мардъхаи сѣдѧше въ вратѣхъ царѧ. И гнѣваꙗ сѧ бѧше
{В}ихванъ и Вафесъ, два тиоуна царева иже стрѣжаста вратъ его, и
оумыслиста ꙁадѣти руцѣ цари Ахасъверосѣ.

2:22 И бы^{сть} вѣсть Мардохаеви, и повѣда Есфири царици и повѣда Есфирь
цареви ° имѧ Мардъхаево.

2:23 И възискана бы^{сть} рѣчь, и възображена, и повѣшена быста на древе ѡба,
и написа въ книгахъ памѧтьныхъ пред’ царемь.

3:1 и по глаголании тѣхъ [всѣхъ] възнесе царь Ахасъверосъ° сына
Амъдафиина Агаги, и възнесе его и постави столъ его превышии всѣхъ
болѧръ своихъ.

3:2 И вси раби цареви иже въ вратѣхъ царѧ припадающ{е} покланѧху сѧ
Амонови, ꙗко тако имъ бѧше ꙁаповѣдь царева. Мардъхаи же не
приклѧкну и не поклони сѧ.

3:3 И рѣша раби цареви еже въ вратѣхъ царѧ°, чьто ради ты преступаеши
ꙁаповѣдь цареву?

3:4 И быс^{ть} егда глаголахуть ему дн҃е дн҃е и не послушаше ихъ и повѣдаша
Амонови, {оуставны ли видѣти быв’шаꙗ гл҃ы Мардъхаевы} и{ж}е повѣда
имъ ꙗко тъ бѣ Июдѣи.

3:5 И видѣ Амонъ ꙗко не быс^{ть} Мардъхаи ни приклѧкаꙗ ни припадаꙗ ему, и
исполни сѧ Амонъ мысли гнѣвныꙗ.

3:6 И въ неврѣдъ ѡчима его быс^{ть} ꙁадѣти руцѣ Мардъхаю единомоу, иже
повѣдаша ему люди Мардохаевы, и волѧ быс^{ть} Амонова погубити всѧ
Июдѣꙗ иже въ всемь царствѣ Ахасъверосовѣ, людии Мардъхаевъ.

3:7 Мѣсѧца 1-го {еже есть ° Н}исанъ (глаголющии сѧ Април), въ лѣт° 12
царю Ахасъверосоу [и] възвьрже †вражду и† жребии предъ Амонъмь ѿ
дн҃и къ дн҃и, ѿ мѣсѧца къ мѣсѧцю 12 иже есть Адаръ (рекомыи Мартъ).

2:19 съброашє G] съброаша S, събирааше W, собирааше V, ʒьбираше Tn, събираше X || дв҃ою дв҃цю QTG, дв҃ою дв҃ицѣ W, дв҃ою дв҃ица SV

2:21 Въ дн҃и ты и G] И въ дн҃и ты SWVTnX || Вихванъ Tn; Бихванъ QSG, Бѣхванъ T, Бихфанъ WV || Вафєсъ SGTn] Вафєсъ marked with dots, + Тєрєшь in marg. W; Вафєсъ Тєрєш V || тивуна QSG, тиоуна T] старостѣ WV, -ы Tn || стрѣжаста SGTn] стрѣжаашєта WVB || вратъ GTn] врата SWV

3:1 прєвышии G] прєвышє SWV; вышє Tn

3:2 припадающа QT, -щє SGWV, -щи Tn || приклѧкноу WVTn] -клѧну TSG

3:4 дн҃є дн҃є] дн҃ь дн҃є SWV, дн҃є дн҃їи G || и{ж}є: и нє QTSGWVTn || тъ SW] то T, тои GVTn || оуставны . . . Мард. Tn only

3:6 въ нєврѣдъ] нєврѣдъ T, нєврєд VTn, нє въ врєд SGW || людии GWV] людиє и T, лю^{д}и S, людьє Tn

3:7 є^{ж} є^{с} Tn, omit QTSGWV || писанъ Q; нисанъ TSGWVTn

2:18 И устроил царь великий пир для всех князей своих и для служащих при нем, тот пир *для* Есѳири, и дал льготу провинциям, и раздал дары, *подобающие могуществу* руки царя.

2:19 И когда во второй раз собраны были девицы и Мардохай сидел у ворот царя,

2:20 не рассказывала Есѳирь ни о родстве своем, ни о народе своем, как велел ей Мардохай; и повеления Мардохая Есѳирь исполняла, как *и прежде,* когда воспитывалась у него.

2:21 В дни те, *когда* Мардохай сидел у ворот царя, вознегодовали Бигѳан и Ѳереш, два царских евнуха из стражи порога, и замыслили простереть руку против царя Ахашвероша.

2:22 И дело стало известно Мардохаю, и он рассказал царице Есѳири, и Есѳирь сказала царю от имени Мардохая.

2:23 И дело было расследовано и найдено *верным,* и их обоих повесили на дереве. И было вписано *об этом* в книгу дел дней пред лицом царя.

3:1 После этих дел [событий] возвеличил царь Ахашверош Гамана, сына Гаммедаѳы-агагиянина, и вознес его, и поставил сидение его выше всех князей, которые *были* у него.

3:2 И все рабы царя, которые *были* у царских ворот, кланялись и падали ниц пред Гаманом, ибо так приказал царь о нем. А Мардохай не кланялся и не падал ниц.

3:3 И говорили рабы царя, которые *были* у ворот царя, Мардохаю: «Зачем ты преступаешь повеление царское?»

3:4 И было, когда они говорили ему каждый день, а он не слушал их, и они сказали *об этом* Гаману, чтобы посмотреть, устоит ли дело Мардохая, ибо он сообщил им, что он иудей.

3:5 И увидел Гаман, что Мардохай не кланяется и не падает ниц перед ним, и исполнился гнева Гаман.

3:6 И показалось ему ничтожным простереть руку против одного Мардохая; *но так* как сказали ему, *из какого* народа Мардохай, *то* искал Гаман истребить всех иудеев, которые *были* во всем царстве Ахашвероша—народ Мардохаев.

3:7 В месяц первый, то есть *в* месяц Нисан, в двенадцатый год царя Ахашвероша, бросали пур, то есть жребий, пред лицом Гамана изо дня в день и из месяца в месяц, *и пал жребий* на двенадцатый *месяц,* что есть месяц Адар.

3:8 И реӵє Аманъ къ царю Ахасъвєросоу, сє соуть людьє° расѣꙗни и
раꙁдѣлєни[є] мєжю людьми по всєи ꙁємли царства твоєго, и ꙁаконы ихъ
иꙁдрѧднѣє паӵє всѣхъ людии, и ꙁакона царєва ѡни нє соуть творѧщє, а
царєви бы нє право пустити ихъ.
3:9 И ащє царєви бы [оубо] доволно [бы] было, абы написалъ погубити ꙗ и
{10 тысѧщь} †капии срѣбра навѣшю къ стр{о}ю дѣла [твоєго и] принєсти
къ полатамъ царѧ.
3:10 И сънѧ царь пьрстьнь свои съ рукы своєꙗ и да Амонови сыну Амъдафину
Агаги, муӵитєлю Июдѣискому.
3:11 И реӵє царь Амонови, срѣбро буди дано тобѣ, и людиє, створити° волю
ѡӵью твоєю.
3:12 И приꙁвани быша писци царєви, {въ} мѣсѧць 1, {въ} 13 дн҃ь, {и бысть}
написано° єжє ꙁаповѣдашє Амонъ къ тивꙋномъ царєвъмъ и къ
пристав{ом} ижє по ꙁємли и по ꙁєм{л}и и къ болѧромъ людии и
людии, ꙁємьлѧ и ꙁємлѧ ꙗко писмѧ єꙗ, и людиє люди ꙗко ꙗꙁыкъ
ихъ, †имѧ царѧ Ахасъвєроса написахоуть и ꙁапєӵатаху пьрстьнємь
царєвъмь.
3:13 И посылаху книгы погоньц{и} по всєи ꙁємли царєвѣ растворити и иꙁб{ити
и погубити} всѧ Июдѣꙗ ѿ дѣтѧтє и до старого, младєнца и жєны, въ дн҃ь
єдинъ 13 дн҃ь мѣсѧца 12 то єсть Адаръ (рєкомыи Мартъ), добытокъ ихъ
къ росполону.
3:14 [гл҃ть] пєӵать грамотнаꙗ дати ꙁаконъ по всѣмъ ꙁємлѧмъ и ꙁємлѧмъ, и
ѿкрыти всѣмъ людьмъ, быти оуготованымъ на дн҃ь сии.
3:15 Погонци жє вынидоша въскорѣ по глаголу царѧ, и ꙁаконъ быс[ть] данъ въ
Сусанѣ градѣ, а царь и Аманъ сѣдоста пити, а градъ Соусанъ въсплака
сѧ.
4:1 И Мардъхаи бѣ вѣдаꙗ всє єжє творѧшє †царь, и раꙁдра Мардъхаи риꙁы
своꙗ и ѡблєӵє сѧ въ власѧницю и †сукно, и вынидє посрєдѣ града и
въꙁъпи въпльмь вєликъмь и горком.
4:2 И придє до вратъ царѧ а то бѧшє нє право прити къ вратом царєвъмь въ
ѡдєжи сукнѧнѣ.
4:3 И всѧка ꙁємлѧ и ꙁємлѧ идєжє рѣӵь царєва и ꙁаконъ єго доидѧшє жєлѧ
вєлика Июдѣѡмъ бѧшє, и говѣниє и плаӵь и нарѣканиє и власѧницѣ и
†сукна постилахоу старѣишинамъ.

3:8 раꙁдѣлениє Q, раꙁдѣльни T; раꙁдѣлєни SGWV, раꙁдѣленїи Tn ‖ ꙁаконы S] ꙁаконъ GWVTn

3:9 .ı̄. тысѧщь срєбра капи Tn; ҂є̄ капии срєбра QT(SGWV) ‖ стръю Q, строю TSGVTn, страю W ‖ принести STn] принєсє и GWV

3:10 да G, да^{с} S, дасть Tn] дамъ V, дам W

3:12 въ Tn; om. QTSGWV ‖ мц̄ь SGTn] мц̄а WV ‖ въ Tn ‖ написано SGWV] бы^{с} писано Tn ‖ ꙁємнїи S; ꙁємьни и къ QG, ꙁємни къ T; ꙁємником WV ‖ и бы^{с} Tn, и *omit* QTS ‖ приставо^{М} Tn, приставу QTSGWV

3:13 погонц{и} : погоньцѣ QT, погонцѣи S, погонници GWVA ‖ иꙁбить и погоубить Tn; иꙁбавити QTG; иꙁбивати SW, исбивати V ‖ .гı. SWVTn] ги T (crossed out by later hand, above line .гı), H '13th'

3:14 гл̄ть QTSWV, гл̄єть G; om. Tn

4:1 И] а Tn; om. TSGWV ‖ вѣдаꙗ SGV, вѣдаѧ W] видаꙗ T ‖ горко^{М} Q, горєкомь T; горкымь S, -кымъ WV, -ки^{М} G

4:3 плаѵь SGW] -ѵє T, -ѵ V

3:8 И сказал Гаман царю Ахашверошу: «Есть один народ, разбросанный и рассеянный между народами по всем областям царства твоего, и законы их отличны от *законов* всех народов, и законов царя они не выполняют, и царю не следует *так* оставлять их.

3:9 Если царю угодно, то пусть будет предписано истребить их; и десять тысяч талантов серебра я отвешу в руки служителей, чтобы внести в казну царя».

3:10 И снял царь перстень свой с руки своей и отдал его Гаману, сыну Гаммедаѳы-агагиянина, угнетателю иудеев.

3:11 И сказал царь Гаману: «Отдано тебе серебро и народ, *чтобы* поступить с ним, как в твоих глазах угодно».

3:12 И призваны были писцы царя в первый месяц, в тринадцатый день его, и написано было все, как приказал Гаман, к сатрапам царя, и к начальствующим над каждою областью, и к князьям каждого народа, в каждую область письмом ее и к каждому народу на языке его: *все* было написано от имени царя Ахашвероша и *скреплено* перстнем царя.

3:13 И посланы были письма через гонцов во все области царя, чтобы истребить, убить и погубить всех иудеев, от молодого и до старого, детей и женщин, в один день, в тринадцатый день двенадцатого месяца, то есть Адара, и имущество их разграбить:

3:14 список с указа отдать в каждую область *как* закон, объявляемый для всех народов, чтобы они были готовы к тому дню.

3:15 Гонцы отправились поспешно с повелением царя. Был объявлен указ и в Шушане-городе, и царь и Гаман сели пить, и город Шушан *был* в смятении.

4:1 И Мардохай знал все, что делалось, и разодрал Мардохай одежды свои, и возложил на себя вретище и пепел, и вышел на середину города, и возопил воплем великим и горьким.

4:2 И дошел до ворот царя, ибо нельзя было входить в ворота царя во вретище.

4:3 И во всякой области, куда *только* доходило повеление царя и указ его, было большое сетование у иудеев, и пост, и плач, и вопль; вретище и пепел служили постелью для многих.

4:4 И придоша дѣвы Есфирины и тивоуни єꙗ, и повѣ{да}ша єи, и оужасє сѧ царицѧ вєлми ѕѣло, и посла риѕы ѡблєщи Мардъхаꙗ и снѧти соукно єго с нєго, и нє въсхотѣ приꙗти.
4:5 И възва Есфирь Афанъ ѡт тивунъ царєвъ, иже стоꙗшє предъ нєю, и ѕаповѣда єму оунє Мардъхаꙗ оувѣдати чєму то є и про что є.
4:6 И в{ы}нидє Афанъ къ Мардъхаєви на оулицю града прѧмо вратъ царєвъ,
4:7 и исповѣда Мардъхаи Афаноу всѧ съключьшаꙗ сѧ ємоу и расповѣданиє сребра єже рєчє Аманъ {н}авѣсит{и} къ полатѣ царѧ на Июдѣихъ погубити ꙗ.
4:8 И пєчать {книга}мъ ѕаконнымъ иже быс^{ть} в Соусанѣ градѣ дана растворити є да єму показати Есфири и повѣдати єи, и ѕаповѣдати єи прити къ царю молити єго и оумилоср҃дити сѧ прєд нимь ѡ людьхъ своихъ.
4:9 И придє Афахъ и повѣда Есфири рѣчи Мардъхаєвы.
4:10 И рєчє Есфирь къ Афахови, и ѕаповѣда єму оунє Мардъхаꙗ.
4:11 [И] вьси раби царєви и людиє власти царєвы вѣдають ꙗко всѧкъ мужь и жєна ꙗко ащє придєть къ царєви къ двору дн҃ѣшнєму дондєже нє ѕванъ будєть єдинъ тъкмо ѕаконъ єго єже †къ оубою† кромѣ ємуже простреть царь проутъ ѕлатъ° , а аѕъ нє ѕвана быхъ прити къ царєви сє оуже 30 дн҃ии.
4:12 {И} повѣдаша Мардъхаєви рѣчи Есфирины,
4:13 и рєчє Мардъхаи вратѧ сѧ къ Есфирии, Нє мни си въ мысли своєи иѕъбудучи сѧ в дому царѧ пачє всѣхъ Июдѣи.
4:14 Ащє мълчиши мълчачи въ годину сию †простєрыи† иѕбавлєниє въстанєть Июдѣѡмъ ѿ мѣста иного, а ты и домъ ѡ^{ть}цѧ твоєго погыбнєть, да кто вѣсть ащє въ годину сию доступиши ли ты царства.
4:15 И ѡтвѣща Есфирь° къ Мардъхаєви,
4:16 Иди, събєри всѧ Июдѣꙗ єже ихъ ѡбрѧщєши въ Сусанѣ градѣ и говѣитє мєнє ради, и нє ꙗдитє ни пиитє по 3 дн҃и, дн҃ь и нощь. И пакы аѕъ сама и дѣвыꙗ дѣвы моꙗ говѣти начнуть съ мною. И по томь поиду къ царєви, ащє си и нє по ѕакону, да ащє погыбну да погыбну.
4:17 И придє Мардъхаи и створи° ꙗкоже ѕаповѣда єму Есфирь.
5:1 И быс^{ть} въ дн҃ь 3-и и ѡблєчє сѧ въ риѕы царьскыꙗ Есфирь и ста †оу дому† царєва дому дн҃ѣшнєго противу дому царєва, а царь сѣдѧшє на столѣ царства своєго въ полатѣ своєи прѧмо двєрємъ полаты.

4:4 повѣша Q, повѣдаша TSGWV
4:5 Афанъ SGWV] Афаха Tn || оунє G] оу WVAB, S om. || оувѣдати SGW] -дѧти T, -дѣти V
4:6 внидє QTSGWVTn
4:7 да вѣситы QTSGV, да виситы W; навѣсиⷮ Tn
4:8 пеѵѧть книгъ Tn, пеѵатьникомъ QTSGWV || ȥаконнымъ SGWV] ȥаконных Tn || є да єму] и да єму GWV, єгⷣаємоу S, єгⷣа гл҃а ємоу Tn
4:9 Афахъ S] Афанъ GWV, Афакъ Tn
4:10 Афахови S] Афанови GWV, Офахоу Tn
4:11 єжє SGWV] иⷢ Тн || днѣшнєму] внѣшнємꙋ SGWV || проутъ SGWV] пругъ T || къ оубою QTSGWV; оубьєноу быти Tn || ȥвана S] въȥвана GWV
4:12 И SWV; om. QTGTn
4:14 простєрыи] прострыи TSG, простри WV || цⷭр҃ства STn] царѧ GWV (added later S)
4:16 .г҃. Q, три TSG || (second) погыбну QSW, погибну V; побну T] G om.
5:1 оу дому SGTn] + домꙋ V: H 'in the court of the house' || дн҃єшнєго Q, дн҃ѣшєньго T, дн҃єшнѧго TV, дн҃єшьнєго W; внѣшнѧго S || дому царєва Tn; д. царєву TSGWV

4:4 И пришли служанки Есѳири и евнухи ее, и рассказали ей. И сильно встревожилась царица, и послала одежды, чтобы облечь Мардохая и снять с него вретище его, и он не принял.
4:5 *Тогда* позвала Есѳирь Гаѳаха, одного из евнухов царя, которого он приставил к ней, и послала его к Мардохаю узнать, что это и отчего это.
4:6 И вышел Гаѳах к Мардохаю на площадь города, которая перед воротами царя.
4:7 И рассказал ему Мардохай обо всем, что с ним случилось, и о деле с серебром, которое обещал Гаман отвесить в казну царя на иудеев, чтобы истребить их,
4:8 и вручил ему список с указа, данного в Шушане, об истреблении их, чтобы показать Есѳири, и сказать ей, и наказть ей, чтобы она пошла к царю, и молила его о помиловании, и просила его за народ свой.
4:9 И пришел Гаѳах, и пересказал Есѳири слова Мардохая.
4:10 И сказала Есѳирь Гаѳаху, и послала его *сказать* Мардохаю:
4:11 «Все рабы царя и народы в провинциях царя знают, что всякому — и мужчине, и женщине — кто войдет к царю во внутренний двор, не быв позван, один суд — смерть; только тот, к кому прострет царь свой золотой скипетр, останется жив. А я не звана к царю вот уже тридцать дней».
4:12 И пересказали Мардохаю слова Есѳири.
4:13 И сказал Мардохай, отвечая Есѳири: «Не думай, что ты *одна* спасешься в доме царском изо всех иудеев.
4:14 Если ты промолчишь молчком в эту пору, то свобода и избавление придет для иудеев из другого места, а ты и дом отца твоего погибнете. И кто знает, не для такой ли поры ты и достигла достоинства царского?»
4:15 И сказала Есѳирь, отвечая, Мардохаю:
4:16 «Пойди, собери всех иудеев, находящихся в Шушане, и поститесь ради меня, и не ешьте и не пейте три дня, ни днем, ни ночью, и я со служанками моими буду так же поститься, и потом пойду к царю, хотя это не по закону, и если мне погибнуть, погибну».
4:17 И перешел Мардохай, и сделал, как приказала ему Есѳирь.
5:1 На третий день Есѳирь оделась по-царски и встала во внутреннем дворе дома царя, напротив дома царя; царь же сидел *тогда* на престоле своего царства, в доме царя, против входа в дом.

5:2 И бысть ꙗко оуꙁрѣ царь Есфирь ° въ дворѣ, [и] бысть [Есфирь] ѡбнесена
милостию предъ ѡчима єго, и простре царь прутъ ꙁлатыи Есфирии иже
имѣꙗше въ руку своєю. И приближи сѧ Есфирь, и ꙗтъ ꙁа конецъ прута.
5:3 И рече єи царь, что ти єсть, Есфири царице, и что мыслиши просити
царства моєго, будєть ти дажь и до полу царства моєго.
5:4 И рече Есфирь, аще бы сѧ цареви оудобрити, да бы пришелъ царь съ
Аманъмь дн҃ес на питву єже быхъ створила єму.
5:5 И рече царь, оубърꙁите по Амана и створите рѣчь Есфиринꙋ. И придоста
царь и Аманъ на пиръ иже створи Есфирь.
5:6 И рече царь Есфирии въ препоихъ виньныхъ, что †еже прошенїє твоє, и
дам ти, и что єсть мысль просьбы твоєꙗ, да{же} и до полу царьства
моєго, {и} створимъ тобѣ.
5:7 И да ѿвѣтъ Есфирь и рече, просьба моꙗ и мысль моꙗ,
5:8 ° милость ѿ царѧ. И аще бы цареви [тако] оудобрѣло [то] дати мнѣ
просьбу мою и створити мысль мою, да бы пришелъ царь и Аманъ на
пиръ иже сътворю [пакы] има, а ꙁаоутра створю ꙗкоже будєть рѣчь
царева.
5:9 И вынидє Аманъ въ дн҃ь ° веселъ и ѡхвотьнъмь сьрдьцьмь, ꙗкоже оуꙁрѣ
Аманъ Мардъхаꙗ° не подвигнуща сѧ ни приклѧкноуща пред нимь, и
наполни сѧ Аманъ на Мардъхаꙗ гнѣва.
5:10 И въꙁдохнувъ Аманъ придє къ дому своєму, и пославъ приведе приꙗꙁнь
свою и Зересъ жену свою.
5:11 И расповѣда им{ъ} Аманъ ч{ь}сть богатьства своєго и множьство
сыновъ своихъ и ° єже въꙁвелича єго царь, и како въꙁнесе и надъ [всѣми]
вельможами своими и рабы царевы.
5:12 И рече Аманъ, и пакы не приведе [ли мѧ] Есьфирь царицѧ съ царемь на
пиръ иже створила бѣ аще не мене и пакы наоутриꙗ аꙁъ ꙁванъ єсмь к неи
съ царемь,
5:13 и все то не вредно †ли† єсть мнѣ въ всѧку годину єже аꙁъ вижю
Мардъхаꙗ Иудѣꙗ сѣдѧща въ вратѣхъ царѧ.
5:14 И рече єму Зересъ жена своꙗ и вси приꙗꙁни єго, сдѣлающе будѣте древо
въꙁвышѣе 50 локотъ, и ꙁаоутра речеши цареви, ать повѣсѧт Мардъхаꙗ
на немь, и при{деши} съ царемь на пиръ веселъ, и оудобри сѧ рѣчь пред
Аманъмь, и створи дрѣво.

5:4 бы сѧ цр̃ви оудобрити G, бы сѧ оу. ц. S] оу сѧ оудобрити цр̃єви T, бы^{с} цр̃єви оудобрити WV

5:6 єсфирии] -ри TSGWVTn || ϒто єже QTSWV, є^{ж} G, ϒто^{ж} Tn || єсть QT] єже є^{с} S || просьбы STn] проситы WV, проситбы G || да{жє} и: дай^{ж} Tn, дам ти Q, дамь ти T, дамъ ти SW, да^{м} ти GV || {и} SGWV, om. QT

5:8 и створити мысль мою SGWV] om. T || тако] om. Tn || то] om. Tn

5:9 приклѧкнуща S, -щи Tn] + сѧ GWV

5:10 въѯдохнувъ STn] -нȣ QWV

5:11 и^{м} Tn, има QTSGWV || ϒасть QGW, ϒѧсть V, ϒьсть ST

5:13 Мардохаꙗ SWV -дах- G] -хаю T

5:14 възвышѣє Q, възвышє T, -шєє GWV; възвышено S; вышє Tn || повѣсѧ^{т}] -си^{т} T, -сить SV, -сѣть W, повѣси G || приш^{д}є G, при^{д}шєши Tn] придєши W, приидєши SV

5:2 И было, когда увидел царь царицу Есѳирь, стоящую во дворе, она обрела милость в глазах его. И простер царь к Есѳири золотой скипетр, который был в руке его, и приблизилась Есѳирь, и коснулась конца скипетра.

5:3 И сказал ей царь: «Что тебе, царица Есѳирь, и какова просьба твоя? Даже до половины царства будет дано тебе».

5:4 И сказала Есѳирь: «Если царю угодно, пусть придет царь с Гаманом сегодня на пир, который я приготовила ему».

5:5 И сказал царь: «Поторопите Гамана, чтобы сделать по слову Есѳири». И пришел царь с Гаманом на пир, который приготовила Есѳирь.

5:6 И сказал царь Есѳири при питье вина: «Каково желание твое? — оно и будет дано [удовлетворено]. И какова просьба твоя?—*хотя бы вплоть* до половины царства, она и будет сделана [исполнена]».

5:7 И отвечала Есѳирь, и сказала: «*Вот* мое желание и моя просьба.

5:8 Если я обрела благоволение в глазах царя, и если царю угодно удовлетворить желание мое и исполнить просьбу мою, то пусть царь с Гаманом придет на пир, который я приготовлю для них, и завтра я сделаю по слову царя».

5:9 И вышел Гаман в тот день веселый и благодушный. Но когда увидел Гаман Мардохая у ворот царя, и *тот* не встал и не дрожал перед ним, исполнился Гаман гнева на Мардохая.

5:10 И сдержался Гаман. И пришел в дом свой, и послал позвать друзей своих и Зереш, жену свою.

5:11 И рассказывал им Гаман о славном богатстве своем, и о множестве сыновей своих, и всем том, как возвеличил его царь и как превознес его над князьями и рабами царя.

5:12 И сказал Гаман: «Да и царица Есѳирь *никого* не позвала с царем на пир, что она приготовила, кроме меня; так и назавтра я зван к ней с царем.

5:13 И всего этого не довольно для меня, доколе я вижу Мардохая-иудея сидящим у ворот царя».

5:14 И сказала ему Зереш, жена его, и все друзья его: «Пусть приготовят дерево вышиною в пятьдесят локтей, и утром скажи царю, чтобы повесили Мардохая на нем, и весело иди на пир с царем». И понравилось это слово Гаману, и он приготовил дерево.

6:1 И въ ту нощь смѧте сѧ царь въ снѣ, и повелѣ принести книгы памѧтныꙗ, и быша проѹтены пред царемь.

6:2 И изобрѣте [в них] написано иже повѣда Мардъхаи на Вигъхвана Вавероса 2 тивуна царева двьрника, иже оумыслиста задѣти руцѣ царю Ахасъверосу.

6:3 И реѹе царь, ѹто створено е ѹьсти и велиѹьꙗ Мардъхаеви за то? И рекоша ѡтроци цареви слугы его, не створено ему ниѹтоже [за то].

6:4 И реѹе царь, кто есть на дворѣ? и [тъгда] Аманъ приде къ двору дому царева вънѣшнего рещи цареви повѣсити Мардъхаꙗ на древе еже створи ему.

6:5 И рекоша ѡтроци цареви к нему, се Аманъ стоить на дворѣ. И реѹе царь, да придеть [сѣмо].

6:6 И приде Аманъ, и реѹе {ему} царь, ѹто створити моужю иже †царѧ волю† ѹьстити его? И помысли Аманъ въ мысли своеи, кому хотѣлъ бы царь створити ѹьсть боле мене?

6:7 И реѹе Аманъ къ цареви, мужь иже царь хощеть ѹьстити его,

6:8 да принесоут пърты царевы в' нѧже царь ѡблаѹить сѧ, и конь на немже царь ѣздить вънѣгдаже възложенъ вѣнець царевъ на главу его,

6:9 и дати пърты и конь на руцѣ мужю боѧриноу цареву сѫдии, и да ѡблеѹемъ мужа егоже царь хощет ѹьстити, и †провести {и на кони} по оулицамъ града, рекуѹе, тако се створи мужеви егоже хощет царь ѹьстити.

6:10 И реѹе царь Амонови, бързо възми свиту и конь, ꙗкоже глаголалъ еси, и створи тако Мардъхаю Июдѣю, иже сѣдѧше {въ} вратѣх царѧ, и не оуими рѣѹи всего еже еси глаголалъ.

6:11 И взѧ Аманъ ризы и конь и ѡблеѹе Мардъхаꙗ, и сътвори поꙗздити ему по оулицамъ града, и бѣ клиѹа пред нимь, тако †створити мужеви егоже царь оулюби ѹьстити его.

6:12 И възврати сѧ Мардохаи къ вратомъ царѧ, и Аманъ иде в домъ свои желенъ и повѣсивъ главу свою.

6:13 {И} исповѣда Аманъ Зереси женѣ своеи и всѣм рабомъ своимъ всѧ съклюѹьшаꙗ сѧ ему, и рѣша ему мудрьцї свои и Зересъ жена его, аще есть племене Июдѣиского Мардъхаи, ꙗко поѹалъ еси падати пред нимь не можеши оуже с нимь быти и [еще же глаголющимъ имъ с нимь] аще падаꙗ падеши пред нимь.

6:2 на Вигъхвана Ваверoса S (with и added later)] но Вихвала и Аверо^{с} WV, и аверєсъ G
6:4 кто SGWVTn] никто T
6:5 сѣмо QTSGWV; om Tn
6:6 цр̄ѧ волю GWV] волю цр̄ѧ ST || ємоу Tn only
6:9 на кони Tn; om. QTSGWV
6:10 свиту S] свиты GWV || оуими SW] оуми TV || въ: во Tn; на QTSGWV
6:11 ѡблеѵє SG] + сє W, сє corrected to сѧ V || мардъхаꙗ S] мардохаю T || створи^{ти} Q, створи TS, сътвори G, сътворити W, сотворитє VTn
6:12 повѣсивъ STn] повѣси GV, -сѣ W
6:13 свои] єго Tn || єщє ... прєд нимь] om. SGWVTn || падєши] падаши T

6:1 В ту ночь сон бежал от царя, и он велел принести книги памяти дел дней; и читались они перед царем.
6:2 И *было* найдено записанным *там*, как донес Мардохай на Бигѳану и Ѳереша, двух евнухов царских из стражей порога, которые замышляли простереть руку против царя Ахашвероша.
6:3 И сказал царь: «Что было сделано *как* честь и величие для Мардохая за это?» И сказали отроки царя, служившие при нем: «Ничего не сделано для него».
6:4 И сказал царь: «Кто на дворе?» Гаман же пришел *тогда* во внешний двор дома царя сказать царю, чтобы повесили Мардохая на дереве, которое он приготовил для него.
6:5 И сказали отроки царю: «Вот, Гаман стоит во дворе». И сказал царь: «Пусть войдет».
6:6 И вошел Гаман. И сказал ему царь: «Что сделать для того человека, которого царь хочет отличить почестью?» И сказал *себе* Гаман в сердце своем: «Кому *другому* захочет царь оказать почесть, кроме меня?»
6:7 И сказал Гаман царю: «Для того человека, которого царь хочет отличить почестью,
6:8 пусть принесут одеяние царства, в которое одевался царь, и *приведут* коня, на котором ездил царь, и на голову его [т.е. коня] *будет* возложен венец царства,
6:9 и пусть передадут одеяние и коня в руки одного из первых князей царя, и облекут того человека, которого царь хочет отличить почестью, и выведут его на коне на городскую площадь, и провозгласят перед ним: «Так делается для того человека, которого царь хочет отличить почестью!»
6:10 И сказал царь Гаману: «Тотчас же возьми одеяние и коня, как ты сказал, и сделай так для Мардохая-иудея, сидящего у ворот царя. Ничего не пропусти из всего, что ты сказал».
6:11 И взял Гаман одеяние и коня, и облек Мардохая, и провел его на коне по площади города, и провозглашал пред ним: «Так делается для того человека, которого царь хочет отличить почестью!»
6:12 И возвратился Мардохай к воротам царя. Гаман же поспешил в дом свой, печальный и покрыв голову.
6:13 И пересказал Гаман Зереши, жене своей, и всем друзьям своим все, что случилось с ним. И сказали ему мудрецы его и Зереш, жена его: «Если из племени иудеев Мардохай, из-за которого ты начал падать, то не пересилишь его, а, наверно, падешь пред ним».

6:14 Єщє же глаголющимъ имъ с нимь, и сє тивоуни царєви приступиша и
оубързиша привєсти Амана къ питвѣ ижє оустроила бѧшє Есфирь.
7:1 И придє царь и Аманъ питъ къ Есфирии царици.
7:2 И рєчє царь Есфирии пакы въ дн҃ь 2 въ питии виньнѣмь, что †просьбы
твоєꙗ†, Есфирии царицє, и дадимъ тобѣ, и что волѧ твоꙗ [и дамь] дажь и
до полу царьства [моєго] и створим' ти [волю твою].
7:3 Ѿвѣща Есфирь царицѧ и рєчє, ащє ѡбрѧку милость прєдъ ѡчима твоима,
царю, ащє царєви оудобрю, †и створиши мысль мою† въ просьбѣ моєи, {и
люди моꙗ в' воли моєи},
7:4 ижє прєпродана быхъ азъ и людиє мои растворити и оубити и погубити.
Ащє бо быхом къ рабом и къ рабынѧмъ прєпродани, мълчала быхъ, нєбо
н{ѣ^{сть}} тѣсноты †в дому† царєвѣ.
7:5 И рє^{чє} Ахасъвєросъ царь Есфири царици, кто то, и ѿкуду єсть, ижє †такы
помыслы помысли †и тако створи?
7:6 И рєчє Есфирь царицѧ, мужь вражьбьныи и нєприꙗзнивыи, Аманъ
възлюблєникъ с{ьи}. И абиє Аманъ въстрєпєта прєдъ царємь и царицєю.
7:7 И царь въставъ съ гнѣвомь ѿ питвы винныꙗ къ ѡградꙋ дн҃ѣшнєму, и
Аманъ ста ° на души своєи ѿ Есфири царицѣ †и оувидѣ ꙗко сконьчала сѧ °
{бѧ}шє злоба ѿ царѧ.
7:8 И царь врати сѧ ѿ ѡграда дн҃ѣшнєго къ дому питвьному, и Аманъ
припалъ бѧшє прєд постєлєю Есфириною, и рєчє царь, †право мука
царицина† съ мною в дому? И вынидє глаголъ из оустъ царєвыхъ и лицє
Амонови спадє.
7:9 И рєчє Харвуна єдинъ тѣх тивоунъ прєд цар^{є}мь, право {ѡноє} дрєво єжє
створилъ бѣ [самъ] Аманъ Мардъхаєви, ижє глаголашє доброє на царѧ и
стоить в дому Амановѣ възвышѣ 50 локотъ. И рєчє царь, повѣситє на
нємь Амона.
7:10 И повѣсиша Амона на дрєвє ижє створилъ бѧшє Мардъхаєви, и гнѣвъ
царєвъ потухну.

6:14 сє SGW] съ V || тивоуни QS, тивуни T, тиоуни W, тиȣни G] тиоуны V; старосты Tn ||
къ питвѣ] на пиръ Tn
7:1 питъ] пити S, пить GWVTn
7:2 волѧ твоѧ SG] волю твоєѧ GWV; om. Tn || и дамь SGWV] om. Tn || волю твою] om. Tn
7:3 ѡбрѧку QT] ѡбрѧщȣ SGWVTn || оудобрю S] оудобрѣю Tn, оудобно GWVAB || цр҃ю
SGWV] цр҃цю T (second ц crossed out) || и люди мои в' воли моєи моєи Tn; om. QTS-
GWV
7:4 прєпродана STn] прєповѣдана GWV || нє QTSGWVTn
7:5 то STn] тои GWV
7:6 въꙁлюблєникъ GV] -нѣкъ T, -ькъ W; въꙁлюблєнъ S; ꙁлокоꙁнивыи Tn || сы QTSGW,
сыи V
7:7 ѡграду Q, ?аграду corrected to ограду T] граду SGWV || дн҃ѣшнєму] днєшьнємоу W,
днєшнємȣ V, днєшномȣ G; внѣшнєму S || бѧшє TSGWV, шє Q || ѿ цр҃ѧ GWV] ѡ̑ цр҃цѣ
T; ѡ цр҃и S
7:8 дн҃ѣшнєго] днєшнєго G, дн҃єшнѧго WV; внѣшнѧго S || есфириною SGWV] -рииною T
|| вынидє] ?вьнидє T; выидє GVWAB; S выидє corrected from внидє; иꙁыидє Tn ||
Амонови SGQ, Аманови ("а" corrected from "о") T] Амоново WVTn
7:9 {ѡноє Tn; бѧшє QTSGWV; болѧшє T || самъ SGWV] om. Tn || на цр҃ѧ SGWV] цр҃ю Tn ||
въꙁвышѣ] -шє TSGWV; вышє Tn
7:10 повѣсиша SGWVTn] повѣси T || мардъхави Q, мардохаєви T

6:14 Они еще разговаривали с ним, *когда* пришли евнухи царя и стали торопить
Гамана идти на пир, который приготовила Есѳирь.
7:1 И пришел царь с Гаманом пировать с Есѳирью-царицею.
7:2 И сказал царь Есѳири также и во второй день во время пира: «Каково желание
твое, царица Есѳирь?—оно будет тебе дано [удовлетворено]; и какова просьба
твоя? Даже до половины царства—она будет сделана [исполнена]».
7:3 И отвечала царица Есѳирь, и сказала: «Если я обрела милость в глазах твоих,
царь, и если царю угодно, да будут дарованы мне жизнь моя по желанию моему и
народ мой по просьбе моей!
7:4 Ибо проданы мы, я и народ мой, на истребление, убиение и погибель. И если бы
мы проданы были в рабы и рабыни, я молчала бы, ибо враг не достоин ущерба
царя».
7:5 И отвечал царь Ахашверош, и сказал царице Есѳири: «Кто это такой, и где он,
который отважился в сердце своем сделать так?»
7:6: И сказала Есѳирь: «Муж враждебный и неприятель—этот злобный Гаман!»
7:7 И царь поднялся во гневе своем от пира винного *и пошел* во внутренный сад.
Гаман же стал умолять о жизни своей царицу Есѳирь, ибо видел, что определена
ему злая участь от царя.
7:8 И царь возвратился из внутренного сада в дом пира. И Гаман припадал к ложу,
на котором была Есѳирь. И сказал царь: «Еще и насиловать царицу при мне в
доме!» Слово вышло из уст царя, и накрыли лицо Гаману.
7:9 И сказал Харвона, один из евнухов при царе: «Вот и дерево, которое приготовил
Гаман для Мардохая, говорившего доброе для царя, стоит у дома Гамана,
вышиною в пятьдесят локтей». И сказал царь: «Повесьте его на нем».
7:10 И повесили Гамана на дереве, которое он приготовил для Мардохая. И гнев царя
утих.

8:1 И въ дн҃ь тъ вдасть царь Ахасъвєросъ Есфири царици домъ Амановъ,
врага Июдѣиского. И Мардъхаи придє пред царꙗ †и повѣда ємоу† ꙋто
бꙗшє єи.
8:2 И снꙗ царь пърстьнь свои ижє бѣ ѡтꙗлъ оу Амана и дасть и Мардъхаєви,
и постави Есфирь царицꙗ Мардъхаꙗ надъ домъмь Амановомь.
8:3 И †наꙋа глаголати Есфирь царицꙗ прєдъ царємь, и падє прєд ногама єго,
и въсплака молꙗщи єго прєвратити ꙁлобу Амановоу Агаги и мысль єго
южє бꙗшє помыслилъ на Июдѣꙗ.
8:4 И простре царь Есфирии прутъ ꙁлатъ, и ѡправи сꙗ Есфирь и ста прєд
царьмь.
8:5 И рєꙋє, ащє царєви оудобрю и ѡбрꙗку милость прєд {нимь и
†провоꙁвѣщю глаголъ пред} царьмь и добра боуду аꙁъ прєд ѡꙋима єго, и
да напишєть книгы вратити мысль Амановоу сына Амдавина Агаги, ижє
бѣ написалъ погꙋбити Июдѣꙗ єжє по всєи власти царєвѣ.
8:6 Нєбо како могоу видѣти ꙁлобу ꙗжє приѡбрѣтє люди моꙗ, и како могꙋ
видѣти пагубꙋ рода моєго?
8:7 И рєꙋє {царь} Есфирии царици и Мардъхаю Июдѣю, сє домъ Амановъ
далъ єсмь Есфири, єгожє повѣсиша на дрєвѣ, им'жє въвьрглъ бꙗшє руцѣ
свои въ Июдѣ{ꙗ}.
8:8 {А вы прєпишє҃т на Июдѣꙗ} ꙗкожє оулюбѣєть ѡꙋима ваю имєнємъ
царєвъмь и ꙁапєꙋатлѣита пєꙋатью царєвою любо †писмєнємь ижє писано
єсть имєнємь царєвъмь и ꙁапєꙋатанѡ пєꙋатию цар҃євою нє [можєть того]
вратити [никтожє].
8:9 И въꙁвани быша писци царєви въ годину ту, въ мѣсꙗць 3-ии, то є҃с
мѣсꙗць Сиванъ (рєкомыи Июнь), {въ} 23 дн҃ь° написаша° ꙗкожє
ꙁаповѣдашє Мардъхаи къ Июдѣѡмъ {и посадникѡ҃м и тиоуно҃м} и къ
вєлможамъ ꙁємнымъ ижє ѿ ѡ[до]ду дажь и до Хусъ 100 и 20 и 7 ꙁємль,
ꙁємлꙗ и ꙁємлꙗ ꙗко писаниє єи, и людиє людиє ꙗко ꙗꙁыкъ ихъ, и къ
Июдѣѡмъ ꙗкожє ихъ писмꙗ и ꙗко ꙗꙁыкъ ихъ.
8:10 И написаша †писмєньмь царєвъмь Ахасъвєроса и ꙁапєꙋатлѣша пєꙋатию
царєвою, и послаша книгы съ приставы коньникы [и] ижє ꙗꙁдꙗху на
бърꙁдыхъ конихъ,°

8:2 ωтѧлъ GW(V); ѿнѧлъ Tn] ѿтѧлъ TS

8:4 оправи сѧ STn] обрати сѧ GWV

8:5 ωбрѧку] corr. to -щꙋ in T, -щꙋ SGWVTn || напишеть STn] напишуть GWVA || нимь . . . гл҃ъ прєд Tn only

8:7 цр҃ь SGWVTn, om. QT || июдѣю QTG; июдѣѧ SWVA; июдѣꙗниноу Tn

8:8 а вы препишеᵀ на июдѣꙗ Tn only || ꙗкоже STn] ꙗко нє GWV || оулюбѣеть QTS, ꙋлюбѣ ѐсть G] оулюби єсть W(V); любо Tn || ҁап҃етлѣита Q, ҁапеѵатлѣита T, -ѣєта S; ҁапеѵѧтано Tn || ҁапеѵатано STn] ҁапеѵатлѣно W, -нно V

8:9 въ Tn only || и посадникωᴹ и тиоуноᴹ Tn only || ѿ ωдоду QTS, ѿ адоду GWV || р҃ и к҃ и ҁ҃ S] .р҃к. и ҁ G, рк҃ҁ WV || ихъ писмѧ GWV] и писмѧ иˣ TSTn

8:10 писмєньмь Q, писмєнємь SGWV, пєсмєнємь T (for {имєнємь} H); имѧ Tn

---

8:1 В день тот отдал царь Ахашверош царице Есѳири дом Гамана, врага иудеев; а Мардохай вошел пред лицом царя, ибо Есѳирь объявила, что́ он для нее.

8:2 И снял царь перстень свой, который он отнял у Гамана, и отдал его Мардохаю; Есѳирь же поставила Мардохая *смотрителем* над домом Гамана.

8:3 И продолжала Есѳирь говорить перед царем, и пала к ногам его, и плакала, и умоляла его предотвратить злобу Гамана-агагиянина и замысел его, который он замыслил против иудеев.

8:4 И простер царь к Есѳири золотой скипетр, и поднялась Есѳирь, и стала пред лицом царя,

8:5 и сказала: «Если царю угодно, и если я обрела милость пред лицом его, и *справедливо* дело это пред лицом царя, и нравлюсь я глазам его, то пусть было бы написано, чтобы возвращены были письма по замыслу Гамана, сына Гаммедаѳы-агагиянина, писанные им об истреблении иудеев во всех областях царя.

8:6 Ибо как могу я видеть бедствие, которое постигнет народ мой, и как могу я видеть гибель родных моих?»

8:7 И сказал царь Ахашверош царице Есѳири и Мардохаю-иудею: «Вот, я дом Гамана отдал Есѳири, и его самого повесили на дереве за то, что он простирал руку свою против иудеев.

8:8 Напишите и вы об иудеях, что вам угодно, от имени царя, и скрепите печатью царя: ибо письма, написанного от имени царя и скрепленного перстнем царя, нельзя отменить».

8:9 И позваны были царские писцы в ту пору, в третий месяц, то есть *в* месяц Сиван, в двадцать третий день его, и написано было все так, как приказал Мардохай, к иудеям и к сатрапам и начальникам и правителям областей, что от Годду и до Куша — ста двадцати семи областей — в каждую область письмом ее и к каждому народу на языке его, и к иудеям письмом их и на языке их.

8:10 И написал он от имени царя Ахашвероша, и скрепил перстнем царя, и послал письма в руках гонцов на конях, на рысаках царя с конных заводов,

8:11 ꙗже дасть царь Июдѣомъ єже [ихъ бѧшє] по всѣмъ градомъ сбирати †и
душахъ† своих, растворити и оубити и погубити всю силу люди и ꙁємлѧ
ижє бѣша мучили {ꙗ} дѣти и жєны, и добыткы ихъ по росполону,
8:12 въ дн҃ь єдинъ въ всѣх ꙁємлѧхъ царѧ Ахасъвєроса, 13 дн҃ь мѣсѧца 12, то
єсть Адаръ (рєкомыи Мартъ).
8:13 Пєчать грамотнаꙗ †даниє ꙁакона† въ всѣх ꙁємлѧхъ и ꙁємлѧхъ и
ѿкрыто[мъ] всѣм людємъ, {быти} [и всѣм людьмъ] Июдѣѡмъ
приготованом {къ} дн҃и тому оумьсти{ти} сѧ ѿ врагъ своих.
8:14 А погоньци иже ѣꙁдѧху на конихъ бърꙁдыхъ° в{ы}нидоша бърꙁо
вънатъщь по рѣчи царєвѣ, и ꙁаконъ быс^{ть} данъ в Соусанѣ градѣ.
8:15 И Мардъхаи вынидє ѿ лица царєва въ свитѣ царьстѣи и въ чєрви и въ
оутринѣ, и вѣньць ꙁлатъ вєликъ [на главѣ єго], и оушьвъ шьлковъ
лєптужьнъ. Градъ жє Сусанъ оуѡхвоти сѧ и възвєсєли сѧ.
8:16 Июдѣѡмъ быс^{ть} просвѣщєньє и вєсєлиє, ѡхвота и чьсть.
8:17 И всѧка ꙁємлѧ и ꙁємлѧ и всѧкъ градъ и градъ, [и] мѣсто идєжє глаголъ
царєвъ и ꙁаконъ єго доидѧшє вєсєльє и ѡхвота Июдѣѡмъ, пиръ и дн҃ь
добръ, и множьство людии ꙁємных жидовѧху сѧ, ꙗко †оумножилъ сѧ
бѧшє страхъ Июдѣискыи на них.
9:1 Въ 12 мѣсѧць то єсть Адаръ (рєкомыи Мартъ) въ 13 дн҃ь, идєжє ащє
постигнѧшє глаголъ царєвъ и ꙁаконъ єго створити въ тъ дн҃ь въ ньжє
{оумыслиша} враꙁи Июдѣистии владѣти ими прєврати сѧ то иже почали
бѧху вра{гы} владѣти Июдѣи.
9:2 И събираху сѧ Июдѣи по градомъ своим [и] по всѣмъ властьмъ царѧ
Ахасъвєроса мьсти творити на всѣх враꙁѣхъ своихъ. И никыижє чл^{овѣ}къ
нє ѡстоꙗшє прєд ними, ꙗко †възидє гроꙁа† ихъ надъ всѣми людми.
9:3 И всѧ вєльможа ꙁємныꙗ и тивуни подъстави и чинѧщє дѣло царєво [и]
възношаху Июдѣꙗ, ꙗко напалъ бѧшє страхъ Мардъхаєвъ на нихъ.
9:4 Ибо бѧшє вєлии Мардъхаи {в дому царєвѣ} и {слух єго хожашє по всєи
ꙁємли ибо мужь Мардъхаи} хожашє вєликъ.
9:5 И оудолѣша Июдѣи всѣмъ врагомъ своимъ раною мєчєвою и оубьєниємь
и погублєниємь и створиша въ [всѣх] враꙁѣхъ своихъ волю свою.
9:6 И въ Сусанѣ градѣ° погубиша Июдѣи 500 мужь,

8:11 ꙗ и^{x} Tn, om. QTSGWV
8:13 быти TSGWVTn, om. Q ‖ къ TSGWVTn; om. Q ‖ оумьсти сѧ QTGWVTn; оум'стити ѿ врагь свои^{x} S
8:14 погоньци Tn, погонцѣ S] погонници GWV ‖ бърꙁдыхъ Q, борꙁды^{x} W] борꙁыхъ TGV, борꙁыихъ S, борꙁы^{x} Tn ‖ внидоша QTSGWVTn ‖ бърꙁо Q, борꙁо TSGV, боръꙁдо W; вборꙁѣ Tn ‖ вънатъщь], внатощь S внатьщє W, оунатщє V; в тои ϒа^{c} Tn
8:15 оушьвъ] оушивъ SWV, оушибъ G; оужє Tn
9:1 оумыслиша Tn; оуслышаша QTSGWV ‖ вра{гы}: враꙁи QTSGWV; враꙁѣ Tn
9:2 и никыижє SG] никыжє T, и никиижє WV
9:4 Ибо бѧшє SGWV] И болѧшє T ‖ в домȣ ц҃рєвѣ TnX; om. QTSGWV ‖ слоух … Мордъхаи TnX; om. QTSGWV
9:5 мєϒєвою STnX] мєϒною GWV ‖ въ SGWV] на Tn
9:6 ·ф· мужь GWV] ·ѳ҃· мужь T, S (with ф in margin)

8:11 о том, что царь позволяет иудеям, находящимся во всяком городе, собраться и встать на *защиту* жизни своей, истребить, убить и погубить все *военные* силы народа и области, которые нападают на них, [убить их] детей и жен, и имущество их разграбить
8:12 в один день по всем областям царя Ахашвероша, в тринадцатый день двенадцатого месяца, то есть месяца Адара.
8:13 Список с этого указа *приказано было* отдать в каждую область, *как* закон, объявляемый для всех народов, чтобы иудеи готовы были к тому дню мстить врагам своим.
8:14 Гонцы, поехавшие верхом на быстрых конях царя, отправились скоро и поспешно с повелением царя. И указ был дан в Шушане-городе.
8:15 И Мардохай вышел от царя в царском одеянии алого и белого цвета, и в большом золотом венце, и в мантии висонной и пурпуровой. И город Шушан возвеселился и возрадовался.
8:16 У иудеев был свет, и радость, и веселие, и почесть.
8:17 И во всякой области и во всяком городе, *во всяком* месте, куда доходило повеление царя и указ его, была радость у иудеев и веселие, пир и праздничный день. И многие из народов страны становились иудеями, потому что напал на них страх перед иудеями.
9:1 В двенадцатый месяц, то есть *в* месяц Адар, в тринадцатый день его, в который пришло время исполниться повелению царя и указу его (в тот день, когда надеялись неприятели иудеев взять власть над ними, а вышло, наоборот, что сами иудеи взяли власть над врагами своими),
9:2 собрались иудеи в городах своих, по всем областям царя Ахашвероша, чтобы простереть руку против зложелателей своих, и никто не мог устоять перед лицом их, потому что страх перед ними пал на все народы.
9:3 И все князья в областях, и сатрапы, и начальники, и исполнители дел царских поддерживали иудеев, потому что пал на них страх перед Мардохаем.
9:4 Ибо велик *был* Мардохай в доме царя, и слух о нем ходил по всем областям, так как этот человек, Мардохай, поднимался выше и выше.
9:5 И перебили иудеи всех врагов своих, побивая мечем, убиением и истреблением, и поступали с неприятелями своими по своей воле.
9:6 И в Шушане-городе убили иудеи и погубили пятьсот человек;

9:7 и Парсанъдас и Далфанъ и Аспасъ

9:8 и Порафа и Адалиꙗ и Аридаса,

9:9 и Парма{с}та и Арисаи и Аридаи и Ваиꙁаса,

9:10 10 сыновъ Амановъ сына Амъдафина врага Июдѣиского оубиша, а въ
полонъ нє простроша рукъ своих.

9:11 И въ дн҃ь тъ придє ҷисло †оубиицъ въ Сусанѣ градѣ прєд цара.

9:12 И рєҷє царь Есфирии царици, въ Сусанѣ градѣ иꙁбиша Июдѣи и погубиша
500 мужь и 10 сыновъ Амановъ [повѣсиша на дрєвє], раꙁвѣ єжє по всєи
ꙁємли царєвѣ ҷто створиша? И проси ты и дам ти, помысли ты и єщє
створимъ тобѣ.

9:13 И рєҷє Есфирь, ащє, царю, тобѣ оулюбѣєть дати пакы ꙁаоутра
Июдѣѡ[є]мъ ижє в Сусанѣ градѣ створити ꙗкожє ꙁаконъ дн҃єшнии, и 10
сыновъ Амановъ †повѣсиша на дрєвѣ.

9:14 И рєҷє царь, створи тако. И быс^{ть} данъ ꙁаконъ въ Соусанѣ градѣ и 10
сыновъ Амоновъ повѣсиша.

9:15 И събраша са Июдѣи ижє въ Сусанѣ градѣ, пакы въ дн҃ь {14} мѣсаца
Адара (рєкомаго Марта), и оубиша въ Сусанѣ градѣ 300 мужь, и въ
полонъ нє подѣша рукъ своих.

9:16 И ѡстаткы Июдѣи ижє по ꙁємламъ цара събраша са и †стоꙗху {на}
покоихъ своихъ {и оупоҷиша ѿ врагъ своих} и оуби[тъ] къждо
нєлюбимого† 70 и 5000 и въ полонъ нє подѣша рукъ своихъ.

9:17 Въ дн҃ь 13 мѣсаца Адара [говѣху] (рєкомаго Марта), и оупоҷиша 14 и
твориша ° дн҃ь питвьныи и вєсєльныи.

9:18 Июдѣи ижє въ Соусанѣ градѣ сбираху са [и] 13 и 14 и поҷиваху 15, и
твораху и тъ дн҃ь питвьныи {и вєсєлыи}.

9:19 Того ради Июдѣи распра{ш}єници ижє сѣдаху по градомъ распрашєным
творащє дн҃ь 14 мѣсаца Адара (рєкомаго Марта), вєсєлиє и питьє и дн҃ь
добръ, и посылающє дары другъ къ другу.

9:20 И написа Мардъхаи рѣҷь сию и посла книгы по всѣм Июдѣємъ ижє по
всѣмъ ꙁємламъ цара Ахасъвєроса блиꙁь и далєҷє,

9:7 парсанъда҇ QW, парсандасъ Tn, -сь X, парса҇дастъ V, порсанъдасть T, -тъ S, парсанъдасть G
9:8 адалиꙗ GWVX] адариꙗ TS; адалида Tn
9:9 пармаста TnX, пармата QTSWV, паръмата G
9:10 сн҃амъдафина Q; сн҃а ам- TSGWV
9:12 .ф҃. GWV] .ѳ҃. T, S (with ф҃ in margin)
9:13 оулюбѣєтъ Tn, -бѣ[е] GX] оулюблѣєть S, оулюбиєтъ W (оубїєть V[!])
9:15 .д. QSWVX, ѵєтвєртыи G; .ıд. T (ı added later); .д҃.и Tn; H ‘14th’
9:16 остаткы] ѡстатокъ TSG, останокъ WV || .о҃. и .҂є. QTGV; .҂о. и. ҂є. S, .о. и пѧ[т] тысѧщь W, .о. и .є. тысоущь AB || на TnX; om. QTSGWV || и . . . свои[x] TnX; om QTS-GWV || оуби TnX; оубитъ QTSGWV
9:17 говѣху S, говѣахоу X; om. Tn] то бѣху GWV || оупоѵиша STn] оупоуѵиша T, опоѵиша X, поѵиша G; полоуѵиша WV
9:18 ижє GTn] жє TSWV || и вєсєлыи WV, Q om.; вєсєлыи T; и вєсєлныи SG; вєсєл҇ѧ Tn
9:19 распращєници QTG, -цы W, распрѧщаницы V, распрѧшєници Tn, распрашєници S || творѧщє GTn] творѧшє TSWV || къ lost in Q because of torn page

---

9:7 и Паршандаѳу, и Далфона, и Аспаѳу,
9:8 и Пораѳу, и Адалию, и Аридаѳу,
9:9 и Пармашту, и Арисая, и Аридая, и Ваизаѳу,—
9:10 десятерых сыновей Гамана, сына Гаммедаѳы, врага иудеев, убили они, а на грабеж не простерли руки своей.
9:11 В тот же день донесли царю о числе убитых в Шушане-городе.
9:12 И сказал царь царице Есѳири: «В Шушане-городе убили иудеи и погубили пятьсот человек и десятерых сыновей Гамана; что же сделали они в прочих областях царя? Каково желание твое?—оно и будет удовлетворено. И какова еще просьба твоя?—она и будет исполнена».
9:13 И сказала Есѳирь: «Если царю угодно, то пускай бы позволено было иудеям, которые в Шушане, сделать по сегодняшнему закону и завтра, и десятерых сыновей Гамана пускай повесили бы на дереве».
9:14 И приказал царь сделать так, и дан был *на это* указ в Шушане, и десятерых сыновей Гамана повесили.
9:15 И собрались иудеи, которые в Шушане, также и в четырнадцатый день месяца Адара, и убили в Шушане триста человек, а на грабеж не простерли руки своей.
9:16 И прочие иудеи, находившиеся в царских областях, собрались, чтобы стать на *защиту* жизни своей и *обрести* покой от врагов своих, и убили из неприятелей своих семьдесят пять тысяч, а на грабеж не простерли руки своей.
9:17 *Это было* в тринадцатый день месяца Адара, а в четырнадцатый день сего же месяца они успокоились и сделали его днем пира и веселья.
9:18 Иудеи же, которые в Шушане, собирались в тринадцатый день его и в четырнадцатый день его, а в пятнадцатый день его успокоились и сделали его днем пира и веселья.
9:19 Поэтому иудеи сельские, живущие в селеньях открытых, проводят четырнадцатый день месяца Адара в веселье и пире, как день праздничный, посылая подарки друг другу.
9:20 И описал Мардохай эти происшествия, и послал письма ко всем иудеям, которые в областях царя Ахашвероша, к близким и к дальним,

9:21 оуставити имъ абыша творили дн҃ии 14 {мѣсꙗца Адара и 15} всꙗкоу
годину и годину

9:22 ꙗкоже дн҃ь въ ньже поѹиша Июдѣи ѿ врагъ своихъ и мѣсꙗць иже
преврати сꙗ имъ ѿ скърбии къ веселию и ѿ желаниꙗ къ дн҃и доброму
створити ꙗ дн҃и питвьныꙗ и веселныꙗ и посылати дары къмуждо другу
своему и помилование сиротамъ.

9:23 И подъꙗша Июдѣи ꙗкоже бѣша поѹали творити и ꙗже бѣ написалъ
Мардъхаи к нимъ.

9:24 Любо Аманъ сынъ Амъдафинъ Аагаги врагъ всѣх Июдѣи [иже]
мыслꙗше на Июдѣꙗ ° погуби{ти} ꙗ.

9:25 Да егда прихожаше пред царꙗ ° [и] съ грамотою ѡбрати сꙗ мысль его
ꙁлаꙗ, иже помыслилъ баше на Июдѣꙗ, на главу свою и повѣшенъ быс^{ть}
съ сынъми на древе.

9:26 И того ради проꙁваша дн҃и ты ° по имени жребиинѣмь, ꙁане{же} всꙗ рѣѹь
си книгамъ симъ и ꙗже видѣша того ради и еже събы^{сть} сꙗ имъ.

9:27 И оуставиша и подъꙗша Июдѣи на сꙗ и на племꙗ свое, и на всꙗ елико их
приступаше къ нимъ, и н^{ы}нѣ того не имуть преступати, ꙗкоже суть
творꙗще 2 дн҃ии си ꙗкоже писмꙗ ихъ и ꙗкоже година ихъ по всꙗ лѣта и
лѣта.

9:28 И дн҃ии сиꙗ поминающе суть и творꙗще ꙗ въ всꙗ {вѣ}кы вѣком, родъ и
родъ, ꙁемлꙗ и ꙁемлꙗ, и всꙗкъ градъ и градъ, и дн҃ье веселии си не
†минуша [николиже] ѿ Июдѣи, и памꙗть ° не конѹаеть сꙗ ѿ ѹадъ их.

9:29 И написа Есфир{ь} царицꙗ дщи Авихаилова и Мардъхаи Июдѣи всю
твьрдь [и] оуставити книгы веселиꙗ сего, другыꙗ.

9:30 Посла книгы къ {всѣмъ} Июдѣемъ къ 127 ꙁемль царства Ахасъверосова
рѣѹи оумиреныꙗ и оувѣреныꙗ,

9:31 оуставити дн҃и веселиꙗ сего въ годы своꙗ ꙗкоже оустави Мардъхаи
Июдѣи и Есфирь царицꙗ и ꙗко оуставиша †душа своꙗ† на ѹада своꙗ,
рѣѹи говѣныꙗ и въплꙗ их.

9:32 И реѹение Есфирино оустави глаголы веселїа сего написа въ книгах.

10:1 И възложи царь Ахасъверосъ дани на ꙁемлю и на ѡстровы морьскыа.

9:21 мц҃а Адара и .єі҃. Tn only
9:22 посылати SGWVTn] послати T ‖ къмуждо] комуждо TTn; кождо SGWV
9:23 ꙗкоже G] ꙗже TSW, й҃ Tn, (V om. 5 words after июдѣи) ‖ бѣ написалъ GWV] бѣша писалъ T, бѧше писалъ S, бѧше написалъ Tn
9:24 аагаги QTGW; агаги V (perhaps a letter erased?), агаги S ‖ мыслѧше SGTn] мышлѧше TWV ‖ погуби Q, погубити TSGWV, погоу Tn
9:26 ꙁане ꙗже QTSG, ꙁанеѧ єже WV
9:27 приступаше Tn] приступиша SGWV ‖ прєступати STn] прєступити GWV ‖ дн҃ии си] дн҃и си G, дн҃и сии TWV, дн҃їи сїи S; дн҃и Tn
9:28 всѧкы Q, всѧ вѣкы TSGWV + вѣкомъ Tn
9:29 И TSGWVTn; om. Q ‖ Есфирии QTS, Есфири WV; Есфирь GTn
9:30 всѣм Tn, om. QTSGWV ‖ июдѣємъ S] -ѡмъ TWVTn
9:31 оустави SGWVTn] оуставити T
10:1–3 in G is translated from Latin, see comm.

9:21 чтобы они установили празднование у себя четырнадцатого дня месяца Адара и пятнадцатого дня его каждый год,—
9:22 дней, в которые иудеи *обрели* покой от врагов своих, и месяца, в который превратилась у них печаль в радость и сетование—в день праздничный,—чтобы сделали их днями пира и веселья, посылая подарки друг другу и подаяния бедным.
9:23 И приняли иудеи то, что уже сами начали делать и о чем Мардохай написал к ним,
9:24 как Гаман, сын Гаммедаѳы-агагиянина, враг всех иудеев, думал погубить иудеев и бросал пур, то есть жребий, об истреблении и погублении их,
9:25 и как *Есѳирь* вошла пред лицом царя, и как *царь* приказал письмом, чтобы злой замысел Гамана, который он замыслил против иудеев, обратился на голову его, и *чтобы* повесили его и сыновей его на дереве.
9:26 Потому и назвали эти дни Пурим, от имени «пур». Поэтому, согласно всем словам сего письма и тому, что сами видели и до чего доходило у них,
9:27 постановили иудеи и взяли на себя, и на отпрысков своих, и на всех, присоединяющихся к ним, непременно праздновать эти два дня по предписанному о них и в свое для них время каждый год;
9:28 и чтобы дни эти были поминаемы и празднуемы во всех родах, в каждом племени, в каждой области и в каждом городе, и чтобы дни эти Пурим не отменялись у иудеев и память о них не исчезла у детей их.
9:29 И написала царица Есѳирь, дочь Авихаила, и Мардохай-иудей со всею настойчивостию, чтобы исполняли это второе письмо о Пуриме.
9:30 И послал *он* письма ко всем иудеям, в сто двадцать семь областей царства Ахашвероша, со словами мира и правды,
9:31 чтобы они твердо соблюдали эти дни Пурим в *названное* им время, какое уставил для них Мардохай-иудей и царица Есѳирь и какое они сами назначали для себя и для детей своих—дела пощения и воплей.
9:32 И повеление Есѳири подтвердило эти слова о Пуриме, и оно вписано в книгу.
10:1 И обложил царь Ахашверош податью землю и острова морские.

10:2 И всє дѣло твєрдї єго и мощї єго и расповѣданїє вєличьа Мардъхаєва
и[мь]жє възвєлїча єго царь и та соуть написана въ кнїгах грамотных [и]
царєвъ Мадѣискыхъ и Фарисѣискыих,
10:3 Ѩко Мардъхаи Июдѣи, другъ царѧ Ахасъвєроса, и вєликъ въ Июдѣ{и}х
и вольникъ множьства братьѩ своєѧ възискаа доброты людєм своим и
проповѣдаа миръ всѣм чадом своимъ. аминь.

10:2 ц҃рєвъ мадѣскыхъ QAB] T om.; ц҃рвъ дѣамьскых [!] WV; мадѣамьскы^{x} и фарисѣискы^{x} 4 (Porfir'ev, p. 5); мадискых и ѳарсиискых 24 (Kopanev, p. 9); фарсїискы^{x} и мидїискыи^{x} S

10:3 вꙁискаѩ, въꙁыскаа S] въꙁыска WV || проповѣдаѩ S] проповѣда WV

10:2 И все дела силы его и могущества его, и рассказ о величии Мардохая, которым возвеличил его царь, не записаны ли в книге дел дней царей мидийских и персидских?

10:3 Ибо Мардохай-иудей *был* вторым после царя Ахашвероша, и великим для иудеев, и любимым для множества братьев своих, *ибо* искал добра народу своему и говорил во благо всего племени своего.

T0.1 The Book of Esther was, for the Orthodox Slavs of up to the 14th century, a part (however marginal) of Christian culture, a concept that automatically was delineated in terms of the Greek Orthodox background. The basic scriptural, liturgical, and hymnodic texts had been translated from Greek by the time Jaroslav Volodimerovič began to consolidate his rule over Rus′ and gained the reputation for fostering monks, churchs, and books that is praised by the chronicler in the entry for 1037 in the PVL. Whether the Slavonic Esther was translated before or after that time, it was intended to fit into patterns that existed c1037, and/or the modifications of those patterns that took place up to about 1350. What did the other translations look like? What is the relation of other OT books in Slavonic to the MT?

T0.2 Translation techniques range from word-for-word agrammatical strings of glosses intended to help readers to read the original language to paraphrases intended to replace the original completely by a restatement in the new language. More generally, critics distinguish literal from free translation. An ideal Bible translation is, in the words of Bruce Metzger, a distinguished textual critic and editor, *as* **literal** *as possible, as* **free** *as necessary.* This view was surely shared by the translators who produced the Septuagint and by the Slavs who labored to reproduce the books in their own language. Yet then, as now, individuals inevitably disagreed as to when a literal rendering of a given phrase in its specific context is possible, and as to just how much freedom is necessary or appropriate. Still, literalism was the rule. A text translated as literally as possible from Hebrew into grammatical Greek will give clues as to precisely what the Hebrew looked like. Similarly, a literal translation into OCS from Greek will tell us a great deal about the Greek wording. It follows that the Slavic that closely reflects a Greek version will still be close to the original Hebrew.

T1.1 Let us look at specific examples of Hebrew, Greek, and Slavic parallels to observe the *linguistic* relationships. The Slavic is from ms W (East Slavic, c1500). We start with the first five verses of 2 Kingdoms (= MT 2 Samuel) 12. The English glosses attempt to show the major characteristics of the H words. ("*A*" means *accusative marker.* The verb-forms are explicitly masculine where we do not provide the pronoun *she.*).

12:1	καὶ ἀπέστειλεν	κύριος	τὸν Ναθαν	τὸν προφήτην	πρὸς Δαυιδ
	wyšlḥ	yhwh	’t ntn		’l dwd
	and-sent	*Lord*	*A-Nathan*		*to David*
	и посла	господь	нафана	пророка	къ давыду

καὶ εἰσῆλθεν	πρὸς αὐτὸν	καὶ εἶπεν	αὐτῷ	ἀνάγγειλον δή μοι τὴν κρίσιν ταύτην
wyb’	’lyw	wy’mr	lw	
and-came	*to-him*	*and-said*	*to-him*	
и влѣꙁе	к нему	и рече		ѿвѣщаи ми царю нынѣ рѣчи сеи

δύο ἦσαν ἄνδρες	ἐν πόλει	μιᾷ	εἷς πλούσιος	καὶ εἷς πένης
šny ’nšym hyw	b‘yr	’ḥt	’ḥd ‘šyr	w’ḥd r’š
two men were	*in-city*	*one*	*one rich*	*and-one poor*
два мужа бѧста	въ единомъ	градѣ	единъ богатъ	а другии оубогъ

Now, we agree, on the basis of the totality of cultural and textological information, that the Slavic was translated from Greek. Let us, however, try to look at these lines with a completely open mind: what clues *dis*prove the possibility that the Slavic came directly from the Hebrew? Further, let us entertain the possibility that the underlying Hebrew might differ somewhat from the MT—a possibility now generally recognized by biblical scholars. The Hebrew in the first two lines represents eight units that might be rendered as units in Gk or Sl.[1] Both versions add a connective (καί/и) at the beginning, but addition or suppression of these little words (whether as connectives or emphatic elements) is ubiquitous and, in most cases, of little importance.[2] More significant is *the prophet* in the first line, and we may hypothesize appositional *hnby'* for the original H. In the second line, Greek and Slavic have slightly different prefatory remarks, "Do tell me this judgement," and "Answer me, king, now this matter," for which H equivalents could be devised.[3] Otherwise the three texts agree, with appropriate grammatical adjustments,[4] except that Sl has transposed *city one* to *one city.*

12:2	καὶ τῷ πλουσίῳ	ἦν ποίμνια	καὶ βουκόλια	πολλὰ	σφόδρα
	l'šyr	hyh c'n	wbqr	hrbh	m'd
	to-the-rich	*was flocks*	*and-herds*	*many*	*very*
	и оу богатаго	стада бѧхути	буволи	мноꙁи	ѕѣло

The three texts agree literally on the expression meaning "(he) had" and on everything else except that instead of *herds (of horned cattle)* Sl has a word perhaps meaning "buffalos," surely to be labelled a mistake.[5]

12:3	καὶ τῷ πένητι	οὐδὲν ἀλλ' ἢ	ἀμνὰς	μία	μικρὰ
	wlrš	'yn kl ky 'm	kbśh	'ḥt	qṭnh
	and-to-the-poor	*is-not all but if*	*ewe-lamb*	*one*	*small*
	а оу оубогаго	ниѵтоже но токмо	агницѧ	единa	мала

ἣν	ἐκτήσατο	καὶ περιεποιήσατο	καὶ ἐξέθρεψεν αὐτὴν
'šr	qnh		wyḥyh
which	*(he)-bought*		*and-nourished-her*
юже	стѧжѧ	и оустрои ю	и въскорми ю

1 Strict literalism might be defined as the translation of each word, or even each morpheme, but the structural requirements of individual languages impose restrictions. The H prepositions *l-* and *'l* are very close in meaning, and at the same time close to the meaning of Indo-European dative case-forms. The former, however, is regarded as a bound morpheme that is part of the following word (*lntn* 'to Nathan') while the latter has orthographical independence (*'l ntn*). The Hebrew accusative-marker is structurally more like a Gk or Sl preposition, but an IE accusative case form can be counted as strict literal translation. The distance from H to either Gk or Sl is about the same, while that between Gk and Sl is shorter.

2 This variation with и and καί has no analogue in H, for *w-* is part of the tense-aspect system and plays a vital role in the syntactical patterning; its presence or absence is important.

3 Cf. Deut. 17:9 ἀγγέλουσι σοι τὴν κρίσιν, 'they will report the judgement to thee'; H *whgydw lk 't dbr hmšpṭ*, 'and they shall show thee the sentence of judgement.'

4 W's spelling is often faulty; бѧстѧ for -ста (expected бѣста or ancient бѣсте) is not surprising.

5 The explanation doubtless lies in the realm of the many problems that can arise as a result of faulty transmission of a translated text, see below. Here the original translator probably took over the Greek word as *воуколи, which was then rationalized (or miscopied) to боуволи (itself a rare word akin to Lat *bubalus*, Gk βούβαλος, cf. Srez sub бивол-, боувол-, бывол-).

καὶ ἡδρήνθη μετ' αὐτοῦ καὶ μετὰ τῶν υἱῶν αὐτοῦ ἐπὶ τὸ αὐτὸ;
wtgdl 'mw w'm bnyw yḥdw;
and-she-grew with-him and-with sons-his together;
и въꙁврастє с нимъ и съ сыномъ его в купѣ;

ἐκ τοῦ ἄρτου αὐτοῦ ἤσθιεν καὶ ἐκ τοῦ ποτήριου αὐτοῦ ἔπινεν
mptw t'kl wmksw tšth
from-bread-his she-ate and from-cup-his she-drank
ѿ хлѣба его ꙗдѧше и ѿ чѧши его пиаше

καὶ ἐν τῷ κόλπῳ αὐτοῦ ἐκάθευδεν καὶ ἦν αὐτῷ ὡς θυγάτηρ.
wbḥyqw tškb wthy lw kbt.
and-in-bosom-his she-lay/rested and she-was to-him as-daughter.
и на лонѣ его почиваше и бѣ ему ꙗко дщи.

The H idiom *nothing but* (first line) is reproduced fairly literally. For H *nourished* (etymologically *caused-to-live*), Gk uses two near-synonymous verbs, to *keep alive* and *nourish* (both of which occur elsewhere in LXX to translate the same H causative).[6] In the last line, both Gk and Sl use dative without preposition for *to-him*. The rest of the verse consists of literal equivalents.[7]

12:4 καὶ ἦλθεν πάροδος τῷ ἀνδρὶ τῷ πλουσίῳ
wyb' hlk l'yš h'šyr
and-came traveller to-man the-rich
и приде нѣкто с пути къ мужу богатому

καὶ ἐφείσατο λαβεῖν ἐκ τῶν ποιμνίων αὐτοῦ
wyḥml lqḥt mc'nw
and-had-compassion to-take from-flocks-his
и не въсхотѣ поꙗти ѿ стад своих

καὶ ἐκ τῶν βουκολίων αὐτοῦ τοῦ ποιῆσαι τῷ ξένῳ ὁδοιπόρῳ
wmbqrw l'śwt l'rḥ
and-from-herds-his to-make for-the-guest
и ѿ буволицъ на створение ѡбиду путнику

ἐλθόντι πρὸς αὐτὸν, καὶ ἔλαβεν τὴν ἀμνάδα τοῦ πένητος
hb' lw wyqḥ 't kbśt hyš hr'š
the-coming to-him, and-he-took A-lamb-of man the-poor
пришедшу к нему, но поꙗтъ агнецю оубогаго

[6] Such "doublets" may arise at the moment of translation or in the course of later copying, see below, T3.12. The Gk gives two valid alternate meanings of the H: *keep from dying, save* and *cause life to continue, feed.* The two verbs in Sl are not really synonyms: оустроити is only marginally appropriate; it has a broad range of meanings including *put in order* and *take care of.* This is perhaps a signal that direct translation from H is implausible.

[7] W's въꙁврастє probably is based on late въꙁърастє (old въꙁдрастє).

καὶ ἐποίησεν αὐτὴν	τῷ ἀνδρὶ	τῷ ἐλθόντι	πρὸς αὐτόν.
wy'śh	l'yš	hb'	'lyw.
and-made-her	*for-the-man*	*the-coming*	*to-him.*
и ʒакла и сътвори ѡбитъ	мужу	пришедшему	к нему.

The Gk verb in the second line is "held back, restrained from," while Sl is simply "did not want," a phrase often used to mean *refuse*. In line 3 Gk again uses dative, but Sl has къ for H *l*. The equivalents of *traveller* were apparently chosen to emphasize the notion of arrival from some other place. The infinitive "(in order) to make/do/prepare" becomes substantivized in Gk by means of the preposed genitive article τοῦ, and in Sl by a verbal substantive; both are reasonable equivalents. Slavic adds an object, *dinner* (normalized обѣд-). H *guest* becomes *foreign traveller* in Gk but only "one who has arrived" in Sl. The laconic *did/made-her* is expanded to *slaughtered and made dinner* in Slavic—is this still within the bounds of the definition *as free as necessary*?

12:5	καὶ ἐθυμώθη	ὀργῇ	Δαυιδ σφόδρα τῷ ἀνδρί.	καὶ εἶπεν Δαυιδ
	wyḥr	'p	dwd b'yš m'd.	wy'mr
	and-was inflamed	*anger-of*	*David on-the-man very.*	*and-said*
	и раʒгнѣва сѧ	гнѣвомъ	ѕѣло давыдъ на моужа того.	и реѵе давыдъ

πρὸς Ναθαν	ζῇ Κύριος,	ὅτι υἱὸς θανάτου	ὁ ἀνὴρ	ὁ ποιήσας τοῦτο.
'l ntn	ḥy yhwh	ky bn mwt	h'yš	h'śh zwt.
to-Nathan	*may-live Lord*	*for son-of death*	*the-man*	*the-doing this.*
къ нафаноу	живъ гд҃ь	ꙗко достоинъ є҇с	мужь тои смр҃ти	створивыи то.

The H expression denotes extreme anger, often translated *(someone's) anger burned,* but it is not a *figura etymologica* because two different roots are used, as in the Gk. The Sl translation, however, becomes an etymological figure (cf. T5, below). The adverb *very* (σφόδρα, *m'd,* ѕѣло) is the only word whose relative position in the sentence changes. Sl carries over the preposition *'l-*/πρός as къ, surely a usage that was established early in OCS. The exclamation "as the Lord lives" is rendered in conventional ways in both Gk and Sl. H *son of death* is replicated in Gk but replaced by "worthy of death" in Sl. W's wording (OB agrees) may well not belong to the original translator, but to a subsequent scribe or editor. (Note that a copula "is" has been added, and that the word *death* is strangely positioned.) In sum, the Slavic wording could well be directly dependent on the MT.

T1.2 Somewhat different problems arise in the versions of Genesis 31:34–5, where Laban, Rachel's father, is looking for his stolen household gods. (The Slavic is from Mixajlov's edition, somewhat normalized.)

Ραχηλ δὲ	ἔλαβεν	τὰ εἴδωλα	καὶ ἐνέβαλεν αὐτὰ	εἰς τὰ σάγματα	τῆς καμήλου
wrḥl	lqḥh	't htrpym	wtśmm	bkr	hgml
And-Rachel	*took-she*	*A-the-images*	*and-she-put-them*	*in-saddle-of*	*the-camel*
Рахиль же	въʒемши	коумиры	положи ихъ	под сѣдло	велбуже

καὶ ἐπεκάθισεν αὐτοῖς.
wtšb 'lyhm wymšš lbn 't kl h'hl wl' mc.'
and-she-sat on-them. And groped Laban A-all the-tent and-not found.
и сѣде връхоу ихъ.

Here Sl and Gk omit a phrase of MT; this is part of a rearrangement of elements interpreted as reflecting variant Hebrew texts. Otherwise the wording differs only in that the Sl presents the hiding-place as *underneath* rather than *inside* the saddle.[8]

καὶ εἶπεν τῷ πατρὶ αὐτῆς Μὴ βαρέως φέρε, κύριε, οὐ δύναμαι
wt'mr 'l 'byh 'l yḥr b'yny 'dny ky lw' 'wkl
and-she-said to father-her, not be-angry in-eyes-of lord-my, for not I-am-able
рече же отцоу своемоу, не имѣи си тѧжка господи, не могоу

ἀναστῆναι ἐνώπιόν σου, ὅτι τὸ κατ' ἐθισμὸν τῶν γυναικῶν μοι ἐστίν.
lqwm mpnyk ky drk nšym li.
to-stand-up from-face-thy for way-of women to-me.
въстати прѣд тобою ѩко вещь женска ми есть.

ἠρεύνησεν δὲ Λαβαν ἐν ὅλῳ τῷ οἴκῳ καὶ οὐχ εὗρεν τὰ εἴδωλα.
wyḥpś wl' mc' 't htrpym.
and-he-searched and-not found A-the-images.
иска же Лаванъ въ всемъ имѣнии и не обрѣте коумиръ.

Rachel's mollifying phrase uses the verb we encountered in 2 Sam 12:5, but with no expressed subject and the semi-preposition "in (the) eyes of my lord" in the sense "as far as you are concerned." The Gk has abandoned literalism in favor of an appropriate idiom that uses entirely different words, "Do not carry heavily" or "with difficulty" (which occurs in LXX only here and in the Maccabees, known only in Gk). The awkward Sl must be recognized as an effort to reproduce the Gk; roughly "do not have for yourself difficult (things)." Not only is it distant from the H, it is unsatisfactory in its own terms. Scribes were unsure what was intended, and distorted the phrase (не смѣи си 'don't laugh'; не смѣси 'don't mix' [?]) or rationalized it (не стѫжиши си 'you will not complain'; не оучини ми 'don't put it right for me' [?]). Rachel's excuse for not standing up, however, is rendered freely and appropriately by Gk and Sl idioms: "for the according-to-habituation of-women to-me is"; "for I have (a) female thing/matter." The rest of the texts consist of perfectly literal and acceptable renderings.

T1.31 The book of Ruth is represented in early Slavonic by two versions, one transmitted only in Croatian Glagolitic breviaries and surely of Cyrillo-Methodian origin (S1), and the other a thorough revision to be ascribed to Preslav in the 900s (S2). Both were published by Mixajlov and later by Vajs. Here is 1:1ab:

[8] The translator (or, very possibly, a subsequent copyist) did not visualize a saddle as a sort of bag stuffed with soft materials, and found *in* inappropriate.

Καὶ ἐγένετο	ἐν τῷ	κρίνειν τοὺς κριτὰς,	καὶ ἐγένετο λιμὸς	ἐν τῇ γῇ,
wyhy	bymy	špṭ hšpṭym	wyhy r‘b	b’rc
and-it-was	*in-days-of*	*judging-of the judges,*	*and-it-was hunger*	*in-the-land,*
S1 бисть оубо	соудещимь	соудиѣмь	и бисть гладь	по ꙁемли,
S2 и бысть	вънєгда	соужахоу соудїѧ	и бысть гладъ	на ꙁемли.

καὶ ἐπορεύθη	ἀνὴρ	ἀπὸ Βηθλεεμ	Ἰουδα
wylk	’yš	mbyt lḥm	yhwdh
and-went	*man*	*from-Beth-lehem-of*	*Juda*
и идє	моужь	от Витлѣома ꙁємлє	Июдови
и идє	моужь	ѿ Виѳлеѥма Іюдина	

Gk and S2 reproduce the introductory H connective, while S1 replaces it with “therefore”—a departure from literalism. The underlying H lacked the *days* of MT, and is to be posited as *bšpṭ* ‘in the judging-of’ with an infinitive construct that cannot be exactly reproduced in Gk or Sl. The Gk here is typical, preposition *in* + article + infinitive; *when* + finite verb is a frequent alternative, and the genitive absolute is possible. S1 uses dative absolute, S2 *when* + imperfect. These Slavic lines could equally well have been translated directly from H. Verse 1c:

τοῦ παροικῆσαι	ἐν ἀγρῷ Μωαβ,	αὐτὸς	καὶ ἡ γυνὴ αὐτοῦ,	καὶ οἱ δύο υἱοὶ αὐτοῦ.
lgwr	bśdy mw’b	hw’	w’štw	wšny bnyw.
to-dwell	*in-fields-of Moab,*	*he*	*and-wife-his*	*and-two sons-his.*
пришалствовати	на село Моавово,	та	и жєна єго	и сн҃а єго.
ѡбитанїѧ ради	въ сєлѣ Моавли,	самъ	и жєна єго	и два сн҃а єго.

The H infinitive construct with *l* ‘to’ corresponds to Sl infinitive of purpose, so the Gk infinitive with preposed genitive article and S1’s infinitive are as literal as possible, and S2’s “for the sake of dwelling” is not too free. Gk παροικῆσαι rather than unprefixed οἰκῆσαι provides a nuance of temporary dwelling that is inherent in Biblical H *gwr*; S1’s *пришьльствовати is more explicitly ‘dwell as a stranger.’ Neither verb is as free as possible. The pronoun *he* is *тъ in S1, but самъ in S2. Hebrew, Gk and S2 specify *two* by means of a numeral; S1 makes an unemphatic specification by means of the unambiguous dual form. Again there is nothing in the two Slavic versions that could be not derived from the Hebrew text.

T1.32 Verse 3:18:

LXX	ἡ δὲ εἶπεν,	κάθου θυγάτερ	ἕως	τοῦ ἐπιγνῶναί σε
MT	wt’mr	šby bty	‘d ’šr	td‘yn
	and-she-said,	*sit, daughter-my,*	*till-that*	*you-know-fem.*
S1	она жє рєѵє	сѣди дєщи,	доидєжє	разумѣєши
S2	си жє рєѵє	сѣди дщи,	дондєжє	оувѣси

πῶς οὐ πεσεῖται	ῥῆμα	οὐ γὰρ μὴ ἡσυχάσει
’yk ypl	dbr	ky l’ yšqṭ
how will-fall	*matter*	for not (he-)will-be-silent
како нападєть ти	глаголь дн҃сь	нє имать бо прѣмлчати
како оулѧжєть	слово	нє оумлъчитъ

ὁ ἀνὴρ	ἕως ἄν	τελέσῃ	τὸ ῥῆμα	σήμερον.
h’yš	ky ’m	klh	hdbr	hywm.
the-man	*but if*	*(he-)ends*	*the-matter*	*today*
мужь	доидєжє	кончаєть	глаголь	дн҃сь.
мужь	доидєжє	съвръшить	слово	днєⷭ.

In this verse the postposed connectives жє and бо are appropriate equivalents of preposed *w-* and *ky*. For *fall* in the sense *turn out, show a result,* S2 has substituted a rare verb apparently meaning “settle down.” The extra elements in the second line of Sl could come from any scribe: the benefactive *to/for you* (before *matter*) serves as clarification, while the *today* (after *matter*) anticipates the end of the next clause. For *dbr* ‘word/matter/affair,’ see L8.2.

T1.4 The Song of Songs is also known in two versions, one old, perhaps even going back to Methodius, and the other a revision made when the biblical verses were embedded in a commentary, probably in Preslav in the 900s.[9] Verse 1:7 illustrates some of the complications a poetic text presents:

LXX	[1] ἀπάγγελόν μοι,	[2] ὃν ἠγάπησεν	[3] ἡ ψυχή μου,
MT	[1] hgydh ly,	[2] š’hbh	[3] npšy,
	[1] tell me	[2] whom she-loves	[3] soul-my
Sl1	[1] въꙁвѣсти ми	[2] єгожє въꙁлюби	[3] душа моа,
Sl2	[1] въꙁвѣсти ми	[2] єгожє въꙁлюби	[3] душа моꙗ,

[4] ποῦ ποιμαίνεις,	[5] ποῦ κοιτάζεις	[6] ἐν μεσεμβρίᾳ,	[7] μήποτε
[4] ’ykh tr‘h	[5] ‘ykh trbyc	[6] bchrym	[7] šlmh
[4] where you-pasture	[5] where you fold	[6] at-noon	[7] lest
[4] гдє пасєши,	[5] гдє лєжєши	[6] в полуднє,	[7] єда когда
[4] гдє пасєши,	[5] гдє почиваєши	[6] в полуднє,	[7] да нє

[8] γένωμαι	[9] ὡς περιβαλλομένη	[10] ἐν ἀγέλαις	[11] ἑταίρων σου.
[8] ’hyh	[9] k‘ṭyh	[10] ‘l ‘dry	[11] ḥbryk.
[8] I-be/become	[9] as wrapping	[10] on/at/by flocks-of	[11] friends-your.
[8] бѫдѫ	[9] ꙗко обходѧщи	[10] по стадѣхъ	[11] дроугъ твоих’
[8] буду	[9] ꙗко одѣвающи сѧ	[10] по стадѣ	[11] оунєць твоих’

[9] The texts were published by Alekseev (1983, 1986). He overlooks the substantial agreement in wording throughout the book and insists that the younger version was produced in Rus′ by the putative native Rusian translators whose existence he takes as a given. Cf. Lunt 1985d. Disputed points cannot be adjudicated without the full context, the commentary in which the verses occur.

The Hebrew means '[1] tell me, [2–3] (you) whom my soul loves, [4] where you pasture, [5] where you cause to lie down [6] at-noon, [7] lest [8] I become [9] like wrapped (fem. sg.) [10] at/by/near the flocks/herds of [11] your friends.' The present of [2] becomes aorist in the versions. The verb [4] does not require an express object; *sheep* or *flocks* is understood.[10] [5] is a causative, /tarbîc/, "you will make to lie down" of a verb that refers to animals, usually four-legged. Omission of a letter yields *trbc*, to be be read as a future, /tirbāc/ 'you will lie down,' which, although inappropriate here, may be what the translators had in mind.[11] The participle [9] is taken to mean "covered" or "veiled." The Greek offers a fairly literal equivalent that can mean 'clothed,' and the same idea is in the secondary Slavic одѣвающи сѧ. The older Slavic text, however, suggests a Hebrew variant with reversed consonants, *ṭ'yh*, meaning 'wandering,' i.e., 'one who strays'; this idea justifies the preposition по. The revised clause, however, is extremely obscure.[12] The shift from plural -ѣхъ to -ѣ might be a later change, a simple failure to copy a superscript [х], or it might be connected with the change from 'friends' to 'young bulls' (оуньци, OCS юньци). Perhaps these significant changes in the biblical wording have something to do with the commentary in which the verse is imbedded; we do not have access to the commentary. In this verse there is nothing that demonstrates conclusively that the Slavonic was not translated directly from the Hebrew.

T1.5 Here is another OT passage, 1 Kingdoms [= MT 1 Samuel] 16:21–23 as recorded in its full context (from ms W), and also portions of verse 23 in the form embedded in the Chronicle of George the Monk, Hamartolos (Istrin 1920 125, lines 20–1), compared to the usual LXX wording and the MT.

LXX	Καὶ εἰσῆλθεν	Δαυιδ	πρὸς Σαουλ	καὶ παρειστήκει	ἐνώπιον αὐτοῦ
MT	wyb'	dwd	'l š'wl	wy'md	lpnyw
	and-entered	*David*	*to Saul*	*and-stood*	*to-face-his*
W	и вниде	дд҃ъ	къ саоулȣ	и пре[д]ста	пре[д] нимъ

καὶ ἠγάπησεν αὐτὸν	σφόδρα	καὶ ἐγενήθη	αὐτῷ	αἴρων	τὰ σκεύη αὐτοῦ
wy'hbhw	m'd	wyhy	lw	nś'	klym
and-he-loved-him	*very*	*and-he-was*	*to-him*	*carrying*	*utensils*
и въꙁлюби {и}	ѕѣло саоулъ	и бысть	ємоу	носѧи	ѿроужиє {є}го

καὶ ἀπέστειλε Σαουλ	πρὸς Ιεσσαι	λέγων	παριστάσθω δὴ Δαυιδ
wyšlḥ š'wl	'l yšy	l'mr	y'md n' dwd
and-sent Saul	*to Jesse*	*to-say*	*stand may/let David*
и пȣсти саоулъ	къ євъсѣєвѣ гл҃ѧ	пре[д]ста нн҃ѣ дд҃ъ

10 Some copies of the younger Sl have not пасеши but спиши, a combination of visual misapprehension and semantic assimilation to the following verb.

11 Marvin Pope's remark about another verse (337) is perhaps applicable here, "An imaginative exegete, of course, need not be frustrated by mere grammatical detail, real or imaginary." Every translator is necessarily an exegete. Commentators through the ages have proposed a broad range of meanings for the individual words and phrases and the overall significance of this verse. See, for example, the survey in Pope 328–32.

12 The notion of *wandering* is in the Vulgate's *vagari* and in the Syriac; its origin is controversial (Pope, *ibid.*). Sl's rendering probably was influenced by the Vulgate, but in theory it could have been engendered by a H form different from the MT.

ἐνώπιον ἐμοῦ	ὅτι εὗρεν	χάριν	ἐν ὀφθαλμοῖς μου.
lpny	ky mc’	ḥn	b‘yny.
to-face-my	*for he-found*	*grace*	*in-eyes-my*
пре^{д} мною	ꙗко ѡ̈рѣтє	блгⷣть	предъ ѡ̈чима моима.

The only deviation from literal translation in these lines is W’s пре^{д}ста нн҃є, an aorist plus the adverb ‘now’ for an expected third person imperative, OCS прѣдъстани. We may conjecture that this form was originally here, but the final syllable was misunderstood and converted to the superfluous adverb.

T1.51 Verse 23:

LXX	καὶ ἐγενήθη		ἐν τῷ εἶναι	πνεῦμα πονηρὸν	ἐπὶ Σαουλ
Ham	καὶ ἐγένετο,	φησὶν,	ἐν τῷ εἶναι	πνεῦμα πονηρὸν	ἐπὶ Σαουλ
MT	wyhy		bhywt	rwḥ ’lhym	’l š’wl
	and-it-was		*in-the-being-of*	*spirit-of God*	*to-Saul*
W	и бы^{с}		єгда быти	дꙋхоу нечистꙋ	в саоулѣ
Ham	бы^{с}	ре^{ч}	ѥгда боудѧшє	дх҃ъ ѕлыи	на Саоулѣ

LXX	καὶ ἐλάμβανεν	Δαυιδ	[a] τὴν κινύραν	[b] καὶ ἔψαλλεν	[c] ἐν τῇ χειρὶ αὐτοῦ
Ham	καὶ λάμβανων	Δαυιδ	[a] τὴν κινύραν	[b] ἔψαλλεν	[c]
MT	wlqḥ	dwd	[a] ’t hknwr	[b] wngn	[c] bydw
	and-took	*David*	[a] *A-the-harp*	[b] *and-played*	[c] *in-hand-his*
W	и приимъ	дд҃ъ	[c] роукама своима [a] гꙋсли [b] и поѧшє		
Ham	и приимъ	дд҃ъ	[a] гоусли		[c] въспѣвашє

LXX	καὶ ἀνέψυχεν Σαουλ	καὶ ἀγαθὸν αὐτῷ,
	(Hamartolos omits.)	
MT	wrwḥ lš’wl	wṭwb lw
	and-rested to-Saul	*and-good to-him*
W	и ѿдохнꙋ саоулъ	и бл҃го ємꙋ бы^{с},

LXX, Ham	καὶ ἀφίσατατο	ἐπ’ αὐτοῦ	τὸ πονηρὸν πνεῦμα.
MT	wsrh	m‘lyw	rwḥ hr‘h.
	and-departed-she	*from-on-him*	*spirit the-evil*
W	и ѿстꙋпи	ѿ него	дх҃ъ нечистыи.
H	и ѿстоупашє	ѿ него	ѕлыи дх҃ъ.

This sentence illustrates several typical problems of translation from Hebrew to Greek to Slavonic. Like Ruth 1:1, it starts with a typical Hebraism, ‘and it happened that’ that is maintained, καὶ ἐγένετο > и бысть/бысть.[13] Then comes a H infinitive construct (*bhywt* ‘in the being/becoming’), translated here, as often, by a Greek preposition plus articulated infinitive ἐν τῷ εἶναι, which must somehow be paraphrased in Slavic. Here, as in most cases, the OCS translator chose a subordinate clause with a highly marked verb form that is fully appropriate for the context. Notice, however, that this Sl clause does not allow us to reconstruct the Greek with any confidence, although we must regard it as a satisfactory

13 Up to this point Ham has been paraphrasing the story, so “they say, it is said” is inserted to denote the beginning of a direct quotation.

equivalent of the Hebrew.[14] The subordinate participle приимъ, on the other hand, implies a similar Gk construction, which in fact is not in this verse; instead we have imperfect καὶ ἐλάμβανε that faithfully reflects the H *wlqḥ*.

T1.61 With these examples in mind, let us turn to the special problems of Esther. Typical relationships of the two Greek texts to the MT and the Slavonic may be seen in 1:4, which is the last part of a long sentence beginning with 1:1.

LXX	[1] καὶ μετὰ ταῦτα,	[2] μετὰ τὸ δεῖξαι	[3] αὐτοῖς	[4] τὸν πλοῦτον
L	[1]	[2] εἰς τὸ ἐπιδειχθήναι		[4] τὸν πλοῦτον
MT	[1]	[2] bhr’tw		[4] ’t ‘šr
	[1]	[2] in-showing-his		[4] A-wealth-of
Sl.	[1]	[2] єгдаже покаꙁа		[4] богатьство

[5]	[6] τῆς βασιλείας	[7] αὐτοῦ	[8] καὶ τὴν δόξην
[5] τῆς δόξης	[6] τοῦ βασιλέως		[8] καὶ τὴν τιμὴν
[5] kbwd	[6–7] mlkwtw		[8] w ’t yqr
[5] glory-of	[6–7] kingship-his		[8] and A-honor-of
[5] чьсти	[6] царьства	[7] своєго	[8] и чьсть

[9] τῆς εὐφροσύνης	[10] τοῦ πλούτου αὐτοῦ	[11] ἐπὶ ἡμέρας
[9] τῆς καυχήσεως αὐτοῦ		[11]
[9] tp’rt	[10] gdwltw	[11] ymym
[9] splendor-of	[10] greatness-his	[11] days
[9] красоты	[10] величьствыꙗ своего	[11] дьньми

	[15] ἑκατὸν		[13] ὀγδοήκοντα	
[13] ἐπὶ ὀγδοήκοντα		[14] καὶ	[15] ἑκατὸν	[16] ἡμέρας
[12] rbym	[13] šmwnym	[14] w	[15] m’t	[16] ywm
[12] many	[13] eighty	[14] and	[15] a-hundred-of	[16] day
[12] мъногыми	[13] 80	[14] и	[15] 100-мь	[16] дьнии.

Moore renders: [1] “and [2] displayed [4] the great wealth of [5–7] his empire [8] and the glorious [9] splendor of [10] his majesty [12] for many [11] days.”

T1.611 Both Greek versions have broken this verse off as a separate sentence, the more usual LXX type (B-text), adding a conventional phrase at the beginning ([1] ‘After these things’) and a pronoun after the verb of the first clause (‘after the showing [3] to them’). The Hebrew infinitive construct [2], ‘in his causing-to-see,’ that is, ‘in his displaying-of’ has remained an infinitive in Greek (whereby the L-text makes it passive, ‘in the being-shown’), but the Slavic has made it a finite subordinate clause with conjunction plus verb. The ornate double object, ‘the **wealth**-of [5] the glory-of [6–7] kingship-his [8] **and** the **honor**-of [9] the beauty/splendor-of [10] greatness-his,’ was apparently excessive for Greek stylistic sensitivity. The translator of B is acknowledged to favor free interpretations that often stray rather far from the MT. Here he chose to emphasize riches: he changed *greatness* to *wealth*

[14] The juxtaposition of H *spirit of God* and Gk *evil spirit* is not to be taken literally, since the context (going back to 16:15) has established a spirit sent by God that has adverse effects on Saul. The implication that God might send something evil disturbed commentators from the beginning.

(position [10]) and substituted *glory* for *honor* ([8]) and *high spirits* for *splendor* ([9]), 'the wealth of his kingdom and the glory of the cheerfulness/merriment of his wealth.' L's modifications retain both *honor* and *glory*, but omit *greatness*: 'the riches of the king's glory and the honor of his boasting (or, of the cause for boasting).' Note that *tp'rt* means 'beauty; splendor; glory; boasting' and thus the range of equivalents in LXX includes ὡραιότης (presumably the source of краснота in our text) and καύχησις, but not εὐφροσύνη. (For καύχησις, OCS uses похвала, похваление, хвала, хваление.)

T1.612 The epithet 'many' [12] was deemed superfluous in the presence of the specific number, as was the repetition of a form of 'day.' The L-text translates to normal Greek numbers, while L sticks to the unusual '80 and 100' that exactly copies the Hebrew.

T1.613 This sample suffices to demonstrate that the Slavonic reflects the MT faithfully except that 'glory' [5] has become 'honor.'[15] The two Greek versions, on the other hand, reproduce the general sense of the Hebrew verse, but with significant differences of detail. Obviously the Slavonic was not translated from either of these known Greek texts. Yet from the elements here and from other passages from the Greek OT one could easily put together a Greek text that corresponds nicely to the MT:

> εἰς τὸ δεῖξαι τὸν πλοῦτον τῆς δόξης τῆς βασιλείας αὐτοῦ καὶ τὴν τιμὴν τῆς ὡραιότητος τοῦ μεγαλειότητος (τῆς μεγαλωσύνης) αὐτοῦ ἐπὶ ἡμέρας πολλᾶς, (ἐπὶ) ὀγδοήκοντα καὶ ἑκατὸν ἡμέρας.

This in turn is a reasonable equivalent of our normalized Slavonic text.

T1.7 We have scrutinized the entire text in this manner, and reached the conclusion that there is nothing in the 167 verses of Esther that demonstrates direct translation from Hebrew to Slavic. On the contrary, a small number of details point definitely to a Greek intermediary translation as the direct source of the attested Slavonic wording. And finally, we maintain, there is no word or phrase that could *not* have come from a Greek version.[16]

Theory of translation

T2 As a preface to our verse by verse analysis, we offer some general observations about translation, chiefly of biblical texts, and in particular about translating from Hebrew to Greek and from Greek to Slavic.

T2.1 An acceptable translation must conform to the grammatical norms of the target language, but flexibility in phraseology and vocabulary is usual. Individual passages in translations inevitably will vary as to the faithfulness of form and meaning to the original,

[15] Some of our mss have и after [4] and all have it after [9]. Reading the phrases accordingly, we may interpret: [4] wealth *and* [5] honors [6–7] of his kingdom [8] and of the beauty (?) *even* [9] of his greatness. Since the addition or omission of и (as an reinforcing particle, 'also, even,' or a connective, 'and') takes place unsystematically in the work of most Slavic scribes, we do not hesitate to excise or interpolate и as dictated by the sense (guided by the Hebrew wording). Cf. n 2 to T1.1.

[16] For passages that have been cited by previous investigators as proof of direct Hebrew-Slavic translation, see especially C9.5 and C9:28; also C1:11, C1:16, C2.3, C2.11.

and critics invariably will disagree as to the correctness or appropriateness of each rendering. When we perceive a deviation, there are two possibilities: error or intention—either the translator simply made a mistake, out of ignorance or carelessness, or else he or she consciously chose an equivalent that raises questions in observers' minds.

T2.11 No two copies of any text in medieval manuscripts ever agree completely; each copy has at least a few tiny deviations from every other copy. We must, therefore, reckon with the probability that the text they provide is not the pristine wording approved by the translator, which almost inevitably has been modified as it was copied and recopied. At each stage, unintentional error or purposeful intention may produce change. A careful scribe may introduce casual changes here and there, or a more thorough revision may be imposed by a systematic editor. The longer the tradition, the more changes will be found in a given text, as a rule. Some of the intentional modifications may arise from attempts to "repair" a perceived defect. Such corrections may be made ad hoc from the immediate context or from parallel passages within the same work. They may be based on another copy of the text that is available to the scribe or editor—a copy in the target-language or in the the original source-language. In such cases, the wording may not correspond exactly to the wording in the model the original translator used. One more complication is that two quite independent translations may have been made, and later they may be blended together, partly or completely.

(Particularly with biblical translations it is difficult to distinguish a new translation from a rigorous and principled revision of an extant translation; thus, e.g., the King James or Authorized Version of 1611 owes a great deal to phraseology used by Tyndale and others.)

T2.12 Many possible combinations of these factors produced such a tangle in the tradition of biblical texts we believe were translated before 885 by the original creators of OCS that A. V. Mixajlov, the astute and prudent investigator of the Slavonic book of Genesis, concluded that it was impossible to retrieve any single early redaction of that important book.[17] Mixajlov's remarks about Ruth imply an original southwestern version (probably with early Macedonian revisions) and a slightly later southeastern redaction, cf. the samples above. The history of the other books of the Slavonic Octateuch, and of the Tetrabasileion, remains to be investigated.[18]

[17] He distinguishes a lectionary portion, surely going back to Cyril and Methodius, and witnessed by *paremejniki* from the 12th–15th centuries, from the larger non-lectionary sections known only from post-1300 manuscripts, mostly East Slavic. The earliest copy (the Grigorovič Paremejnik or Prophetologion) clearly shows it had already undergone revision, probably in Macedonia in the 10th century. (This corresponds to evidence even from OCS Gospels and the Psalter that makes it probable that the earliest retrievable form of these texts as well—apart from a few isolated lexical items—is that approved by Clement and Naum and their immediate successors.) Subsequently, in the late 14th and early 15th century, Serbian editors twice revised Genesis and other biblical texts; some East Slavic 15th–16th century manuscripts reflect this redaction.

[18] Superficial soundings of Joshua, Judges, and the Tetrabasileion from ms W (which generally corresponds to the Ostrih text, though there are significant deviations) lead to the working hypothesis that these books too reflect extremely tangled filiations. Recent studies on the Slavonic Octateuch by Anna Pichkhadze (1991, 1995) and on the Tetrabasileion by Svetlina Nikolova (1995) show that the problems are being examined.

Otto Kronsteiner, Professor of Bulgarian at Salzburg, has recently begun to publish in his journal *Die slavische Sprachen* texts labelled *The Bible of Methodius* (vol 37 [1994] Psalms, 38 [1995] Judges, 40 [1995] Leviticus, 42 [1995] 1 Kingdoms, 45 [1995] 2 Ki). These texts unfortunately appear to be based on haphazardly chosen sources, chiefly the Ostrih and Gennadius Bibles. Some of these volumes provide variants, but they are unsystematic; they are of little or no scholarly value.

T2.13 The role of unintentional error, the work of careless or even incompetent scribes, is significant. Mixajlov repeatedly emphasizes the faulty character of the majority of the manuscripts he worked with. There was a break in the tradition of copying texts. Not a single 13th-century copy of most of the OT books exists. The oldest Pentateuch and codexes with Joshua, Judges, Ruth, the Tetrabasileion and Esther are ascribed to the second half of the 14th century. Multiplication of texts appears to have begun in earnest about 1390 and to have continued through the 15th century.[19] Scribes were neither well trained nor conscientious, and most manuscripts teem with errors that are compounded to become more and more damaging to the meaning. A Kievan editor of 1629 complains that he must correct the Slavonic of the major liturgical texts by reference to Greek, "for all Slavonic books, for however many centuries, have been copied by ignoramuses who only smear ink about, who have no sense, who do not know the language and who do not know the meaning of the words."[20]

T2.14 Since even the major texts were bad, it can be no surprise that such a marginal book as Esther has survived only in lamentably corrupt form. We assume that there should be discrete layers of textual history, but it is extremely difficult to identify them. This working hypothesis was not shared by our predecessors: Roždestvenskij and Meščerskij tacitly assumed that the copies they were able to consult were essentially identical with the original Slavic translation.[21] Roždestvenskij lists a series of items he classes as involuntary mistakes or else intentional decisions by the translator that he finds unsuitable, and another class he clearly views as errors, although he offers no explicit reason for their existence. Meščerskij ignores most of these items, but some phrases impel him to note, "Еврейский же язык переводчик, как видно, знал не очень хорошо" (1956a 211).

We see nothing to disprove the hypothesis that the original Slavonic was a reasonably intelligible version of the MT text, but with some deviations from the original sense. By positing that the Slavic translator had before him a Greek translation, we offer the possibility that some inappropriate items belong to the Greek translator,[22] and some others perhaps to Gk copyists—for it is necessary to assume that the Gk version too had its own history. The mass of omissions, additions, emendations (whether reasonable or inept), and corruptions are—in our view—to be ascribed to the copyists and editors who had a hand in the presumably many re-copyings that led finally to the reconstructible *pervospisok* of about 1350.[23]

T3 In the commentaries to individual verses we will discuss each individual item. Here we will mention some more general categories.

T3.1 The Sl, as compared with MT, has more than thirty additions. Most obvious are the 10 glosses that give the names of the Jewish months in Greco-Roman terms. The first, in

19 Most of the surviving mss are from well after 1450.

20 In simplified orthography, понеже вся книги славенския от колико лѣт преписуются невѣжами токмо чернилом мажущими, ума же не имущими, языка не умѣющими, и силы словес не вѣдущими. See I. Karataev, Описание славяно-русских книг напечатанных кирилловскими буквами, т. I (= *SbORJaS* 34/2), 405.

21 Our contemporary, Anatolij Alekseev, agrees, in explicit, uncompromising terms: "Обилие в славянском тексте Есфири темных мест и гапаксов определенно указывает на то, что это первичный, исходный текст, но не переработка или переделка" (1987a 3).

22 Only in the rendition of three of the exotic personal names can one discern definite misunderstanding of the H: see A2.36.

23 If this is the original translation, then the translator must have been ignorant, careless, and stupid. In our opinion, the haphazard but varied character of the deviations from what we expect in terms of the MT is not compatible with what we find in cases of incompetent translation.

2:16, accompanies the name *Tebeth*, itself part of a gloss defining "the tenth month": for H *hw' ḥdš ṭbt*, 'that is, the month (of) Tebeth,' we find гл̄ющи сѧ Тєвєфъ по жидовьскому, а по греѵьску Декѧбрь. The simple H pronoun *hw'* expands to a rather ornate reflexive participle, and then the phrase labelling the term *Jewish* and adding the Greek name. There is no clear reason for the occurrence of the pronominal desinence with жидовьск- (unique to this verse; otherwise июдѣски- occurs 7x) as opposed to the nominal or short desinence in грьѵьску (a stem found only here in Est). The parallel Hebrew, *hw' ḥdš nysn* 'that is, [the] month [of] Nisan,' 3:7, comes out Нисанъ, гл̄ющи сѧ Априлъ, using the same reflexive participle and omitting the introductory *that is*.[24] Also in 3:7, *hw' ḥdš 'dr* yields the full literal equivalent, иже есть Адаръ (cf. LXX ὅς ἐστιν), plus the gloss—this time expressed by a present passive participle—рєкомыи Мартъ. In 3:13, 8:9, 8:12, and 9:1 *hw' ḥdš* gives *тъ есть (omitting *month*), plus рєкомыи. H has no *that is* in 9:15, 17, and 19, and we find the literal мѣсѧца Адара, plus рекомаго Марта.[25] These glosses obviously were added when the text was translated from Hebrew or thereafter.[26] The disagreement in wording might suggest that they were made at different times. The first two, with гл̄ющии сѧ perhaps were translated from Gk, while the other seven could have been added, not necessarily simultaneously, by any Slav from any region.[27] In any case, these glosses tell us nothing about the language from which the Slavonic was translated.

T3.11 The other twenty-odd additions are extremely varied. Most of them are minor, and probably intended by scribes to emphasize certain words or phrases without really changing the text; at least one may have been in the Greek or even possibly the Hebrew text (2:18). All are discussed in the commentaries to individual verses. Three are *doublets,* two equivalents of a single Hebrew word or phrase.

T3.12 Doublets are a familiar phenomenon in LXX and many other translations, posing problems for textual critics. A doublet may indicate that the original translator was uncertain, or that later scribes or editors were unsatisfied. It is generally assumed that the duplication began by the addition of a marginal note or gloss, and later the gloss was incorporated into the text.[28] Ordinarily, doublets are taken as an indication that the text does not represent

[24] Tn has єж єс but omits the expected 'month' and the gloss is єж толкоуєтьс, introducing a verb that is dubious for OCS and only sparsely attested for ESl before 1400.

[25] Compare Ostromir 210d мсца авгоста рєкомааго ꙁарєва, 256a єноуара просиньца рєкомааго, with apparently South Sl month names.

[26] Sobolevskij 1903 435 seems to consider them a sign of a Gk text underlying the Sl. M56a 208 objects, declaring roundly that "on the contrary, these additions are a strong proof against the hypothesis of translation from Greek. Only a Russian could have made them, and they have nothing to do with the Greek text."

[27] A gloss with the "Macedonian" name is in the L-text of 3:7 (or 6, Hanhart 156), οὗτος ὁ μὴν Αδαρ ὅς ἐστι Δύστρος. Josephus (*Jewish Ant.* XI 286, roughly Est 8:13) defines the "12th month" ὅς κατὰ μὲν Ἑβραίους Ἄδαρ καλεῖται κατὰ δὲ Μακεδόνας Δύστρος 'which is called Adar by the Hebrews, and Dystros by the Macedonians'; he also (290, Est 9:15) uses the Macedonian name alone. (Compare the lists of exotic month names in the Izbornik of 1073, 251c, reflecting a Preslav OCS translation, where дуострос is in the list labelled "по єлиномъ.")

[28] The third stage, elimination of the original translation in favor of the gloss, does not concern us in this section. Examples can be cited from the fraction of the Slavonic Esther tradition that is known to us. E.g. the puzzling срамоту for expected 'honor' of 1:20 is, one can safely surmise, first glossed by the somewhat more suitable word драготу; then we have the doublet срамоту драготу in ms 4 (according to Roždestvenskij 195); then only драготу in the text of V. A fourth stage is illustrated by W, where the text is as in V, but the dubious word is marked by dots, and the alternative is recorded in the margin. See also variants for 1:18, 2:14, 2:19.

the original translation, but has undergone at least one stage of redaction. However, two alternative possibilities must always be kept in mind: (1) that a translator might add glosses, particularly when the chief purpose of the translation is to enable someone to read the original text; and (2) that a translator purposefully uses two words to achieve a close definition of the original single word.

Doublets of phrases may also occur.

T3.121 The simplest doublet in Esther is велми ѕѣло in 1:12 and 4:4 when H has the single adverb 'very.'[29]

T3.122 A complicated set of relations can be seen in the description of the golden vessels at the banquet in 1:7, each one different. The three Hebrew words literally mean *and-vessels from-vessels different.* All our texts have:

и съсоудъ съсоуду нєоуподоблєнъ нъ всє раѕноличь
wklym *mklym* *šwnym*

The idea is expressed twice, but the Slavonic wording is distant from the H. (The neutral form всє surely should be Npm вьси.) In 1:17, there appears to be a doublet for the H phrase "so that they will not look down on (despise) their husbands": ѩко нє оуврѣдити мужь своихъ [и нє въ послухъ] прєд ними. For discussion see the commentary on that verse.

T3.2 The opposite problem may arise when a translator is faced with a doublet or juxtaposition of near synonyms. A literalist of the type we assume for these early translations will ordinarily try to reproduce every word of the original. Confronted with synonyms, he sometimes must resort to introducing words he otherwise avoids, or to stretching or constricting the meaning of words he does use. Thus in 9:27 the words for 'time' and 'year' both occur, and the selection of Slavonic equivalents posed a problem (see L20). A well-known example is *bowels* versus *stomach* and also *womb* and *kidneys* or simply *innards.* For OCS the specific 'womb' was ложєсна (usually *pl. tantum*), while 'stomach' γαστήρ frequently was ѫтроба and 'bowels' κοιλία was ѵрѣво, but these two alternate with each other in a bewildering fashion both with regard to the Greek original texts and within the Slavic textual traditions. When the specific notions co-occur, however, scribes do not make substitutions: thus in Ps. 7:6, all traditions maintain отъ ѫтробы, и[с] ѵрѣва. If one of the synonyms goes beyond the translator's knowledge, he may resort to guesswork; this is perhaps the source of судии in 6:9, see comm.[30]

Hebraisms

T4 The LXX is explicitly a translation, or rather a series of translations of different times and localities, from the Hebrew (or Aramaic). Its language is indelibly marked by a wide

29 Substitution of one word for the other could be a source of error. In SRJaXI, *sub* антраксъ (анфраксъ), 'ruby,' is a citation from a 17th-century *Алфавит*: Анфраксъ камень честен велми зелен образом, a garbled definition that goes back to Izb1073 121d18 ѕѣло ѵрьвєнъ ѥстъ обраѕъмь, cf. Chron 1512 (PSRL 22/1 192) ѕѣло чєрьвлєнъ єсть обраѕомъ. When, or after, ѕѣло was glossed with вєльми, the original color was switched from red to green.

30 An all too common device is simply to leave out a difficult item, e.g., the specifications of the kind of horse used by the king's couriers, see C8:14.

range of Semitic features carried over by literalist translators from the source language. The New Testament has many of the same characteristics, in part perhaps because the earliest form of some of the books may have been written in Aramaic, but also because large numbers of Jews in the Holy Land, Egypt, and elsewhere spoke Greek—a Greek heavily influenced by the Semitic languages recently spoken by older generations or still in use in bilingual and polyglot communities. Bible translations into most languages continue to hold to the precept "as literal as possible" and recreate in language after language phrases and meanings that go back to Hebrew.

T4.01 The LXX paraphrase of Esther has perhaps fewer of the striking Hebraisms than many other books, but Origen obviously revised his text to be more literal and thereby "restored" a number of controversial items. The Slavonic text has its share of Hebraisms, but neither the number nor the quality is impressive by comparison to Genesis, Ruth, or the Tetrabasileion.[31] There are no absurdities such as God speaking *by the hand of the prophet,* where the prepositional phrase in Hebrew means "through the agency of" and the use of *hand* in most other languages should be counted as bad translation (cf. L6.33).[32]

T4.1 Two syntactical Hebraisms will be examined in this section. The question of prepositional phrases is treated in A9 and some other idioms using *hand, face, eyes,* and *soul* are discussed in the sections on these lexical items (L6). Other possible Hebraisms will be mentioned in the commentaries to individual verses.

Distributive repetition

T4.11 The Hebrew repetition of a noun, of the type "day and day" to mean 'each day, every day, daily,' is relatively common in Esther, particularly in the accounts of the king's decrees. Of the 23 instances in the MT, 19 have survived in Slavonic, but *1350 does not reflect any consistent translation technique.[33] Usually the conjunction 'and' remains, except for мужєви мужю 1:8, which may well stand for an older and more consistent мужю и мужю.

[31] Meščerskij made much of these elements, but his comments are meager and often wrong or beside the point, cf. AT 312–15, LT 152. In particular, his use of "и т. п." and "и мн. др." implies a wealth of uncited examples that in fact do not exist. M56a 210, admitting that Hebraisms are common in texts translated from Greek, insists that in Esther there is such an enormous number ("громадное число") that they affirm the hypothesis of direct translation. Earlier (209) he declares that Hebraisms "встречаются в тексте буквально на каждой строке." By our estimate, there are no more than 35 clear Hebraisms; Meščerskij's hyperbole is unjustified whether he had in mind the 167 verses of Esther or the approximately 600 lines of manuscript text (LT n. 38). Alekseev seems not to have read pages 312–17 of AT; he loyally echoes the words of his mentor (1987a 5): "сами по себе гебраизмы могут проникать в славянские тексты и через греческое посредство, но в данном случае их *особенно много*" (emphasis supplied). *Many* by what measure, compared to what texts? We will treat Meščerskij's comments in the appropriate contexts below.

[32] LXX has some 15 instances of ἐν χειρὶ τινὸς λαλῆσαι in 3–4 Kingdoms, and most of them survive into Slavic (and often English). For example 4 Ki 17:23 (W, OB), ꙗкоже гл҃а гд҃ь роукою рабъ своих всѣх пророкъ. Even more absurd is the dual in 4 Ki 21:10: и гл҃а г҃ь роукама рабъ своих гл҃ѧ ("by the hands of his servants"—as though they were using sign language). The oldest attested Slavonic version of this verse (1073 96c12) copies the Gk exactly, въ роуцѣ рабъ ѥго пр°ркъ.

[33] Nine H nouns are involved: *'yš* 'man,' *dwr* 'generation,' *mšpḥh* 'family, kin, clan,' *n'rh* 'maiden,' *šnh* 'year,' *ywm* 'day,' *'yr* 'city,' *'m* 'nation, people,' *mdynh* 'province.' Sl echoes repetition in 1:8 (see comm.), 1:22, 3:4, 3:12 (4), 3:14, 4:3, 8:9 (2); 8:13, 8:17 (2); 9:21, 9:28 (4) Other equivalents are found in 1:22, 2:11, and 8:11. The дв҃ыꙗ дв҃ы of 2:12 is hendiadys in the Sl text as it stands, rather than an unambiguous echo of H repetition (cf. L2.462).

T4.12 When Hebrew has preposed *kl* כל (*kol*) 'all,' Slavic may have 'each' and singular nouns (всѧка ꙁемлѧ и ꙁемлѧ 4:3, 8:17; всѧкъ градъ и градъ 8:17, 9:21; всѧкоу годину и годину 9:21), or 'all' and plural nouns (по всѣм ꙁемлѧмъ и ꙁемлѧмъ 3:12, въ всѣхъ ꙁемлѧхъ и ꙁемлѧхъ 8:13).[34]

T4.13 In 2:11 H has *bkl ywm wywm*, lit. 'in all/every day and day,' и на всѧкъ днь; in 3:4 H *ywm wywm* and Sl дн҃е дн҃е. LXX has καθ' ἑκάστην ἡμέραν for both.[35]

T4.14 In 9:28 въ всѧ вѣкы вѣкомъ is inappropriate. The Hebrew has 'to every generation' and we might expect rather forms of родъ (cf. Ps. 99/100:5). Perhaps въ вьсѣкъ вѣкъ и вѣкъ was the rendering, and the ubiquitous formula 'for ever and ever' was substituted by a careless scribe? See C9:28.

T4.15 LXX Esther occasionally retains the repetition, and it is frequent in the O-mss. Thus LXX κατὰ χώραν καὶ χώραν 8:9, κατὰ γενεὰν καὶ γενεάν 9:28; O, πρὸς λαὸν καὶ λαόν 1:22.[36] Instances where the syntax of such phrases is peculiar will be treated with other problems of individual verses.[37]

Figurae etymologicae

T5 Esther has only six etymological figures, and only one has failed to survive translation; оудолѣша . . . раною меѵевою 9:5 is far from the literal 'smote with a smiting of the sword.'[38] Въꙁъпи въплемь великъмь 4:1 and мысль . . . юже бѧше помыслилъ (8:3, 9:25) present no problems. The аще мълѵиши мълѵаѵи 'if you keep complete silence' has no equivalent in the LXX paraphrase of 4:14, but падаꙗ падеши 'you will surely fall' (6:13) is exactly paralleled by LXX πεσὼν πεσῇ.

T5.1 The appearance of phrases with this sort of word-play need not depend on a Semitic original. Thus Est 6:6 has И помысли Амонъ в мысли своеи where H has 'And Amon *said* in his *heart*.[39] In Joshua 5:10, станомъ сташѧ 'they made camp' (see SJS) is to be

[34] Apparent cases of distributive repetition appear in Slavic translations from NT Greek texts, e.g., OCS Mk 6:39–40, на сподъı на сподъı . . . на лѣхъı на лѣхъı, see Seliščev RES 5 (1925) 50ff., and Старославянский язык, I, 19–20. On the other hand, in a translation from Alexandrian (Jewish) Greek, the *Dialogue of Timothy and Aquila*, ζυγὴν ζυγήν yields по двѣма, cf. Taube 1991.

[35] Note that WV have in 3:4 дн҃ь дн҃е, a sequence that in Gen 39:10 translates H *ywm ywm*. Though *waw copulative* is usual in Esther and Chronicles, and occasionally appears elsewhere (e.g., Ps. 89:1, 4 *ldwr wdwr*, LXX 88:2, 5 εἰς γενεὰν καὶ γενεάν, OCS въ родъ і родъ), in most of the MT the two nouns are simply juxtaposed. Thus Gen 39:10 yields ἡμέραν ἐξ ἡμέρας, with a preposition. The usual Sl. is дн҃ь дн҃е, without preposition and thus seemingly closer to the Hebrew; Mixajlov records rare variants, дн҃ь ѿ дн҃е, дн҃ь до дн҃е.

[36] In 1:22 one ms even has κατὰ χώρα χώρα. See also C9:28.

[37] GorNev 54 quote examples of distributive repetition (from 9:27, 28, with references to 1:5, 16, and 5:2), Ro 196 cites 3:12 (parallel to 9:27–28), M56a notes 1:22, 3:4, 12 (plus 8:13 "etc."). The implication is that these phrases constitute proof of direct translation. None of these scholars really analyzed the full data of Esther, nor did they consider the wider context of Biblical Greek and its reflection in Slavonic OT books.

[38] A variant of the same H phrase in Joshua 10:20 became κόπτοντες αὐτοὺς κοπὴν μεγάλην and then, to judge from Lebedev's laconic remark, 146, сѣкуще ѧ сѣѵемь великомь (distorted in ms. T [and W] to сѣѵь великъ). See also Eckert and Kostov 1986.

[39] M56a 210 cites this example, apparently with some surprise (cf. AT 314–5). He did not realize that H "tautological expressions" that have a noun as the cognate accusative are easily enough translated into other languages and indeed often have native equivalents elsewhere. If the object is an infinitive absolute, however, Greek, Slavic and English (and many other languages) must resort to paraphrase. Biblical Greek commonly uses a present active participle, like πεσών in 6:13, which easily can be replicated in Slavic. Examples of both abound in the Octoteuch. Translators do not always agree. 1 Kingdoms 1:10–11, κλαίουσα ἔκλαυσε . . . ηὔξατο

ascribed to the original lectionary translation; this surely gives us a glimpse of an old idiom, preserved in medieval SC.[40] The phrase is omitted in most LXX manuscripts of Joshua, but the Προφητολόγιον (lectionary) text has simply παρενέβαλον 'they encamped,' translating H *wyḥnw*. In 4 Kingdoms 18:28 ἐβόησαν φωνῇ μεγάλῃ yielded OB вьꙁопи гласомъ великимъ, which corresponds to the text in W. In the replica of the same episode in 2 Chron 32:18 the 15th-century translators created an etymological figure by changing the noun to воплємъ; the sense is now inappropriate, however, since lamentation is not involved. The Sl Hamartolos has гнѣвомъ гнѣваюѵе сѧ in a Christian context (503.22) with no Semitic background; the original has only διαπληκτιζόμενοι.[41]

T6.1 There are peculiarities of translation which depend on the original language. In the case of Hebrew, the nature of the writing system itself may be a source of confusion or error. The consonantal spelling of individual words is frequently ambiguous—in today's newspaper as well as in ancient texts—and at times the context admits conflicting interpretations. For example, the letters רע *r'* may represent /rea'/ friend' or /ra'/ 'evil (man).' Adding two letters produces a plural רעים *r'ym*, to be read as /re'im/ 'friends,' /ra'im/ 'wicked' or /ro'im/ 'shepherds.' Thus Hosea 3:1, dealing with problems of adultery and forgiveness, speaks of a woman who is אהבת רע *'hbt r'*, traditionally /'ahuvat rea'/, lit. 'beloved-of friend,' i.e., loved by a lover. LXX, however, has the phrase ἀγαπῶσαν πονηρά, 'loving [Asf] evil things'; the translator read /'ohevet ra'/, changing the passive participle to active as well as reversing the sense of the second word.[42] The old text as preserved in Croatian Glagolitic corresponds to LXX: жєну любєщоу нєприєꙁнина. The revision (or new translation), probably made in eastern Bulgaria very early, retains the LXX sense, though it has come down to us in garbled form, жєнȣ любѧщаѧ ꙁѣло, with inappropriate desinence and a distorted final word—surely for older любѧщѭѭ ꙁъло.[43]

T6.21 The opposite mistake, translating *friend* where *wicked* is the original sense, is to be found in Esther 7:6, see comm. to that verse.

T6.22 Substitution of *shepherds* for *friends, lovers* occurs in LXX Jeremiah 3:1. MT *w't*

εὐχὴν . . . ἐὰν ἐπιβλέπων ἐπιβλέψῃς, lit. 'weeping she wept . . . prayed a prayer (or, vowed a vow) . . . looking you will look,' yields плаѵющи приплака in W (проплака OB) and аще приꙁрѧ приꙁриши (W, OB). The noun object is omitted in W (помоли сѧ), but rendered помоли сѧ молитвою in OB, later revised to обѣща обѣтъ of current Slavonic bibles.

40 Let us emphasize that the Sl texts of Joshua, Judges, and Kings which we usually cite are post-1450; they often do not preserve the archaisms that occasionally survive in older *Paremejniki*.

41 Note the ESl characteristic -ѵ- in the participle. Compare раꙁгнѣва сѧ гнѣвомъ of 2 Ki 12:5, T1.1 above.

42 This ambiguity of individual verb-forms is very common, but usually the context resolves the difficulty.

43 The end of the same verse gives us a glimpse of regional Slavic intimate vocabulary. For LXX πέμματα μετὰ σταφίδος 'cakes with dried grapes (raisins)' the Glagolitic has мєдваники са оуждєном' виномь 'honey-cakes with dried grapes,' (for *мєдвьникы съ ѫждєномь виномь), implying *ѫдити 'to cure by smoking' and pointing to Moravan/Pannonian words (cf. Cz dial. *uditi,* Slk *úditi,* Sln *oditi, voditi*). The revision shows that in other regions other terms were needed, сковрадники съ сухвами, where the first is rather 'pancake' (cf. сковрада 'frying pan'), while *соухы or соухъва is based on the ComSl root *sux* 'dry.' (OB keeps these words, but Syn. Slav has варєнїѧ с корі́нками; R виноградные лепешки.)

A different problem is illustrated by the English translation in the King James Bible and many later revisions: the last two words are rendered 'flagons of wine.' The word '*šyš* was taken not in its old meaning, but in a different sense (disputed by various exegetes) 'goblet; bottle'; this required that '*nbym*, properly *grapes,* be taken metaphorically to refer to wine.

znyt r'ym rbym, 'and thou played the whore with many lovers,' becomes 'with many shepherds': καὶ σὺ ἐξεπόρνευσας ἐν ποιμέσι πολλοῖς.[44]

T6.3 The situation may be even more complex when homographs represent homonyms. In Esther 4:3, the written word *lrbym* is surely the preposition *l* 'to' and the masculine plural of the adjective *rav*, viz. /lerabbim/. In that particular context, the sense "to many (men)" is unsatisfactory for many readers, and one venerable interpretation has been to understand quality rather than quantity, "to the great (men)," the leaders. This view underlies the Sl старѣишинамъ of our text, cf. C4:3.[45] The Sl phrase reflects a legitimate attempt, anchored in Jewish exegetical tradition, to handle an obscure passage, not, as Meščerskij 1956a 210–11 would have it, a mistranslation. It resulted from a dilemma that faces any translator of Esther, and in no way supports the hypothesis of direct translation from Hebrew to Slavic.

T6.4 A considerably more complex textual puzzle that has plagued commentators and translators is Proverbs 26:10, which begins with the Hebrew *rb* /rav/.[46] It provides a typical illustration of the fact that decisions made by Greek translators from the Hebrew will ordinarily be followed by a Slav who has no knowledge of the original dilemma. The English translators came up with "The great *God*"—a noun is provided, along with a definite article, to make some sort of sense. LXX, on the other hand, keeps the adjective, πολλά, and this of course is what is reflected by OB, много. However, the difficulties are not merely in the first word, but in the whole verse. Suffice it to say that most commentators now start with the assumption that *rb* is not "much, many; large, great," but a homophone "archer."[47]

T7.1 A word in a translation can, in theory, be defined in terms of the original. Thus when we find a Sl word meaning *lamb* in a specific OT verse we expect it to correspond to a Gk term meaning *lamb* in the LXX verse and a Hebrew term for *lamb* in the MT equivalent. Most words occur in enough contexts in OCS or later texts so that we have confirmation of our expections, or at least comparable data as a basis for estimating the degree of deviation of meaning that has occurred in the translation process. When in the OCS codex Supraslien-sis we read телицѧ (As, 359.29, 360.5, 13) and in the corresponding Chrysostom sermon ἀμνάδα (as in LXX 2 Kingdoms 12:3 Ns ἀμνάς, 12:4, 6 As -άδα, cf. T1.1 above, and in MT *kbśh*, 2 Sam 12:3, 4, 6), we see that the 'ewe-lamb' of the biblical anecdote has become a baby heifer. Slavic *tel-ic-a* is a familiar formation based on the root *tel-* 'calf' (cf. тельць μόσχος L 15:27, Is 11:6). There is no evidence that *tel-* meant 'lamb' anywhere in the Slavic world.[48] Since the OCS sermon otherwise is a generally competent translation, and

[44] One expects Sl to reflect LXX, even in this kind of misunderstanding. We would predict, therefore, that *shepherds* would occur in this verse; indeed the modern Synodal text has с пастырми многими. OB, however, has ты же съблудила еси съ любовными многими: this goes back to the Vulgate, for, as F. J. Thomson has pointed out to us, this verse is not attested in Slavonic before it was translated from Latin for the 1499 bible.

[45] Lexicographers disagree on whether to include the substantival use ("master, lord, chief; rabbi") in one lemma with the adjectival senses ("great, large; many").

[46] Meščerskij appends to his comment on 4:3, "(ср. Притч. XXVI, 10)"—his motivation is obscure, for the problem is quite different.

[47] Lexicographers again disagree whether this is to be included with "chief; rabbi" and/or with the adjective. The first clause in the King James version is: "The great *God* that formed all *things*." The translation of LXX reads: "All the flesh of fools endures much hardship" (cf. OB много труждает сѧ всѧка плоть безумных). Modern scholarship has completely reinterpreted the verse, partly on basis of Syriac and Targums. Cf. the wording of the Jerusalem Bible: "An archer wounding all who pass: such is the man who employs a fool."

[48] It is surprising that the editors of SJS define телица as *lamb* with no cautionary note.

this change of lamb to calf is consistent, we must conclude that the translator or a subsequent copyist made a conscious decision. Just why he did so remains a matter for speculation.[49] Su 389.9 ты каинꙗ братооубииства бѣлꙑѧ ризꙑ съвлѣчє means "You took off the white garments of Cain's fratricide." The Gk, however has "the robe of brotherly love," τῆς φιλαδελφίας, fitting the symbolism of treachery required by the context; surely originally братолюбьства stood here, and a careless copyist associated the name of Cain with fratricide and emended the text accordingly.[50]

T7.2 If different copies of a text have variants, we assume that we are dealing with synonyms. Thus Gen 8:20 has на олтарь, на трѣбьникъ, and на жрътвєникъ for H *on the altar.* We may surmise that the variation somehow reflects different regions and/or periods, that the scribes changed the words to fit local taste.

T7.21 There are problems, however. In Gen 35:4 усєрѧꙁѧ 'earrings,' τὰ ἐνώτια, are mentioned; in one ms, however, ꙁлато is substituted, and in another ѡбєдцѧ, i.e., обьдьца. The former clearly has removed the specific term and put in a general indication of value. The latter is a unique diminutive of the rare обьдо 'treasure, item of value.' This means that we need to be cautious: the new word may have quite a different value from the one it has replaced.[51]

T7.22 Estimating the time and place of lexical substitutions may be difficult. In John 12:6, for γλωσσόκομον 'purse, money-bag' OCS has 'little box' with two variants, скриница in Mar and Sav (diminutive of *skrinja*, adapted from Latin and/or OHG) versus ковьчєжьць in Zo and Assem (dim. of ковьчєгъ, probably of Turkic origin). The *text* surely goes back to Cyril and/or Methodius, but the exact wording is more complex. The western word surely is older, but the eastern substitution may well have been made before 900. The Ostromir Gospel has рачица, a diminutive of рака 'coffer, coffin, reliquary' a very early borrowing from Lat. *arca* 'box.' The evidence shows that this variant appeared before 1056, but it could have been made in Bulgaria (cf. ларь in Izb 1076 for ковьчегъ, Veder 1992 330–31), possibly still in the 10th century. The total evidence for OCS vocabulary simply does not suffice to guarantee a firm conclusion.

T7.3 Substitutions for foreign or unfamiliar words require particular caution. In 4 Ki 20:12 (ms W) a prince sends to a king who is ill "книгы и свѣщы" OCS свѣща is ordinarily *candle,* but it may be *source of light* or *light* and render a series of Greek words denoting various kinds of *lamp* or *torch.* In this context, however, LXX has μαναα, transcribing imperfectly H *mnḥh* [minḥa] 'gift.' The same LXX word in 4 Ki 17:3, 4, remains as μανα; the context warrants a translation 'tribute,' and OB appropriately has дань, дани. In 4 Ki 8:8, 9, W and OB agree on даръ. A reasonable assumption is that the original translator cautiously retained the Hebraism in all five instances, and that later editors substituted

49 In the same Su text, 2 Ki 12:1, the H and Gk *flocks* (i.e., sheep, goats) and *herds* (i.e., cattle) are rendered by the vague скотъı (Ap, where стада would have been more accurate) and чрѣдъı, a precise equivalent. The full biblical text (W), on the contrary, has a dubious rendering, see note 5 to T1.1 above.

50 SJS correctly defines братооубииство as 'fratricide' and provides a note to show it is inappropriate as a translation.

51 A closer look discloses further complications: it is probable that there was a different noun, объдо, meaning a fine cloth or a specific kind of fine garment; SRJaXI (sub обдо) cites two examples from Ham. The exact sense of a third, царскы(м) объдъмь, 'with a royal mantle' 373.17 is uncertain because the Gk equivalent χλανίς varies in meaning with time and place. The Sl word was replaced by the scribe of an early copy by the familiar вѣньцемь 'crown; wreath.'

Slavic words. Here, as often in such cases, it appears that the editorial intervention did not apply to the whole of 4 Kingdoms; the person who replaced мана with даръ in one passage presumably left it untouched in two others. A second emendator selected the inappropriate свѣщѧ (we provide archaizing normalization to the form), but not in the tradition underlying the OB. This sort of uneven nativization is found in the oldest layer of OCS, where for example иєреи and архиєреи, "priest, ἱερεύς; chief priest, ἀρχιερεύς" are partly replaced by жьрьць, старѣишина жьрьцємъ; свѧщєникъ, старѣишина свѧщєникомъ, and later свѧтитєль and ѵиститєль.[52]

T8 In principle, variation of vocabulary or phraseology may be part of an original translation, or it may be the result of random intervention by subsequent hands or of purposeful editing. Attitudes toward style vary: sometimes repetition of a word or phrase is regarded as undesirable and therefore to be emended. Some translators try to be as consistent as possible in keeping the wording of their model. Esther is characterized by frequent reprises of phrases and even sentences; the LXX paraphrase seems to avoid repeating such elements, and it varies the phraseology. The Slavonic translation has an unusually large number of multiple renderings. We suspect that some variants come from choices made by the Greek translator and copyists of that version, some more from the Slavic translator, but perhaps even more from the inconsistent copyists and editors in the history of the ancestral copy of attested manuscripts, *1350.

T8.1 Variation may concern one lexeme; thus the same H word 'bed' is reflected in 1:3 by ложє and in 7:8 by постєлѩ. It may include more than one element, e.g., 'Their property [is to be] for plunder' yields добыток ихъ къ росполону in 3:13, but добыткы ихъ по росполону in 8:11; 'to the treasury of the king' is къ полатам царѧ in 3:9 but къ полатѣ царѧ in 4:7. In the first case the H is identical, and the Slavic varies both in the number of the noun and the preposition; in the second, variant prepositions in H ('*l* 3:9 vs. '*l* 4:7) both become къ, while the H *plurale tantum* gives variant numbers in Slavic.

T8.2 'In the books of the things of the days,' i.e., the daily records, in various passages of Kings is translated literally, εἰς τὰ βίβλια τῶν ῥημάτων / λόγων τῶν ἡμέρων. In our text it yields two unexpected phrases, въ книгахъ памѧтьныхъ 2:23, and в книгах грамотных 10:2. (See C2:23, C10:2.)

T8.3 'Every year': всѧку годину и годину 9:21 but по всѧ лѣта и лѣта 9:27. (See also L19.23.)

T8.4 The H construct infinitive 'and in the coming of the turn,' i.e., 'and when her turn came' yields two appropriate clauses, и ѩкожє придѧшє ꙁнамєниє for the general rule applying to any maiden in 2:12, and и вънєгда доступи жрєбии for the specific moment that Esther's turn came, 2:15. Just why all three of the lexical items differ remains enigmatic.

T8.5 The Sl clause ижє стрѣжаста вратъ єго that serves to define two specific eunuchs in 2:21 reflects the participial nature of the H noun, '(those) guarding the threshold,' i.e., 'from the guards of the threshold'; it adds the explanatory pronoun 'his.' Yet in

[52] It appears probable that the original translations contained a substantially larger number of untranslated Greek words, and some post-OCS texts witness items that in the canonical texts have already been replaced.

6:2, the same Hebrew is reduced to a single word двьрника Nom. dual. Notice that 'threshold' becomes the more concrete 'gate(s)' in one place but 'door' in the other; yet the two verses are dealing with the same individuals, and that fact is of crucial significance for the plot. It is therefore especially puzzling that the variation occurs precisely here.

T8.6 The Hebrew phrase "for fear fell/had fallen" occurs in three different verses with three different equivalents, see L14.51.

T8.7 In 6:9, H 'and let them call/proclaim before him' becomes simply рекуѵє, while the very similar 'and he called/proclaimed before him' of 6:11 is the more literal бѣ клиѵѧ прѣдъ нимь. A similar pair in the same verses is 'and let them cause him to ride' провести и, 6:9, and и сътвори поꙗѕдити єму, 6:11.

T8.8 This kind of translation problem will frequently be met in our discussions of specific semantic groups of the lexicon of Esther.[53]

Hellenisms

T9.0 The pervasive Greek influence that shaped Old Church Slavonic phraseology and syntax established patterns that became the norm. The first generations of native Slav writers found it natural to express themselves in terms of the translations which were the basis of their education. Newer translations of course reinforced these patterns. It is, therefore, not easy to identify a given item as a Hellenism, somehow marked as exceptional in its context.

T9.01 Sometimes a phrase that fits the context but deviates from the H suggests a Greek intermediary. In 5:3 будеть ти 'it will be for you' is the precise equivalent of LXX ἔσται σοι, but distant from H *wyntn lk* 'and it will be *given* to you.' See C5:3.

T9.1 The most obvious signals that a Greek text underlies the Slavonic Esther are the proper names, which have been analyzed in detail above, A2.

T9.11 Another indication of direct Gk influence is the inappropriate странамъ of 1:3, which should mean a type of high official and, we maintain, points to a Gk stem adapted to Sl morphology, *сатрапомъ 'satraps'; see A2.3.

T9.2 Mistranslation sometimes provides persuasive evidence: a Slavic word or phrase is inappropriate in its context, but it can be shown to be an inept or erroneous translation of a Greek word. We submit the following examples.

T9.21 Растворити, which elsewhere means 'mingle, dilute, dissolve,' occurs four times in contexts requiring *destroy, wipe out*. This peculiarity rests on a confusion of the Gk stem *ap-ollu-* 'destroy' with *apo-lu-* 'loosen, dissolve,' in at least one of the passages, perhaps supported by a more appropriate translation, разорити, in one or more of the others. See L17.5.

T9.22 The phrase въ мысли своеи 'in one's thought' stands in 4:13 and 6:6 where H has 'soul' and 'heart.' Gk διάνοια is used for both elsewhere in LXX, and is rendered by

[53] Compare, for example, the discussions below on idioms with *hand* (L6.3), *fall down and worship* (L10.11), expressions meaning *wish to honor* (L12.15), *please* (L12.6), *banquet* (L13.74), *smash, kill, destroy* (L17.2).

мысль in Joshua. The assumption that διάνοια was used also in some other passages where мысль appears in Esther helps explain unusual meanings; see L11.2.

T9.23 In 1:20 the wives of the nobles възложать срамоту—will *put shame* (on their husbands)—instead of *giving* the *honor* specified in the original. Kulik (1995) convincingly argues that ἐντροπή, which has both of these polar meanings, must have been in the Greek intermediary text. See L15.3.

T9.24 In 3:9, доволно, *enough, sufficient* (for the king) is far too weak for the context, where H has *is pleasing* (to the king). It surely represents ἀρκέσῃ 'it suffices' instead of the appropriate ἀρέσκῃ 'pleases.' The substitution (*.rk.s.* for *.r.s.*) may have been made by a Greek scribe and thus may have been in the text from which the Slavic translator worked, or it may have been a misreading on the part of the translator. In any case, there are parallels in Greek manuscripts (see L12.61).

T9.25 Въздъхнувъ, 'groaning, sighing,' in 5:10 is semantically plausible in the context, but H has 'restraining himself, holding back (his anger).' This is possibly based on an error in reading or copying: the translator perceived a sequence -φυσ-, [fis] in pronunciation, (perhaps in ἐφύσατο 'was blown up') instead of -φεισ-, also phonetic [fis], (ἐφείσατο 'he refrained, held back'), and selected a form containing the root 'blow, breath'; see C5:10.

T9.26 In 2:15, Esther's *turn* to go in to the king is expressed by жребии 'lot.' This may be explained by misreading κληρός 'lot' for καιρός 'time, turn' (see C2:15).

T9.261 An alternate explanation appeals to the Jewish background and comparable situations. A sentence in the *Apocalypse of Abraham* (1:2) begins въ время прилучения жребии моего, егда сконцевахъ службы требы отца моего Фары, 'at the time when my lot came, as I was completing the services of my father Terah's sacrifice.' Alexander Kulik, in his forthcoming commentary on *ApAb,* cites Talmudic equivalents in which the priests cast lots to determine their turn in the order of sacrifice. This suggests that our hypothetical translator could have used κληρός for 'turn' consciously.

T9.27 In 2:3, да бы приставилъ приставникы surely imitates a Gk phrase using a prefixed verb with the root *stand* and a prefixed noun with the same root: see L2.24.

T9.3 Several items that are calques of Greek idiomatic phrases seem awkward or even opaque in Slavic, but occur in other translations and occasionally in original Slavic works. It is not impossible that they may have been regarded as appropriate in literary Slavonic.

T9.31 The H morphological causative *wyrkybhw* 'and he caused him to ride' becomes, in 6:11, a thoroughly un-Slavic phrase и сътвори поıаздити ему, lit. 'and he made to him to ride,' although the same H in 6:9 is appropriately paraphrased with провести 'escort, conduct.' 6:11 surely calques a normal Greek idiom with ποιεῖν plus infinitive.[54] Similar examples are to be found in many early Slavic translations, indicating that this foreign structure was at least tolerated. (cf. n. 16 to C4:16).

T9.32 Въ дн҃ьшнии дн҃ь 'on today's day' is an exact equivalent of ἐν τῇ σήμερον ἡμέρᾳ, a normal phrase in LXX. Est 1:18, however, requires 'on that same day' in the

54 Emanuel Tov (1982 8) holds the phrase ἐποίησέ με ζῆν 'caused me to live' in one of the additions to the Greek L-text to be evidence for a Hebrew original text with a *hiph'il* form.

future, so the adjective дн҃ьшнии is inappropriate. Moreover, SJS provides examples from various old translations where дн҃ьшнии дн҃ь reflects the single Gk word σήμερον.

T9.33 In 4:7 and 6:13, вса съклюҷьшаꙗ сѧ ѥму 'all (things) that (had) happened to him' has a neuter plural participle, like the πάντα τὰ συμβεβηκότα of LXX 6:13, for MT's relative clause, 'all that happened.' In Gen 42:29 this same H and Gk yields a singular слоуҷьшеѥ сѧ, in accord with native Slavic usage, but one scribe changed it to plural, слуҷившаа сѧ (Mixajlov). The possibility of a Gk singular is shown by LXX 4:7, τὸ γεγονός. See C4:7.

T9.34 In 1:3, и иже ихъ о немь 'and those who (were) around him' has a superfluous initial conjunction and a redundant ихъ 'them' where H has merely 'in his presence' (lit. 'to his face'); it can be explained by an intermediate τοῖς or τῶν περὶ αὐτών.

T9.35 In 7:9, ѥдинъ тѣхъ тивунъ 'one of those stewards' stands instead of H 'one of/from the eunuchs.' Surely it reflects εἷς τῶν εὐνούχων (actually in LXX here), with substitution of the demonstrative 'that, those' for the Gk definite article. It is hard to judge when a native speaker of a language that has no definite article will find it necessary to use a pronoun to translate a definite article. Here the substitution serves to define the Gp case of the noun as opposed to the Ns of the numeral. In any case, the result is precisely equivalent to the Gk, but not the H.

T9.36 Єлико or ѥликоже 'as many (as)' functions as a relative in phrases where H has simply *all who, everyone who* in 1:5, всѣмъ людьмь ѥликоже ихъ ѡбрѣте 'for all the people as many as [he] found (in the city),' and in 9:27, на вса ѥлико ихъ приступаше къ нимъ 'for all (as many as) who had joined them.' This apparent redundancy surely reflects the Gk ὅσοι, which often occurs as an equivalent of the relative οἵ. Thus John 10:8, πάντες ὅσοι ἦλθον 'all who (as many as) came' yields вьси ѥликоже ихъ приде in Zo and Mar, but все ѥлико ихъ приде in Ostromir and Mstislav, and вьсе ѥликоже приде in the Archangel Gospel of 1092.[55] Compare Gen 39:22 вса...ѥликоже ихъ въ темници, πάντας...ὅσοι ἐν τῷ δεσμωτηρίῳ; 2 Ki 18:32 (W) вси ѥлико их въсташа, πάντες ὅσοι ἐπανέστησαν. On the whole, forms of ὅσος are translated ѥлико, with ѥликоже as a common variant; scribes apparently felt free to omit or add the же.

The presence of ихъ is relatively rare, and it surely constituted a special mark.[56] The PVL has ѥлико ихъ in the 912 treaty (елико ихъ приидеть, PSRL 1 36.15) and twice in the 945 treaty (ѥлико ихъ крьщенье приꙗли with plural verb, 47.24; ѥлико ихъ есть нехрещено with singular agreement, 47.27).[57] The treaties surely represent Bulgarian translation from Greek, and we can assume that the original had forms of ὅσοι in these examples.

The unexpected ихъ in еже ихъ ѡбращеши 4:16 and еже ихъ бѧше 8:11 suggests ѥликоже after an explicit or implied 'all'; see C4:16 and C8:11.

55 The quantificational meaning causes difficulties for translators into English. In this example, KJ has 'All that *ever* came'; NEB '*any* who came'; Jerusalem 'all *others who* have come.' In the absence of an expressed antecedent, ὅσοι is usually rendered *all who*, e.g., J 1:12 ὅσοι δὲ ἔλαβον αὐτόν 'all who received him.' Cf. OCS (Assem) ѥликоже ихъ приꙗтъ і.

56 This usage has made its way into an original passage in John the Exarch, ҷл҃вци в'си ѥлико ихъ...прилоуҷаетъ, 'all men who (as many as) happen (to be born in the 7th age)' 235d.

57 In similar fashion, PVL has a defining Gp pronoun in a NT citation, Rom 6:3: ѥлико насъ крьсти сѧ Lav 120.13 (but ѥлико хрьстихом сѧ in the Rusian 12th-century Xristianopol′ Apostol, with 1pl verb as in the other oldest copies of the Apostol), for ὅσοι βαπτίσθημεν.

T9.37 In 4:11, кромѣ емуже простреть (прутъ) 'except for (a person) to whom he extends (the wand)' omits the antecedent, *того* емуже. The phrase corresponds to LXX πλὴν ᾧ ἐκτείνῃ, with attraction of the case of the relative. See C4:11.

T9.381 The generalizing particle аще in еже аще 2:13 'everything whatsoever' and идеже аще 9:1 'wherever' is a common Hellenism, calquing ὅ ἐάν and ὅπου ἐάν (see Vaillant, *Manuel* §258, SJS sub аще). Cf. Mk 6:23 (OCS normalized) и клѧтъ сѧ еи ꙗко егоже аще просиши дамь ти до полъ цѣсарьствиꙗ моего, ὅ τι ἐάν με αἰτήσῃς.

T9.382 In 1:16, аще не 'but also,' and in 5:12 аще не мене 'except for me, other than me' imitate nuances of εἰ μή. L 5:12 indeed has εἰ μή.

T9.39 The redundant ли in 5:12 (не приведе ли мѧ) and 5:13 (не вредно ли) may reflect οὐ μή intended as emphatic 'not at all,' which was taken by the translator to introduce a rhetorical question, 'is it not so that.' Cf. Ruth 3:1, οὐ μὴ ζητήσω σοι ἀνάπαυσιν, 'shall I not seek rest for you': in the early western version не имам ли вꙁискати ти покоища, and the later eastern version не поищоу ли тебѣ покоѧ (Glagolitic and Cyrillic texts from Mixajlov 1907).[58]

T9.4 Taken together, all these details furnish substantial support to the hypothesis that the Slavonic Esther was translated from Greek.

58 Vil 10 (262), translating H *hl' 'bqš lk mnwḥ*, has веджe имаю тобѣ искати покою (Altbauer 1992 100–101).

Commentaries

C0 Our aims in this chapter are to find evidence to determine when, where, and from what language this text was translated. We try to see how each word and phrase in manuscripts Q and T contributes to retrieving the details of each verse of the hypothetical common *pervospisok*. Variant readings from other copies of Esther, as well as other early Slavonic biblical and non-biblical texts, are adduced in an effort to establish the book's place in the development of Slavic written culture. At every step we test our working hypothesis that the translation was made from a now lost Greek version that was a close equivalent of what Jon Levenson aptly terms "the surviving Hebrew form" of the text, the MT.

The 167 verses of the MT constitute the backbone of our discussion, our fundamental term of comparison. The Hebrew text abounds in textual difficulties and linguistic puzzles that have kept generations of commentators busy. An important sample of authoritative opinions was reprinted by Carey Moore (*Studies in the Book of Esther*, 1982), and Moore's own commentary (in the Anchor Bible *Esther*, 1971) has been our major point of reference.[1] A quite different term of comparison is the standard Greek Septuagint (LXX, or Beta-text), especially the Origen-based variants; we cite it (and the Alpha- or L-text, which has proved less important for our purposes) from Hanhart's edition, cf. In2.5.[2] Our discussion includes the details adduced by those who have written about the Slavonic Esther in the past (cf. In7).

Title. The variants are incompatible and we have arbitrarily posited the simplest wording. Q's unexpected книгы иєсиѳли 'the book(s) of Joseph' may well, in the general chronographic context where the book occurs, reflect the association of the "historical" Biblical books, and in particular Esther, with the account of these same events in Josephus.[3] Seven manuscripts (16–22) include extensive chronographic texts, some occasionally associated with the name of Josephus, see E2.2.

T has книгы дєсѧтыꙗ Єсфири, reflecting the normal position of the book as the last unit of the sequence Joshua, Judges, Ruth, the Tetrabasileion, and Esther, frequently written in a single codex that is envisioned as following the Pentateuch (Mathiesen 1983b). The alternate title, Естєрь мудраѧ и цр҃ь, (in at least mss. 20 and 24), apparently is more usual in the later 15th century.[4] For ms 19 Leonid (1883 kn 4. p. 2) reports Книгы глаголємыа Естирь мудрая. The Gennadius Bible (ms 25, G) has simply книга гл҃ємаѧ єсѳєрь (note sg книга rather than the older *plurale tantum*.) The source and exact sense of the heading in S and U (Книгы прѣимѣꙗ и ѡбъдръжитєлно) is unclear.

1 Moore's 1971 commentary will be cited simply as Moore; the *Studies* will be referred to as Moore 1981. Our work was essentially completed in 1996. Revisions made necessary by data from the Tixonravov chronograph (see E4.3) offered the opportunity to add a few references to Levenson's stimulating new commentary (1997); see also note 2, p. 246. "Commentaries" footnotes renumber with each new Esther chapter.

2 The passages in the two known Greek texts of Esther that correspond to the Hebrew of the MT occasionally are useful as parallels in the same sense that translations from Genesis or Ruth can be instructive; they suggest how Greek translators might deal with comparable textual and linguistic problems in a Hebrew text. Arxipov's inchoate effort to demonstrate LXX influence on the known Slavonic Esther is uninformed and off the mark.

3 The forms Иєсифъ, Иєсифль are well attested in Genesis, for usual Иосифъ and Иосифль or Иосифовъ.

4 Meščerskij spells the name in this title "Естири," raising needless questions about syntax; his typically imprecise indication "А и др.," brings up problems of just what is to be found in which manuscript.

1:1 The opening sentence of the H text contains several subordinate clauses and includes the first four verses. In Slavonic, the members of this sentence have been further broken up, in a rather clumsy fashion.

Бы^{с}: H *wyhy,* lit. 'and [it] was,' LXX, L καὶ ἐγένετο; we expect **и** бысть (although we have not provided the usual degree sign to mark the omission). The familiar formula, "and it came to pass," is the first word also in Joshua, Judges, Ruth, among other books. It recurs in 1:8, 3:4, 5:1 and 2.[1] It is a clear Hebraism or Biblicism here, but since equivalents are to be found in Greek and many other languages, it cannot be considered evidence of direct translation from Hebrew.

All copies omit the equivalent of 'the Ahashwerosh who' which in H defines this particular king. The omission could have been made by any copyist in the Slavic, Greek, or even Hebrew tradition.

царствоваше with instrumental object is unexpected, see L9.5.

властии: H *mdynwt* 'provinces'; землъ for the same H in 8:9, 9:30, see L9.321.

1:2 егда сѣде: H *kšbt* 'as-sitting,' the preposition *k* plus infinitive construct. LXX responds with conjunction plus passive aorist, ὅτε ἐθρονίσθη ὁ βασιλεύς 'when the king was enthroned,' while L has preposition plus articulated infinitive, ἐν τῷ καθῆσθαι. Ἀσσυηρον ἐπι τοῦ θρόνου 'in the seating of Assuerus on the throne.' The Sl could reflect either Gk construction; see T1.31, C1:5 and A10.81.

1:3 The adjective 'third' of the H is absent from all copies. Perhaps the phrase was influenced by въ лѣто царьства его in 4 Kingdoms 25:27, which occurs on the last page of the Tetrabasileion, just a few lines before the beginning of Esther in nearly all manuscripts; in Q it is 240v 12–13, the heading of Esther being line 22.[2]

пиръ°: H 'a banquet *for all*'; we expect вьсѣмъ.

фарисѣистѣи и мадѣистѣи: for the shape of the stems expected to mean 'Persian and Mede' see L2.34.

странамъ is inappropriate for 'notables'; we conjecture сатрапомъ 'satraps,' which nicely fits the evidence, see A2.34.

и иже ихъ о немь separates the 'local boyars' from 'those around him' while H has simply 'before him' and refers to all the notables. Thus the и is probably superfluous. The rest, as Sobolevskij 1903 435 noted, probably reflects a Gk article with a prepositional phrase, τοῖς or τῶν περὶ αὐτόν. Cf. Dubrovina 1987, 91, 95.

1:4 Егдаже is a relative, 'at which time.' The Sl as it stands makes sense, although the first use of 'honor' represents H *kbwd* 'glory' (cf. also 5:11). Otherwise, the removal of the two bracketted connectives (cf. p. 56, n. 2) restores the sense of the H: 'the wealth *of* the

[1] The initial И would ordinarily be written large in the margin, preferably in cinnabar, extending down beside two or more lines of text. Adding such decorative (or at least special) initials in a different color of ink was a separate task that was done after the ordinary text had been written; it was often done by a different scribe (or rubricator). It is not uncommon that a letter is omitted entirely (see C2:5), or that an incorrect symbol is used. (This is very likely the origin in S of Добромь instead of Бобръмь, 1:6.) All copies now begin the text with a special marginal Б; the И must have been absent from *1350.

[2] H *bšnt mlkw*: LXX ἐν τῷ ἐνιαυτῷ τῆς βασιλείας αὐτοῦ; Ostrih Bible въ лѣто цр҃ства своего. Compare Malalas, bk 6 в лѣто же цр҃ства его ἐν δὲ τοῖς χρόνοις τῆς βασιλείας αὐτοῦ (Istrin 1911 5), and в лѣто же цр҃ства дарїа, ἐπὶ δὲ τῶν χρόνων τῆς βασιλείας Δαρείου (Istrin 1911 9). The Sl phrase thus corresponds to several possible Gk phrases. It may well be that the superscript "t" in лѣ^{т} should be read as plural лѣта in some cases, but the distinction was not made by the scribes.

*glory of his kingdom' (not 'wealth *and* *glor*ies*), and 'the honor of the *beauty of* his greatness' (not 'the honor of (his) beauty-*and*-greatness'). See T1.611.

красота here *tp'rh* 'beauty, splendor,' LXX τῆς καυχήσεως, but in 1:11 it corresponds to H *ypyh* 'her beauty,' LXX τὸ κάλλος αὐτῆς, (cf. such examples as Ezek 16:14, 15, 25).

величьствье 'greatness,' cf. величье 6:3, 10:2, for the same H noun.

For instrumental in expressions of time, 'during,' cf. Vaillant GC 5 §1311, pp. 95–96.

On the spelling ѡ.п.и.р.мь, surely with *omega* as the first letter of the number, '80,' see A7.4.

1:5 The initial вънегда же 'and when' implies that the intransitive H infinite construct *wbml'wt'* 'and-in-the-fulfilling-of' was translated by a finite passive (cf. LXX ὅτε δὲ ἀνα-πληρώθησαν), but only Tn has an appropriate intransitive aorist.[3] The other mss all have the transitive imperfect исполнꙗше, which seems to entail the king as subject and an action that is continuing or repeated; accordingly 'these days' is in the accusative.[4]

всѣмъ . . . еликоже ихъ: Hellenism, see T9.36.

обрѣте: active, implying the king as subject; H has passive 'who were found'; cf. 4:16, where the same H passive comes out as Sl active.

велика, мала: these short-forms still survive in the R set phrase от мала до велика, which of course is a heritage from the Bible, e.g., 1 Ki 30:2.

даже vs. дажь is not restricted to this text, but the variation has not been identified with any particular time or place.

дн҃овъ in both Q and T, surely intended to spell the recent innovation [dn′ov], doubtless the same as spelled дневъ in Monomax in Lav 1377, cf. A3.11.

The intrusive бысть же 'and it happened, came to pass' separates the verb from its direct object, *feast*, and cuts the sentence off inappropriately. The second half of the verse then becomes an independent sentence. This disruptive addition must have been in *1360; it is absent from Tn.

The abbreviated цртва of T for цр^с ва = ц(ьс)арева of QWVE illustrates the kind of error that may arise from misreading abbreviations.

въ дворѣ ѡграда оутренего царева: on 'inner garden' (cf. 7:7, 8), see L1.231.

1:6 This description of the luxurious court with its exotic furnishings is difficult and corrupt in Hebrew, and syntactically unrelated to the preceding material. Any attempt to translate it requires guesswork; therefore it is not surprising that the Slavonic text is obscure.[5]

The first three nouns, бобръмь, оутринъмъ, чьрвемь apparently refer to fine cloths; their possible meanings are discussed in L5.4–45. In the Hebrew text, they constitute the subject. There is no obvious reason for the instrumental; perhaps they were assimilated to the case of the following 'silken cords' as somehow dependent on the participle.

сниманънъ Q (and сниманъно TWV) is written by the scribes with a punctuation mark (or, in V, a space) after the first ъ, implying two words, a masculine participle сниманъ followed by the conjunction нъ (но GTWV), 'but.' We write a single word on the assumption that it reflects the original, a H passive participle meaning 'held' (and the fact that S has only сънимань). Unfortunately, neither a Sl neuter nor a masculine fits the context, and the adversative conjunction makes the sentence even worse.

[3] For other examples of H infinitive construct, see C3:4.

[4] Tn often uses Ap for Np. A comparable instance is the appropriate imperfect напълнꙗху сꙗ дн҃ье in 2:12 (where Tn has напл'нꙗша^с, an improbable imperfective aorist, with a new Np, дн҃и).

[5] Tn has abridged and changed it.

The 'bands' or 'cords' in H are not explicitly silken; *bwc* (regularly βύσσος, or adj βύσσινος) probably referred to fine linen. The Aramaic Targum, however, has 'held by silken ropes' (*'ḥydn b'šly mṭksyn,* the last word being a loan from Gk μέταξα or μάταξα 'raw silk,' cf. Grossfeld 1983 81, n. 16). The form шьлковыми attests the stem шьлк-, which may well be East Slavic. See L5.45. For лептугъ (and its derivative лептужьнъ 8:15), known exclusively from Esther, see L5.46. The form appears to be nominative, and therefore not a modifier of врьвьми, but a separate item in the series that includes the marble columns and the golden and silver beds.

For главахъ H has a word meaning 'round object' which has been translated both as 'ring' and 'cylinder'; the Slavic implies something rather different. The relationship to the 'marble columns' is unclear.

Блискъ: H *rcph* (*ricfah*) רצפה 'pavement.' We assume that the Greek translator read *ricpah* רצפה as ἄνθραξ, 'glowing coal' (Is. 6:6), and that the Slavic translator selected блискъ as an equivalent (cf. Taube 1986).[6] Ἄνθραξ also means 'ruby' (cf. Izb 1073 121d анфраксъ and T3.121 fn).

Sl. каменига драгаго is a weak echo of the H *bhṭ*, apparently a specific precious or semiprecious stone, but which one is unclear. It is followed by the connective 'and' plus the names of three more precious or semiprecious stones, the first of which is missing in the Slavonic.[7] The words стѣны и оустьꙗ (Q's ѡстьꙗ is aberrant)[8] seem inappropriate, although we can readily translate 'walls and openings (lit. mouths).'[9] Tixonr. 704 (ms 22) has стѣны ѡкр^с^тныꙗ; perhaps this indicates a model with ѡ-. It is just possible, however, that it represents an original reading that reflects the description in the Targum: 'and picturesque hangings surround them on all sides,' *w'yṭwnyn mcyyryn mqpn lhwn ḥzwr ḥzwr.*

1:7 пьꙗху: H causative verb, 'caused to drink.' LXX, L omit.

съсоудъ съсоуду: The Sl roughly maintains the general sense of H 'vessels from vessels different' as 'all different' or, as Moore translates, 'no two alike.' For the H adjective *different,* however, Sl has a doublet; either нє оуподоблєнъ or всє раꙁноличь is an acceptable rendering (though всє might better be Np вси).[10] The conjunction но tends to support Roždestvenskij's contention (198) that но всє раꙁноличь was added "to clarify the meaning." Yet both the structure and meaning of нєуподоблєнъ point to a calque from Gk (cf. A5.23). It may well be the Gk translator who doubled the phrase.

For the indeclinable раꙁноличь 'different, varied,' see A5.11.

[6] The word caused difficulty to translators elsewhere. (The pointing in individual MT examples is not unanimous; we will not attempt here to deal with the problems of vocalization.) In LXX Ezek 40:17, 18 *ricpah,* apparently 'pavement,' is rendered περίστυλον, περίστυλα, and στόαι, OB столпи, столпѣх, and стаѧ. In the Song of Songs that was translated from H in the 15th century (Muz 8222, cf. Alekseev 1981, Taube 1986), 3:10 H *tkw rcwp 'hbh* (usually translated 'its interior is laid out with love') becomes послѣдь єго блєщащи ꙁа любовь. This fits in with Jewish exegetical tradition. Thus Ibn Ezra, commenting on SoS 3:10, notes: "*rcwp*: some say that it is related to *rcpt bht wšš* [Est 1:6] and others say that it means 'burnt,' related to *wbydw rcph* [Isaiah 6:6 'and in his hand a burning coal']." The 1553 (Jewish-)Spanish Bible printed in Ferrara translates SoS 3:10 *su medio abrasado de amor* 'its (or, his) inside *is inflamed* with love.'

[7] If one insists on a direct translation from H to Sl, one should take the four H words (two containing 'and') to be the functional equivalents of four Sl words, in which case драгаго would stand for *wšš* 'and marble.' This is manifestly improbable, and we mention it only to emphasize the distance between the H and Sl.

[8] Possibly a misreading; in some hands "ѡ" looks very much like "ю."

[9] Roždestvenskij (198) attempts an explanation based on the putative etymologies of the Hebrew words, whereby the latter would mean 'doors'—it seems far too strained. Moore translates "on a mosaic pavement of porphyry, marble, mother-of-pearl, and colored stones."

[10] LXX changes the text, while L has ἔξαλλα 'special,' which is used by LXX for the same H adj in 3:8; there Sl has a different paraphrase, иꙁдрѧднѣє, see comm.

сила H *yd* 'hand; capability, power' cf. 2:18. *kyd hmlk* (lit. 'as-hand-of the-king') perhaps means 'according to the king's capability'; in 1:3, 8:11 сила corresponds to *ḥyl* 'army; power.'

1:8 аки вольна: H *kdt* 'as [is] law, as customary.' Ro 199 thought that 'custom, rule' was taken by the translator as meaning 'wish (of each guest)'; it is not clear at all. Вольна generally means 'free.' However, in Slovene and Old Czech it may mean *willing*; perhaps here it may signify 'at will.' Very likely it is based on a rather free interpretation of a passage that was obscure in the original; Moore (and LXX) insert a negation, '*not* according to law,' and some other commentators read *kdt* to mean '(large) flagons.'[11] See also L9.2.

мужєви мужю: we expect 'man *and* man,' cf. T4.1. This surely is a defect of *1350.[12]

такъ: in T there is a superscript ов and correction of ъ to *о*, thus таково.[13] We are unable to judge whether the emendations were contemporary or later.

All mss except Tn have the crippling error до for дому.

1:9 в дому царевѣ иже царь ахасъверосъ H 'the house of the kingdom [= royal palace] which [is of] king Ahashwerosh' i.e., the palace of king A., where иже probably reproduces a Gk definite article, cf. LXX ἐν τοῖς βασιλείοις, ὅπου [98 τῆς] ὁ βασιλεὺς A. The scribe of S attempted to rationalize by adding в дому царевѣ иже [сътвори пиръ] цр̃ь Ахасъверосъ.

1:10 вънєгда . . . цр̃єва: H *kṭwb lb hmlk,* lit. "in the being/becoming good of the heart of the king," that is, 'when the king was feeling good.' See L11.24 on мысль, L12.711 on оудобрѧшє (сѧ).[14]

For the names, see A2.35–36.

In ижє служаху прєдъ царємь, прєдъ corresponds to *'t pny*, which might be an accusative object, lit. 'serving the face of,' cf. Moore's rendering 'who personally served King Xerxes.' Here, however, *'t pny* appears to be an example of the relatively rare semipreposition meaning 'in the presence of,' as, e.g., in 1 Ki 2:18, 2 Ki 12:6, cf. Sollamo 116. The usual LXX has τοῖς διακόνοις τοῦ βασιλέως, while the O-copies insert πρὸ προσώπου.

1:11 людьмъ: H *'mym* 'peoples, nations.'

The final eight words may perhaps be interpreted as "both her beauty and her good looks," provided we take єжє as a sort of article. H is lit. "(to show) her beauty, for good-of appearance she," with no equivalent for either Sl и. Thus и єжє stands for H *ky* 'for, because' and the final єѩ for the H subject 'she.' We might emend to имьжє, or simply єжє.

добрыи възоръ: *ṭwbt mr'h*, which in Gen 24:16 yields καλὴ τῇ ὄψει, whence добра възороу. Here the H phrase might better be rendered добровъзорьна она (see C2:2), cf.

[11] We may offer a conjecture that the consonants *kdt* represent a conjunction, parallel to Aram. *kd'*, meaning 'like this, as follows.'

[12] Ro 196, M56a 210 consider it proof of direct translation from H. Tn has моужєви комоуж^до.

[13] M56a 205 cites the replacement of short pronouns by long, e.g., in 1:8, as a diagnostic criterion separating the two younger groups of mss (Gennadius, other) from QT: таков- does not fit this statement. GWV, like Q and the original text of T, all have такъ here. S and Tn have таков-.

[14] Ro 196 considered the translation of the H construct infinitive *kṭwb* by conjunction plus finite verb as proof of direct translation, although it is a paraphrase. Gk often uses preposition plus articulated infinitive in such cases; L appropriately has ἐν τῷ εὐφρανθῆναι τὸν βασιλέα here. Gk phrases of this type are routinely restructured as OCS conjunction plus finite verb, see Słoński, Istrin 1922 vol. 2, 177–78, and cf. C3:4 and C1:2.

LXX ὅτι καλὴ ἦν. The O-variant has καλὴ τῇ ὄψει; καλὴ τῷ εἴδει would also be acceptable.

1:12 и абие не въсхотѣ: H simply 'and she refused,' cf. L12.3. There is no H equivalent of абие here or in 7:6. This strikingly bookish adverb was surely added by a scribe for vivid narration. Such affective emendations are not uncommon, e.g., Ham 130.8, 526.16.

иже по рукахъ is labelled a Hebraism by Ro 196 and M56a,[15] but διὰ χειρός occurs in this verse in the L-text, and in many passages in LXX. See L6.32.

вельми ӡѣло: a doublet, as in 4:4.

For рѣчи (рѣчѣ T), W has речи, V по рочи.

1:13 иже поӡнаахху годины: a literal equivalent of the H (cf. L20). Those 'who knew the times' were probably 'astrologers,' but this sense is deemed inappropriate by many commentators, e.g., Moore 9 favors not *'tym* 'times' but *dtym* 'laws.'[16]

иже рѣчь царева, H *ky kn dbr hmlk* 'for such [was] the matter [= practice] (or, word [=order]) of the king.' H *dbr* = ῥῆμα = рѣчь 'word; affair, matter.' See L8.21–22. Lack of an equivalent of *kn* (as opposed to *ky kn* 2:12 небонъ тако)—except that Tn has та—and the ambiguity of the noun render this sentence obscure.

1:14 иже сѣдаху: H *hyšbym* is present, lit. 'the sitting [mp],' сѣдащии; the иже might reflect a Gk definite article.

наипьрвѣе: like H *r'šnh* an adverb. Ham 32.9, 33.13 has this same superlative form for Gk πρῶτος in the sense 'first (to do something).' Similar forms are known from Old Czech and from 14th-century Ukr documents, see SSUM.

1:15 иже не створи: 'because,' possibly original имьже, but for the late 14th century we must allow that иже could mean 'because.'

иже по рукахъ старостъ i.e., 'the king's command [which was conveyed] by the officials' (with the common confusion of иже instead of еже): here no 'hand' in the Gk texts. The иже is a quasi-article or relative pronoun; there is no equivalent in Hebrew.

1:16 съкривила (H *'wth,* lit. 'perverted, bent; offended') is Sreznevskij's only example of this verb, but Miklosich implies it is not uncommon. He cites съкривити оубогыѥ жены from a 16th-century Serbian menaion, perhaps a negative allusion to Is 1:17, оправьдите въдовицу 'obtain justice for the widow.' In view of the confusion of the prefixes *съ-* and **ьz-* that is common in Ruthenian manuscripts because the two prefixes (and prepositions) had merged in Ukrainian and Belarusian,[17] we may consider also искривити, which occurs in Josephus (Istrin 1/196.9, M 287.14) 'do something wrong' (clearly opposed to исправити 'correct, set right'), and *Secretum Secretorum* 150.7, стережи сѧ . . . да искривиши ӡавѣтъ свои 'beware lest you distort your covenant' (H different).

15 M56a 210 wrongly writes еже по рукам.

16 GorNev 54 (cited word for word by Ro 196, without mention of the source) give this phrase as the first example illustrating their statement, "Удержаны все обороты речи еврейской и коренные значения слов, иногда вопреки связи речи." They say that *h'tym* "here means *fate*." Literal rendering of the idiom is, of course, no proof of direct translation from Hebrew into Slavic, for it is the exact equivalent of O's εἴδοσι τοὺς καιρούς.

17 Cf. Ham 146.18 иӡбралъ in the oldest copy, c1300, but expected и събралъ in the later copies.

Syntactically, the *king*, the *boyars*, and the *peoples* should be parallel, for the queen has acted against all three. It is the dative of *king* that seems least apt, for на with accusative may denote 'against' in a context implying hostility.[18]

аще нє: Hellenism (AT 316) T9.382, A10.4.

въ всѣхъ° цр҃ꙗ: властєхъ is omitted by all mss but Tn.[19] Ro 195 noted the omission in the mss at his disposal, and that въ всєхъ was modified in ms 5 to въ вєсѣхъ.[20] The phrase recurs in 2:3, but 3:8 has по всєи ꙁємли (NB singular, not plural) for the same H; see L9.321.

1:17 гл҃ъ: H *dbr* 'word, matter'; see L8.21.

внидє (in QTVW) should be present, not aorist. We assume that an early scribe omitted a final superscript т (as attested in Tn, внидєᵀ), although an alternate dialectal present with zero-desinence (of a type attested in OCS and at all stages of ESl dialect) cannot be ruled out. As for the prefix, въ- fits the context, focusing on the arrival of the message; cf. Moore's paraphrase 'When all the women hear the rumor about the queen.' The Hebrew *yc'* 'goes out' would more appropriately be rendered by иꙁидєть (or Gk ἐξελεύσεται). Possibly *1350 had выдєᵀ, or вынидєᵀ, cf. 4:6. See L19.1.

царицинъ formally is innovative: the older language should have цариѵинъ, see A5.14.

на всꙗ жєны: на is inappropriate, for it implies "against"; къ or до might be possible, but simple dative should suffice. The extra little words of the later mss (но, и) do not improve the phrase.

ꙗко нє оувръдити мужь своихъ прєд ними for expected meaning 'so that they will look down on (despise) their husbands'; H *lhbzwt b'lyhn b'ynyhn,* lit. 'to make disrespectful their husbands in their eyes.' прєд ними approximates the H phrase 'in their (the womens') eyes.'

Now, OCS врѣдити and прѣврѣдити mean 'do harm to, damage'; оуврѣдити presumably has a similar meaning, but the negation does not fit the context. We may declare that нє was mistakenly added by a thoughtless scribe, or else emend the conjunction to ꙗко{ж}є to produce a plausible text. (As a parallel, compare the correct ꙗкожє of QT 8:8 and the variant ꙗко нє of GWV.) The SC verb *uvrijediti uvrediti* has the specialized meaning 'offend, insult.' On the other hand, another view also makes sense. A second, presumably homonymous, root *vrěd,* that has the opposite meaning 'worthy, valued' is attested in OCS (but only with negation). It is now common in South Slavic (Slovene, SC, Mac.). Thus

18 M56a 209 considered this sentence an illustration of the slavish imitation of H prepositions; he did not notice that *'l* occurs three times, nor did he look at the overall use of prepositions in Esther, cf. AT 312–13. It is plausible to conjecture that на царꙗ was once in this verse; cf. Ham. 130.11 oldest copy имъ творꙗхоу ꙁлаꙗ, but most mss. на нꙗ = G εἰς αὐτούς. (Cf. also Ham 124.23 Самфирѣ vs. majority reading на Сампфȣрȣ ἐπὶ Σαμφειρας.)

19 Later scribes tried to repair this passage by modifying *all* into *villages,* OCS вьсьхъ. Вьсь was widely used in OCS, but very early was replaced (usually by сєло) in Rus′. If retained, it normally had an invariant stem (вєсь, вєси, вєсью). Here WVE (and 6 and 28) have вєсѣхъ; cf. въ своих вѣсєх (var. вєсєх) in Josephus (Istrin 1938 100.14, Meščerskij 1958 380.4), оу вѣсѣхъ twice in a 1399 gramota of Vitovt (Vytautas) of Lithuania, Peščak 140. (M78a is confused by such spellings; he states that въ всѣхъ is a mistake for "въ вьсѣхъ.") In Malalas older and correct въ вси becomes въ вѣси (Istrin 1911 16.14). Not infrequently it was misunderstood in chronographical texts, e.g. въ всѣхъ приморскых 'in the villages by the sea' was considered incomplete and scribes added странахъ, making 'in all the lands by the sea' Malalas (Istrin 1911 20.12).

20 Note that the same H phrase yields въ всѣх ꙁємлꙗхъ in 8:12 and по всєи власти in 8:5. On власть 'power, authority' and 'province,' see L9.3.

не оуврѣдити would mean 'not value, dishonor' and fit this context without emendation.[21] See L16.1.

The phrase не въ послухъ would seem to mean 'not in obedience,' and surely is a gloss. Perhaps this doublet was added to justify the phrase пред ними. The noun послухъ in OCS and most old texts means 'witness' (see Srez), but the verb послушати means both 'hear' and 'obey'; послушание 'obedience' is OCS. In U and BR послух may mean 'obedience,' cf. P *posłuch*.[22] A 1393 gramota to Boris Aleksandrovič of Tver′ from Vitovt (Vytautas) of Lithuania uses a feminine послуха (быти в моеи послусѣ, *Gram. XIV st.*, Peščak 121), but a 1427 copy replaces it with the masculine въ моемъ послусѣ (Srez, sub послухъ).

иже рекоша should be 'in their saying/reporting' (93 ἐν τῷ λέγειν αὐτάς) i.e., 'when (if) they say'; neither the connective nor the tense is appropriate. Perhaps имьже рекуть?

не рачи прити: H simply 'she did not come' (cf. 93 καὶ οὐκ ἦλθεν; the usual LXX and L have no equivalent). See L12.3.

1:18 рекоша should be future, viz. рекуть; scribal carelessness, perhaps influenced by 'heard' later in verse. Note that the same word in the previous verse is also incorrect with regard to the H.

въ дн҃ьшнии дн҃ь surely is a Hellenism, ἐν τῇ σήμερον ἡμέρᾳ, a normal LXX equivalent of H *hywm hzh*, see A5.61. Here, however, the H means 'that same day.'

болѧрынѣ фарисѣискыѣ и мадѣискыѣ provides the East Slavic *ě tertium*, and Q and T agree in detail; this allows us to posit these examples for *1370 without implying anything about *1350 (cf. A1.2). Variants have only the Slavonic -ѧ, also spelled ıa, a.

1:19 оулюбѣе, see L12.6. GorNev 55, Ro 202 considered it (in the shape оулюбие), a Polonism.

аще изидеть рѣчь црьскаıa: H 'let a royal decree go out,' expected OCS да изидеть, but possible dialectal ать изиде(тъ). The аще simply was repeated by an early scribe from the previous clause; such a lapse would be favored if ать were the conjunction. On the other hand, perhaps Ro 199 is right in seeing simple mistranslation. We might conjecture an interpretation "if the king pleases *that* a decree should go out," with ἄν used as conjunction: the Slavic translator might then naturally use аще.

въ книгахъ фарисѣискахъ и мадѣискахъ, H *bdty* 'in the *laws*,' not 'the books.' Ro 201 plausibly suggests the influence of the preceding напишеть, and analogy to 9:32, 10:2 where we have 'books.' The indefinite endings -ахъ of QT are inappropriate, because the phrase surely is definite; again this allows us only to glimpse *1370, not earlier copies. Indeed, it may be a hypercorrection, an attempt to archaize, on the part of the scribe of *1370. Note that later mss (e.g., E) have a gloss (marginal or added in text) персьскыѧ.

преступи for present: omission of *t* or translation error?

ıако не пришла: H 'that she should not be allowed to come,' cf. Gk ὡς μὴ ἐλθεῖν. Perhaps бы was originally present. Ro 199 sees it as mistranslation.

предасть°: H has *the king* as explicit subject; we assume царь has been omitted.

[21] GorNev 55 (Ro 203) considered увредити a Polonism, "uradzić"—a serious mistake, for this verb means *decide* and is based on the Germanic loan *rada* 'advice.' Perhaps they had in mind *urazić* 'hurt, injure'—but here the root is *raz* and phonologically too remote from врѣд to be helpful. (M56a 215 declares that вредити in the sense of R бесчестить is a typical Russian word.)

[22] SSUM does not have the noun, but the adjective послушенъ 'obedient, subordinate' is known from the late 14th century.

1:20 будеть послушана is the equivalent of the H; QTSG послушание reflects an early scribal lapse, while other copies have an inappropriate definite desinence.

рѣчь repeats the word from v. 19: in 19, H has the very broad term *dbr*, but here the more specific *ptgm* 'decree, edict'; see L8.22.

иже: for Asg юже.

цр҇стви: could be contraction for older -ьствьи, or "и" written for "ъ." Fluctuation of the longer and shorter formations in this word are common from the oldest OCS to the 18th century.

иже силна есть: H 'for it (is) large.' The feminine силна is incongruous with царствье (or царьство), and with иже, taken at face value as a pronoun. It can be construed as referring to рѣчь, but this makes no real sense. We might attribute the gender to the feminine βασιλεία or H *mlkwt*, but there is no other evidence of this kind of exaggerated literalism elsewhere in Esther. We might simply agree with Roždestvenskij 199 that the translation here is bad. The иже is presumably a causal conjunction reflecting ὅτι, cf. 1:15 and A10.62. Most mss of LXX omit the phrase, which surely indicates some problem. O-mss have ὅτι πολλή, some others ὅτι ἀληθής, again showing disagreement, but nothing to explain our variant.

If we take the grammar seriously, then силна agrees with рѣчь. A translation might be, "And the word [pronouncement] of the king (which he made) will be heard in his whole kingdom, because it is powerful." This contradicts the H grammar, for *ptgm* 'decree' is masculine, while *mlkwtw* 'his kingdom' and the adjective *rbh* 'much, abundant, great' are feminine. Yet it is similar to the paraphrase in the First Targum: "And let the king's decree, which shall be executed throughout his domain, be made public because his decree is great" (Grossfeld 44).

възложать срамоту is manifestly inappropriate for H *ytnw yqr* '(they) will give honor' (Ro 201); the substitution of драготу or Tn's друготу does not significantly improve matters. The misunderstanding very likely is based on a Greek intermediary, see L15.3.

на мужь свои might represent an archaic accusative singular, and a singular with distributive sense might be possible in this context. However, we expect *husbands* to be plural, as in SWV. QT's reading might be an inappropriate attempt at archaizing or simply a lapse.

доже и до 'to, even to': newer shape даже, see A8.121.

1:22 The Sl sentence states that the king sent a message (to everyone) *to affirm* (for every man) *authority* (in his own house) *and language* (definition unclear): утвьрдити . . . власть . . . и глаголъ. The MT wording 'to be . . . ruling . . . and speaking' has dissatisfied many commentators; the decisive Sl verb утвьрдити 'affirm' imposes an interpretation—the king is reasserting the established rights of husbands in the face of the potential rebellion of wives. Unfortunately, the Sl verse as it stands is obscure. The word власть occurs thrice meaning 'province' and once meaning 'power, authority (as ruler)'; the last clause is obscure.

властемъ: the younger властелемъ 'rulers' makes sense, but it does not correspond to the H, which has 'province,' see L9.32.

власть: H *śrr* 'master, one who rules'; see L9.31 and fn.

и глаголъ . . . ихъ: the clause is uncertain as to syntax and meaning. The H *wmdbr klšwn 'mw*, can be parsed ('and speaking according to the language of his people'), but commentators have debated at length just what it means; see Moore. LXX has changed the sense ("so that men might be feared in their own houses"), while L omits it. The Sl witness to a purposeful shift from parallel participates (*ruling, speaking*) to nouns (*power, word*) suggests traditional Jewish exegesis (First Targum, Rashi, Ibn Ezra), namely that the home language is to be that of the husband—not the wife's or community's.[23]

2:1 по рѣчьхъ тѣхъ, see L8.21.

гнѣвъ царевъ Ахасверосовъ with possessive adjectives, in contrast to the variants of WV with genitives; cf. 2:7, 3:12. See A9.

створеније еꙗ: H 'and what she did,' L ὧν ἐποίησεν, O καθ' ἃ ἐποίησεν.

осуди: H impersonal passive, *осужено.

2:2 да поискали быхомъ:[1] H 'let them seek' with indefinite 3p subject; we expect быша.[2]

добровъꙁорна: *ṭwb mr'h* 'good-of appearance' (cf. LXX καλὸς τῷ εἴδει, Est 2:2, 3, 7).

2:3 да бы приставилъ: H 'and let the king appoint'; the Sl conditional depends on рѣша in 2:2.

приставникы: see L2.23.

[своихъ и власти]: not in H or Tn. X has свои[X] и въ волости, with pleophony.

да быша събрали: H 'and let them collect'; the Sl is a normal final clause, 'in order that they might collect.'

по руцѣ here and in 2:8 is unclear as to case and sense; see C2:8.[3]

тивунъ: VTnX староста, W has староста in text but тивунъ in margin, U has the opposite while our ms 5 has both, тивунъ староста (according to Ro 195). See L2.2.

дѣву versus дѣвую see L2.46.

хранитель женьскыи "objective genitive" cf. A5.631

даꙗ: H lit. 'and to give,' an absolute infinitive whose function here is to continue the tense-value of the preceding verb, viz. 'and let him give.'

пристрою: H 'cosmetic ointments,' LXX σμῆγμα (cf. v. 9, 12, below); Moore, very freely, 'massage.' Пристроꙗ is not attested in OCS; in Ham and Josephus it means a piece of equipment, referring in a variety of contexts to tools or weapons or regalia (see also C2:9 above).

2:4 дв҃[у] юже in QTW, surely a misreading of дв҃а юже as -вую же; V has дв҃ую юже.

цр҃ь ꙁвати is found in QT (and, according to Ro 195, in 21), and three copies of the Gennadius Bible (GorNev 130), whereas WVX, 5 (R 195), and 20 (M78) have цр҃ити. Srez does not list царити but it is in SJS from "Czech OCS" and appears to be an old western formation. We expect an infinitive 'to rule' here. The simplest emendation is цр҃евати; this verb is well attested in the earliest Rusian copies of OCS texts (Srez). Tn has цр[с]твати, which together with the цр҃ствоваше of 1:1, suggests an alternate, цр҃ствовати. The two verbs co-occur in the extant copies of Ioan-Exarch's *Bogoslovie*; we suggest that both were found in *1350.

улюблꙗше as general statement, 'whomever he might [at any time] like.'

23 Cf. Robert Gordis, in Moore, *Studies*, 418.

1 M78a prints доискали, commenting that ПАВ have да по-: in fact T = WV with the latter; we do not know where M got доискали; App. I, 7.1.

2 A close parallel is 3 Ki 1:3 *ybqšw l'dny hmlk n'rh btwlh,* ζητησάτωσαν τῷ βασιλεῖ παρθένον νεανίδα, but да поище[М] гн҃ꙋ своемꙋ цр҃ю дв҃ца ꙋныи (W); H and Gk *let them seek* becomes Sl *let us seek*.

3 M56a 210 mistakenly considers this a Hebraism that demonstrates direct translation from H, cf. note to L6.33.

2:5 In QWV this verse begins with a large cinnabar initial Ꙟ in the left margin, obviously intended to signal the beginning of a new section of text. The scribe of T forgot to write this letter in, so that the line begins оужь (compare omission of expected И in 1:1). In S and Tn, the verse begins in mid-line, but with a large (probably cinnabar) Ꙟ. This is the only textual subdivision in the whole book that we can ascribe to *1350. Q and T agree in starting 6:1 with a cinnabar И, but W and V do not. The Gennadius Bible, in accord with the Vulgate, signals the traditional chapter beginnings with a large red letter starting a new line, and provides the chapter number in the margin. S gives the chapter numbers in the margin, but makes no effort to start the first verse with a new line; only the initial Ꙟ of 2:5, in the middle of a line, is especially large (and probably red; the photo does not tell us).

аировъ: see A7.

2:6 полонєнъ . . . поло{нє}ни: All 9 instances of the root **peln* have the ESl shape *polon* in QTTnX (and, to judge from M56a, mss 16, 21, 23), although expected *съ полонъмь is distorted in QT (and presumably therefore their ancestor *1370). M56a 205 reports с полономь for 16 (Und. 1); he also reports that the pleophonic forms in this verse (but not elsewhere) in 16 have been corrected by a later scribe to the usual SSl *plěn*. Only плѣн- occurs in the other mss.[4] See A1.54.

поло{нє}ни: the full word is attested in TnX. The form reflects the logical plural inherent in the collective meaning of the referent полонъ 'booty; *prisoners*.'

ѡхониємь: better WV Иѡхониємь, O μετὰ Ἰεχονιου, cf. SJS and A2.32 note 34. TnX have the desinence of the feminine declension: съ Охонїєю.

2:7 бѧшє пѣстуꙗ: Srez cites пѣстовати only from Est, but it is also known in OCz and later WSl, in 16th-century Dalmatia (*pjestovati*) and modern Serbian (*pestovati*). Miklosich has it from an unspecified Prolog. In Slovene it means 'carry in arms, nourish, care for (a child).'[5] The noun пѣстунъ 'teacher, tutor' is OCS, very possibly from Morava.

домаѵадицю сир{у}: surely a doublet; H has the single personal name *Hadassa*.[6] L's ἦν ἐκτρέφων 'was nourishing, raising' is closer to the H *'mn* (a present participle), while LXX shifts the emphasis: ἦν τούτῳ παῖς θρεπτή 'there was to him a child [who was] a slave born in the house.' Like the Sl., both Greek versions lack the H name. Домаѵѧдица (also домо-) and the masc. домаѵѧдьць were probably OCS, calqued from Gk οἰκογενής. The notion of servant is thus common to LXX and our hypothetical Gk, while 'orphan' can be derived from the context. Yet there seems to be no reason for the doublet and the lack of the proper name. The reading from Tn and X is preferable; not сироту (as in QT), but сиру plus the pronoun та (X; таꙗ in Tn). WV affirm сиру and follow it with an explanatory то, which is an acceptable equivalent of the H *hy'* 'this is, she is.' The copula бѧшє probably reflects a Greek addition.

єи as D possessive (in the two oldest mss) is typical of OCS, where it probably is a Hellenism, or a "Balkanism."

добротварна/добротворна: see A5.22.

4 M56a 205 considers polnoglasie forms original, the плѣн-spellings being corrections by later scribes. Roždestvenskij, who used ms. 21 for his study, oddly enough does not mention this root.

5 M56a 215 wrongly calls it a "typical Russian" word. The prefixed verb въспѣстова is in the *Life of Moses* (Tixonravov 242.2), and remains unchanged in later redactions.

6 M56a 210 "explains" the lack of the name by conjecturing it was taken as meaning 'myrtle' but rendered by a common noun rather than a proper noun. He does not account for just why 'servant' or 'orphan' was chosen. Vil. 262 has the expected name Гадасу.

да 'and': a relatively unusual sense for OCS, more common in ESl.

въ дщєрє мѣсто: H 'to him(self) as daughter.' We might rather assume въ дъщерь, which would result from the O-variant εἰς θυγατέρα, comparable to the construction 'take as wife' in LXX.[7] LXX makes Esther Mordecai's wife, εἰς γυναῖκα, while L omits the phrase entirely.

Июдѣи occurs at the end of the verse in all mss but Tn. It has no obvious function; could it somehow be a misplaced gloss referring to Mordecai?

2:8 по руцѣ . . . на руцѣ both represent H *'l yd* lit. 'to the hand-of' with the "metaphorically local" meaning 'into the care/custody of' (Sollamo 218). The use of по (also in 2:14) in this sense is unexpected; подъ рукою might be more appropriate, cf. Moore's rendering 'under the authority of.' LXX uses simply a dative in 2:3, but varies ὑπὸ χεῖρα here for the first with πρός for the second. (Cf. L6.32.)

Q has expected поꙗта; in T, поѧта with ѧ in unblocked positon violates T's orthographic rules; it is a correction, apparently of є (suggesting SSl е for ѧ?) by a later hand.

2:9 This verse is seriously corrupted, for the first part apparently states that the *king* was attracted to Esther. In fact, it is Hegai who is impressed—the king does not see her until a year has passed (cf. verse 16). We may assume a correct Slavic sentence in the original translation, but it was distorted and then, presumably in an effort to repair the damage, restructured with a new and incongruous meaning. Xleb and Tn again provide a better reading; they omit цр҃ь: и оулюби дѣвицю ѡчима своима. Cf. C2:4 and L12.5. We may guess an original reflexive construction, and surmise that сѧ became царь. Once 'king' becomes subject, the object of the preposition 'before' must become 'her.'

In the MT, Hegai made haste to give Esther (1a) cosmetic ointments, and (1b) portions (i.e., delicacies to eat), and to give (2) seven maidens. The infinitive 'to give to her' is repeated. The Sl sentence retains this structure, but there are complications.

оубърꙁи: the verb recurs in 5:5 and 6:14; Srez cites all three examples, and also the Comm. to Amos 7:14 (Upyr′) and the Perejaslavl′ Chron. sub 1111.[8] It is in the *Life of Moses* (Tixonravov 239.11).

пристрою єи: H *tmrwkyh* 'her ointments' as in v. 3 above and 12 below.

дары: H *mnwtyh* 'her portions' (LXX τὴν μερίδα), as also in 9:19, 22; the term is generally agreed to refer to something special to eat, cf. Moore 'her delicacies.' The Sl noun даръ 'gift' fails to express either sense; see C9:22.[9]

A second set of problems involves the phrase describing the seven maidens; H *hr'ywt* agrees with *maidens,* but the exact meaning is disputed. LaSor takes the passive 'seem' to equal 'seemly'; Moore, because of the definite article, translates 'the seven *special* maids.' Another interpretation takes the word to mean 'fitting,' so the maidens are proper to give to her; thus LXX has τὰ ἀποδεδειγμένα αὐτῇ 'the ones designated to/for her' (L omits). Sl иже doubtless reflects ѧже (fem pl); QT's стоꙗху does not fit, but достоꙗшє, attested in WVAX, is appropriate: 'whom it was fitting to give to her.'

QT's second пристрою cannot be the noun that occurs earlier in this verse, but is to be emended to a verb plus feminine pronoun -строи ю on the basis of WVA, while the prefix прѣ- is appropriate to the sense. A similar case is in the PVL sub 1089, where L 208.24 has

[7] For example, Gen 30:4, 9, LXX εἰς γυναῖκα, OB въ жєну.

[8] Note: оуборзи пасти на лици своємъ instead of борзо пади in Hyp. and Xlebnikov copies of this passage, reproduced in Lunt-Taube 1988 162.

[9] The First Targum has 'gifts of necklaces as well as royal garments' (Grossfeld 46).

пристрои ю великою пристроєю, probably to be understood as *restructured it* [the church], i.e., прѣстрои *by means of an additional structure,* пристроꙗ; the other copies have пристрою в неи великую створи 'made in it a big additional structure.' Confusion of при- and прѣ- is found in East Slavic manuscripts even when other examples of confusion of и and ѣ are absent; here the noun пристрою of the clause just above surely exerted some influence.[10] In Ham 277.18 the oldest ms has просто, while the others have прєстрои παρεσκεύασεν 'prepared, made arrangements'; in 280.17 all have прєстроимъ for прєстрои имъ. The meaning 'change arrangements' is apparently only in Esther.

For оудобрѣло (or WVA's оудобрилъ), we expect a noun-phrase 'for the better' rather than a verb form.[11] Tn's оубри ю suggests оудобри ю, perhaps an effort to make better sense of a corruption rather than a reflection of the original translation.

2:10 Neither QG вѣда nor T вѣдѧ is appropriate, and SWVX offer a better form. For problems involving this root in competing lexemes see L21.54, p. 243.

людии: H *'m* 'nation, ethnos,' LXX τὸ γένος οὐδὲ τὴν πατρίδα.

родъ: *mwldth* 'her descent'; in 2:20 reverse order.

любо: *ky,* cf. 8:8, 9:24 and A10.61.

роду: Gs attested for OCS (Lunt Gram §4.142), cf. normal рода 2:20.

2:11 и на всѧкъ дн҃ь: H *wbkl ywm wywm*, distributive repetition. QT have an extra и, while 16 had it but it was erased. This suggests an original и на всѧкъ дн҃ь и дн҃ь, precisely what is in Tn.

въсхожаше: H 'used to go'; the prefix въс- 'up' may show that the palace was thought of as being on the highest point in the city.[12]

T's домȣ жєньскомѹ is acceptable as a "possessive" dative; the construction was completely familiar to East Slavs in the 14th century, but very likely bookish for any nouns but kinship terms. The genitive дому женьского of QWVTnX may, but need not, be original.

увѣдѣти миръ Е: H *ld't 't šlwm 'str.* 'Esther's peace,' whether миръ Есфири or миръ Есфиринъ, is a clear Hebraism, meaning 'health, welfare, well-being.'[13] It is not, however, *pace* GorNev 54, Ro 196, M56a 210, proof of direct translation, for εἰρήνη, the literal equivalent of *šlwm* (*šalom*), is abundantly attested in LXX (cf. AT 314, n. 25).[14]

что быша сотворили еи: H *mh y'śh bh*, 'what shall be done with her?,' an impersonal passive. Moore reduces the clause to the noun 'progress.' LXX τί 'Εσθηρ συμβήσεται, approximately 'what will happen to Esther.' The Sl conditional seems to imply 'what they might have done, what they might be doing.' See also A11.43.

2:12 придѧше: perfective imperfect, fully appropriate to context. H *wbhgy'* 'and-in-the-arriving-of.'[15]

10 Srez illustrates the verb прѣстроити with two examples spelled with при-. For confusion of ѣ and и in other instances, see A1.2.

11 M78a's оудобрѣла seems to be a misprint; Meščerskij does not mention -ло.

12 The prefix in Xleb's исхож^{д}аше is not probative, since through the whole ms the scribe tends to confuse original *iz-* and *sъ-* and *vъs-*. (He also frequently substitutes ж^{д} for native ж.)

13 Xleb has a sense-destroying metathesis, римь есфиринь 'Esther's Rome.'

14 E.g., 4 Kingdoms 4:26 (W) тєцы въ срѣтєниє єи и рцы єи аще миръ тобѣ, аще миръ моужоу твоємȣ, аще миръ ѡтроѵищоу; ѡна ж рєѵє, миръ is an exact equivalent of 2 Kings 4:26 (KJ 'Run to meet her, and thou shalt say, *Is it* well with thee? *is it* well with thy husband? *is it* well with the child? and she said, *it is* well.'), although it surely was translated from LXX, δράμε εἰς ἀπαντὴν αὐτῆς, καὶ ἐρεῖς εἰ εἰρήνη σοι? εἰ εἰρήνη τῷ παιδαρίῳ? ἡ δὲ εἶπεν, εἰρήνη.

15 Xleb has distorted the form to придаша, which makes sense, but removes the notion of repetition: 'when they gave [perfective] the sign.'

пристроꙗ Gsf: H *mrwqyhn* '(of) their [fem pl] massage,' LXX τῆς θεραπείας; пристроꙗхъ just below stands for a different lexeme, *tmrwk* which (as in 2:3, 9) refers to the cosmetic ointments used in the beauty treatment, LXX ἐν τοῖς σμήγμασιν.

ꙁнамєниє: H *tr* 'turn' (but 2:15 жрєбии). A probable Gk σημεῖον 'sign, omen' is to be posited; it is not quite right, but the sense 'when(ever) a *signal* (that the maiden is summoned) would come' does not distort the text.[16] Perhaps the H had *tw* rather than *tr* (or *twr*).[17] See also C2:15.

Presumed Gs дѣвыѧ дѣвы does not quite reproduce H repeated *n'rh wn'rh* 'maiden and maiden.' (Cf. T4.11 with note.)

по нєм'жє бы{сть} єи: H *mqc hywt lh* lit. 'from-the-end-of being to-her,' that is, 'after it had been to her'; Moore 'after having been treated.'

нєбо нє: TSWX introduce an unwanted negation, while QGV's нєбо does not account for the нє of the others; нєбонъ is well known from OCS, and appropriate here.

The omission of the long phrase is important for QT's history; it is to be attributed to *1370.

мастит- is not quite right. In early texts it is purely a psalm word meaning 'fat' with a clear connotation of flourishing and well-being. It is out of place here; H has 'myrrh,' accurately reflected in LXX ἐν σμυρνίνῳ ἐλαίῳ. The phrase въ олѣи маститѣ 'in fat oil' occurs in Ps 91:11 (whereby in many copies the Latinism олѣи, from *oleum,* is replaced by the Hellenism елеи, from ἔλαιον[18]), and въ старости маститѣ 'in fat old age' in 91:15.[19] The only other old example is in the commentary to *Čud.* It survived in Slovenian with the original meaning, 'fat' but is now obsolete.[20]

и [въ] 6 мц҃ь: H 'and six months' has apparently been modified to 'and in the sixth month.' Tn and X emend further, changing the number to '7th' (въ .ꙁ҃и Tn; въ се^д^мыи м^с^ць X).

кандило is properly 'candle' but it is a common replacement for expected кадило 'censing, incense' in early East Slavic copies of OCS texts.[21]

2:13 и в томь: a literal equivalent of *wbzh* (which Zimmermann considers an Aramaism because of the sense needed here, 'and then'). GorNev 54 consider it a Hebraism, but it could easily have come through Greek.

вcє єжє аще: Hellenism, see T9.381.

2:14 The враѵюющи сѧ of Q, Tn, and X apparently would mean 'doctoring' (cf. Srez, SRJaXI) or perhaps 'working spells'; in any case it is a crippling distortion. The agreement of Q with TnX as opposed to T and WV is unique; it suggests at least minor access of a scribe of Q's immediate ancestry to a copy of Esther belonging to the TnX branch, thus complicating the stemma (see above, p. 15).

16 Cf. Judg 20:38, where ꙁнамєниє renders σημεῖον, exceptionally standing for H *mw'd*, which normally is translated καιρός.

17 Note that *tr* 'turn' occurs in the OT only in these two verses of Esther. LXX Ez 9:4, 6 has σημεῖον for *tw*. For Est 2:12 we suggest ἐν τῷ ἐλθεῖν (τὸ) σημεῖον.

18 The word in other contexts often is replaced once more, by масло.

19 From this verse маститая старость came to mean *vigorous old age*, and in 19th-century Russia the adjective acquired the sense *long-lived* and then *venerable; old and eminent.* From standard Russian it was borrowed into Belarusian (масціты) and Bulgarian (мастит). It is absent from Russian dialects (Filin).

20 Srez (followed by SRJaXI) cites only the 1296 Psalter, so unwary readers may not realize that this is surely an original early OCS word.

21 Srez II 1466 (line 3) cites a variant въ ароматахъ instead of въ кандилѣхъ; we do not know what ms he took this verse from.

бѣ приходѧщи . . . бѣ възвращающи сѧ express repeated past actions, see A11.44.

Саазъгазовѣ тивуна царєва хранитєль: it is unclear what case the last form represents; cf. A6.2.[22]

тивуна: according to Ro 195, our ms 5 has a doublet, старосты тиуна (cf. C2:3): W has тивуна in the text marked with dots, старосты in margin. TnX have старосты in the text (see note 48).

ложницѧ: elsewhere 'bedchamber,' so QTSG have 'keeper of the bedchamber,' a reasonable title for a court official. H, however has *concubines*. We would expect Gp or Dp of наложьница; indeed Tn has наложницѧм and X наложница^М. The apparent Gs of W (-ца) and V (-цѧ) surely resulted from omission of a superscript м.[23]

Лапь (always accompanied by negation) means 'not easily, not without cause.' It is not a precise equivalent of the MT 'no longer, not again.' See A8.3.

нъ єгда: H *ky 'm* 'except, unless,' cf. 2:15.

будѧшє волѧ: a perfective imperfect; H has the verb *ḥpc* (see L12.15).

тъгда QW, but ти тогда WV: ти is possibly old, but it may have been added by a late scribe with a taste for archaic style. (X has тъ 'he.')

позвашє is correct in T and G, but confusion with the stem позна- is common to Q and WVX. H has a personal passive *wnkr'h* 'she was called.' The active позвашє entails a change of focus (A13.62–63).

2:15 и вънєгда доступи жрєбии: the H is identical with that of 2:12, but the Sl wording differs completely. For H 'in-the-coming-of' 2:12 has non-temporal ꙗкожє with the imperfective of при(и)д-; here a temporal adverb is followed by the aorist of доступи-. The perfective aorist is entirely appropriate for the single act of 2:15, as opposed to the imperfect of 2:12 which denotes repeated or customary completed acts. The force of the prefix *do-* is unclear; Sreznevskij's example (Dopoln.) and the examples in SRJa have somewhat different meanings.

жрєбии 'lot, κλῆρος' seems more appropriate for 'turn' than the знамєниє of 2:12; though it is not literal, it is not dangerously misleading. In LXX 2:12, καιρός is used; we suggest that it was in our Greek translation, but during its history KAIPOC was distorted to KΛIPOC/KΛHPOC.[24] Cf. the example from Judg. in C2:12, above.

поꙗлъ бѧшє: an appropriate pluperfect. VW omit the auxiliary, while X puts it before the *l*-form: ижє бѣ поѧлъ ю.

собѣ: ESl shape, normal after the 12th century, but сєбѣ remains frequent.

нъ ꙗкожє: H *ky 'm 't 'šr* 'except for what.'

рєчашє: could be either perfective or imperfective.

тивѹнъ QTG, староста WVX: H adds 'of the king.'

слугами: *b'yny kl r'yh* 'in the eyes of all who see her' (cf. 1:14 ижє видѧху лицє цр҃єво), LXX ἦν γὰρ Εσθηρ εὑρίσκουσα χάριν παρὰ πάντων τῶν βλεπόντων αὐτήν.

обнєсєна: see L12.91.

22 The reshaping in Xleb of the sequence по руцѣ саазъгазовѣ to поручи сѧ ахазъверосови 'entrusted herself to Ahashwerosh' is instructive. X frequently confuses "ч with "ц" and "ѣ" with "и"; here these letters have been redistributed to create a meaningful phrase. The verse as a whole, however, does not work, because the next phrase, старосты цр҃єва, remains grammatically isolated. Tn is also bad: о роцє съазъхазовє старости цр҃ства.

23 M78a fails to note наложьница; surely it must be in mss other than W, V, Tn, and the fragmentary X!

24 The cod. Venetus has KAIPOYC for KΛHPOYC in Est 9:26, and the Sinaiticus has KΛHPON for KAIPON in F:8, Hanhart 204, 207.

2:16 быс поꙗта: passive OK, LXX simply εἰσῆλθεν.

своєго of QTS is not fully appropriate, the єго of WVTnX is better. However precise delimitation of the two pronouns is not maintained by medieval scribes and no significance can be attached to the variation.

гл҃ющи сѧ: *hw'*, lit. 'it (sc. month)'; cf. LXX ὅς ἐστιν. On the glosses defining the months see T3.1.

милостью и любовью *ḥn wḥsd*: see L12.91.

2:17 облюби: see L12.72.

створи ю цр҃цю is the old construction with double accusative, while WV have the newer instrumental, which in spelling differs only by one letter, цр҃цєю. H has a morphological causative, *wymlykh* 'made her reign,' O ἐβασίλευσεν αὐτήν.

2:18 H has only 'feast-of Esther,' a somewhat belated apposition to the 'feast' early in the verse; in Sl it is expanded to '[and this] feast [was called the feast] of-Esther.' Ro 198 says, plausibly enough, that the addition was for clarification. Since the First Targum has inserted an equivalent phrase 'and he called it' *whwh qry lyh* (Grossfeld 13, 103), we may attribute the explanatory phrase to Jewish traditional exegesis and conjecture that it was present in the Gk translation.

утѣху 'comfort, consolation, reassurance' stands where H has a hapax *hnḥh,* apparently 'a causing to rest' that is translated ἄφεσιν in LXX, a noun denoting "a letting go" that has very broad use. The First Targum's equivalent is more specifically 'release'; some commentators suggest 'amnesty' or release of prisoners. Moore conjectures 'holiday.' In Ham, утѣха translates ἄδεια, and παραμυθία, either of which denote, among other senses, *relief* or *release (from).*

The H verb 'did, made' follows *provinces*; this is one of the very few cases where the Sl word-order departs from that of the MT.

Дары 'gifts' renders H *mnwt* in 2:9, 9:19, 22, but here *mśt* (from the root *nś* 'carry'). See C9:22.

бѣ: no H equivalent; for the phrase, see C1:7.

2:19 събраше, apparently perfective imperfect, replaced by imperfective сбирааше in A (and съб- X, соб- V). Subject-agent is not specified and is unclear in this context. S and U have the aorist събраша, with indefinite person, that probably was original;[25] the imperfective tense is appropriate, however. H has a passive or intransitive verb, so 'maidens' are the subject; no agent is required.

въ другыꙗ: apparently Ap, but unclear as to reference. In H too, *šnyt* 'second' is puzzling. LXX/L omit it; Moore 30 considers it a misreading; some see it as involving a second harem. The traditional Jewish interpretation (e.g., both Targums) is 'for the second time,' a sense that is not particularly appropriate for the situation. Could the Sl reflect this interpretation?

2:20 The syntactical relationships here are awkward. Verse 20 is a sort of parenthesis between the almost identical final clause of v. 19 and the initial words of v. 21. It affirms that Esther continues to act as in 2:10; some commentators (e.g., Haupt) find it superfluous.

бѧше повѣдающи: compound tense considered by Sobolevskij 1903 434 as "old."

[25] Given събрашѧ, either a SSl or a "West Russian" scribe might substitute "є" for "ѧ."

Such forms do indeed occur in older texts, both translated and those written by East Slavs. Evidence for active usage in the 1300s has not, to our knowledge, been documented.[26] Cf. L11.44.

бѧше оутвердила сѧ: H *b'mnh* 'in (her) upbringing' (related to the пѣстуꙗ of 2:7). The Sl clause 'as she had affirmed with him' seems unidiomatic but passable to mean 'as she had agreed (in advance).'[27] This is remote from the H, first because the connective *k'šr* plus *hyth* 'she was' seems inadequately rendered. The next H word, *b'mnh* can be read as the preposition *b-* plus a noun *'omnah* 'bringing up, tutelage' (as indicated by the vowel-points of MT), but translators prefer an infinitive construct plus feminine suffix *'amnah* which can be interpreted either as accusative or possessive, viz. 'fostering her,' or 'her fostering,' as implied by O ἐν τῷ τιθηνεῖσθαι αὐτήν, cf. Moore, 'just as she had when she was being raised by him.' (The verb is that used in 2:7, бѧше пѣстуꙗ). Working from a retroversion ὡς ἐστήρισε, we might conjecture that the Greek translator interpreted a form of *'mn* in a sense of 'establish, verify, confirm.' We suggest that the translator interpreted *'mnh* as *'amanah* 'covenant'; cf. Neh 10:1 (LXX 2nd Esdras 20:1) *'nḥnw krtym 'mnh* > ἡμεῖς διατιθέμεθα πίστιν, 'we are making a sure covenant,' or 'we are entering into a firm pact.' The Vulgate has *percutimus foedus,* which yields OB полагаемъ вѣру. Or we might venture, on the basis of H, to conjecture ὡς ἦν στήριγμα αὐτῆς, freely interpreted by the Sl translator. In any case, this clause is not a direct rendering of the MT. Its effect, however, is to reassert Esther's continuing obedience to Mordecai, a crucial element in the plot (cf. Moore, Levenson).

2:21 In LXX and L, Mordecai's exposure of the eunuchs' plot is transposed to the beginning of the book and prefaced by a prophetic dream (A:1–11). MT verses 21–23 are paraphrased as A:12–14, whereby LXX and L are very different. In ch. 2, LXX restates the content of 22–23, but L omits it altogether.

бѧше preceeding the two named subjects is grammatical, although an explicit dual бѧста would be possible, see A12.1.

вихванъ in Tn, бихванъ elsewhere: "Б" is unexpected. For a Greek transcription *βιγθαν we would predict *Вигѳанъ; the replacement of ѳ by ф and in western ESl dialect regions the further shift of гф to хв is unproblematical. The initial letter is surely a matter of visual confusion (on the part of the scribe of *1360) because of the similarity of the Cyrillic Б and В. Even in the slender evidence available to us for Esther, two examples occur: вер'бми in 1:6 (for вервьми 'by cords,' Evseev 1898 163), and the intrusive gloss in 9:17, T говѣху, WV то бѣху. For examples outside of the Esther tradition, see A2.83. The same person is Вигъхван- in 6:2.

тивуна: WV have instead the correct Nd старостѣ here. (Cf. L2.2.)

стрѣжаста вратъ: the use of the genitive is old. WVB have the archaic dual imperfect стрѣжаашета but the newer accusative object.

врата for 'threshold' is odd, cf. дверника 6:2; see L7.43.

ꙁадѣти руцѣ plus locative is unexpected (1) because locative without preposition is extremely rare in even the oldest texts and restricted to special contexts that do not include this one, and (2) the same H yields dative in 6:2, as does a similar phrase in 3:6.[28] Ms. 15 has цр҃и Ахасъверосоу, possibly to be read цареви. See also C6:2.

26 An early example is PVL бѧху ловѧща ꙁвѣрь, Lav 9.18.

27 Ro 200 thinks it a mistranslation. Instead of сѧ, WV repeat бѧше; the corrector of ms 16 erased сѧ.

28 M56a 214 lists this as "characteristic," but it is not clear of what. The expected verb is прострѣти, see L6.31.

2:22 и бы(сть) вѣсть: H *wywd‘ hdbr* 'and the thing became known,' LXX (O) καὶ ἐδηλώθη ὁ λόγος (L8). Вѣсть here may be an archaism, an uninflected adjective meaning 'known.' Only vestiges remain in *OCS, for it was being replaced by inflected but suffixless вѣстъ. SJS lists вѣсть бы<стъ> from Is 7:2 sub вѣсть, while sub вѣстъ it cites Acts 28:22 вѣсто намь єсть Hilf Šiš, but вѣсть Mac, γνωστὸν ὑμῖν ἐστιν. In Daniel 3:18, the "Methodius" redaction has вѣсть тобѣ боуди, 'let it be known to you, may you know,' γνωστὸν ἔστω σοι, while the "Cyril" and "Symeon" texts have вѣсто да ти єстъ (Evseev 1905 38). A post-OCS variant is вѣстьнъ: in Ephraim the Syrian the *OCS has вѣсть бысть ѥмоу for ἠκούσθη αὐτῷ, lit. 'it was heard to him' (Usp 301d12, Bojkovsky 2 298), but вѣстно быст in a SSl revision (Bojkovsky 2 299). The imperfect is attested in the *Skazanie* of Boris and Glěb; Usp 11b20 бѧше же ѥмоу и вѣсть (contrast later in the text, 23d4, вѣсто ти буди). In Josephus, бысть вѣсть is frequent, with at least one case of a future, єгда вѣсть ми будєть 'when I find out' (Meščerskij 1978b 229.16). In the dative absolute, however, бывши вѣсти is found, indicating association with the feminine noun.[29] It appears that later scribes favored the archaic usage from time to time.[30]

The final phrase should be '*in* Mordecai's name'; въ has been omitted.

2:23 MT 'And the matter was investigated and found'

рѣчь 'word, speech, matter, affair' is a close equivalent of H *dbr* and of the overlapping Gk terms ῥῆμα and λόγος (L8). Here it could refer to the (verbal) accusation made by Mordecai, the plot, or the whole complex of affairs. In Gk, it is the eunuchs that are investigated (A:14 'the king examined the two eunuchs').

въωбражена for 'was found': we expect обрѣтена or possibly въобрѣтена, or the usual изобрѣтена, cf. изоωбрѣтє 6:2. The participle in -жен- could belong to a verb in *-z-i* or *-d-i*. въобрази- means 'to shape, form, depict,' a sense that does not fit this context. However, Sreznevskij cites a 1207 example from the Suzdal' chronicle (Lav 431.10) that may illustrate a legal usage that could apply here: онѣм же кленущим сѧ и ротѧщим ꙗко нѣ^с^ то тако…кнѧзь же великыи слышавъ ꙗко въображена бы^с^ истина повелѣ изъимати ихъ. The sense seems to be "the truth (true state of affairs concerning the matter at issue) had been depicted."

Now, the H verb implies *find to be correct* (e.g., Moore, "the plot was investigated and its existence confirmed"), and it would not be surprising if a translator imposes a specific interpretation when selecting an equivalent. For Sl, we may conjecture that the original form was обрѧжена, from обрѧд-и-, 'put in order, arrange'; Sreznevskij gives a 12th-century example where it is used of a bishop dealing with the punishment of errant monks and nuns. Spellings with "ра" for "рѧ" are not uncommon.[31] Any subsequent scribe, influenced by the preceding verb, could easily add the prefix to make the appropriate perfective form въображена.

The meaning, then, is that the matter was *investigated and dealt with*. This fits the termi-

[29] The OCS idiom быстъ без вѣсти 'disappeared' implies for the noun a sense 'knowledge' that still exists in Slovene but was almost unknown in old texts.

[30] Competing scribal choices are illustrated in 15th-century texts: 1 Ki 23:7 вѣсто бысть Саѹлу (GB, W), versus вѣсть in J, S, and возвѣсти сѧ in OB; 1 Ki 14:16 и бысть мѣсто (! < вѣсто) Саѹлови (GB, OB), vs. вѣсть (W, J). Srez cites бысть вѣсть from the Novgorod First Chronicle sub 1216. It is from the 18th-century copy of a 15th-century ms that is defective at this point; the other 15th-century ms has вѣсть прииде.

[31] Srez sub образити II 538 and обрѧдити II 556 cites from a single text ображени and обрѧжени in senses that could mean objects or pictures that are *executed, arranged*. In PVL sub 1093, Lav 224.22 has expected обращающа сѧ but Hyp обрѧщающа сѧ. The opposite occurs in приобращєть 'finds' Archangelsk Gospel of 1092, 80v3 Mk 8:36 (cf. оусраѵѫ as a variant of оусрѧщю^т^ 'meet,' Ham 465.18).

nology in Oleg's 911 treaty with the Greeks, where обрѧжєниє is a man's final 'arrangement, disposal,' that is, 'testament, will' and makes reference to урѧжєноє or individual item left to a survivor.[32]

книгахъ памѧтныхъ H *spr dbry hymym* 'the book of the things of the days,' i.e., the daily official record, diary, journal. The Acc книгы памѧтныꙗ of 6:1 recurs in the abridged Esther story of the 1512 Chronograph, with a gloss, сирѣчь лѣтописныꙗ. LXX 6:1 has γράμματα μνημόσυνα τῶν ἡμέρων. Памѧтьнъ is noted by Srez from this verse and from 1076 (6.5, in the one text that appears to have been composed by the 'sinful Ioan' who compiled 1076 in Bulgaria), with the sense 'memorable' that is confirmed by medieval Serbian sources (Mikl). The H phrase occurs in Kings and is rendered in LXX as βιβλία τῶν λόγων τῶν ἡμέρων (4 Kingdoms 14:28 etc.) or τῶν ῥημάτων (4 Ki 14:18), but in Esther the verse is paraphrased and the matters are written down 'for a reminder/memorandum' εἰς μνημόσυνον. Perhaps our Gk intermediary text had some form of μνημόσυνον or μνημοσύνη 'remembrance' as an attribute of 'book.' On the other hand, perhaps this verse has been modified by a Slav with some familiarity of the LXX Esther. In any case, the same book appears in 10:2 as книгах грамотных, another rendering that differs significantly from the H. See C10:2c.

повѣшєна быста: H passive, 'they were hanged (the two of them)'; Sl has correct dual.

3:1 по глаголании тѣхъ [всѣхъ]. Possible as 'after the speaking (Ls) of [all] these (things),' although a Lp глаголании(х) with superscript "х" in an early copy might be conjectured. H 'after these things' as in 2:1, по рѣчьхъ тѣхъ. Perhaps по *глаголѣхъ тѣхъ, then confusion of "ѣ" and "и," and still further confusion? In any case, 'all' is not in H; it could have been added at any time. Here L λόγους, O ῥήματα. Alternatively, we may view it as parallel to Gen 15:1, по гл҃анїи жє сємъ (var. гл҃є симь, Mixajlov; LXX μετὰ δὲ τὰ ῥήματα ταῦτα) and emend тѣхъ to сємь.

The name Haman is omitted; H has "Haman, son of Hammedatha the Agagite." The omission must be ascribed to *1350, and is disturbing because it affects the first mention of this important personage. In the later mss the corruption seems to be slightly more complicated.[1]

The first възнєсє is an error, influenced by presence of the verb in the second part of the verse; we expect възвєличa. The same sequence occurs in 5:11. There the second verb is възнєсє и, with retention of old Asm pronoun; newer єго is used here.

Прєвышии, apparently a long adjectival form, is less appropriate than the adverbial прєвышє attested in SWV.

3:2 припадающа of QT perhaps by attraction to the preceding Gs цр҃ѧ.[2] For terms meaning *fall down, worship* and *kneel*, see L10.

32 The term is attested only in the Radziwill and Academy copies (PSRL 1 34.7; Srez sub обрѧжєниє); Lav is defective and Hyp and Xleb have a misspelling обрѧщєниє.

1 We would predict амана сына *амадаѳина *аагаги (cf. A2.32). The possessive adjective *Hammedatha's* caused trouble. Ms 16 (Und 1) has сына амъдафиина marked with dots and вєл'дахїина in the margin. Ro 195 states that сына вєлдахина амадахина агаги appears in ms 5; вєл- apparently was an early error, possibly corrected from later verses (8:5, 9:24). G and ms 7 (Volok 12) have сн҃а вєлдафїина агагї. V changes the word-order and therefore the sense: вєлдахина сн҃а аминадахиїна агагї. W has вєльдахии сн҃а амадиxина агаги (each letter of the two names marked with a superscript dot) with "a" written over "и." This is an instance where the precise attestation of all known manuscripts might be helpful. M78a cites вєлдафина (ms 20) and вєлдєхїина (ms 31), but in his comments on 3:2 rather than 3:1.

2 M78a wrongly says Q has correct old -є. A more remote possibility is a foretext where perhaps ѧ was written for SSl [e] as a hypercorrection?

тако имъ бѧше ꙁаповѣдь царева: *ky kn cwh lw hmlk*, 'for so the king (had) commanded concerning him.' For *lw*, lit. 'to/for/with reference to him' we expect not the plural имъ, but a singular, ємꙋ or possibly о нємь. The H past-tense verb is represented by a noun plus 'was' in QTGTn. Variants (V ꙁаповѣда, W final -ь corrected to -a, or vice versa) suggest an original l-participle, ꙁаповѣдалъ as in 2:10 and 2:20. (Note that H has *cwh* for both Sl imperfect and pluperfect.)

3:3 Рѣша is a normal archaism (also 2:3, 6:13).[3]

The indirect object 'to Mordecai' is omitted, obscuring the meaning of the verse.

ѵьто ради: normal Rusism, attested since 11th century; ѵєсо ради is relatively rare in ESl manuscripts.

3:4 и быс(ть) єгда гл҃ахꙋть: a normal equivalent of *wyhy b'mrm* 'and-it-was in-their-speaking,' possibly, as Sobolevskij 1903 435 observed, an echo of a Gk phrase such as ἐν τῷ plus infinitive or the like. (For parallel examples, see C1:10, T1.31 [Ruth 1:1a], T1.51 [1Ki 16:23], T1.611 [Est 1:4]).

днє днє, var. днь днє: the case usage is unclear,[4] see T4.13.

QTSGWV have no equivalent of the clause *lr'wt hy'mdw dbry mrdky* 'to see whether Mordecai's words would stand' in the sense 'Mordecai's conduct would be tolerated,' or 'whether Mordecai would persist in his conduct.'[5] Tn fills the lacuna with six words that only vaguely recall the MT sense: оуставны ли видѣти гл҃ы Мардохоєви. A literal equivalent would be *видѣти устоꙗть ли глаголи Мардохаєви, for the verb устоꙗти means both 'persist, withstand' and 'prevail, rule over.' Tn's wording implies the noun уставъ 'regulation, set of regulations.' If we move видѣти to first position, perhaps we may translate, "to see whether Mordecai's affairs which had taken place were in accord with the regulations." There is no way to decide whether this grammatically incoherent clause goes back to an original rendering that was intended to clarify the value of this clause in a laconic verse, or whether it is the result of radical reworking at the hands of the editor of the Tixonravov Chronicle.

и нє повѣда is in all texts, but it contradicts sense; he *did* tell them. Perhaps it arose in part by reminiscence of 2:20 and Esther's silence, but a similar sense-distorting shift of жє to нє is found in WV, see variants to 8:8.[6] In any case the simple emendation of "н" to "ж" makes an appropriate reading.

The phonological replacement of older тъ (QSW) by the ambiguous то in T indicates that the scribe was not concerned with archaizing; such spellings occur in Lav. The extended тои of VGTn is more typical of innovating scribes.

бѣ is unexpected. H has no copula; LXX supplies the usual present ἐστιν.

3:5 Нє быс: seems inappropriate as an auxiliary with the present active participle: бѣ or бѧшє would be more appropriate.

On *fall down and worship* see L10.1.

мысли гнѣвныꙗ: see L11.21.

[3] M78a puts во вратѣхъ in his text, with a note that ms 15 has въ; in fact въ is in QT.

[4] M56a 210 cites дн҃ь и дн҃ь, apparently his own rendering of the H. His 1978 text дн҃е дн҃ь is in error; WV do have дн҃ь дн҃е.

[5] M78a translates the omission чтобы посмотреть устоит ли в славе своей (! for в слове своем); he misunderstood what the subject is. Vil. 262 has видѣти чи ѡстоѧт сѧ рѣчи мордохаєвы.

[6] Careless scribes sometimes insert a нє where it does not belong; e.g., Job 42:5, око нє видѣ as var. of око видѣ or, better, оѵи мои видита, Afanas'eva 30. PVL 128.25, for коли можетє, X has коли нє можетє.

3:6 нєврѣдъ (or two words?) оүима: see L16.
ʒадѣти руцѣ Мардохаю 'send hand': L6.311.
єдиному: *lbdw*, perhaps indicates Gk intermediary, cf. A7.11.
волꙗ бы^{с}: *wybqš* 'and he wished,' see L12.15.

людии мардохаєвъ is apparently Gp in form, but accusative in function. Such usage is improbable before c1400, although it becomes usual toward 1500. Moreover, after c1200, old **ljudьjь* was normally written людєи; an archaic spelling людии might possibly be supported by western ESl dialect forms. Altogether, it seems safe to postulate older Ap люди мардохаєвы here.[7]

3:7 This verse is crucial to the plot of the whole book, even though many scholars believe that it is intrusive (Moore 37).

The key phrases, in Moore's translation, are: "In the first month, which is the month of Nisan, [. . .] the *pur* (that is, the lot) was cast in Haman's presence to determine the day and the month." Only Tn preserves a partial equivalent of 'which (is) the month,' showing that *Nisan* is a definition: є^{Ж} є^{с} 'that is.'

The verse contains the first two of the glosses defining Hebrew months; these glosses may have been added at any time during the history of the translated text, whether in Greek or in Slavonic. It is notable that the wording of the first gloss, гл҃ющии сѧ (cf. 2:16), contrasts with the one at the end of the verse and all subsequent glosses, рекомыи.

Far more important is the key phrase *pwr hw' hgwrl*: in the wording of the King James translation, "*Pur*, that is, the lot." *Pur* was a special word that required definition in the original Hebrew text; it is reasonable that translators might retain the form, translating only the gloss.[8] Yet LXX simply has "he cast lots (κλήρους)"; only O-texts insert φουρ. (L omits the verse entirely.) The attested възвьрже вражду и жрєбии 'enmity and lot' of our text makes no sense. It is one of our general assumptions that an original "normal" and therefore meaningful translation may be distorted by inattentive copyists. We further assume that the original translation should reflect, even at second remove, the Hebrew sense. Therefore we emend the first noun to *вражу, because we find that **worg-j-a* in the concrete sense 'die, lot' fits the context precisely, and this sense is attested in West and South Slavic (AT 308) as well as in 15th-century Belarusian.[9] The hypercorrect "ж^{Д}" for "ж" that produced the inappropriate вражда is to be attributed to a careless scribe, not to a thinking redactor.[10] The phrase was surely вражу иже жрєбии (perhaps with added copula, єсть). Tn garbles it: враж^{Д}оу иже бѣ и. See also A1.3.

7 Addition of a superfluous "и" is also found in 9:29, днии for expected Ap дни.

8 On the vexed origins of the word (Hebrew? Old Persian? Babylonian? Assyrian?) and of the holiday, see Moore xlvi–xlix. See also C9:26.

9 Karskij's very brief glossary to a RNB *sbornik* (Q I 391 [= Turilov 1986 no. 1571]) contains ворожу киноувши киноули жеребьи (Karskij 1962 310); we assume that the passage must concern the soldiers throwing lots for Christ's clothing at the crucifixion. The last two words appear to be a gloss on the first two, implying that ворожу required explanation. The related verb is recorded in Gen 44:5 and 15 where the oldest copy (RNB TSL 1) has ворожениємъ ворожитъ, although most have враж^{Д}єнїємь вражить for οἰωνισμῷ οἰωνιεῖται 'divine with divining.' (It is also used by the 15th-century translators of 2 Chron 33:6, where several techniques of divination are enumerated: [H *w'wnn* >] LXX καὶ ἐκληδονίζετο > OB и вражашє со жрєбїи.) Ham has ворожа in the general sense 'divination, magic, μαντεία, 67.19.

10 Alekseev prefers "the word *вражба*, which has two meanings, 'ворожба' and 'вражда' (cf. Srezn.)" (1987a 3). But the abstract sense 'ворожба' is inappropriate here. (Further, the substitution of hypercorrect жд for ж is very common; it is more likely than ж for жб, and it is attested for this stem in Hamartolos, враждєниє for вражєниє μαντεῖον 502.24 as well as Genesis, see previous note). Alekseev's comment is unclear. "Переводчик . . . был в затруднении . . . [и] перевел его [слово pur] вражба/вражда"—does this mean that the mistake could go back to the original translation? We see no difficulty. The singular *pur* has appropriate

Many commentators (e.g., Moore) consider the MT deficient here and emend to include "and the lot indicated the thirteenth day of the twelfth month." The H from which the Sl is ultimately derived agreed here too with the MT.

3:8 се соуть: H has no explicit equivalent of the introductory particle се; it could have been added by the Greek translator (ἰδού) or by a Slav, cf. 6:14.

людие is fine, but H has 'one people' (*'m 'ḥd*) and the use of the plurale tantum людие has made a modifier 'one' difficult.[11] On the other hand, perhaps even the Gk translator didn't think the 'one' was needed because of the extensive definition that follows; simply no definite article and then the modifiers would do. LXX has ἔθνος, L λαός, with no article or numeral.[12]

по всеи ꙁемли: H 'in all provinces,' which yields въ всѣхъ властьхъ in 2:3; see L9.321.

издрѧднѣе паче: MT is lit. 'and their laws (are) different from all people.' LXX ἔξαλλοι παρὰ πάντα τὰ ἔθνη, using παρὰ with accusative in the sense 'as compared to,' so that the preceding adjective—here ἔξαλλος 'special'—implies a comparative or superlative, therefore, *more special than* or *most special of all the nations.* In Gk, and in the Sl equivalent construction with паче, the adjective may be formally either positive or comparative, e.g., Dan 3:32 (cf. PVL sub 1093, PSRL 2 214.17), (βασιλεῖ) ἀδίκῳ καὶ πονηροτάτῳ παρὰ πᾶσαν τὴν γῆν, lit. 'to the unjust and more crafty (king) compared to all the earth,' цр҇ю неправедноу и лѫкавнѣишю паче всеѧ ꙁемлѧ 'to the most unjust and crafty king of all the earth.' A comparative in Sl may go back to a positive form in Gk, e.g. L 13:2 ἁμαρτωλοὶ παρὰ πάντας τοὺς Γαλιλαίους, KJ 'sinners above all the Galileans,' NEB 'more sinful than,' OCS (Zo) грѣшьнѣиши паче вьсѣхъ Галилѣанъ.

The sequence ꙁдр in иꙁдрѧднѣе represents archaic or archaizing spelling of morphophonemic *z-r*. Иꙁдрѧдьнъ means 'out of the ordinary, exceptional,' where H has simply *different,*[13] with the same lexeme as in 1:7, see comm. In *Čud* and Ham иꙁдрѧдьнъ renders ἐξαίρετος.

не суть творѧще: progressive, see A11.44.

ц҇реви бы не право: here and in 3:9 бы is not justified by the H, cf. A11.434.

не право: H *'yn šwh* 'it is not worth while' (Moore, 'not appropriate').[14] In 5:13 similar H is represented by не вредно, see L16.

3:9 доволно for 'please': probably reflects ἀρκέσῃ 'suffices' by error for ἀρέσκῃ, see L12.61.

The superfluous бы is in all copies known to us, except for Tn, which has no бы at all.

---

equivalents, once in adjectival form, по имени жребиинѣм (9:26) and *вража here in 3:7; either of these could rest on a Greek original. The whole phrase "and they threw *pur*, that is, the lot" is missing from 9:24. The plural form *purim,* the name of the holiday, comes out as *veselij-* (with peculiar grammar) in 9:28, 29, 31, 32.

[11] Vil. 262 has людъ ѡдинъ.

[12] In Gen 11:6, *'m 'ḥd* yields γένος ἕν, which gives Sl родъ единъ (Mixajlov). In principle, *jedin-* may appear with a non-singular noun, cf. Gen 11:1, with a *duale tantum*: и бѣ всѧ ꙁемлѧ оуста едина, χεῖλος ἕν, *śph 'ḥt*.

[13] Nor is LXX ἔξαλλος 'special' an expected equivalent of the H. It is a rare word; oddly in 2 Ki 6:14, στολὴν ἔξαλλον (2 Sam 6:14 *'pwd bd* 'a linen ephod') becomes ѡдеждꙋ бѣлꙋ (W).

[14] The бы can be read as aorist, 'It *was* not'; compare а то бѧше не право in 4:2, where H has no express past tense.

The construction абы написалъ might be interpreted as 'that he should write,' but seems strange after a conditional clause. H has a passive 'let it be written.'[15]

5000 капии срѣбра QTSGWV; ї тысѧщь сребра капи Tn: MT 10,000 *kkr ksp*. The usual Gk translation of *kikar* is τάλαντον, and here LXX O-mss have the expected μύρια τάλαντα ἀργυρίου '10,000 talents of silver.' The majority Sl is not a translation, but an interpretation; it adapts the sum by calculating that one *kap*' of silver equals two *kikar* or talents.[16] Tn's variant has the literal equivalent of the H number, but the unit, *kap'*, of the converted sum. It is likely that this shows an intermediate step: an original талантъ has been replaced with капии (reduced by an extremely common type of haplography to капи in Tn). By *1360, the sum was properly determined. See L16.4.

навѣшю: H *'šqwl* 'I'll weigh,' denotes *measure out, pay over* in this verse (as does the infinitive *lšqwl* in 4:7). See L16.43.

къ строю дѣла: *'l ydy 'śy hml'kh*, lit. 'to the hands of those who do the work(s),' i.e., to the officials. O ἐπὶ χεῖρας τῶν ποιούντων τὰ ἔργα.[17] Surely строю should be rather строѧщю, or possibly строителю. Cf. 9:3, чинѧще дѣло царево, and L2.41.

къ полатамъ царѧ: *'l gnzy hmlk* 'to the king's treasury.' It is puzzling that the plural is used here but sg in 4:7 for the same meaning. (H has *'l* in 4:7.) The use of полата as 'treasury' seems to be late ESl, attested with reference to churches. In 5:1 полаты and полатѣ mean 'palace'; the H is not quite the same in the two instances; see L1.12.

3:10[18] пьрстьнь, also 8:2; see C3:12 and, on печать, C3:14.

да for дасть is normal late OCS 3s aor; the absence of an explicit object 'it' (viz. ring) is probably admissible.

мучителю: H *crr* 'oppressor'; LXX, L omit.

3:11 срѣбро буди дано тобѣ: H *hksp ntwn lk,* (lit. 'the money (is) given to you') provides no equivalent of the 3 sg imperative буди. A Gk δοθήτω might underly the Sl. LXX, L use active imperative, τὸ μὲν ἀργύριον ἔχε. Perhaps буди дано (rather than да будеть) is a sign of antiquity.[19]

створити {имъ, съ ними?} волю? Omission of 'in it, with it [sc. the Jewish people]' (H *bw*) does not seriously affect the sense.

3:12 и призвани быша: *wyqr'w*, but the same H in 8:9 corresponds to възвани быша. Both verbs are good OCS.

и бысть attested only by Tn (which, however, has the imperfective писано).

еже: *kkl 'šr,* literally 'as all who/which.'

писци цареви = 9:9 *spry hmlk*, Moore 'the king's secretaries.'

Tn furnishes the plural приставωм, agreeing with H against all other Sl mss; see L2.2 for terms denoting officials.

людии и людии, землѧ и землѧ: syntax odd, we expect datives.

писмѧ; compare the following phrases:

15 In this verse M78a prints погубити и, claiming that ms 2 (Q l.2) has -ти ꙗ; both in fact have ꙗ.

16 M56a 215 claims that капь is "typically Russian," adding, mistakenly, in the accompanying footnote that "*20* капий" = 10,000 talents.

17 This same phrase occurs in 2 Chronicles 34:10, paraphrased by the 15th-century translators of OB as дѣлателїе.

18 M56a 205–206 says that his two first groups of manuscripts have a lacuna at end of this verse, while his "third group" of mss provides all the words. In 1978a *ad locum* he claims his text was reestablished by later mss, not including "П" (Q 1.2); in fact it is Q and T that preserve the full text.

19 M78a prints на, noting дано from 2, 20, 31; in fact it is in T as well as Q.

3:12	ꙗко	писмѧ	єꙗ
8:9	ꙗко	писаниє	єи
1:22	ꙗко	писаниє	ихъ
9:27	ꙗкожє	писмѧ	ихъ
8:9	ꙗкожє	ихъ	писмѧ

H has ‘as-writing-her’ for the first two and ‘as-writing-their’ for the last three. The Slavic has variation in all three elements: genitive vs. dative possessive pronoun, ꙗко vs. ꙗкожє, the shape of the nouns, and even the order of elements. Tn has ꙗко^{ж} писмѧ и^{ж} [sic, instead of их] also in 8:9; писаниє is only in 1:22.

имѧ for expected въ имѧ; seriously misleading, because “they wrote the name of king A” is quite different from “wrote *in* the name of.” So also in 2:22.

написахуть and ꙁапечатаху (no -ть) are nonspecific 3p; H has passive. They are imperfects because this is an explanatory clause, as opposed to the perfective narrative form написано earlier in the verse.

пьрстьнємь: possibly ESl form with original -ен- replaced by morphophonemic -ьн-, as in standard Russian, cf. перстень перстня. However the BR variant Gs перстеня and Uk перстінь перстеня mean that here the fluctuation may be purely orthographic (cf. раꙁдѣльни with “ь” for “є” in T 3:8).

3:13 погоньцѣ illustrates the rather erratic use of “ѣ” instead of “и” that leads us to suspect such usage for *1350. We interpret this form as instrumental, because the H has ‘by the hand of the couriers.’ In 3:15 the form погоньци, spelled with expected и, is nominative; see L2.44 on stem and meaning.

иꙁбити is to be restored from Tn иꙁбить, along with и погубити, which is missing from all other copies. The imperfective избивати of WV surely underlies the mistaken избавити of QTG; this glaring blunder illustrates how poorly the scribe of *1370 understood (or cared about?) the text he was copying.[20]

On the three near-synonymous H verbs meaning *kill* here, 7:4, and 8:11, see L17.

добытокъ ихъ къ росполону: the same wording is attested by Tn in 8:11, but slightly modified in the other mss—добыткы ихъ по росполону.

*Добытъкъ meant primarily ‘property’ in the form of ‘cattle, domestic animals,’ but also ‘profit’ and ‘booty,’ see L18.11.

The noun росполон- is unique to these two verses of Esther, although the corresponding verb is attested, in more conventional SSl shape, расплѣни-. See A1.44.

3:14 The extraneous глть is absent from Tn, but was apparently in *1360; we can find no convincing reason for its presence.

печать грамотнаꙗ (also 8:13). H ‘copy of the writing’; Moore translates ‘the contents of the document.’ LXX τὰ δὲ ἀντίγραφα τῶν ἐπιστολῶν ‘the copies of the letters.’ Печать (masc in OCS, fem in ESl copies) chiefly means ‘seal.’ We may suppose that, like σφραγίς, it could mean ‘impression made by a seal.’ We may surmise that a phrase грамота съ печатью (or perhaps печатьнаꙗ грамота?) could mean a certified official document, and (on the basis of two unclear examples in Srez) that печать metaphorically means such a document. In any case, this phrase is not a literal translation of the MT; see also C4:8.

20 A contrary error is in the *Third Capture of Jerusalem.* One copy (RNB, OLDP F.33) reads, surely correctly (although unfortunately there is a lacuna at this point in the unique Hebrew manuscript) и оускориша храбрїи єго и иꙁбавиша єго; a second (BAN 33.8.13) has иꙁбиша єго, an obvious corruption; and another (Tn) changes the last two words to иꙁбивати ихъ, a sense less appropriate for the context.

(Note that in 8:8 and 10 печатью цр҃евою involves the king's ring: H has 'ring' not 'seal.')[21]

дати ꙁаконъ: H *lhntn dt* '[the content of the letter is] to be given as law,' Moore 'promulgated.' The Sl syntax is unclear; the sense of the H passive infinitive has been lost. In 8:13, данис ꙁакона for same H is equally unsatisfactory.[22]

открыти lit. 'to uncover, to open': H *galui* נגלוי 'published'; LXX προσετάγη, cf. 8:13, where the same H yielded открыто[м].

оуготованым **на** дн҃ь сии: versus **при**готованом **к** дни тому 8:13 for the same H.

3:15 погоньци: H *rcym* lit. 'runners' (also 3:13, 8:14),[23] see C8:10 and L2.44.

Compare the wording of 8:14 (except for Tn):

3:15	погонци же	[1] вынидоша	[2] въскорѣ	[4] по глаголу царѧ
	hrcym	[1] yc'u	[2] dḥwpym	[4] bdbr hmlk
8:14	hrcym	[1] yc'u	[2] mbhlym [3] wdḥwpym	[4] bdbr hmlk
	погонци ..	[1] в(ы)нидоша	[2] бърꙁо [3] вънатъщь	[4] по рѣчи цр҃евѣ

dḥwpym 'urged on' and *mbhlym* 'being in haste' are participial forms; our text has adverbs. Thus въскорѣ = вънатъщь for 'being urged' and бързо for 'hastening' (Tn has скоро and вборзе, with distorted в тои час).[24]

In [4], note the contrast in vocabulary and syntax: по рѣчи + possessive adjective versus по глаголу + G of possession.

бысͤ данъ: M78a gives данъ бысть, an order attested, as he asserts, in n. 11 (erroneously under 3:14) in mss ПА (= 2, 20), but in fact П (i.e., Q) has exactly the same spelling as T.

сѣдоста пити: a supine питъ would be possible here.

въсплака сѧ: *nbwkh* 'was perplexed' (Moore 'was thrown into confusion') correctly rendered in LXX ἐταράσσετο. The translator of our text from H into Gk interpreted the verb as belonging to the root *bky* 'weep' rather than *bwk* 'be perplexed,' an interpretation reflected in other Jewish translations.[25] The verb is good OCS, used for translating a series of Gk verbs.

4:1 бѣ вѣдаꙗ: no obvious reason for continuous tense; H has simple past *yd'*, LXX ἐπιγνοῦς, L ἐπέγνω.

творѧше {сѧ} would be a plausible equivalent of the H passive; on the other hand the extant phrase, 'everything the king did,' fits perfectly into the context.[1] Gk substitutes 'what was done': LXX τὸ συντελοῦμενον, L τὰ γεγονότα.

[21] GorNev 56, Ro 203 consider печать грамотнаꙗ as a vernacular, recent expression. Tn has печѧт и грамоты here and печѧт и грамота in 8:13.

[22] Ro 200 suggests mistranslation for "содержание закона было, чтобы дан был закон."

[23] GorNev 56 consider it a late, vernacular word. GWVA have instead погонници; this is surely secondary.

[24] 2 Chron 26:29 also juxtaposes the two verbs, *dḥp* and *bhl*: *wybhlwhw mšm wgm hw' ndḥp lc't* > LXX καὶ κατέσπευσαν αὐτὸν ἐκεῖθεν καὶ γὰρ αὐτὸς ἔσπευσεν ἐξελθεῖν > Ostrih изгнаша его ѿтѹдѹ но и тои оубо т'щა сѧ изыити.—Let us note that the Origen texts have [2] (ἐπι)σπεύδοντες [3] καὶ διωκώμενοι [4] τὰ λεγόμενα ὑπὸ τοῦ βασιλέως.

[25] Cf. the Second Targum: *hwt bky'* 'was weeping.' Jerome followed suit, but with more freedom: *et cunctis qui in urbe erant flentibus,* 'while all who were in the city wept.'

[1] M56a 208 "explains" that царь was a self-evident addition of a subject when active was substituted for passive. The problem is why the substitution was made. A possibility is that a superscript сѧ went unnoticed in an early copy.

посрєдѣ града: H *btwk h‘yr*; посрєдѣ is quite normal OCS, implying ἐν μέσῳ. LXX elaborates, διὰ τῆς πλατείας τῆς πόλεως, L different.

власѧницю и сукно: H "sackcloth and *ashes*"; Ro 202 sees this somehow as "mistranslation" due to the verb. See L5.3.

въꙁпи въпльмь: both въпити/въꙁъпити and въпль are good OCS, very likely Moravan to start with, but rooted in psalms and gospel texts. The H equivalents are based on the root *z‘q,* and the Sl reproduces a common etymological figure. In LXX this figure is usually lost; at best κραυγή and κραζεῖν are used. See T5.1.[2]

The non-definite desinences in вєликъмь and горком may perhaps point to an old translation, as Sobolevskij (1903 434 [=M56a 208]) thought. On the other hand this is the sort of phrase that might sound better this way: the disappearance of short adjectives is by no means easy to date, and we know of no serious study of the question. Note that T has -омь in both words.

4:2 до вратъ царѧ: H *‘d lpny š‘r hmlk,* lit. 'up to the face of the gate,' i.e., 'right up to' LXX, like Sl, has no equivalent of 'the face of' (but adds 'and stopped'): ἕως τῆς πυλῆς τοῦ βασιλέως καὶ ἔστη. Sl до = ἕως = H *‘d.*

а то бѧшє нє право прити: *ky ’yn lbw,*' Moore 'for no one . . . was allowed'; LXX οὐ γὰρ ἦν ἔξον αὐτῷ εἰσελθεῖν, L οὐ γὰρ ἠδύνατο εἰσελθεῖν. H is general, LXX somewhat more personal, L definitely personal. Sl is closer to H. SJS нєправо 'incorrect(ly).' Cf. Ham 229.4, where нє право renders ἀθέμιτον 'unlawful.'

Sobolevskij 1903 434 cited къ вратомъ царєвъмь, from Q, as "old"; he is correct that Q's -ъмь and T's -омь probably represent the normal older nominal desinence -омъ. The question, however, is whether this desinence was already obsolete c1400. Had it been definitively displaced by adjectival -ым?

4:3 всѧка ꙁємлѧ и ꙁємлѧ perhaps a "casus pendens," unusual for Slavic; H has a preposition, *bkl mdynh wmdynh* (LXX ἐν πάσῃ χώρᾳ); the same H and Sl in 8:17 (LXX κατὰ χώραν, O +καὶ χώραν).

идеже: *mqwm ’šr,* 'place where,' LXX οὗ, L zero. (The *’šr* of 9:1 is temporal, see comm.)

	’šr	*dbr*	*hmlk*	*wdtw*	*mgy‘*
4:3	идєжє	рѣчь	царєва	и ꙁаконъ єго	доидѧшє
8:17	идєжє	глаголъ	царєвъ	и ꙁаконъ єго	доидѧшє
	’šr	*hgy‘*	*dbr*	*hmlk wdtw*	
9:1	идєжє ащє	постигнѧшє	глаголъ царєвъ и ꙁаконъ єго		

On H *dbr* and Sl рѣчь/глаголъ, see L8.1.

The perfective imperfects are appropriate if we allow the meaning 'on every occasion the word reached a destination' and expect a completed result each time.

жєлѧ: *’bl* 'mourning'; LXX, L omit. Tn has жалость. See L14.1.

говѣньє 'fasting': the meaning seems to be ESl, see L18.8.

нарѣканиє: *mspd* 'weeping'; perhaps κοπετός. SJS does not record the stem and нарѣкати (Srez, Efr korm) means 'называть' and thus is irrelevant here. See L14.2.

[2] A similar figure with H *c‘q* is lost in LXX and therefore Sl, in Gen 27:34 (Mixajlov), и въспї жрєломь вєлїємь (var. глаⷭмь вєликомь) и горкомъ for LXX καὶ ἀνεβόησεν φωνὴν μεγάλην καὶ πικρὰν σφόδρα, H *wyc‘q c‘qh gdwlh wmrh.*

власѧницѣ: apparently Ap, although one might expect the singular as an equivalent of 'sackcloth' *śq*.

и сукна, expected 'sackcloth and *ashes*': as in 4:1, see L5.3.

постилаху старѣишинамъ: *yc' lrbym*, 'was spread out to most of them (lit. *many*).' The phrase poses two questions: why has the H passive yielded a Sl active, and why has the nominal been rendered as it was? The interpretation of *lrbym* as 'for important men' is surely an effort to clarify an obscure phrase.[3]

4:4 велми ѕѣло: doublet, *m'd* (as in 1:12).

сукно, cf. 4:3.

не въсхотѣ приѧти: H simply 'did not accept' *l' qbl*, see L12.3.

4:5 Афанъ QTSGWV is an error for accusative Афаха, correctly written in Tn. M56a 214 saw it as a non-personal Acc, an ancient feature. Unfortunately it is merely another illustration of scribal carelessness.

стоꙗше: H causative, Moore 'whom he (sc. the king) had appointed to wait upon her.' The Sl removes the appointing agent and merely describes the eunuch-chamberlain's customary position, as does LXX παρειστήκει αὐτῇ and the Second Targum, *dy hwh q'ym qdm'h*. (L omits the clause).

уне Мордъхаꙗ: H 'about Mordecai,' LXX καὶ ἀπέστειλεν μαθεῖν αὐτῇ, 4:10 same. WVAB have у for уне, see A9.4.

чему то є и про что є: *mh zh w'l mh zh*; O τί τοῦτο καὶ περὶ τινὸς τοῦτο. про does not occur in OCS, but is normal in E and W Sl.[4]

4:6 вниде: H *yc'* 'went out.' The prefix can be justified as a shift in point of view, "he *came* out." A literal rendering of the H produces ἐξῆλθε, but simple ἦλθε would be acceptable in the context. LXX mss usually omits the whole verse, but O provides a version we may normalize to ἐξῆλθε δὲ Ἀφαχ πρὸς Μαρδοχαῖον εἰς τὴν πλατεῖαν. Mechanical addition of a prefix under the influence of the following preposition would give εἰσῆλθε(ν) > въниде. All mss have вниде (as far as we know), but H and the context justify вы-. The similar problems in 1:17 and 8:14, the equivocal spelling in 7:8, and the clear attestation of вын- in 4:1 etc. makes вы(н)иде in a foretext probable.[5]

Афанъ for Афахъ (cf. 4:5); here Tn has a different error: Ахахъ.

улица: not OCS, but occurs in the Hexameron with a rather unclear meaning of 'corridor' or 'anteroom' apparently within a palace. Srez (1076, PVL) illustrates general sense of a narrow passage, indoors or outside. The sense 'street' seems clear in Malalas (Istrin 1911a, 22.18), по улицамъ. Cf. L1.1.

[3] Ro 200 opines that the translator took *lrbym* as the pl of *rb* "большой, великий человѣкъ, начальникъ." (M56a 210–11 repeats the idea without mentioning Ro.) The interpretation may have been individual or traditional, but it in no way demonstrates direct translation from Hebrew to Slavonic. It is found in Jewish exegesis. Thus the 16th-century *ywsp lqḥ*, ad loc., says "or it would seem also that the word *rbym* here means *gdwlym* 'great ones,' as in *rby hmlk* [Jer 39:13, 41:1]." Neither instance is in the main LXX recension of Jeremiah (A-text, B-text, Q-text), but 39:13 (LXX 46.13) is in the Origen recension (Ziegler 413), attesting μεγιστάνες, with variants ἡγεμόνες, ἐπιστάται, μεγάλοι, διδάσκαλοι. In OB, which is based on the Vulgate, not LXX, 39:11 has воеводы цр҃ѧ (*et omnes optimates regis babylonis*), and 41:1 велможи цр҃евы (*et optimates regis*).

[4] GorNev 1855 56 = Ro 203, M56a 214 consider it a Russism.

[5] In the *Third Capture of Jerusalem,* H 'he went out into the street of the city' also comes out и вниде в оулицю града. GorNev 56 = Ro 203 see вниде на улицю as vernacular and late, but it is not clear whether they mean the verb, the noun, or the whole phrase.

прѧмо вратъ: H 'which (is) before the gate.' OCS прѣмо occurs with either G or D, cf. 5:1 прѧмо дверемъ. Reflexes of *prěmo* have survived only in SC (but cf. adj. R прямой etc.).

4:7 Афану for Афаху: H has a pronoun, 'to him,' not the name. Tn has only Мордохаеви (for Мордохаиему?), as in v. 6 just above.

вса съклюъшаıа са:[6] the neuter plural, 'all (the things) that happened,' for H singular *'t kl 'šr qrhw,* is probably a Hellenism (see T9.33). In this verse LXX uses a singular τὸ γεγονός.[7] When the phrase recurs in 6:13, however, LXX has the usual Gk plural, πάντα τὰ συμβεβηκότα αὐτῷ (a cliché, cf. Gen 42:29, Josh 2:23, Job 42:11, I Mac 4:26), precisely echoed by the Slavonic. In OCS, приключити са and unprefixed ключити са are well attested in the sense 'happen, befall,' but the very rare съключити means 'shut in, confine' (obviously calquing συγκλείειν). Съключити са 'happen' is certain for 11th-century Rus', but it may well replace сълучити са приключити са, прилучити са, ключити са, or лучити са, all of which are known from OCS, but are essentially interchangeable in copies of gospel texts or histories. Thus in the PVL случи са (Lav 164.23, 1064) is in a citation from Hamartolos, where ключи са is written (200.16).

расповѣданиє срєбра: *pršt hksp* 'sum of money.' The H *pršh* occurs only twice in the bible, both times in Esther, and is taken to mean 'exact, detailed account,' here the precise amount of silver, and in 10:2 the official record of Mordecai's greatness (Moore: "an exact account of the influence of Mordecai"). The noun расповѣданиє is unknown except for these two passages. Srez failed to note it, but he did list the aorist расповѣда 'told (at length).' Cf. L8.31.

да вѣситы QTSGV and виситы W, so -ы seems to go back to *1360. The verb corresponds in sense to H 'weigh' *lšqwl* (like навѣшю 3:9; see L16.43).[8] We might conjecture an earlier да вѣсить и = jь, with 3s masc pronoun, but the gender is inappropriate. The attested sequence of letters makes sense as a short phrase да вѣси ты, 'and you know': perhaps this is why scribes simply copied what was before them. Tn has навѣсти.

къ полатѣ: *'l gnzy hmlk*, LXX τῷ βασιλεῖ εἰς τὴν γάζαν, var. γαζοφυλάκιον (L zero); cf. къ полатамъ 3:9 same meaning, but H preposition *'l*. For other meanings of полата, see L1.2.

погубити ıа: *l'bdm* = 3:9.

4:8 Tn's печать книгъ законных is preferable to the majority reading печатьникомъ законнымъ, which perhaps is derived from a variant with a dative, книгамъ законнымъ. (Srez cites печатьникъ from the 13th century, but the sense, 'keeper of the seal' is not appropriate here.) The H noun *ptšgn* 'copy' occurs in the MT only in Esther 3:14, 4:8, 8:13. The phrase *ptšgn ktb hdt* means 'copy of the book of the law; copy of the legal document.' How did the notion of *copy* shift to *seal*? O has τὸ ἀντίγραφον γράμμα τοῦ δόγματος; in Ham 247.3 печать reflects ὑπογραμμός '(an ideal) type, model (to be copied).' Elsewhere ὑπογραφή may mean *copy,* and even 'copy of legal proceedings, legal decision.' Cf. 3:14 *ptšgn hktb* - печать грамотнаıа. Somehow our Slavic translator and later copyists/editors were involved in this vague set of associations of words, although we cannot reconstruct a clear path.

растворити є: H plural object, so we would expect Slavonic ѧ, or ESl ѣ (*ě tertium*).

[6] M78a omits the prefix, ключьшаıа са, and falsely states that "П" omits са.

[7] Tn has всє ключивше са.

[8] M78a prints вѣсити by error, but remarks "очевидно следует читать повѣсити, ср. III,9 порча текста во всех списках."

Using ѥ or є for *ję̆* is not uncommon in the 1300s (e.g., in Lav), and implies an older ѣ. We assume that here it reflects an archaic spelling in *1350.[9]

вѣдаютъ: the thematic present is late and regionally marked. See L21.54.

умилосьрдити сѧ means "have mercy" and is inappropriate. See L12.141.

4:9 Афахъ: later mss generalized Афанъ. Tn has a different error, Афакъ.

4:10 унє Мардохаѥа:[10] cf. 4:5.

4:11 The initial и of QTSGWV is redundant, but Tn has ѥако; see A10.11.

ѥако аще, perhaps 'in whatever manner': H simply 'who,' LXX ὅς.

дондеже: the temporal meaning 'while' or 'until' is absent from the H, 'who is/was not called.' LXX condenses it to ἄκλητος 'unsummoned.'

днѣшнему = 5:1, cf. 7:7,8. Later scribes tend to substitute the more familiar внѣшнему, thereby changing the sense from 'inner' to 'outer.'

къ двору днѣшнему: a literal equivalent of H *'l ḥḥcr hpnymyt* 'to the inner court,' exactly reproduced in LXX εἰς τὴν αὐλὴν τὴν ἐσωτέραν (cf. L1.231). The adjective is solidly though sparsely attested for early ESl (Srez), but apparently dubious for post-1400 scribes (in part, surely because of its closeness to днешнии from older дьньшнии 'today's').[11] In SGVW 4:11 it has become внѣшнии 'outer'—a serious change of meaning. S consistently has in all occurrences. Tn has purposefully changed all four instances to денниѵныи, which is entirely out of place. The adjective дьньниѵьнъ is attested for *OCS as a derivative of дьньница 'day-star, morning star'; even if we take the metaphorical sense 'Lucifer, Devil,' it does not fit in Esther.

тъкмо 'only' is not in H: it was surely added by a translator or editor—Gk or Sl—to emphasize the importance of this law for the story.

къ оубою vs. оубьеноу быти: H causative infinitive, 'to put to death, kill'; the preceding еже could stand for a Gk article. An articulated infinitive (such as τὸ or τοῦ θανατῶσαι, θανατοῦν) could underlie either the noun-phrase (although the preposition къ is unexpected), or Tn's passive infinitive (cf. бысть ѡбнесена, C5:2). Is this an unmotivated change made by the scribe of *1360, or a rational "correction" from a copyist in the history of Tn (or Tn's editor)? (Compare p. 262, §6.2.)

кромѣ емуже простреть: this looks like a Hellenism, attraction of the case of the relative, *jemuže* for *togo jemuže,* LXX πλὴν ᾧ ἐκτείνῃ. Compare Malalas (bk. 10, Istrin 1913 21), да не влаѕѧть къ нему раѕвѣ емоуже повелѣваеть Симонъ εἰς τὸ μηδένα ὡς ἔτυχεν δίχα τοῦ τὸ Σίμωνα κελεύειν τῷ κυνὶ καὶ συγχωρεῖν τὸν κύνα παριέναι, οὓς ἠβούλετο ὁ Σίμων.

прутъ: H *šrbyṭ'* 'scepter, wand, rod,' a late word, only in Esther (also 5:2, 5:4) in MT, where it yields LXX ῥάβδος, from which we would expect OCS палица or жьѕлъ. Gk βακτηρία, a LXX word, also yields жьѕлъ, as do the related βακτήριον and βάκτρον in Hamartolos. We must posit прѫтъ for all early Slavic dialects, but its meaning generally appears to have been a thin branch suitable as a switch or whip. SC *prut* as the rod, staff, or scepter symbolizing the authority of a ruler is well attested in Dalmatian writers, particularly Čakavian; this sense surely imitates that of Latin *virga.* Such use is inappropriate in ESl; the abbreviated Esther in the 1512 Chronograph adds a gloss, сирѣчь посохъ (PSRL 22/1 166), itself not quite right.

9 WV have и, possibly a Ukrainian replacement for ѣ, but perhaps for the contemporary их, often written иˣ, G's editor saw a new clause, beginning with the archaic conjunction єда 'lest'; he "updated" the spelling to єгⷣа, which destroys the sentence completely.

10 M78a misprints унє мардохаю (although QT have -аѥа).

11 *SRJaXI* omits днѣшний (дьнѣшьнии) altogether, though it lists днешний (-ый).

4:13 врат҄ѧ сѧ: H inf. *lhšyb* "told [the servant] *to return* [a message] to E"; LXX πρὸς Ἀχραθαιον πορευθῆτι καὶ εἶπον αὐτῇ Ἐσθηρ, L καὶ ἀπέστειλε πρὸς αὐτήν Μαρδοχαιος; Lat *rursum mandavit Hester dicens.* Compare 4:15 *wt'mr 'str lhšyb 'l mrdky,* и отвѣща Есфирь къ Мардохаеви, where there is no equivalent of 'return.'

не мни си въ мысли своеи изъбудуѵи сѧ: H *do not think in your soul to escape.* The benefactive dative reflexive си 'for yourself' seems superfluous; the phrase 'in your thought' probably reflects ἐν τῇ διανοίᾳ σου (for мысль = soul = self, see L6.43). In OCS, изъбѫд- 'avoid, escape' is non-reflexive. Srez cites this example (sub изъбытисѧ), while GorNev 56 = Ro 203 consider it a vernacular, late expression (note the unusual ESl ѵ, cf. 4:14). It survives with the changed prefix *z-* in U збутися. The nominative participle governed by мьнѣти probably reflects a Gk infinitive, as in Luke 24:37 мьнѣахѫ дх҃ъ видѧщте 'they thought they were seeing a ghost' (cf. Růžička 257).

4:14 (Moore says this is a difficult verse.)

мълѵиши мълѵаѵи: an etymological figure (cf. T5). The composition and order of elements differs from the H *hḥrš tḥryšy*, where a non-finite element (an "absolute infinitive") is followed by a finite verb. Slavic has first the finite verb and then the non-finite element which, as usually in Gk renderings of H etymological figures, is a present active participle. (In this particular example, O has reversed the order as well as shifting the verb to 'ignore, refuse to listen': παρακούσασα παρακούσῃς.)

Note ESl ѵ in мълѵаѵи.[12]

простерыи избавлениє Q, TSG простры и, WV простри.[13] H has two nouns, *rwḥ whclh,* Moore "relief (lit. *space*) and salvation'; LXX βοήθεια, L βοηθός. This surely allows us to posit просторъ, well attested in Rusian copies of originally OCS works (Srez) with the sense 'latitude, freedom, lack of constraint.' In Ham it translates ἄδεια, which also is rendered тишина, небоꙗзнь, оутѣха. A subject просторъ и избавлениє would require a dual verb, въстанета, see below.

доступиши: H past, "if you reached the kingship"; Moore "it's possible that (*lit.* who knows if) you came to the throne." A genitive object of доступи- was no longer current syntax after 1300, but it was so familiar that it was used by East Slavic writers through the 17th century, and it therefore has no diagnostic value for dating our translation.

погыбнеть: "you and your father's house" should add up to dual, or possibly plural, therefore -ета or -ете: Possibly an old abbreviation -е^{т} (as it is written in V and Tn) failed to specify the final vowel.

4:15 H has the same idiomatic infinitive "said to return" *'mr lhšyb* that is in 4:13; here Sl condenses it into one word, ѿвѣща 'replied.'[14]

4:16 еже ихъ ωбрѧщеши, lit. 'what of them you will find': H *hnmc'ym* "those who are found." The use of the neuter relative plus the explicit accusative plural of the third person pronoun instead of the explicit Ap relative ѧже is not old, but neither is it easy to locate as a dialectism. Perhaps it represents a miscopying of the Hellenism we noted in 1:5, viz. е{лико}же ихъ. A more literal rendering would be вьсѧ Июдѣѧ обрѣтъшихъ сѧ въ Соусанѣ, based on πάντας τοὺς Ἰουδαίους τοὺς εὑρεθέντας ἐν Σούσοις.[15] It is quite possible that such a clause could have been reshaped to the attested form.

[12] GWV have distorted this form to молча сѧ, S to молѧщи. Tn has аще не [!] молчиши молчанїемъ.

[13] M78a prints простыи, with the comment "вероятно простъръ и избавление." Tn has простъ. и.

[14] M56a 210 cites къ here (erroneously labelled 4:2) as a Hebraism rendering H *l-*; in fact *'l* is here, see A9.52, and Taube 1985 p. 207.

[15] Compare equivalents of the H singular *hnmc'* in the Ostrih Bible: 2 Chron 34:32 И постави всѣхъ иже ωбрѣтени бѧхꙋ во Іерꙋсалимѣ; καὶ ἔστησεν πάντας τοὺς εὑρεθέντας ἐν Ἰερουσαλημ; *wy'md 't kl hnmc'*

д҃нь и нощь: H 'night and day.' This is one of the rare instances where the word-order of *1350 differs from MT. This banal phrase is known in both orders in H, Gk, and OCS.[16]

наѵнуть H 1s: a simple error called forth by the plural "my maidens." If the maidens are included in the action, the verb should be 1p, наѵьнемъ. The phrase съ мною stands where H has only *kn* 'so, likewise.' The resulting sentence is awkward. (Cf. A12.4.)

и по томь: H *wbkn* lit. 'and in thus.' Slav is more appropriate to mean 'after that' than H. Perhaps Sl reflects a traditional interpretation of this verse; thus the First Targum has *wbtr kn* 'and after that.'[17] Compare 2:13, where similar H (*wbzh*) comes out и в томь, though the sense should be 'after.'

4:17 и приде: H has *wy'br* 'crossed,' which creates exegetical problems (crossed the street or square or river? transgressed? cf. Moore 51), but suggests *прѣиде, which could come from παρῆλθε or διῆλθε. LXX has βαδίσας. The prefixes при and прѣ are confused in many ESl mss that otherwise do not confuse the letters и and ѣ. Cf. A1.53.

ıакоже: H *kkl 'šr* 'according to everything that.' The phrase in 8:9 also lacks the expected pronoun вьсе.[18]

5:1 въ ризы царскыıа: not a literal equivalent of the MT, for a word for *garments* is missing in the H, although it is to be inferred as the object of the transitive verb *wtlbš*.[1] Sl requires an overt noun, as does Gk; the translation made from H by the editors of the Complutensian edition, 1514–17 (Hanhart 42), however, is rigorously literal, ἐνεδύσατο 'Εσθηρ βασιλικοῖς.[2]

H 'stood in the inner court of the king's house,' surely въ дворѣ дому царева дънѣшьнемь, textually corrupted within the Slavic tradition. Perhaps first the locative desinence -ѣ was attracted to -у of дому, then въ became оу (perhaps a southwest Rus' phonological feature?); finally двору дому became the дому домȣ attested in V, then simplified to a single дому.

въ полатѣ своеи H *bbyt hmlkwt* 'in the house of kingship.' (Moore contends that this means 'the throne room, facing the building's entrance.') The repeated *house* in this verse (along with the unclear relationships of the structures and spaces) may have caused trouble

---

byrwšlym. 34:33 и сотвори всѣхъ ѡбрѣтшихъ сѧ во Іерȣсалимѣ и во Існаили слȣжити г҃дȣ; καὶ ἐποίησεν πάντας τοὺς εὑρεθέντας ἐν 'Ιερουσαλημ καὶ ἐν 'Ισραηλ τοῦ δουλεύειν κυρίῳ; *wy'bd 't kl hnmc' byršlym wbyśr'l l'bd 't yhwh.* (Notice that the H causative in v. 32 yields a Gk transitive, whence Sl постави, but in 33 ποιεῖν appears.)

16 In the Gk Gospels, *day and night* occurs once, *night and day* three times. OCS agrees only once, Mk 4:27 (*night and day*); in L 18:37 дьнь и нощь corresponds to ἡμέρας καὶ νυκτός, while in L 2:37 and Mk 5:5 the same Slavic stands for Gk *night and day.* In Acts, Gk *day and night* is reflected in OCS 9:24, but 20:31 and 26:7 change the order. This kind of variation is unpredictable. The *day and night* of OCS and LXX psalms 1:2, 31:4, 41.4; 54.11 agrees with MT (1:2, 32:4, 42:4, 55:11). MT 13:13 = LXX 12:13 with day, but OCS adds *and night* as do some Gk mss.

17 Zimmermann 86 says that H here is mistranslation, or a rather literal morph-by-morph translation of Aramaic *bedain* 'in this,' which indeed means 'and then.'

18 M78a asserts that after the last word of this verse, Esther, "in all copies" is a rubric for the beginning of a new chapter. There is no rubric in QT or SWV. G gives the chapter number in the margin.

1 The omission is permissible, indeed good style; in the First Targum it reappears, *wlbšt lbwšy mlkwt,'* cf. Haupt 139.

2 5:1–2 in LXX is replaced by the additional text Hanhart subdivides as C:1–30, a long prayer attributed to Esther, and D:1–16, an expansion of the two MT verses. In D:1 this phrase is doubled: ἐξεδύσατο τὰ ἱμάτια τῆς θεραπείας καὶ περιεβάλετο τὰ ἱμάτια τῆς δόξης 'she took off her dress of service [everyday clothing] and put on her dress of glory [glorious apparel]'; the latter phrase reflects the H of 5:1. See also L5.11.

to translators and editors. Yet the problems of *byt hmlk* 'king's house' and *byt hmlkwt* 'house of kingship' are mixed up with defining *treasury*:

4:13	*byt hmlk*	въ дому царѧ
1:9	*byt hmlk*	въ дому царєвѣ
2:16	*byt hmlkwt*	въ домъ царства своєго
5:1	*byt hmlkwt*	въ полатѣ своєи
3:9	*'l gnzy hmlk*	къ полатамъ царѧ
4:7	*'l gnzy hmlk*	къ полатѣ царѧ

противу and прѧмо: both *nkḥ* 'in front of, against, opposite, facing' ; cf. 2:11 and 4:6, also A9.53.

5:2 H has 'saw Esther the queen *standing* in the court.'

быс обнєсєна: H *nś'h* lit. '(she) raised, carried' (active). See милость L12.91.

The explicit subject Esther comes from *1360; it is not in H or Tn.

5:3 мыслиши просити: H 'your request.' Ro 202 thinks this indicates "will of the translator to express the sense more clearly," see L11.22.

просити царства моєго makes sense if 'my kingship' is understood as an imperial term for 'me.' It does not belong here, however. From H we expect (what is your request) + (up to half of my kingdom) + (it will be given to you). The words *up to half* were omitted and then the whole middle clause was tacked on at the end, probably by a later scribe, perhaps in a later copy.

будєть ти: H 'and it will be given to you' *wyntn lk*. Perhaps дано has been omitted. Alternatively, this might be a Hellenism, reflecting the same sort of translation we find in LXX, ἔσται σοι 'let it be (so) for you.' The same H in 5:6 and 9:12 yields a personal active, дамь ти 'I will give (it) to you.'[3]

5:4 Neither the аще бы сѧ of mss QWVAB, nor T's аще оу сѧ оудобрити is satisfactory in terms of OCS or PVL usage, while Tn's аще бы цр҃ь хотѣлъ мєнє оудобрить seems to be an editorial attempt to repair a poor text rather than a reflection of the H. The conflicting wording of passages containing this clause makes it difficult to adjudicate the issues, see L12.711. T's wording more likely reflects a false start by the scribe, who then failed to cross out the superfluous оу, than a mistake for оубо, as M78a suggests.

удобрити сѧ 'please': Srez attests this meaning only from Est, 5:4 and 14,[4] see L12.711.

съ Амановь: H 'and Haman.' This use of *with* for *and* is North Slavic, common in ESl and Polish.

быхъ створила: H, LXX and L have simply future, and створю might be expected. Cf. A11.43.

5:5 оубърꙁите: H causative 'make Aman hurry.' The по is probably secondary, but the change of meaning is tolerable: 'hurry after Aman.' M56a 214 (doubtless influenced by Buslaev 1861 col. 187, n.) assesses по Амана as a typical Russian feature. However, *po* + A is well known in OCS and many modern dialects to mean 'after' in the sense 'to get' (cf., e.g., Kopečný 1, 182, item 21).

[3] The First Targum converts the passive in 5:3 to a first person singular active.

[4] M56a 215 calls "удобритися" a "typically Russian" word.

и створитє: WV have simply сътворити, which corresponds exactly to the H infinitive. The meaning is not significantly different.

5:6 мысль просьбы, see L11.22.
дам . . . створимъ: compare

5:6	и дам ти	. . . створимъ тобѣ
7.2	и дадимъ тобѣ	. . . и створимъ ти
9.12	и дам ти	. . . створим тобѣ

In ESl mss of about 1400, the дам can stand for older 1s дамь or 1p дамъ, although by 1200 the plural could be spelled дамы. Дадимъ in older texts is 1p imperative ('let us give'), but by 1400 it could serve as present ('we will give').[5] Створимъ must be 1p ('we'll do' or 'let us do'). The three passages in *1350 therefore imply 1p *we* as subject. The context, however, guarantees that the king is speaking; yet the king does not speak with the "royal we" in any other passage.[6] The first verb in H has an impersonal passive (*wyntn* 'and it will be given') in 5:6 and 9:12 and a 3sf passive (*wtntn*, agreeing with the noun *request,* i.e., 'it will be granted'). The second verb is 3sf passive, *wt'ś* '(your request) will be done.' It is probable that the impersonal of the H in the first verb was shifted to 1s, yielding дамь in Sl.[7] It would appear that a later copyist interpreted the *give* as 1 pl and changed the second verb (perhaps from створить сѧ?) to agree; he then "harmonized" the passages in the other two verses. Tn has сотворю тобѣ in 5:6; see App III, p. 262, §6.2.

The enclitic pronoun ти alternates with the full ESl shape of the accented form тобѣ.

The second дам ти of the mss stands where we expect 'up to' and we believe the original text had "дажє (or дожє) и."

въ прєпоихъ виньныхъ: GorNev 56 (= Buslaev 1861 col.188 = Ro 203) see this as a late vernacular expression. We agree, since the word is known, as far as we have been able to ascertain, only in Ukrainian, and surely it is new to our text, see L13.71. Srez cites прєпои only from Esther.[8]

5:7 и да ѿвѣтъ 'and gave answer': H simply 'and answered,' cf. Malalas, bk 14 (Istrin 1913 24) въспусти ѿвѣ ἀντεδήλωσεν. Possibly the phrase дати отъвѣтъ is intended to specify the perfective aspect; отъвѣщати was ambiguous (cf. Ham ѿвѣтъ давъ for ἀπολογησάμενος).

5:8 The first words of the verse are missing, so the sentence links to the preceding words. We would expect аще обрѣтохъ, cf. discussion in L12.6. Tn substitutes быс ми, which is unhelpful.

5:9 въ днь ° : H. *bywm hhw*' 'on *that* day.' Tn в тои днь.

[5] The last word in LXX Gen 34:11 means 'we will give,' and the next clause has 'I will give'; Mixajlov's base text (Und 1, our ms 16, c 1483) has дамъ for both. The second oldest copy, late 1400s, has дамы for the first but the innovative (and textually inappropriate) дадимъ for the second; all other ESl copies have дадимъ for both.

[6] In 5:6 Tn has сотворю; this seems to be a random correction rather than a relic from *1350. In a 14th-century Serbian ms, створим(ь) could be a new 1s form. The possibility of a SC stratum in the recent history of Esther, however, seems too remote to be acceptable.

[7] Note that the *wyntn* of 5:3 was translated with 1s active in the First Targum.

[8] In Ruthenian Vil. 262, перепои stands for H *mnwt* 'portions' in 9:19, 9:22.

The superfluous тако and то are not in Tn.

и охвотнъмь срдцмь: *wṭwb lb*. The adjective is generally recognized as "western"; the root-shape *xvot* is Belarusian, see L13.4.[9] The word order follows the H construction, which literally would be 'good of heart.' See A5.51.

After Мардъхаıа, 'at the king's gate and' is omitted.

The construction 'saw Mordecai not rising or kneeling' makes an excellent sentence, but the Hebrew is different: 'when Aman saw Mordecai . . . and he did not stand up or move (aside).' LXX omits it, but cf. O: καὶ οὐκ ἐξανέστη οὐδε ἐτρόμασεν ἀπ' αὐτόν.

приклѧкну- (called a Polonism by GorNev) is not the same as H *z'* 'shake, tremble'; see L10.2.

5:10 и въздъхнувъ 'having sighed': H *wyt'pq* 'he contained himself.' The aorist of GWV corresponds grammatically. O's ἐνεκρατεύσατο is appropriate (L om.); it stands in Gen 43.31 for the same H verb-form, yielding въздрьжаше сѧ in Sl (and in Gen 45:1 has LXX ἀνέχεσθαι, Sl. оудрьжати сѧ [var. дрьж-] (Mixajlov). We might expect въздьржа сѧ.

A possible explanation involves an error in the Gk transmission of the text. Conjecturing ἐφείσατο (from φείδομαι, usually 'spare' but also 'hold back'), we suggest a misreading ἐφύσατο (from φυσάομαι 'be puffed up,' active φυσάω 'blow'). The Sl translator, faced with a strange collocation of verbs, perceived the root *fus* as equivalent to Sl *dъx/dux/du* in such examples as Ham 88.15 въдъхноувъша в нихъ дхъ живъ 'who had breathed into them the living spirit' ἐφυσήσαντα; Su 520.6 доунѧ 'he blew [on]' ἐνεφύσησεν; Ham 537.13 доуноув 'having blown' [the wind] φυσήσας. His choice of *sigh* offers a plausible reaction for Aman in the context, cf. T9.25.

приıазнь свою: H. 'his friends.' This may be the unique attestation of приıазнь as a collective (so Srez), but it is more probable that it is an early scribal lapse for the plural (cf. 5:14) and should be emended to приıазнѧ своѧ. The word is more common in the sense of *friendship, amity, devotion.*

5:11 и расповѣда: H 'recounted, told.' Although Srez cites this verse (and the 11th-century Cyril of Jerusalem) for the sense 'proclaim,' here the Slavic *raz-* surely emphasizes completeness, cf. расповѣдание 4:7, 10:2 'complete account.' GorNev 55 = Ro 203 see the verb as a Polonism; Buslaev 1861 (col. 188) calls it "local dialect, for повѣдалъ." In fact it is Ukrainian, Polish, and Czech, 'tell, narrate.' Cf. L8.31, L21.54.

има: Perhaps the collective приıазнь + Zeresh = dual, but more likely this is an error for plural имъ. Tn in fact has и^{М}.

чьсть, as in 1:4, vs. H *kbwd*, for expected 'glory.'

еже: H 'everything that'; with "all" added before вельможами.

възвеличa . . . възнесе cf. 3:1. Direct object 'и' Asm is archaic, but here probably merely bookish usage. The addition of всѣми is not significant; this is a context of superlatives.

5:12 и пакы: H *'p*, Moore 'besides all that' RSV 'even.'

The second пакы is *gm* 'again'; cf. 1:9, *gm* и пакы.

приведе: 'caused to come,' i.e., 'invited'—"not invited . . . except me" = invited only me. ли мѧ is absent from Tn and H, but it is not wholly extraneous, even though аще не

9 GorNev 55 = Ro 203 and Sobolevskij consider it (as spelled in their sources охот-) a Polonism.

contains the same notion.[10] Indeed, it might represent Gk εἰ μή as in L and as variant in LXX. A LXX variant, ἀλλ' ἢ ἐμέ, seems to provide motivation for Sl ли; see T9.39.

ꙁванъ єсмь: an acceptable equivalent of H passive.

5:13[11] нє врєдно: H *'ynnw šwh,* lit. 'is not worthy for me' ('fails to satisfy me' Moore).[12] Compare неврєдъ 3:6, неправо 3:8 and perhaps 7:4. The positive meaning of *vrěd* is not ESl, see L16.1. No equivalent of ли is in H. Yet again as in 5:12 it seems to make a rhetorical question that is not out of place in the context if we attribute the usual negative meaning to *vrěd*; 'Is this all not harmful to me?'

5:14 жєна своꙗ: OCS uses свои in sense of 'not alien, one's own' where the reference is not necessarily to the grammatical subject of the sentence, cf. Mt 27:19 (Vaillant 1964 117).[13] Compare Malalas book 6 (Istrin 1911 15) и нє приꙗша єго гражанє ни болѧрє свои.

сдѣлающе будѣтє as imperative is exceptional, despite parallels in Supr, see A11.441. H has 3p impersonal 'let them make.'

въꙁвышѣє is an adverb meaning 'in height, to the height of.' In 7:9 Q spells it въꙁвышѣ, but the other mss all have въꙁвышє, which is the usual form (e.g., PVL 150.18, Ham 141.3, cf. воꙁвышє, 1406 Paleja 51a25, c6). Yet Lav at 90.20 has въꙁвышиє (RA -шє), and perhaps -ѣє in this verse is an example of "ѣ" for "и." (X has въꙁвы^ш^; this may correspond to the въꙁвышь of the 1477 Paleja, 58a21 [but воꙁвышь 58d2], and represents a newer shape.) OCz had *vzvýši* (mod. *zvýši*) and OPol had *wzwysz, wzwyszą*.

локот ESl for лакътъ: same form and phrase in 7:9.

ать is quite appropriate here. Tn has a pharaphrase, повєлѣть повѣсити.

пришє^д^ in QTG and пришє^д^ши in Tn, for придєши of SWV, illustrate how superscript letters in abbreviated forms can cause misunderstandings.

6:1 смѧтє сѧ цр҃ь въ снѣ 'the king was troubled in his sleep' differs fundamentally from H 'the sleep of the king wandered off (departed, fled).' None of the ancient versions reproduces the personification, although it is quite translatable (cf. LXX Gen 31:40 ἀφίστατο ὁ ὕπνος ἀπὸ τῶν ὀφθαλμῶν μου 'my sleep departed from my eyes'; OB и ѿхожаше сънъ ѿ очїю моєю). Moore (and the Vulgate) have simply 'could not sleep.' The Gk versions attribute the insomnia in 6:1 to divinity (e.g., LXX ὁ κύριος [L δυνατὸς] ἀπέστησεν τὸν ὕπνον 'God [the Powerful One] caused the king's sleep to depart'). The Sl has changed both the focus and the idea, since the king is now subject and sleep is in the background; the important event concerns confusion. This is squarely in Jewish exegetical tradition. The First Targum has an elaborate tale implying that the voice of Esther has reached the Lord, and he "commanded the angel who was in charge of disturbance to descend and disturb Achashwerosh, whereupon the sleep of the king became unrestful and he rose in the morning troubled in appearance" (Grossfeld 61). We may confidently posit

10 Tn has a new sentence: паки не приведе Єсфирь ср^д^ца со ц^с^рмъ на миръ, perhaps "Esther again has not brought her heart to peace with the king"? This kind of half-meaningful modification, possibly the work of successive scribes, is all too typical of the intervention of copyists and/or editors in the history of this text.

11 M78a mistakenly всего instead of все то.

12 LXX has καὶ ταῦτά μοι οὐκ ἀρέσκει 'these things please me not,' surely by error for the correct ἀρκέσει 'suffice not' of one ms., plus the Old Latin *non sufficiunt mihi.*

13 M56a 213 considers this "characteristic" of the language, but without specifying why. He refers unhelpfully to the Ostromir Gospel, which, as usual, agrees with OCS texts.

ἐταράχθη as the basis for смѧте сѧ.[1] At any rate, the Slavonic sentence is grammatical and apposite to the context, even though it does not reproduce the MT.

книгы памѧтныꙗ: Tn has книгы сонныꙗ, apparently *dream books*, surely an *ad hoc* change introduced by a scribe at this point. Tn agrees with the other mss in 2:23 and 10:2, see C2:23.

и быша проѵтены: H *wyhyw nqr'ym,* lit. 'and-they-were being-called-out,' i.e., read aloud. LXX ἀναγινώσκειν, L ἀναγινώσκετο.

6:2 в них 'in them' is a harmless addition from *1360; it is not in H or Tn.

The H is almost identical in 2:21, but the Sl wording differs considerably.

вавероса lacks the preceding conjunction we expect not only from the Hebrew but also from the context. In origin, the initial *va-* quite possibly represents the *wa-* 'and' of Hebrew, but the explicit mention of 'two eunuchs' surely requires 'and' before the modified name. Tn has added the connective in the wrong place: на вигъфа и на вафероса. See also A2. The dual of verbs and nominals is appropriately used here, as in 2:21.

двьрьникъ implies 'door-keeper'; H is rather the 'guardian of the *threshold*.' The same H in 2:21, referring to the same individuals yields Sl 'who guarded the *gate*.' Cf. L2.43.

ꙁадѣти руцѣ here takes dative, cf. locative in 2:21. Srez gives special place to this idiom, citing Est 6:2 and 3:6 but not 2:21; SRJaXI follows suit. Задѣти in other meanings is OCS. See L6.311.

6:3 ниѵтоже: normal East Slavic for expected G of OCS.

ꙁа то: no H equivalent, but it could have been supplied by any editor or scribe.

6:4 и тъгда Аманъ приде: a highly appropriate equivalent of H *whmn b'*, where word order plus tense imply a "circumstantial" or "simultaneous" or "background" action a translator might render by means of an adverb. Тъгда might have been mediated by τότε.

на дворѣ here and 6:5 but въ in 1:5 and 5:2. See A9.

къ двору is perhaps an old error for въ двору, see L1.22.

6:5 да придеть сѣмо: H *yb'*, 'let him come,' without specifying 'hither.' Tn lacks сѣмо.

6:6 єму attested only in Tn.

цр҃ѧ волю: H 'the king wishes.' Possibly царѧ волꙗ 'the king's wish' or 'царь воли(ть)' 'the king desires.' See L12.15. Tn rationalizes: иж цр҃вꙋ волю дѣєть, 'who does the king's will.'

помысли въ мысли своєи: H 'said in his heart,' see L11.1, 23.

боле менє: H *ywtr mmny* , lit. 'more than me,' Moore 'besides me' (cf. LXX εἰ μὴ ἐμέ, OB развѣ мене), KJ 'more than to myself.' We assume that a literal Gk rendering (perhaps * πλέον or μεῖζον ἐμοῦ) underlies the Sl.

6:8 конь as non-personal accusative persists well into the 1500s, see A3.

въньгдаже 'when': H *w'šr* 'and which.' Note, however, that the temporal conjunction

[1] Compare Nebuchadnezzar's dream in Daniel 2:1 and particularly his memory of it in 4:2, сънъ видєхъ и оустраши мѧ, и съмѧтохъ сѧ [ἐταράχθην] на ложи моєм,' и видѣниѧ главы моєѧ съмѭтаахѫ мѧ. The unprefixed imperfect of the verb is used in Josephus in the context of a bad dream, И душа его мятешет ся в немь, M58a 196.7, a passage with no Gk equivalent. In Ps 63:9, съмѧсѧ (съмѧтошѧ) сѧ for ἐταράχθησαν rendering a form of H *ndd.*

and the coreferentiality of 'head' and 'horse' are supported by Jewish traditional exegesis, e.g. Ibn Ezra *ad loc.*: 'a golden crown on the head of the horse when the king is riding on it' (*wktr zhb 'l r'š hsws k'šr hmlk rkb 'lyw*).

Note that the пърты of 6:8, 9 become свиту in verse 10 and ризы in 11. See L5.1.

6:9 мужю болꙗрину цареву судии: lit. 'to a man, a noble of the king, a judge,' apparently three alternate definitions that fit together nicely. Although this sort of string is stylistically awkward and may create difficulties for translators, it is grammatically acceptable. The first noun might be taken as a sort of pronoun, "a certain noble."[2] The MT syntax is more explicit: *'yš mśry hmlk hprtmym*, lit. "(to) a man of the princes-of the king, the distinguished (ones)." Moore translates, "to one of the king's most noble princes." Sl does not retain the notion of selection from a group that is the crux of the H phrase. LXX reproduces the syntactic pattern, ἑνὶ τῶν φίλων τοῦ βασιλέως τῶν ἐνδόξων, but replaces *man* with the numeral *one* and *princes* with *friends*. L makes the individual subject, and changes the order, εἷς τῶν ἐνδόξων τῶν φίλων τοῦ βασιλέως 'one of the notable friends of the king.' As it stands, the Sl phrase differs from the MT both in syntax and meaning: *hprtmym* surely are not judges, although this term is more appropriate as an indication of high status than the "nations" of 1:3. For судии we might expect something like сатрапу,[3] see L2.

ѡблеүемъ: QTSGWV agree on 1p 'we will dress him'; H indefinite 3p 'let them dress the man,' with explicit object. Tn has ѡблеүе^т^, thus agreeing with LXX and L (cf. Moore's comment) in implying that the special noble "judge" mentioned earlier in the verse is the subject. The 1p form is a reasonable substitute for an unspecified 3p in some contexts, but it is inappropriate here. The shift from -еть to -емъ probably was facilitated by a superscript spelling, -е^т^.

H 'have *him* ride *on the horse*.'[4] We restore и from the context and на кони from Tn.

рекүүе has ESl *č* for standard *šč* < **tj*. This local trait is intermittently attested in the orthography of present participles from the 12th century on, and scribes admitted sporadic

2 On the other hand, a translator might choose to emphasize the noun *man,* even at the cost of changing the original order of elements. Compare the definition in Acts 8:27 which starts out with three nouns plus an adjective and a descriptive noun-phrase that itself contains two nouns in apposition and a third serving as attribute: καὶ ιδοὺ [1] ἀνὴρ [2] Αἰθίοψ [3] εὐνοῦχος [4] δυνάστης [5] Κανδάκης [6] βασιλίσσης [7] Αἰθιόπων. The early Slavic translator was literal: и се мѫжь Моуринъ каженикъ [4] сильнъ [5] Кандакии [6] цѣсарици [7] Моуромъ (spelling normalized). The King James version shifts the emphasis by making the ethnic identification an attributive phrase: "And behold, a man [2] of Ethiopia, an eunuch [4] of great authority under Candace queen of the Ethiopians." The *New English Bible* paraphrases: "he caught sight of [2] an Ethiopian. This [1] man was [3] a eunuch, [4] a high official, of [5] the Kandake, or [6] Queen, of [7] Ethiopia." (Notice that the adjective, [4], has become a noun [justifiable if one posits δυναστής, with word-final accent], the people, [7], are replaced by their country, and—a substantive matter of interpretation—the proper name has become a title. This illustrates a free style of translation that, in our opinion, is alien to the history of the Slavonic Esther. An even greater freedom, emphasizing *eunuch* and *man,* but omitting the explicit *powerful,* is shown in the *Good News for Modern Man* Bible: "Now an [2] Ethiopian [3] eunuch was on his way home. This [1] man was [8] in-charge-of-the treasury of the [6] Queen, or [5] Candace, of [7] Ethiopia.")

3 Keeping the lexical oddity, we may conjecture earlier мужю болꙗръ цѣсаревъ судии, with Gp forms in accord with OCS syntax, the case sufficing to express the notion of selection from a group. A scribe could easily accomodate the two middle words to Ds, and the last automatically will be understood as dative. The conjectural Greek might have been ἀνδρὶ τῶν ἀρχῶν τῶν σατράπων. A Gp сатрапъ, unknown to a scribe or editor, would then be "rationalized" by means of a known and plausible term.

4 GWV (and 7) omit from и провести through the end of the verse. Ro 197 implies that mss 5, 6, 10 and 20 also omit the whole clause. M78a, on the other hand, defines the omission in 20 ("в списке А и подобных ему") as extending only to the word града.

examples in any text they copied (cf. A1.4). The Hebrew is somewhat more explicit, *wqr'w lpnyw*, 'and let them proclaim before him.'

тако сє створи: H passive 'thus [it] shall be done.' The same H produces тако створити in verse 11, a rendering that is quite adequate. T agrees with Q in 9, but has тако створи in 11. We might see the last as an old 3s imperative, or a present-future with habituative sense. The сє is most probably a Sl addition: scribes could parse the adverb with the preceding verb, "crying out in this manner," and put in an explicit subject ("*This* is to be done.") or object ("Do *this*!"). Tn has тако сє створитє in both verses, either imperative or future. Another strong possibility is that scribes understood the adverb тако as belonging with the preceding verb, "crying out thus," and the сє was added as an explicit object, "This do!"—whereby the following verb could be imperative, as in Tn.

6:10 'who sat at the gate': a reasonable but free translation. The presence of на in most copies is odd, cf. въ in 2:19, 21; 5:13. If we expect full conformity with H, ижє сѣдѧшє should be an agreeing participle, сѣдѧщю, or else a relative clause with present tense, ижє сѣдить.

The parts of the king's command възми...и створи have been separated; thus створи appears to have been taken as a aorist, starting a different sentence, 'And he did (it) that way.' The 'sitting' adjusted to the past reference. It is unlikely that the sentence had its present form in the original translation.

6:11 сътвори поѩздити ємоу: H *wyrkybhw* 'caused him to ride'; the same H causative yields провєсти in 6:9. This is a clear Hellenism; see T9.31.

бѣ клиѵа: H *wyqr'* 'called, proclaimed,' with verb that yields рєкуѵє in 6:9.

тако створити: H as in v. 9. T's створи might possibly represent an old 3s imperative, or a present-future with habituative sense.

6:12 идє: this fails to reproduce the notion of urgency expressed in H passive *ndḥp*, approximately 'was hastened'; cf. C3:15 on this verb.

'sad and hanging his head' makes good idiomatic sense, but the H apparently signifies 'despondent and (with) his head covered' (in any case a pointed contrast to 5:9 вєсєлъ и ѡхвотнъмь ср҃дцмь).[5] The H 'cover' as a sign of sorrow or disgrace recurs in 7:8, see L14.4.

6:13 исповѣда: H 'and he told.'

рабомъ: H 'lovers' or 'friends.' The same H in 5:10 has приѩзнь as a collective and 5:14 приѩзни as plural.

мудрьци свои, with emphatic свои meaning 'not someone else's,' leads us to expect жєна своѩ, but here we have normal єго. Cf. 5:14.

нє можєши оужє с нимь быти is not clear: H *l' twkl lw*, lit. 'you will not be able to him,' means 'won't succeed against him.' Surely the last three words represent original съ нь, where съ plus accusative has the sense of 'equivalent to, equal to'; see L9.61.

ѩко...прєд ним H 'who (*'šr*)...before him'; possibly ὅς (ижє) misread by the Slavic translator as ὡς.

аще: H *ky* after negation means 'but.' The discrepancy between H and Sl perhaps goes back to Gk εἰ μή rendered as ащє нє (as in 1:16), with subsequent loss of the negative particle. See A10.4.

5 Vil. 262 too has повѣсил голову.

и еще же (Т ещ^е^) глющимъ имъ с нимь QTG is out of place, and QT repeat it appropriately as the first clause of 6:14.[6]

падеши: M78a prints пада/е/ши, and his note states that the words аще падаеши пред ним are missing from all mss but T; in fact both Q and T have the words, but after the misplaced dative absolute (which is mistakenly put in verse 13 after с нимь быти as well as in its appropriate place in 14). It seems that only the later mss (like VW) omit the words. T's падаши could be a dialectal form for -аеш(и) from any of several different regions.

6:14 G omits the whole first clause.

се: no corresponding element in H; perhaps a Hellenism, ἰδού (cf. 3:8).

къ питвѣ: Tn на пиръ; see A9.22.

7:1 приде цр҃ь и Амонъ питъ къ Есфирии: preposed verb is sg in H; there is no need for dual in Slavic either. The supine is justified.[1] On къ for *'m* 'with' cf. LXX συμπιεῖν τῇ βασιλίσσῃ. See A9.232.

7:2 просбы твоеꙗ: genitive is puzzling, possibly for мысль просьбы as in 5:6, cf. L 12.11.

дадимъ: H passive, 'it will be given'; the Sl form is 1p active, either imperative or present, surely a mistaken replacement for older 1s дамь. See C5:6.

дамь is superfluous.

створим': H 'it will be done' passive; O ποιηθήσεταί σοι.

ти: not MT, but Moore adds "from several LXX and O[ld]L[atin]."

7:3 отвѣща normal for *wt'n,* but 5:7 same H yields да отвѣтъ.

обрѧку in QT, for usual Slavonic обрѧщю (or potential ESl обрѧҷю) is an egregious deviation from expected norms, see A1.41.

мысль мою: H 'my soul' = 'my life'; L11.221.

The final clause is attested only by Tn. All other copies go back to the work of a scribe who skipped from моеи to a second моеи.[2]

7:4 иже for H *ky* 'because, for,' cf. A10.62.

растворити и убити и погубити = *lhšmyd w lhrwg w l'bd*: there is no syntactic signal that these transitive infinitives are to be interpreted as passive. For these verbs see L17.

препродана быхъ: H *nmkrnw* first person plural; LXX ἐπράθημεν, var. 1sg ἐπράθην.[3] The prefix прѣ- is unexpected; перепрода- is good modern ESl for '*re*sell,' but no appropriate form is to be found in Srez. The pronoun in the defining phrase 'I and my people' easily leads scribes to change the plural verb to singular; it could have been in the Gk version used by the Slavic translator or have arisen during the transmission of the Slavic text.

небо нѣ(сть) тѣсноты в дому цр҃евѣ: H *ky 'yn hcr šwh bnzq hmlk*. Moore (70) calls

6 M78a 154 says that these words are crossed out in T; if so, the cancellation does not show up in photocopies: nor is there any cancellation visible in our copy of Q.

1 Sobolevskij 1903 434 cites сѣде питъ to illustrate the supine in Esther. Perhaps he had in mind 3:14 сѣдоста пити, a phrase in which the supine might well be used.

2 The text of this verse is somewhat corrupt and the copies seem to provide different readings. M78a fails to mark the lacuna and his notes are confused and confusing. (Both textual notes I and K are out of place and, it would seem, inaccurate. Notes 16 and 16a are unclear.) Perhaps variants in this verse might help establish families of manuscripts.

3 An inappropriate variant преповѣдана is in ms 7 (Vlk 12) and, as a correction, in ms 16 (Und 1).

it "undoubtedly the most difficult clause to translate in all of Esther, primarily because the meanings of three of the six words in it are uncertain"—*hcr* has been read as 'enemy,' 'distress' and 'deliverance'; *šwh* is a participle with a variety of meanings; and the *nzq* of the prepositional phrase *bnzq* is extremely rare, and its meaning was not always agreed upon.[4]

We may therefore hypothesize that the Slavonic version was obscure, and that it deteriorated under the hands of uncomprehending scribes. We assume that *ky 'yn* 'for there is no(t)' was originally небо нѣсть, whereby the last word was shortened to нѣ and then misspelled. This yields a comprehensible sentence—'For there is no crowding (lack of space) in the king's house'—but it does not fit the context. An alternative conjecture, that the first two syllables represent the two H words, is possible.

The Slavonic seems to have no equivalent of *šwh* (usually 'is worthy' cf. 3:8, 5:3). In the Hebrew MT *nzq* is a *hapax legomenon*; however, it occurs in the Aramaic part of Daniel, 6:3, and also in the Talmud, as an Aramaic word, meaning 'damage.'[5] Here it apparently goes with Sl домъ, which is reminiscent of LXX's 'court.'[6]

7:5 и рєчє А. цр҃ь *: H has *wy'mr* initially and at *. Moore suggests *wymhr* 'hastened' for the second. LXX and L both simplify in different ways. The Sl may have been translated from a Gk text that omitted the second 'said,' or a later Slavic copyist may have suppressed the apparently superfluous verb.

The unreinforced то from older тъ (*my hw' zh,* LXX τίς οὗτος, L τίς ἐστιν οὗτος) may be an archaism or an artificial literary mannerism.

и откуду есть: H *'yzh,* (lit. 'where this') functions as an interrogative, as in O, ποιός ἐστιν. LXX/L omit.

такы помыслы помысли и тако створи:[7] *ml'w lbw l'śwt kn* 'his heart filled him to do thus,' LXX ἐτόλμησε ποιῆσαι τὸ πρᾶγμα τοῦτο 'he dared to do this thing,' L ἐτόλμησε ταπεινῶσαι 'he dared to make low [= humble].' Perhaps this complexity represents layers of scribal confusion; it may well be that Tn's variant is original: тако помысли сотвори[T]. See L11.1, L11.25.

7:6 мужь вражьбьныи и неприꙗꙁнивыи:[8] The determined adjectives seem out of place; surely short forms are to be expected. In any case, the H has three nouns plus an adjective and demonstrative pronoun apposite to the initial *man*: *'yš cr w'ywb hmn hr' hzh,* lit. "a man, oppressor and enemy, Aman, the bad (one), this (one)," forming a complex definition (as in Acts 8:27, see C6:9). The two descriptive nouns are near synonyms, and LXX

4 Thus interpretations come out with extraordinarily different sense. For example First Targum (Grossfeld 64), "for the enemy does not value the king's loss"; LXX "for the slanderer (διάβολος) is not worthy of the king's court"; Haupt (50), "The enemy is not equivalent to the annoyance of the King."; Moore: "for our problem would not have been worth bothering the king"; Levenson (99) "for then the adversary would not have been worth the king's loss." Authorized Translation: "But I did not want to announce it so that I would distress my lord." In view of these complications, Roždestvenskij's remarks (200) "mistranslation for 'ибо не стоит враг (*hcr*) убытка царского"; "тѣснота stems from the translator's taking *cr* in its primary meaning" are not altogether helpful.

5 As a verb, it occurs also in Aramaic passages in Ezra 4:15, 4:22, 13:4. The Theodotion Gk of Dan 6:3, has ὅπως ὁ βασιλεὺς μὴ ἐνοχλῆται 'that the king not be damaged.' The "Methodian" Sl renders да быша цр҃ю агавиꙗ нє дѣꙗли, the "Simeon" version has да цр҃ю нє ꙁаꙁлаѭть (Evseev 1905 94 [where the verse is numbered 6:2]). The агавиꙗ of this passage reflects a common misspelling of OCS огавьє 'annoyance' (cf. огавиє творѣахѫ ми Ps 34:13).

6 Zimmermann 90–91 offers stimulating but extremely conjectural explanations for the difficulties of the Hebrew text, including a possible reason for the notion of 'court.'

7 M78a prints такое помыслI.

8 M78a says that неприꙗзливыи occurs in "П"; he is mistaken.

uses only one equivalent—the other is restored in O-mss—otherwise translating literally, ἄνθρωπος [O + ἐπίβουλος καὶ] ἐχθρός, Αμαν ὁ πονηρὸς οὗτος.[9] L turns *the bad* into 'your friend the false (one) this-very-one' and changes the word-order to emphasize Haman: Αμαν ὁ φίλος σου ὁ ψευδὴς οὑτοσί, ὁ πονηρὸς ἄνθρωπος οὗτος.

The noun неприꙗꙁнь meant *The Evil One, The Enemy,* viz. Satan. The rare and ancient adjective неприꙗꙁнивъ seems not to have been quite so specific.

възлюбленикъ: H *hr'* הרע [hara'] 'the evil (one),' read as [harea'] 'the friend, neighbor.'[10]

с{ьи}: H *hzh.* The mss spellings imply сы or сыи 'being,' but the sense requires сь or the reinforced сьи 'this (and no other).'

7:7 въставъ...от питвы винныꙗ къ ограду is elliptic exactly as in H and LXX ἐξανέστη ἐκ τοῦ συμποσίου εἰς τὸν κῆπον. An aorist въста (Tn воста) is better.

оградъ дънѣшьнии here and in 7:8 is 'inner garden': the same H, but оградъ оутрьнии in 1:5. (Many commentators hold that the H means 'garden of the palace,' but obviously this view was not shared by the person who translated our text from Hebrew to Greek.)[11] LXX only κῆπος, but O 7:7 κῆπον τὸν συμφύτον.

The second part of the sentence is corrupt both by omission and by the unexpected prepositional phrase от Есфири царици. First, we expect 'stood up *to plead for* his life' (where H 'soul' is used for 'life'), possibly ста *молити* на души своеи.[12] Further, if the preposition is отъ (which might be deemed a Hebraism), then the noun should be G, царицѧ/царицѣ, while царици fits the preposition o. We might propose that оу + G would be idiomatically appropriate, but this requires further emendation. The confusion goes on into the final phrase, where the king and the queen get mixed up.

†и surely for имьже or иже, H *ky*, cf. 1:15.

Prefixed увидѣ is unusual before 1400. OCS uses unprefixed видѣ or else уꙁьрѣ as aorist, 'saw [visually].' Examples of увидѣ(ша) in pre-1400 ESl texts such as the PVL nearly all represent the root вѣд 'know' in the sense 'come to know, perceive.' Here H has the explicit verb of visual apperception (*r'h*), but scribes could easily confuse the two Slavic roots.

скончала сѧ (на немь) бѧше ꙁлоба от царѧ would be literal *klth 'lyw hr'h m't hmlk.*[13] Here an idiom 'there was evil determined against him from the king,' i.e., 'the king

[9] Note that ἐχθρός is common both as noun, *enemy,* and adjective, *inimical*; ἐπιβούλος 'plotting, treacherous' is adjectival.

[10] M56a 211 believes this proves direct translation from Hebrew into Slavonic, although of course this kind of misinterpretation could be made by anyone translating from Hebrew into any language (see T6.1–2). Alekseev did not understand this simple point, and continues to repeat the fallacy (1987a 7). As we noted above, L has "this false friend of yours" precisely here, cf. Moore 71. In 5:4, Haman is defined as ὁ φίλος σου both in L and in the Old Latin translation, made from LXX. This misunderstanding tells us nothing about *direct* translation from Hebrew to Slavonic. *Pace* Alekseev, Greek mediation is possible. Tn has ꙁлокоꙁьнивыи, surely a new editorial emendation.

[11] M56a 215 considers both дьнешний and утрьнии in the sense of внутренний to be "typically Russian."

[12] Thus Gk O: ἐξανέστη καὶ παρῃτεῖτο τὴν βασιλίσσαν Εσθηρ περὶ τῆς ψυχῆς αὐτοῦ.—Ro 197 noted that 'plead' was missing. M56a 210–11, attempting to see here the H idiom 'stand on one's soul' (with the sense 'defend self'), failed to notice the omission and the different intent of this verse.

[13] Sl съконьчати is a calque of συντελεῖν 'bring to an end, finish.' Compare 1 Sam 20:9, *d' ky klth hr'h m'm 'by,* LXX 1 Ki 20:9, γνῶθι ὅτι συντετέλεσται ἡ κακία παρὰ τοῦ πατρός μου, 'know that evil is determined by my father'; W раꙁумѣи ꙗко [аще не] сконуѧ сѧ ꙁлоба ѿца моего (OB sim., but еще instead of аще). The same H and Gk in 20:7 yields съвръшить сѧ in W and OB.

had decided to punish him,' cf. the paraphrase in LXX, ἑώρα γὰρ ἑαυτὸν ἐν κακοῖς ὄντα 'he saw that he was in bad (troubles).' L omits.

7:8 припалъ бѧше: H simply *npl* 'he fell,' but LXX ἐπιπεπτώκει, var. ἐπεπτώκει, L προσέπεσεν ἐπὶ τοὺς πόδας Ἐσθηρ τῆς βασιλίσσης ἐπὶ τὴν κοιτὴν ἔτι ἀνακειμένης, Moore 'was prostrate on the couch.'

предъ постелею: H 'on the bed,' LXX ἐπὶ τὴν κλίνην.

Есфириною: H *'šr 'str 'lyh* on which Esther (was).

The words право мука царицина съ мною въ дому seem to mean, "Indeed the queen's torment (is) with me in the house." This is far from the laconic but lucid Hebrew. Право corresponds to *hgm* (*gm* 'actually, even' [as in 7:9] with question-introducing *h-* prefixed), and the last four Sl words reproduce the H. The noun мука with the possessive adjective царицина stand in place of H inf. 'force, violate, rape' plus 'the queen.' Moore translates, "Would he actually violate the queen while I'm in the building?" LXX is similar, but uses 2nd person: ὥστε καὶ τὴν γυναῖκα βιάζῃ ἐν τῇ οἰκίᾳ μου? "Wilt thou even force my wife in my house?" L, however, has a longer text: οὐχ ἱκανόν σοι ἡ ἁμαρτία τῆς βασιλείας, ἀλλα καὶ τὴν γυναῖκά μου ἐκβιάζῃ ἐνώπιόν μου? "Is your sin against the kingdom not sufficient for thee, but thou wilt force my wife in front of me?" Rather than conjecture that the *queen's suffering* of the Slavonic goes back to a lost H variant, we suppose that this is the result of a misdirected editorial effort to correct an early scribal error.[14]

и вынидє: H has no 'and,' cf. O-text ὁ λόγος ἐξῆλθεν ἐκ τοῦ στόματος τοῦ βασιλέως.

спадє лицє Амонови 'Haman's face fell' fits the context nicely. The H phrase, however, 'and the face of Haman they covered,' is troublesome, because 'face' (*pnym*, a plurale tantum) lacks an accusative marker and might be construed as subject.[15] Further, although covering the head as a sign of sorrow or shame is known even in Esther (6:12, see also 2 Sam 15:30, Jer 14:4), there is no clear parallel to covering the face in such a context.[16] Taking *face* as subject, scholars have suggested emending the verb *ḥpw* to *ḥprw* 'grew red' or *ḥwrw* 'grew pale,' to produce a more plausible meaning. The verb съ-пад-є suggests συν-ε-πεσ-ε, and indeed the phrase 'face fell' with συνέπεσε occurs in Gen 4:5 and 6 as a literal translation of H.[17] More important, it is used in contexts indicating sorrow or shame in LXX 1 Ki 1:18 and Ju 6:9 where the Greek paraphrases Hebrew expressions that do not have both 'face' and 'fall.' From there it became known in other texts, cf. лицє ємоу съпадє Usp 274c23 in a sermon of Chrysostom.[18] Just how it came to be in verse 7:8 remains purely conjectural. Could the H before the Greek translator have been *nplw* (instead of *ḥpw*)? In any case, the clause is controversial; the L-text omits it, while LXX has διετράπη τῷ προσώπῳ 'he was confounded in the face.'

Аманови as possessive dative and Аманово as a possessive adjective are equally suitable for this context.

[14] A similar puzzle, with a not-quite-right noun (къ оубою) where we expect an infinitive, may be solved by Tn's variant, see C4:11.

[15] Vil. 262 has и лице гаманово накрыли.

[16] Moreover the action of covering one's head is ordinarily done by the person who feels sorrow or shame; here the unnamed minions of the king must be envisioned as performing the action.

[17] Mixajlov gives the Slavonic here as испадє лицє єго (var. и испадє). This very likely reflects older и съпадє.

[18] It may also have slightly different meanings, cf. Est 7:6 in Latin, *cecidit vultus ejus*, where Sl has въстрєпєта, LXX ἐταράχθη. In the *Skazanie* of Boris and Glěb, Usp 12b25, възрѣвъ къ нимъ оумиленама оүима и спадъшємь лицьмь, the sense is surely literal: the face has 'fallen in,' is emaciated.

7:9 Харвуна: *u* for expected *o* very likely reflects a change within the Gk tradition.

єдинъ тѣхъ тивунъ might be a Hellenism, but the 'of' that signifies a group may also be represented by a preposition in Greek and отъ or из in OCS.

право: *gm* as in 7:8.[19]

Tn's ωноє probably represents оно, a plausible equivalent of H *hnh* 'lo, R вот!'; Moore "Then, too." LXX ἰδοὺ καὶ ξύλον, L ἰδοὺ ξύλον. The majority variant, бѧшє, is puzzling.

самъ is not in H, but the addition is appropriate as emphasis.

иже глаголаше доброє на царѧ: *'šr dbr ṭwb 'l hmlk*, LXX τῷ λαλήσαντι (O ἀγαθὰ) περὶ τοῦ βασιλέως. L Μαρδοχαιον τὸν λαλήσαντα ἀγαθὰ περὶ τοῦ βασιλέως.

иже глаголаше and доброє are fine, but на цр҃ѧ seems inappropriate, for на with accusative of a person normally means 'against.' Perhaps the Gk rendered H *'l* by ἐπί or κατά, which then was carelessly translated as на. Tn has the simple dative цр҃ю, which then is "to/for the king."

възвышѣ: cf. 5:14, A8.42.

повѣситє *и: H has a direct-object pronominal suffix. Greek uses passive, LXX σταυρωθήτω, L κρεμασθήτω. In Sl (*1360) the explicit name Амона has been substituted; Tn lacks it.

7:10 гнѣвъ царєвъ потухну: H *škkh*, Moore 'abated.' LXX ὁ βασιλεὺς ἐκόπασεν τοῦ θυμοῦ, L om.[20] The verb is known in OCz in the sense 'lose brightness' (cf. SJS for CzOCS) and in early Rus′ as 'be extinguished' (Srez; cf. Tixonravov 1863, 23.4), a fitting term if *anger* is metaphorically a flame. The morphological variant in Tn is потоуше, an obsolete shape that argues for a date well before 1300.

8:1 домъ амон*овъ* враг*а* июдѣиск*ого*: see A6.3.

и повѣда єму что бѧшє єи seems to say 'and he [Mordecai] told him [the king] what was to her,' whereby the last clause, which lacks an explicit subject, may be interpreted in several ways. MT, however, has significantly different wording: 'for *Esther* (had) told what he to her'; in context this final phrase is readily taken to mean *what Mordecai's relationship* to her was. A literal equivalent of the H would be имьже повѣда Есфирь чьто онъ єи. (LXX spells it out: ὑπέδειξεν γὰρ Εσθηρ ὅτι ἐνοικείωται αὐτῇ, 'for Esther had revealed that he was related to her.') An early scribal substitution of єму for Єсфирь in this sentence presumably destroyed the context and led to further modifications. The verse as it stands fails to express that Esther's previous silence about her identity (2:10, 20) has been broken and *therefore* Mordecai is brought even closer to the king.[1]

бѧшє: H *mh hw' lh* 'what he to her'; the copula has been added (cf. 2:7).

8:2 бѣ ωтѧлъ (which could also be spelled отъѧлъ ѿѧлъ):[2] H causative *h'byr* meaning simply 'removed, took away (from)' (but see C8:3).

[19] For право as an equivalent of аминь in OCS and in early Rus′, see SJS and Srez *sub voce*; it is also in the Serbian Vlkan Gospel of c1200. In the Sl *Third Capture of Jerusalem, by Titus* право renders *'mnm* 'truly, indeed.'

[20] M56a 211 cites this verse among those that contain mistranslations, but does not specify the error; apparently this is another of the frequent instances when he gives the numbers incorrectly.

[1] The garbling continues in Tn: и бѣ повѣдаıа емоу^ж^ что бѧше еи. The superscript ж converts the unwanted masculine personal pronoun to a relative.

[2] T by error has ѿтѧлъ, which would represent older ωтътѧлъ 'cut off,' from the verb тьн-, not from -ьм- 'take.' M78a prints the mistaken spelling without comment. Tn has the younger form ѿнѧлъ.

The apposition *Esther the queen* occurs 14 times in MT. Sl omits "queen" (and the following word) in 5:3, but adds it here and in 8:3.

дасть и: old Asm pronoun, also in WV.

8:3 и нача глати: H *wtsp ldbr* 'she continued to speak,' Moore 'she again spoke'; LXX προσθεῖσα ἐλάλησα, lit. 'adding on, she spoke.' The Sl 'began to speak,' without indicating a new start or a continuation, fails to reflect the H idiom.[3] Similarly in the *Third Capture of Jerusalem*: *wtwsp kl h'yr lbkwt* и нача весь градъ плакати.

превратити: H *lh'byr* 'cause to cross over; remove' (LXX ἀφελεῖν, KJ 'put away,' Moore 'frustrate'). (In 8:2 the H verb yields бѣ отѧлъ, LXX ἀφείλατο.) Превратити elsewhere means 'turn *around,* turn *over,* upset' or else 'turn *into*' i.e., change, cf. 9:1, 9:22. Unprefixed вратити reflects the same H verb in 8:5.

8:4 прутъ ꙁлатъ should be definite, as in 5:2; H *hzhb*.[4]

оправи сѧ: H simply 'stood up,' cf. LXX ἐξηγερθῇ (ἀνέστη would be all right).[5] Since Esther is prostrate (as medieval readers surely would conclude from verse 3) and then takes a standing position (ста), her intermediate action must be to get up. The GWV variant ѡбрати сѧ suggests that at some point a scribe disapproved of оправи сѧ, but the sense of *turning* remains inappropriate.

Ordinarily, *prav* means 'correct, straight,' and the verb *o-prav-i-* accordingly means 'make right, justify, fix, cure.' We might conjecture that Gk used a verb with the root *orth*, cf. Ham ис-прав-и and у-прав-и for κατ-ορθ-οῦν. For this verse, we might allow that the Sl "anticausative" reflexive signifies 'recover (from her distraught state).' The modern R and BR sense 'recover (from illness)' is listed in *SRJaSXI* as late 17th century, but an example is attested in chapter 13 of Maimonides's *Book of Asthma* which is interpolated into the Slavic version of the pseudo-Aristotelian *Secretum Secretorum* (Тайная тайных), translated from Hebrew into Ruthenian Slavonic in the 15th century: а не может сѧ оправити—*wl' yqwm tqwmh šlmh* '(the sick man) would not recover completely (from his illness),' Speranskij 1908, 227, line 17. It is possible that this sense was known to the scribe of *1350, but we must admit that оправити сѧ in this verse is at best marginally appropriate.

8:5 Q обрѧку, T обрѧщꙋ: the last two letters in T are clearly a later correction over a partial erasure, probably -кю. VW and, to judge from M58a, the mss he used, have the expected standard Slavonic form as in the corrected T. Cf. A1.4.

The words of Tn that fill the lacuna of all other copies should include an equivalent of *wkšr hdbr* "and [if] the matter [is] proper"; Tn's провозвѣщю "I prophesy" stands where we expect the simple adjective правъ.

напишеть . . . вратити мысль:[6] in place of напишеть H has 'let it be written'; cf. A13.521 and note.

Although he is dead, Aman's written orders were affirmed by the king's seal and will remain valid: the story insists (counter to the historical plausibility established by historians) that the king cannot cancel the decree except by issuing new and different orders. In the

[3] One solution is to imitate the Gk Hebraism, προστίθημι plus infinitive (Gehman 144–45), e.g., Deut 3:26 'Do not continue speaking,' μὴ προσθῇς ἔτι λαλῆσαι, OB не приложи к сему глти; Judg 9:37 'and Gaal spoke again and said' καὶ προσέθετο ἔτι Γααλ τοῦ λαλῆσαι, W и приложи и еще глати.

[4] M56a 215 calls прут "вм. жезл" a typical "Russian" word. The remark is meaningless.

[5] A correct equivalent of H *qm* is въста[въ] in 7:7, and somewhat less appropriate is двигнуща сѧ in 5:9, see comm.

[6] Alekseev 1987a 11 opines that вратити мысль here signifies 'отвратить Амана'; this makes no sense, for Aman was hanged in 7:10 (cf. LT fn. 78).

Hebrew, ‘ꙁамысл Амана’ is grammatically in apposition with ‘книгы.’ In *1350, the word-order has shifted (1234 → 1324), but the sense has not seriously been altered:

yktb	*lhšyb*	*’t-hsprym*	*mḥšbt*	*hmn*
да напишеть	книгы	вратити	мысль	Амонову

8:6 нєбо како: H *ky ’ykkh* ‘for how,’ LXX πῶς γὰρ ‘how therefore.’

приѡбрѣтє ‘gained, acquired’: H *ymc’* ‘finds, will find’; lit. обрѧщеть. The Sl tense is wrong, and the sense added by при- is not quite right.

8:7 QT июдѣю would refer to ‘Judea,’ not the Jews; the mistaken letter can be assigned to the scribe of *1370.[7] G adopted the inappropriate variant.

8:8 All mss but Tn lack the beginning of the verse, ‘And you write concerning the Jews.’[8] This is surely homoioteleuton (Jews . . . Jews), and it apparently occurred in *1360. The prefix in прєпишє^{т} is dubious, and the desinence is uncertain. H has simply ‘write’ (not ‘write again, copy’). The dual is expected, and the superscript “т” ought to represent -та (and for a really ancient text, the pronoun might be ва). The preposition на is inappropriate for ‘about, concerning’ (H *’l*), cf. A9.52.

любо писмєнємь: H *ky ktb* ‘for a writ.’ On любо ‘because’, see A10.61. A scribal misunderstanding of любо in the familiar sense ‘or’ led to the association with the following noun *seal* and the inappropriate instrumental case, instead of N писмѧ.

8:9 ꙗкожє: H ‘according to everything that’ as in 4:17.[9]

After дн҃ь, H has ‘of it,’ sc. of thc month.

After Июдѣѡмъ, ‘to the satraps and officials’ is omitted except in Tn: и посадникѡ^{м} и тиоуно^{м}.

ѡ[до]ду, хоусъ, according to M56a 205, is glossed in some mss, and further corrected to индѣи, кушь in others, a point NM takes as defining certain groups of manuscripts. 15 and 17 have this sort of gloss/correction; cf. also M78a *ad versum.* Compare W’s gloss in 1:1.

8:10 писмєньмь, -ємь ‘writing’ instead of имєнємь ‘name’ in all mss except Tn, which has the phrase имѧ ахашвороша цр҃ѧ, but lacks the verb написаша, cf. also C3:12.

съ приставы коньникы: H *byd hrcym bswsym* ‘by-the-hand-of the-runners on-horses.’ съ stands for expected ‘by the agency of,’ and in most Slavic dialects is therefore superfluous. (Tn has erroneously collapsed the words: со приставни^{к}.)

The H text here and in 8:14 has a fuller description of the horses:

8:10	ижє ꙗꙁдꙗху	[2] на бърꙁдых коних	*[3]*
8:14	ижє ѣꙁдꙗху	[2] на коних бърꙁдых	*[3]*
8:10	[1] rkby	[2] hrkš	[3] h’ḥštrnym bny hrmkym
8:14	[1] rkby	[2] hrkš	[3] h’ḥštrnym

7 Meščerskij’s chaotic remarks about this verse are discussed in App I, 7.2.

8 M56a 204 points to this omission (which he unfortunately locates in v. 16) as the defining feature uniting all copies known to him as descended from a single *pervospisok*.

9 GWV have the distorting error ꙗко нє.

H *rkš* is a rare 'collective term denoting some special type of horse, presumably fast' (Moore). The words in phrase [3] are also rare and their meanings not really certain. LXX makes whole thing simply διὰ βιβλιοφόρων, 'by letter-carriers,' O-mss add ἐν ἵπποις τοῖς ἐπιβάταις τῶν ἁρμάτων οἱ μεγιστάνες υἱοὶ τῶν ραμαχειμ. In 8:14 LXX οἱ ἱππεῖς. O-mss add καὶ ἐπιβάται τῶν πορίων (var. πυρίων) οἱ μεγιστάνες. Tn has на борꙁы[X] коне[X] in v. 14.

Preposition of adjective is rare in Esther, see A5.53.

On бързд- for бърз-, see Al.51.

On older конихъ QT vs. newer конѣ[X] WV, see A3.5.

8:11 єже ихъ бѧшє: simply relative 'who' in H; possibly a Hellenism, perhaps є{лико}жє, cf. 1:15.

We expect сбирати {сѧ} и {стоꙗти на} душахъ своихъ; cf. L6.41.[10]

ижє бѣша мучили: H 'those who had been tormenting *them*.' We posit the Ap pronoun ꙗ in accord with Q's orthography, although it is missing from all copies except Tn (which has the new form и[X]). Without it, the *children and wives* must be perceived as the only objects. Мучили is apparently the only imperfective l-participle in a pluperfect formation.

по росполону: Tn has к, as do all copies in 3:13.

8:13 Cf. 3:14, 4:8 'copy of writing'

даниє: 'to be given,' same H as 3:14. Perhaps we might conjecture δοθῆναι in Gk (A13.61).

оумьсти{ти} сѧ. The prefix is unusual, but known from Serbian Slavonic (Mikl); the usual prefix is отъ- (M78a wrongly attributes it to Q), but Srez lists also въꙁ-, по-. ѿ seems inappropriate for the object.

8:14 погоньци: see C3:15, L2.44.

внидоша surely must be emended to выидоша/вынидоша, cf. C4:6, L19.11.

вънатъщь is attested only here, see A8.22.

8:15 оутринѣ cf. C1:6 and L5.44.

уѡхвоти: a marked Belarusian root-shape, see L13.3–4.

вѣньць: H '*ṭrt*, not the royal crown, *ktr*, of 1:11, 2:17, 6:8; see L5:21.

ушьвъ шьлковъ лєптужьнъ: see L5.2, L5.45–6.

8:16 просвѣщениє "illumination, enlightening, φωτισμός": MT ’*wrh* 'light'; cf. LXX φῶς.

охвота: see L13.41.

8:17 дьнь добръ: not, *pace* M56a 210, a Hebraism, nor is людии ꙁємныхъ; both may reflect possible literal translation from H to Gk, cf. L9.321, note.

жидовѧху сѧ: the verb is unique because the idea is unique; it merely demonstrates the productivity of *i*-verbs.[11] The scribe of ms Tn misunderstood, and wrote дивѧхоу сѧ.

умножилъ сѧ страхъ: 'fear fell (on)'; same H, different Sl in 9:2, 3, see L14.51.

10 M78a offers no comment. M56a states that the phrase goes with 7:7 and 9:31; the passages, in fact, are different. Note that H 'stand on soul' = 'defend self' is corrupt also in 9:16, see comm.

11 M56a 215 calls it, for no good reason, a typical "Russian" word. In 78a he prints живодяху ся.

9:1 As it stands, the Sl verse loses the thread of action entirely and makes the whole story unclear. (LXX omits more than half the verse, from ȥаконъ to the end.) The general H conjunction *'šr* 'that,' preceded by 'day,' has a temporal sense, 'when'; Slavic has locational 'wherever' (идеже аще, a Hellenism, implying ὅπου ἐάν/ἄν).[1] LXX has παρῆν without any conjunction.

постигнѧше implies repetition, cf. C4:3.

умыслиша: a reasonable equivalent of H *śbrw*. The majority reading, услышаша, demonstrates the sort of vague visual and semantic associations that led inattentive scribes to miscopy words in ways that ruin a phrase or sentence.

враȥи июдѣистии: 'enemies of the Jews' must be understood, cf. A5.632.

владѣти ими is a good equivalent for *lšlwṭ bhm*.

превратити сѧ то: *wnhpk hw'* 'it reverted, overturned'; Moore 'the opposite occurred.'

иже: literally H *'šr* 'that'; we expect neuter еже. Moore translates 'that is to say.'

At this point the Sl departs from the H. To be sure, поѵали бѧху враȥи владѣти июдѣи is a sort of reprise of the earlier part of the verse, 'the enemies had begun to rule the Jews,' and as a phrase it makes sense. However, it is the diametrical opposite of the meaning of the underlying Hebrew, 'the Jews themselves dominated (gained power over) their enemies.' The nominative враȥи destroys the original meaning; it must be emended to Inst врагы. As the text stands, the ambiguous form Июдѣи is surely instrumental; if it is to fit the whole story, however, it has to be nominative.

Note that the first враȥи renders H *'yby,* while *врагы corresponds to *bśn'yhm,* 'on those that hate them.' The sense 'begin' has no correspondence in H, and the compound pluperfect поѵали бѧху is thoroughly unjustified.

враȥи	июдѣистии	владѣти	ими
'yby	*hyhwdym*	*lšlwṭ*	*bhm*
enemies-of	the-Jews	to-dominate	on-them

[1a] поѵали бѧху	[4] вра{гы}	[1b] владѣти	[2] Июдѣи
[1] *yšlṭw*	[2] *hyhwdym*	[3] *hmh*	[4] *bśn'yhm*
[1] they-dominated	[2] the-Jews	[3] themselves	[4] on-the-hating-them/-their

9:2 Both the initial И and the next и are inappropriate: MT 'in the cities in all provinces.'

мьсти: presumably Ap. Мьсть творити is normal Slavonic and usually means 'avenge.'[2] On the other hand, many old citations are based on Luke 18:7, where мьсть сътворити is 'vindicate.'[3] Here MT has the idiom 'send hand' (Moore translates in this case 'to kill'), see L6.31.

на всѣх враȥѣх: *bmbqšy r'tm* 'on them seeking their evil' (Moore 'who sought their ruin'). На 'against' would be appropriate to the context only if we emend the noun to the accusative врагы; still, it is not the same as H *b-*.

и никыиже ѵлъ: H *w'yš l'* (*'md*) lit. 'and man not (stood),' where *man* together with the negation on the verb means 'no one'; никътоже (не) would suffice.

не остоıаше предъ: H lit. 'no man stood before them' in the sense 'could withstand them.' The предъ corresponds to the relatively rare semipreposition *bpny*, typically used

[1] Cf. SJS sub идеже **1**, e.g., Mk 14:14 идеже аще вънидетъ ὅπου ἐὰν εἰσέλθῃ, 'wheresoever he shall go in' (cf. T9.37).

[2] Cf. in the *Čudov Ps* мьсти такыимъ творѧ δικὰς τοῦς τοιούτους εἰσπραττόμενος (Lépissier 318).

[3] In OCS, L 18:8 has сътворитъ месть ихъ in Mar, мьсть Assem, but милость (!) Zogr.

with verbs denoting resistance, Sollamo 119. The verb о-стоꙗ- is well known as a variant of объ-, обь-, оби-стоꙗ- 'surround,' usually more narrowly 'besiege' cf. OCS, Srez, Ham, Mikl; or it might be a variant of отъ-стоꙗ-, meaning 'be distant (from).' OCS also has оу-стоꙗ- 'dominate, have mastery over, win out,' and *-stoj-a* also occurs in OCS and many Slavic dialects with a variety of other prefixes and correspondingly varied senses. The desired sense *withstand, resist* is found only in OCz *ostáti* (mod. *obstáti*) and Polish *ostać.*

въꙁиде гроꙁа 'the threat (?) came up': *npl pḥdm,* lit. 'their fear fell' (meaning 'fear *of them*'—Moore 'since everyone feared them,' LXX φοβούμενος αὐτούς, L ὁ γὰρ φόβος Μαρδοχαίου ἔπεσεν ἐπ' αὐτούς 'for the fear of Mordecai fell on them'; see L14.51.

9:3 Translators use a variety of terms for the array of officials in this verse; here is a selection from standard English bibles and from Moore:

вельможа ꙁемныꙗ: *śry hmdynwt* : rulers of the provinces; provincial officials
и тиуни: *wh'ḥšdrpnym* : lieutenants; satraps
подстави: *pḥwt* : deputies; governors
чинѧще дѣло царево: *'śy hml'kh 'šr lmlk* : officers of the king;
those who conduct the king's affairs.[4]

For discussion, see L2 (esp. L2.23).

въꙁношаху 'elevated, bore up': *mnś'ym,* Moore 'supported/helped,' LXX, L ἐτίμων. H *nś'* apparently yielded ὑψοῦν which in turn yielded OCS въꙁ-нес-/въꙁ-нос-и-

ꙗко напалъ бѧше страхъ Мардохаевъ; see 9.3 and L14.51.

9:4 Our principle witnesses have a drastically shortened verse: и бѧше велии Мардъхаи и хожаше великъ.

Fortunately, Tn and a fragment of X preserve the missing text:

ky	*gdwl*	*mrdky*	*bbyt*	*hmlk*	*wšm'w*	*hwlk*
for	(is-)great	Mordecai	*in-the-house-of*	*the-king*	*and-fame-his*	*goes*
ибо	бѧше велии	Мардъхаи	{в домѹ	цр҃евѣ}	и {слоу^{х} его	хожаше

bkl hmdynwt	*ky*	*h'yš*	*mrdky*	*hwlk*	*wgdwl.*
in-all the-provinces	*because*	*the-man*	*Mordecai*	was-going	and-was-becoming-great.
по всеи земли	ибо	мѫжь	Мордъхаи}	хожаше	великъ.

Clearly this is a case of homoioteleuton in a crucial early copy of *1350, with a subsequent attempt to make better sense by adding 'and' between what now look like identical statements.[5] The form велии is archaic even in OCS, but is retained in many phrases down to modern Synodal texts; here it is no proof of an early origin of our translation.

The H *hwlk w-* 'go and' in the final phrase is a sort of auxiliary denoting increasing intensity, 'continued to grow great, became ever greater'; the Sl phrase does not reproduce this meaning. LXX/L omit the clause, but O has ἐμεγαλύνετο γὰρ Μαρδοχαιος πορευόμενος.[6] Otherwise the verb *gdl,* in the causative *pi'el* formation comes out as въꙁвелича, cf. 5:11, 10:2 (and the erroneous въꙁнесе of 3:1), see L15.2.

4 Чинити has a general meaning *do, make,* with a more specific transitive sense *complete, carry out,* in Ukr (see the ample documentation in SSUM sub чинити, оучинити), Bg and SC (but not BR). (M56a 215 wrongly calls чинити in the sense делать указанное "typically Russian.")

5 The Xlebnikov version departs from the H in the imperfect хожаше (for expected present ходить) and singular по всеи земли (cf. всѣхъ землѧхъ in 8:12, 13).

6 This idiom 'go and . . .' = 'continue *X*ing more and more' requires translators to adapt various approxima-

9:5 The whole verse was omitted by LXX and L, though it was restored in the O-text. Gorskij and Nevostruev cite the full Sl and H, together with the Vulgate, to demonstrate the dependence of Sl on H and contrast it with Latin (53), and by default with LXX.[7] Here is the O-text, the Latin, the Slavonic, and the Hebrew, with glosses.

и оудолѣша	Июдѣи	всѣмъ	врагомъ своимъ
wykw	hyhwdym	bkl	’ybyhm
and-smote	*the-Jews*	*in-all*	*enemies-their*
καὶ ἐπάταξαν	οἱ Ἰουδαῖοι [πληγὴν]	ἐν πᾶσι	τοῖς ἐχθροῖς αὐτῶν
itaque percusserunt	Judaei		inimicos suos

раною мечевою	и оубьениемь и	погублениемь
mkt ḥrb	whrg	w’bdn
with-smiting-of sword	*and-slaying*	*and-destroying*
πληγὴν μαχαίρας	καὶ ἀναιρέσεως	καὶ ἀπωλείας
plaga magna	et occiderunt eos	

и створиша	въ [всѣх] вразѣхъ своихъ	волю свою.
wy‘św	bśn’yhm	krcwnm.
and-did	*in-those-hating-them*	*as-wish-their.*
καὶ ἐποίησαν	ἐν τοῖς μισοῦσιν αὐτούς	κατὰ τὸ θέλημα αὐτῶν.
reddentes	eis	quod sibi paraverant facere.

"Thus the Jews smote all their enemies with the stroke of the sword, and slaughter, and destruction, and did what they would unto those that hated them."

As can be seen, the Sl is indeed close to the MT wording, but it is not fully accurate and there is nothing that could not have come through a Greek intermediary.[8] See also A5.12.

удолѣша всѣм врагомъ своимъ: Sobolevskij thinks that the dative object demonstrates that the text is old. However, the old government was by no means unknown after 1400, and in any case it could be used in imitation of older texts, e.g., Ps. 9:26 вьсѣмъ врагомъ своимъ удолѣетъ (OCS PsSin; Kiev Ps of 1397). More importantly, удолѣ- does not correspond to H 'strike, smite'; удариша would be more appropriate.[9]

---

tions according to the context; not all are successful. Compare I Chron 11:9, *wylk dwd hlwk wgdwl* 'and David continued to increase' KJ ('David steadily grew stronger' NEB), LXX καὶ ἐπορεύετο Δαυιδ πορευόμενος καὶ μεγαλυνόμενος, Ostrih Bible преспѣваше Давидъ їдѹщи и растѹщи. Cf. also Gen 8:5, *wylkw hmym hlk wḥsr* 'and the waters decreased continually,' LXX τὸ δὲ ὕδωρ πορευόμενον ἠλαττοῦντο > Slavonic вода же оуходѧщи малѧше сѧ or revised оуходѧщи оскудѣваше (Mixajlov). Judges 4:24 *wtlk yd bny yśr'l hlwk wqšh* 'and the hand of the sons of Israel prevailed more and more,' LXX καὶ ἐπορεύθη χεὶρ τῶν υἱῶν Ισραηλ πορευομένη καὶ σκληρυνομένη, whence и поиде роука сновь иїзлевъ идоущи же стоужающи (? < жесточаиши?) W fol 104v7, cf. Ostrih: и поиде рука сновъ іилевъ и оукрѣписѧ стѹжающи. From a translation made directly from H, the *Life of Moses* (Tixonravov 1863 237.16–17) и поиде рука фараонова болши и жесточаиши, H *wtlk yd pr'h hlk wqšh* (Shinan 1977 109).

7 Though GorNev cite Usher's edition of the O-text (London, 1655) for other purposes on p. 54, they ignore it for this verse. The space they devote to this sentence constitutes nearly 10% of their treatment of Esther. Cf. C1:12.

8 The Latin is quite free, and a literal translation into another language would therefore be recognizable as not directly from Hebrew. For a further sample of Jerome's style of translation, see C10:1, with the corresponding Sl provided by East Slavs in the 1490s.

9 One might even speculate that an original ударишѧ was replaced by оудолѣша under the influence of the familiar psalm verse. Ms 15 has ѡдолѣша, in accord with the 13th-century Simeon Psalter (GIM, Xlud. 3) and others.

раною мечевою is problematical; it most likely reflects πληγὴν μαχαίρας, as in O. H has the etymological figure 'strike with a striking' that usually is lost in the common LXX idiom πατάσσειν πληγήν, as in ἐπάταξεν πληγὴν μεγάλην. Рана does translate words meaning 'blow,' but it usually denotes the result—the wound caused, rather than the blow which causes. Πληγή (like H *mkh*) does for both.

мечев- is a distinctly odd formation, because we don't expect a possessive for a non-animate: see A5.12.

волю свою: *krcwn* would be well expressed by волею своею. Contraction of the dissyllabic desinences is common enough in South Slavic texts, but rare in East Slavic. It may well have happened in these two words.

9:6 погубиша: H 'killed and destroyed.' T, with ѳ instead of ф (here and in 9:12), has a mere "9" victims instead of "500" as correctly in QWV. The two letters have equivalent *phonetic* value in ESl mss from the very beginning, but the failure to discriminate the *numerical* values constitutes another error of T that shows how careless the scribe was.

9:7 H *pršndt'* by the usual rules should yield παρσανδαθα (actually attested in the Complutensian Bible), and *Парсандаѳа. If Θ was replaced by C (in Gk or Sl, cf. note 33, p. 149), we would expect *Парсандаса. The variants may well go back to a careless abbreviation -д^{с}а, perhaps in *1350, plausibly understood as -дас(ъ) by some (e.g., Tn), but—by association with the verb дасть in its frequent shortened spelling -да^{с}—as даст(ь) by TG. Abbreviations with superscript letters are often ambiguous (cf. E11.31); in names they can cause serious misunderstanding.

9:8 и порафа и адалиꙗ и аридаса: ф in first name surely for older ѳ, and с in last name for expected ѳ.[10]

9:9 The majority spelling Пармата perhaps arose from a superscript letter that was omitted; otherwise the history of the name follows the expected steps: *prmšt'* > *παρμαστα > пармаста (TnX only) > ?парма^{с}та > пармата.

9:10 10 сыновъ амоновъ сына амъдафина[11] врага июдѣиского: the interaction of possessive adjectives and possessive genitives doesn't work out here; this phrase specifies Hammedatha as the enemy of the Jews, see A6.3.

9:11 оубиицЬ: H 'those killed, victims'; Xleb оубїець suggests original оубиенъ, precisely the appropriate form. A similar example with the actor-noun where we expect a passive participle denoting victims is in an early 16th-century copy (ms RNB Sof. 1462) of a 15th-century translation from a Hebrew version of *Yosippon* in the subdivision called the *Story of Zorovavel*: множи^{ж} ѹбиици ею сѹ^{т} for *w'yn mspr lhrwgyh* 'and there is no number to *those who were killed* because of her.'

9:12 повѣсиша на древѣ: not justified by H or LXX (H mentions ten sons, LXX does not, L has neither hanging nor sons). On the other hand, strictly speaking, it does not really

[10] M78a omitted the last two names from 9:8, along with и пармата of 9:9, and therefore he misplaced the verse-number "9" and left "10" out altogether.

[11] Instead of амъдафина M78 prints амдавина; is it a lapse or possibly from a different manuscript? See 8:5.

contradict 9:6 and 9:10, but merely remarks once again that they had been hanged before this speech.

раꙁвѣ єже по всеи ꙁємли: H ‘in the rest of the king’s provinces.’ The first two words apparently mean ‘except for (?those),’ but the phrase remains obscure. We might conjecture either раꙁвѣ ѧже with a relative pronoun signifying people, or раꙁвѣ аще (as an equivalent of πλήν or ἐκτός εἰ μή, cf. SJS), but it remains distant from the MT. The H syntax is unusual, but understandable; it has little to do with the Slavic text in our manuscripts.

проси ты: cf. 5:3, 5:6, 7:2, L12.11

створим: the plural desinence -м is puzzling; see A11.12.

9:13 оулюбѣєт: see L12.6.

The originally impersonal sentence, ‘If it please the king,’ was reshaped when a scribe interpreted the old D цр҃ю as vocative and he or a subsequent copyist then added тобѣ to strengthen the direct address.

ꙗкоже законъ днєшнии: H *kdt hywm,* lit ‘according to the law-of today’; LXX merely ὡσαύτως, ‘in the same way.’

дати: H *yntn* ‘let it be given’; see passive A13.61.

повѣсиша: should be future or conditional, so Xleb’s повѣсѧ[т] is appropriate.[12] The confusion in part comes from the sense of the H text, for the ten sons have already been killed in verse 10; commentators assume that “hanging” now refers to a shameful public exposure of the corpses.[13] The aorist form in most copies seems to be an echo of the erroneously included phrase in 9:12 and the correct form of 9:14, perhaps mediated by superscript spellings—повѣсѧ[т] > повѣсѧ[иш].

дати . . . створити: H ‘may [it] be granted . . . to do,’ that is ‘permitted to act’; LXX δοθήτω χρῆσθαι . . . ὧστε . . . κρεμάσαι; L ὡς . . . κρεμασθῆναι.

9:14 створи: an imperative is possible in this context, but H has a passive infinitive, ‘said to be done thus’; perhaps we should conjecture створи{ти} .

9:15 H has ‘on the 14th day,’ but QWV have д҃ ‘4’; T originally agreed (as does Und 1), but a later hand modified it to ıд҃. The ‘ten’ usually follows the ‘unit’ in numerals, so this correction is somewhat unusual.

9:16 The middle part of this verse is hopelessly corrupt in most copies, but even with the valuable data from Tn and X, serious problems remain. The phrases corresponding to H ‘stood on their soul [= defended themselves][14] and rested [= gained relief] from their enemies’ are usually reduced to и стоꙗху на покоих своихъ. Tn and X allow us to restore

и стоꙗху	на покоих своихъ	и оупоѵиша	ѿ врагъ своих
w‘md	*‘l npšm*	*wnwḥ*	*m’ybyhm*

A plural of покои ‘rest’ is improbable, and we would emend to на покои своємь.[15] A lit-

[12] Tn has посидѧ[т], with the expected 3p present form but a mistaken root, ‘will sit.’

[13] LXX has in 9:14: ‘he gave up to the Jews of the city the bodies of the sons of Haman to hang.’

[14] The same idiom occurs in MT 8:11, but only the noun душахъ survives in Sl, without preposition or verb. See L6.4.

[15] In the sense ‘place of rest; chamber, room’ attested in WSl, a plural would be normal. Note that H *nfš* ‘soul’ is based on a root meaning ‘rest.’

eral rendering into Gk would use a form of ψυχή. We suggest that a copyist, influenced by the next word *rested,* wrote instead ἀναψυχή; the Sl translator rendered this noun by покои, cf. Ps 65:23 (LXX εἰς ἀναψυχήν, OCS въ покои).

The verbs *stand* and *rest* of the previous clauses are followed in MT by *kill,* an unusual series of three absolute infinitives. The form оубитъ of nearly all copies cannot be old.[16] It could be a post-1400 ESl past passive participle (Nsm or possibly Gp); or, perhaps, we might read оубить (taking into account the final -т' of T) as an infinitive, but it still does not fit with the following incoherent words. Tn and X have a coherent phrase, but it does not fit the context.

QTSGWV	и оубитъ къждо	нєлюбимого	70 и 5,000
TnX	и оуби къж^{д}о и^{х} нєлюбимого своєго		70 и 5
H	*whrwg*	*bśn'yhm*	75,000

H has "and-kill in-haters-their 75,000," that is, 'and they killed 75,000 of those that hate them [= their enemies]'—оубишѧ нєнавидѧщихъ ихъ 75,000. How did the expected active participle *hating* (or an equivalent noun *enemies*) get converted to the passive *un-beloved* preceded by an inappropriate pronoun?

70 and 5,000 is a usual way of expressing 75,000. Ms 15 is clearer: ҂о и ҂є.

9:17 говѣху 'they fasted' has no equivalent in MT or Tn. It may be a note indicating that Jews were supposed to observe the Fast of Esther.[17] The то бѣху of GVW is inappropriate. The substitution of letters (in either direction) is common enough.[18] Perhaps in fact то бѣху implies an original explanation 'that is,' cf. 3:13, 8:19 where this sort of definition occurs in glosses of month names.

9:18 и тъ (G reinforced form тои): in effect a doublet. The enclitic Asm object-pronoun **jь* 'it' (spelled и, here meaning 'the day') tends to motivate use of the optional desinence -ть. Thus творѧхуть и could be copied as творѧху^{т}и, then—because a superscript letter is often ambiguous as to position in the sequence of letters—reinterpreted by a later scribe as emphatic particle и plus a clarifying deictic pronoun тъ, 'made it too a day of . . .'[19]

9:19 распрашєници: spelled correctly only in S; Tn has распрѧшєници. QTGWV have "щ": распра[щ]єници (with variation in other letters, see variants), but the participle распрашєным fits OCS распрашити 'disperse, scatter' (e.g., распрашєни Su 442.16 = Usp 213d9; Srez) cf. also распрашат сѧ ἐξολοθρεύσονται in the *Testament of Shem* (Tixonravov I.155). Compare the related verbal substantive in по распрашании in an excerpt from Malalas (in the Biblical collection of 1507 [ms BAN 24.4.28], Lavrov 1933, 93). This verb is presumably based on **porx* 'dust.' The original Malalas passage has по распрошанїи жє цр҃ства Людска, μετὰ τὸ ἀπολέσθαι, Istrin 1911 9.15 (cf. note to C1:1).

16 M56a 213 notes the ending -тъ but fails to label it a hypercorrection in оубытъ but an archaism in ꙗтъ. On scholarly confusion about this kind of aorist, see Lunt 1990 15. Older ppp forms could be replaced at will by scribes, cf. e.g., PVL sub 945: князь нашь оубьєнъ, 56.21 (LRA), but оубитъ (HX).

17 In an early *responsum* a gloss on 9:15–16 reads, "they gathered, i.e., fasted." See Kulik 1995.

18 M56a 208 believed that the fact that говѣху separates the gloss рєкомаго марта from адара showed an old marginal note inserted in the wrong place within the text; he failed to notice that the verb was textually superfluous, AT 309. Volok 12 writes адара^{г} | бѣхѹ.

19 Tn lacks и тъ. M78a omits the тъ without comment; did he in fact know a manuscript without it?

9:20 рѣчь сию: H plural *hdbrym h'lh*.

The first example of по is surely an erroneous anticipation of the second, and represents ко for standard къ: ко всѣмъ . . . по всѣмъ. Orthographical ко does not occur in Q, but it is in T (4:11), and is not uncommon in Lav. The use of къ instead of prepositionless dative is probably artificial, foreign-flavored syntax, but it is unremarkable in Slavonic texts.

9:21 H 'the-day 14-of month-of Adar and (-the) day 15 in-it'—two specific days to be celebrated. The Sl majority reading днии 14 surely is intended as "14 days," with Gp of the noun—a two-week celebration. Tn has 14 днь plus the full definition of the month, omitted by the other mss; except for the order of *14* and *day*, this mirrors the MT.

годину meaning 'year' in Srez only from Esther and Ham; in Ham it occurs (214) in a discussion of the lunar versus the solar year, otherwise ἐνιαυτός comes out годъ or лѣто in Ham. See L20.

9:22 дары: H 'portions, delicacies' (cf. C2:3). This rendering of *mnwt* is consistent with earlier verses (2:3, 9:19), but here the MT adds *mtnwt l'bynym* 'gifts for the poor' (using the general noun derived from the root 'give'). The usual equivalent would be дары; instead we have помилование. The context suggests the meaning 'alms' (not found in canonical OCS, but assured by examples from Srez), though it usually means 'compassion, mercy.'[20]

сиротамъ: H 'to the poor.' For this meaning Srez cites only Est. Moore notes that OLatin adds 'orphans and widows': perhaps our Gk text had some similar wording. Tn has сиротамь и худымъ.

9:23 подъяша (cf. 9:27). H simply 'accepted,' i.e., приꙗти or възꙗти; подъ- implies the notion of support.

9:24 любо represents H *ky* 'because,' cf. 2:10, 8:8. M56a 215 sees no difficulty, remarking "Всегда подчинительное значение причины свойственно союзу *любо* (IX,24; X,1 [sic!])." GorNev also appear to accept this meaning, but we found it hard to verify; see A10.61. Most of the final clause is missing from all mss: "and had cast *pur* (that is, the lot) to discomfit and [destroy them]" (cf. Moore 92).

Verses 9:24–26 are a summary of the previous events contained in Mordecai's letter to the Jews; therefore the tenses are different, see below.

9:25 The Slavic is very close to the MT, but the H text displays, as Levenson (127) puts it, "an awkwardness of phrasing and an obscurity that are uncharacteristic of the book of Esther."

да егда прихожаше is a reasonable equivalent of the initial infinitive construct (*wbb'h*), where the imperfect functions as pluperfect, approximately 'had been [and still was] coming' (a resumé). Sl has no explicit subject. In H, the feminine suffix *h* is usually assumed to refer to Esther, so 'in her coming' means "when Esther came" before the king. Then the masculine verb *'mr* '(he) said' is followed by *'m hspr* 'with the book.' The subject is taken to be the king, but it is unclear *what* he said and just what *with the book* has to do

20 Thus дары stands for two different H nouns (*mnh*, usually implying special food or delicacy, in 2:9, 9:19, 9:22; *mś't*, a rare word, in 2:18), but the generic term *mtnh* ends up as помилование. Vil. 262 has ѡброк in 2:18 for *mś't*, дары in 2:9 for *mnwt*, and in 9:22 for *mtnwt*, but, puzzlingly enough, перепои in 9:19, 22. LXX has no equivalent in 2:18, but uses μέρις 'portion' in the other three verses. L has the notion only in 9:22, with μέρις.

with speaking. Moore conjectures 'he gave orders in writing.' Slavic omits *'mr* 'he said,' and renders *'m hspr* as съ грамотою. The extant Slavic sentence seems to mean 'When he (sc. Haman) came before the king, even with a/the letter, his wicked thought was turned back on his own head.' Both the verb *come* and *turn/take back* raise questions. As to the first, it is significant that LXX has refashioned the sentence, with Haman as subject, and with no reference to Esther or the king. Scholars have conjectured that the underlying H text had *bb'* with no affix to indicate gender, so that by default the action is Haman's. We may posit the same H for the history of the Slavic version. As to *turn*, the H has rather 'should return' for Sl 'be turned,' обрати сѧ; however, the H masculine verb does not correspond to the feminine subject *mḥšbh* 'scheme, thought.' (The reflexive свою is inappropriate, though contextually it can refer only to Haman.) We postulate a causative *yšyb* for MT's *yšwb* (an easy conjecture); this produces the transitive sense "he turned" (i.e., the king [?] turned his [Haman's] wicked scheme on his [Haman's] own head) and helps explain the form of the sentence as it stands. In the final analysis, however, this verse remains unclear in Slavic.

The Sl. и повѣшєнъ бы^{с} съ сынъми corresponds to a Hebrew clause that normally would signify 'and they hanged him and his sons,' but it may also be read to mean 'that they should hang him and his sons.' As Moore points out (94), interpretation depends on one's view whether it is chronology or the fact of execution that is important to the context.

In this summary account ("so highly compressed that it seems cryptic," Levenson 127), the reader is assumed to be familiar with the events, and the actions are repeated as a reminder.

Note that Slavic 'with his sons' rather than the 'and his sons' of H corresponds to North Slavic idiom (which is also in 5:4).

9:26 GorNev quote the H of this verse at some length to show identity with Sl, especially the repetition of nouns. The problem is that H is not clear to start with: the translator(s) rendered each phrase as literally as possible, ending up with a Sl text that isn't clear either.

[и] того ради: H *'l kn* 'therefore, accordingly' (cf. 9:19).

The H word *Purim*, so vital to this verse—and to the Jewish significance of the whole scroll—is missing here, though it is represented by вєсєлиє in 9:29, 31, 32 and perhaps 9:28. It may have been lost during either the Sl or Gk transmission.

We have provided no punctuation in this verse because the extant Sl offers no real clues as to what scribes thought it might mean. Commentators on the MT text generally agree that with the word 'lot' (жрєбиинѣмь) a sentence—even a paragraph, vv. 26b–28—ends (cf. Levenson 128). The new sentence or paragraph also begins with *'l kn*, for which both ꙁанє and ꙁанєжє are possible. What follows is incoherent, although each phrase is close to the H. Всѧ рѣчь си книгамъ симъ should mean "concerning/because of all the words of this letter" (*'l kl dbry h'grt hz't*, LXX διὰ τοῦς λόγους τῆς ἐπιστολῆς) perhaps *ꙁа всѧ рѣчи к. с. Tn has за тыа речи всѧ книга^{М} всимъ. Here and in 9:29 the *plurale tantum* книгы reflects H *'grt* 'letter.' и ꙗжє видѣша того ради 'and what they saw concerning this' fits the H (того ради = *'l kkh*), though a perfect would be preferable to the aorist.

єжє събы^{с} сѧ им: H *wmh hgy' 'lyhm.* The H, lit. 'and what reached them,' has troubled some commentators, but the Targums are compatible with Moore's rendering, 'what had happened.'

9:27 уставиша и подъꙗша: H 'agreed and made it customary.'

племѧ: *zr'* 'seed'; LXX ἐπὶ τῷ σπέρματι. Otherwise *zr'* comes out чад- in Est.

на вса елико ихъ: surely a Hellenism, * καὶ ἐπὶ πάντας ὅσοι, see T9.36.

приступаше: H a participle, approximately приступающи, with the sense 'all future converts,' cf. LXX καὶ ἐπὶ τοῖς προστεθειμένοις ἐπ' αὐτῶν. While Sl imperfects may in certain contexts indicate a relative future, here the clause indicates a summary past, 'those who have already joined.'

и нн҃ѣ того не имуть преступати: H *wl' y'bwr* 'and it will/should not pass,' i.e., 'so as not to fail, without fail.' The adverb 'now' is an addition. Perhaps the Sl 'and they shall/may not trangress [this agreement]' goes back to the H that Moore suggests, *y'brw,* 'they will/should not pass [it] by.' The H is a regular reference to an immutable law, cf. Ps 148:6, *ḥq ntn wl' y'br,* πρόσταγμα ἔθετο καὶ οὐ παρελεύσεται, повелѣние положи и не мимоидетъ; Job 14:5 *ḥqw 'śyt wl' y'br,* εἰς χρόνον ἔθου, καὶ οὐ μὴ ὑπερβῇ, ОВ въ летѣ положилъ еси и не прест8пи[т].

ꙗкоже суть творѧще: in H this continues the agreement; they took it on themselves *to do* these two days, viz. to celebrate them. The Sl, with its added ꙗкоже, has a quite different meaning 'as they (regularly) are doing.' This sense was imposed also on the next verse, which in H continues to spell out the terms of the agreement.

днии си: presumably for dual дни си.

година here for *zmn,* лѣта for *šnh,* reduplicated, see L20.11.

9:28 поминающе суть и творѧще ꙗ: H passive, '(are being) remembered and done' see on translation of passive, A13 (esp. A13.62).

не минуша николиже: 'never passed' makes sense in this narrow context, but H has 'will not pass,' LXX οὐ μὴ ἐκλίπῃ.

днии: for дни Ap.

дньe веселии си seems to be 'these merry days' Np; the three words correspond to H 'these days of Purim,' so that веселии appears where we want 'Purim.' Perhaps дньe веселии сихъ might be possible (cf. the pl in standard LXX αἱ δὲ ἡμέραι αὗται τῶν Φρουραι). As it stands the phrase is not good. The equivalence of the word веселие and *Purim* seems guaranteed by 9:29, 31, and 32.[21]

This verse is particularly rich in replicas of H distributive repetitions (see T8), and Gorskij and Nevostruev cited it at length because they saw these phrases as proof of direct translation from Hebrew. The Origen-influenced Greek of ms 93, however, reproduces the MT very closely: αἱ δὲ ἡμέραι αὗται μνημόσυνον ἐπιτελούμεναι κατὰ γενεὰν καὶ γενεὰν, πατριὰν καὶ πατριὰν, χώραν καὶ χώραν, πόλιν καὶ πόλιν. αἱ δὲ ἡμέραι τοὺς φουρουρειμ αὗται ἀχθήσονται τὸν ἅπαντα χρόνον, καὶ τὸ μνημόσυνον αὐτῶν οὐ μὴ ἐκλίπῃ ἐκ τῶν γενεῶν.

въ вса вѣкы вѣком: H *bkl dwr wdwr* 'in every generation.' The conventional Sl phrase means 'for ever and ever' and is surely the result of thoughtless emendation by scribes from expected всакъ вѣкъ и вѣкъ. The usual equation is *'wlm* > αἰών > вѣкъ.

родъ и родъ: H *mšpḥh wmšpḥh* 'every family/clan.' The use of вѣкъ for *dwr* 'generation' is to be explained in part by the fact that both *dwr* and *mšpḥh* are often rendered by γενεά, so that if both occur in the same context, another equivalent must be found. Copyists sometimes are influenced by phrases they know by heart, especially psalms and hymns. Here perhaps Ps 100:5 played a role: въ вѣкъ милость его и до рода и рода истина (PsSin рѣснота) его, εἰς τὸν αἰῶνα τὸ ἔλεος αὐτοῦ καὶ ἕως γενεὰς καὶ γενεὰς ἡ ἀλήθεια

21 M56a 208 remarks, "Примечательно, что систематически пропускается еврейское название праздника Пурим." In what way is it significant? The omission is *not*, in fact, systematic, but one time, 9:26, out of five.

αὐτοῦ, MT 99:5 *l'wlm ḥsdw w'd dr wdr 'mwntw*. Родъ has an extremely broad semantic range, see SJS,[22] and the phrase γενεὰ καὶ γενεά recurs in the psalms.[23] Slavic seems not to have had a specific term for *generation,* i.e., H *dwr*; поколѣние is late (not in SJS or Srez).

ꙁемлꙗ и ꙁемлꙗ: H *mdynh wmdynh* 'every province'; see C1:16.

памѧть: H 'their memory,' i.e., memory *of them.*

ѿ чадъ их 'from their children': H 'from their seed.'

9:29 is "a most confusing verse" (Levenson) whose message is confirmation (or reconfirmation) of decrees.

всю твьрдь: H 'all power.' In the whole MT, *tqp* occurs only here, in 10:2 (again твердь) and in Daniel.[24] Sl is a literal equivalent of H *wtktb . . . 't kl tqp*, "she wrote . . . all authority/affirmation" if *'t* is taken as the mark of accusative (as it was interpreted in the First Targum); many scholars view it as the preposition 'with.'[25] Sl твьрдь ordinarily means 'foundation, firmament; fortress' and repeatedly stands for στερέωμα. LXX has a somewhat different wording in this verse, but στερέωμα (+ Gen) is used where Sl has the phrase твьрдь уставити (+ Acc), surely with equivalent meanings, *ratification* or *confirmation* (of the letter) and *to ratify* or *confirm* (the letter). In our opinion, therefore, the Slavonic of 9:29 probably represents a Greek text with στερέωμα. Srez has твьрдь in this sense only from Esther.

The last two words stand for H 'this second [letter]' which Moore calls "a troublesome phrase" that some commentators consider a gloss. Sl reproduces the MT word-order, with the pronoun and adjective somehow postponed. We assume that the original had Apf сьѧ (сиѧ) другыѧ to agree with книгы, but *1350 indicates that someone mechanically changed the pronoun to agree with Gsn веселиꙗ.

9:30[26] H 'to *all* Jews'; only Tn has всѣмъ. The two participles in the concluding phrase surely are errors for verbal substantives in the genitive, that is, "ыꙗ" has replaced "ьꙗ" or "иꙗ." Рѣчи оумирениꙗ и оувѣрениꙗ, 'words of reconciliation and assurance' still is not equivalent to the direct 'words of peace [or, health] and truth' of H *dbry šlwm w'mt*. Cf. Deut 2:26 *dbry šlwm* LXX λόγοις εἰρηνικοῖς. Λόγοι εἰρηνικοί occurs in Judith and I Maccabees, as well as Esther D8, that is in original Biblical Greek. In Ps 118 [H 119]:43 *dbr 'mt* becomes As λόγον ἀληθείς, OCS Gs словесе истиньна. Perhaps Sl речи мирьны и вѣрьны was original, but for some reason was made more elaborate and then distorted to the attested inappropriate forms.[27]

22 In 2:10 and 2:20 it corresponds to *mwldth* '(her) descent,' another word that yields γενεά in LXX, though in Est 2:10 it is γένος.

23 It is worth noticing that in some cases a Slavic translator rendered the Gk γενεά by племѧ (a meaning not recorded by Sreznevskij). Thus Deut 23:4 καὶ ἕως δεκάτης γενεᾶς, Warsaw Jewish Chron. до 10 племене; 23:9 γενεὰ τρίτη, племѧ третьее. In Job 42:16, LXX γενεάν yields родъ in Usp., колѣно in OB, but поꙗсъ in the Gennadius Bible!

24 Dan 11:17 has *btqp kl mlkwtw* 'in/with the strength of his whole kingdom,' ἐν ἰσχύϊ πάσης τῆς βασιλείας αὐτοῦ, older Sl съ крѣпостию всего ц^срствиѧ его, but with reassignment of 'all' in the revision, вьсеѩ силы ц^срства своего.

25 The H syntax is awkward, and the sense of the whole verse is controversial, cf. Haupt 76–77. Relying on the usual interpretation (e.g., Moore 'with full authority'), we might conjecture вьсею твьрдью as original, but the evidence is not firm enough. Alekseev's comment (1987 10) on твьрдь is off the mark; this noun has nothing to do with the adverbial use of твердо in any other text.

26 M78a begins this verse with другыя, which in fact ends 29.

27 Malalas, bk 6 (Istrin 1911, 7 n. 20) мѣренїе versus мѣрнаꙗ (морѧ), μέτρα θαλάττης, 'the measures of the sea.'

9:31 веселиꙗ: cf. 9:28.[28]
душа своꙗ: for {на} душѧ своѧ {и}. H 'they established for themselves and for their seed'; see L6.42.[29] The на is attested in Tn.

9:32 реѵение, глаголы, see L8.23, L8.41.
написа: H passive, 'it was written.' As it stands, this sentence is incoherent.

10:1 From here to the end, the text in Q was added by a later hand, in somewhat different orthography.[1] The text may well be slightly updated in contrast to the rest. These final verses very probably were on the last folium in various codexes; the final folium is most likely to be damaged or lost.

In the Gennadius Bible these three verses have been replaced by the translation newly made from Latin; for the text, see below.

10:2 тверді, cf. 9:29.
мадѣискыхъ: Porfir′ev's description of ms 4 provides the variant мадѣамскыхъ, which helps explain the spelling in WV. This form very likely is associated with the confusion of Μαδαι and Μαδιαμ, illustrated for example in Malalas, въ мадїамли странѣ, ἐν τῇ Μηδῶν χώρᾳ (Istrin 1911 39). See also A2.34.
грамотныхъ: see C2:23.

10:3 другъ царѧ: H 'second to the king,' i.e., viceroy. As it stands, the Sl can mean only 'friend of the king.' The determined form другыи (or въторыи) is required. Thus in 1 Ki 23:17 Jonathan says to David, и ты имаши цр҃ствовати въ Iи҃ли и ꙗзъ ѹ҆дѹ по тобѣ другыи (W, GB, OB) for καὶ ἐγὼ ἔσομαι σοι εἰς δεύτερον, H *w'nky 'hyh lk lmšnh*; the Warsaw Jewish Chronograph and S have вторыи.
вольникъ: probably an error, see L12.22. H 'accepted' or perhaps 'favored.'

Gennadius Bible. Esther, Chapter 10:1–3

Here are the three verses of chapter ten in the new translation made in the 1490s from the Vulgate for the Gennadius Bible (in the fifth line), together with (1) the LXX, (2) the older Slavonic translation, (3) the Hebrew (with literal English glosses), and (6) Jerome's Latin.[2]

(1) Ἔγραψεν δὲ ὁ βασιλεὺς ἐπὶ τὴν βασιλείαν τῆς τε γῆς καὶ τῆς θαλάσσης
(2) и възложи царь Ахасъверосъ дани на ѕемлю и на ѡстровы морьскыа
(3) **10:1a** *wyśm hmlk 'ḥšrš* *ms 'l h'rc* *w'yy hym*
(4) and-put the-king Ahashwerosh tax on the-land and-islands-of the-sea
(5) цр҃ь бо Ассоуеръ всю землю и всѣ морскыа островы сътворил данникы
(6) Rex vero Asuerus omnem terram et cunctas maris insulas fecit tributarias;

καὶ τὴν ἰσχὺν αὐτοῦ καὶ ἀνδραγαθίαν,
и все дѣло тверді егои моцї его
2a *wkl m'śh tqpw* *wgbwrtw*
and-all act-of power-his and-might-his
ему же крѣпость и цесарьство
cujus fortitudo, et imperium et

[28] Ro 202 sees веселиꙗ as a substitution (apparently arbitrary) for the unfamiliar term *Purim*.
[29] M56a 211 says that уствити [!] душа своя is one of three different renderings of "a'mad a'l nepheš" [!] with 7:7 (he writes 6:7) and 8:11. Here in fact is not *'md* 'stand' but *qymw*, lit. 'caused to stand,' meaning 'placed/took (upon themselves). [See above, p. 10, note 28.]
[1] M78a omits царь and has острови for -вы.
[2] Roždestvenskij 203–204 printed these lines in a somewhat updated spelling, with the Latin.

πλοῦτόν τε καὶ δόξαν τῆς βασιλείας αὐτοῦ,
и расповѣданїє величьа Мардъхаєва имьжє въꙁвєлїча єго царь
2b *wpršt* *gdlt* *mrdky* *'šr* *gdlw* *hmlk*
and-account-of greatness-of Mordecai which exhalted-him the-king
и въꙁвышении[M], иже възвысилъ Мардохая,
dignitas atque sublimitas, qua exaltavit Mardocheum,

ἰδοῦ γέγραπται ἐν βιβλίῳ βασιλέων Περσῶν καὶ Μήδων εἰς μνημόσυνον.
и та соуть написана въ кнїгах грамотных [и] царевъ Мадѣискыхъ и Фарисѣискыих
2c *hlw' hm* *ktwbym 'l spr* *dbry hymym* *lmlky* *mdy wprs*
(are-)not they written on book-of affairs-of the-days to-kings-of Media-and-Persia
написана суть въ книгахъ Медеискых и Перскых
scripta sunt in libris Medorum atque Persarum

ὁ δὲ Μαρδοχαῖος διεδέχετο τὸν βασιλέα Αρταξέρξην
ꙗко Мардъхаи Июдѣи, другъ царѧ Ахасъвероса
3a *ky mrdky* *hyhwdy* *mšnh* *lmlk 'ḥšwrwš*
for Mordecai the-Jew second to-king Ahashwerosh
И како Мардохеи Іудеѧнинъ родомъ, вторыи ѿ цр҃ѧ Ассѹера бы[с]
et quomodo Mardorchaeus Iudaici generis secundus a rege Asuero fuerit;

καὶ μέγας ἦν ἐν τῇ βασιλείῃ καὶ δεδοξασμένος ὑπὸ τῶν Ιουδαίων
и великъ въ Июдѣих и вольникъ множьства братьꙗ своєѧ
3b *wgdwl lyhwdym* *wrcwy* *lrwb* *'ḥyw*
and great to-the-Jews and-liked to/by-multitude-of brothers-his
и велик предъ Іюдеи, и ѹгодникъ народѹ братїи своеи,
et magnus inter Iudaeos, et acceptabilis plebi fratrum suorum,

καὶ φιλούμενος
въꙁискаа доброты людємъ своим
3c *drš* *ṭwb* *l'mw*
seeking good to-people-his
ищѹщи бл҃гаѧ людемъ своим
quaerens bona populo suo,

διηγεῖτο τὴν ἀγωγὴν παντὶ τῷ ἔθνει αὐτοῦ.
и проповѣдаа миръ всєм чадом своимъ.
3d *wdbr* *šlwm* *lkl zr'w.*
and-speaking peace to-all seed-his
и гл҃ющи та, иже въ мирѹ сѣмени своему пристоѧт.
et loquens ea quae ad pacem seminis sui pertinerent.

Commentary

10:1 ассоуеръ is marked with superscript dots, and аха[з]веросъ is in the margin. Otherwise in this chapter only the Latinate form occurs.[3] Notice that the Latin is fairly free with regard to the Hebrew, but the Gennadian translation slavishly follows the Latin.

[3] The Latin shape is based on a Greek transcription of Hebrew where ח (ḥ) is omitted, contrary to the rule that

2a възвышении[M]: the case is inappropriate.

2c The traditional rhetorical question in MT, "are the deeds of X not written in the book of Y?" (e.g., 3 Ki 22:39, 4 Ki 8:23), has been modified in LXX ("Lo, it is written") and made a simple statement in Latin.

Conclusions

The earliest retrievable text of the Slavonic book of Esther, based chiefly on the two oldest copies (Q and T, of about 1400) with a significant contribution of lacuna-filling words and phrases from the late and aberrant text of Tn (1500s; cf. E7.2) and some significant variants agreed on by W and V, abounds in incoherent phrases, inappropriate grammatical combinations, and outright incomprehensible clauses. As we struggled to understand items that do not fit within the bounds of a fairly literal reflection of the MT phraseology, we continually wondered at the number and complexity of the difficulties, and were led to speculate about how many layers of copying, that is, how many successive scribes and/or editors, it took to produce so many faults.

Only four of the 167 verses seemed to require no comment at all. For many verses, notes concern only minor lapses in spelling or unexpected grammatical or semantic details. Many comments deal with problems of translation. Yet perhaps a quarter of the verses have more serious defects in number or tense or person, or in meaning. Often each phrase in a passage will make sense by itself, but the whole sequence fails to cohere. The universal inventory of routine scribal errors—omissions, additions, replacements—can be illustrated from this text, which is further damaged by perverse misreadings and arbitrary editorial changes.

The lamentable state of the text must have made it difficult to comprehend, and sporadic efforts to repair or improve individual bits and pieces only made things worse. It would seem that the bare outline of Vashti's fall and Esther's rise comes through, as does the basic position of Mordecai and Haman as rivals for the favor of the king. That the intentions of the evil Haman are frustrated and that Esther and Mordecai triumph and the Jews rejoice and vow to celebrate every year seems clear enough. Esther's path from Mordecai's house via the harem run by her protector Hegai to her crucial position in the King's household is far less clear, and the role of casting lots in determining Haman's actions is quite hazy. Toward the end, the sense of much of the action is lost. The special name of the lot, *pur*, and the holiday *Purim* are gone without trace.

Contradictions in attestation are not always easy to assess, much less resolve (cf. E10.1). Some solutions are obvious. In 9:1 оуслышаша is flat wrong for H 'hoped, expected,' and from the outset we conjectured умыслиша for the original translation; we were jubilant to find that Tn guarantees this reading for the reconstructible *pervospisok*. (On the contrary, the unfamiliar adverb or adverbial phrase вънатъщь 'in haste,' carefully written not only in QT but also in U, was "rationalized" in Tn to в тои ѵа[c], 'that moment, at once,' cf. A8.22.) The drift from correct perfective изъбити 'kill' to imperfective изъбивати to a totally con-

---

χ is the equivalent, A2.32 (6): **aasweros* yields ασυηρος. The last two letters are interpreted as Ns desinence, so the stem is shortened to ασυηρ- (*asuer-us* in the Vulgate). Josephus uses both the transcribed Hebrew name and the translated Gk equivalent (*Jewish Ant.* XI 184), εἰς τὸν υἱὸν Ἀσύηρον, ὅν Ἀρταξέρξην Ἕλληνες καλοῦσιν 'to his son *'ᵃḥašwērôš*, whom the Greeks call Artaxerxes.' The L-text regularly uses the transcribed and shortened stem, conventionally accented Ἀσυῆρος, Ἀσυήρου. (Contrast A2.32, note 38.)

trary иꙁбавити 'save' is, fortunately, documented (3:13). Some solutions are probable but nonetheless speculative. The phrase бѧшє ꙁаповѣдь '(such) was (the king's) command' in 3:2 may well have originally been бѧшє ꙁаповѣдалъ '(thus) had (the king) commanded,' but since the sentence is otherwise peculiar it may be that the variants from V and W are editorial "improvements," and the evidence of QT and Tn suggests that the oddities were indeed present in *1350. There the attested variants document arbitrary scribal intervention but permit unambiguous decisions as to the form to be ascribed to *1350. In 9:4 прєпродана and прєпродани have an unexpected prefix, but surely fit the H sense 'sold.' The first, however, was changed in some copies to a well-formed word прєпровѣдана that might mean 'preached about,' but is unknown elsewhere and manifestly inappropriate here; the changed sentence has one action affect Esther and a different action apply to her people. Such examples neatly illustrate the processes that corrupted the text.

The adjective дънѣшьнии is entirely appropriate to describe the 'inner' court of the palace complex (4 times), but post-1400 scribes, by changing a single letter, rendered an unfamiliar word comprehensible, вънѣшьнии 'outer,' but damaged the text. Tn exhibits another purposeful editorial intervention; in all 4 verses we find an exotic word, дѣнничьн-, 'belonging to the day-star' (?) that is utterly out of place. Such cases show that editors can generalize a mistaken reading, even when it garbles sentences. Consistent oddities (like сукно 'rough cloth' for 'ashes'—3 times) that are in QT, WV, and Tn must be ascribed to the *pervospisok*, but it is unreasonable to assume that the unanimity of attestation guarantees that such an egregious misunderstanding comes from the Slavic translator. Some items remain mysterious. The two words мука царицина in 7:8 stand for two H words: *to-force the-queen*. Zealous interpreters might construct a tortuous equation of raping and suffering, of infinitive and substantive, of direct object and possessive adjective; we have curbed our speculation in this and many other instances. The bare fact is that this sentence, though reasonably grammatical, does not fit its context.

The MT Esther is artfully constructed in language that abounds in repetitions, near-repetitions, and polar reversals. The Slavonic text has lost much of this careful wording by varied—but reasonably literal—translation of one and the same word or phrase (e.g., C3:15, C4:3, C5:1; more complex cases in the chapter on lexicon, e.g., L0.42, L12.15, L12.6). Precisely how much of this can be attributed to our hypothetical Greek intermediary (and its own internal history), and what has happened at the hand of scribes between the pristine Slavic translation and our faulty *pervospisok* remains conjectural.

In spite of all the unsolved puzzles, we are confident that the unsatisfactory text we can reconstruct is derived from a decent—if imperfect—translation from a Greek intermediary text that in turn reflects a reasonably competent literal translation from the standard Hebrew, the MT. Several passages indicate traditional Jewish exegesis, one verb shows a misreading of the Hebrew consonantal text (3:15), and others may be the result of similar misinterpretation (2:12, 2:20, 7:8, 9:25).

Linguistic Analysis

A0 The grammar of Esther follows the patterns of OCS with the primary modifications introduced by Rusian orthography[1] and a number of further alterations that appear in East Slavic manuscripts of the twelfth to fourteenth centuries, whether copies of older texts or new compositions. In the following sections we assume OCS as the fundamental basis of comparison, and focus on innovations and deviations from that norm.[2] The primary evidence is from Q and T.

Phonology

A1 The orthographies of Q and T indicate the normal ESl standard of the period from c1350 to c1450. Middle Common Slavic **tort* is always written *trat*; MCoS **tert* is *trět* or *tret*. (Q rather prefers рє, T рѣ). MCoS **telt* occurs only in the root **peln,* and comes out *polon* in QT (see below). The prefix **orz-* is written раꙁ- (рас-), except for the doubly Rusian form росполонъ. Word-initial **olt-* is represented only by ESl локотъ (Gp). Initial **je* is only in єдин-, єжє. There are no cases of the roots **jug-* or **jun-*. The adjectival formant -ѣн-/-ѧн- has the expected ESl shape in мраморѧнъ and сукнѧнъ.

A1.1 All of these features are fairly stable from the earliest Rusian manuscripts; it is the historical jers that are most variable. For any time after 1200 we must assume that all ESl dialects had *o/e* for strong ъ/ь and no vowel at all for weak jers. Yet the traditional orthographic habits persisted, and word-final and many internal weak jers continued to be written, while jer-letters for new *o/e* were frequently maintained fairly well. Q's conservative orthography is relatively correct in terms of the pre-1200 norms, while the scribe of T was far more innovative. Yet neither is consistent. Compare a phrase from 4:1:

Q въꙁпи въпльмь вєликъмь и горко^М
T воꙁъпи воплємь вєликомь и горєкомь
* въꙁъпи въпльмь вєликъмь и горькъмь

Q omits weak internal jers in the first and last word and the final jer is lost by the convention of superscribing word-final consonants. T's spelling is surely more indicative of pronunciation, but the weak internal ъ in the first word is correct historically, while the weak ь of the last word is written with a hypercorrect "є." Similarly, 11th-century Rusian *tъrt, tьrt,* and *tъlt* (< both MCoS **tьrt* and **tъlt*) are usually spelled etymologically in Q but with є/о in T.[3] *Tense ь* (i.e., ь before a vowel-letter) alternates with и: милостью 2:17, милостию

1 See Lunt 1974, 1988b.

2 OCS represents a series of written variants of the SouthEastern Late Common Slavic macrodialect that is presumed to have existed approximately from 800 to about 1100 in Macedonia and Bulgaria. Rusian is the (North)Eastern Late Common Slavic macrodialect that seems to have survived as late as 1150. Both developed from a stage here called Middle Common Slavic, generally familiar from the formulas posited in standard works on Slavic etymology. For more detail, see Lunt 1997.

3 Mss W, V, and G (in ch. 1–9) generally have "є/о" here. E.g., 1:6 G чьрвемъ, вервьми шолковыми, столпы, WV червемъ, верьми [!]; GWV 4:14 молчиши, 9:29 твердь, 6:10 борзо. In the newly translated ch. 10–16, G alternates between терт/торт spellings and трът.

2:15. T and Q often disagree; we follow Q. *Tense* ъ is spelled with ы, except in стръıа (2:7, T стрыıа), but строıа 2:15 (Q=T). (For тъ 'that,' see below A4.1.) The same sort of spelling can be documented from passages in Lav (1377) and other mss of this period. This kind of variation between Q and T rarely—if ever—provides real phonological information; for the most part we ignore it. See also E11.32–34.

A1.11 In OCS, excrescent jers are occasionally written in consonant clusters in borrowed stems (particularly names), and by 1350 the presence or absence of a jer in a particular stem seems to have been subject to scribal whim. Thus Саазъгаз- surely reflects older *сг that by assimilation has become [zg], cf. A2.32 (5). The fact that the stem Ахасъверос- regularly has the jer in Q and T allows us to attribute that spelling to *1350, but it tells us nothing about the pronunciation of the original Slavonic translation. We will not comment specially on jers in names.

A1.2 On the whole, **ě* is promiscuously confused with *e* in Q, but spelled more etymologically in T. All mss have a few instances of confusion of **ě* and **i*, probably a matter of the taste of individual scribes. We see no patterns that might be attributed to *1350. Initial *ě* in East Slavic develops like any other *ě* (or **jě*), so that the spellings ıадитє in 4:16, поıаꙁдити in 6:11 and ıаꙁдѧху in 8:10 are surely to be attributed to the tenacity of a South Slavic tradition. The expected native spelling ѣꙁдѧху is also found.[4] The special North Slavic Gsf, Npmf and Apmf soft desinence -ѣ where SSl had -ѧ appears three times in a single Ap phrase (a noun and two adjectives) in QT, being represented by normal Slavonic -ѧ (or -ıа, -а) in later copies, see C1:18. Ap власѧницѣ (see C4.3) is also maintained in QT, but Gs царицѣ in Q contrasts to цр҃ци in T (see C7:7). This desinence is implied for Ap of the 3rd person pronoun **jě* by є in QT (and и in WV); see C4:8.

A1.3 In the consonantism, QT write "ж" for MCoS **dj*; there are no cases of **zdj* or **zg* before front vowel.

A1.311 The words вражду 3:7 and вражьбьныи 7:6 are inappropriate in their contexts; they pose problems of etymology and spelling. The first we see as a spelling error for вражу, As of вража 'throwing dice, casting lots' or perhaps 'lot, die,' and discuss in C3:7.

A1.312 The second stands where we expect *hostile, inimical*: it implies a noun вражьба, which, however, means *sorcery, divination.*

A1.321 The root **werg *wьrg* underlies the OCS verb врѣщи врьгѫтъ 'to throw.' Its apophonic variant **worg* appears in several words connected with divination and spells—originally surely associated with casting lots—such as OCS вражєниє 'divination' (Euch), *OCS вражити 'divine, work magic, foretell,' from **worg-i+*; вража 'divination, μαντεῖον (and OPol *wroża* 'lot, divination by lot; magic, wizardry'), from **worg-j-a*. ESl copies attest native shapes such as ворожити, ворожєниє, ворожа (Ham). Cautious etymologists posit a second Late Common Slavic root **worg* 'evil, wrong' for the noun врагъ 'enemy, adversary,' frequent in OCS, where—as surely in the dialects ancestral to Slovene,

4 Though the shape *jazd-* (and the related *jaxa-*) is well represented in South Slavic, spellings with "ıа" are so common in 14th–16th century ESl texts that they cannot be taken as significant indicators of SSl origin. Initial *ě* occurs in only two roots, **ěd-* 'eat' and **ě- /*ěd-/*ězd-/*ěx-a* 'ride,' and it was therefore easy for scribes to remember that such words (particularly the latter, which has *ja-* in many SSl dialects where 'eat' has the local reflex of **ě*) should or may be spelled with "ıа."

Serbo-Croatian and Macedono-Bulgarian—it often referred to Satan, *The Enemy*, the devil. Here too belongs the abstract вражьда 'enmity.'[5] East Slavic shapes, ворогъ, ворожьда, are attested, though rare.

A1.322 Theoretically the two sets of words were distinct, and those meaning *casting of lots, divination, soothsaying, fortune-telling* were separate from those meaning *enemy, enmity, hostile.* However, Christianity frowned on soothsayers and the casting of lots was deemed pagan. For this reason, words of the first group are rather rare, usually appearing in contexts that call forth pejorative connotations. It is not surprising that the original lines between the two semantic fields were blurred or erased. Thus Old Polish *wróg* 'enemy' also meant 'lot, omen,' and sometimes specifically 'evil omen.'

A1.323 The story of Esther involves decisions made on the basis of casting lots. The H used a special term, *pur,* that is glossed at its first two appearances by the normal word *goral* (3:7, 9:24). A careful translator would keep the first and translate the second; so KJ "they cast Pur, that *is,* the lot," Origen ἔβαλεν φουρ, τουτέστιν κλήρους. A translator (or subsequent editor) unaware of the importance of the special term could eliminate it, so LXX ἔβαλεν κλήρους 'he cast lots.' Another translator (or editor) could decide that both items should be comprehensible; we conjecture that the Slavonic of 3:7 originally, or at least early, had въꙁвьрже вражѧ иже (есть) жрѣбии.

A1.331 Orthographical fluctuation between SSl жд and ESl ж (from Middle Common Slavic **dj*) in such words as между/межю, нужда/нужа and хождаше/хожаше was frequent in 11th-century Rus′. The phonetic sequence [žd] was foreign to East Slavic, but presumably it was used in this kind of word by teachers from Bulgaria and at any rate was ubiquitous in the imported model manuscripts. Scribes tended to favor the native spellings with "ж," however, and from the early 1100s to the late 1300s ж was the norm.

A1.3311 Words that originally contained a sequence *žьd*—chiefly the generalizing particle -жьдо (as in къждо or кождо, 'each one'), the verb жьда- 'to wait,' and the noun stem вражьда—in late OCS and in 12th-century Rusian came to have a new phonetic [žd]. In Rus′ from the early 12th to the late 14th century, the sequence жд on the whole represented older жьд, e.g., ждати, кождо for жьдати, къжьдо. After c1450 SSl между, хождаше, and the like reappear and even become the norm for some scribes.[6] Under these circumstances, some relatively rare words or forms seem to have confused scribes and led to odd spellings.

A1.3312 Even in the OCS codex Suprasliensis we find стражда (91.29) for expected As of the usual стража 'guard' or its rare synonym стражьба (from **storg-j-a, *storg-ьb-a,* ESl сторожа). A similar error, стражденю, is in the Rusian early 12th-century *Efr. korm.* In the 11th-century Rusian *Čudov Psalter* the Gs стражьбы of Ps. 76:5 is spelled correctly,

5 Perhaps the two meanings go back to a much older **werg worg*; however the sense 'evil' is well attested in Germanic but confined to the early Slavic nouns **worgъ* and **worgьda* (with derivatives created on Sl patterns), which may be seventh or eighth-century borrowings from Germanic (cf. Vaillant GC 4, 493).

6 The 1377 Laurentian and the Hypatian (c1425) copies of the PVL offer scarcely an example of жд for **dj*, but it is fairly common in the Radziwiłł and Academy copies, and usual in the Xlebnikov copy. In Lav, the sequence жд is in the items mentioned above, and in the rare reflexes of **zdj* or **zg+front vowel*, such as дожд 'rain (Gs),' иждену 'I will drive away' or **šьd* as in многажды 'many times.' The Academy copy has at least two hypercorrect spellings, възлож^{д}ьше (L 162.4 въꙁожьше) and торж^{д}ьство (L 16.6 торжьство).

but when it is repeated in the commentary, it comes out страждьбы. This may reflect confusion with the root **strad,* as in страдати 'to suffer,' 3pl pres OCS страждѫтъ, ESl стражуть; here ESl scribes had the choice between native ж and SSl жд. A somewhat different hypercorrection was made by the second scribe of the *Izbornik* of 1073 when he wrote враждюѭштаꙗ with the "ю" that is appropriate after SSl жд instead of the "оу" normally used after д.[7]

A1.34 The well-formed derivative adjective враж-ьд-ьн- 'hostile, inimical' is amply attested for *OCS (*SRJaXI sub* вражедный). A second adjective, враж-ьб-ьн-, though it is in the 12th-century *Efr. korm.* (*SRJaXI sub* вражебный), raises questions. The passage is describing the beliefs and practices of a group of heretics—items very likely to be repugnant to right-believing Christians. It speaks of пьрю вражьбьноую (As) between body and soul, Gk μάχην ἄσπονδον. Now, μάχη is *battle, war,* while пьрꙗ is a verbal dispute or argument, usually a reasonably orderly process before a judge or witnesses. The Gk then speaks of an 'unremitting war'; we suggest that the Sl translator has misunderstood or else purposefully changed the phrase to something like *magical dispute, sorcerer's debate.*[8]

A1.4 MCoS **tj* is regularly "щ." There are four exceptions. Three are banal, with ESl *č*: the present active participles мълүаүи, иꙁбудуүи сѧ, рекуүе. The fourth is strikingly anomalous: обрѧку, 'I will find.'

A1.41 The Middle Common Slavic present stem **obrętjǫ *obrętje-* is regularly spelled обрѧщ- in early East Slavic. We assume the possibility of a rare alternant обрѧүю обрѧүе-, but the only evidence we know is a 3p form with a different prefix: оусраүѧ (var. оусрѧщю[T]) Ham 465.18, δέχωνται 'meet.' The unequivocal обрѧку twice in Q and once in T, with the obviously secondary spelling обрѧщу in T where the last two letters are written over earlier letters that might have been ку or кю, is unique. Sreznevskij, suprisingly, included this deviant 1s in his lemma обрѣсти, although its appearance in Esther seems to be the sole evidence for such an East Slavic form.[9] Even more surprising is that Vaillant GC 3 183–4 undertakes to explain the example (whose extreme rarity he does not mention) as "confusion des alternances *t* : *č* et *k* : *č*"—without any motivation as to why this analogy should apply to only the first person singular, not to mention just why it should apply at all.[10] Only in the Southwest area can we be sure of a development of **tj* to a palatal *ḱ* that is written "k" in the pre-Slovene Freising texts (*chokú *xotjǫ* 'I want') and, from the earliest

7 Older, chiefly Glagolitic, OCS writes мєждю, but the later tradition that shaped Rusian orthography has мєждоу. Rusian scribes preferred мєжю but allowed мєждю (1056, 1076, Usp.) beside мєждѫ, мєждоу (1073). This verb should in theory be *враждовати. In any case, the participial stem is correctly spelled вражьдоуꙗ *Usp* 184d25. The jer is absent in another Rus′ ms of similar age, враждоуꙗи (*Lěstvica*, RGB Rum. 198 83a3 but present in the work of a scribe a generation or so later, Rum. 199 72a4 вражьдоуꙗи).

8 Another problem is Monomax's statement to Oleg, аꙁъ нѣсмь ти ворожбитъ ни мєстьникъ (PSRL 1.254.20), usually interpreted as 'I'm not your *enemy* or avenger.' Yet when it reappears after 1350, and in modern dialects, ворожбит means only 'sorcerer, shaman, soothsayer,' clearly related to ворожба, 'divination, fortune-telling' (not attested before 1350). It is possible that in 12th-century Rus′ it had a specialized meaning in such contexts, "agent alloted by fate to deliver retribution, nemesis"; a meaning close to, but distinct from, *OCS мьстьникъ or мьститель.

9 Vostokov, in his 1858 dictionary, VI:2 col 21, cites it for Est 7:3 and also Ruth 2:2 from a copy made for the Rumjancev Museum from an unspecified 16th-century Kirillobelozerskij ms, probably our ms 5. Sreznevskij, who took over most of Vostokov's information, did not include these citations (though Mikl did); we assume he had reason to omit them.

10 Valentin Kiparsky gives a similar account, 1967 202.

SC texts (late 12th century), is often spelled simply "к."[11] Thus a document of 1254 (Stanojević 27) has хок8 in one copy and more standard хоцп8 in another for OCS хоштѫ, which in Rusian standard was хоцпю, with an infrequent variant хоץю.

A1.42 In the light of recent information on Pskov dialects, it is possible that **tj* developed to **ḱ* also in northwestern Rus′ (cf. Nikolaev 1988, Zaliznjak 1991, Krys'ko 38–9 and fn. 18); if this is so, perhaps we may attribute the examples of обрѧку to a scribe from that area who wrote *1370 or *1350.

A1.5 There are a few special cases:

A1.51 The sequence *rz* in the root *bъrz* becomes *rdz* in much of Polish and Belarusian, and the cluster may then be reshaped to *rzd*. In T the spelling борꙁ is maintained in all instances, but in Q we find the adverb бърꙁо twice and the verbal stem оубърꙁи- three times, but the adjective бърꙁдыхъ twice.[12] This detail cannot be ascribed to *1370, but only to Q (and individual later copies).

A1.52 The old root **xot/*xъt* appears in the stem **oxot-* 'desire' in the unusual shape *-xvot-*; these spellings are found in QTWV, and we are inclined to ascribe them to *1350. This feature is known only from northern Ukrainian and adjacent Belarusian regions, and therefore places the *pervospisok* in the West. Its presence in Esther tells nothing about the origin of the Slavic translation, however. See L13.4.

A1.53 The appearance of "и" instead of etymological "ѣ" is of importance in 2:9, where we conjecture that in *1350 (or an ancestor) прѣстрои ю 'set her up in alternate circumstances' is to be read for the пристрою of extant copies. A second example is 4:17, where QTSGWV have приде for the expected прѣиде 'crossed.' In T there is confusion of ѣ and и in other instances; 4:1, also рѣץѣ 1:12, възлюбленѣк-. In 3:13 both Q and T have погоньцѣ, see comm.

A1.54 The root **peln* is regularly плѣн/плен in Rusian manuscripts, but more often than other similar formulas it appears in East Slavic form with polnoglasie. Thus in QT it is exclusively *polon* (although with a garbling in the form *полонъмь 2:6 possibly in *1370). The noun росполонъ 3:13 is unique to this text. It provides the only *ro-* or North Slavic form for ComSlav **ort-* (unmarked or "circumflex") in the text; the many instances of the prefix **orz* are all spelled раꙁ/рас as is normal from the beginning of East Slavic literacy. The corresponding verb is attested in more conventional SSl shape, расплѣни-, see L18.12–.23. Just why **peln* appears more frequently in marked East Slavic phonological shape than other roots is a puzzle; we may conjecture that the spelling полон had something to do with meaning. In any case, it cannot be taken as proof that a text in which it occurs was translated in Rus′.[13] It is found not only in Esther in QT, but in T it is also in

[11] The oldest writ (August, 1189, Stanojević 2) has, for example хоке for OCS хоштѧ, ESl хоץа (not attested, so far as we know), and тис8ка for OCS тысѫшта or тысѧшта, ESl тысѧץа.

[12] SSUM I 465 cites боръздо from a 15th-century document.

[13] One need not go beyond the evidence Srez provides sub полон- to demonstrate that scribes in Rus′ felt free to modify the плѣн- spellings in their models, though further examples are to be found in manuscript after manuscript. It is difficult to understand why Istrin and Meščerskij, among others, pay no attention to the facts and maintain that the only source of полон- spellings has to be the original translator, who therefore must have been an East Slav. Istrin's own notes, for example, show that Ham 279.12 has плѣненомъ in the oldest ms, but полоненомъ in the younger, more markedly Rusian, mss (more examples in Istrin 1922 327, fn.).

Joshua 8:2 (Lebedev 13; cf. Srez sub полонъ).[14] In the Izbornik of 1073 the root *plěn* occurs 32 times: it is spelled плѣн 15 times, in Rus′ hybrid style плєн once, and полон 8 times. О полонѣ is in the oldest copy (13th century) of the Закон судный людем, a text translated very early into OCS, see SJS sub плѣнъ. A rarer shape, reminiscent of Polish, is плониша, in the 11th-century Sinai Paterikon, 80.12 (cf. Srez s.v.).[15] Moreover, this root is subject to hypercorrect Slavonicization and written план-, e.g., планѥниє in what may be the oldest ESl manuscript (Sermons of Gregory Nazianzus, RNB Q.п.I.16; cf. Srez s.v.) and the Čudov Psalter (GIM, Čud. 7).[16]

A1.6 The word изд̧рѧднѣє, 3:8, with inserted *d*, may possibly be an archaism, but it could be simply a conscious archaization on the part of scribes. Some local Slavic dialects still automatically require [zdr], while others require [zr]; how to write individual words is a matter of convention. Even in OCS the [d] was omitted at least once, изърасти, Supr 388.11.[17]

A2 Excursus on the Spelling of Names

A2.1 Esther contains sixty proper names, fifty-six of which go back to the MT, while four are glosses giving the normal names of the months (cf. Wutz 1915, esp. 1036ff.).[18]

A2.2 The terms *Jew, Jewish, Judaean,* and *Babylonian,* appear in the form normal in OCS: июдѣи, июдѣискыи (жидовьскыи), июдинъ, вавулоньскыи. *Jerusalem* has lost the first letter: ерс̄лма Gs.[19] The name of the Babylonian king Nebuchadnezzar,

[14] Even in ms W, a relatively late copy (c1500) with SSl-influenced orthography, the passage reads полонь жє и скота єѧ да плєниши собѣ, καὶ τὴν προνομὴν τῶν κτηνῶν προνομεύσεις σεαυτῷ, 'and you shall take spoil of the cattle for yourself' (the MT is somewhat different). Ms W also has полона in Judges 8:25.

[15] The root is normally плѣн- in this ms, too, and no полон- is found. Examples of spelled ТлоТ for **tolt* are ꙁлотьник- 9x 'gold-piece' (and ꙁолотьник- 5x) beside normal ꙁлат- and the infinitive повлоѹи 'drag, pull' 57v18 (but normal ниꙁьвлѣщи 'drag down' 57v14), cf. Dumitrescu.

[16] Ms W has бѧху полонєни in 1 Ki 30:4, but in the next verse бѣша планєни (should be fem. dual). Ham 481.14 has планникъ, планнѣкъ as variants of плѣнникъ. In the first redaction of the Life of Aleksander, планеника (As) 'captive' appears; the second redaction has further distorted it to платежьника or платоникъ (Istrin 1897, App., 15, 138).

[17] Examples of morphophonemic *z-r* without inserted *d* are rare in early mss, but for the 14th century, spelled "ꙁр" is commonplace. The 12th-century Uspenskij sbornik has иꙁдрѧдьнѣє, иꙁдраꙗ, and even иꙁдростова 'from Rostov,' indicating that *d*- insertion was an active process in Rus′. (Srez reports иꙁрѧднѣє from the 11th-century Pandekty; in fact the ms has -ꙁдѧ- with a small superscript р added by the scribe.) In the 14th century, Lav (1377) has иꙁ раꙗ, иꙁрѧди, иꙁ Руси, while Ham has иꙁрѧднии. Yet for some 14th-century East Slavic scribes the ꙁдр-spelling may well have been considered desirable. (Tvorogov 1975 61 has посла август иꙁд-Рима from the early 15th-century *Troickij Chronograph,* RGB TSL 728.)

[18] Evseev (followed by Meščerskij and Alekseev) insisted that the shape of the names showed direct dependence on the Hebrew, while Sobolevskij maintained that the Slavonic spellings demonstrated Greek mediation. The discussion in Evseev 1898 (esp. 341–42) and Sobolevskij 1903, 435–36, is incomplete (and not improved by the notes of Meščerskij 1956a 209 or Alekseev 1987a 5–6), but on the whole Evseev was wrong and Sobolevskij right. Evseev failed to distinguish the "translation" of names that is characteristic of LXX and L (chiefly *'aḥašweroš, wašti,* and *šušan* become Ἀρταξέρξης, Ἀστιν, and Σοῦσα or Σοῦσοι) from transcription (reproduction of the sounds in terms of a different spelling system, Αχασβερος, Ουαστι, Ουασθι or *Βαστι, *Σουσαν), see below. *Jerusalem* and *Moscow* are "translations"; *Yerušalaim* and *Moskva* are transcriptions (the latter being also a transliteration).

[19] The spelling implies initial *jer-*, for normal *i(j)er-*, with the sort of loss of non-Slavic initial *i* before vowel that occurs in other names. For example, the river Jordan Ἰορδάνης, иордан-, becomes иєрдан- and then both ордан- and єрдан-, see SJS. In the name of the holy city, however, the initial и remains not only in canonical OCS but also in most later writings. It was usually abbreviated, им- (in Glagolitic often with a ligature, "l" over

Навъходъносоръ, shows vowels that surely reflect a Slavic adaptation of the normal Greek spelling, Ναβουχοδονοσορ, of other texts.[20]

A2.3 For the rest, we find that, if we start from MT forms, the names are rendered generally in the spellings expected for transcription of the Hebrew written forms in Greek, and then further transcription into Slavonic.[21] Of course it is to be expected that unfamiliar names will be distorted somewhat in the course of any manuscript tradition,[22] and indeed the complications here are of the sort known from the idiosyncratic treatment of personal and geographic names in LXX, for example in Joshua.

A2.31 Transcription of vowels is not easily predictable, even with well-known names whose vocalism is well established; in the case of unusual or unique names it is probable that variant traditions existed.[23] Thus H *'estēr* 'Esther' should have η in the second syllable, and apparently this spelling is maintained in the Greek tradition; the є of some Slavic examples suggests, however, that there was variation.[24] The diphthong [ai] is usually reflected as "аи" (Мардъхаи, Арисаи, Ваиѕаса), implying Gk "αϊ"; "ѣ" also occurs (мадѣискыхъ), perhaps suggesting Gk "αι."

A2.311 The a/o variation in Аманъ/Амонъ and Мардахаи/Мардохаи which occurs apparently in all the manuscripts (with further variants, especially Мардъхаи in Q) must be regarded as an internal Slavic problem. It should be noted that Амонъ is in the earliest

"m"). We do not know when spellings without и- occur, but they are normal in the 1377 copy of the Chronicle (9x єр- vs. 4x иєр-), a manuscript slightly older than TQ. The usage is obscured by haplography, e.g., in the Mstislav Gospel, of 1117, where "and Jerusalem" єр°слма 73c9, 164a15, 174b7, єрȣсалима 201b9, all Luke 6:17 but in a variant of the same verse "and from Jerusalem" ї отъ иєр°слма 73c25, see also n. 34 below.

[20] It shows normal [s] as expected for the H emphatic sibilant "ṣ" (which we transliterate with "c," see below). Evseev overlooked this example when he remarked (1898 341) that no possible "ṣ" is found in names in Esther.

[21] The details of the complex problems of the vowels in these names are glossed over here because the many variables seem on the whole irrelevant to our discussion.

[22] Many examples could be cited from the five chief witnesses to the PVL. Thus from Greek Αιολιδα expected *єолидоу appears as салиду (Lav), солидоу (Hyp), and солиуду (Radz). From local traditions норова (Lav 11.11), морома (Hyp, probably correct), нерома (Radz, Akad), and even морава in the lost Troickij copy. From other Slavic, хорутане (Lav 6.6), хутанѣ (Hyp), хобутане (Xleb), for expected *Корутанє. A Greek tradition yields to local prejudices when амазоне (Lav 16.2) becomes мазонѧне in Akad. From 15th-century copies to 1512, in the *Third Capture of Jerusalem* the Ammonites shift from амонє to камонє to команє and finally куманє; if we had only the 1512 copy, we might argue that the Cumans existed in the Holy Land in the first century CE. (Indeed, this is implied in the index, PSRL 22/1 553, where the mythical Куманє appear in a single entry with the real Cumans.)

[23] The Greek texts of Esther have an extraordinary variation in the names that surely demonstrates lack of unity in the early Semitic texts and several divergent developments within the Greek tradition. The remarkable series of transformations of these names in the LXX tradition is recorded in Hanhart's apparatus; for a more general summary of the unpredictable variation in other traditions, see Moore 1971 pp. XLII–XLIII.

[24] The name Есфирь, originally Есѳирь, is rare outside this book. In the list of canonical books in the *Изборник* of 1073, it is in a passage that is repeated, appearing first as ѥсѳєръ, then ѥсѳиρ́ (252d3, 11). In John the Exarch's translation of John of Damascus's list, the two books of Ezdras (counted as one) are joined with Esther, which is rendered as an adjective: тажє ѥѕдръı пьрвъıѩ и вторъıѩ єдинъı книгъı сълагаемъı съ есфирьскъıми, Sadnik 3.64. (Earlier in the list, reference is made to 'poetic,' стихирьскъıѧ, books—Job, the Psalter, etc.; the 16th-century scribe who copied this text into the VMČ, Dec. 1–5, 253, altered this word to єсфер'скыѧ, thereby confusing the text badly.) In Hamartolos 189.23 the name is ѥстира. In copies of Esther from the 15th–16th century, several combinations of ѳ/ф/т and є/и seem to occur, but the stem is usually soft, -рь. (The editor of Tn wrote Астиръ instead of Васти in 1:9 and 1:11, and no name at all in 1:12; did he really have a single queen in mind?)

copy of Hamartolos (c1300); there may be some confusion with the Αμων of Matthew 1:10, a text known to scribes because it is in the lectionary.[25]

A2.32 For consonants, six general rules apply: (1) Hebrew sibilants 'samekh,' 'shin,' 'śin' (the two last always spelled in manuscripts with undifferentiated ש), and 'tsade' all come out 'sigma' and therefore Cyrillic "с": H *meres, zereš* > μερες, *ζερες[26] > Мересъ, Зересь.

(2) H 'beth,' 'daleth' and 'gimel' ב ד ג > β δ γ > в д г, so Hebrew [b] is normally "в" [v]: Вигъфану, Виꙁъсану.

(3) H 'pe,' 'tav,' 'kaph' פ ת כ, normally are rendered by φ θ χ, but sometimes the plain stops π τ κ appear. Usage obviously differed in time and space; the traditional Hebrew pronounciation does not provide a reliable guide.[27] The φ/π and χ/κ ordinarily are reproduced in Slavonic, e.g., H *dalfon (*spelled *dlpwn)* *δαλφον Далфанъ; Есфирь; *kuš* Χους, Хусъ.[28] The theta was surely also spelled ѳ, but within Slavic this sometimes was replaced by т, or, in the East Slavic tradition, by ф, e.g., Θωμᾶς 'Thomas' is Тома in OCS Glagolitic texts, but Ѳома in Sav, eventually Фома in Rus′.[29] The sound [f] was variously pronounced, often being replaced by [v][30] or (particularly in Ukrainian and Belarusian areas) [xv] or [xf];[31] the phonetic variants give rise to spelling variants. Hence Порафа, Афахъ, Сефаръ, Тевефъ; Амдафинъ and Амдавинъ; Вигъхвана; Зъвихфаръ.[32] Unexpectedly [s] appears in the names of four of Haman's sons (Аридаса, Аспасъ, Ваиꙁаса, and Парсандаᶜ [which has further problems]), and of one eunuch, Виꙁъсану.[33]

[25] This name further brings up the question of names where the traditional Greek form differs from the usual Hebrew. Here we expect Αμως, and indeed it occurs in important old manuscripts, although not those that underlay the Slavic translations.

[26] The printed *Complutensian Polyglot Bible* (1514–17) provides a number of Greek spellings that seem to reflect pronunciations close to the MT. In these examples, μερες is in *Compl.*, while Josephus has an accusative form Ζαρασαν which demonstrates the consonantal structure but with typically deviating vocalism. Cf. Vulgate *Zares*.

[27] These three letters could represent, in different phonetic environments and under certain morphophonemic conditions, stops [p t k], geminate stops [pp tt kk], or spirants [f θ x]. The Greek alphabet provided letters that could represent these sounds. The parallel alternations of voiced stop [b d g] and spirant [v δ γ] could not be expressed by the unmodified Greek alphabet, a fact that resulted in rule 2.

[28] Χους 'Ethiopia' is the same as the name of one of Ham's sons, Cush (LXX Χους Gen 10:6–8), compare Χουσια, defined in Hesychios as 'Ethiopian' in psalm 7:1, where the Bologne Psalter has Хоусиꙗ.

[29] In Esther 1:14 is a personal name *Taršiš,* which in most copies of our text is Тирисъ, but Тарсисъ in Tn. The same Hebrew form, but as the name of a precious stone, occurs in the Song of Songs 5:14, LXX Θαρσις, Slavonic Тарсисъ (Alekseev 1983, 254) in the older translation but Фарсиса Gs in the Preslav revision for the exegetical translation (see Alekseev 1981, 121); cf. also SJS sub таръс-. For Esther, we assume Θαρσις (*Compl.*) > Тарсисъ, and then distortion to *Тирсисъ > Тирисъ. This in no way precludes the possibility that the original translation had Ѳарсисъ, since ѳ can become т within Slavic traditions, particularly in the early period. The same H and LXX name in Gen 10:4 (Θαρσος in Josephus) has become Фарсисъ (often Афарсисъ) in most surviving mss, but Атарсисъ in the Archive Chronograph and Тарси in another copy (Mixajlov).

[30] Perhaps this is indicated in Gen 46:11, H *qht* > LXX κααθ > каѡѳъ, var. каавъ (Mixajlov).

[31] Thus the Ostrih Bible occasionally has hypercorrect spellings even for fairly familiar words, e.g., волфованїємъ, волфы for волхв-, 2 Chron 33:6. In the *Secretum Secretorum,* фворы (var. хворы) occurs (Speranskij 1908 176.11).

[32] For the location of the names and more details, see the Index of Names at the end of the lexicon.

M56a 209 notes that for *tav* we find five variants, т, ф, с, хв, хф; "Это объяснимо особенностями живого еврейского произношения того времени." This statement is meaningless, first because it is unclear what period he is referring to, and second because the five different variants cannot all be subsumed under a single heading.

[33] This may represent misreading of Θ as C, a mistake that could occur in Cyrillic *ustav* or, if we assume that part of the transmission of our hypothetical Greek Esther was in uncial copies, by confusion of theta and a

(4) Consonantal 'yod' and 'waw' > ι and ου/υ/β: *ya'ir* > ιαιρ > иаиръ;[34] *wašti* > ουασθι/ουαστι/*βαστι > Васти.[35]

(5) Hebrew 'aleph,' 'ayin' and 'he' א ע ה [' ' h] are normally lost: *haman* > αμαν > Аманъ,[36] *ha'agagi* 'the Agagite' > *ααγαγι > аагаги; *ša'ašgaz* > *σαασγαζ > саасгаꙁ-.

(6) Hebrew 'teth,' 'qof,' and 'cheth' ט ק ח [ṭ q ḥ] > τ κ χ > т к х: *qiš* > Κις (with a poss. adj. Κισαιος) > *Кисъ, кисовъ;[37] *'aḥašweroš* > Αχασβερος > Ахасъверосъ.[38]

A2.33 An effect of rules 1 and 2 is that no ш or б is expected in Hebrew names (or other words) that have come into Slavonic via Greek.[39] Tn has the expected name Вихванъ in 2:21, but other copies have бихванъ (var бѣхванъ, бихфанъ), a fact that has aroused comment. This same eunuch appears in 6:2 under the name вигъхвана (accusative). Part of the difficulty goes back to Hebrew, for בגתן [bigtan] of 2:21 becomes בגתנא [bigtana'] in 6:2, so we may expect *βιγθαν and *βιγθανα—with uncertainty about a possible case ending. This variable name has been conflated with another, בגתא [bigta'] of 1:10, Ds Вигъфану (< *Виг‍ѳан- < *βιγθα[ν]). For the isolated б in бихванъ, then, it is certain that it was a careless post-*1350 scribe who replaced original Cyrillic "В" with "Б."[40]

'lunate' sigma. Cf. 4 Ki 24:24 H *trpym* 'idols,' LXX θεραφειν,var. σεραφειμ; G, W серафими, but OB ѳераѳимъ. There are confusions within the Slavic tradition, however, e.g. Русь for Руѳ in a 17th-century "South-Russian" Chronograph (Popov 1866 285), or a variant for Θαμαρ in Gen 38:26 Самаръ, for Фамаръ or Ѳамаръ (Mixajlov). In Josh 13:6, *mśrpt mym* (*maśrefot mayim*) > μασερεφωθ μαιμ > масрефоѳъ маима (OB), but масерефосъ маима (W). The well-known Ashkenazic [s] for ת is not definitely unique; it might well have been shared with the pronunciation of Greek-speaking Balkan Jews. Moreover, there is no way to date just when this pronunciation arrived in Eastern Europe. Although Ashkenazic and Sephardic pronunciation has been studied in some depth, little is known about the traditions of pre-Sephardic Jews in the Balkans and in Byzantium. In any case, assuming weak *tav* ת as the direct source of Sl [s] fails to explain the other variants, т, ѳ, ф, хв, and хф.

34 The initial OCS и before vowel was phonologically unusual and easily lost. The NT Jairus, OCS Иаиръ, became аиръ in Assem (see SJS) just as *иаировъ in Esther became аировъ. (Indeed, a different Ιαιρος/Ιαρος has a fluctuating name in Slavonic translation; for example in Sinai 39, fol. 46v, it is ιєорос, and a related copy, RNB Muz 6, ιєрєос; see Taube 1988.) Jechonia Ιεχονια Iехониꙗ first modified the second syllable, producing Иохониꙗ, and then even in OCS Охониꙗ (Sav, Mt 1:12). As a reaction, the initial *i* frequently is "restored" where it does not belong, e.g., OCS иеꙁекиꙗ (Sav, As; also Mst, Lav 199.2), beside expected еꙁекиꙗ.

35 By Greek phonetic rules, [sθ] would ordinarily become [st], as well-known fluctuations in spelling throughout medieval Greek manuscripts demonstrate.

36 In cases of direct translation, H [h] may result in "г," as it is consistently in Vil. 262; this sort of spelling may be carried over into other texts, e.g., ms 22 (Tix 704), Гаманъ, Агаманъ, and in the *Third Capture of Jerusalem* Годоуи for *hdw* 'India.'

37 The adjective кисовъ stands for undeclined Κις functioning as a genitive in Ham, сн҃а кисова 125.8, and also in the Ostrih Bible, ослѧта кисова 1 Ki 9:5, which probably goes back to a much older translation.

38 Names in LXX often remain with a final consonant not in accord with normal Greek morphology, but sometimes an appropriate declensional ending is added. In the 14th-century Jewish translation *Graecus Venetus*, this name becomes Αχασβερωσος, Dan 9:1. The excrescent jer in Ахасъверосъ has no phonological significance, cf. A1.11. See also C10:1. For a different Gk pronunciation of this name and its written forms, see p. 139, fn 3.

39 In post-1450 mss., examples with ш and б begin to appear as glosses, surely added by scribes with some knowledge of Hebrew.

40 Such confusion is found in the common name Abraham in Ham (Абрама, Абрамлѧ 94.13, but normal Аврам- elsewhere, even on the same page), in the Academy copy of the PVL Британию (Вротанию Lav, Вританию Rad, Hyp, Xleb), and occasionally even in normal Slavic words (e.g., белми in the Paremejnik of 1271). Replacements of в by б are particularly easy in unfamiliar names, but they may also occur in straightforward Sl sentences and cause serious textual corruption. Thus a very poor copy of a sermon by Cyril of Alexandria has біеми бо домми бѧхꙋ 'for the houses were (being) beaten' (?); a better copy has биеми водими

A2.331 The complete absence of ш in any of the names in Esther unquestionably demonstrates Greek mediation, *pace* Evseev, Meščerskij, and Alekseev.[41] The reappearance of 'lost' names in forms like Тереш (in 2:21) or Куш (for Хоусъ) in 15th-century manuscripts signals intervention by someone who knew at least a little Hebrew.[42]

A2.34 Where LXX has Περσῶν καὶ Μήδων, 'of the Persians and Medes,' the Slavonic Esther usually has фарисѣискыи и мадѣискыи. Here we must assume first that our hypothetical Greek did not use the normal "translations" of these names, but transcribed them (by rule 3). The Persians may well have become Φαρσι, cf. Εθι, Φερεζι in LXX 2 Ezra 9:1. This presumably gave rise to a Slavic adjective фарсиискъ, although it is attested only in a small minority of cases: Tn provides some examples; S has фарсїистѣи 1:3, фарсїискы[x] 10:2 (ms 24, according to Kopanev, p. 9, has ѳарсииских 10:2) along with фарсєискыѧ in S 1:18;[43] from such a form to фариискыѩ T 1:18 or the familiar but incongruous фарисѣиск- is no great distance.[44] As for the Medes, the usual Greek has Μηδ-, with corresponding Slavic Мид-. However there are cases (apart from the μαδαιοι of the [possibly Jewish] Greek *Graecus Venetus*) with the vowel *a*, e.g., Gen 10:2 LXX Μαδαι, yields Мадаи,[45] or the Chronicle of Malalas, Bk 6, въ Мадїамли странѣ ἐν τῇ Μήδων χώρᾳ, Istrin 1911 39: cf. the variants to 1:18 and 10:2.[46] Therefore we may conjecture a Gp Μαδαιων, which would easily yield an adjectival *Мадѣискыи.

бѧхоу, lit. 'beaten, they were (being) led,' i.e., as they were led (off to captivity, the Jews of Jerusalem) were (constantly) beaten (Istrin 1893, App. 348, with note 2, p. 356). This is surely a matter of visual confusion because of the similarity of the two Cyrillic letters.

Sobolevskij's comparison (1903 436, n.) with the unique OCS form рабби (Zogr Mk 14:45) instead of normal равви is out of place, since it involves another complex of problems (that do not occur in Esther), viz. the possible phonetic [b] in Greek words spelled with ββ or [mb] spelled μβ. Examples of the latter are ємболъ for ἐμβόλων in Malalas, Istrin 1913 22, and самбоука (самъбукы, самъбукыинъ) for σαμβυκᾶς in all old versions of Dan 3:5, 7. The prophet Habbakuk, Gk both Ἀββακούμ and Ἀμβακούμ, is normally Амбакоумъ, from the Glagolitic OCS PsSin (Амбакоумма, 2/N fol 18.1, Tarnanidis 88, 266) on, but see SJS for early variants. The fact that this oldest example has -мм- at the end of the stem illustrates the arbitrariness of the spelling of many names. Another source of -μβ- in Gk is epenthesis, e.g., Zimri (*zmry*), king of Israel (3 Ki 16), is consistently Ζαμβρι in LXX, whence ʒамбрїи in GSW; OB corrects it to Замъврїи.

41 It is deplorable that Meščerskij states in a textbook that the forms Ахашверошъ and Шушанъ градъ appear in Esther (1978b 30). Nowhere in his earlier writings does he hint at even a single instance of such spellings. For the name Ахашворос-, Ахасворош- (along with Гаман-, Гоман-, Агаман-) in Tn, see Appendix III.

42 Problems of transcribing Hebrew in non-biblical texts and in various regions and periods after 1400 are not relevant to this particular translation of Esther. Alekseev 1987 6 confuses a number of different questions without saying anything helpful. In particular, distinctions possible by specifying שׂ versus שׁ, *ś* vs. *š*, are not normally marked; scribes use the ambiguous ש, which provides no phonetic information whatsoever. Arxipov misunderstands the questions in similar ways; he ignores what we have written on these topics (AT 1984, LT 1988).

43 Cf. also ц҃рвъ . . . фарьсѣиискихъ in 10:2 in ms 22 and фарсиистѣи in the Esther passage in the Chronograph of 1512 (*PSRL* 22/1 165).

44 Indeed, if we start with *Φαρσων and a hypothetical *Фарсьскыи, the conflicting attested forms are within the limits of the kind of wild fluctuation that can be documented for many names of persons and places (e.g., Tn 1:16 Моу[р]доуха, for Моумоуханъ).

45 In echoes of this passage stating that the Medes are descendants of Madai, we find a more usual form in Izb 1073, 138d, мадаи отъ нєгожє мидѹ (!), and in Ham 131.7, соущи ѿ Мадаиѩ Мидѧнє.

46 Some of this variation is doubtless because scribes tended to substitute a known name for an unknown one, thus mixing up names of different places: *Midian*, Gen 25:2, 4, Exod 2:15,16 becomes Μαδιαμ Мадиамъ; scribes doubtless were completely familiar with the зємлѩ мадиамьска of Canticle 3 (Habakkuk 3:7, cf. SJS) without having the slightest idea whether it had anything to do with Esther or not.

A2.35 Some corrupt forms imply several stages of distortion. Thus H *mehuman* > *μεουμαν > Ds *мєуманови > (рєчє) ємууманови. In T, the letter-sequence оу marks the beginning of a word, so the spelling ємуоуманови shows that the scribe envisioned єму Оуманови. Tn's рє[ү] Моуханови creates a different name (more like the Мумуханъ of vv. 14, 16, 21). Longer names are particularly subject to change, e.g. H *ḥarbonah* (7:9) > *χαρβουνα(ν) > харвуна but *ḥarbona*' (1:10) > dative *χαρβονανῳ > variants харвунанови, харнунановѣ > нарнунановѣ. For other examples, see the table below.

A2.351 An unexpected stem-final *n* may well be, as Sobolevskij pointed out (1903 435–6), a trace of a Greek accusative desinence, or perhaps a Greek addition to keep the stem from ending in a vowel.[47] Hence the datives Виꙁъсану, Ваавахфану of 1:10 and the nominative Адамафана of 1:14 (H *bizta,*' *wa-'avagta*' [see below], '*admata*'). With further misunderstanding, for expected *Аѳах-, from probable Ἀθαχ (*Compl.*) from *hatax*, we have Афахъ, Афанъ Ns, Афанъ As (thus no 'animate' desinence), and Афахови, Афану Ds.[48] Cf. Харнунанови above.

A2.36 The H copulative *waw* was interpreted as the first syllable of a name in three instances.[49] Two are in the list of the seven eunuchs in 1:10, where the names are unique and exotic. It is understandable that the initial *wa-* of the fourth item could be taken as part of a foreign name rather than a rather oddly-placed 'and.' That the seventh item should be perceived as lacking a connective is somewhat stranger. The third case involved the second of two eunuchs who appear in 2:21 and 6:2; the fact that the names should be the same in both verses has been all but erased by the copyists. It is possible that some distortion occurred during the Greek history of the text. In any case, the attested shapes are unpredictable.

H *wa-'abagta*' > *βααβαγθα(ν) > *ваавагѳан- > Ds ваавахфану 1:10
H *we-xarkas* > *βαχαρκας > Ds *вахаркасу > варкохасу 1:10
H *wa-tereš* > *βαθερες > *ваѳєрєсъ > Вафєсъ 2:21, but As *ваѳєрєса > Вавєроса 6:2.[50] This sort of misunderstanding is demonstrable from many translated texts.[51]

47 Thus in a 16th-century glossary, we find земла . . . въ июдехъ жє адаманъ (Kovtun 1975 265), surely reproducing the H word 'soil' '*dmh* ('*adama*) from a Greek source.

48 On the evidence of later manuscripts (WV), the stem Афанъ appeared to be replacing the more correct Афах-. The same substitution of "n" for "k" in this name occurs in the Syriac text of 4:5.

49 With different vocalism before labial consonant, *waw* in Ex. 6:19 'and Mushi' *u-muši* > LXX καὶ Ομουσει > OB и Омꙋси. On the other hand, in 2 Ki 17:27, 'and Shobi,' H *wšby* > Ουεσβει, but the incorrect initial vowel has been changed to 'and' in Sl, и єсвѣ W, и єсви OB. Sobolevskij knew that initial ва- came from Hebrew (1903 435) and took it for granted that it accounted for the hypothetical Greek shape. Meščerskij, on the other hand, mistakenly believed that it proved direct translation into Slavonic, 1956a 209, fn. 2.

50 The context specifies two individuals, and 2:21 has и вафєсъ in QTGWV. In 6:2 the expected *и Ѳєрєса appears as и авєро[с] in WV, and и авєрєсъ in G and 7. See also C6:2.

51 In the Izbornik of 1073 in the account of the division of the earth among the sons of Noah, some conjunctions and prepositions are included in the names, as Franklin 1982 8–9 points out, for they were unrecognized by the Bulgarian translator of this passage from a Greek work attributed to Anastasius of Sinai. Thus Anastasius: καὶ βιζακηνοι 138c21, ἀφ'οὗ Ασταβαροι 138d8, ἀφ'οὗ Εσεβεχθενοι 138d10, Αρμενοι 138d10, Βαστρανοι 'and the Bizakeni; from whom [are descended] the Astabari; from whom the Esebechtheni; Armenians; Bastrani.' 1073: кєвиꙁакину афуаставару афусєвєхфину рамєнє вавъстрану. (Note that expected армєни has been "Slavonicized" by the East Slavic scribe to рам-). Further copying gave rise to new variants (see Franklin); the Armenians even became Romans, римлꙗнє! Gk prepositions may become part of a Sl name: Ham 177.15 (and PVL 97.75) render ἐν Δαν, from 3 Ki 12:10, as въ єнданѣ. LXX 1 Ki 1:1 ἐξ Αρμαθαιμ σιφα is єксармафєма сифьскаго in W, whereas the editors of OB added a preposition, ѿ єꙁармаѳєма сиѳъскаго.

The table below gives sample names, with the rules which have applied; a plus (+) indicates further complications. The full material is given in the list of names in the lexicon.

Hebrew	Greek	Expected Slavonic	Actual Slavonic	Rules
'aḥašweroš	Αχασβεροσος	Ахасвєросъ	Ахасвєросъ	1, 2, 6
'ester	Εσθηρ	Есѳирь	Есфирь	1, 3, 5
wašti	*βασθι	*Васѳи	Васти	1, 3, 4
mehuman	*μεουμαν	*Мєуманови Ds	р[ѵ]є ємоуоуманови	5+
		*рєѵє Мєуманови	?єму Оуманови	
zētar	*ζηθαρ	*ꙁиѳар-	ꙁъвихфару Ds	3+
taršiš	θαρσις	тарсисъ	Тирисъ (var.)	1, 3+
ḥarbona	*χαρβουνα(ν)	харвуна	харвуна 7:9	
			харвуванovѣ 1:10	
		*харвунанови Ds	харнунановѣ	2, 6+
			нарнунановѣ	
hatak	αθαχ	афахъ	афахъ	3, 5
			афанъ	+
wa-'abagta'	*βααβαγθα(ν)	*ваавагѳан-	ваавахфану Ds 1:10	2, 3, 5+
we-karkas	*βαχαρκας	*вахаркасу Ds	варкохасу 1:10	3, 4+
wa-tereš	*βαθερες	*ваѳєрєсъ	Вафєсъ 2:21	1,3+
		*ваѳєрєса As	Вавєроса 6:2	

A3 Nouns

A3.1 The substantives in Esther illustrate neutral standard Slavonic morphology, with two exceptions.

A3.11 Particularly striking is the innovative genitive plural desinence in дн҃овъ in 1:5 in both of the oldest witnesses, beside дн҃ии, which is normal for post-OCS Slavonic, in three other verses. This agreement in innovation is probably to be ascribed to the immediate common ancestor of Q and T, *1370. The spelling with "o" is unexpected, but surely represents the desinence attested in 1377; сихъ дневъ, in a passage of Monomax's, Lav 241.6.[52] The Gp цр҃евъ of 10:2, on the other hand, could have arisen in any type of Slavonic after c1100.

A3.12 Otherwise in the anomalous declension, the Gs of дєнь is дни, while дщи forms дщєрє. It is no surprise that мати has матєрє in Q and матєри in T; fluctuation in this paradigm existed in classical OCS and has persisted down to modern East Slavic dialects.

[52] It is more common about a century later, cf. in Josephus, мало дновъ in the *Archive Chronograph* (Istrin 1934 4, line 19), and днѣвъ in the *Vilnius Chronograph,* Meščerskij 1958a 169.2.

A3.2 One example of a soft twofold noun with *ě tertium* in the desinence is the nominative plural болѧрынѣ, which is accompanied by adjectives that also have this markedly East Slavic morphophonological element, see C1:18. A second is власѧницѣ 4:3, although the reason for plural is not clear. A likely third is the Gs цр̃ицѣ, although the syntax is not entirely clear, see C7:7.

A3.3 M56a 214 lists this unmarked accusative as "characteristic" of this text's language, but he does not specify just what he believes it to mean.[53]

A3.4 At the end of the 14th century, the old Npm desinence *-i* was obsolescent if not obsolete, and the two scribes of Lav often wrote -ы for nominative and sometimes -и for accusative. QT make no clear errors of this sort, but WV do, e.g. столпы мраморѧни for QT Np стълпи мраморѧни. In Tn the forms are interchangeable.

A3.5 The difference of "soft" and "hard" stems with appropriate twofold desinences is generally maintained in Q and T. Sobolevskij 1903 434 mentions Lp конихъ as an archaic feature, which is somewhat misleading. It is the normal old form, and survives in many traditions well after 1400, and thus is expected in Q and T. In Lav it occurs 9x, vs. 2 конѣ^x. This shows that the replacement of "soft desinence" by "hard," part of the general reduction of the "twofold" character of the declension, was already in progress; these forms are therefore normal in W and V. Elsewhere, it is clear that конь tended to be treated as an i-stem, so older коньхъ, коньмъ may be expected to be spelled конєхъ, конємъ. The Dp in Lav indeed is конємъ (154.1, 278.26). Like many other features in Esther, конихъ is conservative, and implies an origin older than c1370—but in fact it is no help in dating or localizing the text.[54]

A3.6 The Gs роду, permissible in OCS, is used in 2:10, but more usual рода in 2:20.

A3.7 The Ds царю (well attested beside царєви) was apparently reinterpreted in 7:3 as a vocative, with consequent reshaping of the sentence. Both мужю and мужєви occur in 6:9. In 1:8 мужєви мужю stands where we expect the Hebraism 'man and man.'

A3.8 Vocatives, only царицє and царю, are used normally, in accord with East Slavic usage of c1400.[55]

A3.91 In terms of derivational morphology, Esther's array of substantives offers nothing unusual. The complete semantic equivalence of царьство and царьствьє, or вєличьє and вєличьствьє illustrates the same sort of competing formations known from OCS. We might note просьба with the formant *-ьb-* that was of limited productivity in most dialects; this seems to be a western or "Moravan" lexeme, see L12.

A3.92 Only one compound noun occurs, домачадица/домочадица, see C2:7.

53 M56a 214 mistakenly considers As конь a sign of ESl antiquity. In fact, the use of Gs form for accusative function in the singular was characteristic only of personal nouns, *not* of nouns referring to animals, as late as 1550, cf. Unbegaun 1935 227.

54 Kiparsky II 60 remarks, misleadingly, that the form конихъ is "a rare exception" in the Novgorod Chronicle of the 14th century. This tells us about local usage, not the age of the text.

55 Sobolevskij 1903 434 states that the vocative is an ancient feature. This is perfectly true, but the vocative was a living category in much of East Slavic long after 1400. It is highly probable that these were living forms for the scribes who wrote our mss.

A4 Pronouns

A4.1 The demonstrative тъ is freely used. In Q and T, тъ often remains or is replaced by то, with the ъ behaving as strong. This trait, with no reinforcement (as opposed to тои **toj* < *тъjь*) is possibly an indication of early origin.[56] The parallel pronoun сь, however, is not preserved, and the variants in 7:6 only suggest **сьjь*, a form that is rarely spelled сьи (e.g., in the 11th-century Sinai Paterikon) but usually сии.[57] The pronouns къждо, инъ, такъ,[58] вьсѧкъ, мои, твои, свои,[59] вьсь, and самъ all occur in normal shapes. The interrogatives что and кто call for no special comment; the negative никтоже and ничтоже are also normal. The relative иже uses the shapes иже and еже for various genders, numbers and cases; this failure to distinguish the full array of forms began in late OCS and became more and more common in early Rus′. In 2:13 все еже аще 'whatever' occurs, surely a Hellenism.

A4.2 The personal pronouns have their expected forms. Only the Slavonic азъ occurs.[60] The genitive is only мене, an old form that survives in a number of ESl dialects. The accusative form мѧ occurs, but in a corrupt passage (5:12) where syntactically a genitive should stand. Second person ты has a short D ти beside the long тобѣ, with the native ESl form that occurs sporadically from the 11th century on. Similarly, си parallels собѣ; сѧ is clearly As 'self' only in 9:27, otherwise it must be construed as a particle that expresses verbal voice.

A4.21 The third personal pronoun онъ has the usual suppletive forms with **j-* and **nj-*. Accusative и is found twice, and нь once, while его functions as A five times. Его as accusative is OCS, but it is uncommon in Rus′ until after 1200. Accusative и is probably an archaism after c1350 (although variation continues, cf. Klenin 65–66). In the plural, accusative ѧ is normal, but native ѣ is possible. In Est, ѧ occurs five times, and е for **jě* once, see C4:8.

A4.22 The genitives его, ею, ваю (second person dual), and ихъ function as possessives, as expected.

A4.221 The dative also expresses possession ei 'her' (2:7, 2:17, 8:9), and ему (имѧ ему Мардахаи 'his name [was] Mordecai' 2:5). Such usage is relatively common in Bulgarian texts, but not excluded for East Slavic. For competition between dative and genitive pronouns in Est, see C3:12.

56 It could still be used by Novgorod bookmen in the 1490s, however, cf. дн҃ь тъ for *dies illa* in G Est 11:8 (LXX A:7 only ἡμέρα), 11:5 (A:4) и то его сонъ, *et hoc eius somnium,* beside да и тои *ut et ipse* 14:3 (C:24) and тои иже *ipse qui* 16:18 (E:18).

57 Scribal confusion of these NAsm forms with the present active participle сы is not uncommon, e.g., сы in the 11th-century Čudov Psalter, fol. 9d. In some cases it may be difficult to determine whether *сьjь* 'this' or *sy* or **syjь* belonged in the original text; occasionally the context admits either meaning.

58 M56a 213 remarks on такъ (1:8) and такы (7:5), apparently finding the "short" forms old. As far as we could ascertain, they are routine for c1400, although такой and такие are common in the 1500s. See also C1:8.

59 For свои meaning 'one's own; not alien,' see C5:14.

60 Keep in mind that this lexical item, which is easy to remember, is also the name of the first letter of the alphabet. Any barely literate person could manage to use it. The native forms ꙗзъ and ꙗ are remarkably rare in all of early East Slavic writing.

A4.23 The text does not require plural first or second personal pronouns or possessives (expected мы, вы, нашь, вашь). Вы as nom dual (8:8) is in a phrase attested only in Tn.

Adjectives

A5 Of the 71 lexical adjectives in Esther, six call for special comment.[61]

A5.11 **Раꙁноличь** 'different' is striking because of its archaic uninflected form and its compound stem. In terms of the MT, the раꙁноличь (with the doublet нє оуподоблєнъ) of 1:7 and the иꙁдрѧднѣє of 3:8 represent the same adjective, *šnh*. Srez lists раꙁьноличь from 1096 (разнолиць, used adverbially) as well as Esther, and it occurs in Ham (5.15, in the index), so it clearly was known at an early date.[62] Yet it is unusual; more common is раꙁличь, solidly attested for "Preslav" OCS (Supr, 1073, Usp) and surviving in 14th-century copies of OT books. The normal OCS was clearly inflected раꙁличьнъ (see SJS, Srez), while раꙁьноличьнъ seems to be a post-OCS innovation.[63] In Esther, therefore, раꙁноличь may indicate considerable antiquity, but we cannot rule out the possibility that it represents conscious stylization by a later editor or scribe. (More discussion in L21.5.)

A5.12 **Мєчєвъ** 'of a sword' exceptionally contains the *-ov-/-ev-* suffix that ordinarily is reserved for stems denoting persons, or else materials. It is attested under 1231 and 1232 in the Hypatian copy of the Galician chronicle (768.25, 769.6, cf. Srez) and in the Tver′ chronicle's text of the *Life of Alexander Nevskij,* as well as in one of the versions of the account of the capture of Azov in 1637 (cf. *SRJaXI*). The meaning is precisely that of the more usual formation мєчьнъ, which is attested in later copies of Esther (WV, the Gennadius Bible) and in works that surely go back to OCS.[64] Мєчєвъ in QT may reflect a connection with 13th-century Rus′, or an idiosyncratic trait of *1350.[65] An exact equivalent of раною мєчєвою is in the Cz Olomouc Bible of 1417, *ranú mečovu* (Num 20:21, where OB has сѣченїем мечным).

A5.13 **Вражьбьнъ** 'of sorcery, divination' is doubtless an error for вражьдьнъ 'hostile, inimical'; see A1.3.

[61] For purposes of derivation, we class 13 participles (such as рєкомыи and приготованомъ) not as adjectives, but as members of verbal paradigms. On *увѣрєныꙗ and *умирєныꙗ, see C10:1.
[62] M56a 215 considers it "typically Russian."
[63] Another inflected equivalent was apparently раꙁличьи, reconstructable from John the Exarch's Hexameron (e.g., 5b24 раꙁличиими гласы, 34a28 дѣлъ раꙁличиихъ) and *Bogoslovie* (150b раꙁличьꙗ поучинъı Ap 'various seas'), and the *Lěstvica* (e.g. ражличиихъ RGB Rum 198 91d3). Some forms in Hex, however, have been modified in the oldest copy, 1263 (e.g., 82a9 раꙁличаа красота, for -чиꙗ), and replaced by the usual stem in -ьн-.
[64] Indeed, the phrase звукь от мечеваго сѣченія in the Tver′ chronicle—which is a 17th-century copy of a 1534 adaptation of earlier chronicles—reflects отъ мечнаго сѣчениа of the First Novgorod Chronicle (Nasonov 1950 296, 450; with reversed order, сѣчения мечнаго, in the Second Pskov Chronicle, Nasonov 1955 13), and also at least one 16th-century non-chronicle copy of the *Life of Alexander* (SRJaXI s.v. мечный). Was the suffix -(ь)н- replaced by -ев- in 1534 or in the 17th century? (Notice that since the root was *mьč-* in SC, Miklosich lists his examples s.v. мьч-).
[65] Although the suffix *-ov-/-ev-* occasionally is used with stems denoting materials (such as шьлк-ов- in Esther), it sometimes apparently is intended to anthropomorphize the reference. This surely the case in the OCS phrase сынъ громовъ 'son of thunder' Mk 3:17, while the normal громьнъ is used to refer to sounds and the like. Could the sword here not be envisioned as animate? The phrase до солнцева восхода in the 1795 translation of Racine's *Esther* (1689) was objected to by the poet and critic A. A. Bestužev-Marlinskij (1819), who insisted on солнечного (cf. Jurij D. Levin, ed., Русские писатели о переводе XVIII–XIX вв., Leningrad, 1960, pp. 137–45).

A5.14 The possessive 'of the queen,' derived from the stem we conventionally write цариц-а, is царицинъ, in violation of the rule that requires mutation of *c* to *č* before a suffix beginning with a front vowel, cf. OCS богородичинъ 'of the theotokos,' from богородица, пьшеничьнъ 'wheaten' from пьшеница. Miklosich has a lemma **царичинъ**, with references to several manuscripts; this is the historically correct spelling. Sreznevskij's lemma, however, is "цѣсарицинъ = цьсарицинъ," despite the fact that one of his two examples is цьсаричина порода. This suggests that the -ицин- form was so firmly established in ESl texts that Sreznevskij took the spelling with "ц" as normal.[66] Yet this word is twice spelled цсрчин- in the 12th-century Uspenskij sbornik, surely a Kievan (or in any case non-northern) manuscript.

A5.141 The normalization with ц is to be found in the Laurentian copy of the PVL (111.13, 22; 117.20), but the later Radziwill and Academy copies write out царичины correctly according to the old norm.[67] Quite possibly our *pervospisok* of Esther had -рицин-, but any scribe could change the form to -ичин-.[68]

A5.21 The two compounds **добротварьна и добровъзорьна** in 2:7 illustrate a regular formation ((adjective + noun) + adjective formant), although the first is unique to this verse and the second is known only from Est (2:2, 3, 7) and a 16th-century copy of a saint's life (Srez), where it may be an addition made by a Slavic scribe. The underlying phrase добрыи възоръ occurs in 1:11 (see comm.), but not as a description. See, however, Gen 24:16, дѣвца же бѣше добра възору (var. взоромь Mixajlov) велми, καλὴ τῇ ὄψει, for H *ṭbt mr'h* 'good to-look-at.' Such phrases are often converted into adjectives in Greek, e.g., Gen 12:11, where the same H becomes εὐπρόσωπος (lit. "good-faced"), whence добролична. The relationship of adjective and phrase in both Slavic and Greek is productive, and conversion in either direction is possible; thus Mixajlov records a variant добра еси жена въ лице.[69]

A5.22 Добротварьнъ is not so simple, because of the meaning: if the epithet is to fit appropriately into the context, we must allow the Czech or Polish sense 'face' for the second element *-tvar-*. In SSl and earlier ESl sources it means 'creation, creature,' and, perhaps, rarely 'figure.'[70] T's variant, добротворьна, is not helpful. The root *tvor* is verbal and the compound-pattern is therefore ((noun-object) + (verbal root) + adjectival formant); the word should mean 'good-doing,' (cf. ѧзетворьнъ 1073 'disease-making, νοσοποιός,' 14th-century грѣхотворьнъ 'sin-creating').[71] Mikl gives добротворьнъ (which he appar-

66 Perhaps he viewed ч-spellings to reflect the northern dialect feature of cokanie.

67 Possessives from words in -иц-а are rare in the texts; Srez gives блудьницинъ сынъ 'son of a harlot' from a 16th-century ms (and another hapax, блудьничищь from the same source), while SRJaXI has блудьницыны ризы from a different 16th-century ms. It would be interesting to see what other derivatives of this type exist and how they are spelled in various times and places. Anomalies in other *-in-* possessives are also found. Thus for Ольг-а we expect Ольжинъ, but Lav has ѡльзины, opposed to the normal ол(ь)жины of the other copies.

68 Vil 262 has слово црчино both in 1:17 and 1:18.

69 In Job 1:3 Gk εὐγενής 'noble, well-born' is usually reflected by the literal доброродьнъ (Afanas'eva 14); the variant добра рода surely was devised by a Slavic scribe.

70 Compare, in Malalas, bk 2 (Istrin 1902 471), the phrasal epithet, дѣвцю соущю и добра твари, παρθένον οὖσαν καὶ εὐπρεπῆ. (*Pace* Istrin, this cannot be a compound noun; it is adjective plus Gs of a noun.) Although Srez has nearly three columns to illustrate тварь, no example means 'face.' He does not list добротварьнъ.

71 The first member may also be verbal or adjectival (OCS животворьнъ 'life-creating, ζωοποιός'). In Epi-

ently took from Vostokov), with no citations, defined as 'εὐποιός, beneficent.' In similar vein, Srez notes that this adjective is derived from добротворие, εὐποιΐα, yet his sole illustration is this example. However, the meaning required is 'well-formed, beautiful in shape,' H *ypt t'r*, rather like добровъзорьна 2:7 (or OCS доброобразьнъ εὐσχήμος, 1076 καλὸς τῷ εἴδει), cf. comm. to 2:2.[72] This very common type fits the formula: (adjective) + (noun) + adjectival formant. The morpheme *tvor* indicates a different pattern: (noun-object) + (verbal root) + adjectival formant (cf. ѧзетворьнъ 1073 'disease-making, νοσοποιός,' 14th-century грѣхотворьнъ 'sin-creating') but the first member may also be verbal or adjectival (OCS животворьнъ 'life-creating, ζωοποιός'). In Epifanij Premudryj's *Life of Stephen of Perm'* we find радостьнотворьнъ on the old pattern, but also красьнотворьнъ in a sense perhaps parallel to our example (see Srez), i.e., simply 'beautiful.'

A5.23 Неуподобленъ is transparently the negated past passive participle of a causative verb, уподобити, etymologically "make similar" (cf. подобьнъ 'like, same,' подоболичьнъ 'of similar shape, shaped like' [Su]), but well attested in the sense 'compare' (with сѧ, 'be similar, be like; imitate, pretend to be'). The usual Gk source of this verb is ὁμοιοῦν, cf. ὅμοιος 'like, similar.' Negative неподобьнъ 'different, dissimilar' is known from *OCS, cf. SJS (but far more commonly, in OCS and later, (не)подоб- and derivatives denote *(im)proper, (un)fitting, (un)timely, (in)convenient.* Negated passive participles of this type tend to be ambiguous: *not (having been) done* may also mean *cannot be done, undoable.* Thus OCS неиздреченъ is both 'unspoken, not spoken' and 'unutterable, ineffable,' ненасыщенъ 'unsated; insatiable.' The negative in Gk is regularly *alpha privative* (an inseparable prefix, *a-* [*an* before vowel]). The adjective ἀνόμοιος 'unlike, dissimilar' is matched by a causative ἀνομοιοῦν 'make different,' with a passive participle ἀνομοιούμενος 'dissimilar.' We suggest that неоуподобленъ reflects this Gk form; the meaning for subsequent Slavic readers may well be 'not comparable.

A5.31 In terms of structure, only nine adjectives are underived stems: **бърз-**, **добр-**, **драг-** (*dorg-), **друг-**, **злат-** (*zolt-), **зъл-**, **мал-**, **стар-**, and the dissyllabic **весел-**.[73]

A5.32 The largest derived group has the suffix **-ьn-**

(a) added to simple stems:

весел-ьн-, **вин-ьн-**, **вол-ьн-**, **вред-ьн-** (*werd-), **гнѣв-ьн-**, **грамот-ьн-**, **жел-ьн-**, **зем-ьн-**,[74] **сил-ьн-**, **сребр-ьн-** (*sьrebr- or *serbr-), and perhaps **лептуж-ьн-**;

(b) added to derived stems:

(1) with prefix: **до-вол-ьн-**, **за-кон-ьн-**, **из-д-рѧд-ьн-**, **о-хвот-ьн-**, **па-мѧт-ьн-**

(2) with suffix: **враж-ьб-ьн-** (*worg-ьb-), **жреб-ьj-ьн-**(*žerb-), (perhaps **лептуж-ьн-**, with *-ug-?), and **пи-тв-ьн-**;

(3) compound: **добр-о-((въ)зор)-ьн-**, **добр-о-твар-ьн-**

A5.33 Derivatives from adverbs are (1) **ближ-ьн̑-** 'near-by,' **утр-ьн̑-** 'inner'; (2) **вън-ѣ-ш-ьн̑-** 'outer,' **дън-ѣ-шь-н̑-** 'lower,' and **дьн-ь-шь-н̑-** 'of today.'

---

fanij Premudryj's *Life of Stephen of Perm'* we find радостьнотворьнъ on the old pattern, but also красьнотворьнъ in a sense perhaps parallel to our example (see Srez), i.e., simply 'beautiful.'

72 Sreznevskij also has the adverb доброутворьно, apparently meaning 'skillfully,' from a text of 1193. Uncompounded възорьнъ περιβλέπτος 'admired' occurs in Prov 31:23 (quoted in PVL, Lav 81.15), while Ham attests възраѵьнъ for the Gk compound εὐειδής 549.3.

73 Formally, дѣваꙗ 'virgin' belongs here, but functionally it is a substantive; see L2.461.

74 The form земл̑ьн- of the later mss, GWV, is also well attested in OCS.

A5.34 With **-ьск-** are **грьѵ-ьск-**, **жєн-ьск-**, **жидов-ьск-**, **июдѣј-ьск-**, **мор-ьск-**, and **ц(ьс)ар-ьск-**, along with **вавулон-ьск-**, **фарисѣј-ьск-** and **мадѣј-ьск-**.

A5.35 Derivatives denoting materials are **мрамор-ѧн-** 'marble' and **сукън-ѧн-** 'sack-cloth,' **шьлк-ов-** 'silken,' and **маст-ит-** (for *maz-t-it-*) 'of oil.' The use of these three suffixes **-ѧн-** (ESl *-än-*), **-ов-**, and **-ит-** is unexceptional.[75]

A5.36 The possessive sense of the suffix **-ов-/-єв-** is found in **ц(ьс)ар-єв-** 'of the king' (for мєѵєвъ see above) and derivatives from proper names: **Авихаиловъ**, **Аировъ**, **Амановъ/Амоновъ**, **Ахасъвєросовъ**, **Вєниаминовъ**, **Саазъгазовъ**, **Єгаєвъ**, **Мардохаєвъ**. The distinction between царєвъ 'belonging to the king' and царьскыи 'royal, regal, kingly' is not strictly maintained, cf. вѣнєць царьскыи 2:17, but царєвъ 6:8.[76] Besides царицинъ (treated above), only the possessive **Єсфиринъ** is derived from a feminine name; from a-stem names of masculine gender are **Амадафинъ** and **Июдинъ**. **Симаинъ** 'referring to Simai' is not entirely clear; it may be envisioned as derived from *Симаꙗ and therefore regular, or as simply irregular from *Сима, or even possibly as *Симај-ьн-ъ.

A5.37 Other derivational suffixes in Esther are illustrated by the forms **вєлии** and **вєликъ**; **горькъ**; **нєприꙗзнивъ**; **нєлюбимъ**; the comparatives **лꙋчьшии** and **издрѧдьнѣє**, and the superlative **прєвышии** (although the desinence is not quite clear).

Inflection

A5.41 Adjectival inflection in Esther includes both nominal and historically compound forms. On the whole the distinction in nominative and accusative is correctly maintained, but the short form occurs where determination should be expressed. For example, the phrase прутъ златъ 'a golden wand' occurs on the first mention of the object, 4:11, then as this known quantity recurs in 5:2 it is appropriately прутъ златыи '*the* golden wand'; yet in 8:4 the now familiar scepter incongruously is again merely златъ. In въ книгахъ фарисѣискахъ и мадѣискахъ 1:19, the short feminine desinences also are inappropriate, for the phrase is determined (the fact that it does not correspond to the Hebrew text is irrelevant for this issue).[77] The short forms in oblique cases are normal for possessive adjectives such as царєвъ (see glossary), but restricted for other adjectives (Gs ѿ вєлика дожє и до мала; Is въпльмь вєликъмь и горком, охвотнъмь ср҃дцьмь). The short Dp of приготованом in 8:13 is in the same context as the оуготованымъ of 3:14. Scribal uncertainty about the use of the desinences is found also in the Laurentian chronicle (e.g., плачємь вєликомь 68.3, п. вєликымь 260.18).

A5.42 The long Gsmn balances **-аго** (драгаго, рєкомаго [внѣшнѧго T]), the persistent traditional spelling that survived into the 20th century, with **-ого** (старого, июдѣиского, днѣшнєго, утрьнєго), which became normal in Middle Bulgarian proba-

75 Alternate formations occur in early texts for some words, e.g., Ost трьновъ and трьнѧнъ like Zo трьновъ, Sav трьнѣнъ.

76 On the use of possessive adjectives versus an adnominal genitive (e.g., царєвъ vs. царꙗ, see below, A6.2.

77 No conclusions about the antiquity of the original text can be based on the "correct" use of short forms; it is simply by chance that WV have the appropriate срєбрєнах 1:16, while QTG have the expected post-1200 "long" desinence, срєбрєныхъ.

bly in the 12th century, and in Rus′ after c1200.[78] Dative **-ому/-єму** is exclusive; it goes back to c1050 in both regions. Mutation of -ьск- is only -ьст-, in accord with conventional ESl spelling from 1200 on (Lsm женьстѣмь, Dsf фарисѣистѣи, мадѣистѣи, Npm июдѣистии).

A5.43 The early phonetic differences in OCS and ESl desinences, such as Asf **-ѫ** and **-ѭѭ** or Ism **-ъмь/-ьмь** cannot be expected in 14th-century orthography (becoming **-у**, **-ую**; **-омь/-ємь**), and the only remaining contrast is "ě tertium": ESl **-ѣ** versus OCS **-ѧ**. A single phrase provides two examples of -ыѣ (Np болѧрынѣ фарисѣискыѣ и мадѣискыѣ 1:18), as opposed to the normal -ыꙗ (7x, all Gsf).[79]

Word order; predicative adjectives

A5.51 In OCS and early Rusian, adjectives may stand either before or after the noun they modify. In Esther, of about 120 cases, only four have a preposed adjective, one short (охвотьнъмь с҃рдцмь 5:9) and three long (добрыи въꙁоръ As 1:11 [which could possibly be interpreted as predicative], въ д҃нєшнии д҃нь 1:18, на бърꙁдыхъ конихъ 8:10).

A5.52 Just what range of semantic values the various combinations *short* vs. *long* and *preposition* vs. *postposition* may express is a matter for speculation.[80]

> It is hard to delimit attributive from predicative senses of the adjectives in specific contexts. For example, in the PVL вєлику ҹесть приꙗлъ (Lav 10.6) can be interpreted simply as 'received a great honor,' while на ҹесть вєлику (Lav 56.18) perhaps is more complex, '(Olga invites you) to an honor which [I must also inform you] is great.' Idiomatic usage may be suspected in some phrases: thus вєликъ дьнь normally specifically refers to Easter (as in the dative absolute вєлику дни, Lav 217.26), while the phrase в вєликую суботу 269.29 '*the* great Saturday' appears to be an equally specific reference to the day before Easter. Postposition of a definite adjective may also be interpreted as predicative, e.g. город вєликыи (Lav 151.19) 'the great citadel, viz. the one which [as of course we all know] . . .' In view of the possibility of such subtleties, it is not surprising that scribes could change a long form to short, or the word order; as the grammatical system slowly eliminated the contrast between long and short morphological forms, the semantics doubtless changed somewhat. For the PVL, we assume that our manuscript witnesses go back to a uniform 12th-century original.

78 The assumption that *-ago* must disappear at the same time as *-umu* is widespread in the literature, but it is not justified by the facts, cf. Lunt 1987 252. Examples of *-ogo* citable from manuscripts before 1200 are so rare that it is probable they illustrate that most common of scribal mistakes, anticipation of the vowel-letter of the following syllable. Dative *-omu* is found four times in rubrics in the OCS Assemanianus, written somewhat after 1050, a single time in a rubric in Ost, but in the Vygoleksa sbornik from after 1150 it is exclusive.

79 M 56a 213 writes, "Флексии в членных прилагательных преобладают русские, но наряду с ними встречаются и славянские на *я* (юс малый) в род. пад. ед. ч. жен. р. и вин. пад. мн. ч. муж. р." This sentence is incorrect. Apart from the Rusian ѣ in 22% of the possible cases of *ě tertium,* ALL desinences of the adjectival paradigms are neutral in Esther—neither "Russian" nor "Slavonic."

80 In analyzing the categories of definite versus indefinite adjectives, we must keep in mind that languages with obligatory definite articles vary in the details of usage, although the overall system may be fairly uniform (e.g., Eng. *my house*, Greek σπίτι μου, French *ma maison* without article, but Italian ***la*** *mia casa*, Macedonian *moja**ta** kuḱa* with article). Ideally, one might hope for an analysis of early Slavic texts made by a team of Slavists whose native languages have articles, say an Italian, a German, a Greek, a Bulgarian. In any case, dicta from many Slavic analysts tend to be based on theoretical considerations that are, for this complicated material, unrealistic.

For Esther, we can only observe that the somewhat erratic usage *may* reflect a similar early system, or any of the variant systems that arose after c1200.

A5.53 Meščerskij (1956a 213) notes the preponderant postposition of adjectives, but cites only the last two counter-examples.[81] He opines that preposition took place when an adjective was added by the "Russian" translator, for otherwise postposition is dictated by the word order of the Hebrew text. Again, he fails to consider the fact that this sort of literalism is typical of most LXX books, and therefore to entertain the probability that the Slavonic reflects an intermediate Greek translation.

Special cases

A5.61 Verse 1:18 in H has *hayom hazeh*, literally 'the day the this,' i.e., 'this very day,' a phrase often rendered ἐν τῇ σήμερον ἡμέρᾳ. The Gk adverbial attributive must be given adjectival form in Slavic; въ дьньшьн҃ии дьнь surely reflects this Greek phrase (cf. SJS sub дьньсьн҃ь)—the Slavic translator followed the word order of his model, inventing nothing.

A5.62 Both добрыи въꙁоръ and охвотнъмь ср҃дцмь correspond to the order of the Hebrew units involved, but not to the grammatical constructions (see C1:11 and C5:9). Finally, на бърꙁдыхъ конихъ, as Meščerskij implies, is by no means a literal equivalent of the Hebrew (see C8:10); the same complex Hebrew wording recurs in 8:14, but in our text it comes out as на конихъ бърꙁдыхъ, a fact not mentioned by Meščerskij. Without speculating on the exact shape of this phrase in the hypothetical Greek translation, we may assume that it meant simply 'on fast horses.' If this is so, we may surmise that the Slavonic faithfully, perhaps even slavishly, follows the Greek order, which in turn was based on the Hebrew. There remains only the problem as to why на бърꙁдыхъ конихъ is opposed to на конихъ бърꙁдыхъ. (The late and idiosyncratic Tn has на борзы^{X} коне^{X} both times.)

A5.631 The adjective женьскыи 'female, feminine' also means 'of/for women' (пиръ женьскыи 'banquet for the women,' домъ женьскыи 'house of/for women [=harem], cf. Supr женьскыи манастырь 'convent'). In хранитель женьскыи it obviously must be interpreted 'guarder of (the) women' as an "objective genitive" rather than an epithet, cf. H *šmr hnšym,* φύλαξ τῶν γυναικῶν.[82]

A5.632 Similar adjectival representatives of Gk objective genitives are the possessive adjective in 'the fear of Mordecai'—meaning that people fear him, not that he possesses fear—страхъ Мардохаєвъ 9:3. This is a variant on the страхъ июдѣискыи 8:17 that is familiar from OCS gospels (e.g., J 19:38, διὰ τὸν φόβον τῶν Ἰουδαίων). Similarly враꙁи июдѣистии 9:1 (not Jewish or Judean enemies, but those likely to attack or harm the Jews), cf. мучителю июдѣискому 3:10 (also 8:1, 9:10).

[81] He mistakenly locates дн҃ьшнии in "I, 8."

[82] Neither Srez nor SRJaXI specifies this meaning. In SRJaXI the first entry, from the 1096 *minei*, is б҃ъ сн҃ъ женскый. *Pace* SRJaXI, the meaning can hardly be simply 'female, feminine'; it must be 'the son of woman,' and indeed the Gk has precisely that—θεὸς υἱὸς γυναικός (theotokion of 8th ode in second canon to the Theotokos, Mēnaion for Sept. 8). Compare the noun adjunct that presumably was in the dative for 'keeper of the concubines,' хранитель наложницам.

A5.633 The dative in adverbial phrases meaning "in X language" is nominal in по грєѵьскꙋ 'in Greek' and pronominal in по жидовьскомꙋ 'in Jewish,' 2:16. This conflicting usage provides no helpful clues as to what might have been in the original translation.[83]

A6 Possessive genitive and possessive adjectives

A6.11 Possession is expressed in OCS, and presumably in other early medieval Slavic dialects, by the formant of possessive adjectives (*ov/ev, -in-, -j-*) and may be expressed by the genitive case of a noun.[84] The normal rule was that a possessive adjective was used if the possessor was not further defined by an adjective or pronoun, or else an appositive noun. Thus мати Иисусова 'Jesus's mother,' сєло Иосифово 'Joseph's dwelling,' проповѣдь Ионинѫ 'the preaching of Jonah (As)' (Luke 11:32), прємудрости Соломонѧ 'Solomon's wisdom (Gs)' (Luke 11:31); имѧ пророѵє 'the name of the prophet' Mt 10:41, пророѵьство Исаино 'the prophesy of Isaiah' Mt 13:14, but словєса Исаиѧ пророка 'the words of Isaiah the prophet' J 12:38.[85]

A6.12 Various combinations occur. In отъ Витаниѧ, градьца Мариина и Марты сєстры єѧ "from Bethany, the city of Mary and of Martha her sister" (J 11:1), *marij-in-a* contains the notion of possession in the formant *-in-*, while the genitive case-ending is required because the word is in apposition with the genitive градьца and therefore depends on отъ; in "of Mary, her sister" the possession is signalled by the genitive case. Compare молитва иєзєкилєва цѣсарꙗ июдѣиска 'the prayer of Ezekiel [by error for Hezekiah], king of Judea' (Ps Sin, Tarnanidis 88), молитва Анина матєрє Самоилєвы 'prayer of Hannah, mother of Samuel' (*ibidem*), оусъпєниє свѧтыѧ Аннъı матєрє богородиѵинъı 'the dormition of St. Anna, mother of the theotokos' (SJS sub богородиѵинъ), молитвами свѧтыѧ богородицѧ 'through the prayers of the holy theotokos' (Euch 63a7).

A6.2 The rules are not always followed, and Esther illustrates some uncertainty. A long definition in 2:15 shows expected usage: жрєбии Єсфиринъ дщєрє Авихаиловы строꙗ Мордохаєва ижє 'the lot of-Esther = daughter of-Abihail = uncle of-Mordecai = who'; also 2:5 Мардахаи, сынъ Аировъ, сына Симаина, сына Кисова, моужь Вениаминовъ 'Mordecai = son of-Jair = son of-Simai = son of-Kis = man [of the tribe] of-Benjamin.' In 2:14 the syntax in the final link of a complex definition fails to agree: по руцѣ Саaѕъгаѕовѣ тивуна царєва, хранитєль 'at the hand of-Saazgaz = steward of-the-king' is all right, but the nominative 'keeper' has no marker to show that it refers to Saazgaz = steward. When the phrase 'king Ahashwerosh' is possessor, it should be two genitives, as in имѧ царѧ Ахасъвєроса, 3:12. QT, however, have гнѣвъ царєвъ

[83] For OCS, adverbs in -ьскы are usual, cf. 4 Ki 18:26 and 28 (W) июдѣискы 'in Jewish.'

[84] The unmodified dative was also used widely in OCS and later SSl medieval texts to express possession, but it was less favored in Rus′. [In Est it occurs only in pronouns, in two passages: with kinship terms, отьць єи и мати єи, 2:17 QT (GWVX єѧ), and имѧ єму Мардъхаи, 2:15.] Competition of possessive dative with possessive adjectives is rare.

[85] For an overview, see Vaillant, *Manuel* §88. Cf. modern Russian possessives with *-in*: сестра Сашина "Sasha's sister" or сестрина Саша "sister's Sasha," but сестра маленького Саши, the sister of little Sasha, or сестра Саши, моего соседа "the sister of Sasha my neighbor." In earlier Russian, possessives in *-ov-/-ev-* also functioned in this way, e.g., послѣ Петрова дни 'after (St.) Peter's day' (cf. Unbegaun 1935 328). Examples abound in the PVL and other chronicles.

Ахасверосовъ in 2:1; we may conclude that this is an inappropriate innovation of *1370, the common source of Q and T, for WV have the expected two nouns in the genitive.

A6.3 In 8:1 домъ амоновъ врага июдѣиского '(the) house of-Haman = enemy Jewish' is effective except for the problem of ambiguity in the final adjective. A more complex definition in 9:10, however, becomes even less satisfactory. 10 сыновъ амоновъ сына амъдафина врага июдѣиского '10 sons of-Haman = son of-Hammedatha = enemy Jewish,' if taken literally, identifies not Haman, but his father Hammedatha as the enemy. However, in this instance the original Hebrew is overloaded with appositions, 'sons-of Haman, son-of Hammedatha, enemy-of the-Jews,' and only the reader's memory makes it possible to understand that Haman is the enemy.

A7 Numerals

A7.1 Although there are more than fifty passages using numbers, the scribes rarely wrote the words out in full; they usually used alphabetical symbols as numerals. For the mixed notation "ωп" for "80" see A7.4 below.

A7.10 The evidence for numerals is sparse: седмью и **двѣма десѧтьма** и .р҃.мь властии 1:1 and два тивуна 2:21 and **ωба** 2:23 provide the expected Ad and Id of the intrinsically dual numeral **дъва**, the Nd of 'both,' and the instrumental dual of десѧть, in accord with the generally correct use of the dual number throughout the text. In седми старостъ 1:10, седмью . . . властии 1:10; and по три дн҃и 4:16 we see the Ds and Is of the grammatically singular **седмь** (not the East Slavic phonetic shape семь) and the A of the logically plural **трье**.[86] Only the masculine Ns and As of 'one' occur, **единъ** (4x).

A7.11 (The two instances of единому 'only, sole' go back to Hebrew *lbdw*, surely by way of μόνος.)[87]

A7.21 The preposing of units to tens and of tens to hundreds (7+20+100) is found in 1:1, and 80+100 in 1:4, Q ω.п҃.и.р҃.мь дн҃ии (.п҃.и.р҃. дн҃ии TV).[88] This order is normal in Hebrew and acceptable in Greek;[89] it occurs in the Origen-influenced manuscripts of Esther in both of these examples (plus some Latin manuscripts), and also in 8:9, where QT have р҃ и к҃ и ѕ҃[90] In 8:9 LXX has '3+20th'; T writes .к҃.г҃. дн҃ь. For Hebrew 'five and seventy thousand' in 9:16, Josephus (*Antiquities* XI 291) has 'seventy thousand and five thousand' (LXX reduces the number to 15,000). Correspondingly T writes .о҃ и .҂е҃ '70+5000.'[91]

86 Sobolevskij 1903 434 considered Gp after oblique cases of '7' as "древний синтаксис." This is true, but the problem is when the "new" usage appeared: was it current before c1350?

87 OCS единъ 'only, sole' normally represents μόνος; Hebrew *lbd* + suffix usually is μόνος in LXX. Est 1:16 LXX, L μόνος; 3:6 is paraphrased, but O has μονώτατον.

88 For the "ω" of Q, see A7.4 below.

89 From Greek texts with no Semitic background it is rendered faithfully into Slavonic, e.g., четыри и ·л҃· и ·р҃· словъ '134 *slova*' τεσσάρων οὖσα καὶ τριάκοντα λόγων πρὸς τοῖς ἕκατον in the Life of Theodore of Studios, *Vyg. sb.* 83.11.

90 Further, QT have р҃.к҃.ѕ҃ (VW .рк҃ѕ.) in 9:30, where LXX abridges the sentence and omits the number. M56a 216 believes the unusual order demonstrates direct translation from Hebrew. He cites the two examples (erroneously adducing 9:30 instead of 1:1, and adding an unjustifiable 'etc.'), failing to mention the counterexamples or the presence of similar order in Greek in general and in the known versions of Esther in particular.

91 X omits the symbol for 'thousand(s),' ҂, and thus reduces the number to 75. Meščerskij's edition omits the symbol both in 3:9 and 9:16 (M78a 144, 162).

A7.22 M78a 162 notes for 9:16 the variant о и є тысоущ in mss A and B. This reflection of тысѫщь rather than the normal East Slavic (and possibly eastern OCS) тысѧщь is striking. A detailed study of the occurrence of тысоущь in East Slavic mss might well be instructive.

A7.31 In 1:14 the ordinal 'first' is used as an absolute superlative in adverbial form: иже сѣдѧху **наипьрвѣє** въ царствѣ, 'foremost, in the most prominent position.'

A7.32 **Другыи** 'another' may function in OCS as an ordinal, 'second.' In 2:14 and 9:29 it could have either meaning; in both cases the H is not fully clear. In 2:19, въ другыꙗ can only mean 'for a/the second time'; this idiom does not appear in OCS, but it is in Lav *sub* 1152 (вдругыѣ, col. 337).

A7.4 In 1:4, Q's notation of the instrumental of the numeral 180, written ѡ.п.и.р.мь, surely intends *omega* as symbolizing the first syllable of the number, followed by the п that stands for '80' (ѡ[смью десѧтъ] и [сто]мь), although ·п· should have sufficed. In the photos of T we can see .'п҃.и҃р҃.мь: apparently a letter has been erased from the place corresponding to Q's ѡ, but the diacritic above it remains visible.[92] In the Miracles of Boris and Glěb, a 12th-century original Rusian text, a wall was built до о.п҃. локоть възвыше (Usp 22d16) 'to the height of 80 cubits.' In East Slavic manuscripts, the omega might indicate the [wo] or [vo] of various regions. Yet it occurs also in the 12th-century Macedonian Grigorovič Parimejnik, Dan 3:1: въ ѡ.и҃ı. лѣ^{T} i.e., въ осмоєнадесѧте лѣто, ἔτους ὀκτωκαιδεκάτου, 'in the 18th year.'

A7.41 An example from the Ruthenian translation (from the Hebrew) of de Sacrobosco's *De Spera* suggests rather a device for distinguishing the value of the symbol "*и восьмеричное*" from "*і десятеричное*." Sobolevskij's edition of the text (which for lack of better identification he named *Cosmography*, 1903 409–413) twice has "78 круговъ" for the expected "8" (p. 410). The lone manuscript (16th century, Chełm, cf. Taube 1995 190, fn. 13) has been lost; we assume that it had иныхъ ои круговъ (probably with a titlo over the letters "ои"), to be read осмь. This combination unfortunately signifies a different value, as Sobolevskij's edition attests; with knowledge of the H original, however, we may confidently assume that an earlier copy had the letters "ѡи."[93]

A8 Adverbs

A8.11 Two adverbs formally equivalent to neuter adjectives are **зѣло** 'very,' from the poorly attested *OCS ѕѣлъ 'violent, furious,' and **бързо**, 'swiftly,' 6:10 and 8:14.

A8.12 Зѣло occurs in Esther only in the doublet вельми зѣло, 1:12, 4:4. There is no way of establishing which word was in the original translation. OCS ѕѣло/зѣло is overwhelmingly favored (being exclusive in the gospel mss), but вельми is well attested. In the PVL, however, зѣло is clearly a stylistically marked literary word, appearing in nine pas-

[92] In ms 16 (Und 1), copied from T, there is an erasure in the same place, and in the margin о҃п и р҃ has been added.

[93] Moldavian and ESl mss of the Song of Songs use the same mixture of phonetic and numerical notation, according to Alekseev (1980 1 24), 6:8: ѡ·п· женимъ '80 concubines.' Since the Greek precedes the number with 'and,' Alekseev wishes to interpret the omega as a misreading of a Croatian Glagolitic "i" and therefore a proof of a Croatian link in the transmission of the text (1983 247) The suggestion is thoroughly improbable in cultural terms; in any case it is quite unnecessary (cf. Lunt 1985d 308, n. 70).

sages, while вєльми is in 29. In two they overlap: 28.5 LRA ꙁѣло vs. HX вєльми,[94] and 220.25 (1093) пєчаленъ ꙁѣло L vs. вєлми RAHX.

A8.121 The adverbs **дожє и** or **дажє и** or **дажь и** preceed the preposition до in seven out of nine cases (and another has и до, see A9.32). MT offers no reason for providing this apparent emphasis (perhaps '*all the way* to, *even unto*'), but early Sl examples translated from known Greek texts usually correspond to ἕως or μέχρι, in a spatial or temporal or quantifying sense. OCS surely had the first two (although the variant дожи и is more securely attested), and дажє и became normal in early Rus'.[95] After about 1300 ESl scribes begin to use дажь, which often is written да^{ж}, and occasionally даж^{д}ь.[96] The superfluous дамь ти of 5:6 is probably a misreading of a spelling with this sort of superscript letter.

A8.21 **Бърꙁо** is semantically close to the phrasal **въскорѣ** 3:15. Both are OCS.

A8.22 Another near-synonym is the adverbial phrase **вънатъщь** 'in haste,' which is unique to Esther 8:14.[97] The presumed root **tъšč* 'speed, haste, zeal' is known from the uncommon but solidly attested OCS тъщати сѧ 'hasten,' тъщаниє 'haste, speed,' and тъщьно 'speedily,' supplemented by *OCS тъщьнъ and натъщьнъ' 'speedy, zealous' (Srez, Ham), but it did not survive into modern dialects (except via Slavonic in R).[98] The Greek equivalents are nearly always based on the root *spud* (e.g., σπουδαιος 'speedy, with haste, with zeal, zealous,' περισπούδαστος 'much desired'). The stem на҃тъщ- is to be ascribed to tenth-century Bulgaria, but it soon disappeared. The adverb вънатъщь in Esther is thus to be regarded as Bulgarian and relatively old.[99] U like T and Q, carefully writes the correct jers, while S updates to внатощь (only the first letters внат show in our photo of G). The внатъщє of W (with Ruthenized оунатщє in V) possibly were understood as 'in vain, with no result,' by association with the far more familiar stem тъщ-ь 'empty' and derived adverbs тъщє, вътъщє. Tn has a somewhat more appropriate innovation, в тои ча^{с}, 'at once'; this does involve a shift in meaning.

94 This is in a paraphrase of the *Life* of Methodius, which has посажь дъва попы скорописьцѧ ꙁѣло (Usp 108c10–11, where, as Mathiesen pointed out, три попы makes better grammar and an even more plausible situation), PVL посади 2 попа **скор**описца **ꙁѣло** L, **скор**описца **вєлми** X, **борꙁ**описца **вєлми** H, **борꙁ**описца **ꙁѣло** RA. In Usp, incidentally, the next phrase is 'he translated rapidly' въбързѣ—another old synonym of the terms discussed in A8.2.

95 OCS gospels do not have дожє и, but the Mstislav Gospel of 1115–17 has it in two passages. Izb 1073 has both дажє и до and дожє и до, with one дожи до. Usp. has 6 дажє и до to one дожє и. The six occurrences in the PVL (five of them from Ham) all have variants in different copies. A more distinctively Rusian equivalent ωли и до is at 192.16.

96 Thus PVL 40.13 (where Lav is defective), Hyp (and Ham 305.23) дожє и до нынѣ, RA да^{ж}, X даж^{д}ь. In five other passages дажє and дожє are variants. L has no дажє in this sense, but дожє и до only once (25.23), **т**ожє и до once (1:4), simply до twice (2.3, 7.8). Hyp has дожє и до five times, and дажє до at 2.3, where X has дожє до and LT merely до.

97 Srez cites it from Vostokov as a single word, and sub натъщь as a phrase. Vostokov further cites не бѣ бо натощь οὐ γὰρ ἦν περισπούδαστον from the 1434 ms of the *Učitel'noe Ev.* of Theophylactus of Ohrid (cf. *SRJaXI*).

98 Cf. obs. тщание; тщательный 'careful, painstaking' is a relatively modern formation. The homonymous root **tъšč* 'empty' was far more common and tenacious, e.g., OCS тъщь, SC *tašč* (*našte srce* 'on an empty stomach' < *na tšte*, cf. R натощак, U на́тще́ or нащесе́рце), OP *tszczy*, mod. *czczy* 'empty' (cf. R тощий 'gaunt,' тщета 'emptiness, vanity'). In OCS, there was at least one parallel formation тъщивъ 'quick' and 'pusillanimous'; Srez also 'empty, vain.'

99 For the formation, compare SC *unazad* 'back' beside older *nazad.*

A8.3 Лапь in 2:14 is difficult. The MT says that after a night with the king a concubine "never again will come" to the king, unless the king desires her especially. LXX uses a present, οὐκέτι εἰσπορεύεται, "no longer enters." With this knowledge, lexicographers take *1350's не прихожаше лапь къ цареви to mean "did not come any more (again)" (Srez, SRJaXI). However, other examples of лапь suggest *suddenly, abruptly,* a sense congruent with the verbal root in *lapati, lapiti* 'pounce suddenly, grab, capture.' With negation, ESl лапь and (Old Czech *lap*) mean *not immediately, not without difficulty, not without reason*: реклъ бо Кесарь ꙗко не лапъ пристроꙗет чюже грады (Josephus), 'For Caesar said that it was not without reason (for no cause) that he was equipping alien towns';[100] не лап ти велита брата крстъ цѣловати (Hyp 542.16, sub 1170) 'It is not for nothing (for no reason) that your brothers are telling you to swear (friendship) by the cross'; а лапь не доити до тѣхъ мѣстъ поганыхъ ради (Daniel Palomnik), 'it is not easy to (not without difficulty can one) reach those places because of the infidels.'[101] This sense is plausible for Esther as well; the next clause specifies the possible difficulty and how it may be overcome, но егда будѧше волѧ царева на неи, 'but when(ever) the king's wish be for her.' This, then, is not a literal equivalent of the MT (like O ἐὰν θελήσῃ αὐτὴν), but an interpretive paraphrase.

A8.31 ESl лапь and OCz *lap* preserve an old adverbial format *-ь, while P dial. *łapie* and U dial. лапі show the newer formant *-*ě*.[102]

A8.41 The superlative form наипьрвѣе 1:14 denotes "most honorable" in terms of seating rank.

A8.42 възвышѣ 7:9 and its alternate възвышѣе 5:14 look like comparatives, with the preposition/prefix въз-; in any case they have the special sense 'in height.' The usual shape is възвыше (e.g.Usp 22d16, PVL 150.18, Ham 141.3, cf. возвыше, 1406 Paleja 51a25, c6). Yet Lav at 90.20 has възвышие (RA -ше), and perhaps -ѣе in Est 5:14 is an example of "ѣ" for "и." (X has възвы^ш^; this may correspond to the възвышь of the 1477 Paleja, 58a21 [cf. возвышь 58d2], probably a newer shape.) The usual adverbal phrase with this meaning is въ высоту, e.g., in Ham 140.19, 141.4, Gen 6:15 (SJS), PVL 5.14. OCz had *vzvýši* (mod. *zvýši*) and OPol had *wzwysz, wzwyszą.*

A8.43 Далече, although comparative in form, is generally positive in OCS, 'afar, at a distance'; in 9:20 it is contrasted with **близь** 'nearby.'

A8.44 Боле, an irregular comparative, appears only in the somewhat inappropriate phrase боле мене 6:6, "in preference to me," see comm. For развѣ 'except for,' see C9:12.

A8.5 Єлико ихъ 9:27 and **еликоже ихъ** 1:5 preceded by 'all' appear to be redundant equivalents of relative pronouns, "all [as many as] who." They surely reflect forms of the Gk ὅσοι.

100 Vaillant correctly defines '*pas pour rien*' and Pascal translates '*pas sens intention*' (in Istrin 1934–38 II 263, resp. I 67), but Meščerskij 1958 545 mistakenly gives "больше не" (which does not fit the context).

101 Cited by SRJaXI from a 1496 copy, with a variant, впростѣ. The wording in Srez is different, лапь до тѣхъ мѣстъ не ѹдобь доити—older лапь не is reinforced by the more familiar удобь 'convenient.' The explanatory *because of the infidels* makes it easier to interpret the obsolescent word.

102 Trubačev ES has only the lemma **lapě* and he omits OCz examples, even though some were included by Sreznevskij. M56a ignores Srez and calls лапь "typically Russian."

A8.6 On **нєврѣдъ** 3:6, see L16.1.

A8.7 **Како** 'in what way,' and **тако** 'thus, in this way' are normal OCS.

A9 Prepositions

A9.0 The use of prepositions in European languages varies considerably from one regional dialect to the next, and standard languages perforce allow some variation. In OCS, variations occur on the one hand in the competition of different prepositions in essentially identical phrases and, on the other, in the competition of case-forms without preposition with prepositional phrases. With all this in mind, we see that the use of prepositions in Esther generally fits patterns known from OCS and pre-1400 East Slavic evidence.[103]

A9.1 Esther has the ordinary OCS prepositions **бєꙁ**, **въ**, **до**, **ꙁа**, **иꙁ**, **мєжю**, **на**, **надъ**, **о**, **от**, **по**, **прєдъ**, **съ**, **у**, along with the postposition **ради**, the somewhat less usual **противу** and **прѧмо** (the ESl shape of OCS прѣмо), the 'improper preposition' **посрѣдѣ** and the phrase **въ . . . мѣсто** 'instead of.' It also has one instance of **про**, which is not OCS but rather North Slavic (OCz and early ESl), and finally the rare **унє**, which occurs only in certain East Slavic mss.

A9.21 The preposition **въ** is frequent (105x) and requires little comment. Three instances of **въ . . . мѣсто** are discussed below. The contrast въ вратѣхъ (5x) to на вратѣхъ 6:10 seems unmotivated; both refer to the same unspecified position 'at the gate.' As for на дворѣ 6:4, 5 vs. въ дворѣ in 1:5, 5:2 for *bḥcr*, we must assume that dialects differ in the nuances of meaning denoted by the variants; we see no basis for the actual distribution in the text that has come down to us.[104] The use of **на** (53x) is quite ordinary.[105]

A9.22 The preposition **къ** occurs 54 times, chiefly in phrases that need no comment. With verbs of speaking, the dative, surely the native Slavic construction, alternates with къ plus dative e.g., и рєчє царь Амонови 6:10, but и рєчє Амонъ къ цареви 6:7. This use of къ is apparently foreign to any Slavic dialect, and it has long been considered as a calque, intended to reflect with utmost fidelity the Greek contrast of simple dative to πρός

[103] Meščerskij claims that the peculiar use of prepositions betrays literal translation from Hebrew, but his examples are anecdotal and without merit. His entire treatment consists of a single sentence (1956a 209–210): "Буквальная передача еврейского предложного управления: напр., I, 16—'Не црю [1] единому съкривила Васти црца, еще [2] не *на* вся бояры и *на* вся языки [3]' (евр. 'al [4]—'против'; II, 2 [5]—'Еже осуди *на* ню; IV, 2 [6]—'И отвеща Есфирь *къ* Мардохаеви' (евр. le); VIII, 7—'Иже [7] повергль [8] бяше руце свои въ июдея [9]' и мн. др." The bracketed numbers indicate problems: [1] the dative reflects the H prep. *'al*; [2] is аще in Meščerskij's edition and all sources we know; [3] is mispelled by T's rules, which require -кы; [4] the H prep. is *'al*; [5] this is 2:1; [6] this is 4:15; [7] им'жє in T; [8] ввєрглъ in TQ (= "П"), по- is not in any ms we could check; [9] questions concern both preposition and case, see comm. to 8:7. The problem with 1:6 is why the three prepositional phrases of H did not come out with parallel constructions in Sl., but with a dative and then two instances of на. In 4:15 къ is probably a Hellenism, see below.

Meščerskij then (214) asserts that three uses of prepositions are "typical Russian syntactical features" or "Russisms": по with accusative signifying goal 5:5, про plus A in sense of reason 4:5, and къ, "в смысле цели назначения" (with unlocated examples which in fact are from 3:13 and 4:11, and will be mentioned below). He is mistaken or confused, or both.

[104] From the point of view of Hebrew, въ usually reflects *b-* (83x = 79%). It also occurs for *'l* 5x, *l-* (4:14, 10:3)

[105] На usually reflects *'l* (30x = 56%), but also *b-* (9x), *'l* (7x), and *l-* (2x); 4x the H has no preposition and in 9:12 на is in a superfluous addition.

plus accusative.[106] Perhaps this artificial phraseology is responsible for the unexpected ȥаповѣдаше Амонъ къ тивуномъ (and other officials) of 3:12 and the parallel 8:9. Otherwise this verb takes a dative in Esther (2:10, 20; 4:5, 8, 10, 17) and elsewhere.

A9.231 Different prepositions in identical contexts may reflect scribal whims. Most texts appear to oppose къ росполону 'for plunder' (3:13) to по росполону (8:11), but Tn has к in both. For the recurring phrase 'to the banquet' QTWVSG agree on the unexpected къ питвѣ in 6:14 against a more normal на питву in 5:4, but Tn has на пиръ in both verses (as well as the five times where the others agree on this wording).

A9.232 In 34 instances (63% of the total), къ goes back to the Hebrew preposition *'l* אל, in 14 (26%) to *l-* -ל, and in three to *'l* על.[107] In 4:11, къ оубою is an inadequate equivalent of the H infinitive 'to put to death' (see comm.). In 8:9, one instance of къ occurs where H does not repeat the preposition in a parallel series. In 7:1, приде царь и Амонъ питъ къ Есфири, H has 'with Esther'; the Sl construction implies going *to* Esther's (place), which in fact may rest on a legitimate interpretation of *'m* as French *chez* or R *y*, taking къ as the proper equivalent to express goal of motion.[108]

A9.24 Въ Вастии мѣсто in 2:17 is normal Slavonic, for 'instead of Washti' *tḥt wšty*, ἀντὶ ουασθην. In 2:7 and 15, however, where Mordecai took Esther 'as a daughter,' въ дщере мѣсто is not accurate translation. Both H and G have simply 'to daughter' *l-bt*, εἰς θυγατέρα, and instances where LXX εἰς γυναῖκα becomes Sl въ жену (e.g., Gen 30:4, 9) allow us to expect въ дъщерь.

A9.31 As usual, the picture is clouded by many instances of what must be considered poor translation, with inappropriate prepositions and/or case-forms; the difficulty is that no sure criteria exist whereby we can decide with confidence whether variation illustrates native usage from different dialects (or styles, with subtle shades of meaning), or foreign usage. With a text like our *pervospisok*, the problem of possible regional dialects is complicated by various possible temporal differences, and the foreign influences may come from two stages of translation.[109]

A9.32 **До** 'to, up to' functions alone in 4:2 (до вратъ царѧ 'to the king's gate') where H has *'d* עד ' up to' plus the semipreposition *lpny* לפני 'to the face/presence of' (cf. L6.1). Usually it is buttressed by a preceding и (3:13) or доже/даже/дажь и (7x). H has merely *'d* (2:13, 5:3, 7:2) or *w'd* 'and to' (1:1, 5, 20; 3:13, 8:9). These preposed elements have little or no semantic weight; see A8.121.

A9.33 **Отъ** (23x) and иȥ(ъ) (4x) are not clearly differentiated, but the usage follows patterns familiar from OCS and other early texts.[110]

106 Whether or not this use of къ with *rek-* and other verbs of saying had any roots in a Slavic dialect at the beginning, its ubiquity in OCS translated texts made it acceptable for original texts written in various areas in the earliest period. In 14th-century Slavonic it is perfectly normal anywhere in the Orthodox Slavic world.

107 For a case where one H phrase *'l yd* results in semantically differentiated по руцѣ and на руцѣ 2:8, see note 82 to L6.32.

108 LXX συμπιεῖν τῇ βασιλίσσῃ expresses 'with' in the verbal prefix.

109 Lebedev points a number of difficulties in the use of prepositions in the Slavonic book of Joshua, including variants from ms to ms.

110 **Иȥ** always stands where the H has *m-*, and отъ usually does (20x = 87%). In 7:7 H has 'from Esther' as is appropriate to the idiom; the Sl text is somewhat corrupt, and although T has ѿ, it seems to be an error for о, see

A9.34 **Предъ** is used appropriately with the accusative for motion (6x) and the instrumental for rest (31x); for its relation to the H text, see L6.11, 6.2.

A9.35 **Противу** and **прѧмо** 'opposite' each occur twice; in 4:6 прѧмо takes the genitive вратъ, while in 5:1 it takes a dative, дверемъ. Both cases are used with прѣмо in OCS, but this variation within such a small body of examples seems odd.[111]

A9.36 **По** occurs with accusative (3x), locative (12x), and dative (23 [or 24, see C9:20]). See L20.41 and C2:8 for unusual uses. Unsurprisingly, по stands for a broad range of Hebrew constructions: *b-* 18x (49%), *'l* 6x, *'l* 2x, *'ḥr* 'after' 2x, *m-* (in the improper preposition *mqc* lit. 'from the end,' по немьже, see C2:12), twice in glosses and six other passages where H has no preposition.

A9.37 **Съ** with instrumental, 'with,' occurs once in an addition to the Sl text (4:16), twice for H 'and' (5:4, 9:25), once to express agent (8:10, H 'by the hand of'), once for H *b-* 'in' (7:7), once in an idiom (see C6:13), and 9x for H *'m* 'with.' Twice it occurs with genitive, '(down, away) from' in accord with H *m'l* (3:10, 4:4). The preposition ꙁа in the idiomatic sense 'took hold *of*' occurs (ѩть ꙁа конець 5:2, H *b*) and ꙁа то 'in return for' in 6:3 (H *'l zh*, see comm.) The postposition ради reflects H *'l* once (4:16); того ради is *'l kn* in 9:19, 26 and *'l kkh* also in 9:26; ѵто ради goes back to H *mdw'* 'why?'

A9.4 The preposition **уне** (probably phonologically /uňe/) is known only from East Slavic manuscripts; it takes the genitive case. In mss Q and T of Esther 4:5 = 4:10 ꙁаповѣда ему уне Мардохаꙗ corresponds to H *wtcwhw 'l mrdky* in 4:5 'she commanded him *concerning* Mordecai' (LaSor) but, with a different preposition, *'l* 'to' in 4:10 (La Sor 'to go tell it to').[112] The two H prepositions על and אל often overlap in meaning, and interpretations depend on context. Moore thus translates 'ordered him *to go* to Mordecai' and 'gave him this message *for* Mordecai.' LXX renders 4:5 as 'learn *from*' (ἀπέστειλεν μαθεῖν αὐτῇ παρὰ τοῦ Μαρδαχαίου), while 4:10 becomes a direct command 'go to!' (πορευθῆτι πρὸς Μαρδοχαῖον). Thus it is unexpected that the Slavonic treats the two verses identically. The уне in 4:10 is not appropriate.

A9.41 In the *Life* of Theodore of Studios in the 12th-century *Vygoleksa sbornik,* оунѥ occurs in a sentence that illustrates the difficulties of interpreting the translation: мълъѵю оунѥ стражь посмисани и пороугании. By following the Greek word-order and not providing any equivalent for the definite articles, the translator has produced a sequence of words that surely will be misunderstood by a reader who does not have the Greek at hand. It should mean 'I will not speak of the scoffs and mockings of the guards,' i.e., оунѥ should

---

comm. Otherwise, отъ represents the improper preposition *mtwk* (lit. 'from among' 9:28), and semiprepositions: *mlpny* in 1:19 and *b'yny* in 5:8. 8:2 'took from Haman' uses у in appropriate Slavic fashion; Hebrew has *m-*.

111 These two prepositions show no dependence on the Hebrew usage. Противу 2:11 corresponds to H *lpny* 'in front of,' usually прѣдъ, as does прѧмо in 4.6. (But *'d lpny* comes out simply до (вратъ) in 4:2.) H *nkḥ* 'opposite, across from' occurs twice in Esther, yielding противу 2:11 but прѧмо 5:1.

112 Mss W and V (and apparently all other mss) have оу.

In his Josephus book, Meščerskij speaks of уне with accusative (1958b 117), citing Esther "оуне Мардахан" (corrected in errata sheet to Мардахаи). Later, in his edition (1978a), he misprints in 4:10 уне мардохаю (although QT have -аꙗ), with a note "следует читать Мардохаи /вин. пад./ как в П" (= Q 1.2). Thus he has invented a spurious example of an Acc = Gen form that also is supposed to demonstrate that this rare preposition takes the accusative.

be construed with Gp посмисани{и} и пороугании, while стражь denotes the source of these actions. For our purposes, the important point is that унѥ (*uňe*) plus genitive means 'concerning.' The Life of Theodore is surely another Rusian heritage from eastern Bulgarian OCS.

A9.42 A second example is in an answer to a question about canonical law put to Bishop Nifon of Novgorod (died 1156), unfortunately in a sentence that is somewhat obscure. It concerns what is permitted for children (отроци) in church, and includes the clause нє велми ѿлоуҷають сѧ оунє приҷащєньꙗ, 'they indeed should not be excluded *regarding* communion.'[113]

A9.43 Sreznevskij also cites the two examples from Esther, two from an unidentified 16th-century chronograph (one of which is in the episode of the *Third Capture of Jerusalem (by Titus)*, with a wording different from that of PSRL 22), and two from the Paleja of 1494. One we cannot verify: и постави свои^{х} ꙋнѣ ·п҃· му^{жь}, where Sreznevskij sees the meaning 'approximately.' The other is found in the Solomon and Queen of Sheba episode, in the repeated phrase унє мудрости твоєꙗ, Pypin 3, 54 and 55, cf. Proxorov 1981 74, taken from 3 Kingdoms (1 Kings) 10:6 = 2 Chron. 9:5, where LXX has περὶ τοῦ λόγου σου and περὶ τῶν λόγων σου.

A9.44 In the *Third Capture of Jerusalem* (ms RNB OLDP F.33) there are six examples that render H *'l*, 'about, concerning, for': и даша римлѧнє дш҃а своѧ къ смр҃ти оунє приҷины дѣла ѡвновъ, fol 243v; А Титъ боѧшє сѧ бг҃а оунѣє [for оунє] ст҃аꙗ ст҃ых, fol 251v; нє всꙋє даша жидовѣ дш҃а своѧ къ смр҃ти оунѣ домꙋ сєго *ibid.*; възыскати живота оунє дш҃ь своих 252r; а нн҃ѣ молитє сѧ оунє дш҃ь ваших, *ibid.*; и розсмѣꙗ сѧ Титъ и возвєсєли сѧ оунє храборьства є^{г}, *ibid.* The second is apparently accusative (so Srez), but the *Holy of Holies* may well be an idiomatic indeclinable unit; the rest show the expected genitive.[114]

A9.51 Examples already mentioned make it clear that there is no correlation between the Hebrew and Slavonic prepositions that could demonstrate direct translation. A few more details will show how complex the relations are. The most frequent Hebrew preposition in Esther is -ב *b-* 'in, at,' 178 times. Of these, 4 are omitted in the Slavonic text as it has come down to us and 6 are in corrupt phrases; 5x it is merged into the infinitive ҷьстити, 7x it is part of a conjunction; 40x it is reflected in case-forms; 116x it yields a preposition (въ 83x, по 16x, на 8x, прєдъ 6x, съ 2x, за once).

A9.52 The Hebrew preposition על *'l* occurs 76x in Esther. Of these, 5 are not represented in the Slavonic text, two are in *'l 'šr*, lit. 'on which,' meaning *for which reason, because* (им'жє 8:7, ижє 1:15), and 13 are expressed by the dative case. The usual equivalent is на (19x with L, 20x with A, total = 54%), but we find also ради 4x, надъ 3x, къ and по each twice, and once each въ, за, о, прєдъ, про and унє. The compound *m'l* twice yields съ with G, and once is submerged in the comparative прєвышии (see C3:1).

113 For the text, see Goetz 310. The answers to the questions asked by Kirik, Sava, and Il′ja may well have been revised by a 13th-century editor. Any interpretation depends on unspoken assumptions about the complex background of the question. Srez sees the meaning to be "кроме" (*outside of*? *except for*?). Goetz opts for '*from* communion.'

114 A seventh example, *ibid.* И видѣ и оудиви сѧ велми оунє дѡмє бг҃а велика^{г}, is uncertain because the text is faulty. From the H, we expect "he looked [at the temple] and he was astounded, and he wondered and he (finally) *believed that this was* the house of the great Lord."

A9.53 The preposition אל *'l* is found 59x, of which two are lacking in the Slavonic. The usual equivalent is къ (35x = 61%), but въ, на, and по each occur 6x; prepositionless dative occurs twice, genitive once.

Conjunctions

A10 The conjunctions of Esther are on the whole those of most Slavonic texts, but there are some unusual cases and a number of obscure points. There is some evidence of a Greek background, but no demonstrable influence of the ultimate Hebrew original.

И, **а** 'and'

A10.1 The normal connective is **и**, clearly the most frequent word in the text. The elements it connects range from identical nouns in a distributive phrase (ꙁємлꙗ и ꙁємлꙗ, cf. T4.1) to synonymic elements in a doublet or hendiadys (весєлъ и охвотнъмь срдцмь 5:9) and on to large syntactic units. We have made no attempt to separate out the many nuances which may be expressed by this ubiquitous little word, for the examples all seemed to fall well within the normal range of usage as measured either by OCS (cf. the meticulous distinctions made by the Czech syntacticians who edited SJS) or the Повесть времен и лет.

A10.11 It is well known that scribes are prone to add an и or omit one at any time in the history of a text;[115] it is doubtful that we could reconstruct the exact distribution of и in our hypothetical *pervospisok*, not to speak of the more remote original translation. Our text prints [и] for some instances of redundant и, and sometimes {и} where и (expected from the MT) is not in QT. Our decisions favored the sense of the attested text rather than strict adherence to the Hebrew. **И** is by far the most frequent word in the text; we have not attempted to list the occurrences in the dictionary.

Some 430 examples have и for *w*-; in another 70 the expected и does not appear, and 59 times the и attested in Q is superfluous. In negative contexts, the appropriate ни is found 6 times where H has *w*- (plus one justifiable addition, 3:5). 115 MT verses (69%) begin with *w*-; of these the Slavic omits 4, has **а** and **жє** each twice. 12 times Sl adds verse-initial и so that 127 verses (76%) begin with this conjunction. An added и may change the meaning of a phrase (cf. C1:4, C9:2), thus opening the way for further deterioration of the text. On occasion an unexpected и seems to replace some other element; thus the redundant but harmless initial и of 4:11 QTSGWV corresponds to LXX ὅτι, serving to introduce a direct quotation. It turns out that Tn, and therefore possibly *1350, has the appropriate ꙗко here.[116]

A10.2 The seventeen examples of the conjunction **а** also fall within the normal Slavonic range of usage, and we have not tried to separate the simple additive sense from the more contrastive or even adversative nuances. See also C1:19 and C4:2.

[115] Greek scribes deal with καί in similar fashion. Hebrew *w*- is more stable, particularly when it denotes a morphological-syntactic element rather than a simple connective, cf. p. 56 fn. 2, p. 65 fn. 15.

[116] Arxipov (1994 114 = 1995 252) believes that the treatment of *w*- in "biblical textology" is exceptionally important, but his treatment hardly scratches the surface of the material in Esther. In 4:11 he overlooks ὅτι, seeing the и as opposed to zero in both MT and LXX (and disregards the following words entirely). We may suspect this ꙗко of being a Hellenism, but since none of the other direct or indirect quotations has this conjunction, it is to be regarded as an interpolation during the history of the hypothetical Greek translation.

A10.3 We follow the convention that **a** plus conditional is written as a single word: абы, абыша. See A11.43.

Да; ать

A10.31 Of the fifteen instances of **да**, four mean ‘and,’ perhaps with the continuative nuance separated out in SJS as meaning 5. Once, ꙗко да has a clearly final sense (1:19 ‘so that he will give’). Five times it is followed by conditionals, indicating purpose, and five times it is the introductory particle denoting first or third person imperative (e.g., да ѡблеүем 6:9). (A scribal error in *1360 produced a да-clause that could be interpreted as indicating a confident relative future (4:7 реүе Аманъ да вѣсит{ь} ‘that he will/would weigh out’). Tn’s навѣси^{T} points rather to an infinitive, corresponding exactly to the H.)

A10.32 **Ать** is attested in 5:14 (ать повѣсѧт Мардохаꙗ) and is to be conjectured for 1:19, where the manuscripts have аще, possibly a careless repetition from the initial clause in the verse.

аще ‘if’

A10.4 Twenty-one examples of аще occur.[117] In ten (1:19, 4:14, 4:16, 6:13 [2], 7:3 [2], 8:5, 9:13) it means ‘if’ in an autonomous conditional clause, and in one embedded conditional clause it means ‘whether’ (4:14, ‘and who knows whether . . .’); the accompanying verbs are in the present tense, perfective or imperfective. As variants of the phrase ‘if it please the king,’ **аще** is followed by **бы** plus *l*-participle (3:9, 5:8) and once by бы plus infinitive (5:4).[118] Once аще is followed by the conditional auxiliary and past passive participle in a contrary to fact condition (7:4 аще бо быхом . . . препродани, ‘for if we had been sold’). These fourteen examples are all appropriate as equivalents of G εἰ or ἐάν. In 4:16 **аще . . . и** is concessive ‘even though’ (cf. εἰ καί, ἐὰν καί). The аще не мене of 5:12 has a sense well attested in OCS, ‘other than me, except for me; εἰ μή, ἐὰν μή in the sense ‘but (Ger. *sondern*).’ In 1:16, however, аще не stands after ‘not only,’ so that ‘but also’ is to be expected (cf. LXX, L ἀλλὰ καί).[119]

A10.41 Three times аще is a generalizing particle: все еже аще реүаше ‘everything (no matter what) that he said’ (2:13); идеже аще ‘wherever’ (9:1), and the dubious ꙗкоже аще придеть ‘however’ or possibly ‘whenever’ (where a personal relative ‘whoever’ would be more appropriate, 4:11). These surely are calques from Gk πάντα ὅτι ἄν, ὅπου ἄν, and ὅς ἄν or the like.[120]

117 The second аще in 1:19 is inappropriate, surely an error for ать, see comm.

118 The structural variation in this recurrent formula (4x present, 3x бы) is accompanied by lexical variants: see L12.6.

119 Cf. Job 42:8, where the H survives literally into the GB, *ky ’m pnyw ’ś*; ὅτι εἰ μὴ πρόσωπον αὐτοῦ λήψομαι; ‘for I will accept only him’ (lit. ‘his face’) GB ꙗко аще не лице его прїимȣ (but OB точїю бо).

120 In the MT, *’m* ‘if’ occurs 16 times, of which ten correspond to аще in the Sl (and two are omitted: in 8:5, before обрѧку, where it is textually superfluous, and at the beginning of 5:8, where there is a textual gap). H *’lw*, introducing a contrary to fact condition, also corresponds to аще, in 4:16. Otherwise аще stands where H has *ky* (6:13, аще падаꙗ); *ky ’m* (аще не in 1:16, 5:12) and *wk’šr* (4.16, where the rather vague sense of time is easily interpreted as conditional). In 4:14 *ky ’m* is not concessive, but means ‘for if.’

The generalizing particle corresponds to the H relative *’šr* (2:13, 4:11; 9:1 [see comm.]), while the inappropriate аще не of 1:16 corresponds to simple *ky*. H *ky ’m* comes out нъ егда in 2:14 and нъ ꙗкоже in 2:15.

***Ли** interrogative marker*

A10.42 The enclitic ***ли*** occurs with аще in 4:14 to specify an indirect question, 'whether (or not)'; H has no equivalent. *Ли* in 5:12 and 5:13 appear to mark rhetorical questions, not explicit in H, see T9.38.

Нъ 'but'

A10.5 The contrastive нъ (often spelled но after about 1150) occurs alone in 1:17, but нъ егда 2:14 'but when, except when' and нъ ꙗкоже 2:15 'except as.'

Бо, ибо, любо, нєбо, нєбонъ, имьжє, ижє, занєжє 'for, because'

A10.61 The *pervospisok* has a number of puzzles concerning causal conjunctions that can usually be solved on the basis of the context and the sense of known Slavonic words. **Бо, ибо, нєбонъ**, and **имьжє** are known from OCS, while **нєбо** has been plausibly established for *OCS with this same sense (SRJaXI).[121] **Любо**, on the other hand, surely to be read meaning 'because' in 2:10, 8:8, and 9:24, has not been identified as a causal conjunction elsewhere.[122]

A10.62 Both **ижє** and **єжє** function as causal conjunctions (cf. SJS) through a complex process involving mechanical translation of the Greek ὅτι as though it were the relative ὅ τι,[123] and then the formal confusion of ижє and єжє within Slavic. *Ижє* 'because' is certain in Esther 1:13, 1:15, 1:20, 3:6, and 7:4, and possible in 3:4, 6:6, 7:7 and 8:1, where there are complex textual corruptions.[124] The unsatisfactory reading ꙁанє ꙗжє of 9:26 surely represents the normal OCS **ꙁанєжє**. This brings the number of causal conjunctions in Esther to eight, to which must be added the polysemantic **ꙗко**. It is an impressive number for so short a text.

ꙗко, аки, ꙗкожє, како (тако)

A10.7 The broad range of meaning of both **ꙗко** (31 examples), with the variant **аки** in 1:8, and **ꙗкожє** (21 examples) gives rise both to ambiguity and to scribal substitution of

121 The sequence of letters нєбонє occurs in 2:12 and in 7:4. Emending the first to нєбонъ is unproblematical because of the meaning. The second is less certain, since the H sentence is difficult and the Slavic is unexpected and unclear; since H contains a negation, we read нєбо нѣ(сть), see C7:4.

122 One possible exception is adduced by Srez and glossed as 'может быть' (Hypatian Chron. sub 6790, *PSRL* 2 891.20), but the meaning 'for, because' is not implausible: Сыну мои Юрии, не ходи самъ с Литвою; оубилъ ꙗ кнѧꙁѧ ихъ Воишєлка; любо восхотѧть мьсть створити.

GorNev 56 enumerate the three occurrences as part of their list of non-ChSl vocabulary; M56a cites 9:24 (and, mistakenly, 10:1) in a context implying that this usage is typically "Russian." Ro 201 includes любо in 8:8 in his list of mistranslations.

If we assume that любо, like Gk ὦς, covers the range of 'that' and 'for,' we can cite an example from the 1st Novgorod Chronicle (Syn. sub 1149; Nasonov 28) и услышавъшє новгородьци любо въ 500 съ Водью идоша по нихъ. (Later copies revise the sentence, omitting this word, Nasonov 215.) The meaning is uncertain, but we suggest: "And when the Novgorodians heard that they were (approximately) 500, including the Vod′, they went after them."

123 Keep in mind that the space between the two syllables is provided by modern editors, not the manuscripts.

124 Perhaps in some cases an older имьжє was written и^{М}жє and then was mis-copied. Note that both ижє of 1:15 and имжє of 8:7 correspond to the composite *'l 'šr* of H.

The Gennadian translators actively used causal иж(є) for *quod* (Est 11:12 = A:11, 13:5 = B:5), *quia* (15:15 = C:8, 15:2), and *nam* (16:13 = E:13).

one for the other.[125] Overlapping is particularly apparent in Esther in the meaning 'as, according to,' where ꙗко occurs eight times. As a general connective 'that' ꙗко is normal (5x). It may introduce quotations (3x), express temporal relationships ('when' 2:1, 5:2, ꙗко аще 'whenever' 4:11), cause (5x) and purpose (twice).

A10.71 Similarly, ꙗкоже means 'as' (7x, plus 2:15 нъ егда 'except as'), 'according to' (10x), and 'when.' In 9:22 it is a simple connective, 'that.'

Егда, вънѣгда, вънегдаже 'when'

A10.8 More explicit temporal conjunctions are **егда** (6x) and **вънегда/вънѣгда** (3x); **вънегдаже** conveys no obviously different meaning. Relative егдаже 'at the time that' is in 1:4. In 2:8, вънѣгда . . . и ꙗкоже introduce clauses that are entirely parallel in Hebrew; the Slavonic text is not clear.

A10.81 The relationship between Slavonic temporal and causal conjunctions and Hebrew constructions is varied and indirect. Thus H *k* plus infinitive construct ends up as егда (сѣде *kšbt* 1:2) 'when he took his seat,' ꙗко (уꙃьрѣ *kr'wt* 5:2) 'when he saw,' and ꙗкоже (уꙃьрѣ *wkr'wt* 5:9). H *b* plus infinitive construct shows the same sort of variation: егда (глаголаху *b'mrm* 'in their speaking' 3:4), егдаже (показа *bhr'tw* 'in his showing' 1:9), и вънегда (доступи *wbhgy'* 'and in arriving' 2:15), и ꙗкоже (придѧше *wbhgy'* 2:12). This kind of rendering is common for Gk articulated infinitives and for clauses with ὅτε, ὅταν, which in turn are usual translations for H infinitive constructs. Cf. C1:5, C3:4.

A10.91 **Како** is found as a conjunction (5:11, LXX ὡς), and an interrogative (8:6, LXX πῶς). The parallel adverb **тако** is more frequent (9x, LXX usually οὕτως).

A10.92 **Доньдеже**: 4:11 **дондеже не ꙃванъ будеть** clearly enough means 'as long as he is not called' or 'until he is called.' This sense, however, is not congruent with the context, which requires a descriptive 'who is not (has not been) called.'

A10.93 **идеже** in 4:3 and 8:17 mean 'where' in almost identical contexts specifying the goal of a motion, see C4:3. H *mqwm 'šr* underlies both. **Идеже аще** in 9:11 (see A10.14 above) is locational; the H context requires a temporal conjunction, see comm.

A11 Verbal forms and their uses

A11.1 Conjugation

The verb-forms in Esther conform to old patterns, with a few deviations known from other texts written down in the 14th century or earlier. Thus the verb 'to rule' contains the classifier *-ěj-*, rather than the older *zero*, so владѣти (not власти). Two old forms of вѣдѣ- 'know' are found, unprefixed 3s pres вѣсть and prefixed оувѣдѣти. Otherwise the classifier *-aj-* is present, e.g., вѣдають, оувѣдати. In OCS the *aj*-variants are well attested beside the older irregular forms with prefixed stems; in Esther only the regularized forms appear (повѣдати, заповѣдати, исповѣда, расповѣда).[126] See L21.54.

[125] Perhaps one should distinguish a unit ꙗкоже, with a relative meaning parallel to that in **jьže*, from ꙗко же, including the meaning 'and' as a separate component; we have not found that possible to do.

[126] The *ě* of the aorist-infinitive system seems to have been replaced by *a* very early, cf. unprefixed вѣдати in the 11th-century Rus' *Sinai Patericon* (42v3), вѣдахъ in the 12th-century Usp Sb (93a24). Evidence is more abundant for prefixed stems, and the *Izbornik of 1076* has повѣдаѥть and повѣдають. In Lav, only two unprefixed forms are attested (вѣдаꙗ 146.3, аще быста вѣдала 178.22)—along with вѣдаеть in Monomax's "autobiography" (254.24). The younger copies of PVL all have *aj*-forms in greater number.

A11.11 The first-person singular обрѧку is found twice in the two oldest manuscripts (7:3, 8:5), though it is corrected in T 8:5 by a later hand to the normal southeastern SSl shape (by origin OCS) in ESl orthography обрѧщꙋ.[127] This form is strikingly exceptional in an East Slavic context; for discussion, see A1.41.

A11.12 A similar problem is raised by the unexpected створимъ of 5:6, 7:2, 9:12, where the king is promising to grant Esther's requests. For normal Slavonic, this form is first person plural, but otherwise, including precisely these verses, the king speaks in the singular. On the other hand, створимь is entirely possible as 1s in a Serbian manuscript of c1300: could this be an indication of a Serbian layer in the history of Esther? The problem is complicated by the fact that the H in these expressions is impersonal, 'let it be done; it will be done.'[128] See A13.72–73.

A11.13 The 2s падаши of 6:13 of T is probably a simple error for Q's perfective падєши, which nicely fits the Greek equivalent πεσῶν πεσῇ. On the other hand, if we take it seriously because it is in the oldest manuscript, it could be the imperfective падаєши, either by simple omission of the є or as contraction of the *-aje-* to *-a-* that was common very early in numerous South Slavic dialects, but much later in East Slavic. With the items mentioned above, this might support an argument for a Serbian stratum in the text, but it cannot be considered strong evidence by itself.

A11.14 The perfective and irregular stem *da-/dad-* and the imperfective *daja-* over the centuries gave rise to redistribution of the allomorphs using *dad-* and *daj-* along with a new imperfective stem *davaj-*. Thus old дадимъ is 1p imperative, but in 7:2 it apparently functions as a present/future as in modern ESl.The present participle or gerund даꙗ of 2:3 belongs historically to даꙗ-ти; in modern dialects to has been replaced by давая, to давать.

A11.2 As in OCS and Rusian, there is no explicit future tense. In 4:16 the auxiliary 'begin' probably expresses a simple future: говѣти начнуть 'I/we will fast.' In 2:4 the notion of beginning may be more significant, начнєть цар{є}вати, 'will rule' or 'will begin to rule.'[129] In 9:27 того нє имуть прєступати again we may see simply future ('they won't transgress'); however, a more forceful sense 'they should not, are not to transgress' is equally possible.

A11.3 The preterites occur only in third-person forms, and they call for little comment.

A11.31 The aorist forms are mostly well-known from other texts of the 1400s and earlier.

127 Meščerskij's note to this form in 7:3 is numbered 15a, indicating that it was something of an afterthought. Puzzlingly enough, it reads "обрящу A. обрящю A." We assume that one of spellings represents manuscript B or another of the manuscripts he refers to haphazardly. Sobolevskij 1903, 435, also notes these forms in Q.

Alekseev in effect sweeps these forms under the rug, saying that обрѧку occurs only once in one manuscript (1987 3). Even if this were so, the form needs to be explained.

128 Freidhof 1984 351, following GorNev, cites similar forms from the Gennadius Bible to demonstrate the influence of SC through the Dominican Venjamin: сътворимъ 'faciam,' пиємъ 'bibam,' учтємъ 'recenserem,' благословимъ 'benedico.'

129 In any event, H has no *begin* in these two verses with начати. In 6:13 and 9:23 поучати corresponds to H *hḥl* 'begin, start.' In the context of 9:1, *yšlṭw* 'they dominated,' marks a vivid change of affairs that justifies a translation "began to rule" (though not the pluperfect поучали бѧху).

The old unproductive aorist рѣша is retained three times, against normal рєкоша four times, as a special relic that survived in eastern OCS and then Rusian and was widely used down into the 18th century. The 3s приꙗтъ 2:7 and ꙗтъ show the -тъ desinence that was probably borrowed from OCS, but is acceptable in East Slavic texts well into the 16th century. Beside them are the normal снѧ 3:10, 8:2, and наҹа 8:3, with the zero-desinence which was usual in eastern OCS and also in "Middle Bulgarian" texts. (For hypercorrect оубитъ, see C9:16.)

A11.311 One variant aorist in Tn stands out, потушє 'dwindled away, was extinguished' (7:10), as opposed to потухну in all other copies. Both forms fit 10th-century paradigms (cf. Lunt 1974 113), and the verb seems to have existed in most areas at the time. Which form was in *1350? Would a 14th-century ESl scribe or the 15th-century editor of Tn generate the highly-marked alternative shape потушє?

A11.32 Imperfect forms show the usual patterns of East Slavic copies or original texts of the 14th century. Spellings show the East Slavic imperfect-marker *-ä-* (contracted from older *-äa-*) in consonantal stems—будѧшє, дадѧшє (2x), доидѧшє, придѧшє, постигнѧшє—and *ě*–verbs—видѧху, сѣдѧшє (2x), сѣдѧху (2x)—where OCS or later SSl would have -ѣ-, дадѣшє, сѣдѣхѫ/сѣдѣху, and the like. In *i*-verbs, five in both Q and T show SSl mutation (in ESl orthography)—хожашє, въс-, при- (2x); въꙁношаху—and three the non-mutated stems of a type known from the beginning of East Slavic literacy—жидовѧху сѧ, ꙗꙁдѧху and, with different spelling of the root, ѣꙁдѧшє.[130] Disagreement appears in two other forms. In 2:4: Q оулюблѧшє, with the normal SSl shape, but T оулюбѧшє, the characteristic ESl form. In 9:24, conversely, Q has the ESl мыслѧшє, while T has SSl мышлѧшє. The third person desinence -ть, sporadically used by East Slavic scribes since the 11th century, is found only twice, гл҃ахуть 3:4, написахуть 3:12.[131]

[130] Freidhof 1984 351 appropriately cites GB могашє, могаху to illustrate SC influence, but the forms ходѧшє, приходѧху, иꙁводѧху, трудѧху are not convincing, precisely because they correspond to the native Rusian tradition.

[131] The glaring inadequacies of Meščerskij's discussion of verb forms in his remarks about the "русский язык перевода кн. Есфири" illustrate his carelessness with exposition and details, compounded by his uncertainty about OCS and pre-modern East Slavic grammar. In reproducing this short passage, 1956a, 213–14, we insert bracketed numbers for ease of reference:

> [1] Настоящее время третьего лица всегда с русскими окончаниями, довълѣеть, вѣдають и т.д. [2] Будущее сложное употребляется только с вспомогательным глаголом начнеть[2]. [[The note cites S. P. Obnorskij's remark that this is a "typically Russian feature".]] [3] Имперфект встречается свыше 80 раз с типично русскими наращениями в глаголах мн. числа: написахуть (III,4); глаголахуть (III,12). . . . [4] Только два раза форма аориста употреблена с наращением *тъ* (оубитъ, ятъ). Во всех остальных случаях 3–го л. ед. числа без окончания: сня, нача. Систематическое употребление таких форм Соболевским отмечается также как типично русская черта языка."

[1] says only that the manuscript is East Slavic. [2] refers to a total of two examples (2:4, 4:16; the second in a garbled phrase), but the qualifying "only" is wrong because there is a future with имуть (9:27). In any case, *načęti*-futures exist in OCS (Vaillant 1964, §245); Obnorskij is not a reliable source. [3] apparently reflects a mix-up in NM's notes. The total number of imperfect-tense forms is 80 (81 if we include the unexpected говѣху inserted in the gloss in 9:17), of which 22 are plural and have the suffix *-xu*, while only the two words NM cites have the typically East Slavic person-suffix -ть, i.e., 4.5%—a not unusual proportion. [4] The third person singular aorist suffix -тъ in *ятъ* is unexceptional, see above. The form *оубитъ*, however, is a blunder in a badly corrupt verse (9:16) that does not correspond to the Hebrew text; in any case, the root *bi-* does not admit aorists in *-тъ*. Xleb attests the correct оуби. [The example cited by Weingart II/2 448 from a Serbian ms of

A11.321 The third person dual is correctly written in стрѣжаста 2:21. It is striking that manuscripts W, V and B have the variant стрѣжаашєта, with the distinctive desinence -шєта that was losing ground to the aoristic -ста even in OCS. This archaism in three manuscripts may indicate that the *pervospisok* contained ancient features which were not retained in T and Q, the oldest surviving copies. Traces of similar forms are found in the oldest copy of Hamartolos (Tr., c1300), but eliminated in the later copies (post-1400).[132] Since Old Czech also preserves examples suggesting this old formation of the imperfect desinences, we may hypothesize that they survived longer in some north Slavic dialects than in South Slavic.

A11.33 The past active participle of *i*-verbs is represented by Nsm повѣсивъ 6:12 and Apn съключьшаꙗ сѧ 4:7. In 10th-century Bulgaria the innovative untruncated type (*-i-vъ[š]-*) was clearly productive (Lunt, *OCS Gram,* §11.14), but in early Rus′ the older, truncated, type (*-*j-ь[š]-*) was familiar enough from OCS models,[133] to be used actively.[134] We may conjecture that it had support in some local dialects. By the 14th century, *iv*-forms were normal; it is possible that the shorter and more complex formation had special value.[135] It is clear that the shorter formation cannot be regarded as a significant archaism in Esther.

A11.4 Periphrastic verb forms

A11.41 Perfects occur in only five examples; the sole instance of 3s omits the auxiliary, see A13.3.

A11.42 Pluperfects are found with both the old imperfective aorist бѣ 3s, бѣшѧ 3p and imperfect бѧшє 3s, бѧху 3p as auxiliary with no apparent distinction, e.g., и снѧ царь пьрстьнь свои иже бѣ ѡтѧлъ оу Амана 8:2, but и повѣсиша Амона на древє иже створилъ бѧшє Мардохаєви 7:10. Only one of the 18 pluperfects has an imperfective *l*-participle, the exception (иже бѣша мучили) being in a corrupt verse, 8:11, see comm.

1386 (GIM, Sin 148) оубить и, Gk only ἀπέκτεινε, must be deemed a scribal error (though without context it is hard to assess the possibilities). The past pass. part убитъ may replace убьєнъ in ESl copies after 1400; e.g., PVL sub 945, LRA кнѧꙁь нашь убьєнъ, but HX убитъ.] Moreover, forms of the type *сънѧ*, with zero desinence, need no comment (Vaillant 1964, §154); they cannot be called upon as proof of any regional origin of a translation. (As indicated above, our *pervospisok* has, in all, five aorists of this type: three with zero-desinence, two with -т.) Unfortunately, this passage is typical of Meščerskij's presentation of all the subjects he treats in the article.

[132] Thus имашьта 254.26 (no variants given), but творѧшта 253.17 only in Tr (MDA 100), творѧста in all others.

[133] In Ost, the truncated type is regular, with 8 exceptions, all Nsm (e.g., научивъ сѧ 227c Mt 13:52, оставивъ 160a Mt 26:44); a ninth exception, сътворивъшѧ 268d Mt 20:12 is textually awkward, for we expect 3p aorist сътворишѧ, as in Assem (but Mar has the truncated participle сътворьшѧ).

[134] In the 12th-century Uspenskij sbornik, the two types occur approximately equally in the texts inherited from Bulgaria, but in the original Rusian compositions the truncated type is clearly in the minority, about 18.5% of possible cases.

[135] In Lav, alternate forms are well represented; e.g. створшє 200.14, 265.4 (1078, 1097) but створившє 45.14 (1093); възложьшє 130.23 and вължоживъшє 134.15 (both 1015). Examples with mutation of the root-final consonant are less common: e.g. рожьшаꙗ Gsf 124.15 (996) but родивши Dsf 155.10 (1044). Epifanij Premudryj has frequent *iv*-forms, but does not hesitate to show off his knowledge of the truncating type (e.g., о приключших сѧ, оступльшимъ, прєставльшю сѧ in the first long sentence of final section, плачеве и похвала, of the Life of Stephen of Perm).

A11.43 The old western OCS distinctive conditional forms do not occur in Esther, but as in eastern OCS and early East Slavic, the old perfective aorist forms of быти serve with *l*-participles to form conditionals. Thus in 7:4 Аще бо быхомъ...препродани... мълчала быхъ 'If we had been sold... I would have kept silence'; 5:8 аще бы цареви [тако] оудобрѣло 'If it should [so] please the king.' However, there are many inconsistencies. The same Hebrew clause that underlies this straightforward Slavonic occurs in five other shapes (see L12.6): in three variants аще plus present tense makes a real condition, in two (including 5:8) аще plus бы plus *l*-form produces a normal hypothetical condition, and 5:4 has аще бы plus infinitive for another nuance of *irrealis*.

A11.431 In an independent question (6:6 кому хотѣлъ бы царь створити чьсть 'to whom *might* the king *like* to do honor'), the conditional expresses possibility. A similar meaning appears in a relative clause (5:4 на питву єже быхъ створила єму 'which I *might* [or, *would like to*] give'), but here neither the context nor the Hebrew provides any reason for this note of doubt. For the unexpected conditional in 2:11 (оувѣдѣти...что быша створили єи), see C2:11.

A11.432 After verbs of commanding, the conjunction **a** plus conditional is normal: 2:10 ꙁаповѣдалъ єи абы нє повѣдала 'ordered here not to tell'; 9:21 оуставити имъ абыша творили 'established for them that (these days) should be made.'

A11.433 The usual OCS hortative or jussive consists of да plus present tense, a construction that appears four times: 4:16 да погыбну 'let me die, may I die'; 6:5 да придєть сѣмо 'let him come here'; 6:8 да принєсоут пърты 'let them bring garments'; and 8:5 да напишєть книгы 'let him write a letter.' The obsequious language used to address the king uses conditionals as indirect requests, 3:9 абы написалъ "let him write" in the sense "you might write, why don't you write." Again there is a variant, 5:4 да бы пришєлъ царь 'let the king come' (or 'why don't you, o king, deign to come').

A11.434 In 3:8, цр҃єви бы нє право, the бы might be an aorist ('it was not right') or a 14th-century Ruthenian conditional indicator ('it might not be right'); in any case, H has no equivalent.

A11.44 The Slavonic Esther has an unusually large proportion of verb-forms that combine a present active participle with a present or preterite form of *byti* as auxiliary. In part this is due to the high number of participial forms, some of them compound, in the Hebrew text (a feature of late Biblical Hebrew and also of Aramaic).[136] This kind of periphrastic usage is common in Biblical Greek and also in translated Slavonic texts. Moreover, it appears in original early East Slavic texts. Whether or not it was originally a result of imitation of Greek, it is widespread enough so that we may accept it as part of the book-language, if not indeed a native usage.[137] Thus, with a present auxiliary, и ꙁакона царєва нє суть творѧщє 3:8 (cf. also 9:27, 28); with imperfect auxiliary нє бѧшє Есфирь повѣдающи рода своєго 2:20 (cf. also 2:21): with imperfective aorist auxiliary и бѣ клича прєд ним 6:11 (cf. also 2:14, 4:1, possibly 2:7). The perfective aorist in и видѣ Амонъ ꙗко нє бы[с] Мардохаи ни приклѧкаꙗ ни припадаꙗ єму 3:5 is to be ascribed to the general loss of the older three-way contrast between бысть, бѣ, and бѣ(а)шє/бѧ(а)шє.

136 This is one of the features cited for the hypothesis that the book was originally written in Aramaic.

137 It may have been reinforced by Latin-influenced examples in the early western texts, e.g., будита въ молитвахъ вопиюща Nik 82.19 *eritis in orationibus clamantes.* Many of the examples in Nik, however, seem quite foreign to normal Slavic syntax, see Vaillant 1968 xvi–xvii.

A11.441 The peculiar compound imperative, съдѣлающє будѣтє древо 5:14, with perfective auxiliary and perfective participle, is surely some sort of corruption (see comm.). Near-parallels in Su 165.8 (вѣдѫштє бѫдѣтє, 299.15 вѣдѫшти бѫди) translate normal Gk imperatives γνώσκετε, γίνωσκε (addressed to a woman). In the *Izbornik* of 1073, however, и сє жє бѫдѣтє вѣдоуштє 81d27 reflects the unusual compound ἔστε γινώσκοντες; compare 99b11 боудоу владоушти 'I'll be ruling, I'll rule' ἔσομαι ἀρχοῦσα.[138]

A11.442 The present active participles творѧщє 'doing' and посылающє 'sending' 9:19 are not accompanied by an auxiliary, though суть might be expected.

A11.443 These forms may have resulted from the general usage in the particular kind of Greek used in the hypothetical text we propose; it is important to note that only six of the examples cited above correspond to periphrastic forms in Hebrew, while six do not (2:21, 6:11, 2:14, 4:1, 5:14, 9:19). In this feature, too, there is no direct relationship between the Hebrew and the Slavonic.

A12 Agreement of subject and verb

A12.1 When more than one subject is placed after the verb, the verb may remain in the singular: и придє цр҃ь и Аманъ 7:1; и написа Есфїрь . . . и Мардъхаи 9:29; оустави Мардъхаи Июдѣи и Есфїрь царицѧ 9:31; гнѣваѩ сѧ бѧшє Вихванъ и Вафєсъ, 2:21. This is normal in Hebrew and Greek, as well as OCS and native early Rusian texts; it often appears to indicate that the first-named subject is more important than the additional subject or subjects. On the other hand, the verb may agree: и придоста царь и Аманъ 5:5 (H here has singular verb). It is not expected for a marked personal form: прєпродана быхъ азъ и людиє мои, 7:4; here H has a plural verb, cf. LXX ἐπράθημεν. The Sl (and Old Latin and important LXX mss ἐπράθην) represents sensible adaptation to native usage.

A12.2 Still a third possibility is the North Slavic idiomatic use of the singular representing the most important subject and a prepositional phrase, 'with x,' for the secondary subject or subjects, as in 5:4 да бы пришєлъ царь съ Аманомь, where Hebrew has a singular verb plus 'the king and Haman.'

A12.3 A special case is perhaps represented by 2:6, where the noun 'booty' (съ полонъмь) was interpreted as the collective group of prisoners who were captured (полонєни). In H the singular prevails, *'m hglh* (sg) *'šr hglth* (fsg); this agreement is also in Gk O-mss (standard LXX differs), μετὰ τῆς αἰχμαλωσίας ἧς αἰχμαλωτίσθη.

[138] Genesis provides several forms of *bǫd-* plus present participle. (Examples from Mixajlov 1900–08, normalized spelling.) In 1:6, a third person imperative: и да бѫдєть раꙁлѫчаѭщи (sc. твьрдь), 'and let it (sc. the firmament) be dividing (i.e., a division),' καὶ ἔστω διαχωρίζον, *wyhy mbdyl*. In 4:12 a prophetic continuative future: стєнѧ и трѧсы сѧ боудєши, στένων καὶ τρέμων ἔσῃ, 'thou shalt be groaning and trembling'—NOT equivalent to H *n' wnd thyh* 'a fugitive and vagabond shalt thou be' (or, interpreting as hendiadys, 'a restless wanderer'). In 37:8 it mirrors the H emphatic absolute infinitive in a rhetorical negative question: єда цьсарьствоуѧ боудєши над нами или владыи боудєши нами?, 'shalt thou indeed reign over us, or shalt thou indeed be lord over us?' μὴ βασιλεύων βασιλεύεις ἐφ' ἡμᾶς ἢ κυρεύων κυρεύσεις? *hmlk tmlk 'lynw 'm mšwl tmšwl bnw*? In 18:18 the absolute infinitive of 'to be' *hyw yhyh* 'shall surely become' yields γινόμενος ἔσται, боуды боудєть.

A12.4 If the subject comes before the verb, we expect agreement. Therefore in 4:14 (ты и домъ отьцѧ . . . погыбнєть) we expect rather a dual (-та) or, if 'your father's house' is given its logical value as denoting many individuals, a plural (-тє). In 4:16, 'I and my maidens' is accompanied by говѣти наѵнуть; surely the -ть is an old scribal mistake.

A13 Usage of verb-forms

A13.11 The simple preterites, aorist and imperfect, provide most of the verbal forms in this narrative text, and their use is generally appropriate. Aorists predominate over imperfects (about 5:1), and ordinarily denote single events that move the plot along. Thus 1:12, нє въсхотѣ царица . . . и раӡгнѣва сѧ царь . . . и гнѣвъ . . . ражьжє сѧ . . . и рєѵє . . . and many other passages. Often aorists occur in subordinate clauses to specify previous events. Thus, for example, in 1:2–3 єгда сѣдє . . . сътвори пиръ . . . ; 2:1 ꙗко оустави сѧ гнѣвъ царєвъ . . . въспомѧну.

A13.12 The familiar biblical "and it came to pass" (H *wyhy,* καὶ ἐγένετο) uses the perfective aorist, и бысть, 2:8, 3:4, 5:1, 2 (and with omitted и, 1:1).

A13.21 The imperfect demonstrates the expected range of incomplete or repeated, habitual, or durative actions in main or subordinate clauses. Many of the imperfects correspond to H nominal forms, viz. present participles (both attributive and predicative), infinitive constructs and absolute infinitives. For example, H predicate participial *whmlk yšb*, lit. 'and the king sitting' а царь сѣдѧшє 5:1; attributive *hyšbym* ижє сѣдѧху 1:14, 9:19; infinitive construct *wbb'h lpny hmlk* да єгда прихожашє прєд царѧ 9:25; infinitive absolute *wnḥ . . . w'śh* и поѵиваху . . . и творѧху 9:18.

A13.22 Not only the common imperfective imperfects are used, but also perfectives, which occur as expected in conditional or temporal clauses denoting punctual but repeated action, i.e., whenever action A is completed, action B also is/will be repeated. Thus 2:12–14 provides the rules for selecting the king's new concubine or potential queen: и ꙗкожє придѧшє (P) ӡнамєниє дѣвыꙗ дѣвы прити к царю . . . нєбонъ тако напълнѧху сѧ (possibly P) дньє пристроꙗ . . . и в томь дѣваꙗ дѣва придѧшє (P) . . . и всє єжє ащє рєѵашє (P) дадѧшє (P) єи . . . нє прихожашє (I) лапь . . . нъ єгда будѧшє (P) волѧ царєва . . . и тогда поӡвашє (P) ю имєнємь. The rarity of perfective imperfect forms in early Slavic texts is determined by the fact that passages of this sort are rare: the notions inherent in the form are not required by most narratives; indeed there are scarcely any examples in classical OCS.[139] The usage they attest, however, fits nicely not only with such early East Slavic texts as the Life of Theodosius (Uspenskij sbornik, 12th century),[140] but also with Old Czech texts dating from after 1300. Therefore, it is safe to assume that they reflect the system of Late Common Slavic. [141]

[139] Compare Lunt 1974 § 21.20, esp. note 3.

[140] For a detailed examination of the early East Slavic data, see Van Schooneveld.

[141] An example cited by Vaillant (GC 5 161–2) from the Olomouc Bible of 1417 shows perfective imperfects where the same situation in Ham also has at least one such form. In I King. (I Sam) 16.23 the Czech, translated from Latin, reads, *kdyžkoli duch zlý nadlapieše* (arripiebat) *Saula, David vzhudieše*; Ham, citing LXX, has и бысть (рєѵє) ѥгда *боудѧшє* доухъ ӡлыи на Саоулѣ, и приимъ Давыдъ гоусли, въспѣвашє. The clause ѥгда боудѧшє reflects a Gk articulated infinitive, ἐν τῷ εἶναι, and the form thus was independently generated by the original Bulgarian translator. For a discussion of translation problems of this sentence with somewhat more context, see T1.5.

A13.3 This system gradually became less complex as the simple preterites became rarer, eventually disappearing altogether. As in other cases of linguistic change, we must assume that there were significant regional differences in the development of new relationships. East Slavic scribes copying older manuscripts in the 14th century sometimes maintained older usage, and sometimes we must assume that they up-dated the forms. Although the fine points have not always been maintained by later scribes, the PVL and many other texts surely composed before 1200 allow us to show reasonably consistent usage in a variety of passages.

A13.4 The present tense-forms function in the usual manner, including future denotation for perfective presents. The stem *bud-* provides the (relative) future for 'to be,' добра буду аꙁъ 8:5, and is also used with a passive participle: и будєть послушана рѣѵь царєва 'will be heard' 1:20; as a relative future, дондєжє нє ꙁванъ будєть 'until he is/will be called' 4:11 (cf. also 5:8). For the expression of future in 4:16, possibly 2:4 and possibly in 9:27, see above (under conjugation).

A13.5 Passives, impersonal expressions, and unspecified person

A13.51 The Hebrew book of Esther contains an extraordinarily large proportion of passive verbs, particularly in impersonal constructions.[142] The Slavic text retains many of the passives appropriately using a passive participle, usually with an auxiliary. One example is correct only in Tn and X; ижє полонєни 2:6 for the Hebrew sense '(the exile) which had been exiled'; all other copies reflect an old error, полони, by omission of a syllable. The plural of the Sl indicates that the referent, полонъ, could have a collective meaning, "the captives." In 6:9, perhaps сѧ might have been used to form a non-transitive construction with passive meaning, тако сє створити, for H 'thus it shall be done'; by emending сє to сѧ, a more natural construction results. Yet, in view of the fact that сѧ-passives are avoided in Esther, and because many verses have bizarre phraseology and unusual syntax, we cannot be sure that this emendation is needed.

A13.521 Our text represents some Hebrew passives by active forms. In some instances the change seems slightly peculiar, but can be justified by equivocal forms in H, e.g., въпишєть 1:19, reflecting *wyktb* read as active *weyixtov* 'and let him write' or passive *weyikatev* 'and let it be written.' [143]

A13.522 We also find the unspecified personal form, where 3p stands for a generic person-subject, as in E 'they say' or R говорят (NB *without* они!). Thus in 3:12 написахуть corresponds to the explicit H passive *nktb*, while in 8:9 написаша stands for the ambiguous *wyktb* (traditionally read as passive *wayikatev*).[144] This same passive may

[142] This fact has been used as an argument for the thesis that the original text was in Aramaic, cf. Zimmermann 85.

[143] In 8:5, either напишєть (QT) or напишуть (GWV) is admissible for the passive *wayikatev.* Similar cases are написа 2:23 and иꙁобрѣтє 6:2. The construction абы написалъ is rather more complicated, see C3:9.

[144] See also и запєѵатаху, *wnḥtm* 3:12, посылаху 3:13 for *wnšlwḥ*, постилаху for *yc'* (*yuca'*). Similar rendering of Gk passives, particularly when they do not have an explicit agent, by the generic 3p active is frequent elsewhere, e.g., in Malalas, cf. Istrin's list, 1914 41–42.

result in a Sl. passive, и написано 3:12 (compare створено *n'śh* 6:3). The generic 3p active appears for H 3s impersonal passive in 2:11 as well, оувѣдѣти...ѵто быша створили єи (cf. C2:11).

A13.61 The passive infinitive of H, though it can be expressed by a morphological equivalent in Gk, sometimes comes out strangely; thus дати ʒаконъ for *lhntn dt* 'to be given as law' 3:14 but даниє ʒакона 8:13.[145]

A13.62 Both active and passive H infinitive constructs may be rendered in LXX Gk and consequently in Slavic by temporal subordinate clauses. Thus 1:4 *bhr'tw* 'and in his showing' appropriately becomes єгда жє показа, while the passive *wbhšm'* 'and in the being heard' is и въньгда услышанъ бысть 2:8. In Esther, however, the H passive more often corresponds to a Sl active, e.g., for H *wbhqbc* 'and in the gathering' (intrans.) we find и ꙗкожє събра 2:8 and и ꙗкожє събрашѧ 2:19 (accepting the var. from U and S).

A13.63 Attributive passive participles apparently caused difficulties. In both instances of *hnmc'ym* 'those being found,' i.e., 'those present,' active constructions are used: всѣмъ...єликожє ихъ обрѣтє 1:5 and всѧ...єжє ихъ ѡбрѧщєши 4:16. The use of обрѣсти сѧ 'be found; be' is common in OCS.[146]

A13.62 In contrast, predicative passive participles generally come out correctly, e.g., *wymc' ktwb* 'and it was found *written*' 6:2 и изоѡбрѣтє в них написано 'and he found in them written.' On the other hand, [the days] 'are being remembered and kept' *nzkrym w n'śym* 9:28 is turned around to и днии сиꙗ поминающє суть и творѧщє ꙗ, approximately 'and [they = the Jews] are remembering these days and doing *them*,' with the 3p verb governing an accusative object; the construction was unclear enough to require the addition of a pronominal object, ꙗ, to the second verb. Similarly in 2:14, 'she was called'—where the context implies that the call will come from a servant at the order of the king—is позвашє ю, with an explicit pronominal object 'her' and an implied subject-agent, the king.

A13.63 Substitution of active for passive constructions affects the relationship between the logical subject and object, sometimes bringing about a change of focus and perspective. Thus in 2:1, when the king rembers his former queen Washti, apparently with some regret, the MT has *w't 'šr ngzr 'lyh* 'and that which was adjudged on her.' The Slavonic ижє осуди на ню makes the king the express agent of judgement, 'what he had judged against her,' which may emphasize his possible remorse. Similarly въпишєть 1:19, събра 2:8, поʒвашє 2:14, събрашє 2:19 (but see comm.), абы написалъ 3:9, изоѡбрѣтє 6:2 implicitly present actions ascribed to the king, against the equivalent passive forms without explicit agent in H.

145 Cf. створити for *lh'śt* 'to be done' 9:1, but створи for the same H in 9:14. Thomson 1994 318 remarks that the Gk passive inf δέδοσθαι was rendered дано in a 10th-century Bg translation, but дати сє in a 14th-century Serbian version.

146 There are non-Biblical examples of 'be found' in the sense 'prove to be, turn out to be' or simply 'be,' yet the frequency of this meaning in Biblical Greek surely reflects Semitic idiom. In turn, we may surmise that early Slavic usage is strongly Hellenistic, but there is no way to demonstrate the limits of native use. SRJaXI, s.v. обрѣсти ся cites the Gennadius Bible, Daniel 5:11, a verse that goes back to Aramaic, and parallels from early Slavic authors. Compare the 15th-century translation of 2 Chron 31:1: *kl yśr'l hnmc'ym l'ry yhwdh*, LXX πᾶς Ἰσραηλ οἱ εὑρηθέντες ἐν πόλεσιν Ἰουδα, OB весь і҃ль иже обретенъ бысть въ градѣ[x] Іoудиныхъ. In the 17th century найтися/находиться in this sense is attested, and its use becomes normal in the 18th century, possibly because it was reinforced by Fr *se trouver* and Ger *sich befinden, sich (vor)finden.*

A13.64 The lack of clarity of such sentences may have caused someone to add an explicit subject; thus the impersonal H 'everything that was done' 4:1 becomes все еже творѧше царь 'everything the king did.'

A13.71 Reversal of roles in active/passive constructions also occurs, particularly in expressions of pleasing, e.g., verses 2:4 and 9; see L12.52, C2:9.

A13.72 The indefinite passive leaves the actor unclear, whereas an active construction makes the actor explicit. E.g. the impersonal promises 'it shall be granted thee . . . it shall be done' have become first-person statements и дамь ти .. и створимъ тобѣ in 5:6 and 7:2.[147]

A13.73 The generic agent of a suggestion in 2:2, when the king's servants advise him, 'let there be sought young virgins,' or 'let one seek,' 'que l'on cherche' becomes explicit in да поискали быхомъ цареви дѣвыхъ дѣвиць 'let *us* seek.' Similarly, Haman's advice about the man to be honored starts with an unspecified 3p equivalent of a jussive, да принесоут пърты 6:8, but goes on in 6:9 with the generic 3p 'and let one dress the man' which in Slavonic is specifically 1p и да ѡблеѵем мужа, 'let *us* dress the man'; further, 5:14 'let one make' yields a somewhat unusual imperative сдѣлающе будѣте. In 4:5, the causative *h'myd* keeps the king in the foreground as it defines the eunuch (тиоунъ) 'whom he caused to stand before her,' i.e., to wait on her. LXX removes the king, making the eunuch the subject ὃς παρειστήκει; similarly our version, иже стоꙗше.

A13.81 There are other ways in which a change of focus comes about in the translation. At the crucial dramatic point of the plot, between the two drinking feasts, the MT tells us that 'on that night the sleep of the king wandered off/departed,' but in our text смѧте сѧ царь въ снѣ 'the king was disturbed/confused in his sleep/dream.' (See further C6:1).

A13.82 A change from verb to noun also shifts the focus. Thus 'for so had the king appointed' 1:8 becomes ибо бѧше такъ оуставъ царевъ 'for such was the decree/appointment/ of the king.'

A13.83 'For she was of good appearance [= fair to behold]' 1:11 is replaced by '(to show) her good appearance' и еже добрыи възоръ еꙗ. See comm.

A13.84 'Except the king delighted in her' 2:14 becomes нъ егда будѧше волѧ царева на неи 'except when the king's will/desire was on her.' Perhaps in this case the Gk translator took the unvocalized *ḥpc* to be a noun instead of a verb.

A13.85 'For so had the king commanded concerning him' 3:2 becomes ꙗко тако имъ бѧше заповѣдь царева, 'for thus was the king's command to them,' whereby the singular pronoun 'about him' is replaced by a plural имъ which has to denote the recipients of the command.[148]

A13.86 'Haman sought' 3:6 is transformed to и волѧ бы[с] Амонова, 'and it was/became Haman's wish.'

A13.9 Hebrew morphological causatives (*hif'il*) are, on the whole, rendered by semantically appropriate Sl lexemes.

147 The form створимъ looks plural, though the sense would be more appropriately singular, cf. A11.12.
148 Compare the wording of V: тако имь баше заповѣда цр҃ѧ, perhaps for заповѣда[л] цр҃ь.

A13.91 Only once do we find a periphrastic equivalent to a *hif'il* form: in 6:11 'and he caused him to ride' *wyrkybhw* comes out створи поѥздити ємоу. GorNev (with Ro, M56a 210) cite this as proof of direct translation from Hebrew to Slavic. It is, rather, a literal translation of a form of Gk ποιεῖν plus infinitive, a clear Hellenism (see T9.31). The same Hebrew verb in 6:9 comes out with the appropriate lexeme провести.

A13.92 In 2:17, створи ю царицю, with double accusative, corresponds to the H hif'il *wymlykh* 'he caused her to rule.' There are instances where Sl shows no trace of the H causative, e.g., пьѩху 1:7 for H 'to cause to drink,' не оуврѣдити 1:17 for H 'make disrespectful,' стоѩше 4:5; such examples will be noted in the commentaries to individual verses.

A14 Syntactical observations

A14.1 Subordinate clauses in Esther nearly always begin with a conjunction. In OCS Gospel texts and other narratives, it is common that an active participle may function as a clause subordinate to a main clause with a finite verb-form. In Esther there are only three such clauses, two in a single sentence. И *въздъхнувъ* Аманъ приде къ дому своєму и *пославъ* приведе приѩзнь свою 5:10;[149] всплака *молѧщи* єго 8:3. (A fourth instance is dubious, for the participle stands where a finite verb would be expected, 7:7 и царь въставъ . . . и Амонъ ста; H has *qm* 'stood up.' For a possible fifth, the attributive повѣсивъ главу of 6:12 is semantically different from the Hebrew, see comm.) A second subordinating device is the dative absolute; it occurs only once in Esther: и єще же глаголющимъ имъ с нимь и се тивуни цареви приступиша 6:14.

A14.2 In all of these cases the Slavonic reflects the relatively simple syntax of the Hebrew. The LXX, despite the fact that its paraphrase of Esther often adds syntactic and phraseological embellishments, tends to avoid the use of participial subordinate clauses. Precisely where the Slavonic has the exceptions, LXX usually agrees: 5:10 καὶ εἰσέλθων . . . [O-text] ἀπόστειλας ἐκάλεσεν.[150] Yet LXX, and L, do permit introductory participles in some instances, e.g., 4:17 καὶ βαδίσας Μαρδοχαιος ἐποίησεν, but и приде М. и створи = H *wy'br. . . wy'ś*; 4:16 βαδίσας ἐκκλησίασον, but иди, събери = H *lk, knws!*[151] It is also striking that the lone genitive absolute in the LXX text that corresponds to the MT is precisely in 6:14, ἔτι αὐτῶν λαλούντων. This is a natural equivalent for the H participle which must be construed as referring to the people of the previous sentence, not the eunuchs in the following main clause.[152] The syntax of the additions tends to be more complex, and the very first sentence starts with a dative absolute, βασιλεύοντος Ἀρταξέρξου A:1, and others occur, e.g., B:3. It is plausible, therefore, to presume that our hypothetical Greek intermediary translation followed Hebrew syntax in the use of these forms, so that our text remains faithful to the original.

149 Semantically, въздъхнувъ presents a puzzle, see C5:10.

150 In 8:3 LXX omits the verb 'wept' and has 'and besought'; one O-ms, however, substitutes the present participle, now dependent on the previous aorist, 'fell': ἔπεσεν . . . ἀξιοῦσα.

151 LXX is more likely to have a participle than is L, e.g. 3:5 LXX ἐπιγνοῦς Ἀμαν . . . , but L ὡς δὲ ἤκουσεν (и видѣ Аманъ); cf. 4:1 LXX ἐπιγνοῦς, L ἐπέγνω (бѣ вѣдаѧ).

152 The OCS and early East Slavic dative absolute need not be regarded a calque from the Greek genitive absolute. There is no reason to deny older Indo-European syntactic structures for Late Common Slavic simply because they later were lost in the attested forms of individual dialects. It may well be that the dative absolute was relatively rare in spoken dialects by the 11th century, and that their use in writing does have a flavor of bookishness, but this in no way makes it foreign.

A14.3 The perfect tense, i.e., *l*-participle with a present auxiliary (or zero in 3s), is used: далъ єсмь 8:7; ꙗкоже глаголалъ єси . . . єже єси глаголалъ 6:10; ꙗко поꙋчалъ єси падати 6:13; съкривила 1:16. These examples illustrate the typical function of the perfect as a weak predicate, when the focus is on another part of the sentence (as in 1:16), as a non-narrative form (6:10, 13), or as a statement (8:7) opposed to the narrated fact (8:1, where the king performed the act expressed by an aorist form, дасть).

A14.4 In 1:19, ꙗко нє пришла is unclear. From H the sense is '(she) is not to come,' and it is possible that the translator had a conditional with бы, but the context is uncertain and any conjecture must be extremely speculative.

Lexicon

L0.11 Vocabulary as a rule varies regionally; different dialects of a language ordinarily have characteristically individual lexicons. Standard languages must be selective; not all dialect words can be admitted for general use. As a standard evolves over time, the written vocabulary may retain words or meanings that no longer correspond closely to ordinary every-day speech in any living dialect. The greater the area and dialectal diversity the standard is intended to cover (and the greater the time over which the written standard has developed), the more difficult it is to assign regional significance to any lexical item or even a short list of items.

L0.12 The language of the Slavs in the ninth century surely was not uniform over the vast region from the Baltic to the Mediterranean and the Black Sea, but the dialect divisions that can be discerned in the phonological and morphological systems are minor indeed.[1] Our oldest body of Slavic texts, the Old Church Slavonic manuscripts, were written at unknown times and places: we believe most of them to date from about 950–1050, probably written in what is now Macedonia, Bulgaria, or northern Greece. They preserve texts of different origins—some going back to the work of Constantine-Cyril (863–69) and its continuation under Methodius (c872–85), others translated after 890 in the southwest (Macedonia, with the major cultural center in Ohrid) or the southeast (with a major center in Preslav). The phonology and morphology of all the OCS texts is fairly homogeneous; it is the vocabulary that exhibits the greatest variation. It shows, no doubt, regional preferences. Unfortunately, there is no set of reliable criteria that allows us to classify individual words, or particular meanings of words, by region. Matters are complicated by the probability that in our oldest texts regional differences stand side by side with temporal differences.

L0.13 More than a century of study of OCS and related manuscripts has produced lists of words that are believed to typify a more conservative or western lexicon ("Moravan" plus "Macedonian" or "Ohrid") versus a more innovating or eastern ("Preslav" or "East Bulgarian") type. Yet even the oldest surviving texts show that western and/or archaic words could be tolerated in a predominantly eastern text, while an occasional eastern innovation could find its way into a faithful copy of an older western work. This sort of variation is typical of an evolving standard language. When this written language was adopted in Rus′ in the 11th century and its texts were read and copied by East Slavs, the new users had their own perception of the semantic and stylistic value of possible variants and added (or substituted) local words and meanings they felt appropriate. Lists of this kind of "Russisms" have also been compiled. Unfortunately, much of this work has been haphazard and criteria for selecting and evaluating words have been imprecise or even contradictory. It is obvious that the vocabulary of a text is a possible clue to the time and place it was written (or translated into Slavic), but this kind of evidence must be used with caution.

L0.21 In the commentary we have treated words in their specific contexts, with attested variants and concern for the sense to be expected from the Hebrew text. Here we examine words as part of the systematic lexicon of Esther against a broad background—the vocabu-

[1] On the relationships among early historical Slavic dialects and written evidence, see Lunt 1950, 1982, 1985a, 1990, 1996.

lary known from standard Old Church Slavonic and later medieval manuscripts that contain modified copies of originally OCS texts and newer works (including translations) by a variety of later hands. We pay particular attention to Rusian and later East Slavic works because the Slavonic Esther is known only from ESl copies, and all the variants and alternations must be presumed to have been introduced by East Slavs. The arrangement of items and topics grew from our intuitive associations of Hebrew, Greek, and Slavonic materials—semantic, derivational, textual—and the scholarly literature about Esther. The ordering is of necessity arbitrary, as is the placement of major or minor treatments; we hope that cross-references will allow readers to establish complex relationships we could not fit into the linear sequence of chapter-verse comments.

L0.22 We start with the external scene—the city and the palace, with its complex subdivisions and spaces, and the furnishings—and move to the background human beings, officials (from princes and governers to scribes) and servants, friend, enemy, and kin. Then we treat clothing and the cloths from which they are made. Terms for *face, eyes, hand* and *soul* are important because of special idioms that in part go back to biblicisms that are well known in Greek. The ubiquitous general verb *to do, make* leads to the concern for speech acts and their results—the close relationship of *word, matter* and *deed. Speaking* and *recounting* are related to *commanding, law,* and *power.* The manifold uses of the root *mysl* involve not only thought, but *query* and *request*; these lead to *desire* and notions of *pleasing. Feasting* and *celebration* alternate with *lamentation, fear, anger,* then *shame* and its antonym *honor,* then the important themes of *killing* and *destruction* and *plunder.* Finally we discuss certain verbs denoting *motion* and words expressing *time.*

L0.23 It is not our intention to examine every lexeme, for many of them are normal in old and new texts.

L0.31 The vocabulary of Esther is the chief criterion that has led investigators to the conclusion that it is an East Slavic translation. The problems are not simple and it is clear that the lexicon of many more works, in particular chronographs and related historical pieces, must be investigated before some questions can be meaningfully formulated, let alone answered satisfactorily.

L0.32 The running text of Esther, as we have printed it, is close to 4100 words; the lexicon of Esther includes just under 600 words, excluding the proper names. Most of them are known from the oldest layers of attested Slavic, but many are unusual and some are unique.[2] A measure of the special quality of this vocabulary is the fact that Sreznevskij's Материалы use Esther in more than 50 entries, without exhausting the unusual items or meanings.[3] Twenty-three of these entries cite only Esther, while 8 adduce Esther for special sub-meanings. Twenty-two lemmas include citations from Esther that supplement evidence from other texts.

[2] In rough calculation, 70% are found also in the OCS Gospels, another 10% from other OCS manuscripts, and perhaps 6% more from mss we symbolize as *OCS (copies, chiefly made in early Rus′, that, we believe, preserve characteristics of originally OCS texts). Still others surely belonged to early language and are not attested because they were not, by chance, required for the texts which have survived, e.g., ꙗздити/ѣздити 'ride (on horseback).'

[3] Six lemmas provide a word that is in Esther, but not the appropriate meaning (бобръ, врєдно, въображєна, жєланиє, остоꙗти, пєѵатьникъ). Five items are not in Srez (нарєканиє, прєпродана, расповѣданиє, оудобрити/оудобрѣти, оумьстити сѧ). One word (навѣшю) has no separate lemma but occurs in an illustration of another (конобъ, a word not in Est).

L0.41 Evaluation of the age and stylistic value of lexemes requires a point of view. We have framed our discussion to allow a range of hypotheses to be tested: that Esther might have been translated before about 1050 in the South Slavic area, or in either the South or East Slavdom as late as the 14th century (cf., e.g., the note to L5.12). The fact that some rare items are shared by Esther and 15th-century texts that certainly are translated from Hebrew has been cited as proof that Esther too is a direct translation from the MT; in our opinion it merely demonstrates that the manuscripts were copied by scribes—or perhaps were new products of translators—who shared the same traditions, viz. the Ruthenian culture of the 14th–15th century.[4]

L0.411 On the whole, the lexicon contains words that are known from OCS and the manuscripts ascribed to 11th–12th century Rus′. A single morpheme, *vrěd,* in нє оувредити, въ нєвредъ, and нє врѣдно, has a positive meaning 'value, worth' that is otherwise known only from western South Slavic (see L16.2).[5] Most of the other words are to be found in East Slavic, and the less common ones are usually registered in Berynda's lexicon (1627, 1653).

L0.42 Esther is remarkable on the one hand for multiple equivalents of one Hebrew lexeme (or by our hypothesis one or two Greek words), and on the other for consistency in error or idiosyncratic usage. Thus there are four terms for 'banquet' (L13.7), and 'garment' (L5.1). The second noun in 'sackcloth and ashes' has twice been converted to a near-synonym for sackcloth, surely a mistaken generalization (L5.31). Less clear is растворити, thrice as first member of the formula 'to wipe out, slaughter, and annihilate,' where раȥорити seems more appropriate (L17), yet there is some indication that растворити indeed meant 'destroy' in a Ruthenian tradition (L17.63). The most striking and unexpected stem is *oxvot-* 'glad' (L13.3–6), where *rad-* might be expected.

L0.43 Some of the unique or unusual words denote exotic objects (блискъ, бобръ, лєптугъ, лєптужьнъ, утринъ, ушьвъ) or persons (сатрапъ [?], подъставъ) that are not called for in most texts. Others are made of familiar morphemes, combined in ways not attested elsewhere (подѣти, вольникъ, въnатъщь) or with meanings that are special (оудобрити сѧ). The absence of such common lexemes as кънѧѕь 'prince' (L2.01), слово (L8.11), and радъ 'glad' (L13.5) adds to the special atmosphere of the Slavonic Esther.

L0.5 Our chief sources for comparable words (attested in OCS and/or *OCS, cf. note 2, p. 186) are Sreznevskij's fundamental Материалы, the Prague OCS dictionary (SJS), *SRJaXI,* the word-indexes to the *Izbornik* of 1073 (Dinekov 1993), the *Izbornik* of 1076 (ed., Kotkov 1965), the *Sinai Patericon* (Dumitrescu 1973–76), the *Uspenskij sbornik* (ed., Kotkov 1971), John the Exarch's *Hexameron* (Aitzetmüller, vol. VII), the *Chronicle* of George the Monk, Hamartolos (Istrin 1930 vol. 3), and Josephus's *Jewish War* (Hansack 1990–91). We have also consulted the published glossaries to various sorts of medieval texts and drawn from our own notes on published and unpublished Slavic manuscripts.

[4] E.g. the preposition оунє 'concerning' (A9.4), the verb растворити 'destroy' (L17.6), and the nouns просьба 'request' (L12.13) and нарѣканиє 'lamentation' (L14.2).

[5] Taken together with the striking anomaly of обрѧкю (not OCS обрѧщѧ or early Rusian обрѧѵю, cf. A1.41), створимъ for expected 1s сътворю (cf. C5:8), and perhaps another detail or two, this might tempt one to hypothesize a Serbian or Croatian origin.

L1 Structures, spaces, furnishings

L1.1 The MT distinguishes *h'yr šwšn* 'the city of Shushan' (8:15), usually referred to simply as 'the city,' from *šwšn hbyrh* 'Shushan the acropolis' (e.g., 1:2, 8:14), the royal part of the capital which was separated from the city (Moore 5, Bickerman 208). The loanword *bira* occasionally is rendered in LXX by βάρις, understood as a large house, tower, or palace. In Esther, however, it comes out as πόλις, except that in 8:14 most Origen texts have ἐν Σούσοις τῇ βάρει. The Slavonic text has only **градъ**; this must reflect a Gk text with πόλις in all instances. H *rḥwb* 'street' is represented by улица (3x); the mediating word was probably ῥύμη, as in Isaiah 15:3.[6] The gates, **врата**—presumably to the city—were doubtless fixed with a passage through thick walls: Mordecai and others customarily sit (LXX says 'serve') *in* the gates.

L1.2 The palace of Ahashwerosh within the acropolis of Shushan must have been an elaborate structure far beyond the experience of most writers and readers of the Jewish and Christian scriptures. The description of the banquet room in verse 1:6 (see comm.) was garbled very early, and just where other events took place is not always clear. The Hebrew text has no specific words for *room, chamber.*

There is no special designation for the palace: H 'king's house' *byt hmlk* comes out simply as **домъ** царевъ (or царѧ) eight times. The less usual 'house of kingship' *byt hmlkwt* also is въ дому царевѣ in 1:9, but more literally въ домъ царства своего in 2:16. In 5:1, however, is въ полатѣ своеи, with a more specific word for 'palace'; it is repeated at the end of the verse where H has the unmodified word 'house' but clearly refers to the same structure, прѧмо полаты, see comm. (Since **полата** may denote a single room or chamber, a palace is usually referred to by the plural, полаты.)

L1.201 The use of полата in 3:9 and 4:7 gives no hint that H has a specialized term, *treasury* (LXX γάζα, var. γαζοφυλάκιον); the context of paying money is not sufficient to establish this meaning for the Slavic lexeme. Sreznevskij does give examples, exclusively from Rusian sources, for полата in the sense of treasury, but the connection with this text is not clear.

L1.21 The palace also contains the домъ женьскыи, lit. 'female house,' surely calqued from οἶκος γυναικῶν representing 'house of the women,' H *byt hnšym*, often rendered in this context as 'harem' (cf. Moore 18).[7] This harem has a court, 2:11. In 2:14 къ дому женьскому другому affirms the 'second harem' of MT (*'l byt hnšym šny*, cf. LXX εἰς τὸν γυναικῶνα τὸν δεύτερον) that puzzles commentators, cf. Moore 23.

L1.211 The scene of Esther's party for the king and Haman is a 'house of drink,' дому питвеному, 7:8; LXX omits it, but the O-mss have εἰς τὸν οἶκον τοῦ πότου τοῦ οἴνου, approximating H 'house of the party/banquet of wine.'

6 LXX usually translates *rḥwb* with πλατεία (incl. Est 6:9, 11), which ordinarily comes out стъгна in OCS and related texts (cf. SJS sub стьгна; the normalization with ь is questionable). The notions of *street, lane,* and *crossroads,* as opposed to *public open space, square, market-place* are not clearly distinguished in medieval Slavic usage. In 1073 (683.9) and Malalas, по улицамъ (Istrin 1911 22.18) renders κατὰ (τὴν) ἀγοράν. The earliest attestations of улица (e.g., the *Hexameron*) may well denote *corridor* or *narrow passage* either within a building or between buildings.

7 LXX uses the rare word γυναικών; elsewhere a harem or other areas set aside for women may be γυναικωνῖτις.

L1.22 **Дворъ** regularly corresponds to the H 'court,' except that in 5:1 it is confused with домъ, see comm. The 'inner court' in 4:11 and 5:1 is дворъ дънѣшьнии, and in 6:4 there is an 'outer court' (H *bḥcr byt hmlk hḥycwnh*, lit. 'in court-of the-house-of the-king the-outer,' where the feminine adjective unambiguously goes with the noun 'court'). The syntax of the attested phrase къ двору дому царєва вънѣшнєго unambiguously dictates the meaning 'to [the limts of] the court of the king's outer palace.'[8] This shift of meaning has no bearing at all on the story, but it is another instance where the Slavonic text does not correspond to the MT.

L1.221 Within the palace are open spaces and/or other structures. They may be separated by **двьри** 'doors' or врата 'gates' (both formally *pluralia tantum*, see also L2.43).

L1.23 In the banquet-chamber of 1:6 are **стѣны** 'walls' and **оустиꙗ**, presumably 'openings'; see C1:6.

L1.231 The term **оградъ** 'garden' occurs three times, corresponding to H *gnh* in the phrase *gnt bytn.*[9] In 1:5 *bḥcr gnt bytn hmlk* comes out въ дворѣ ѡграда оутрьнєго царѧ,[10] while in 7:7 and 7:8 *gnt bytn* yields къ ѡградȣ днѣшнєму and ѿ ѡграда днѣшнєго. Both **утрьнии** and **дънѣшьнии** mean 'inner' (cf. 4:11), therefore reference appears to be to an inner garden (which in 1:5 somehow has a court). Modern commentators take *bytn* as a structure, a sort of open pavilion or summer house (cf. Moore 7), but early translators saw it rather as an adjunct to the noun *garden.* Thus, while LXX has simply κῆπος, the Origen-influenced texts add ὁ σύμφυτος, perhaps in the sense 'thickly wooded,' compare Vulg *arboribus consitum* 7:7, *nemoribus consito* 7:8. The Sl corresponds rather to the Jewish interpretation embodied in the Targum rendering *gynt' gw'h/gww'h* 'inner garden' (1:5, 7:7, 8). It is justified by Ibn Ezra in his commentary to 1:5. He analyzes *bytn* as derived from *byt* 'house' and mentions the metaphorical use of *byt* in the adverbial pair *mbyt/mḥwc* 'within'/'outside.'[11]

L1.3 In the banquet scene in 1:6, beds are mentioned, and **ложє** is used. In 7:8, Esther's bed is **постєлꙗ**. H has *mṭh* for both. While LXX uses κλίνη twice, L has it in 1:6 but κοίτη in 7:8. We may conjecture that our Greek translator also used two different words. OCS commonly uses одръ and ложє, while постєлꙗ stands for στρωμνή; in terms of etymology both Sl and Gk refer to the bed-clothes or material *strewn* for lying on.[12] H *ks'* 'chair' yields **столъ**, normal for θρόνος (cf. O-copies and L) or σκάμνος in OCS and general in medieval texts.[13]

[8] It is understandable that a correct dative form внѣшнєму might have been miscopied by an inattentive scribe, so this "mistake" cannot be attributed to the translator. In a comparable case, a dative desinence was substituted by the scribe of T for a genitive one, двору дому жєньскому 2:11.

[9] In T the prefix is omitted twice, leaving град- 'fortress, city' and thereby obscuring the sense of the passages.

[10] T's variant, града creates an "inner fortress" that is entirely out of place.

[11] This tradition is still valid for Vil. 262, 7:17 кь палате нȣтренои and 7:8 ѿ полаты нȣтреное.

[12] Less clear is the function of the "sackcloth" власѧницѣ и сукна, that 'they spread for the elders'; see C4:3.

[13] *Pace* M56a 215, столъ meaning 'седалище' is in no way "typical Russian." Specialized terms for *seat, bench, chair, throne* and *table* developed at different times in different Slavic regions.

L2 Officials, positions; social relationships, kinship terms.

L2.0 Part of the background of the story of Esther is an array of courtiers, officials, and subordinates, whose precise positions are unimportant to the narrative. Our text has (apart from the central **царь** and **царица**) the terms **вєльможа**, **болѧринъ** (and **болѧрынꙗ**), **сатрапъ** (a conjecture), **старѣишина**, **староста**, **тиоунъ**, and **судии**. There are also lesser functionaries such as **подставъ**, **приставникъ**, **приставъ**, **чинѧщє дѣло**, **погоньци**, **конникы**, **писци**, **двьрникъ**, **хранитель**, as well as **отроци**, **слугы**, **раби**, **рабынѧ**, **домачадица**, **дѣвы**, and **наложьницы**.

L2.01 Two aspects of this array of terms are striking; first, the unusual or unique terms that have attracted scholarly attention from the beginning, and second—and of great importance for the questions of the origin and history of the Slavonic text—the *absence* of normal early Slavic terms.

L2.02 At the time the Slavs began to assimilate the higher culture and more complex social organization of their neighbors, they appear to have had little or no terminology designating leaders. The inherited господь has become the supreme, if rather vague, ruler.[14] In the civil sphere кънѧѕь (a loan from Germanic **kuningaz*) and владыка (with a suffix *-ūk-* that may well indicate borrowing) are not clearly specified in terms of responsibilities, while the usual military chief was the воєвода, a word made of native morphemes, but suspiciously similar to OHG *herizogo* and related Germanic forms that in turn imitate Gk στρατηγός 'general,' lit. 'army-leader.' A lesser ruler was властєль; вождь in old texts is usually *guide* rather than leader. None of these lexemes appears in Esther. Nor does начальникъ, solidly attested in OCS, though somewhat marginal. Nor do we find such less common but well established terms as къмєтъ, known from Monomax (Lav 250.38) as well as early Serbian and Czech texts, or жюпанъ (see SJS), or the *гъпанъ we must posit to account for OCz *hpán*, later *pán*, used also by other West Slavs and exported into Belarusian and Ukrainian regions. It must also be stressed that Esther lacks any of the imported terms like игумєнъ or стратигъ that were common in the oldest translations and reappear in 13th–14th century translations.[15] In sum, the array in Esther is unusual. It is also inconsistent, even contradictory.

L2.1 Болѧринъ and вєльможа are, as in OCS, essentially synonyms for 'noble, prince, notable.' (Болѧрынꙗ is the wife of a *boljarin.*) In all instances, H has *śar* in the corresponding verses.[16] Болѧрє or вєльможа ȥємныꙗ are provincial people of importance. Старѣишина, a word of wide applicability in OCS for leaders of all sorts of groups, in 1:8 refers to officials in charge of a feast, for its meaning is specified by домоу and it corresponds to H *rb bytw* רב ביתו (LXX οἰκονόμοι). In 4:3, however, *rb* should have the more usual meaning 'many' (LXX omits), so we expect *множьствоу rather than старѣишинамъ, see C4:3.

14 That neither господь nor богъ occurs in our text is no surprise, since none of the twoscore H words or phrases that evoke κύριος 'lord' in LXX is to be found in the Scroll of Esther (see Moore's remarks, The Absence of Religious Elements in the Book of Esther, xxxii-xxxiv). The additions in LXX (cf. In2.5) attempt to repair this defect by providing prayers addressed to the Lord.

15 Like Esther, Daniel also requires an arsenal of terms for Persian court officials. In Dan 3:3 LXX has [1] οἱ τοπάρχοι, [2] ὕπατοι, [3] στρατηγοί, [4] ἡγούμενοι, [5] τύραννοι μεγάλοι [5a] οἱ ἐπ' ἐξουσιῶν, καὶ [6] πάντες οἱ ἄρχοντες τῶν χωρῶν > Slavonic [1] мѣстъни кнѧȥи єго, [2] ипати [ѵпати, ѡпати] и [3] воєводы и [4] владыкы и [5] моучитєлє вєлии [5a] (var. ижє) надъ властъми и [6] въси кнѧȥи странъни [странъ, страньнии].

16 H *śr* occurs 15x; вєльможа corresponds to it 6x, болѧрє 8x, болѧринъ 1 (6:9).

L2.2 Староста and тиоунъ (or тивунъ) refer to various sorts of stewards. Despite the statements of Russian scholars, neither word is exclusively East Slavic. The presence and frequence of the two terms in Esther (in fourteen different verses, from 1:10 to 9:3) surely was a major factor in persuading Russian scholars that the book was translated by an East Slav. The distribution is the same in Q and T, but sometimes where both have тиоунъ/тивунъ ms V and/or W replaces it with староста. Did both words occur in much earlier copies, or was one gradually replacing the other? Perhaps evidence from other manuscripts will help answer this question.

L2.21 In general usage, староста is well known in Old Czech and Polish as well as East Slavic; it occurs in the Novgorod First Chronicle s.a. 1016 and the PVL s.a. 1018.[17] The loan from Scandinavian, тиоунъ, is not attested in the PVL,[18] but is in Monomax (Lav, 246.4).[19] Both terms were in active use in the Ukrainian-Belarusian lands in the 14th–16th centuries (cf. SSUM). In the 1400s it is well attested in Latin documents from Poland, *tywn, thyn, cywun.*

L2.22 Староста and тиоунъ scarcely occur in other translated works.[20] In Esther they account for all twelve instances of H *srys* (*saris*) סריס 'chamberlain, eunuch.'[21] This word is usually rendered εὐνοῦχος in LXX, and in turn εὐνοῦχος becomes каженикъ or скопьць in OCS and such other early translations as Hamartolos. Yet it also appears as δυναστής (Ham вельможа 320.15), and we must assume that readers were able to decide that in certain contexts the words *saris* or εὐνοῦχος emphasized the status of trusted official rather than the individual's physical integrity. An early replacement of каженикъ is known from the Izbornik of 1076. In the *Life of St. Niphon*, the personage is a divine messenger, but the editor who adapted the Sozomenus episode for the princely miscellany found каженикъ inappropriate, and wrote оуношѧ красьнъ ѕѣло 'a very beautiful youth' instead (p. 690, l. 10). The substitution was most probably made in Bulgaria, as William Veder has established (1992, esp. pp. 362 and 331).

L2.23 Тиоунъ in 3:12 and 9:3 stands for H *'ḥšdrpn* (*'aḥašdarpan*) אחשדרפן, a loan from the Persian word represented by Greek σατράπης.[22] In both verses several officials are enumerated, and the next term is *pḥwt* (*paḥot*) פחות 'governors': it is represented by приставъ in 3:12 but подъставъ in 9:3 (without the preceding 'and' expected from H). In 8:9 the

17 Both examples refer to Jaroslav and are connected with Novgorod. After 1200 староста is well attested in *gramoty.*

18 Sub 1093 the discussion of the young men who misbehaved surely justifies the reading ти оунии (Lav, col. 417) as 'the young men,' rather than (*pace* Šaxmatov) previously unmentioned тиоуни 'tiuns, thanes, officials'; Hyp тивунѣ is surely a scribal misunderstanding.

19 Perhaps the chroniclers had no occasion to speak of any official with the specific title of *tiun*. There is no way to discover the precise duties of either a *starosta* or a *tiun*; surely they varied with different groups in time and place.

20 Староста is in the Life of Andrej Jurodivyj (Srez), a text that needs closer analysis than it has been given. The absence of a lemma староста in SJS indicates that the word is not in the Parimejniki. Sreznevskij's 16th-century example from Gen 19:4 represents a late, inappropriate substitution for старьць in the sense 'old man.' Тивунъ is in the 14th-century Пчела, an inappropriate rendering of δοῦλος, 'slave, servant.'

21 M56a 205 makes тивун "IV,21" a criterion for the old group of mss (1, 2, 16, 21, 23) versus староста in the two newer groups. This does not fit the facts: the word is not called for in 4:21, but in 2:15 and 2:21 G and Volok 12 agree with QT on тивунъ, while in 2:3, QT, G, and Volok 12 have тивунъ, and W has both, see variants.

22 The plural, with prefixed 'and' plus definite article, *wh'ḥšdrpnym* 9:3, is said (La Sor) to be the longest word in the Hebrew Bible. LXX 9:3 translates it οἱ τύραννοι.

same sequence is missing from all mss but Tn, which has и посадникѡ^{М} и тивоунo^{М}. It seems probable that Tn has changed the word-order—as it has in a considerable number of phrases—and safe to assume that *1350 had тиоунъ in first position, representing a single Gk word that stood consistently for *'ḥšdrpn*. Приставъ is an ESl word used for a wide variety of minor officials, but attested no earlier than 1270. Подъставъ, however, is unknown elsewhere with such a meaning (Srez defines 'наместник (?)'). Tn's посадникъ is well known from native Rusian sources, but it is probably not original in 8:9. In 9:3, QTSGVW's подъстави и чинѧщє дѣло has become поставиша оучинѧщи дѣло in X, and оуничиниша дѣло in Tn—both gibberish.[23] The apparent verb forms beginning with постав- may be relics of a noun (поставъ?, поставникъ?, see next paragraph). Подъставъ is unknown elsewhere with such a meaning. Приставъ, however, is an ESl word used for a wide variety of minor officials, but attested no earlier than 1270. In 8:10 съ приставы коньникы approximates H 'by means of couriers on horses' (see C8:10).

L2.24 In 2:3, приставникъ is an undefined 'official,' H *pqyd* פקיד. This seems to be a native word, used in OCS to denote a steward or overseer, a person appointed to a definite supervisory post. It renders several Gk terms, chiefly οἰκονόμος (which often remains as икономъ, see SJS)—also rendered as строител҃ь. Приставьникъ in Exodus and Ham, however, translates ἐπιστάτης. The parallelism of verb and noun приставилъ приставникы in 2:3 (which might seem to imitate H *wypqd pqydym*), could go back to a form of ἐφιστάναι and ἐπιστάτας.[24] In Ex 1:1, however, ἐπίστησεν ἐπιστάτας yields постави приставникы (Srez), while the поставникъ 36,000 постави of Ham 139.9 is based on non-parallel ἐπιστάτας 36,000 προστησάμενος. In any case, the Sl noun and verb surely are near-calques of Gk prefixed derivatives of the root *stand*.[25]

L2.3 Another Persian loan in H is *prtmym* (*partemim*) פרתמים 'nobles, notables' (etymologically 'foremost, first'), which occurs in Est 1:3 and 6:9.[26] When these vaguely understood words appear in sequences, a translator must decide what sort of equivalents to provide. In 6:9 is 'man from the nobles of the king, the nobles,' using first the native *śrym* (*śarim*) שׂרים and then the foreign *partemim*.[27] Our text has мужю болѧрину цареву судии, an impressive phrase that emphasizes this person's importance. In fact, the high status is all that matters for the story; the exact socio-political definition is of no particular significance. Verse 1:3—a part of a long and complicated sentence (cf. C1:1)—includes a ten-word listing of the categories of guests at the king's fabulously opulent banquet. Again the precise definitions are subordinate to the total effect of superior power and status. LXX and L both have equivalents of this sentence which are very likely based on somewhat different Hebrew wording, but the MT as it stands tempts translators to emend and paraphrase (cf. Levenson 42). The Slavonic clearly results from word-by-word literalism; L removes a bit, while LXX elaborates, though ignoring the final word:

23 Complex errors like this are not unheard of. Tn has ungrammatical so приставни^{к} for съ приставы коньникы predicted by the other mss in 8:10. The other mss all have печатьникомъ ꙁаконьнымъ in 4:8, with a dubious noun that is explained by Tn's печѧть книгъ ꙁаконныхъ, where the defining phrase is genitive rather than dative.

24 LXX chooses a different prefix and unrelated noun, 'governor': καταστήσει ὁ βασιλεὺς κωμάρχας.

25 A more accurate calque of ἐπι-στά-τ-ης 'preceptor, teacher' (in Luke) is на-став-ьник-ъ.

26 Otherwise, *partemim* occurs only Dan 1:3.

27 For discussion of this phrase, with the equivalents from LXX and L, see C6:9.

	сътвори	пиръ	{вьсѣмъ}	вельможамъ своимъ	и рабомъ своимъ
	'śh	*mšth*	*lkl-*	*śryw*	*w'bdyw*
LXX	δόχην ἐποίησεν			τοῖς φίλοις	καὶ τοῖς λοιποῖς ἔθνεσιν
L	ἐποίησεν ὁ βασιλεὺς πότον				τοῖς ἄρχουσι τῶν χωρῶν

	силѣ	фарсиистѣи	и мадѣистѣи	**странамъ**	и болѧромъ ꙁемнымъ
	ḥyl	*prs*	*wmdy*	*hprtmym*	*wśry hmdynwt*
LXX	καὶ τοῖς	Περσῶν	καὶ Μήδων	ἐνδόξοις	καὶ τοῖς ἄρχουσιν τῶν σατραπῶν
L		Περσῶν	καὶ Μήδων		καὶ οἱ ἄρχοντες τῶν χωρῶν

	иже ихъ о немь
	lpnyw
L	κατὰ πρόσωπον αὐτοῦ

The king gave a banquet "for all his nobles (*śarim*) and his servants, the army of the Persians and Medes, the nobles (*partemim*), and the nobles (*śarim*) of the provinces." In the position occupied by *partemim* in the H, Slavic has the incongruous form странамъ 'countries, nations.'

L2.31 AT proposed an original *сатрапомъ, which in turn suggests that σατραπαῖς was used in the hypothetical Greek text underlying the Slavonic translation. L has no equivalent, because the guests have been reduced to "the leaders (rulers, princes) of the court of the Persians and Medes and the leaders of the provinces (regions)." LXX is in effect quite different, because the equivalent word syntactically must refer to the Persians and Medes (and the neighboring terms have been changed): "for the (his) friends and the other (rest of the) nations and the distinguished (notables) of the Persians and Medes and the leaders of the satraps." The adjective ἔνδοξος 'of high repute' corresponds to the *partemim* of MT in LXX 6:9 as well, and it is used to describe Haman in LXX A:17. L omits it in both. The feminine noun-form странамъ is attested in all the mss and must be ascribed to *1350, but it does not fit semantically. The masculine *сатрапомъ seems to us a reasonable conjecture which would account for later scribal emendations. Thus *сатрапомъ seems to us a reasonable conjecture which would account for later scribal emendations.

L2.32 A second possibility involves the confusion of 'satrap' and 'satrapy': σατραπαῖς would become σατραπίαις/σατραπείαις, which the Slav then rendered by a more general term странамъ.[28] Either of our proposals favors a Greek intermediary text between the original Hebrew and the existing Slavonic Esther. Still a third possibility is some sort of distortion of the variants attested in Daniel.[29]

L2.33 While 'satrap' is common enough in historical works like Hamartolos, the untranslated word has been cited only from Daniel (6:1, 2, 4, 6, 7), the 16th-century Serbian copy of the *Alexandria* (Mikl), and the chronicle of George Syncellus.[30] A derivative сатрапьство is attested in 1 Kingdoms 6:4, but only in one manuscript, as far as we

28 Compare LXX variants in Est 8:9: τοῖς ἄρχουσιν τῶν σατράπων/σατραπίων, σατραπείας/σατράπαις (> Armenian, cf. Hanhart). A similar variation occurs in LXX E:1.

29 In Dan 3:3 οἱ ἄρχοντες τῶν χωρῶν are кнѧꙁи странъни in the oldest layer of translation, modified to кн҃ѕи странъ in the early revision (with corresponding accusative forms in 3:2).

30 In Hamartolos, σατράπης is rendered воевода or старѣишина воеводамъ; the translator understood it to signify a military leader, as did the glossator to Syncellus, see below.

know.[31] The rarity of сатрапъ means that it was unfamiliar to most Slavic readers; scribes distorted the forms in Daniel from сатрап- to сотрапи and сътрапи (Evseev 1905 92, 94).[32] We suggest that *сътрапомъ or even *страпомъ in Esther was "rationalized"—by one of the careless scribes we must posit for the history of this puzzling text—to a familiar if incongruous странамъ.[33] The meaning was also unclear to Slavs, and a copyist of Syncellus added a gloss, сатрапє, єже суть воєводы (Istrin 1922, 287). This illustrates again that we should not expect consistency of translation of words denoting foreign officials or objects, nor should we be surprised at arbitrary substitutions made by later scribes. Modern scholars know that σατράπης is the best equivalent of *'aḥašdarpan*, and indeed that is the equation in Daniel. But LXX σατράπας also appears for *paḥot* (which, as we saw in L2.23, caused difficulties in Esther) and *śar* (Esther вельможа/болѧрє) and some other words not used in Esther.[34]

L2.34 Be that as it may, another text provides a parallel. An inferior copy of a sermon by Cyril of Alexandria has началникы странамъ 'leaders/commanders of the nations' for ἄρχοντας τῶν σατράπων, while a superior copy has началникы сатрапомъ (and a third copy has сатарпомь).[35]

L2.41 Also undefined as to duties are the чинѧщє дѣло of 9:3, a faithful equivalent of the H phrase *'śy hml'kh*, which occurs several times in LXX as οἱ ποιοῦντες τὰ ἔργα.[36] In 3:9 къ строю дѣла stands for the same H in the phrase 'into the hands of them that do the works of the king'; surely emendation is required, perhaps строѧщю or строитєлю.[37]

L2.42 The писци 'scribes' of 3:12 and 8:9 are unproblematical, although the lexeme письць does not appear (except in compounds, cf. A8.12 fn) in OCS or early ESl mss.

L2.43 The two eunuch 'guardians of the threshold' appear as двьрника in 6:2 but ижє

31 Perhaps the phrase по числоу сатрапьствωхь, for LXX κατὰ ἀριθμὸν τῶν σατραπῶν [var. -πείων], in the 1418 Serbian ms Odessa DNB 6 (#125 in Mathiesen 1983a) is the work of a 15th-century editor; in any case, for all other known mss (RNB F I 461, 15–16th century Bulgarian [RM 27]; Q 1 2 [2 in our list], Gen. Bib. 1499 [our G], RGB Rum 29 [RM 62], 1537 Russian, RGB Grig. 1 [Muz 1684, RM 50], 16th century Serbian) Kul'bakin 1901 29–30 reports по числоу (чисмене) воеводъ (-дь); W has по чисмєни воєводъ, J по чисмєнє воєводъ.

32 In the oldest copy of Ham (c1300), *Socrates*, usually Сократ-, e.g., 248.10, also appears as скрат- 248.14 and as сєкратъ 260.8, where a variant from other manuscripts is съкрат-. The first syllable of the unfamiliar word is treated as if it were the variable prefix съ- со- с-, as in съкратити or сътворити.

33 The mechanical confusion of Cyrillic н and п is common, particularly in unfamiliar words, especially names. Thus Q has писанъ for the H month Nisan. Cf. *Izb 1076* крѣность for крѣпость (174v12), Malalas, Bk 6, Канетолїана for Καπιτωλῖνον, Istrin 1911 26.

34 Alekseev's strenuous objections to our conjecture (AT 1984 307) resulted in an obscure proposal (1987 4–5) that seems to us no better than Roždestvenskij's tortured hypothesis that the translator first omitted an equivalent for *partemim*, but then inserted странамъ in an effort to produce a meaningful sentence (cf. LT 153). Alekseev's 1993 ruminations (51–53) are equally muddled. He appears on the point of agreeing that a сътрапомъ from original сатрапомъ might have become странамъ, as we have suggested, but is unable to abandon his postulate that the common ancestor of all known copies (our *1350) represents the pristine Slavonic text. (He seems also to believe that *because* this was an East Slavic translation, its transmission could not depend on a single, relatively late and faulty, copy.) Therefore странамъ, he insists, belongs to the translator, who decided to use a word equivalent to H *gwy* '(foreign) nation' instead of a term for 'nobles.'

35 See Istrin 1893 350, with note 8 on p. 356; we are grateful to F. J. Thomson for locating the Greek original of the sermon and providing the third variant.

36 In LXX and L 9:3 *'śy hml'kh 'šr lmlk* have become οἱ βασιλικοὶ γραμματεῖς, 'the royal scribes.'

37 Origen 3:9 has the literal ἐπὶ χεῖρας τῶν ποιούντων τὰ ἔργα.

стрѣжаста вратъ in 2:21. Both are reasonable equivalents, but in one the H 'threshold' has apparently become двьри and in the other врата.[38] See commentary on the two verses. The 'guardian of the women' is хранитєль жєньскыи (2:3, 8, 15), where the adjective seems to be a mechanical rendering of an adnomimal Gp (LXX [φύλαξ] τῶν γυναικῶν), while the хранитєль ложница of 2:14 keeps a noun. For the variants ложница 'of the bedchamber' versus наложницамъ 'of the concubines,' see L2.47 below.

L2.44 'Couriers' are погоньци (later variant погонници VWG) apparently 'pursuers'; in 8:14 they are explicitly on swift horses. The term погоньць is known in this sense only in Esther. Unprefixed гоньць is attested after 1300, and becomes normal in later centuries. The H word in Esther is *rcym* 'runners.' The literal equivalent οἱ τρέχοντες (cf. 3:15 in the O-texts [cf. also LXX 2 Chron 30:6, 10]), would probably yield текѫщии. LXX paraphrases in 3:13, διὰ βιβλιοφόρων 'by letter-carriers'; in 3:15 the couriers are not mentioned; and in 8:14 they are ἱππεῖς 'horsemen, riders.' In 8:10, for H "by the hand of runners on horses" Sl has a paraphrase, съ приставы коньникы, see comm.

L2.441 The verb *po-gon-i-* is transitive, and погоньць occurs in Exod 5:6 (14th-century copy) as a variant of погонячь 'taskmaster' (here with the connotation of 'slave-driver'). The underlying Gk ἐργοδιώκτης is literally 'work-pursuer' with the morpheme διωκ 'chase, pursue' that corresponds to Sl. *gon gъn žen*. Although both in Greek and Slavic these roots occasionally imply hasty movement,[39] the verbs погонити, погънати 'chase, pursue' ordinarily specify or imply a goal; this transitivity is part of the meaning of погонячь, also attested as 'driver, charioteer.'[40] It is unexpected that погоньць should signify simply 'swift messenger' rather than 'pursuer.'

L2.45 Designations for servants are various. The отроци of 2:2, 6:3 and 6:5 are 'youths' in H. In the first two examples they are defined by the appositive noun слугы; H has a defining participle 'serving.'[41] The Origen version has οἱ διάκονοι οἱ λειτοῦργοι αὐτοῦ in 2:2, with a non-participial rendering, but in 6:3 τὰ παιδάρια τῷ βασιλεῖ οἱ ἐκ τῆς διακονίας. The Slavonic предъ всѣми слугами своими of 2:15 is grammatically flawless, but semantically dubious, and the H means 'in the eyes of all who saw her,' LXX παρὰ πάντων τῶν βλεπόντων αὐτήν.[42]

L2.451 Рабъ corresponds to H *'bd,* 'servant, slave' seven times,[43] but in 6:13 it stands for 'friends.' The problem is not one of simple mistranslation or careless copying, but of interpretation of the personal relationships. Highly placed subordinates may at the same

[38] In LXX, H *sp* 'threshold' is rendered by θύρα and πύλη, among other words. Vil. 262 uses порогов- in both verses.

[39] Thus in 8:14 in the Origen-texts, H *mbhlym* 'being in haste' is rendered διωκόμενοι. In the *Third Capture of Jerusalem,* in a context of pursuit and battle, погон'ници, погон'ци renders H *hprycym* ('robbers, outlaws'), normally нечьстивии but also ʒлонасил'ници. In Josephus (and Jewish historiography generally) the leaders of the revolt against the Romans in Jerusalem were viewed negatively.

[40] Cf. *Aleksandrija* 98, where the singular погонячь of older mss is replaced in a 16th-century copy by the plural погонци, cf. SRJaXI sub погонецъ.

[41] The same participle in 1:10 yields иже служаху (but LXX τοῖς διακόνοις); no other verb meaning 'serve' occurs.

[42] Note that σκοπός 'lookout' in 2 Ki 13:34 is rendered in the more general meaning of 'attendant' as слуга, GB, W, OB.

[43] In 7:4 it clearly implies slavery, otherwise merely subordination.

time be trusted advisers and therefore friends. In any case, LXX has 'friends' rather than 'servants' in 1:3 and 2:18.[44] Female slaves appear once, рабынѧ Ap 7:4. Unexpectedly, instead of the name 'Hadassah,' домаѵадица appears (see C2:7).

L2.46 For *maiden, virgin, maid-servant* we find дѣва, дѣвица, дѣваꙗ, дѣваꙗ дѣвица. SJS opines that дѣва may originally be a short-form adjective; the long-form дѣваꙗ is almost certainly an archaism, and the copyists tend to distort its forms. In 2:3 дѣвую дѣвицю seems a good equivalent of the Hebrew 'virgin maiden.' In T, however, we find всѧкую дѣву и дѣвицу, as though the copyist were trying to differentiate between two nouns. Yet the court officials did not want to gather *every* virgin *and* maiden, but every *virgin*, as the Hebrew specifies.

L2.461 In OCS the noun дѣва is the usual term for 'virgin,' but in competition with the rarer дѣваꙗ, as SJS and Srez illustrate. Later texts not infrequently juxtapose two stems with the root *děv-*. Thus дѣваꙗ дѣвица occurs here both in contexts where the MT has *n'rwt btwlwt* 'maiden virgin' (2:2, 2:3) and where it has only 'virgin' (2:17, 2:19). Дѣвица alone always corresponds to 'maiden' (2:7, 8, 9 ter), as does дѣва, whether alone (2:4, 4:4) or as дѣваꙗ дѣва (4:16). The adjective plus noun in дв҃уꙗ дв҃ы 2:12 is surely hendiadys, a single semantic unit, even though it corresponds to the Hebrew idiom 'maiden and maiden,' i.e., 'every maiden.' This distribution surely tells us little about the original Slavonic translation.

L2.462 The confused attestation of the desinence of the first member of this phrase continues a long history. Very early the instrumental дѣвоѭ began to be used in a quasi-adverbial manner, sometimes reinforcing the related noun (дѣваꙗ дѣвоѭ, дѣвица дѣвоѭ), but often enough functioning as a frozen-form noun or adjective. Vostokov provided a separate lemma, while Sreznevskij gives дѣвою special status sub дѣва. The earliest example (from the 11th-century Rusian *Sinai Patericon,* 151v4)—if it is not a scribal lapse with "o" instead of "oy"—refers to a male, functioning as a personal Acc sg: имѣ сн҃а говѣина и дѣвою '[he] had a son (who was) pious and a virgin,' παρθένον. (SRJaXI rashly invents an improbable **a**-stem noun to accommodate the anomaly, "дѣвоя" sub дѣвая 4.197b, and other examples are sub дѣва 4 197a.) A 12th-century example from the Rusian *Christinopol' Apostol* (SJS, Srez, SRJaXI) refers to young women (Acts 21:9): Сегоже бѧхоу дв҃ою дъщи ѵетыри, 'and the same man had four daughters, virgins,' θυγατέρες τέσσαρες παρθένοι. (It is also in the 13th-century Serbian *Šišatovac Apostol.*) Here дѣвою functions as Np; elsewhere it may stand for Ns, e.g., in Malalas, Bk 2, where we find срѣтє и ѡтроковица єдина дв҃ою дв҃ица. (In fact the translation is wrong, for, as Istrin 1902 447 stresses, the Gk has κόρη χωρικὴ 'a country girl,' misread as κορική.) Examples abound in copies of OT books, cf. next note.

L2.463 In LXX 2:2–3 the notion of virginity is important for the context and it is expressed (κοράσια ἄφθορα/παρθενικά); otherwise παρθένος apparently specifies 'virgin,' while κοράσιον (var. γυνή, παῖς) is the general 'maiden.'[45]

44 LXX otherwise renders *'bd* עבד as παῖς or omits it; the expected δοῦλος occurs in a single ms in 1:3.

45 In at least one instance in Genesis, 24:16, παρθένος is for both 'girl' and 'virgin': *whn'rh ṭbt mr'h m'd btwlh* > ἡ δὲ παρθένος ἦν καλὴ τῇ ὄψῃ σφόδρα, παρθένος ἦν > дв҃ца же бѣше добра възору велми, дв҃ою же бѣше (Mixajlov).

L2.47 *Concubine* does not occur in surviving OCS data, but surely женима was usual in an old stratum of texts and наложьница in another, with подъложьница (Mikl), мьньшица, хоть and кавка (Srez, from Vostokov: a 1583 ms) as alternate possibilities. Наложьница became normal in Rus′ and in SSl. We assume it for 2:14, see comm.

L3 Words expressing social relationships are приꙗꙁнь, другъ and подруга, въꙁлюбленникъ (and вольникъ), and the opposite, врагъ (with вражьбьныи and неприꙗꙁнивыи).

L3.1 For *friends,* we find both the singular приꙗꙁнь (5:10) and the plural приꙗꙁни (5:14); they refer to the same people. This sense (as opposed to the abstract 'friendship') is rare, but it is attested in OCS. Both the underlying verb *prijaj-*, and the stem *prijazn-*, appear to be western and southwestern Slavic, imported early into Kiev and later into the Polish-Lithuanian Commonwealth. Другу (Ds 9:12) is 'friend,' going back to *rea'*, ordinarily ὁ πλησίος = OCS искрьнии, ближьнии; LXX has φίλοις. In 10:3 другъ equates with *mšnh* משנה 'second, next' where the H means 'second to the king,' i.e., *viceroy* (see C10:3);[46] LXX paraphrases. As for 'а иже ближнии ему' (1:14), it surely was read by Slavs as 'friends, neighbors,' and it may well represent οἱ πλησίον/πλησίοι, but here H has *hqrb* (*haqarov*) הקרב 'the next/close.' The feminine подруга 1:19 (cf. OCS m. подругъ 'companion, friend') is not attested in canonical OCS. It corresponds to H (*re'ut*) רעות (f. of רֵעַ *rea'*).

L3.2 Въꙁлюбленикъ 'beloved' is based on a misreading of רע; intended *ra'* 'evil [man]' was seen as *rea'* רֵעַ, see C7:6. Formally it is flawless, with the suffix *-ik-* added to the past passive participle (like мѫченикъ 'martyr,' оученикъ 'student, disciple'). It is rare, however, and we have found it only in originally OCS texts, including two examples in Su. Far more common is the participle, въꙁлюбленъ, or unprefixed любленъ (SJS, SRJaXI).[47] Still another ancient synonym is the present passive participle, любимъ. The old derived noun любимикъ is found over 100 times in Ephraim the Syrian (always vocative, любимиче or любимици) and once in another *OCS text (in Usp).[48]

On вольникъ 'favorite' (?), see L12.22.

L3.3 Врагъ 'enemy' is appropriately used (but see C9:2), as are the adjectives вражьбьныи 'inimical' and неприꙗꙁнивыи 'unfriendly' (cf. приꙗꙁнь). The root *vrag-* corresponds to H *'yb* 'enemy,' *śn'ym* 'those that hate,' and *cr, crr* 'harasser, oppressor' (for which the more specific мучитель appears in 3:10, and иже бѣша мучили in 8:11).[49] On нелюбимого see C9:16.

L4.1 Ordinary kinship terms are мати, отьць, стръи 'father's brother,' дъщи, сынъ,

[46] LXX 2 Chron 28:7 more appropriately for *mšnh hmlk* has τὸν διάδοχον τοῦ βασιλέως, OB втораго ѿ царѧ. For διάδοχος, Ham has наслѣдьникъ, прѣимьникъ, прѣѩтель, приꙗтель.

[47] Unprefixed любленикъ is active in meaning (twice in Su ἐραστής 'lover' and in a few *OCS examples, SRJaXI).

[48] Once in one manuscript люблениче appears where the others have expected любимиче, Bojkovsky 2 26.7; Srez cites this surely erroneous text to affirm the active meaning.

[49] Τύραννος could become OCS мѫчитель even when used in the old sense 'powerful ruler,' see SJS; cf. Dan 3:3, cited above in note 15, p. 190. In the OB, the editors ineptly substituted мучителницы жены for Maksim Grek's correct властели жены (Taube and Olmsted 103).

чада 'children, descendants,'[50] дѣтѧ 'child, young person,'[51] дѣти, and жєна 'wife,' along with the collective братьꙗ. Младєньць is 'baby.'

L4.2 Broader groups are плємѧ, ꙗзыкъ (1:16), людьє, and the very general родъ (see C2:10). H *'m* 'people, nation, ethnos' occurs 31 times in Esther, often in the singular. This distinction is lost in our text, where only людьє, a *plurale tantum,* is used, apart from ꙗзыкъ in 1:16. Вѣкъ represents H 'generation,' see C9:28 and L20.

L5 Garments

L5.1 In Esther, clothing appears chiefly as a symbol of high status, and no specific garment is singled out. Ordinary apparel is implied when Mordecai tears up his clothes in grief (4:1) and puts on penitential sackcloth (4:2), whereupon Esther sends replacements (4:4); otherwise the raiment is explicitly regal. In 5:1, Esther dresses въ **ризы** цр҇скыꙗ, and in 8:15 Mordecai goes out въ **свитѣ** цр҇стѣи. Haman's proposal to honor someone who has served the king well is to dress him in royal apparel: in 6:8 **пърты** цр҇євы, and in 6:9 simply пърты. But then the king commands, 'възми свиту' 6:10, whereupon Haman взѧ ризы 6:11. Nothing in the context allows us to discern semantic nuances distinguishing the three lexical items, though the singular form свита may imply a special garment. Otherwise, Mordecai in anguish раздра ризы своꙗ 4:1, and Esther посла ризы 4:4 to replace the sackcloth he had put on. Finally, it is forbidden for anyone to enter the palace в **одєжи** сукнѧнѣ (4:2) 'in clothing of sackcloth.'

L5.11 In OCS, both одєжда and риза are normal, but свита is listed in SJS only from the noncanonical *Besědy* of Gregory. The presence of свита in the *Izbornik* of 1076, the *Sinai Paterikon*, the *Life of St. Niphon* of 1219, and the earliest Rusian original works, means that it can safely be ascribed to eastern OCS. *Пъртъ was surely known in the south, but usually in the meaning of 'linen' or, in derivatives, 'poor cloth, rag' (cf. въ прътиштихъ Supr 192.3).[52] Still, the preference for the plural пърты to mean 'clothing, apparel' may well be a mark of Rusian usage. Thus we find the normal съ ризами of John 20:7 replaced by пърты in the Halič Gospel of 1144 (Sreznevskij).[53]

[50] In all 3 occurrences, this word goes back to H *zr'* 'seed,' which twice is reflected by плємѧ (6:13, 9:27). LXX has the literal ἐπὶ τῷ σπέρματι αὐτοῦ in 9:27, γένος in 6:113, γενεά in 9:28, and ἔθνος in 10:3 (no equivalent in 9:31). Progeny, generations, and tribes are not kept strictly separate in biblical translations, see also L4.2.

[51] Common as it is in later texts and modern dialects, дѣтѧ (singular) is not attested in OCS and is rare in early ESl texts (the plural дѣти is ubiquitous). The explicitly masculine дѣтищь is normal, and отроѵищь and отрокъ are also used (both may also mean 'servant'). In PVL, дѣтѧ occurs twice (bolstered by three examples in Monomax), while дѣтищь (var. дѣтищє) is found in 6 clear examples.

[52] In Mt 12:20, пръта нє вънємъша сѧ нє оугаситъ 'he will not snuff out a smouldering wick'—a piece of flax fiber or cloth [λίνον] used in an oil lamp—is in Zo, Mar, Sav (by error прьста) and Ost, while Assem has плата and some later mss (including the Halič Gospel of 1144) have льна.

[53] Ham. lacks свита, but has singular пъртъ in a positive sense, в' то сѧ одѣвъ пєрвѣѣ портъ ѿ прапрꙋда, καὶ οὕτω πρῶτος φορέσας ἐκ πορφύρας ἱμάτιον 'and first donning garment of purple' 37.19; also на пъртѣ[х] ѵлѵ[с]кы[х], 'on men's garments' (as opposed to priestly garments). It also has гъдовабль, presumably 'fine clothing' or 'silk' 145.15; see below.

In Josephus, ἀντὶ τῶν βασιλικῶν 'instead of royal [garments]' comes out въ цр҇скых портъ, 214.24; the preceding clause has ризы (ἐσθῆτα), clearly the usual term for clothing (besides одежа [одѣжа, -жда] and одѣꙗниє). The lone example of свита (183.26) also stands for ἐσθῆτα.

L5.12 Hebrew uses the two words, *lbwš* 'clothing, garment' six times, and *bgd* in 4:1 and 4; there is no correlation between the H and Sl usage here. Gk ἱματισμός usually stands for *bgd* and ἔνδυμα for *lbwš*, but the opposite is possible, and στολή and περιβόλαιον also occur for both, along with some rather rare lexemes. There is no obvious reason for the distribution of the words in our text.[54]

L5.2 In 8:15 the silken **оушьвъ** corresponds to a Hebrew word *tkryk* that is a hapax, usually taken to mean 'cloak.'[55] The Slavonic word occurs elsewhere in early texts: in Kiril of Turov it apparently means a covering for the head, 'cap, bonnet,'[56] while the diminutive *ушьвьць is attested with various spellings in Ham 545.4 translating ἐπιρριπτάριον, a monk's *cowl*. In LXX, the golden *tkryk* is στέφανος, while *'ṭrt* is διάδημα, surely in the sense of 'cloth head-band'; L has only one item, διάδημα. Otherwise LXX and L have διάδημα for the kingly *ktr* in 1:11 and 2:17, omitting the item in 6:8. One might conjecture a prefixed formation of the root *šьj-/šьv-* 'sew,' or possibly the root *ux-* 'ear' with a suffix.[57]

L5.21 Also in 8:15, **вѣньць** should be something like a *turban*, if we judge on the basis of the H *'ṭrt*, which means a headdress (cf. II Sam 12:30) and not the royal crown *ktr* that also is вѣньць in 1:11, 2:17, 6:8.

Cloth

L5.31 Garments are often implied by using nouns denoting specific kinds of cloth. Thus mourning garments may simply be *sackcloth*. The early Slavic texts reflect the difficulties of choosing among the meanings of σάκκος: (1) 'rough cloth (usually of hair); (2) garment made of sackcloth; (3) bag made of sackcloth, any bag.' OCS врѣтище (Mt 11:21, Lu 20:13) uses a word for (3) to render sense (1) and/or (2).[58] Greek often specifies τρίχινος σάκκος for the cloth; thus Rev 6:12 (in a 12th-century Rusian copy) has вретище власяно (with the usual ESl phonetic-orthographical substitution of -ıан-/-ѧн- for SSl -ѣн-), while in OCS we find власѣномъ сукномъ (Supr 213.11, cf. SJS). **Соукъно** was a native word for homespun material, apparently usually woolen. A new noun, **власѣница** (built on the model багър- 'purple, crimson,' багър-ѣн-, багър-ѣн-ица 'purple cloth'), was widely used in Rusian texts. For Esther, we may conjecture that originally въ одежди соукънѣнѣ stood in 4:2, and соукъно in 4:4. Verses 4:1 and 3, however, are corrupt, for they have въ власѧницю и сукъно and власѧницѣ и сукна where we expect 'sackcloth and *ashes*.' We suspect that originally the translation had *vlasěno sukъno* plus an equivalent of *ashes*, but that for some reason the adjective was converted to the new noun; then 'ashes' simply was lost. It is remarkable that this happened in two different verses, and we can only guess that someone thought that the two should agree. It is impossible to estimate how many different scribes or editors were involved in this process; we can only affirm that the final results must be assigned to the hypothetical *pervospisok*.

54 If we assume that the translation was early, we might speculate that the Slavonic Esther had only ризa and одежда, while the variant свита appeared early. Later, пърты was substituted in two cases, probably by a Rusian copyist.

55 In Vil. 262 it is rendered кафтан. The same root, *krk*, is known in Aramaic with the notion of *winding*; the derived noun means 'shroud.'

56 Thomson 1992 214.

57 M56a 215 gives the flat definition "ушьвъ (шапка)" with no hint of the difficulties this word entails. In ms 17 (Volok 12) and G, the word has been changed to оушивъ.

58 In Dan 9:3, sense 2 is expressed by вретище in the older translation, but въ ıаризѣ in the Preslav revision. In Gen 37:34, the oldest ms (TSL 1) has рыкъ.

L5.4 Words that apparently denote kinds of cloth are found in 1:6, with more specific reference to garments in 8:15. At the beginning of 1:6, the three words *ḥwr, krps wtklt,* חור כרפס ותכלת apparently refer to kinds of fine cloth, but the exact meanings are not known.[59] Both *ḥwr* and *krps* seem to be white cloth, while *tklt* is more certainly in the purple-violet-blue range.

L5.41 The latter occurs in both 1:6 and 8:15, and is rendered both times by **ѵьрвь**, a word that appears in Ham with the expected meaning 'red cloth, κόκκινος.' This ties in nicely with ordinary OCS and other Slavic ѵьрвь 'worm' and the associated notion of 'crimson.' It is reasonable to equate it with H *tklt*, which denoted a dye extracted from a mollusk or snail (probably violet-blue rather than crimson).

L5.42 More difficult are the relationships with the other two words and the Slavonic translated forms. Hebrew *ḥwr* seems to correspond to **бобръ** in 1:6, but to **утринъ** in 8:15; but, puzzlingly, утринъ in 1:6 stands in place of *krps.*[60]

L5.43 **Бобръ** is listed by Srez only as 'beaver.' A variant in some medieval texts and in modern dialects is бебр.[61] It would appear that there was a different word, possibly *бьбр-, meaning 'silk' or some other fine cloth. Thus in Josephus, Istrin printed въ ризахъ бъбрѧнѧх, and conjectured "perhaps for багрѧнах = σηρικαῖς" (Istrin 1938, 214 fn. 3, also 215 fn. 5). Although his base manuscript in fact has багрѧных, Meščerskij chooses the variant бебрянях for his text, noting the variants бьбрьнах, бъбрѧнах (1958b 445 fn. 46); the lemma in his word-list is бъбрянъ (with alternate бебрьнъ that seems unwarranted by the evidence) and the gloss 'шелковый.'[62] Further evidence is to be found in the Повесть об Акире: одѣхъ и бєбромъ и браѵиномъ, whereby the Arabic parallel has 'silk,' the Armenian 'byssus' and the Syriac 'fine cloth' (for браѵиномъ all agree on 'purple'); and in a second passage одѣвша а въ бєбєръ и браѵину[63] where the Arabic has 'silk and purple' but the others (and some Slavonic variants) have 'mourning clothes,' surely from a variant reading of some common ancestor of these texts. Altogether, it would appear that the general meaning of elegant and expensive garments could be expressed by a rare word referring to a fine and unusual cloth, perhaps silk, or by a more familiar word referring

59 To determine the exact meaning of any of the words for 'fine cloth' is difficult precisely because standards of excellence varied with time and place, and scribes often felt it necessary to change the words to fit their own views. Thus, for example, H *bwc* and βύσσος (either a borrowing or a cognate to the Semitic form), probably originally a sort of fine linen, is translated in a variety of ways, cf. C1:6.

60 Ms 15 has Добромь in 1:6 (possibly from a copy where the "Д" was originally in cinnabar, cf. C2:5, note). Cf. Добромъ in Srez's citation (from Vostokov), sub ѹтрьнъ, of Est "1:5" in a 16th-century copy.

61 Sreznevskij in fact gives no medieval examples of бебръ and we could not find justification for his references to Ukrainian dialect. A wide range for old **bebr-* does seem assured by Bulgarian, Slovenian, and Sorbian examples, however, cf. Trubačev (ES), and it is attested in Novgorod birchbark documents as a rare variant of *bobr-* (Zaliznjak 1995 201).

62 Meščerskij opines that *бъbr–bobr–bebr* meant both 'beaver' and 'fine silk cloth' (1958b 118), stating that Arabic and Persian sources use *xaz* for both. (He offers a variant version on p. 528.) It is more probable that two stems were originally involved, and scribes confused them. Meščerskij wants to connect this all with the Khazars and direct knowledge of Hebrew in Rus′ (although he refers on p. 118 to the item "в древнерусском переводе книги «Есфирь», сделаном непосредственно с греческого [!] не позднее XII в.").

63 These passages are cited in SRJaXI, from Grigor′ev in ČOIDR 226, ч. 2, p. 11 and 230, ч. 2, p. 133 [SRJaXI's references are misleading]; the last word is printed by Grigor′ev as бранїну. Grigor′ev prints also Serbian variants of the text, one providing сребром и брачиномь for the first and вь багрени брачне for the second, and the other вь добре и вь брачьне for the second. To posit **bьbr-* as the common denominator seems justified. SRJaXI has another example "[бебрь]²" with a false reference; we could not verify its meaning.

to the luxurious fur of the beaver. The odd spellings make it difficult to reconstruct the exact shape of the rare word, but we suggest бьбр-, with derivatives бьбрьн- and бьбрѣн-/бьбрѧн-.[64]

L5.44 Утриномъ is unique to Esther 1:6 (*krps*) and 8:15 (*ḥwr*), with a variant утрьномъ cited by Srez from Vostokov. (There is some doubt about the form, for other copies offer утромъ and удромъ.) A possible parallel is the noun утрьницѧ Gs in the Sinai Paterikon, 43v12, 'κουσσούλιον' (defined by Lampe as a monastic garment). This requires that we assume a root **utr-* meaning some sort of cloth; since the context in the Sinai Paterikon gives no indication of fine or expensive cloth, and the rare Greek word looks suspiciously like the humble *košulja* 'shirt' of far-flung Slavic dialects (see Trubačev for forms from the Baltic to the Aegean), this equation is rather dubious.

L5.45 Hebrew *'rgmn* in 1:6 and 8:15 means simply 'purple' but in many contexts it implies *purple cloth*.[65] Its exact reference in 1:6 is obscure, but the Slavonic provides a word unknown from any other text: **лєптугъ**. With admirable consistency, the derivative лєптужьнъ appears in 8:15, surely referring to the color of the silken (шьлковъ) item, the mysterious оушьвъ. Since this stem лєптуг- is so isolated and the history of this translation is so uncertain, we have to be cautious about assigning the unequivocal meaning *purple*; we can state only that it probably refers to a kind of cloth that may be characterized by a special color.[66]

L5.46 The noun *silk* does not appear in any early manuscript. The adjective шьлковъ 'silken' appears in Novgorod shortly before 1200 (Goetz 168); this fits the presumed Scandinavian influence in the phonetic shape of the stem (Vasmer, sub шелк). Its presence in Hamartolos may indicate considerable age, but as in other cases, we must admit the possibility that it replaced an earlier and no longer acceptable word from an older text.

L5.461 For early dialects it is probable that *silk* was known under two names, свила and коприна. Attestation of the noun свила and adjectival свильнъ (Srez) allows us to ascribe them, and possibly also свилꙗнъ, to *OCS; cognates abound in modern South Slavic. Коприна too has survived in some SSl dialects (cf. Srez, Trubačev 11 24). It was surely in the PVL description (PSRL 1, 32) of the rude Словѣни who aided the Varangians in attacking Constantinople and were rewarded with 'silken sails' which proved to be useless; the mss have кропиньныꙗ for *копринньныꙗ.

L5.462 The lone instance of 'silk' in the New Testament is in Revelations 18:12, σιρικον/σηρικον. In the Bosnian tradition, the transcription сирика appears (сырька in the Hval Codex, c1400, but сирика/сѣрика later). In the oldest known copy (BAN, Nikol′skij 1[SK 223]) it has been shortened to сика (later to appear in the 14th-century Rumjancev copy [SJS] and the *Macarius minei* as шика, Srez sub шикъ).[67] The printed Synodal text has шелк. As for the Old Testament, the *mšy* (*meši*) of Ezekiel 16:10 and 13 is believed to

64 Whether the бебрянъ рукавъ of the *Slovo o polku Igoreve* is to be interpreted as 'silken' or 'beaver' remains one of the many puzzles of that enigmatic text.

65 The normal Greek rendering is πορφύρα/πορφυροῦς, usually taken over into OCS as порфура/порфира, which then may be replaced by прапрѧдъ or by багъръ or derivatives (e.g., in Song of Songs 3:10 and 7:6, where the older translation has порфира and the Preslav variant has *багър-).

66 It may well be that this unique Sl word corresponds to the περιπόρφυρον 'edged with purple' of L, rather than the banal πορφυροῦν of LXX. (Perhaps it is a somewhat distorted loan from OHG **lîp-tuoh* 'body-cloth.')

67 The detailed information about Revelations was provided by Tom Oller; cf. SJS under сиръка.

refer to silk, but LXX renders τριχαπτός 'woven of hair,' retained as трихаптъ in G and OB.[68]

L5.463 Another early Slavic word for *silk* was **gъdъwabjь,* the ancestor of OCz *hedvábie,* mod. *hedvábí.* It occurs thrice in Ham. At 145.15, гъдовабль stands for ἱματισμός 'clothing' (translated in 3 Ki 10:25, the source of Ham's information, as ризы [W]).[69] At 428.5, it is provided with a gloss: свиты растоѵєны ѿ годовабла г҃лємаго ѡкъсию, in a sentence whose Gk equivalent is unknown to us, 'embroidered (?) robes of silk, i.e., *oksija*.'[70] At 511.2 it is itself part of a gloss: въ скараманитіи, (рєкшє драга годовавла) сана своѥго '(dressed) in the *skaramangion*, that is expensive silk, of his rank.'[71] An archaizing 1492 south Rusian copy of a sermon of Ephraim the Syrian provides a derivative adjective, in годоваблени ризы for σηρικὰ ἱμάτια (Bojkovsky 4 392, cf. Srez, SRJaXI; the desinence should be -ы, but the ms not infrequently confuses "и" and "ы"); the SSl revision of the originally OCS text has substituted свѣтлы 'festive' for this obsolete adjective. Miklosich cites a variant годовабьнъ from a 15th-century Serbian copy of a saint's life.

L5.464 The source is Germanic **gudawabi,* with the roots *god* and *weave*, the original sense being material made for God, i.e., suitable for priestly robes; it is well attested in the sense of 'fine, precious cloth or clothing made from such cloth' (e.g., OEng *godwebb*). The term was surely borrowed early in the Czecho-Slovak regions, where the second vowel must have been **ъ,* but the spelled "o" of all known examples may indicate a second borrowing, perhaps in the south. We postulate both **gъdъwabjь* and **gъdowabjь* for this name of a new and valuable commodity.[72]

L5.465 All in all, we have no evidence to date the appearance of шьлк- in any Slavic dialect; its presence in Esther may be part of the original translation, but equally probably it may represent an innovation introduced by a subsequent editor.

L5.47 The general verb for 'dress, clothe' is облѣк- (облєк-) (сѧ), облаѵити (сѧ), as in OCS and early Rusian.

L6 Face, eyes, hand, soul

L6.0 A particular characteristic of LXX phraseology is the use of words meaning *face* and *hand* (and, to a lesser extent, *eyes*) in expressions that are closely equivalent to normal Greek prepositions: πρὸ προσώπου σου 'before thy face' = 'before/in front of you,' Exod 23:20. Such phrases generally reflect Hebrew combinations of preposition plus noun, and in Hebrew the noun may retain its full value, may be somewhat weakened (often metaphori-

68 Srez, sub въркоѵь, cites this verse from Upyr′, where the Gk word has been glossed in the margin by a word otherwise unknown in old SSl or ESl mss, cf. Cz *vrkoč* 'braid.'

69 Normalized OCS and early Rusian would be гъдъвабль. Vasmer (sub годовабль) chose the form with initial "год-" from Istrin's word-list (vol. 3), and Trubačev follows; Istrin's text, however, has "ъ" from the oldest copy.

70 Srez cites it from a later copy, sub годовапль and, probably inappropriately, sub растоѵити (though *растъѵєнъ is more probably from *raz-tъk-(nǫ)-* 'punch'); he omits the gloss. SRJaXI has it from that same copy, sub оксь, a dubious lemma.

71 At 511.22 Istrin prints дроуга; the variant драга is only in his comments on the gloss, 2.208.—The Gk has only μετὰ σκαραμαγγίου, with no mention of rank. Lampe defines the Gk noun as a variety of *kaftan*–a specific kind of garment, not a sort of material. The phrase не багряницею ся украсивъ, ни годовабльмь, in a sermon on Elevation of the Cross (VMČ Sept. 14, 733; cf. SRJaXI), surely denotes material.

72 Near the end of the 1300s we find шида (with adj. шидѧный, шидный, see Srez). It goes back via Old or Middle High German to Lat *seta.*

cal), or it may have simply fused with the sense of the preposition into a "new" preposition. This range of meaning, from prepositional phrase to "semipreposition" or preposition, has received much attention in scholarly literature, in particular because of problems faced by translators. Our treatment draws heavily on the meticulous and comprehensive analyses presented by Raija Sollamo (1979).[73]

L6.1 ***Лице*** 'face' occurs only three times in Esther, twice in mildly metaphorical references (1:14, important servitors 'who saw the face of the king'; 7:8, 'Haman's face fell'), and once in a use approaching that of a preposition (8:15 ѡт лица цр҃ва 'from [the presence of] the king'). Perhaps 1:14 and 8:15 might be considered Hebraisms, but their equivalents are quite usual in LXX. All three of these do go back to the Hebrew noun 'face,' but the other thirty examples in the Hebrew text correspond variously to прєдъ (24x), прєд оѵима [твоима] 8:5, отъ [нєго] 1:19, и иже их о нємь 1:3, противу 2:11, прѧмо 4:2, or до 4:6, and one is omitted (6:9).

L6.11 In the MT the noun *pnym* 'face' functions as an independent substantive only twice, in 1:14 and 7:8, noted above. In 1:10 (where the Slavonic has simply прєдъ, see comm. to that verse), the first element of *'t pny* may be interpreted either as the *nota accusativi* or as a preposition that goes with *face* to constitute a semipreposition. Otherwise *pnym* is part of the prepositions *lpny* (lit. 'to the face of' 29x), or the compound *mlpny* (lit. 'from to the face of' 4x, including 8:15, the only case 'face' survived into our translation), and *bpny* (lit. 'at/on the face of' 9:2, see comm.).

L6.2 **Оѵи** 'eyes' occurs only in metaphorical references, partly in phrases denoting 'be pleasing to' (2:9, 3:11, 8:8),[74] once in 'be valueless for/to' (3:6), and three times combined with прєдъ to mean 'before the countenance of, in the presence of' (5:2, 7:3, 8:5). These seven instances all can count as Hebraisms, and all are normal in LXX. In terms of the Hebrew text, 'eyes' has been eliminated in favor of the simple preposition прєд five times (1:17, 1:21, 2:15, 7:3, 8:5), and of the dative case once (цр҃єви 2:4).[75]

L6.31 **Рука** refers literally to a physical hand or hands only twice (3:10, 5:2). Seven times it occurs in phrases meaning 'move, raise one's hand (against),' that is, *do harm to* (a person), or *get possession of* (things). With the king as target, ꙁадѣти руцѣ is used in 2:21, 3:6, and 6:2, and with the Jews въвьрглъ бѧшє руцѣ свои in 8:7. With property as potential plunder нє простроша рукъ своих appears in 9:10, but нє подѣша рукъ своих in 9:15, 16.[76] These all reflect ultimately a Hebrew idiom 'to send a/the hand' which is usually rendered 'stretch out a/the hands' in Greek.[77] The idiom is lost entirely in 9:2,

73 Meščerskij's second category of alleged "syntactical and phraseological Hebraisms" (1956a 210), is the "literal rendering of Hebrew figurative metaphorical expressions formed with the words *hand, eyes, soul*, in combination with various prepositions"—a definition that muddles together the semiprepositions and other kinds of idioms.

74 Sollamo's work shows that some Hebraisms persist more tenaciously in phrases where several cooccur; cf. the discussion of expressions of pleasing in L12.4.

75 Thus прєдъ goes back to H phrases using 'face' 26x (*lpny* 22x, *'t-pny* 1:10, *mlpny* 4:8, 7:6, *bpny* 9:2), using 'eyes' 3x (1:17, 1:21, 2:15; also прєдъ оѵима 3x, cf. above), and to prepositions twice (*mmnw* прєдъ нимь 5:9; *'l* прєдъ постєлєю [not an accurate equivalent] 7:8). This distribution is entirely in accord with the hypothesis of an intermediary Greek text; the number of Hebraisms is minimal.

76 The two-way contrast of QTS becomes three-way in WV, with нє повєдоша (вєдоша G) рукы своими in 9:15, but uniform in X (нє повєдоша). Tn has нє подѣша 9:10, нє нє [!} побѣдиша 15, нє побѣша 16, suggesting a previously uniform нє подѣша. See also L18.212.

77 M56a 211 incorrectly says the literal meaning is протянуть руки. He cites the variety of translation of this idiom to show that the "Russian" translator was *not* bound by the exact wording of his alleged Hebrew origi-

where, as part of the paraphrase of a larger context, the idea is expressed by мьсти творити.

L6.311 This common H idiom is sometimes rendered literally in LXX and other translations, and sometimes other verbs are used. The slavish imitation ἀπόστειλον τὴν χεῖρά σου (i.e., reach your hand out) of Job 1:11 was carried over into early Slavic as посъли руку свою,[78] which persisted through OB into the modern Slavonic Bible. It is replaced by простри руку свою in the Russian translation. One important O-ms reproduces the H of Esther 9:16, οὐκ ἀπέστειλαν τὰς χεῖρας αὐτῶν. On the other hand, 8:7 in LXX has τὰς χεῖρας ἐπήνεγκεν τοῖς Ἰουδαίοις. The verb here, ἐπιφέρειν, means 'put, place on' and it is used in non-biblical Greek with *hand* precisely in the sense illustrated by Gen 37:22, а роукы не възложите на нь, 'but do not lay a hand on him,' i.e., 'do him no physical harm.'[79] Now, the idiom ꙃадѣти руцѣ is cited by Srez (and SRJaXI) only from Est. Otherwise the verb means 'put, put on, impose' or 'cause, make (someone do something)'; the first meaning overlaps with that of възложити. Though poorly represented in canonical OCS (SJS), it is widely documented in *OCS (Srez) and in medieval Croatian; it has survived chiefly in Slovenian. Its appearance in the first three instances of this idiom in Esther perhaps indicates that it was in the earliest form of the translation. The next example uses въврѣщи 'throw in(to),' a verb that is common enough in OCS, though its directional sense seems inappropriate for the context of 8:7.[80] Then comes the reasonable example with 'stretch hand,' and finally the two with подѣша, a verb that is unknown elsewhere.[81]

L6.32 Twice на руцѣ means 'into the hand(s) of, into the care of' (2:8, 6:9). Three times по руцѣ signifies merely 'through the agency of' (2:3, 8, 14),[82] while much the same idea is expressed twice by по рукахъ (1:12, 15); the former refer to single agents, the latter specify plural agents. Both of these usages are equivalents of Hebrew semiprepositions, but both are quite common in Greek, where they are not necessarily foreign elements.[83]

---

nal. This of course means that the lack of correspondence cannot provide evidence of the wording of the original language.

78 See Usp. 84c29; also Job 2:5 посълавъ, Usp. 85c5.

79 Seven passages in 1 and 2 Ki use forms of ἐπιφέρειν for H "send hand"; it is significant for our discussion that they evoke four different Sl verbs (at least in ms W): възложити in 1 Ki 22:7 and 26:23, положити in 26:11; въꙃдвигнѹти 'raise, lift' in 1 Ki 24:7 and 2 Ki 1:14; and простръти 'stretch out, extend' in 1 Ki 24:11 and 26:9. Despite the generally literalistic character of the translation of these books, in this phrase the translator(s) made choices.

Awareness of the underlying idiom and variant possibilities of translation apparently influenced the choices translators and editors made in individual passages. Jerome, in translating from the MT, kept *manus/manum mittere* in 3:6 and 8:7, but paraphrased in the other five instances. Thus in 6:2 (where LXX has "put the hands on"), he renders "send hand on" as *iugulare* 'smother, kill.' In 12:2 (Hanhart A:13), however, he chose to reinstate the hypothetical Hebrew by using *manus mittere* for τὰς χεῖρας ἐπιβαλεῖν. The Gennadian translators, in a rare departure from slavish literalism, wrote руцѣ възложити, as though they had the Greek in mind.

80 The verb **werg/*wirg* is widely used with various prefixes in OCS and Middle Bulgarian (e.g., the mid-14th century Chronicle of Manasses). In Rus′, however, it was apparently purely a book-word; it is hardly attested in native writings before 1350, and after that it is clearly a mark of elevated style.

81 Подѣти is not in SJS, and in Srez only from Esther; SRJaXI adds a 1644 citation. Perhaps подѣша is a distortion of подъѧша 'they lifted up, raised'.

82 In 2:8, the same H *'l yd hgy* results in both по and на руцѣ Егаевѣ, with appropriate differentiation of meaning; LXX ὑπὸ χεῖρα Γαι but simply πρὸς Γαι.

83 Phrases using *hand* as expressing instrument, intermediary, custody, and the like exist in Greek and most other languages. Thus in early Rusian вьдавъ ему сынъ свои Игорѧ на руцѣ (PVL s.a. 879, Lav 22), in Lixačev's translation отдав ему на руки сына Игоря (1950 216). For careful discussions of many examples and categories of examples, see Sollamo. On misuse of this kind of idiom, cf. T4.01.

L6.33 In Esther 3:13 the instrumental погоньци and in 8:10 the phrase съ приставы коньникы stand where Hebrew has 'at/by hand of riders,' with the semipreposition *byd* (*beyad*) ביד. This expression, denoting agent or intermediary, is often rendered in LXX by prepositions (διά or μετά). In 3:9, where MT has 'to the hand of those who have charge of the king's business,' *1350 has only къ строю дѣла (see C3:9).[84]

L6.34 Finally, for the somewhat obscure Hebrew phrase *kyd hmlk* כיד המלך 'as the hand of the king,' *1350 uses the noun сила (1:7, 2:18); LXX and L have no equivalents.[85]

L6.4 **Душа** 'soul' occurs only in three passages, all somewhat corrupt. As a preliminary, we must note that the Hebrew word *npš* (*nefeš*) נפש (from the root *npš* 'rest') means not only 'soul, spirit,' but 'one's own soul, spiritual essence, being, life, self.' Thus in the dramatic scene when Haman sees himself in mortal danger, 7:7, Амонъ ста ° на д҃ши своєи, we expect 'stood *to beg* for his soul,' i.e., his life. LXX paraphrases, 'entreat the queen,' but the Origen-influenced mss have the literal ἐξανέστη καὶ παρῃτεῖτο τὴν βασίλισσαν περὶ τῆς ψυχῆς αὐτοῦ.

L6.41 In 8:11 и д҃шахъ своих is isolated; a verb and a preposition are missing. We expect 'and to stand for/to their souls,' reflecting the Hebrew idiom meaning 'defend their lives, themselves'; LXX paraphrases 'help themselves' βοηθῆσαί τε αὐτοῖς (no Origen variant). The same Hebrew phrase occurs in 9:16, where all of our major sources have only стоꙗху.[86] Yet ms 22 and Xleb provide a literal, indeed etymologizing, equivalent of the H: и стоꙗху на покоꙗхъ (Xleb покоихъ) своихъ. We suspect that the text of this verse was modified during the history of the Greek transmission, see C9:16.

L6.42 In 9:31 we expect уставиша {на} душѧ своѧ {и} на ѵѧда своꙗ, 'established for themselves and their seed.' Tn supplies на, but the connective и is not attested. LXX has the first part, ἔστησαν ἑαυτοῖς καθ' ἑαυτῶν and one Origen-text has ἑαυτούς (for ἑαυτῶν) plus a conflated τῶν υἱῶν αὐτῶν καὶ ἐπὶ τοῦ σπέρματος αὐτῶν.

L6.43 The Hebrew *bnpšk* בנפשך 'in your soul' in the sense 'in yourself, privately' comes out въ мысли своєи in 4:13. This example, as well as the corrupt text of 7:3, where from Hebrew we might expect 'soul,' is discussed with other instances of мысль, L11.221.[87]

84 M56a 210 gives four illustrative examples of this "category," followed by "и мн. др." He cites (1) 1:12, "Речи . . . еже по рукам [*sic*] старость [*sic*]" (евр. bhejad [*sic*], то есть переданные через их евнухов)"—which does not correspond to any ms, but no matter—an excellent example of the H semipreposition with expressions of speaking. (2) 2:3, 8, "«По руце Егаеве» (евр. bhejad [*sic*] Hegai)," where in fact H does not have *beyad*, but *'el yad* אל יד and means 'into the hand/custody of.' (3) "III, 1"—in fact 3:11—"«Створити волю очью твоею» (евр. e'neikh [*sic*])," a corrupt phrase which stands for H 'to do to/with it/them as [is] good in your eyes'—this is precisely the sort of combination of an idiom meaning 'please' plus a semipreposition (here *be'eynexa* בעיניך where 'eyes' = 'judgement') that is likely to be rendered slavishly into Greek. The fourth example "VIII, 7" (for 7:7) is also in a corrupt passage, see below on 'soul.' (Meščerskij's H "a'mad a'l nepheš" should read *'amad* (levaqeš) *'al nafšo*.) See p. 10, fn. 28.

85 In terms of the Hebrew text, 'hand' is missing once in the idiom 'send a hand' (9:2), once in *'l ydy* 'into the care/custody of' (къ 3:9, perhaps *προς + A), twice in *byd* 'through the agency of' (3:13 inst. case, 8:10 съ + I), and twice in *kyd*.

86 Here LXX has καὶ ἑαυτοῖς ἐβοήθουν, but O expands to ἐβοήθουν ἑαυτοῖς περὶ τῆς ψυχῆς ἑαυτῶν 'helped themselves concerning their (own) souls.'

87 In terms of the H text, 'soul' is represented three times by душа (7:7, 8:11, 9:31), once by покои (9:16), and twice by мысль (4:13, 7:3).

L7 To do, make

L7.1 The general verb *to do, make* in Esther, as in OCS, is **творити/сътворити**, nearly always with an expressed object and therefore the sense *set up, make, complete.* Once—сътвори поѩꙁдити, 6:11—it serves as an auxiliary in the sense of Gk ποιεῖν in the sense 'cause,' where H has a causative verb, see comm. Exceptionally in 6:14, **устроила бѧше** refers to a banquet, although сътворити is normal (cf., e.g., 5:4, 1:3). Perhaps строити underlies the equivalent of 'doer of the (king's) work' in 3:9, *стро{ѧщ}ю дѣла. The same sort of employees are **чинѧще** дѣло in 9:3. Finally, in the unexpected imperative of 5:14 **сдѣлающе** будѣте древо "make a tree [gallows]" is contrasted to створи древо in the same verse.[88]

L7.11 The 44 instances of сътворити and 10 of творити are entirely compatible with possible usages of ποιεῖν, which in turn is the most common equivalent of H *'śh.* In the H Esther, *'śh* 'to do, make' (44x, plus the passive *n'śh,* 12x) is the most frequent verb. For '*doers* of the king's work,' LXX uses ἐργάζειν, whence perhaps чинити in 9:3 and possibly строити in 3:9. (On ποιεῖν rendering a H causative, see C6:11.)

L7.2 The notion of changing or restructuring in 2:9 was surely expressed by the aorist **прѣстрои**, although the text is slightly corrupt, see comm.

L7.3 In 9:2, **мьсти творити** 'make vengeances' (see comm.) stands for the H idiom "send (one's) hand," see L6.31.

L8 Speech acts and their results: глаголъ, рѣчь, дѣло

L8.0 Many of the most frequent nouns and verbs expressing notions from the broad semantic fields of *speaking, type and effect of speech, act,* and *result of action* in Slavic, Greek, and Hebrew are etymologically linked in parallel ways; semantic overlap is very common and the resulting ambiguity poses problems of translation that may be solved in many different ways.

L8.1 The Slavonic noun **рѣчь** is etymologically associated with the verb *rek-* (OCS рек-ѫтъ рещи) 'say' and usually means 'word, speech, statement'; it also, however, may mean 'deed, matter, fact, thing.' Near-equivalent and relatively unambiguous nouns in the first sense are **глаголъ** and **слово** 'word.' In Esther, рѣчь occurs 20 times, and глаголъ 8 times.

L8.11 It is notable that the more usual term слово does not occur in Esther. Глаголъ and глаголати apparently attest a regional stem that became impregnably established in OCS during the earliest period on the basis of "Moravan" dialect. As bookish words they continued to be used among South Slavs and in Rus′, despite their absence in local dialects. Рѣчь 'thing' was probably also a heritage from the Moravan OCS period, but it is widely attested—in Slovene plus West Slavic, and, through more recent Polish influence, in Belarusian and Ukrainian.

88 In H, both instances have forms of the general verb *'śh* 'do, make,' as does 7:9, but the building of the same "tree" in 6:4 and 7:10 is expressed by the more explicit verb *hkyn* 'set up firmly, establish, prepare.'

L8.2 Both Gk ῥῆμα and H *dbr* share the range of meaning from 'thing said' to 'thing spoken about,' with extension to 'fact, thing'; λόγος, though its major sense is 'word,' means also 'utterance, discourse' (not to mention the *Logos* of theology). Hebrew *mlh* 'word' does not occur in Esther. Translators have a range of choice.[89]

L8.21 In the MT Esther, *dbr* is used 36 times. In the corresponding Sl verses, рѣчь appears 20x, and глаголъ 8x. There is no discernable pattern to the selection.[90] In 1:12 and 8:14, for example, 'on/at the king's word' is по рѣчи царевѣ, but in 3:15 по глаголу царѧ (cf. C3:15; for comparable variation of 'the king's word/declaration,' see C4:3). In 2:1 'after these things/events' is по рѣчьхъ тѣхъ, but 3:1 по **глаголании{хъ}** тѣхъ.[91] In 2:15 *l' bqšh dbr*, lit. 'not she-asked thing' is не проси рѣчи, and in 6:3 *l' n'śh 'mw dbr*, lit 'not was-done with-him thing' is не створено ему ничтоже. For a seeming shift of 'word/thing' to **вѣсть** 'message, news,' see C2:22. On H 'book of the things of the days,' see C2:23. Phrases containing *dbr* in H are omitted from 3:4 and 8:5.

L8.22 In 1:20, рѣчь царева corresponds to 'the king's decree' *ptgm hmlk*. LXX has rather ὁ νόμος 'the law' (O replaces it with λόγος; L paraphrases, referring to the king's *voice*, φωνή). The Sl wording suggests an underlying Gk sentence with ῥῆμα or λόγος, in accord with Jewish tradition. Dan 3:16 has *ptgm* in an Aramaic context usually translated 'matter.' The usual LXX text has ἐπὶ τῇ ἐπιταγῇ 'according to the decree,' while the Theodotion version has περὶ τοῦ ῥήματος τούτου, yielding о глаголѣ семь. In Dan 4:14 (Gk 4:17) *ptgm*' 'the matter' is ὁ λόγος (LXX has a different sentence).

L8.23 The LXX Esther sometimes paraphrases *dbr* to 'what was said' (λεχθέντα 1:18, λεγόμενα 8:14) or more specifically 'affair' (πρᾶγμα 3:15) and sometimes selects an explicit interpretation—'writings, letter' γράμματα (4:3, 9:1), 'command' πρόσταγμα (2:8, 8:17). In many OT verses, LXX varies between ῥῆμα and πρᾶγμα; similarly 'word' and 'deed' may be distinguished in H by *m'śh* 'deed, doing' or *m'lkh* 'business, work' and in Sl by **дѣло**. In Esther, *m'śh* is only in 10:2, *wkl m'śh tqpw* 'and every act of his power': Sl все **дѣло** тверди его. Дѣло also is found in the equivalents of the phrase *'śy hml'kh*, lit. '(those) doing the work,' *w'śy hml'kh 'šr lmlk*, и **чинѧще дѣло** царево 9:3; see also C3:9.

L8.3 The two verbs *rek-* and *glagola-* 'speak, say' generally correspond to forms of H *'mr*,[92] while *povědaj-* 'tell, recount' corresponds to *hgyd*. In 2:22 the sequence *became*

[89] In LXX, ῥῆμα = H *dbr* has in some passages a variant reading with πρᾶγμα 'deed, affair' and in others with λόγος. In Daniel 6:14 ῥῆμα yields молбу in the older translation and слово in the Preslav revision. A borderline example is Luke 2:15, when the shepherds have seen angels singing and say to each other, "Let us go to Bethlehem and see this thing that has happened, that the Lord has made known to us"—καὶ ἴδωμεν τὸ ῥῆμα ὃν ὁ κύριος ἔγνώρισεν ἡμῖν—OCS и видимъ гл҃ъ сь бывъшии иже господь съказа намъ.

[90] LXX Est prefers λόγος to ῥῆμα, but many verses use paraphrases. In Ruth, ῥῆμα is found twice (in 3:18) and yields глаголъ in the older Glagolitic version but слово in the Cyrillic (see T1.32). In 4:7 *dbr* more clearly means 'word': LXX λόγος yields слово in both versions.

[91] OB 2 Chron 32:1 has по словесехъ сих, for LXX μετὰ τοὺς λόγους τούτους, *'ḥry hdbrym [wh'mt] h'lh*, 'after these things [and their establishment].'

[92] For рекуче meaning 'call out' see C6:9; 6:11 in a similar context with the same H verb, *qr,*' has клича. The H verb occurs in 9 other instances: 'read aloud' appropriately is прочтены 6:1; 'call, summon' is ʒъвати 3x, поʒъвати once, въʒъвати 2x, and призъвати once (приʒвани 3:12 and въʒвани 8:9 reflect identical H phrases in the same contexts). In 9:26 проʒваша should mean 'named,' but the name, *Purim,* is omitted. In a gloss not in MT, **ʒвати сѧ** 'be named' occurs, see C2:18.

known . . . recounted . . . told (*wywd' . . . wygyd . . . wt'mr*) has become быс вѣсть . . . повѣда . . . повѣда in *1350. The first H verb is a passive of 'know';[93] the second is usual for *povědaj-*, while the third might well be expected to yield рєчє. (H *hgyd* corresponds to *povědaj-* 13x, to исповѣда once.)

L8.31 **Исповѣда** reflects *wygd* in 4:7 but *wyspr* 'and he counted, recounted' in 6:13; the latter H in 5:11 comes out **расповѣда**, a western word, see comm. On the related noun **расповѣданиє** 'complete account,' see C4:7.

Command, order

L8.41 In 6:1 и **повєлѣ** is stronger than *wy'mr* 'and he said,' but appropriate for the context. The verbal substantive **повєлѣниє** in 1:15 and 2:20 stands for H *m'mr* (etymologically from *'mr*) 'order, command,' which yields **рєчєниє** in 9:32. The explicit **ȥаповѣда-** 'command' corresponds to H *cwh* 8x and the noun **ȥаповѣдь** to the H derivative *mcwh* in 3:3; in 3:2, the noun replaces a verb-form, see comm.

L8.42 The phrase бѧшє **оуставъ** царєвъ 'was the king's edict' reflects the H verb *ysd* 'established, decreed.' Otherwise the verb **уставити** appears appropriately 8 times to mean *enact, establish* a decree, where H has the causative *qym* 'set up, establish.'[94]

L8.5 **Законъ** 'law' occurs 17 times in Esther, always reflecting H *dt*. The corresponding adjective appears once, и печать {книгамъ} ȥаконнымъ, 4:8; the H here refers to the *book* of the law. In 1:19, on the contrary, where H has 'in the laws,' Sl has въ книгахъ (see comm.). The H phrase *kdt*, lit. 'as law' is reflected appropriately as по ȥакону 4:16. More detailed phrases use adjectives: ꙗкожє ȥаконъ жєньскыи 'according to the rules/regimen for women' 2:12, and ꙗкожє ȥаконъ днєшнии in 9:13 (Moore, 'in terms of today's edict'). In 1:8 and 1:15 the precise meaning of *kdt* is unclear in H; it may be 'regarding.' The Sl of 1:8, аки вольна is also unclear (see comm.).[95]

L8.51 The phrase *dt wdyn* 'law and judgement' (although in later Hebrew *dyn* means rather 'religious law, faith' as opposed to civil law) comes out ȥаконъ и **судъ** (1:13), the equivalent of LXX νόμος καὶ κρίσις, 'law and judgement (or judging).' **Судии**, normally 'judge' stands in place of *prtmym*, denoting a high official, see L2.3.

L9 Power, rule

L9.1 Nouns meaning 'power' are **сила** (see C1:7), **мощь** (which reflects H *gbwrtw* 'his strength, might, valor' in 10:2), and apparently **твьрдь**, usually 'firmament,' in 9:29 and 10:2, where H has a rare word translated ἰσχύς in LXX (see C9:29).

[93] H *yd'* 'know' usually comes out with forms of *věd*: old irregular вѣсть (4:14)—with perfective оувѣдѣти (2:11)—or newer regularized *vědaj-* (бѣ вѣдаꙗ 4:1, вѣдають 4:11; perfective оувѣдати 4:5). In 1:13, however, поȥнаꙗху twice indicates special or deep understanding, although поȥнати usually specifies 'come to know, recognize.'

[94] The reflexive оустави **сѧ** гнѣвъ царєвъ, 2:1, means 'subside.' See L14.71.

[95] In terms of MT, *dt* 'law' occurs 20 times; Sl has ȥаконъ 17 times, ȥаконьнъ once, and other equivalents twice (1:8, 1:19).

L9.2 **Нужа** 'force, necessity' occurs in беꙁ нужа, 1:8, for H *'yn 'ns* 'there is no one compelling, forcing.'

L9.31 **Власть** in the normal OCS sense of 'power, authority' occurs only once in Esther, 1:22: *to affirm for every man* power (authority, dominion) *in his own home,* власть в дому своємь. It goes back to H *śrr* 'master, ruling.'[96]

L9.321 The other 9 instances of власть correspond to H *mdynh* 'province' (once in distributive repetition, къ власти и власти 1:22). One superfluous case, 2:3, has this meaning. Thus it functions as a synonym of ꙁемлꙗ, which corresponds to *mdynh* in 28 instances (8 times in distributive repetition; 3:12 bis, 3:14, 4:3, 8:9, 8:13, 8:17, 9:28). The adj ꙁемьнъ is used in 2 phrases (for *provincial chiefs*–вельможѧ/болꙗре ꙁемьнии) where H has *mdynh*.[97]

L9.322 The usual LXX translation of *mdynh* is χώρα (as in Est 1:1, 3:11, etc.), but in Est 8:9 we find σατραπεία 'satrapy,' i.e., a special kind of province. And 4:11 has ἐπαρχία, denoting another sort of province, a term that in Ham yields страна, область, and in one passage (279.11) a doublet, по странамъ и властємъ. In late OCS область and власть were essentially interchangeable, although earlier they were regional variants. The inconsistent use of ꙁемлꙗ and власть in Est suggests that власть was substituted for some instances of ꙁемлꙗ during the history of the Slavonic text.

To rule

L9.4 Two roots underlie verbs meaning 'rule, have power (over).' **Владѣти** (twice in 9:1) is an innovating shape (cf. A11.1) of a verb that is common in OCS and other early texts, and similar in meaning to the H verb *šlṭ*. At least two stems based on *cěsar-* or *cьsar-* are to be ascribed to *1350, **царьствовати** surely, and **царєвати** probably (cf. C2:4). Царити appears to be a correction made by scribes for the corrupted form царь ꙁвати of 2:4.

L9.5 What is unusual is the instrumental object with царствоваше in 1:1. While such verbs of governing as владѣти take instrumental, цѣсарьствовати in OCS takes D, на plus L (Euch 56b1), or надъ plus Inst (Luke 19:14),[98] cf. Vaillant *Manuel* 191. We have found parallels in post-1400 ESl OT books,[99] Chronographs,[100] and the Gennadius Bible.[101]

96 Note that QT's correct властємъ 'provinces' early in 1:22 was replaced by властєлємъ 'rulers' in SGWVEA. It would be more appropriate to replace the apparent accusative власть near the end of the verse with властєлємъ, to be read as instrumental sg, meaning 'master, ruler.'

97 H *mdynh* means *region* or *province*: it occurs 39 times in Esther, yielding власть 8 times, ꙁемлꙗ 27x, and adjectival ꙁемьныи 4x. The word *'rc* means *land, earth, soil,* and appears only twice in Esther. In 10:1 it yields ꙁемлю, while in 8:17 *wrbym m'my h'rc* 'many from the peoples of the land'—i.e., many individuals from the common people—comes out множьство людии ꙁемныхъ. In Gen 23:7, H (*wyšthḥw*) *l'm h'rc* yields LXX τῷ λαῷ τῆς γῆς, Sl (поклони сѧ) народу селному (Mixajlov).

98 Su 10:5, in a citation of Rom 5:4 has **о** plus L, where the old copies of theApostol have на, which surely is better.

99 In Judg 9:10 (W) прииди цр҃ств ꙋи нами (but OB над нами), δεῦρο βασίλευσον ἐφ' ἡμῶν. 2 Ki 3:21 (W, J, GB, OB) и цр҃твовати имаши всѣми, καὶ βασιλεύσεις ἐπὶ (var. ἐν) πᾶσιν. 4 Ki 8:13 (W) показа ми тѧ г҃ь цр҃ствꙋющи (OB -щa) сꙋрїєю), cf. PSRL 22/1 145 показа ми г҃ь тебе цр҃ствꙋюща сириею.

100 One example is attested in two forms, (1) the extracts published by Istrin from the "Jewish Chronograph" and (2) a chronographic insertion in the Biblical collection of 1507 (BAN 24.4.28, from Suprasl'; Mathiesen 1983a p. 19, no. 16), Lavrov 1933, 93. Neither Lavrov nor Alekseev and Lixačeva 1978 (who described the Suprasl' *sbornik*) noticed that the passages are identical. It is from book 6, Istrin 1911 9: по распрошании же

Contend with, stand up to

L9.61 Нє можєши оужє съ нь is to be hypothesized for 6:13 as the original of attested нє можєши оужє с нимь быти. The H *l' twkl lw* is literally 'you will not be able to him' and means 'won't succeed against him.' It seems safe to conjecture an original съ нь, съ plus accusative in the sense of 'equivalent to, equal to'; compare Vaillant *Manuel* 202, and the PVL sentence that can be reconstructed as нє вѣдѣ могу ли съ нь 'I don't know whether I'll be up to him (able to be his equal in fighting).'[102] That the relatively unusual accusative with съ has been changed to a "normal" instrumental by the scribes is not surprising.[103] After this first change, someone added быти in a vain attempt to provide a rational sentence. Another emendation is found in Tn: нє можєши востаᵀ прєᴰ нимъ.

L9.62 Нє остоıаше прєд ними 9:2 expresses a similar idea, see comm.

Oppress

L9.7 **Мучитель** 'tormentor' stands for H *crr* in 3:10, and the noun phrase иже бѣша мучили in 8:11, see L3.3. On the noun мука 'torment, pain' in the enigmatic phrase право мука царицина see C7:8.

L10 Fall down, worship, kneel

L10.1 Everyone *falls down and worships* Haman except for Mordecai. Hebrew has three parallel phrases using the same pair of verbs *kr'* and *hštḥwh.* Sl also uses two verbs (each in two aspects), but *1350 shows inconsistent variation:

3:2a	*kr'ym wmštḥwym*	припадающа		поклонаху са
3:2b	*l' ykr' wl' yštḥwh*	нє приклакну	и нє	поклони са
3:5	*ky 'yn mrdky kr' wmštḥwh*	нє приклакаıа	ни	припадаıа

It would appear that the phrase припадающє поклонıаху са is an innovation made during the Slavic history of the text.[104] Very possibly the forms of *pripadaj-* are not original,

цр҃ства людска (μετὰ τὸ ἀπολέσθαι) . . . цр҃ствовахѹ странами тѣми. A second example from Malalas is in book 1, цр҃ствова єгуптом, Istrin 1897 19; it might however be a misspelling of the expected єгуптаномъ, for ἐβασίλευσε τῶν Αἰγυπτίων. A third example comes from the unpublished St. Petersburg copy of the *Troickij Chronograph* (ms RNB NSRK, 1918 F.27, fol. 290): и црˢтвова вавилономъ и асоуриєю сєлєвкїи.

[101] In the part translated from Latin, 13:2 (B:2): егда многими азыкы цр҃твовахъ, *cum plurimus gentibus imperarem.* This might be somehow influenced by the Latin ablative; in the same verse is владѣти повинных, with accusative like *gubernare subjectos.*

[102] Sub 992; PSRL 1 123.7, A has со нь, which is updated in HX to с нєго, but L has garbled it to са и и and R has моли єᴳ нєго. The same H idiom yields προς in LXX, and Sl translators treat it variously: Gen 32:25 (26) εἶδεν δὲ ὅτι οὐ δύναται πρὸς αὐτόν, видѣвъ жє ıако нє можєть противу єму (Mixajlov), but Judges 16:15, *bmh nwkl lw*, LXX ἐν τίνι δυνησόμεθα πρὸς αὐτόν, W, OB чимъ възможємъ на нь.

[103] Elsewhere, Sl быти съ plus instrumental renders Gk expressions meaning 'have intercourse with,' e.g., Gen 19:6 (5) да боудємъ съ нима, from LXX ἵνα συγγενώμεθα αὐτοῖς, from H *wnd'm*; Gen 19:32 и боудєвѣ съ нимъ, καὶ κοιμηθῶμεν μετ' αὐτοῦ, *wnškbh 'mw.* Neither Srez nor SJS list this usage, but Mikl has it both sub быти (быти съ отроковицєѭ, Supr 521.17 προσφθαρῆναι τῇ κόρῃ) and sub съ (быти съ роусьскою, Perejaslav chron.).

[104] Note that WV have и поклонающє са бахѹ, which is grammatically more consistent. LXX omits the first verb, but O restores it: κάμπτοντες προσεκύνουν 'bending their knees, they worshipped him' (NB, no 'and'). Similarly in 3:5, O: οὐ κάμπτει καὶ οὐ προσεκύνει αὐτῷ.

but rather *приклѧкаѭште for the first (3:2a) and *прикланꙗѧ сѧ for the second (3:5).[105] Both *pokloni-/poklanjaj- sę* and *pripadaj-* are normal OCS verbs.

L10.2 For *kneel,* 3:2 has *priklękno̧-/priklękaj-*: it is not in OCS and Sreznevskij attests it only from Esther.[106] Mikl notes *priklękno̧-* from the Bg 14th-century Mihanović Paterikon. T's omission of root-final *k* is unexpected, cf. OCS исѧкнѧ 'dried up'; *kn, gn* and *xn* are permitted at the boundary between a root and the *n* of this verbal suffix.

L10.21 In 5:9, ни приклѧкнуща occurs where we expect 'and did not tremble.' Textually this verse registers Mordecai's refusal to *bow down and worship* by specifying that he 'did not stand nor tremble.' Somewhere in the long history of translation and redaction, the association with verses 3:2 and 3:5 led to a substitution of verbs, along with a complex reorganization of the verse, see C5:9.

L10.3 The unprefixed stative клѧчати (*klęk-ě-*) occurs in OCS, *Izb. 1076*, and other ESl copies of originally OCS texts, meaning either 'kneel' or 'limp.' Cognates are found in West and South Slavic, along with numerous other formations of the type *klęk-no̧* and *klęk-aj* (see Trubačev s.v. *klęčati, klękati, klękno̧ti).*[107] Поклѧкъ 'having knelt' is attested in Judg 7:5 (W, VMČ I.75, cf. Srez sub поклѧчи [another ghost-form!]).[108] The imperfect поклѧцаше 'he limped' is found in some good copies of Gen 32:31 (Mixajlov), but in most ESl copies the form is distorted, very likely because it was unfamiliar to the scribes. Apart from WUkr клячіти 'kneel in prayer,' very likely an adaptation of P *klęczeć* (including a 17th-century example клячала, Trubačev 10 29), verbs with this root are absent from modern East Slavic (*pace* Trubačev ibidem).[109]

L11 Mental states

Мысль 'thought, intention, desire; mind, mood'
 помыслъ 'intention, plan'
 мыслити, помыслити 'intend, frame a request'
 умыслити 'intend, plan'

L11.1 The root *mysl* is suprisingly frequent (nouns, **мысль** 11, **помыслъ** 1; verbs, **мысли-** 2, **помысли-** 5, **умысли-** 2 [or 3]). Only six of these cases correspond to the Hebrew root 'think' *ḥšb* חשב (three verbs, 8:3; 9:24, 25; three nouns, 8:3, 5; 9:25), while at least seven respond rather to 'seek, request' *bqš* בקש, two represent 'soul' (4:13, 7:3), two 'heart' (1:10, 6:6), and some are unclear.

105 Perfective припалъ бѧше 7:8 has the literal sense 'had fallen (near).'

106 GorNev 55 consider the verb a Polonism. M56a 215 ignores them and calls it "typically Russian."

107 The infinitive клѧчити (Srez, SRJaXI) is surely a ghost-form; the stative **klęk-ě-*, with *i*-present, would yield *клѧчати. The participle клѧчюща as Sreznevskij belatedly realized, belongs to *клѧцати (Дополн. 140–1); SRJaXI's lemma "клячити" should be replaced by "клячати" for the first two meanings, and "кляцати" for the third. All cited examples are from originally SSl translations.

108 A variant is поклонь сѧ, perhaps reflecting LXX variants from κάμπτειν and κλίνειν.

109 Vil. 262, however, has клекаеть in both 3:2b and 3:5. Further, the Muscovite account of the Ferrara-Florence Council of 1438–49 in the Московский летописный свод of 1479 (PSRL 25 [1949]) uses приклекнет 'genuflects' (257.17) and клечит, клячат 'kneel(s)' (257.32, 34, 36) in describing Catholic church services. No glosses or explanations are given, so we must assume that the chronicler believed that these verbs were understandable to his intended readers.

L11.21 The lexeme мысль occurs eleven times, with a range of meaning that in part is determined by phraseology. The meaning 'intention' is obvious in 8:3, 5; 9:25, and possible in 3:5 where Gs мысли гнѣвныꙗ appears (Hebrew has merely 'anger,' see below, L14.7; LXX and L both paraphrase). In 8:3 and 9:25 the noun is defined by a clause with the aorist помысли.[110]

L11.22 The Hebrew joins the near-synonyms 'query' and 'request' six times. The king is in effect asking two questions, "What can I give you?" and "What can I do [or have done] for you?" The Hebrew words used in the variations on these two facets of the broader question ("How can I please you?") have troubled translators. Should the different passages be worded alike, or is it better to vary the elements? The uneven decisions of a translator can be complicated by later editors.[111] The text we can establish for *1350 is uncertain; in a number of places the Slavonic clearly departs from the literalism that is normal for most of the book. In 5:7, 8 the two nouns are просьба and мысль, but in 5:6 the first is прошениє and the second is doubled, мысль просьбы твоєꙗ. In 5:3 and 9:12 the Slavic again paraphrases, this time with verbs, present tense in 5:3 ҷто мыслиши просити, but imperative in 9:12 проси ты . . . помысли ты. This suggests that in these verses the hypothetical Greek had αἴτημα . . . ἀξίωμα (with perhaps ἀξιοῖς in 5:3), interpreted by the Slavic translator not simply as 'request, petition,' but with the nuance of 'think worthy.' The distribution of ἀξίωμα and ἀξιόω in LXX and L is somewhat different, but illustrates the sense needed for the use of мысль and мыслити in these contexts.

L11.221 In 7:3 MT again has both 'question' and 'request,' and Slavic offers мысль and просьба, but the sense is quite different. Створиши мысль мою can be understood as 'you will fulfil my request' and perhaps the Greek had ἀξίωμα here too. On the other hand, Hebrew has 'let my soul [= life] be given me.' In 4:13 въ мысли своєи corresponds to Hebrew 'in your soul,' and in 6:6 to 'in his heart.' If we assume that H 'heart' and 'soul' could be rendered by διάνοια (as they are in Joshua, cf. Lebedev), these examples become explicable. It seems most improbable that the extreme variety in our text is the work of a single translator; surely more than one editor had a hand in some passages.

L11.23 Parenthetically, we might note that the word оумъ does not occur in Esther, although it might be expected. For example in Genesis, where H has 'said in his heart' and LXX responds with εἶπε ἐν τῇ διανοίᾳ, 17:17 comes out помысли въ оумѣ, and 27:41 реҷє въ оумѣ (Mixajlov). Est 6:6, for the same H, has помысли . . . въ мысли.[112]

L11.24 Finally, the мысль царєва of 1:10 also represents 'heart of the king' in Hebrew (and our hypothetical διάνοια τοῦ βασιλέως), but similar Hebrew yields 'heart' in 5:9. See L12.711.

110 OB and GB have помыслихъ на нѧ in Josh 7:21, for ἐνθυμηθεὶς αὐτῶν, *w'ḥmdm,* 'and I desired (coveted) them.' Ex 20:17, 'thou shalt not covet thy neighbor's wife' is οὐκ ἐπιθυμήσεις τὴν γυναῖκα τοῦ πλησίον σου, нє помысли на жєноу ближьнѧаго си in 1073, 252.12 (sim. GB, but друга своєго), while OB has нє пожєлаи жєны искрєнєго твоєго.

111 The very different distribution of these phrasal variations in LXX, L and MT (and our text) is striking in the three-column array Karen Jobes presents in her thoughtful book on the L-text (1996). It implies quite different selections from a small group of (Hebrew) formulas, with further linguistic complications added by translators into, and editors of, the resulting Greek redactions. Levenson 108 elaborates on the literary effects of the variations.

112 In the *Life of Moses,* the same H, *wy'mr blbw,* yields the literal и рєҷє въ ср҇ци своємь (Tixonravov 243.16).

L11.25 The noun помыслъ appears only in 7:5, такы помыслы помысли, which departs from the MT, see comm.

L11.3 The dual aorist умыслиста of 2:21 and 6:2 also denotes 'intend.' (LXX, L offer no equivalent.) The inappropriate оуслышаша of most copies in 9:1 corresponds to умыслиша of Tn; it is surely old, although Hebrew does not have 'intended,' but 'hoped' (i.e., expected оупъвашѧ/оуповаша or надѣꙗша?).

L12 Request, desire, favor

Просьба, прошєниє, просити 'request'

L12.11 The correlated 'query . . . request' (cf. L11.22) has просьба as first member four times (5:7, 8; 7:2, 3), but in 5:6 прошєниє co-occurs with the conflated мысль просьбы твоєꙗ. In 7:2, что просьбы твоєꙗ, the genitive case is puzzling;[113] perhaps here too an earlier copy had мысль. For the same Hebrew question, the noun becomes a double verbal expression in 5:3, ӵто мыслиши просити, while in 9:12 it becomes an imperative, проси ты.

L12.12 In 2:15 нє проси рѣӵи is 'she did not ask for anything,' precisely as in Hebrew (Greek has paraphrases, but O includes the expected noun ῥῆμα).

L12.13 Просити and прошєниє are normal lexemes in OCS. Просьба, on the other hand, is absent from canonical OCS (except for the still only partially deciphered Glagolitic missal recently discovered on Sinai, Tarnanidis 104) and all of South Slavic (except as a modern inter-Slavic borrowing in Slovene). Its presence in the Sinai missal (and also in a service to St. Cyril in the Croatian Glagolitic Ljubljana Breviary of ca. 1400, cf. SJS) is one of the elements that point to a "Moravan" origin for the texts. The word is well attested for Old Czech, and normal for Polish; it appears in Ukrainian documents from 1347 on.[114] Sreznevskij's only examples of просьба are from Esther, 5:7, 8. (He notes that "other copies" have прошєниє; we cannot document that statement.) Просьба then is relatively new in an East Slavic manuscript from before 1400.

L12.14 The root *pros* is fairly well correlated to the Hebrew 'question' *š'l* שאל, but extends also to 'search, seek favor, ask for' *bqš* בקש (more usually *mysl* in Esther) in 2:15. The latter Hebrew root occurs in 2:2 and 2:23, with the appropriate eventual response поискали and въӡискана бы{сть}; in 3:6 and 7:2, however, волꙗ appears, see L12.15. In 9:12, 'on them that seek their hurt' becomes на всѣх враӡѣх своихъ.[115]

L12.141 In 4:8 H has two synonyms, *lhtḥnn lw wlbqš* (Moore "intercede and beg"; KJ "make supplication unto him and to make request before him"). We may conjecture

113 Srez has a lemma проситва, the sole example being Est 5:6, from Buslaev: Buslaev 169.10 prints проситвы твоєѧ. *Prositva* is attested in Slovene, and проситба is a plausible formation for SC, cf. Lunt 1996.

114 Peščak 1974 25; SSUM, s.v. прозба. A more literary example is the *Secretum Secretorum*, повиннєнъ єсмь испол'нити прос'бȣ твою, Speranskij 1908 138.5, for H *lml'wt š'ltk.*

115 LXX changes the sentences, and even the Origen-influenced text has ἐν τοῦς μισοῦσιν αὐτοῖς. On the basis of the parallel phrase in Psalm 70 (71):24, we might expect ἐν τοῖς ζητοῦσιν τὰ κακὰ αὐτοῖς and на ищущихъ ӡъла имъ.

молити и умолити, with the possibility that an abbreviated spelling оум^{л}ти was misread as оумилосьрдити, which then requires addition of сѧ. A parallel perhaps is Ham 133.12, умилоср^{д}и сѧ stands for παρακληθείς 'having been persuaded'; cf. Su 1.18 оумолена быв'ши παρακληθεῖσα. Alternatively, we may hypothesize молити и мила сѧ дѣти (cf. Euch 61b5 тебѣ сѧ мили дѣемъ, тѧ молимъ, σοῦ δεόμεθα καὶ σὲ παρακαλοῦμεν, and Srez *sub* милыи). From миласѧдѣти, perhaps written мила^{с}дѣти, to милоср^{д}ити is not too far. H *lhtḥnn* in 8:3 yields молѧщи.

Волꙗ 'will, desire, request,' **хотѣти** 'want,' **не въсхотѣти** 'refuse,' **не раꙋчити** 'refuse'; **вольникъ** ?'desired one, chosen one.'

L12.15 The use of волꙗ as 'request' (ἀξίωμα, בקשה) in 7:2 must be associated with the phrase волꙗ бы(сть) Амонова 3:6 'it was Haman's desire,' ultimately ויבקש 'Haman sought' on the one hand, and егда будѧше волѧ царева 2:14 'when it was the king's delight' on the other, where Hebrew has a verb, 'pleased, delighted, desired' *ḥpc* חפץ. This verb is used in the repeated phrase 'a/the man whom the king wishes/desires/delights to honor,' which appears in the following shapes:

6:9a	мужа	егоже	царь	хощеть	ꙋс̃тити
6:9b	мужеви	егоже	царь	хощеть	ꙋс̃тити
6:7	мужь	иже	царь	хощеть	ꙋс̃тити его
6:11	мужеви	егоже	царь	улюби	ꙋс̃тити его
6:6a	мужю	иже	царѧ	волю	ꙋс̃тити его
6:6b		кому	хотѣлъ	бы царь	створити ꙋс̃ть

The first two and the last are good Slavonic sentences.[116] The third uses an indeclinable relative plus a marked accusative pronoun—not normal for pre-1250 Slavic syntax, but acceptable in various more modern dialects. The fourth, with улюби, has two accusative pronouns, while the fifth, lacking both subject and a suitable verb, is corrupt.[117] Possible emendations might be (1) царь воли(ть), or (2) царꙗ/царю (е) волꙗ, both possible in OCS.

L12.151 Волꙗ thus goes back to a range of H expressions: (a) 2.14 and 6:6 *ḥpc*, (b) 3:11 волю ѡчью твоею *kṭwb b'ynyk*; (c) 1:8 and 9:5 *krcwn(m)*; (d) 3:6 and 7:2 *bqš*; (e) 7:2 no Hebrew equivalent. 8:8, see below.

L12.2 The phrase створити волю occurs twice, 1:8 and 9:5, where H has 'do *according to* one's desire,' *l'śwt krcwnw*. LXX 1:8 ποιῆσαι τὸ θέλημα, agrees with Sl, though the broader context has been paraphrased (LXX omits 9:5). A more literal rendering is found, e.g., in Dan 11:36, *w'śh krcwnw*, καὶ ποιήσει κατὰ τὸ θέλημα αὐτοῦ, и сътворить по воли своеи. The distinction between the accusative τὸ θέλημα and the preprositional phrase κατὰ τὸ θέλημα (or волю and по воли) was apparently ignored by some translators and/or copyists. A third example of створити волю, in 3:11, corresponds (with omission of a prepositional phrase) to quite different H, 'to do with/to them as is pleasing in your eyes' (an idiom that in 8:8 yields улюбѣеть, see L12.62).

116 The final infinitive phrases in the first five correspond to H *byqrw*, lit. 'in his honor'; the last is a literal equivalent of H 'to do honor.' See L15.1

117 T's order is волю царѧ, which is no improvement. Tn adds дѣеть, producing an appropriate phrase 'who does/executes the will of the king,' but the idea of honoring is lost.

L12.21 The adjective вольна is treated in the commentary to 1:8.

L12.22 The noun **вольникъ** in 10:3 stands where we expect 'accepted, favored,' cf. LXX 'honored,' L 'loved.' It is a plausible noun, representing the pattern corresponding to Late ComSl **volj-ьn(-)ik-* that is potentially available for any dialect; this example, however, is apparently unique in pre-modern works.[118] It is far more probable that it is a distortion of early **изволѥникъ**, 'chosen one,' whose attestation places it in 10th–11th century Slovene and Czech regions (see SJS), later Cz *zvoleník*, OPol *zwolenik*. It is formed quite regularly from the past passive participle of изволити 'like, desire, choose,' which was firmly established in OCS and continued in use in Rus′. The noun, however, was early displaced by a similar formation from *iz-bьra-* 'select, choose,' изьбраникъ.[119]

L12.3 Unprefixed хотѣти is only in the four examples above. The negated perfective occurs twice. In 4:4 нє въсхотѣ приꙗти is a free equivalent of Hebrew '(he) did not accept.' In 1:12, Hebrew has simply *wt'n* 'and (she) refused'; Sl adds an emphatic adverb 'at once': абьє нє въсхотѣ 'she at once became unwilling.' In 1:17 H has 'and-not-come (f)'; the Sl has changed the tone by providing an emphatic subject and an explicit negated verb of volition, ѡна жє нє раѵи прити 'and/but she did not deign to come.'

L12.31 In Esther, the H verb *refuse* appears only in 1:12. OT Gk lacks a literal equivalent and resorts to negated forms of various stems. In 1:12 LXX has καὶ οὐκ εἰσήκουσεν αὐτοῦ 'and did not obey (listen to) him'; L καὶ οὐκ ἠθέλησεν 'and did not wish.' The spare wording in 1:17 apparently did not express the importance of this repetition of Vashti's defiance of the king strongly enough for some translators. Both LXX and L paraphrase to emphasize her disobedience, and only the O-mss have the literal καὶ οὐκ ἦλθεν. In 4:4 LXX paraphrases, ὁ δὲ οὐκ ἐπείσθη 'but he was not persuaded,' while L selects the more usual ὃς δὲ οὐκ ἤθελεν 'but he did not wish.'[120]

Нє раѵити 'be unwilling, refuse' is attested in western and presumably early OCS, and in the Suprasliensis and several Rusian copies of what is believed to be eastern and later OCS, but it is absent (purged?) from the Psalms and the New Testament, as well as from such translations as Hamartolos and Josephus. It is known in OT translations—only those known in Rusian copies (cf. Srez. who cites Est 1:17)—and the Life of Feodosij Pečerskij, but is not found in Ilarion or the PVL nor yet the translations of Hamartolos and Josephus. It seems to have gone out of active use soon after 1100.

L12.4 The elaborate formality of the Persian court required many terms for 'be pleasing.' Apparently the sycophantic phraseology seemed excessive to some translators, and parts could be omitted. For example, in verse 8:5 Esther prefaces a request thus: 'If [1] it please

118 *Voljnik* or вольник is ephemerally attested in Croatia (1678, 'person who has right, power [to do something],' *Rječnik*), Russia (1691, 'person who acts willfully,' SRJaXI), and Bulgaria (c1871, 'volunteer [for armed forces],' Ilčev), but none of these nonce-words has the meaning appropriate for the last verse of Esther. GorNev 181 say it is Polish, but we could not find it in P sources.

119 An active agentive, изволникъ 'lover, admirer' (Srez) is to be attributed to *OCS. The 16th-century изволницы are also (for Srez) 'admirers.' It is possible to infer from the context that they are 'chosen ones' (as SRJaXI states), but in that case the form must be emended to изволеницы.

120 In Gen 39:8, сьи жє нє раѵааше (with a secondary variant хотѣашє) goes back to *wym'n* 'and he refused' via ὁ δὲ οὐκ ἤθελεν. Cf. Gen 48:19 *wym'n 'byw* 'and his father refused' > LXX (with omission of subject) καὶ οὐκ ἠθέλησεν > и нє раѵи. The нє раѵи of some ES copies of the Life of Constantine-Cyril vies with нє хотꙗшє or нє въсхотѣ of others, cf. SJS sub раѵити.

the king and if [2] I have found favor in his sight and [3] the thing seems right before the king, and [4] I be pleasing in his eyes.' LXX omits the last two phrases. Except for Tn, our text omits the third: аще цареви [1] оудобрю и [2] обрѧку милость...предъ царьмь и [4] добра буду азъ предъ оѵима его. (Tn's wording, провозвѣщю гл҃ъ, is peculiar, see C8:5.) The Slavonic has a wide variety of renderings for such terms, chiefly using the roots *dobr* and *ljub*, in addition to *xot*, in stems not usual elsewhere.[121]

L12.5 The stem *uljub-* apparently underlies two verbs, *uljub-i-* and *u-ljub-ĕj-*, but identification is uncertain because the *pervospisok* and all copies apparently have some degree of confusion of и and ѣ. Moreover, at least T has a variation of люб and лоб, each of which occurs thrice. Since *lob* is not independently attested elsewhere, we assume that the confusion is based on an earlier copy with лѫб or лѹб (or лоıб with the reversed ю-letter known from some Middle Bulgarian mss and Novgorod birchbark texts), and treat the examples together.[122] It is possible that the H intransitives came out intransitive also in Slavic, but then, because of dialect differences in interpreting specific verbal formants, individual sentences were misunderstood and emended in an inconsistent manner. In theory, we would expect the *i*-verb of this type to be transitive, the *ĕ*-verb to be intransitive, but dialect usage varies, and the examples in Esther remain unclear. (For улюби in a corrupt passage, see C2:9.)

L12.51 Улюбити 'desire' occurs in the Novgorod Chronicle s.a. 1216, a Smolensk gramota of 1230, and a Riga gramota c1300 (according to Srez), but the sense 'please' is unique to Esther and then later Ukrainian, as far as we have been able to ascertain.[123]

L12.52 In 2:4 дѣв{а} юже оулюблѧше царь reflects essentially 'the maiden who is pleasing in the king's eyes,' showing transitive улюбити. Similar phrases come out оулюбѣ рѣѵь цареви (also in 2:4), but in 1:21 и добра бы[с] рѣѵь предъ царемь, and 5:14 оудобри сѧ рѣѵь пред Аманъмь (where пред stands where H has the usual preposition *lpny* לפני, etymologically 'to the face of').

L12.6 A H phrase that occurs seven times, *'m 'l hmlk ṭwb* 'if on the-king (it is) good,' corresponds to six Slavonic clauses (variants from Tn are on the right):

1:19	аще цареви	оулюбѣе	аще цареви	оулюбѣеть
9:13	аще царю тобѣ	оулюбѣеть	аще цареви тобѣ	оулюбѣеть
7:3, 8:5	аще цареви	оудобрю	аще цареви	оудобрѣю
5:8	аще бы цареви [тако]	оудобрѣло	аще бы цареви	оудобрѣло
5:4	аще бы сѧ цареви	оудобрити	аще царь хотѣлъ мене	оудобрити
3:9	аще цареви бы [оубо]	доволно [бы] было	аще цареви оубо	доволно было

[121] The pattern of causative and stative verbs made from adjectival stems, of the type *u-krot-i+ti* 'tame, cause to become tame' and *u-krot-ĕj+ǫtъ* 'be tame' (along with the "anti-causative" *ukrotiti sę* 'become tame') was productive in many regions.

[122] Compare, in different copies of I Cor 6:13, люблодѣıанию, *Šišatovac Apostol,* лоıбодѣıаниоу Sof. Nat'l Lib. 880, лобъдѣıаниꙗ Sinai 39. The last two manuscripts, both of the 13th century, are unpublished.

[123] Cz *líbiti se* 'be pleasing' is old, but it does not occur with the prefix *u-*. Quite different is the usage in the late 15th-century translation of the *Third Capture of Jerusalem,* и оулюби єдинъ жидовинъ именемь Ахананъ, и скры сѧ пωд сн҃ωм; he 'volunteered,' H *wytndb.*

9:13 reads well, but surely it shows the old dative reinterpreted as vocative, with 'to thee' inserted for clarity. Tn's variant seems to have normalized what the scribe read as a dative, producing an unsatisfactory sentence. (We must leave the interpretation of Tn's version of the rest of these examples to our readers.) The same tendency to shift this sort of sentence to direct address is found in L's version of 5:8: εἰ εὗρον χάριν ἐναντίον σου, Βασιλεῦ. Similarly in 7:3 and 8:5, but with a change of verb (whether *i*-verb or *ě*-verb is impossible to tell). 5:8 and 5:4 are impersonal, one with the intransitive *ě*-verb and one with the "anti-causative" *i*-transitive plus сѧ.[124]

L12.61 Still impersonal, but without an explicit verb, 3:9 faces us with a choice of two positions for бы; the notion 'satisfactory' seems weak. We suggest that the problem comes from a Greek text with ἀρκέσῃ 'suffices' by error for ἀρέσκῃ 'pleases.' A comparable lapse is attested in LXX, in Est 5:13, καὶ ταῦτά μοι οὐκ ἀρέσκει, with the variant ἀρκέσει (a variant affirmed by the Old Latin translation). In Joshua 17:16, some LXX copies have the opposite error, ἀρέσκει for ἀρκέσει (or ἀρκεῖ).[125] The тако 5:8 and убо 3:9 could have been added by the Greek or the Slavic translator, or any copyist.

L12.62 In a different context, we find ꙗкоже оулюбѣет ѡчима ваю 'as you please' 8:8, with essentially the same H as 3:11 створити волю очью твоєю. Cf. 8:5, cited above, (аще) добра буду азъ пред ѡѵима его.

L12.711 Удобрити сѧ is used fairly concretely in 5:14, и оудобри сѧ рѣчь пред Амономь. Less clear is 1:10, вънегда сѧ оудобрѧше мысль царева; the Hebrew (lit. *in-the-being/becoming-good-of the-heart-of the-king*) means 'when the king was (became) in a good mood.'[126]

L12.712 Sreznevskij records удобрити in the sense 'improve, make beautiful or correct,' with удобрити сѧ only from Esther. A more suitable meaning is found in a Novgorod birchbark letter of about 1400: не можемъ ницимъ єму оудобрити сѧ 'we cannot please him by anything (in any way)' (Zaliznjak 1995 497–8). Several meanings found in other and later sources are unhelpful.[127]

L12.72 The unequivocal 'fall in love' here is ѡблюби 2:17. In the sense 'come to love' облюбити is attested in the Life of Methodius, in Dalmatian literature, and in modern Czech (usually *oblíbiti si*) and Ukrainian.[128] Mss WV "normalize" by substituting възлюби, with the prefix ordinarily used for this sense.[129]

L12.8 The phrases with *god* (годѣ or оугодьно быти, оугодити or оугодьнъ) that commonly mean 'be pleasing' do not occur in Esther.

124 T's оудобрило in 5:8 makes for a more complicated situation. See also 1:10 (and L12.711).

125 'The hill *is not enough for* us' (*hhr l' ymc' lnw*) becomes 'does not please us.' The Slavonic Joshua was based on manuscripts with 'please' and has годѣ есть (later годна есть, GB, J, W), corrected in the Ostrih Bible to довольно, which Lebedev (1890 381) mistakenly glosses as 'pleases.'

126 Mss GWV replace сѧ with же, implying an intransitive *udobrě-*. S, however, has же сѧ.

127 SC *udobriti se* 'ingratiate self' does not seem to be attested in really old texts.

128 The sense 'have intercourse; rape' is also found in SC. The feminine Voc *oblubienico* 'betrothed' occurs in SoS 4:11 (H *klh*, L *sponsa*, Gk νύμφη) in 16th-century Polish Bibles (the Leopolitana [Cracow 1561], the Radziwiłł or Brest Bible [Brest 1563], Wujek [Cracow 1599]) where ESl versions have невѣсто.

129 Alternatively, WV may reflect *1350, while QT show a deviant emendation of *1370. Tn's полюби is late (cf. PVL 10.8, LH възлюби, but RA полюби).

милость 'favor, grace'
възнести, възносити, обнести 'favor, support'

L12.91 The familiar biblical 'find favor' and 'gain favor' use милость in Esther. In 7:3 аще обращу милость пред очима твоима the full Hebrew phrasing is retained, while in 8:5 'eyes' are omitted in favor of the normal пред царемь. (In 5:8 most of the phrase is omitted.) A more active role of the subject is shown in възнесе милость 2:9,[130] even in passivized phrases, обнесена милостью 2:15, 5:2 (extended in 2:17 by и любовью, the only example of this noun in Esther). Otherwise, възнесе is used with a direct object in 3:1 and 5:11, cf. the corresponding imperfect възношаху in 9:3. (See also C3:1.) The възнесе милость of 2:9 is unique. Обнести in these verses is also unique.[131] Notice that the Hebrew root *nś'* 'carry, raise, lift' in these phrases is reflected by the Sl root *nes*.

L12.92 The phrases with милость deviate somewhat from OCS usage and they do not correspond appropriately to the Hebrew.

L12.921 The H terms *ḥn* 'pity, mercy' and *ḥsd* 'favor, grace' ordinarily yield LXX ἔλεος and χάρις, which in turn become OCS милость and благодѣть (often replaced in Preslav and Rus′ copies by благодать, nearly always obscured by abbreviation блгдть). The two H terms both come close to the sense of 'benevolence, favorable attitude.' The phrase 'find favor (in someone's eyes)' is *mc' ḥn*, lit. 'find mercy' three times in Esther (5:8, 7:3, 8:5), while 'obtain grace or good will' is *nś' ḥsd*, lit. 'lift up grace' once (2:9), 'lift up mercy' *nś' ḥn* twice (2:15, 5:2), plus one instance where both nouns are used, 2:17 *wtś' ḥn wḥsd* 'she won his favor and devotion' (or, taking the phrase as hendiadys, his devoted favor,' Moore).[132] LXX regularly has εὑρεῖν χάριν, although literal translation would produce ἔλεος; this phrase is used in the NT and the Church Fathers. Therefore обрѣсти благодѣть is well attested, e.g., in Genesis (or in the NT echoes of the H phrase, Luke 1:30, Acts 7:46, Heb 4:16). The use of милость, except in 2:9, and of любовью in our text is therefore unusual in the Slavonic tradition.[133] The extension from *pity, mercy* to *tolerance, clemency* and then *grace, favor* is not apparent in early texts; it is a Ruthenian innovation.[134] The required positive nuance is particularly clear in SC, where 'find favor' is *naći (iznaći, nahoditi) milost* from Dalmatian literature to Daničić's translation of the OT.

130 It is irrelevant that the subject here, through textual corruption, is incorrect for the context, see C2:9.

131 Srez cites only Est 5:2 from GB. SRJaXI adduces also post-1400 examples meaning 'surround.' In Joshua 6:11 OB has обнесше 'having carried around,' but this is a paraphrase; LXX has περιελθοῦσα 'when it (the ark of the covenant) had gone around (the city),' GB обишедш(е)–the last letter is not visible in the photo.

132 'Find favor' *mc' ḥn* occurs 35 other times in the OT; 'lift, raise' *nś'* with *ḥn* is only in Esther. The juxtaposed *ḥn wḥsd* also is found only in Est 2:17, although it is known in post-biblical Hebrew. Both *nś' ḥn* and *nś' ḥsd* 'gain favor' are also common in post-biblical texts.

133 Srez cites the combination обрѣсти plus милость only from Est. It occurs also in the *Third Capture of Jerusalem*, кто вѣсть ѡбращемъ ли милость предъ очима его. Милость is in fact good Ruthenian (cf. Pol *miłość* and Cz *milost*). In Vil 262 наити милость 10x in Esther, twice in Ruth.

134 SRJaXI posits meaning 2, 'благосклонность, особое расположение, любовь'; it is not warranted by the two examples. The 11th-century citation shows a translation of φιλανθρωπία in the sense of 'clemency, милосердие'; the context is specifically concerned with *mercy* and *charity* (OCS both милость and милостыни). The sentence from the Novgorod First Chronicle, sub 1141, illustrates the same meaning. Both fit nicely under SRJaXI's meaning 1.

L13 Joy, rejoicing

вєсєлъ 'happy'; **вєсєлиє** 'happiness,' **вєсєльныи** 'of rejoicing'
възвєсєлити сѧ 'rejoice'
охвота 'gladness,' **охвотьнъ** 'glad,' **уохвотити сѧ** 'exult'

L13.1 The adjectives вєсєлъ and вєсєлныи are used to refer to days of celebration and are not clearly distinct. Examples in the 11th-century *Čudov Psalter* and the Parimejnik (SJS) allow us to date *vesel-ьn-* to OCS, and indicate that it signified 'of joy, of rejoicing.'[135] Thus the formal distinction from unsuffixed *vesel-* implies a difference in meaning.[136]

L13.2 The noun вєсєлиє corresponds to H *śmḥh* 'happiness, joy' four times. In 9:29, 31, 32 вєсєлиꙗ сего makes sense as 'this happiness,' but they (and an example in the corrupt text of 9:28) stand where the Hebrew has *Purim*, the name of the specific holiday which is so important for the Jewish interpretation of the Scroll of Esther.[137]

L13.3 The phrase възвєсєли сѧ 'rejoiced' is found in 8.15. It is preceded by уохвоти сѧ и, corresponding to H 'shouted and.' The verb уохвоти сѧ is unique to Esther.[138] Buslaev, GorNev 55 called it a Polonism; Sobolevskij 435 said it was "West-Russian."

L13.4 The characteristic Belarusian morpheme *xvot*—a narrowly regional variant of *xot* 'wish'—occurs in *oxvot-* also as a noun, охвота, and an adjective in the descriptive phrase, охвотьнъмь ср҃дцмь. The dialectal root vocalism is attested in the Hypatian Chronicle, 437.15, sub 1151, нє ѡхвотивъ єсмь былъ на кровопролитьє 'I have not been eager for bloodshed';[139] in Josephus (охвотимыа на брань 184.24, 'eager for battle') and in a 15th century BR ms (RNB Q I 391, Karskij 298 provides no definition for the adverb ѡхвот'но). Mod. BR ахвота 'desire,' ахвотны 'desirous, willing' correspond to other ESl derivatives of *oxot-* with meanings that fall in the range of *willingness, desire, eagerness.* The same range is found in the corresponding noun and adjective of Polish, Slovak, and Czech. Only Old Cz *ochotný* seems to include *happy, joyful, glad* in its meaning.[140] Yet this is the sense охвот- should represent in Esther.

135 Isaiah 61.3 has помаӡаниѥ вєсєлно ἄλειμμα εὐφροσύνῃ 'anointing of joy,' a not altogether felicitous rendering of H *šmn śśwn* 'oil of rejoicing, better translated in Ps. 44:8 (MT 45:8) ἔλαιον ἀγαλλιάσεως, which became олѣмъ радостı in Ps. Sin, and масломь радости in *Čud.*
136 Compare OP *wiesiele, wesele* 'joy'; mod. 'wedding' with adj. *weselny,* from which U весілля 'wedding,' весільний, BR вяселле, вясельны. For the broader semantic field *drinking–celebrating–rejoicing–festival –wedding,* see L13.62, note.
137 The combination дн҃ь добръ, 8:17, 9:19, 9:22, reflects what in later Hebrew came to mean 'holiday'; LXX has omitted it in 8:17, while in 9:19 it too has the literal equivalent ἡμέραν ἀγαθήν (cf. AT 314, n. 25). Esther has no word explicitly meaning *holiday.* A Slav wanting to express the notion might use праӡдьникъ or тържьство (for πανήγυρις 'fair, festal gathering, holiday').
138 LXX and L reduce the two H verbs *chlh wśmḥh* 'shouted and was happy' to ἐχάρησαν 'rejoiced'; O-texts add καὶ εὐφράνθησαν.
139 Cf. the normal vocalism in на млⷭтню зѣло ѡхотивъ 'very willing/eager/ready in giving alms,' Lav 368.6, sub 1175. In Esther, G has only охот-, but the glaring phonological dialectism (presumably [vo] from a diphthong [uo]) remains in the other copies available to us.
140 The lexemes defined in the Old Czech dictionary, SčS, are profusely illustrated by examples meaning the "willing, desirous, eager, anxious to," and a small number classed as meaning "glad." The Prague Bible of 1488 has Esther conceal the fearful agitation of her heart *ochotnyma očima*, 'by her cheerful (?) eyes.' Jerome turned LXX's *cheerful face* τὸ πρόσωπον ἱλαρόν to *shining/sparkling eyes—nitentibus oculis* (Hanhart D: 5 = Vulgate 15:8), which G renders appropriately свѣтлыми очима. A second Esther example is 1:10 in early 15th-century Bibles (see SčS); *když král bieše ochoten* for *cum rex esset hilarior* 'when the king was merrier.'

L13.41 In 8:16, the festive mood of the Jews is described as просвѣщєньє и вєсєлиє, охвота и чьсть, H 'light and gladness and joy and honor.' In 8:17 again вєсєльє и охвота, the Jews had 'joy and gladness' according to the MT. In 5:9, Haman left the king вєсєлъ и охвотьнъмь ср҃дцмь, in the MT 'joyful and good of heart.'[141]

L13.42 The MT and the New Testament often combine near-synonyms. Thus Ps 9:2 въӡвєсєлѭ сѧ и въӡдрадоуѭ сѧ εὐφρανθήσομαι καὶ ἀγαλλιάσομαι 'I will rejoice and be glad'; радоуитє сѧ и вєсєлитє сѧ, χαίρετε καὶ ἀγαλλιάσθε 'rejoice and be glad.' Biblical Greek uses three terms – ἀγαλλίασις (ἀγαλλίαμα), ἀγαλλιάω; εὐφροσύνη, εὐφραίνω; χαρά, χαίρω – for a considerable range of Hebrew terms. OCS reduces this further to two: вєсєлъ, вєсєльє, [въӡд]радовати [сѧ]. What is important is that the two sets existed throughout Slavdom.[142]

L13.5 The absence of радъ, радость, радостьнъ, (въӡ[д])радовати is as striking as the presence of *oxvot*. Indeed, we may posit a relationship. If *rad*-derivatives are substituted for *oxvot*—радость 8:16, 17; радостьнымь 5:9; въӡ[д]радова сѧ 8:15—the text becomes normal Slavonic, with no regional or temporal overtones. The phrase радостьнъмь ср҃дцмь is appropriately used in an original Rusian text in precisely the meaning suitable for 5:9, 'with a glad heart, in an exuberant mood.'[143] In Skaryna's Belarusian translation from the Vulgate by way of Czech (Prague, 1517), the verbs of 8:15 are возвесели сѧ и возрадова сѧ. The colloquial translation from the Hebrew a few years earlier (Vilnius 262) has adjectives, радостен и веселъ.

L13.6 A literal translation might be expected to distinguish three roots to reflect the H (5:9 'good of heart, in a positive mood' vs. 8:15 'shout [joyfully]' vs. 8:16, 17 'joy'), but LXX and L (and the Vulgate) show that with such conventional expressions literalism is easily neglected in favor of clichés. We might conjecture that the original Slavonic Esther indeed had normal derivatives of *rad* in one or more of these phrases, and that an editor of the *pervospisok* systematically substituted the *oxvot* forms (or an earlier editor put in *oxot*- and the editor of *1350 changed the spelling). We might conjecture that охот- was original in one phrase, then generalized to the rest. Or we might posit that the original Slavic translator chose to use this North Slavic stem in four different verses in an extreme sense that is poorly attested for 14th-century Czech and not at all elsewhere.

Banquet: Пиръ, питьє, прєпои, питва, питвьныи.

L13.71 In Esther, the *banquet* plays an important role as the background for major actions, and at the end the new holiday of Purim is designated as two days of rejoicing and

[141] This is similar to the H of 1:10 (cf. previous note), the source of a quite different Sl phrase (see L12.711). Охвота corresponds to H *śś(w)n* 'joy, merriment, rejoicing.' The verb уохвоти сѧ stands where H has *chlh* 'shouted,' a verb that does not specifically denote joy (Moore's 'cheered' is not "as literal as possible"). All nine examples of the root *vesel* (noun, adjectives, verb) correspond to H derivatives of the root *śmḥ* 'glad, happy.'

[142] The very limited records of Polabian do not contain *vesel*-; the cognate of радость meant 'wedding'; cf. P *wesele* (note 136 above).

[143] It refers to Prince Boris whose grief for his murdered brother and fear for his own life (стонаашє горестию ср҃дьчьною 'he groaned with the bitterness of his heart') has been dissipated by prayer and he sets off to meet his fate. (The oldest copy has hypercorrect ъ in the suffix *ost*, радъстьнъмь, Usp 10b21 (cf. кротъкъ 10b5 for кротъкъ).)

feasting. All twenty references in the Hebrew text use the noun *mšth* משתה (four times with the specification 'of wine' *hyyn* היין), but Slavonic has four nouns and a derivative adjective: пиръ, питье, препои, питва, питвьныи. The normal word is **пиръ** (11x), well attested from OCS. **Питье**, an OCS verbal substantive 'drinking' is used with 'rejoicing' in 9:19, веселие и питье and въ питии виньнѣмь 7:2. H *hštyh* 'drinking' appears once in Est, 1:8, here **питва**. As 'banquet' питва is found three times (на питву 5:4 = къ питвѣ 6:14, ѡт питвы винныꙗ 7:7); otherwise it occurs in this meaning only in the apocryphal Testament of Judah, 8:2 створи ми [!for 'us'] питвꙋ (Tixonravov 1, 177.11), i.e., ἐποίησεν ἡμῖν πότον. Sreznevskij cites it from a 12th-century *Zlatostruj* and 16th-century texts, where the meaning is apparently 'beverage, drink,' as it is in modern western South Slavic (Croatian, Slovene). The derivative adjective *pitv-ьn-* appears in normal East Slavic form as питвен- in two 14th-century examples Sreznevskij cites, beside Esther.[144] Here it stands in three passages where 'of feasting and rejoicing' is required (9:17, 18, 22), and one where Hebrew has the 'house of the feast of wine' (7:8).[145] H 'feast of wine' results in въ **препоихъ** виньныхъ in 5:6; we have not found this noun in any old source, but its equivalent перепій is known in Ukrainian to denote a portion of certain wedding ceremonies, presumably involving drinking.[146]

L13.711 The description above deals with QTWVSG. Tn has a series of variants, and we have no way to decide what *1350 might have had. Питьба for питва 'drinking' 1:8 is a reasonable Slavic formation, but it is not attested anywhere we could find. We believe that it is secondary, but we do not wish to guess what might have been in *1350. Tn 9:19 has питвоу, not питье; пиръ (not питва) stands in 5:4 and 6:14 (see L13.74). Tn 5:6 has в перепоꙗ[X]. In short, the inventory of lexemes is essentially the same, but the distribution in Tn differs from that of the other manuscripts.

L13.72 In the LXX Esther we find δοχή, πότος, συμπόσιον, and even γάμος 'wedding' for *mšth*.[147] Elsewhere in LXX πόμα and πόσις are also used for *mšth*.

L13.73 We may conjecture that two or more words were used in the Greek translation underlying the Slavonic and that, on the other hand, препоихъ represents a fairly late substitution in the Slavonic text for something else.

L13.74 Note the variations of preposition, noun, relative, and verb in the Sl equivalents for H 'to the feast which she/I made' (the verb is 3s fem in the first two, and 1s in 5:4); the left-hand examples are from the majority of copies, the right-hand examples from Tn:

144 Srez (followed by SRJaXI) gives a separate lemma to the phonological variant питовныи.

145 M78 mistakenly attributes a variant пивьномy in 7:8 to Q .

146 Interestingly enough, перепои is found in the Jewish Belarusian translation of Esther in Vil 262 (early 16th century), in 9:19, 22 (Altbauer 1992 173), for H *mnwt*, where our text more appropriately has дары 'gifts.' See also C2:9, C2:18.

147 The connections between *feasting* and *drinking* with the more general *festivity* easily extend to *holiday* on the one hand and the specific *wedding* on the other. In Genesis, *mšth* is rendered as γάμος (21:8, 26:30, 29:22) which can come out бракъ or гоститва, with variants including пиръ (Mixajlov). In OCS and Ham, веселие translates εὐωχία 'festivity,' which in turn is translated as пиръ in Ham. Compare веселие as 'holiday,' where we expect the specific name 'Purim' in 9:29 (see comm.), with its more modern connotation 'wedding' in western ESl and WSl.

'l hmšth	*'šr*	*'śth / 'śyty*				
на пиръ	иже	створила бѣ	5:12	на миръ	и^{ж}	баше створила
къ питвѣ	иже	оустроила баше	6:14	на пиръ	иже	баше створила
на питву	еже	быхъ створила	5:4	на пиръ...	юже бо	бы^{х} створила

If we accept the feminine relative юже as original, we may posit the noun питву as belonging to *1350. In view of the instability of form of the relative pronoun, however, we may wish to believe that the common word пиръ is more likely to be original.

L13.8 *Fasting,* the opposite of *banqueting,* is expressed by the noun **говѣнье** (4:3, 9:31) and the verb **говѣти** (4:16). This meaning is clearly documented only in East Slavic; in OCS (and generally) the sense is 'reverence, piety; revere, be pious.' The earliest attestation is in the responses attributed to the metropolitan John of 1080–89 (in fact datable only to before 1280) ("иже...в великою говѣнью масо ѧдать," κατὰ τὴν μεγάλην τεσσαρακοστήν, 'during the Great Fast'; Goetz 123).[148] The old meaning (SJS, also говѣѭтъ 'be pious, live piously,' говѣинъ 'pious, god-fearing'), often extends to 'be humble toward, defer to, strive to please' in Bg, SC, and Cz *hověti*, cf. R благоговеть. Bulgarian говея also means 'fast; abstain from eating certain foods,' but we have found no pre-modern examples. Far more common in OCS and most regions are the noun постъ 'fast' and the verb постити сѧ (with *OCS пощенье, Srez), borrowed from OHG *fasto.*

L14.1 *Sorrow* or *mourning* in 4:3 in most copies is the ancient and unusual **желꙗ** (for H *'bl*, LXX and L omit), attested marginally in OCS (Su, θρῆνος; cf. Joel 2:12 с желею ἐν κοπέτῳ).[149] The verbal substantive **желание** 9:22 (also H *'bl* LXX ἀπὸ ὀδύνης) surely is an error for желѣние; this form is not attested as 'sorrow, grieving' in OCS, but, to judge from the citations in Srez, it was used in this sense in Preslav OCS.[150] A parallel phrase (ѿ скърбии *mygwn* LXX ἀπὸ πένθους 9:22) uses a near-synonym that is abundantly attested in OCS (скръбь) and early Rusian. Tn, in contrast, uses жалость instead of желание.

The adjective 'sad, sorrowing' in most mss is **жельнъ** (6:12 желенъ), an unusual word that probably goes back to OCS (cf. Srez), while Tn uses the ubiquitous печаленъ. Which one are we to assign to *1350?

L14.2 *Weeping* is **плачь** 4:3, a normal word.[151] *Lamentation* is **нарѣкание** 4:3, H *mspd* 'mourning'; perhaps κοπετός. SJS does not record the stem and нарѣкати (Srez) means 'называть' and thus is irrelevant here.[152] The meaning 'lament, weep for (the dead)' is western: Cz *naříkání,* U нарікання P *narzekać*; cf. Slk *nariekati*; Sln and East Croatian

[148] Srez cites this example, but glosses it *fletus* 'weeping'—a misunderstanding. He gives the Latin as *luctus et fletus et planctus;* in fact it is *planctus... ieiunium, ululatus et fletus*: говѣние = ieiunium.—M56a 215 speaks of говѣино 'пост'; it does not occur in QT.

[149] M56a 215 lists желѧ among the typically "Russian" words.

[150] Compare also желѣтва πένθος, Su twice, and the early EBg OCS attestation documented by Srez. Older variation between *žel* and *žal* meaning both 'desire' and 'sorrow' was early resolved in favor of *želaj-* for the former and *žalь, žalěj-* for the latter. SRJaXI demonstrates желѣние in the Lithuanian Commonwealth in the 16th century. There seems to be no local dialectal basis for this usage, and we suspect it was literary imitation of old models. GorNev 207 note жалѣнїе as the name of the book of *Lamentations* in a 16th-century ESl ms of the 16 prophets.

[151] Local differences in meaning show clearly in variations attested in Gen 50:3–11. Плачь, жалѣние, желꙗ, and жалꙗ (and also желѣтва) are used in different copies.

[152] In the *Hexameron* of John the Exarch, presumably composed in OCS in the 9th century, нарѣковати means 'define, distinguish,' akin to the adjectives нароучитъ 'distinguished' and нароучьнъ 'definite, special, marked.'

dial. *narekati*; SC *naricati* allows this sense.[153] Beside this passage in Esther, we have found it in pre-modern East Slavic only in the *Third Capture of Jerusalem,* translated from Hebrew probably in the Lithuanian Commonwealth in the 15th century: и нарекаѧ Iωсиѳ нарекан҃їє сє (RNB, OLDP F.33, f. 239) and in Vil. 262, Est 4:3 нарѣканьє. It is apparently unknown in modern Russian (cf. Filin). Perhaps the juxtaposition of synonyms (*wbky wmspd*) brings out the potential for an unusual use of the word; плаѵ- has already been used.

L14.3 **Въсплака** 'wept' corresponds to H in 8:3 (but not in 3:15, see comm.). Sorrowful outcry is **въпль**, used in 4:1 with **въӡъпи**.[154] These (and the imperfective *vъpij-*, not used in Est) are surely by origin Moravanisms, well established in the Psalms and a few Gospel passages, but often replaced by (въ)ӡъвати, ӡъваньє.[155] The words remained very much a part of normal literary vocabulary. Въпль is particularly likely to appear when near-synonyms are used together, as in плаѵь и рыданиє и въпль многъ Mt 2:18 (AsSavOstMst), θρῆνος καὶ κλαυθμὸς καὶ ὀδυρμὸς πολύς.[156]

L14.4 In 6:12, повѣсивъ главу 'hanging his head' seems appropriate to express Haman's shame and apprehension, but does not correspond to the H wording, '(with) covered head.' The Jewish custom of covering one's head as a sign of mourning seems not to have been understood by Slavic scribes. The same H appears twice in 2 Ki 15:30, and is reproduced by LXX, ἐπεκάλυψεν τὴν κεφαλὴν αὐτοῦ, and τὴν κεφαλὴν ἐπικεκαλυμμένος. Slavic bookmen, however, emended the phrases to specify '*un*covered': S, G, and J have ѿкровенома главама, and главою ѿкровеною. OB has returned to the original: покровенома, and покрывше главȣ свою.

L14.51 The Hebrew phrase *for fear fell/had fallen upon* occurs in 8:17, 9:2 and 9:3; the Slavonic has three different equivalents:

9:3	ꙗко	напалъ	бѧшє	страхъ Мардохаєвъ
8:17	ꙗко	оумножилъ сѧ	бѧшє	страхъ Июдѣискыи
9:2	ꙗко	въӡидє		гроӡа ихъ.

The expected Gk is found in L 9:3: ὁ γὰρ φόβος Μαρδοχαίου ἔπεσεν.[157] Otherwise the known Gk versions vary, without introducing new notions like *multiply* or *go up* instead of *fall*. LXX 9:2 changes 'fell' to 'lay (had been placed)' ἔκειτο. In 8:17 L paraphrases, ἐφοβοῦντο γὰρ αὐτούς and LXX makes a nominal phrase, διὰ τὸν φόβον τῶν Ἰουδαίων; L omits. L omits 9:2, and LXX has merely φοβούμενος αὐτούς.

L14.52 **Страхъ** is normal OCS for φόβος; for the accompanying adjectives denoting the agents causing the fear, see A5.632. **Гроӡа** meant 'horror, a fearsome thing, threat; φρίκη' in old texts; the exact nuance must have varied in different dialects.[158] The connection of

153 BR наракаць, нараканне mean 'accuse, blame.'

154 Gen 50:3 has желѣша and плака сѧ as variants. In verse 10 'lamented for him' is плакашє сѧ and плаѵа въпльствиша єго, while the noun is плаѵь великъ or плаѵь вопльствиємь.

155 In Ps 5:2 and 9:12 all old psalters have ӡваньє but in 101:1 and 143:14 въпль; it will be interesting to see whether the still unpublished late-OCS or early post-OCS Glagolitic Sinai mss 5N (Tarnanidis) has the same distribution.

156 Cf. Joel 2:12 (Glag, SJS): καὶ ἐν νηστείῃ καὶ ἐν κλαυθμῷ καὶ ἐν κοπετῷ: пощениємь и рыданиємь и плаѵємь и въпльствиємь, where three Gk nouns yield four Sl nouns.

157 The literal equivalent of the H phrase is perfectly comprehensible in Slavic. Thus in a section of the Три пленения Иерусалима derived from the *Yosippon* and translated from H (Academy Chronograph, ms 20, cf. Istrin 1905 329) we find и падє страхъ єго на всѣх людєхъ.

158 In Hamartolos, ἀπειλή is reflected as гнѣвъ at 399.11, and гроӡа at 431.10.

възиде 'went up' with the following locational 'over all people' (H here is explicitly 'all the peoples/nations') is tenuous.[159]

Other expressions of emotional reaction

L14.6 The verb of 4:4 и **оужасе сѧ** царица 'was astonished' or 'alarmed' is very common in OCS, but not quite equivalent to the extremely rare H form *wttḥlḥl* which Moore translates 'was shocked,' suggesting also 'was perplexed.' In 7:6, reacting to the king's wrath, Haman 'trembled' **въстрепета**, where H has rather 'be startled'; Moore 'was dumbfounded.' LXX has the aorist ἐταράχθη 'became disturbed, alarmed' for both.[160] The Sl often evoked by this Gk verb is **съмѧте сѧ**; it occurs unexpectedly in 5:10, which is quite different from the MT, see comm. In 3:15, H *nbwkh* 'was confused, became perplexed' quite properly is rendered with the imperfect of the same verb, ἐταράσσετο. In Sl., however, we find въсплака сѧ, see comm.

Anger

L14.7 For 'anger,' only the morpheme *gněv* is used in Esther; **гнѣваıа** сѧ, **разгнѣва** сѧ; **гнѣвъ** 6x, and **мысль гнѣвнаıа** 3:5. Hebrew uses two morphemes (*ḥmh* חמה 6x, *qcp* קצף 3x), which might be expected to elicit ὀργή and θυμός, among other possibilities. Hebrew frequently juxtaposes two or more words for 'anger,' and LXX responds with phrases like ὀργὴ θυμοῦ or θυμὸς ὀργῆς (not infrequently attested as variants in individual passages), hence OCS гнѣвъ ıарости ps. 77:49, ıарость гнѣва 68:25. In the apocryphal *Testaments of the Twelve Patriarchs* is the phrase "пьıаньство . . . влагаеть гнѣвную мысль" (Tixonravov 1.116, 180), which reflects ὀργὴν ἐπιθυμίας, properly "the impulse of desire," with a different sense of ὀργή which was not understood by the Slavic translator. We may conjecture that in Esther 3:5 our Slavic translator found a doublet ὀργῆς θυμοῦ, the second member of which he chose to regard not as repeating the sense of the first, but as something like ἐνθύμημα or ἐνθύμησις. In any case, the doublet in Slavic is not a literal translation of MT; it may well reflect a peculiarity of the Greek text.

L14.71 The king's anger in 1:12 is *enkindled*, **ражьже сѧ**. In 7:10 **потухну** (var. **потоуше** Tn) 'was quenched,' a term used of fire or light; the verb is not attested in OCS but cognates are wide-spread in the Slavic world. The H verb is based on a root meaning 'calm.' In 2:1 essentially the same phrase yields **оустави сѧ** гнѣвъ царѧ, from a verb that in eastern OCS meant 'stop, bring to an end' (cf понеже ни сърмьтиѭ гнѣва уставишѧ Su 440.18, cf. Usp 212d21, 'because not even through death did they halt their anger'). Ham offers a precise parallel (420.20): абие оустави сѧ гнѣвъ божии, ἔπαυσεν ἡ ὀργὴ τοῦ θεοῦ, 'God's anger ceased at once').[161] It should be noted that this sense is rare after c1100, and it is not characteristic of native Rusian usage.[162]

159 Dan 7:15 ἔφριξεν τὸ πνεῦμά μου 'my spirit shuddered' is in the older translation гроза обиде дхъ мои 'fear surrounded my spirit.' The Preslav revision has възъгорѣ сѧ, 'caught fire, flared up,' removing the notion of fear entirely; we might conjecture that it is an error for *възгрози (or угрози?) сѧ. An appropriate change in one tradition was оусьтраши сѧ (Evseev 1905 110). Compare Nik 34.21 (Lat. *obstupuerunt* 'they were astonished, terrified'), оугрозиша сѧ, with variants оустрашиша сѧ and оужасоше се. (In northern Macedonia, *ugrozi se* 'be terrified' survives, see *Rječ.*)

160 The translator of Vil 262 used 'tremble' in 4:4, оуздрижала, and 'was frightened' in 7:6, оуполошил сѧ.

161 Cf. the active use, Josh 7:26 (W) и оустави гь ıарость гнѣва своего.

162 Sreznevskij's last example sub ȣставитисѧ is allegedly from the First Novgorod Chronicle, sub 1204; it

L14 Honor and shame

L15.1 The noun **чьсть** occurs six times; four times it corresponds to H *yqr* 'honor' (1:4; 6:3, 6; 8:16) but twice it stands where H has *kbwd* 'glory' (cf. C1:4),which might be expected to yield слава (a word that does not appear in our text). The verb **чьстити** occurs in a single phrase that repeats five times, reflecting *byqrw,* 'in his honor'; see L12.15.

L15.2 **Величье** 'greatness' in 6:3 and 10:2 and its variant **величьствье** in 1:4 are appropriate for H *gdwlh*, Gk μεγαλωσύνη. The verb **възвеличати** 'make great, promote' (5:11, 10:2, and originally, surely, 3:1—probably μεγαλύνειν) is associated with the adjective великъ in the sense of social and political standing, see C3:1, C9:4.

L15.3 **Срамота** 'shame' is used appropriately in 1:18. In 1:20, however, възложать **срамоту** stands where H has *yqr* and therefore чьсть would be expected. The verb may mean 'bestow' or 'put on' and implies, in our view, a Gk verb other than ordinary 'give.'[163] LXX has τιμὴν παριθήσουσι, and Ham uses възложити for περιτιθέναι (as well as ἀνα-, ἐπι-). For the noun, we would expect чьсть (< τιμή), in agreement with other passages in Esther. The appearance of *shame,* as Aleksander Kulik suggests (1995 72), is perhaps the result of a free rendering using Gk ἐντροπή in the positive sense 'respect, reverence.' In biblical Greek this noun has only a negative sense (once in Job and six times in the psalms it translates H *klmh* 'reproach, insult'; twice in 1 Cor it means 'shame'), but in the Church Fathers it has both meanings. OCS срамота often goes back to ἐντροπή; it surely was the primary sense for Slavic translators. Note that срамота in v. 18 correctly reflects H *bzywn* 'shame, dishonor.'[164] The obvious disruption of the sense of the verse (for readers who had followed the story more carefully) led later scribes to add a gloss, драготу, which then in even later manuscripts replaced срамоту in the text itself.

L16.1 This set of misunderstandings involves also the interpretation of the three phrases involving the root *vrěd*:

1:17: ꙗко **не оуврєдити** мужь своихъ [и не въ послухъ] пред ними *lhbzwt b'lyhn b'ynyhn.* The literal sense of the Hebrew in the larger context is "[the story of the queen, when heard by the women of Persia and Media, is likely] to make their husbands unworthy in their eyes" (cf. L6.2). Moore renders it, 'They will look down on their husbands'; LXX omits the phrase, L omits the verse. The bracketted words seem to be a doublet, added by an editor or scribe as a clarification.

3:6: и **въ неврѣдъ** очима его бысть, *wybz b'ynyw*. The Hebrew may be either a subjectless impersonal construction, lit. "(it) was despiteful in his eyes," or a masculine personal with Haman as subject, as Moore renders, 'he hated [to kill just Mordecai],' with note

---

is not there. On the contrary, the only time the verb occurs in this text (cf. Dietze), it has precisely the opposite meaning, 'begin,' and it is adduced by Srez. However, остави сѧ 'cease' does occur, sub 1165 (see Srez).

163 In 2:17, възложи вѣнець 'he placed the crown' on her head; in 10:2 the same aorist means 'imposed' (taxes, tribute). Both reflect H *śm* 'put, set.'

164 It is possible that *shame* is the result of a conscious emendation by a scribe who was thinking of the past situation rather than the future, and considered that a negative word was required. The opposite occurs in 2 Ki 10:5, where 'dishonored' becomes 'honored': ἦσαν οἱ ἄνδρες ἠτιμασμένοι (ἠτιμωμένοι) σφόδρα >(G, W, OB) бѣша мѹжи ти чтомы ѕѣло. Here too a scribe may have misunderstood the passage and considered the negation incorrect. Random reversals of sense do occur; cf. Supr 389.9 with братооубииство 'fratricide' instead of братолюбьство 'brotherly love.' Interpreters may consciously reverse a meaning, cf. C1:8.

" 'he despised in his eyes,' cf. 1:17." LXX simplifies to "and he wished"; L expands, "and Aman, provoked to jealousy (παραζηλώσας) and moved in all his anger, became red, turning him away from his eyes, and with a bad heart he said evil things to the king about Israel."

5:13: **нє врєдно** [ли] єсть мнѣ *'ynnw šwh ly* : Moore 'But all this fails to satisfy me,' lit. "is not sufficient for me."[165] LXX/L "this does not please me." The extra ли after negation, making the statement a rhetorical question ("Is it not harmful to me?"), is surely a Hellenism, see T9.38.

L16.2 The obvious difficulty is that the morpheme *vrěd/vered,* well attested in OCS and Rusian in a variety of nominal and verbal derivatives, means 'harm, damage.'[166] In all three Esther examples, however, *vrěd* has a positive meaning, something like 'value,' which is negated: the women will *not-value* their husbands; it was *not-valuable* in Haman's eyes; it is *not-valuable* for me. This sense is normal in many Slovene, SC, and Macedonian words, and slightly less common in Bulgarian; it is absent from West and East Slavic. This root was surely borrowed into a central western dialect of Late Common Slavic just before the historical period from Old High German *werd* 'worth.' In OCS, we may see it (cf. SJS, врѣдъ²) in the rare phrases невръду [-дъ] сътворити or имѣти (1). 'consider useless, inadequate; reject, despise'; (2). 'deceive, mislead.'[167] Apart from these phrases, the root seems not to be attested until c1390, when the adjective {vrěd-ьn-} 'worthy' begins to appear in SC texts.[168]

L16.31 In Mar, Mt 21:42, we find, камєнь ижє нєврѣдоу сътворишѧ ꙁиждѫштєи, сь бысть въ главѫ ѫгълоу 'The stone which the builders rejected has become the head *stone* of the corner.' It is a citation from ps. 117:22 and PsSin agrees with Mar (with correct сь), as does the oldest dated Slavic ms, the Rusian Ostromir Gospel of 1056. The two OCS lectionaries, however, present variants: Sav, probably not much older than Ost, has нє вь рѧдъ and Assem, possibly even younger than Ost, нє въ рѧдоу. This surely represents *ręd-* 'row, order'; 'not in the row/rank' signifies 'unsuitable.' Jagić (1913 331) rightly considered these two phrases as secondary modifications caused by scribal unfamiliarity with the positive sense of *vrěd.* A. S. L′vov (1966) takes the opposite view: the Sav and Assem phrases preserve an original but inept translation that was corrected when the whole text was revised and expanded to produce a full tetraevangelion.

L16.32 Here we must insist on a methodological assumption: scribes surely were familiar with the whole Psalter and the Gospel readings of the shorter (Saturday–Sunday) lectionaries, both of which have been preserved in OCS copies that provide the closest approximation of the Cyrillo-Methodian translations that we are likely to get.

L16.33 Further, they knew the psalms as a store of pre-Christian sacred hymns that con-

[165] Note that the same H construction in 3:8 is represented by нє право plus infinitive, see comm.

[166] Cf. SJS *sub* врѣдити, врѣдъ¹), врѣдьнъ. This morpheme was MCoS **werd* and is known in all regions.

[167] Examples in SJS *sub* нєврѣдованиѥ, нєврѣдовати, нєврѣдоуѥмъ (also Srez), нєврѣдьно, нєврѣдьнъ with the sense 'negate worth' are all from the Dialogues of Gregory, believed to have been translated in Bohemia in the 10th century, although the text is known only from Rusian copies no earlier than c1250.

[168] The old noun has not survived; *vrijednost* 'worth, worthiness' is known from c1440, followed by other derivatives from the adjectival base. The verb *vrijediti* 'be worth, be valid' does not appear until c1750. Its Mac equivalent, вреди, may well be a borrowing; no similar form appears in standard Bg.

tain many prophecies about Christ. Psalm 117:22 is just such a prophecy about Jesus. It is cited not only in Mt 22:42, which occurs twice in the lectionary (13th Sun after Pentecost, and on the Feast of St. Stephen, Dec. 27),[169] but also in two other passages that are in at least the oldest longer lectionary, the Rusian Mstislav Gospel of c1115–17 (Mk 12:10 [written out twice, the second being Aug. 2, Translation of the Relics of St. Stephen], Luke 20:17).[170] The small number of attestations of невръдоу in an identical phrase as entered in SJS may seem marginal, but the importance of the verses in which they occur means that they must have been known to ordinary pious Slavic Christians. Attestation in Mar, Ost (1056) and the older part of Arx (1092) and all the oldest psalters[171] guarantees its ancient status. Elimination of the unfamiliar word seems to have taken place earlier in Gospel passages than in the Psalter.

L16.34 The shift of врьдоу to въ рѧдоу shows a reinterpretation based in part on the confusion of ѣ and ѧ that becomes more common in post-OCS Macedonian and western Bulgarian mss and indicates that the front nasal vowel usually merged with *ě* before the latter merged with *e*. The phonetic uncertainty encouraged a respelling involving the root {rẹd} 'row, order.'[172]

L16.35 The verb уврѣдити occurs only in Est 1:17; Srez defines it 'dishonor,' tacitly including the force of the не.[173] Perhaps we are dealing with a distortion of the OCS idiom, *не въ врѣдъ имѣти. The въ could become [u] before [vr] in various Slavic areas, particularly SC and U, and the failure to write a syllable in имѣти easily produces -ити.

L16.36 The positive sense of *vrěd* in these three verses seems to point to the southwestern region of Slavdom.

Wealth, *kap'*

L16.41 Allusions to the wealth, **богатьство**, of Ahashwerosh and Aman occur in 1:4 and 5:7, but only 3:9 is there specific reference to a measure; there Aman pledges ten thousand silver *kikar* or *talents*, terms that may refer to weight or to coins. In MT Haman says,

[169] It also occurs in the short Apostol lectionary, in I Peter 2:7, unfortunately preserved only in post-OCS copies that are much less certain reflections of 9th-century translations.

[170] Mst has невръдоу only in Mt 21:42 (132a), in the lection for Monday matins of Holy Week, not a position that uses that reading in the shorter lectionaries. Otherwise Mst has небрѣгошѧ three times but 203b (Aug. 2) потрѣбоваша, without negation and therefore with opposite meaning. The Serbian Vlkan Gospel of c1200 preserves невръдоу in Mt 21:42, but небрѣгоше in Luke 20:17. The late 12th-century Mac Dobromir tetraevangelion has the former in both verses, but the latter in Mk 12:10. The later western Bg or eastern Mac Banica tetraevangelion has не врѧдȣ сьтворишѫ Mt 21:42, небрѣгошѫ Mk 12:10, and the hybrid небрѣго сьтворишѫ Luke 20:17.

[171] In the early 12th-century Sin 6 (cf. Altbauer-Lunt) the scribe wrote невъдѫ, later inserting р between ъ and д; the mid-12th century Hofer Psalter (Houghton Library, ms Typ 221), the next-oldest witness to the Preslav redaction of the Psalter, has невръдоу. After c1350 the secondary небрѣгошѧ becomes widespread.

[172] L′vov (1966 189–91) mistakenly starts with the premise that Sav and Assem are to be preferred to Mar and the overwhelming body of Rusian and other early post-OCS evidence. He apparently relies on the unquestioned hypothesis that any difference between lectionary and tetraevangelion text is to be resolved in favor of the tetra. It is a simplistic hypothesis. More alarming is L′vov's seeming belief that the Psalter passage depends on the tetra (189, 295); here, as in most cases, the Psalter is tenaciously conservative.

[173] SC *uvrijediti* 'wound, insult' is not found before c1490; if we conjecture this negative meaning here, we must suppress the negation.

"I shall weigh out." Sl навѣшю implies weighing on a hanging scale, see C3:9. The Sl text—except for Tn—apparently converts in terms of weight: *5000 kapii*. Thus one *kap′* of silver equals two *kikar* or talents. The results of this calculation were in *1360; Tn perhaps shows an earlier stage, see C3:9.

L16.421 The lexeme **капь** is well attested: Sreznevskij sees three synonyms. Капь 'shape, figure, statue, idol,' and капь 'container, case, sheath, scabbard' are attested for OCS and *OCS (ten examples in John the Exarch's *Hexameron* indicate that both senses were common in Preslav). Specifically Rusian sources show капь as a measure of volume and weight, used in particular for wax and grain, and also as a kind of scale on which items were weighed; it occurs in Latin and Middle Low German documents (*cap*) concerning trade with East Slavs. Etymologists (e.g., Vasmer) point to Turkic *qab* 'vessel, container, sheath, sack, leather bag' as the origin, but Hunno-Bulgarian **qapi* (> Chuvash *хупă* 'container')[174] provides a closer phonetic model as well as plausible cultural connections. From Proto-Bulgarian it became part of eastern OCS in two senses, and from Khazar contacts it entered the language of Rusian commercial life. It was used, apparently, chiefly in Novgorod, Smolensk, and points of contact with Baltic traders.[175]

L16.422 The presence of the word *kap′* in Esther tells us nothing about the original Sl translation. The purpose of the somewhat unclear wording in Tn as well as the modified phrase we attribute to *1360 is to make readers understand what an enormous sum Haman pledged.[176] A different equation underlies the meaning of капь in a tale about Solomon (Tixonravov 1 271), where the queen of Sheba принесе ему ·к҃· капии злата; the corresponding passage in 1 Kings (3 Kingdoms) 10:10, has '120 talents,' so a *kap*' of gold = 60 talents. This is based on an editor's taking капь as an equivalent of the term копа, a measure of 60 units (also apparently spelled капа, SRJaXI s.v.), in his desire to make the text vividly meaningful.[177] The 1512 *Xronograf* explains Sheba's gift by a gloss, 100 и 20 талантъ злата–единъ талантъ 500 рублевъ (PSRL 22/1 128.22), i.e., 6000 gold rubles.[178] This equation is based on the notion of coins rather than weight.

174 Pritsak 1998 57–58.

175 In a birchbark *gramota* of c1200 from Staraja Russa, according to Zaliznjak's reading (1986, 208, 279), it means both the weight (the physical object) that is put on the scales, and the amount measured, воскоу коуплены 3 [ка]пи).

176 Moore 39 enumerates attempts to express the sum in terms of modern currencies, and finds more meaningful an estimate that Haman's offer represented almost two-thirds of the annual income of the Persian empire, and another that the booty Alexander the Great brought to Susa was at least five times the value of Haman's offer.

177 A капь was defined in 1269 as equal to 8 Livonian pounds, i.e., 65,520 grams. A 13th-century Rus′ reader of the two passages—if they both existed in their present form at that time—would try to imagine Haman's pledge as 326,000 kilograms of silver, and the queen of Sheba's gift as 1,310.4 kilograms of gold.

178 The same sum was paid to Solomon by Hiram of Tyre (3 Ki 9:14); 1512 states (PSRL 22/1 128.10), И несе Хирамъ Соломану 100 и 20 толантъ злата и образъ яже сътвори Соломанъ, a reading affirmed by the biblical passage in ms W. In terms of LXX, we would expect not *image*, but *ship*, корабль. (The LXX, which skips from verse 15 to verse 26, but has slightly adapted the initial phrase of 26 to a rather strange clause that is adequately rendered by the Slavonic except for this noun.) We suggest that корабль indeed followed злата и in the OCS translation of the Sl 3 Kingdoms, but later a gloss was added to explain *talant*, капь (or perhaps ·к҃· капии). A subsequent copyist mistakenly took the gloss as a replacement for *ship*; after that another scribe replaced the obsolete word капь by a synonym, образъ. The feminine яже would agree with капь, but it is not appropriate for образъ. GB has и обра^з ѩко^ж бѣ створилъ ц҃рь Соломонъ, which is not entirely clear.

L16.423 In Josephus, a stone weighing a talent becomes трькапьныи камень in one passage (301.14) and, as a collective, камение капное in a second (374.33); apparently either a "three-kap' weight" or a "(one-) kap' weight." Vaillant (in Istrin 1934 223) explains the first as a textual error, and posits for both passages a single adjective капьныи equivalent to ταλαντιαιος; he translates it *quintal.*[179] Sreznevskij cites passages from two different translated works where капь occurs in one copy but кентинарь in another. Κεντηνάριον is a sum of money whose value is not now known; again, a translator or editor has tried to produce a more meaningful passage by using a measure familiar to his audience.

L16.43 Payment of this fabulous sum is expressed in MT by the verb *šql* 'weigh,' and this association survives in навѣшю 3:7 and what can be read as навѣсити (or навѣсить) in 4:7 (see C4:7). Srez has no entry for навѣсити, but adduces it sub конобъ, from Ezek 24:3 (probably originally OCS): навѣси конобъ, for ἐπίστησον τὸν λέβητα 'put the cauldron on.' The H and Gk verbs are general, 'set, put,' while the Sl surely specifies hanging the vessel on something (above the fire).[180] In Ham 555.20 навѣсивше ꙁапоны ꙁлатоисткаными apparently means 'draping with hangings interwoven with gold,' although περιστείλαντες πέπλοις has rather the sense 'wrapping with coverings' (referring to new upholstery rather than curtains). Unprefixed вѣсити 'weigh' is rare but surely old. However, we could find no early attestations of any prefixed form with this sense.

L17 Kill, destroy

L17.0 A crucial theme in Esther is Haman's plot to destroy the Jewish people, which brings about the bloody retaliation by the Jews. Three verbs occur in the MT to express different aspects of killing and destruction: *hrg* 'kill,' 9 times plus the related noun; *'bd* (*'ibbed*) 'destroy,' 10 times plus the related noun *'bdn* twice, and *hšmyd* 'destroy, annihilate' 5 times.

L17.1 In the corresponding Slavonic verses, *hrg* is represented by forms of **иꙁбити / иꙁбивати** twice, **убити** six times (of which two are corrupt, 9:11, 16) and the noun **убьєньє**, and **погубити** once; moreover, its past passive participle, **оубьєнъ** or **оубиєнъ**, is represented in 9:11 by the obviously inappropriate noun оубиицъ 'killers' (surely by way of оубїєць, attested in X, with erroneous "ц" for "н"). 'Destroy' *'bd* comes out with forms of погубити 7 times (and perhaps the equivocal 9:6, cf. C9:6), while the noun is погублениє in 9:5 but **пагуба** in 8:6; in 3:13 and 9:24 there is no equivalent. The most emphatic verb, *hšmyd*, is represented by погубити in 3:6 but, puzzingly, by **растворити** the other four times. A fourth verb, *hmyt* 'put to death' (the causative [hif'il] to *mwt* 'die'), is represented by the not altogether appropriate noun phrase **къ оубою**, in all mss but Tn, which has a passive 'to be killed' оубьєну бити, see C4:11.

L17.2 In three of the four examples of растворити 'wipe out' the corresponding Hebrew verses have a formulaic juxtaposition of the three synonymous verbs, 'to destroy, to kill, and to cause to perish' (Moore 'wipe out, slaughter, and annihilate'):

179 Compare the *талантьскъ (cf. SJS) hail-stones of Rev 16:21, "about the weight of a talent" in the King James translation, but "weighing perhaps a hundredweight" in the New English Bible.

180 This wording survived into G (SRJaXI). G also uses the verb in Esther 13:18 (C:11 in Hanhart): того ради что имъ истиннаꙗ смр҃ть навѣшаше сѧ, a painfully literal equivalent of *eo quod eis certa mors impenderet,* 'because certain death was impending for them.' LXX Esther C:11 has simply 'for death (was) before their eyes'; OB (=Maksim Grek) ꙗко смр҃ть пред очима ихъ есть.

	lhšmyd	*lhrg*	*wl'bd*
3:13	растворити	и иꙁби{ти	и погубити}
7:4	растворити	и оубити	и погубити
8:11	растворити	и оубити	и погубити[181]

L17.21 In 3:13 LXX uses only ἀφανίσαι, but the O-texts add καὶ φονεύσαι καὶ ἀπολέσαι to conform to the MT. The last two verbs are posited on the basis of Tn; apparently *1360 imperfectivized the second (иꙁбивати) and omitted the third. (The scribe of *1370 transposed two letters, producing иꙁбавити 'to save'—with a devastating change in meaning that remains in QTG, see C3:13.[182]) LXX in 7:4 uses nouns, εἰς ἀπολείαν καὶ διαρπαγὴν καὶ δουλείαν 'for destruction and pillage and slavery'—a very free rendering of the MT.[183] (L has only a single noun, εἰς δούλεσιν 'into slavery.') In 8:11 LXX omits all three verbs, but the O-copies provide ἀφανίζειν καὶ φονεύειν καὶ ἀπολλύειν.[184]

L17.3 From the concordances we know that ἀφανίζειν often renders MT *hšmyd*, but the shaky equation of ἀφανίσαι and *'bd* is only Est 3:13 (where three H verbs yield only one Gk verb) and 9:24 (where O-texts have ἀπολέσαι). LXX ἀπολλύειν usually stands for MT *'bd*, but precisely in Esther 9:11, 12, 16 it is equated with *hrg*. The usual equivalent to *hrg* is ἀποκτείνειν; φονεύειν is a relatively rare verb and generally does not equal *hrg*. Ἀποκτείνειν appears in OCS and other early texts as иꙁбити, убити, and погубити. Φονεύειν also yields иꙁбити and убити. Hebrew *hšmyd* is rendered by LXX ἀπολλύειν, ἀφανίζειν and ἐξολοθρεύειν; all three may be translated into OCS by погубити (погублꙗти).

L17.4 Obviously there is no one-to-one relationship between the MT and our Esther in these words. The problem is how растворити, which normally means 'dissolve,' came to be used where we expect the meaning 'destroy.' The verb is not common in early texts, but it occurs in OCS and *OCS (Srez., Exarch), as 'combine, mix together, mingle, temper, dilute, dissolve.'[185] In the Suprasliensis, ростворивъ is 'having opened (wide).'[186] These nuances are easily comprehensible from the meanings of the prefix *raz-* and the root *tvor* 'do,' along with the influence of отворити, ꙁатворити 'open, close.' The most obvious conjecture is that it was originally раꙁорити, a well attested OCS verb meaning *destroy.*

L17.51 We have seen that the general Greek verb for *destroy* is ἀπολλύειν (*ap-ollu-*), with aorist infinitive (Sl. perfective) ἀπολέσαι, passive ἀπολέσθαι. There is a different verb

181 Tn shifts the order in 8:11: и оуби^т и погоуби^т и растворити. The fourth example, растворити {ѧ}, is in 4:8, where MT has *lhšmydm*.

182 The omission of a syllable in V converted 'pleased' (оулюбиеть) into 'killed' (оубїеть) 9:3; the changed verb does not fit the syntax, thus hinting to readers that the sentence is somehow suspicious, cf. L12.6.

183 See below for Sl nouns meaning *pillage, booty.*

184 Thus O-mss have:

3:13	ἀφανίσαι	καὶ φονεύσαι	καὶ ἀπολέσαι
7:4	εἰς ἀπωλείαν	καὶ διαρπαγὴν	καὶ δουλείαν
8:11	ἀφανίζειν	καὶ φονεύειν	καὶ ἀπολλύειν

185 The last meanings in particular are preserved in SC. The same semantic range is also illustrated by the noun растворъ 'mixture, solution, temperament' and the imperfective растварꙗти. In Slovene *raztvoriti* means 'zerlegen, de-compose.'

186 Notice initial *ro-* for normal SSl *ra-* for unmarked ("circumflex") **or-*. This is one of 17 examples in this eastern OCS manuscript of the late 10th or early 11th century, in texts otherwise showing no reason to view this feature as a Moravian archaism. They constitute part of the evidence that the isoglosses that now separate South from East Slavic may well have located in very different regions c1000.

ἀπολύειν (*apo-lu-*), with aorist infinitive ἀπολύσαι, passive ἀπολύσθαι. The root here is 'loosen, dissolve' and it may have a sense of *destruction*; in OCS раꙁорити translates, among other verbs, unprefixed λύειν and also κατα-, δια-, ἀπο-, παρα-λύειν.[187]

L17.52 The Greek translator of Esther seems not to have adhered to a single Greek verb for each of the three Hebrew verbs, but allowed some variation to suit various contexts. One of the verbs was surely ἀπολλύειν (*ap-ollu-*), but the forms may well have been miscopied by subsequent scribes. It is possible that the Slavic translator of Esther found ἀπολύειν in his text, illustrating the common Greek error of confusing single and double lambda, or else ἀπολύσαι by error for ἀπολέσαι.[188] Whether the unjustified form occurred in all four verses (3:13 = 7:4 = 8:11, 4:8) originally or not, we may presume that a later editor harmonized the verb растворити in all cases. Be that as it may, we submit that the complex of form and meaning in the two Greek verbs offers fertile ground for confusion and at the same time a justification for the translation растворити.[189]

L17.61 Further attestation of раꙁорити beside variant растворити is attested the *Life of Moses*, a text that surely was translated directly from Hebrew in the 15th century.[190] The later redactions have и растворить все царство египетское for H *wyḥryb kl 'rc mcrym* (Shinan 1977 107), 'and he will destroy (devastate, lay waste) the whole land (> Sl kingdom) of Egypt.'[191] In the older redaction, however, the more usual verb раꙁорити is used.[192] In a number of instances, the younger redactions of the *Life of Moses* clearly provide better readings; it may be that растворить in this passage is one of them (cf. Taube 1993 93).

L17.62 In the *Third Capture of Jerusalem,* translated from Hebrew in the 15th century, we find каковь бѣ растворенъ (var. adds градъ) люди твоихъ, in a passage missing from the unique H ms with corresponding text,[193] but reconstructable from the *Yosippon,* on which the story is based. There, ch. 73 has the equivalent lamentation, with the expression, *'ykh nšḥth 'yr 'mk,* 'How the city of your people has been laid waste!' Here too раꙁоренъ fits nicely.

187 Cf. also OCS раꙁарꙗти. Among the near-synonyms SJS lists об-ор-ити and сън-ор-ити. The latter is probably a ghost, for сънорѧтъ Su 385.14 is to be corrected by Usp Sb 188c16 съронѧть, 'throw down,' which fits ἀπορίψωσιν, thus implying съ-рон-ити.

188 Random errors involving ε for υ or vice versa are found in LXX manuscripts; the plausibility of a lapse is surely greater in this pair of verbs which might have similar meanings.

189 A comparable shift of forms is noted by Tov 94, in 1 Sam 9:24—ὕψωσεν 'raised' > ὕψησεν: instead of 'the cook lifted the shoulder up' of H, important witnesses of LXX (I Kingdoms 9:24) read 'the cook boiled the shoulder.' The shifted meaning is not disruptive in the sentence, and the phrase is not vital to the meaning of the larger context; therefore the error survived. (It presumably underlies the very free rendering in ms W: вꙁѧ приставникъ жрътвенаѧ.)

190 Alekseev 1993 64 states that the earliest ms of the Paleja containing the *Life of Moses* is GIM, Barsov 619. It was written by a single hand, he reports, and has watermarks dating from 1397 through 1419; he does not say whether the pages containing *Moses* have watermarks. We must conclude that the codex was written about 1419.

191 It is in the Paleja of 1477 (GIM, Sin. 210 [OLDRP 93, 1892] f. 189v), in Pypin's main text (RGB, Rum 453), p. 39, in the Великие Минеи Четии (Sept 1–15, 1868, col. 165), and in the 15th-century Krexiv Paleja, Franko 1896 225. For a schema of redactions, see Turdeanu 1967 [RES 46] 39ff. Notice that the Hebrew verb is not *hšmyd,* as in Esther, but *hḥryb*, which in LXX yields (ἐξ)ερημοῦν, Sl. искаꙁити, Judges 16:24, 4 Ki 19:24.

192 Tixonravov 1863 234.2 раꙁори[т], var. in Pypin, 39. The Serbian version of the *Paleja* (16th-17th century copies), interestingly enough, has растворить here, cf. Speranskij 1960 72.

193 Bodleian ms Hunt. 345 lacks perhaps six folia between f. 219 and 220.

L17.63 These two examples illustrate that in the Lithuanian lands the verb растворити could mean *destroy.*[194] On the evidence of Esther, this meaning may be postulated for the 14th century. Might we assume that the three examples of растворити in this egregiously exceptional meaning imply a 14th-century Ruthenian translator? Or are we to conjecture that the original translation had раȥорити three times, later modified (by one or more copyists) to *rastvoriti*?[195]

L17.7 An open question remains as to just why there is consistency in the Hebrew/Slavonic equivalents of *rastvoriti* in Esther, when so many other words (e.g., *fear, clothing*) exhibit inconsistent relationships. Was this verb part of the literary vocabulary of the original translator? Or was it substituted by a later editor for the commonplace *razoriti*?

L18 plunder, booty, spoils

L18.0 The slaughter is naturally followed by looting in two of these verses. The Hebrew of 3:13 and 8:11, *wšllm lbwz,* uses near-synonyms, lit. "to pillage their plunder," i.e., to take whatever spoils are possible (Moore 'to plunder their possessions'). Sl has slight grammatical variation but the same lexemes: добытокъ/добыткы ихъ къ/по росполону. The first noun is unusual and the second unique.

L18.11 ***Добытъкъ** must be assigned to late Common Slavic, although it is not attested, directly or indirectly, for OCS. It meant *something gained, attained,* therefore *property,* whether *inanimate* (household goods, utensils, fabrics, jewelry, money) or *animate* (domestic animals, especially cattle; slaves) acquired by labor or industry, by hunting or by conquest. The sense *cattle* apparently was universal, and this is the only meaning that has survived in Macedonian and Bulgarian dialects. Moveable property is at the same time potential *booty, spoils, plunder,* and it is not uncommon that a word may have both meanings. In East and Southwest Slavic **dobytъkъ* was so used in early texts.[196]

L18.12 The noun **росполонъ** (or a potential equivalent расплѣнъ) is known only from these two verses of Esther, as far as we have been able to determine.

L18.13 The H near-synonyms for *booty, spoils* are both translated in LXX by two words, σκῦλα (pl.; also NT) and προνομή. The former yielded користь (see SJS) and both yield OCS плѣнъ.[197] Hamartolos, in a citation from Ezek 29:19 has both words in Hebraic for-

194 Another possible Ruthenian witness is the Song of Songs, 2:15, where the little foxes *spoil* the vines, H *mḥblym,* LXX ἀφανίζοντας, usual Sl лисица малы казѧщѧ винограды (RNB F I 461). The Ruthenian copy RGB Muz 8222 of a translation from the Hebrew (Alekseev 1981) has лисицѣ малы затворяют винограды, apparently a further distortion of растворяють of a "West Russian" word. The translator of Vilnius 10 (262) used Muz, correcting it wherever necessary (cf. Taube 1985); he wrote лисенѧта которыи казать винограды, using a conventional word.

195 The *Słownik staropolski* records a figurative meaning 'spoil' for *roztworzyć* 'dissolve' and it lists *roztrwożyć* 'disperdere,' 'destroy, ruin, spoil.' Perhaps scribes working in the Grand Duchy of Lithuania might have confused *roztrwożyć* and *roztworzyć* to produce растворити.

196 In SC *dobitak* now is only 'profit, earnings, income.' Pol. *dobytek* is 'belongings, property' and also 'livestock'; in BR дабытак means 'property.' R has добыток only marginally, in the sense 'profit.' Filin does not report it from dialect sources. M 56a 251 lists добыток among his "typically Russian" words. The current word, добыча, is not attested before 1560 in any sense. Only Ukrainian still has добиток 'prey, booty' (along with newer добича).

197 Користь, though impeccably attested in OCS, is avoided or eliminated in East Slavdom in this sense, and used in the more benign meaning *profit, benefit* (with a shift of spelling to корысть). This sense is possible in

mulas; only the second remains a *figura etymologica* in Sl: створить користь ꙗѩ и плѣнить плѣнъ ꙗѩ, σκυλεύσει τὰ σκῦλα αὐτῆς καὶ προνομεύσει τὴν προνομὴν αὐτῆς, *wšll šllh wbzz bzh,* 'and he shall plunder her (Egypt) and take her prey.'[198] In LXX, the recurring notion of possessions (or their possessors) declared subject to plunder is either εἰς προνομήν or εἰς ἁρπαγήν (διαρπαγήν).[199] Ohrid OCS preferred въ расхъıщение, Preslav OCS sometimes substituted въ раȥграбление (see SJS),[200] as in the older versus revised wording of Dan 3:96 (MT 3:29).[201]

L18.211 The root **peln* means broadly *take by force* and frequently applies to people, so плѣнити is 'make prisoner' and плѣнение is 'captivity'; it also may denote the object, animate or inanimate, so плѣнъ is 'prey, captives, prisoners; plunder, spoils, booty.' It appears in marked East Slavic phonological shape, *polon,* both in works obviously inherited from OCS and in texts we believe to have originated in Rus′. Why this is so is a matter for speculation, but the fact is indisputable, although Russian scholars tend to ignore it. What is important is that полон-spellings cannot be taken as proof that a text in which they occur was translated in Rus′, see A1.54.

L18.212 Both полоненъ 'taken captive' and полонъ '[animate] captives' occur in 2:6. Полонъ '[inanimate] booty' appears in 9:10, 15, 16, in variants of the formulaic 'and they did not stretch out their hands for the booty' (9:10, 15, 16), a comment on the restraint of the triumphant Jews, cf. L6.31. (It is notable that in 9:10 both LXX and L omit the negation, thus implying that the Jews were vengeful: LXX simply καὶ διήρπασαν 'and they pillaged,' but L adds πάντα τὰ αὐτῶν 'all their possessions.' In 9:15 and 16 L omits the clause, while LXX reflects the H negation, καὶ οὐδὲν διήρπασαν 'and they pillaged nothing.')

L18.22 The North Slavic shape of the prefix makes росполону doubly marked as East Slavic. The sense of the prefix is the same as in the more usual terms in this sort of context расхыщение and раȥграбление. There is no reason to attribute the form or even the lexeme to the original translator, however. A related noun, расплѣнение, appears in the second translation of the *Откровение Мефодия патарского,* known from 16th-century Serbian copies.[202] The related verb, расплѣнити, is known from the 14th-century Bulgarian

---

Psalm 67:13 and 118:162, and the word remains. [SRJaXI wrongly defines it in the citation of 118:162 in the Izbornik of 1076, 3v2; it is not clear that the author intended a modified interpretation.] Monomax uses it as 'prey' (Lav 249.26) yet during the same decade it is replaced in Luke 11:22 in the Mstislav Gospel of 1115–17 by плѣнь. Користь is used for λάφυρα, a relatively rare word (rendered by плѣнъ in Su 512.6) in the 14th-century Bulgarian translation of the Chronicle of Constantine Manasses, where плѣнъ regularly represents σκῦλα.

198 OB echoes only the first figure, и плѣнитъ плѣненїе ѥѧ, и повоюютъ села ѥѧ.

In Dan 11:24 a third term 'property' ὕπαρξις is added, 'he will scatter among them plunder, and spoils, and wealth.' The older Sl translation has плены и корысть и имѣние и^{X} [for и^{M}] растоѵить, while the Preslav revision has totally changed the verse, which after successive recopyings yielded плѣнениемъ и плѣнении миръ раȥдѣлить. Just what share East Slavic scribes had in producing this unsatisfactory result it is impossible to say.

199 LXX omits these phrases, but the O-mss supply καὶ τὰ σκῦλα αὐτῶν εἰς διαρπαγήν in 8:11.

200 Cf. Izb 1073, 96c12, 2Ki 21:14: и боудоуть на раȥграбление и въ плѣнъ врагомъ ихъ.

201 Variants to the latter include въ граблении, a word attested elsewhere, and въ граби with an otherwise unknown noun (or a simple error).

202 Istrin 1897b, app. 109, lines 24, 25, 27, вь расплѣнѥнїе; the corresponding passages of the older translation have плѣнение, *ibid.* 94, lines 3, 7, 8. All represent αἰχμαλωσία, 'captivity.'

translation of the *Chronicle* of Manasses, the early 15th-century *Troickij Xronograf* (расплѣнь градъ, Tvorogov 1975 61), and a 1468 Croatian Glagolitic copy of an older apocryphon—as well as the Old Czech chronicle of Dalimil (spelled *rozpleniti*). Srez records it only from a 17th-century ms.[203]

L18.23 Perhaps a fore-text of Esther had расплѣну or simply плѣну; no solid basis for conjecture exists.

L19 Verbs of motion

Verbs denoting movement from place to place are the familiar stems *id-, xodi-, ězdi-, stǫpi-, stignu-*, along with *nes-* and *ved-* 'carry, convey' and *vrati- sja* 'return,' with familiar prefixes.

The prefix **вы**- *and the stem* **вынид**-

L19.11 One exception requires comment: the stem *vynid-*, attested clearly 5 times (выниде in 4:1, 5:9, 7:8, 8:15 and вынидоша in 3:15) and presumed in 3 more verses where the mss write внид- but the sense required is not 'enter, go in,' but 'exit, go out' as affirmed by the explicit H verb *yc*'. Two of the latter can be construed as original *въниде (see C1:7, C4:6), but this entails the assumption that the translation departed from the Hebrew sense. Another possibility is original вънъ ид-, as in Nik 8.18 вонъ иди *exi* 'go out, leave!' but 26.4 внити surely from вънъ ити (cf. Vaillant 1968 xviii). Canonical OCS usually postposes вънъ. Scribes obviously made choices stressing different aspects of the notion, as in the PVL variants sub 1097 (Lav 259.20): иде вонъ LX 'he went out (of the room),' H лѣзе вонъ, but RA выиде вонъ.[204]

L19.12 The presence of verb-forms with the prefix *vy-* has traditionally been cited by Russian scholars as proof positive that a text in which it occurs must have been translated in Rus′ (see esp. Istrin 1922 278–79 on Hamartolos). It is true that **вы**- is only marginally attested in OCS, and it appears that an early isogloss separating southern dialects without *vy-* from more northerly dialects with it ran somewhere in Croatian territory, so that early Alpine (pre-Slovene) dialects were joined to Czech and other North Slavic in this feature. The rare examples in OCS (including a few in post-OCS copies) probably are relics of the Cyrillo-Methodian texts that were based on Pannonian dialects. However, close analysis of вы-verbs in Rusian texts demonstrates that East Slavic scribes occasionally changed an изъ- of their models to вы-.[205] Indeed, вы-verbs were stylistically appropriate in historical works.

[203] The text is the second redaction (13th century?) of the *Life of Alexander*,: не вниду бо во градъ вашь [ни ра͡зплѣню,] Єллинъ [сы милосьрдъ] нъ побѣжю єгоже сѧ боите Дарьѧ цр҃ѧ. The Gk has 'I will not enter your city *until* (ἕως) I conquer King Darius whom you fear,' but the translator apparently misread εἷς 'one, alone' and wrote єдинъ, adding 'but' to provide a transition to the next verb. First-redaction mss all have єлинъ or єллины, which of course makes no sense. The editor who produced the second redaction therefore created a wholly new statement, depicting Alexander as a benevolent Greek. See Istrin 1897b 174 and app 51.16, 166.23).

[204] This is from the secular story of the blinding of Vasilko. Compare, from the more ecclesiastical context of the stories about monks of the Caves Monastery, аще братъ етеръ вънъ идѧше изь манастырѧ 'if a brother went out of the monastery' H, but L (188.32) выидѧше из манастырѧ (RA omit the text; X changes the meaning, въ иныи идѧше манастырь 'went to another monastery'). In the *Paterik* this has become и аще нѣкии братъ отхождаше от (or изыдяше изъ) манастыря (Abramovyč 1930 94).

[205] Particularly pertinent is the вынити adduced from Ham by Srez; the corresponding sentence in Istrin's

L19.13 The examples of вынид- in Esther are to be ascribed to ESl scribes and editors; they stand in contrast to the one иꙁиде (1:19, also H *yc*'), which is normal in texts written or copied by East Slavs. Further, the epenthetic *n* in this verb is unknown in East Slavic dialects, and yet it occurs widely in Polish and Czech dialects. It is normal in many East Slavic texts, but almost exclusively in mss written in the western zone of East Slavic territory after c1350; выиде and выидоша are well attested.[206] It is highly probable that forms with -н- rest on a scribal tradition that was influenced by OPol *wynić wynidzie* (forms supported by central dialects), in turn possibly introduced into Pol writing from OCz *vyníti vynide*. In sum, these forms tell us nothing about the history of the translation of Esther, but only strengthen the characterization of *1350 as typical of the work of "West-Russian" scribes of the time.

Other verbs

L19.2 Otherwise the verbal inventory is unremarkable. Unprefixed **иди** 4:16, **хожаше** 9:4 (twice), and **ѣзди** 6:8 (with ѣздѧху 8:14 and ꙗздѧху 8:10) are found; they stand where H has *lk* 'go' or *rkb* 'ride.' Prefixed forms are usual. При- is preferred by far: прид- 27x, приходи- 3x, приступи- 1x, and **приступај**- 1x. The more specific до- is in доид- and доступи-, each twice, which go back to H *hgy*' 'arrive.' The verbs with при- go back to H *b*' 'come,' except that приде in 4:17 is probably a scribal error for *прѣиде, 'cross,' H '*br*. *Прѣ- in преступаеши 3:3, преступати 9:27, and преступи 1:19 also go back to '*br*, and so does unprefixed минуша 9:28 (for tense see comm.) The sense of arrival is contained in the root of **постигнѧше** 9:1.

L19.3 **Привед**- and **принес**- 'bring' both correspond to the H *hby*' 'cause to come,' the first being used with personal objects (5x) and the second for objects (clothing, money, book) in accord with Sl usage. The H *hrkyb* 'cause to ride' underlies провести 6:9 and the Hellenistic phrase створи поꙗздити 6:11. **Поиду** 'I shall go' (4:16), entirely appropriate in context, stands where H uses *b*' 'come.'[207] Въсхожаше 2:11 is lit. 'went up'; H *mthlk* is simply 'walked.' **Въꙁиде** гроꙁа 9:2 stands where H has 'their fear fell,' see comm.

L19.4 For 'return,' H *šb*, **врати сѧ** 7:8,[208] **обрати сѧ** 9:25, **въꙁврати сѧ** 6:12, and **въꙁвращающи сѧ** 2:14. For прѣвратити 'overturn, change' see C8:3.

L19.5 The noun **погоньци** goes back to the H participle 'running,' in the sense 'couriers'; see L2.44. For adverbs denoting speed, see C3:15.

L19.6 For varied equivalents of identical H phrases, see C2:15 (different verbs and tenses) and C4:3 (different verbs).

---

edition, 400.12, has иꙁити, from the oldest manuscript. Istrin notes вынити from three of the later manuscripts, вынѧти (which we may count as containing the н) from one, and выити without -н- from three. For more discussion, see Lunt 1996.

206 For QT вынide in 7:8, SGWVAB have выиде, whereby the form in S is a correction from вниде. GWV offer no other examples of вы-, but S has выиде also in 5:9 and agrees with QT on вынид- in 3:15 and 8:15.

207 In terms of H, 29 cases of *b*' yield 25 прид-, 3 приходи-, and one поиду. H *hgy*' 'arrive' comes out приступи- once (6:14), доступи- twice (2:25, 4:14), доид- twice (4:3, 8:17) and постигнѧше (9:1).

208 In 4:13, вратѧ сѧ is inadequate for the idiomatic use of H *lhšyb* 'cause to return' in the sense of '(spoke) in return, responded.' Transitive вратити in 8:5, 8:8 (also H *hšyb*) means 'turn (something) back.'

L19.7 The usual old term **въставъ** 'having stood up' is the normal equivalent of H *qwm* 'rise, stand up.'[209] The same H lexeme is also represented by two unexpected verbs: **оправи сѧ** in 8:4, and **подвигнуща сѧ** in 5:9. The first means '(she) made (her)self straight/correct,' which in the context has to mean 'stood up' (see C8:4). The second was presumably intended to mean "raise self up" but it could be interpreted as 'move, budge' (the meaning assigned to this verse by Srez) or 'make effort; hasten' (see SJS).

L19.8 *Fall* is expressed by the Sl root *pad,* usually corresponding to MT *npl.* In 6:13 Haman's wife and friends warn him: 'you have started to fall (почалъ еси **падати**)' so you can do nothing, but 'will fall completely (падаѥ падеши).' In 8:3 Esther fell (паде) at the feet of the king; LXX uses a prefixed verb that is often implies supplication, προσέπεσεν. In the confused emotional scene of 7:8, when the king finds Haman in a compromising position with Esther, Sl has припалъ бѧше, using the prefixed stem *pripad-* that usually denotes obeisance, but may also be interpreted as specifying 'fall near.' (Here LXX has a prefixed stem meaning 'fall upon, attack' ἐπιπεπτώκει.) The forms of *pripadaj-* denoting worship (cf. L10.1) correspond to MT *kr'* 'bend' and may well be reminiscent of phraseology from the psalms, esp. 94:6 придѣте поклонимъ сѧ и припадѣмъ ѥмоу from δεῦτε προσκυνήσωμεν καὶ προσπέσωμεν αὐτῷ, MT 95:6 *b'w nšthwh wnkr'h* (cf. припадѫтъ προπεσοῦνται Ps 21:29, 71:9, from MT 21:29, 72:9 *ykr'w*). In *fear fell* 9:3, the majority напалъ бѧше seems inferior to Tn's unprefixed палъ бѧше (see L14.51 for other equivalents of the phrase).

The causative *hpyl* is regularly used in the phrase *cast lot(s),* and comes out въврьже 'threw' in 3:7 (but is omitted, by homoioteleuton, with the whole clause in 9:25). In 6:10 the king commands, "Omit nothing," lit. 'let no thing fall'; Sl departs from literalism, не уими рѣчи 'take nothing away.'

Haman's *face fell* (спаде, 7:8) as a sign of fear or shame, but the MT has no *fall,* see C7:8.

L20 Time expressions

Words distinguishing *time* in general from a specific *moment* or a suitable *occasion* overlap in many languages with more precise concepts like *season* or *year* or *hour*. Hebrew *zmn* is, for the Scroll of Esther, a relatively new word probably meaning *occasion*, while *'t* could be general or specific and *šnh* is explicitly 'year'; the exact meaning of course varies according to the context.[210] For early Slavic, it is impossible to establish any consistent usage; we can only state that obviously there was variation from region to region—as indeed there still is. The general врѣмѧ 'time, season' was contrasted to часъ 'hour, moment, time' and derivatives of *god* 'suit' (cf. *u-god-ьn-* 'suitable') such as годъ and година on the one hand, and to лѣто 'year; summer' on the other. It is striking that neither часъ nor врѣмѧ occurs in Esther.

L20.11 Two Hebrew words meaning 'time' and the word for 'year' correspond to three Slavic words **годъ**, **година**, and **лѣто**, but the relationships overlap.

[209] Встанеть in 4:14, lit. 'stand up,' means 'come to be, appear'; H has *y'mwd* with precisely the same sense.

[210] The Hebrew and Greek words, like the Slavic, obviously display different relationships in different epochs.

zmn	9:31	годы
zmn	9:27	година
't	4:14	годину
't	4:14	годину
't	5:13	годину
't	8:9	годину
šnh wšnh	9:21	всѧку годину и годину
šnh wšnh	9:27	по всѧ лѣта и лѣта
šnh	1:3	лѣто
šnh	2:16	лѣто
šnh	3:7	лѣто

L20.21 In Old Church Slavonic, the notion 'year' was not attached to годъ or година, according to SJS and the materials adduced by Jagić 1913. For numerous post-OCS works, however, and many modern dialects, this meaning is to be found, cf. Trubačev ES, sub *godъ, godina*. Miklosich notes година 'year' for SerbSlav, and Daničić cites it from a Serbian document of 1358; it is now normal in Bg, Mac, and SC. Though it occurs in Moldavian Ukrainian documents (1471, 1499, SSUM) it is not usual in ESl.[211]

L20.22 'Year by year, every year' occurs in 1 Kingdoms (1 Samuel) 1:7, LXX οὕτως ἐποίει ἐνιαυτὸν κατ' ἐνιαυτόν; ms W тако творѧше ѿ года до года; Warsaw Jewish Chron. тако творѧше ѿ годища до годища. In 7:15, GB, W, J, and OB agree on ѿ года до года.

L20.23 The contrast between 9:21 and 9:27 may in part be explained that in 9:27 ꙗкоже година их (H 'and according to their time') immediately preceeds 'from year to year' = 'every year': whenever two near-synonyms occur in the same context, a translator may assign slightly different semantic nuances to the words than he would use in other contexts.

L20.24 The use of година, годъ, and лѣто in *1350 cannot be ascribed with certainty to the original translation; the lack of consistency is rather more likely a reflection of varying decisions by successive editors and scribes during the transmission of the text.[212]

L20.3 **Вѣкъ** 'age, αἰών' occurs only in 9:28, where, puzzlingly, it corresponds to H *dwr* 'generation.'

L20.4 Expression of time by means of cases or prepositions is for the most part unexceptional. The instrumental дн҃ьми многыми 'during the course of many days' (1:4) is not unparalleled (e.g., J 2:20, четырьми десѧтъı и шестиѭ лѣтъ...трьми дьны (дьньми)), but it is unusual. One of the revisions made by the scribe or editor of the late OCS codex Assemanianus is to shift отъ мъногъ бо лѣтъ (Luke 8:29 ZoMarSavOstMst) to многы бо лѣты, surely to approximate more closely πολλοῖς γὰρ χρόνοις.[213] In the

211 It is not mentioned SRJaXI. In R dial it means 'anniversary, годовщина' which is not far from the meaning here. M56a 215 lists година, without definition, as "typically Russian."

212 In the PVL, годъ twice means 'fixed time, hour' (годъ молитвы 170.17; в годы обычныя 153.9 'at the customary times [for church services]'); otherwise it is in the phrase ѿ года до года in two different senses: 'every year' (130.5, on paying taxes); 'from one year to the next' (дни бо есть ѿ года до года 365 'from the beginning of a year to the end is 365 days' 184.24; отъ года бо до года 'from the time [he arrived] to a year later [the day of his death].' Година occurs but once, 227.26 заутрени сущи годинѣ 'it being the hour for matins.'

213 The scribe's awareness that the passage was somehow controversial is indicated by the diamond-pattern of dots he used to mark questionable phrases, cf. Lunt 1982 410 and 413.

14th-century Serbian translation of Hamartolos, the Лѣтовникъ, πολλῶν ἡμέρων > дн҃ьми мноꙃѣми, Weingart 1922–23 2 379.

L20.41 The use of по to indicate ‘during’ in по 7 дн҃овъ 1:5 and по 3 дн҃и 4:16 is unusual;[214] SJS quotes Acts 19:8 (по 3 мѣсѧць, ἐπὶ μῆνας τρεῖς), Srez cites a single example from 1073, and SRJaXI adds one from Novgorod that is contemporary to our oldest Esther mss. The distributive sense in по всѧ лѣта и лѣта, on the other hand, is normal, cf. SJS. The дн҃е дн҃е ‘daily’ (or its variant дн҃ь дн҃е, VW) of 3:4 looks very much like an echo of the H distributive repetition *ywm wywm* ‘day and day,’ the case presumably being locative, see T4.13.

L20.42 Like other uses of cases and prepositions, this sort of temporal expression varies enormously from dialect to dialect in observable Slavic languages and we must assume variation in the past as well. None of the details here is helpful in establishing the time and place of the original Slavonic Esther.

L20.51 Beside the usual adverb дн҃есь ‘today’ 5:4, the phrase въ дн҃ешнии дн҃ь is found, see C1:18. Заутра ‘in the morning’ denotes ‘the next day’ in the past context of 2:14 and ‘tomorrow’ in the present contexts of 5:8, 5:14, and 9:13. Наутриꙗ occurs only in the latter meaning, 5:12. Both are found in OCS, with no difference that allows conclusions about time or place of translation. (Modern editors disagree on spelling; наутриꙗ or на утриꙗ or variants like на утрие).

L20.52 The usual нынѣ ‘now,’ тъгда ‘then,’ николиже ‘never,’ уже ‘already,’ and еще ‘still’ require no comment. For the unusual (не) лапь ‘(not) easily,’ 2:14, see A8.3.

L20.53 Пакы ‘again’ occurs alone 3x where H has *gm* and once (5:8) where it is an added emphatic element. И пакы in 9:15 goes back to *wgm*, in 1:9 and 4:16 to simple *gm*, and in 5:12 to *’p*. (Право corresponds to *hgm* in 7:8 and *gm* in 7:9.)

Conclusions

L21.1 Close analysis of each word and phraseological unit affirms the initial impression recorded by Gorskij and Nevostruev: the retrievable text of Esther is 14th-century Ruthenian Slavonic, but with a relatively large number of unique or unusual lexemes along with unexpected meanings for many known words. Since the major outlines of the lexicon of 14th-century East Slavic manuscripts are established by the OCS and early Rusian works we mentioned above (L0.5, p. 187)—texts whose vocabulary has been studied in some detail—the earlier data is of prime importance. As our work progressed, it became increasingly apparent that Esther is separated in various ways from the biblical works with which it is associated, the historical books of the Old Testament. The Ruthenian characteristics (as opposed to the older more generalized Rusian Slavonic and emerging Novgorodian and Muscovite variants of written language) have more in common with works which seem to have appeared in the late 1300s or early 1400s. Esther is the first witness to certain words or meanings that are known from (or even common in) Ruthenian texts of the 15th century and later.

214 In Judg 14:10 Samson also “made a banquet,” створи пиръ, for seven days, and W, VMČ, GB have по, but the Warsaw Jewish Chronograph lacks any preposition.

L21.11 Many of these texts are in manuscripts that have been neglected or only superficially utilized by lexicographers. Taube's work on translations made from Hebrew has drawn our attention to a group of texts that have revealed certain lexical parallels with Esther. Here belong the *Life of Moses* (Житие и восход Моисея), first attested in the Barsov Paleja, said to be datable to c1420,[215] the *Third Capture of Jerusalem, by Titus* (Пленение Иерусалима 3-е Титово) in the second redaction of the *Hellenic and Roman Chronicler*,[216] the excerpt from *Yosippon* about Alexander in Jerusalem in the Hypatian Chronicle *sub* 1110 (see LT 1988), and another excerpt from *Yosippon* in the *Academy Chronograph*.[217] A sub-group belonging to the later 15th century includes the nine OT books in a Belarusian-Ruthenian translation preserved in Vilnius codex 262 (Song of Songs, Ruth, Lamentations, Ecclesiastes, Esther [published in Altbauer 1992]; Psalms, Job, Proverbs, Daniel [unpublished]); portions of Al-Ghazali's *Intentions of the Philosophers*;[218] Moses Maimonides' *Logical Vocabulary* (see Taube 1997); Iohannes de Sacrobosco's 13th-century *De Spera* (called Космографиа by Sobolevskij 1903; based on H translation, *Book of the Sphere*, see Taube 1995); Emanuel Bar-Yakov's *Six Wings* (see Taube 1995); and Pseudo-Aristotle's *Secret of Secrets*, with interpolations from Maimonides.[219] The relationships among the language of these manuscripts, that of Esther, and variant Belarusian and Ukrainian Ruthenian chancery styles from c1350 to c1500 remain to be investigated.

L21.2 Within the attested history of the Slavonic Esther certain shifts in lexicon can be discerned. Disagreement in the witness of QT, WV, and Tn shows that scribes changed the vocabulary here and there; sometimes there seems to be a pattern in the changes (дънѣшнии > вънѣшнии in VW but денничныи in Tn) and sometimes the process is still operating (староста versus тиоунъ). It is reasonable to surmise that this is not a new dynamic and therefore to assume that our *pervospisok*—whether we put it at c1350 or c1390—differed from the original translation (whether completed c900 or c1380) in some lexical items.

L21.21 Some editorial decisions may be very old. Thus the opening of 6:1, 'the king was troubled in his sleep' departs from literalism in favor of a paraphrase based on Jewish tradition (cf. C6:1), but was the change made by the Gk translator, a later Gk editor, the Slavic translator, or a later copyist? We must ascribe the unique noun лептугъ and its related adjective лептужьнъ to *1350, but leave open the question of their presence in the original Slavic translation. Either way, they do not help locate the translation in time or place. Similarly unhelpful are the familiar-looking words with unexpected meanings (облюбити, оправи сѧ, удобрити). The positive sense of *vrěd* 'worth,' plus the meaning 'scepter'

215 A translation of the Hebrew *Chronicle of Moses Our Teacher* (Sl text in Pypin 1862, Tixonravov 1863), see Taube 1993.

216 Translated from an abbreviated Hebrew reworking (known from a single 15th-century ms) of the *Yosippon* (a 10th-century H adaptation, made in Italy, of the Latin *Hegessipus*, itself an adaptation of the Greek *Josephus*). Mostly unpublished, although short Sl excerpts are in Meščerskij 1958a and Taube 1989. An edition of both the Hebrew and the Slavic is being prepared by Taube.

217 This chronograph is a 15th-century compilation, see Istrin 1905; some of the texts are treated in Taube 1992.

218 The earliest Slavonic text, translated from the anonymous Hebrew translation, is in a ms of 1483; an edition is being prepared by Taube.

219 The Hebrew was published by M. Gaster in 1907–08 in the *Journal of the Royal Asiatic Society*, the Slavic by Speranskij in Памятники древней письменности и исскуства 171 (1908); the two scholars seem not to have known each other's work.

(not 'twig, wand') for прутъ, hint at southwestern Slavic dialects, and encourage speculation that вольникъ stands for a distorted SW иꙁволѥникъ: this is far from sufficient evidence to prove a Croato-Slovene background.

L21.3 The fundamental difficulty is that the canonical OCS texts are too meager to establish a reliable point of departure. Though the four Gospels are primarily narratives, their scope is limited; only the saints' lives from the Suprasliensis offer a greater variety of action and diversity of background that demand a broader lexicon. The conventional lists of western or Ohrid opposed to eastern or Preslav lexemes are useful in discussing very old manuscripts, but later scribes revalued many items as stylistic variants to be used freely in new works. The surviving manuscripts written in Rus′ before c1150 do provide a great many words we can attribute to OCS, but the homiletic and hymnological vocabulary is often remote from the more concrete lexicon of narratives. The oldest copies of biblical stories from Genesis and Exodus are in *paremejnik* (prophetologion) manuscripts written after 1200; we can agree that the original translations go back before 900, but inevitably will argue about which details are ancient and what is to be ascribed to subsequent editors (where? when?). By 1100, Rusian bookmen were producing historical work. They drew on a Slavic version of the Chronicle of George the Monk (Hamartolos), but was it part of the heritage of Bulgarian OCS (as we believe) or the work of early Kievan translators (as many Russian scholars, including Meščerskij and Alekseev) insist?[220] Even more disputed is the provenance of the Slavic version of Josephus Flavius's *History of the Jewish War*, known only from East Slavic manuscripts of the 15th–16th centuries. Again we believe, contrary to Meščerskij and many others, that this text originated in Bulgaria, but we suspect that the oldest retrievable stage results from many generations of East Slavic copyists. With this in mind, we must be skeptical about labelling individual words from these texts as typical of any time or place. There are words which seem to have been favored by early Rusian bookmen, but for lack of evidence we are unable to pick out specific items that were unknown in Bulgarian OCS.

L21.4 Another major hazard is that some individual problems have too many variables. Decisions about details may be fraught with difficulties. The adjective раꙁноличь 'different' of 1:7 has two notable characteristics: it lacks an adjectival formant (and, presumably, a gender-number-case desinence), but is a compound with an adjectival first member, (*raz-ьn*)-*o*+*lič*-. OCS has indeclinable раꙁличь (considered archaic) along with regularized раꙁличьнъ, but no раꙁноличь or раꙁноличьнъ.[221] Разꙁноличь might seem assured as OCS by its presence in the October Menaion datable to 1096 (Srez, SRJaXI), съ маслъмь раꙁноличь, '(wine poured into a vessel) with oil of a different kind [εἶδους τε ἑτέρου].'[222]

[220] This extraordinarily rich but problematical translation is known from a copy of about 1300 (that unfortunately lacks the last quarter of the text) and from seven copies written after c1450. It includes additions concerning events from 842 to 948 and could possibly have been translated before 1000. The 572 pages of V. M. Istrin's edition (1920) have not been systematically analyzed. Istrin's own lists of mistranslations, scribal errors, compound words, and other important elements (1922) suffice to establish the major outlines characterizing the translation and its transmission, but they are far from complete and often raise questions that Istrin does not answer satisfactorily (or does not address at all). The dictionary (1930) is an indispensable work, especially valuable for its Greek-Slavonic half, but only a single reference is given for each Gk-Sl equivalent. The controversy about time and place of translation may well be insoluble; scholars must be cautious in evaluating the data from this edition.

[221] Post-1100 orthography is unreliable for distinguishing the up-dated *raz-ьn-* from the archaic *raz-n-* that is plausibly discernable in OCS and earliest Rusian spelling.

[222] SRJaXI defines 'отличающийся внешним видом (?)' and states that the Gk is different, citing a variant ἕτερόν [*sic*] τε εἶδος '*и еще кое-что*.' There is no reason for this gloss.

But this ms is a faulty copy of a mediocre translation of difficult poetic texts; the obscure and sometimes incoherent lines surely show Rus′ influence here and there—but where exactly? The preceding troparion begins врача раꙁличьно нєдоужьныхъ 'healer (Asm) of those who are sick in various ways [ποικίλως].' Just what is the syntax? Is it likely that different stem-shapes of one adjective/adverb would be used in consecutive troparia? What compounds with *razno-* are known?

Looking through dictionaries for parallels, we find in SRJaXI разноокый (from a 17th-century *Алфавит*) 'having different eyes' and разноочный, with the same meaning, from Ham 47. The example turns out to be a variant, разнооченъ, for въꙁороучєнъ of the oldest copy, c1300. The passage is instructive. A few lines earlier Candace, queen 'of India,' investigates what Alexander of Macedon looks like. (Gk περιειργάσατο 'investigated' comes out исписа 'wrote,' implying that the translator [whether in Preslav or Kiev] perceived -γρα- and understood some form of γραφ.) 'He is short, having teeth [that are] big and prominent (φαινομένους), and one blue eye and one black.' The Slavic translator assumed that the heroic Alexander must be handsome, so the teeth that 'make themselves show' must be good-looking. He chose въꙁрачьн- (or the ESl shape въꙁороучьн-);[223] but did he add the Ap desinence to refer back to ꙁѫбы? In any case the oldest copy has the Nsm въꙁороучєнъ, syntactically pointing to Alexander. A scribe whose work is reflected in all other copies of Ham (the oldest was written in 1456) decided that this odd word must anticipate the next statement and invented a new compound, разнооч(е)н, based on a pattern that surely included раꙁноличьнъ, доброличьнъ, доброꙁрачьнъ (see A5.2) and perhaps раꙁличноѡбраꙁныи (Ham 475.8, referring to a leopard, ποικιλότροπος 'of variegated shape').

In this case we have evidence to separate въꙁрачьнъ (въꙁороучьнъ) as belonging to the oldest attainable text of Ham, and it is reasonable to equate it with φαινόμενος (though perhaps a note that the translation is not exact is called for). We regard it as one lexeme with optionally varying spelling, and attribute it to a Bulgarian translator, as part of the original translation, which seems to belong before 1200. SRJaXI-XVII gives "взорочный" and "взрачный (возрачный)" as separate entries (in vol. 2, 1975), with no cross-reference, indicating the date of the copy as 13th–14th century and the original as 11th century. The lemma разноочный (vol. 21, 1995) cites Istrin's edition, noting that разнооченъ is a variant, and dating it 13th–14th ~ 11th century. In fact, this adjective is unknown before 1450: it is indisputably a 'Rusism.'

As for раꙁноличь in Esther, an archaic раꙁличь from a pre-1050 translation might have been reshaped by a Rus′ editor, *or* an original compound adjective разноличєнъ was written by a post-1300 translator and modified by an archaizing editor or sloppy scribe. Any decision is speculative.[224]

223 The SSl shape въꙁрачныи appears at Ham 145.24, for εὔοπτος 'good-looking,' at 549.3 (with hypercorrect spelling, въꙁдрачныи, Apm) for εὐειδής, and twice as an epithet distinguishing one king from another, for ἐπιφανής 'prominent, distinguished': Антіохъ Въꙁрачныи 299.7, Птоломѣи Въꙁрачьныи 300.1 (but spelled right only in one late copy; въꙁврачныи in the oldest copy, възᵈрастныи in the other six). The word is not attested in other early texts, as far as we could discover.

224 V. V. Kolesov provides pages of examples of lexemes that characterize texts originating or copied in Rus′, but nothing is clearly stated, much less demonstrated. A list of lexical Russisms comparable to (соотносимые со) the West Slavic languages includes 'разнолич(ный)' with a note that it occurs in Esther (among other texts such as Josephus) and is deemed a Russism by all scholars who have mentioned the word (1991 131). The stem **orz-lič-ьn-* was surely Common Slavic (e.g., Cz, Slk *rozličný* P *rozliczny,* Slk, SC *različni*), but compound forms with *razno-/rozno-* do not occur in West Slavic. The evidence for use of such compounds in early Rus′ is strong, but there is nothing to prove that they were not also part of the heritage from Bulgaria.

L21.51 Many texts are known in variant shapes that are difficult to evaluate—at least in the present state of scholarship. For example, the compilation known as the *Explanatory Paleja* is attested from c1350 (published from the Kolomna copy dated 1406), and from 1477 in a markedly different form; these are called the first and second redactions. Among the components are the apocryphal *Testaments of the Twelve Patriarchs*: a long version corresponding to the Greek text is in the second redaction of the *Paleja,* while an abridged version apparently made by an East Slav is incorporated in the first edition.[225] Logically, then, (1) the whole text was translated into Slavic, (2) a Rus′ editor shortened it, and (3) it was made part of the Paleja. Finally, perhaps as much as a century later, (4) the full text was substituted for the abridgement in the second redaction of the Paleja. If this is so, the oldest witness (c1350 but abridged text) should be less archaic than the younger (1477 but long text). Here is a fragment (Testament of Issachar, 4:2b–3) containing two items that showed varied lexemes in Esther:

1406 (221a)	1477 (167ab)
и питаниꙗ раꙁлична нє ищєть	пищь раꙁличных нє ищєт
и одѣниꙗ красна нє рачить	свитамь краснымь нє хощєт
и лѣт долгыхъ нє желаєть	лѣтъ долго жити нє ищєть

4:2b βρωμάτων ποικίλων οὐκ ἀφίεται, ἐθῆτα διάφορον οὐ θέλει. 3. χρόνους μακροὺς οὐχ ὑπογράφει ζῆν.

'He does not seek varied foods, he does not desire remarkable clothing. He does not plan to live long years.'

Одѣниє is impeccable OCS for 'clothing, garb,' along with одєжда; свита denotes rather an outer garment or robe (cf. L5.1), and is not—very likely by chance—known from canonical OCS. Рачити 'love, be fond of' is plausible as *OCS, though this sense seems rather strong in this context. A dative object with хотѣти is normal OCS but rare in Rus′. (The first cited clause contrasts the all-purpose word for 'food' with the *OCS питаниє, which might be a replacement for older питѣниє.) The third clause goes back to a Gk verb used in an unusual sense and might well have caused the original translator difficulty; the 1406 version is an adequate paraphrase, while the 1477 sentence is not quite coherent: which (if either) is original?

L21.52 Current reference works often send incompatible messages. SRJaXI rightly attempts to specify the date a lexeme is attested, often supplemented by a hypothetical date for the postulated original text. Thus items from Ham are ordinarily classed as "13th–14th ~ 11th century," meaning attested c1300 but reflecting a hypothetical original in the 1000's (an estimate contested by many). Sub питаниє, cited from the first clause above, SRJaXI gives the source as *Testaments,* as printed in Tixonravov, "14th century"—that is, the date of earliest attestation.[226] Sub рачити, however, the three above lines are cited without mention of

[225] On the *Testaments* see Charlesworth (vol. 1) for general information; on the Slavic versions, see Turdeanu 1971 (he points out that the most important manuscript has not been published). Comparison of full and abridged versions makes it certain that the latter was made in Rus′. The drastic revision of Josephus's *Jewish* (more properly, *Judean*) *War* (Meščerskij 1985a) may have been made by the Slav who translated it (in Bulgaria before 1000? in Rus′ after 1050?), but much of the abridgement could have been made in a Greek redaction.

[226] The lemma питаниє[2] (defined "поиск, разыскание (?)") cites a sentence from Усп, "12th–13th century." Indeed, this spelling is in Усп, but the text is an OCS sermon found also in Supr—where the misspelling питан- for пытан- also occurs. Since we have the Gk original, we gloss the noun 'question.' Supr was probably copied in the 11th century, but the text was surely translated before 975. *If* misspelled words are to be listed in such a dictionary, then they should be explained; SJS does not mention this example. In any case, the OCS ori-

the *Testaments* from the first redaction of the Paleja, "1406 ~ 13th century." Now, the second line is absent from the older copy (Tixonravov 1 121); are we to understand that it was added in 1406, or perhaps during the 13th century? In any case, what facts and assumptions underlie the 13th-century dating? We see no reason for not ascribing the *Testaments* to 10th-century Bulgaria, but neither can we deny the plausibility of Turdeanu's estimate that they were translated in Bulgaria (including Athos and Macedonia) in the last part of the 12th or first part of the 13th century. There simply are no criteria that allow us to handle the multiple variables in our effort to classify these words by time, space, and linguistic or sociolinguistic group.

L21.53 We could easily cite scores of similar examples of conflicting assumptions and opinions, based on dubious readings from manuscripts whose character is unknown, but there is no point. The primary evidence, in the form of careful editions of many major texts, is not available. The lists of alleged East Slavic words—as opposed to South (particularly Bulgarian) or West Slavic—that are supposedly distinctive for East Slavic translations, whether made a century ago by Sobolevskij or Istrin or recently by Kolesov, prove nothing at all. Whether a meticulous reexamination of the available materials will produce meaningful criteria for dating these texts (many of which have not yet been analyzed seriously) is a question for the rather distant future.

L12.531 A few details may support the notion that Novgorod was involved somewhere in the history of Esther. The preposition унє, the conjunctions ижє and любо 'for, because,' the verbs удобрити сѧ and улюбити 'please' are affirmed in part from Novgorod sources, but no systematic patterns emerge.

L21.54 The shifting forms of common lexemes may obliterate clues to age. In OCS the root *věd* in the basic sense 'know' had a suffix -ě- in the aorist-infinitive system, and an egregiously irregular present with zero present marker (athematic) and a special set of person-number desinences: вѣдѣти, вѣдѣхъ, вѣдѣлъ, etc.; вѣмь (or вѣдѣ), вѣси, вѣдѧтъ, etc. The prefix *po-* modifies the meaning to 'cause to know, tell, recount'; the irregular morphology (повѣдѣти, повѣмь, повѣси, etc.) is abundantly attested. Beside it was a regularized stem, *po-věd-aj-* (повѣдати, повѣдалъ, повѣдаѭ, etc.), with the same range of meaning. Similarly, исповѣдѣти and исповѣдати are apparently interchangeable. Yet the unprefixed regular вѣдати is unknown in canonical OCS. It is cited by the editors of SJS only from texts they believe to demonstrate a Czech recension, though they are preserved only in post-1200 East Slavic mss. Though the evidence is sparse, the regularized forms were apparently normal by c 1400.[227] The retrievable text of Esther offers two innovative forms (вѣдаѩ 4:1, вѣдають 4:11) four neutral examples (исповѣда 4:7, 6:13, повѣда 2:10, оувѣдати 4:5) and two archaic forms (вѣсть 4:14, оувѣдѣти 4:11). The contrast may be ascribed to an erudite scribe at a relatively late date, but there is ample reason to allow the possibility that it represents partial "normalization" by a post-1100 scribe (or series of scribes).

L21.55 Despite the puzzles and paradoxes, the lexicon on the whole is compatible with

---

gin must be noted, if only by giving the 10th-century date. (It is sad that, as of 1997, SRJaXI continues to repeat the faults pointed out by reviewers of the early volumes, e.g., Lunt 1976, 1979, Keenan 1978.)

227 See note 126, p. 173, and note 93, p. 208.

the hypothesis that Esther is a 14th-century Ruthenian translation; it has undergone editorial reworking (perhaps including intentional archaization) when it was integrated into an East Slavic biblical compilation in the last quarter of the century, perhaps not long after it was translated. The lexicon is perhaps less compatible with the thesis that the translation goes back to 10th-century Bulgaria or pre-Mongol Rus′; the language was repeatedly updated, but inevitably deteriorated as it was copied by indifferent scribes.

L21.6 Before Meščerskij's 1978 publication of Esther it was known that the vocabulary was unusual and puzzling. Our examination of every word has clarified the nature of individual deviations and demonstrated in detail just how idiosyncratic the text is. Yet to account for the special usages (and for the avoidance of expected lexemes) has proved beyond our reach.

Summation and Outlook

Our work has been guided by three questions: from what language, when, and where, was the Book of Esther translated into Slavonic? A fourth question, intimately bound to the first three, had to be faced: why was Esther needed?

Only the first question can be answered beyond reasonable doubt. The Slavonic Esther was translated from Greek. The thesis of direct translation from Hebrew to Slavonic rests chiefly on the fact that the 167-verse shape of the text corresponds closely to the Hebrew MT. Yet this thesis, first enunciated by Gorskij and Nevostruev in 1855 (see p. 8, In7.1, above) does not withstand scrutiny. The transcription of personal names reflects Greek, not Hebrew. The detailed phrase-by-phrase correspondence of the Slavonic and Hebrew wording does not prove direct translation. It can result from the customary method of literal translation, used first to produce a Greek version and then a translation into Slavonic. The number of Semitisms is (*pace* Gorskij and Nevostruev) well within the stylistic limits of original Slavic works written from the 9th to the 14th centuries. Hellenisms abound, many of them apparently motivated by literal interpretation of Greek phraseology. We agree with A. I. Sobolevskij that the evidence points to the existence of a 167-verse Greek Esther.

Unambiguous answers to the other three questions have eluded us. Solid conclusions about the time and place of translation seem to be precluded by the lamentably unsatisfactory state of the reconstructible text, compounded by the fact that comparable texts (such as the Chronicle of George the Monk, Hamartolos, Josephus Flavius's *Capture of Jerusalem*, and the *Testaments of the Twelve Patriarchs* [see L21.5, above]) have not yet been analyzed with sufficient rigor. The Slavonic Esther has the air of a 14th–15th century Ruthenian (that is, Ukrainian or Belarusian) Slavonic work; the dates of the oldest and best extant copies, just before or after 1400, guarantee that it existed by about 1390. The internal contradictions (in vocabulary, phraseology, and syntax) of the presumably mid-fourteenth century ancestral *pervospisok* can be attributed to careless scribes and inconsistent editors who ruined an originally acceptable translation.

How rapidly can a reasonably intelligible text deteriorate? Are we to compare Esther with the apocryphal *Gospel of Nicodemus,* which was apparently translated from Latin in 10th-century Croatia, but survived only in post-1400 copies that are badly garbled?[1] Or is the *Third Capture of Jerusalem, by Titus*, apparently translated from Hebrew in the 15th century perhaps in Novgorod and integrated into the second redaction of the *Hellenic and Roman Chronicler* (EL-2) a better parallel? The several manuscripts containing this text show a wide variety of editorial hands that demonstrate that scribes "standardized" according to their individual view of proper written Slavonic. They often introduced lexical and grammatical archaisms, but carelessness and misguided emendations produced unintelligible sentences and incoherent passages.

The 167-verse shape of the Slavonic Esther is rooted in Jewish tradition. It is improbable that Methodius or any other Byzantine Christian would have chosen it instead of the normal

[1] Unlike Esther, *Nicodemus* is known in both East and South Slavic copies, and tangible archaisms have survived the damaging errors and misguided revisions contributed in various times and places. The fact that the translation was made from Latin, not Greek, is a crucial argument for the time and place of translation, see Vaillant 1968, esp. xxvi–xxviii.

Septuagint version. Historians take it for granted that Greek-speaking Jewish communities existed in the Byzantine Empire during the first centuries of Slavic written culture, although evidence is sparse. We conjecture that a Greek version of Esther was available in some of these communities.

As linguists, we have been primarily concerned with the linguistic expression, seeking a coherent text from the welter of conflicting detail; we were content to establish the immediate meaning of each verse. After we began our collaboration in 1984, a wave of interest in Esther produced several comprehensive commentaries and literary studies. Special attention has been directed to the individual integrity of the four ancient accounts of Esther: the standard Hebrew, the standard Greek LXX (or Beta-text), the shorter L-text (or Alpha-text), and (mentioned but not really analyzed) the still shorter (but longer than the Hebrew) tale told by Josephus (cf. In2.3).[2] The information these authors provide includes a great many details of Greek and Hebrew linguistic affinities and translation strategies in the intricate relationships among these texts. They require us only to emphasize once again that the Slavonic is so intimate a reflection of the 167 Hebrew verses of the MT that our hypothetical Greek intermediary differs only in language, not in important redactional characteristics. The absence of the name *Hadassah* (see C2:7) and the substitution of *rejoicing* (веселье) for *Purim* (C9:29, L13.2) are more likely to be faults in the textual transmission than evidence for special sectarian exegesis.

The earliest known manuscripts present Esther as one of a group of historical texts. Perhaps the Slavonic version was introduced into the Christian tradition by a writer of history. The tangible evidence of manuscripts shows that in the late 1200s East Slavs were actively involved in compiling comprehensive histories that would (like the translated Chronicle of George the Monk) include the major events of the Old Testament. Was this indeed a new intellectual venture of East Slavs, or was it based on a tradition going back to the Bulgarians at the court of Symeon (893–927) or Peter (927–69)? Or perhaps Ivan Asen II (1218–41) or even one of his successors? Whatever the original purpose and site of the original translation may have been, it is clear that the translator worked from a Greek, not a Hebrew, original, but that the Greek was none of the three Greek text-forms known to us from elsewhere (LXX, L, or the Josephus version). What was this Greek text? Perhaps, as we suggested above, it was a newer Jewish translation of the MT Esther first made for the use of Greek-speaking Jewish communities in the Byzantine Empire. At some point this text found its way into the hands of someone who wished to render this "Jewish" (and therefore deemed more "authentic"?) Esther into Slavonic. The exact details of the process must remain unknown.

One might argue that two or three individuals were involved: a Jew whose liturgical language was Greek, but whose home language may have been some sort of Slavic; a Slav who wanted to use the text for his own purposes (probably writing about history); and perhaps a scribe to record it properly. (Maksim Grek's Slavonic translation of the Psalms was described as this kind of sequence: Maksim dictated in Latin, which was turned into "Russian" by Dmitrij Gerasimov, alternating with Vlasij, who dictated to a scribe.) The immediate translation might have been a colloquial kind of Slavic with lexical oddities that were

[2] *1984*: David J. A. Clines, *The Esther Scroll: The Story of the Story.* (Journal for the Study of the Old Testament Supplement Series 30) Sheffield, England; *1991*: Michael V. Fox, *The Redaction of the Books of Esther.* Atlanta, GA; *1996*: Karen H. Jobes (see bibliography); *1996*: Frederic W. Bush, *Ruth, Esther* (Word Biblical Commentary, vol. 9) Dallas, Texas; *1997*: Charles V. Dorothy, *The Books of Esther: Structure, Genre and Textual Integrity.* (Journal for the Study of the Old Testament Supplement Series 187) Sheffield, England. [Cited often from his 1989 dissertation.]; *1997*: Jon D. Levenson (see bibliography).

only in part adapted to a more literary style by the original scribe and his immediate successors. Such speculation fits the skimpy scenario but again fails to hint at time and place.

Both Esther and Ecclesiastes are known only from East Slavic manuscripts, but no one (to our knowledge) has claimed that Ecclesiastes was translated in Rus′. The linguistic criteria that form the basis for the claims that a wide range of works that have survived only in East Slavic copies must be "Russian" translations have not withstood scrutiny; in our opinion there is no credible evidence that East Slavs produced translations from Greek before about 1250.

In the end, choice among alternatives depends on varying linguistic traditions. Our analyses rest chiefly on comparisons with Old Church Slavonic, in part because that is the traditional way to treat medieval Slavonic texts, and in part because one must test the possibility that the translation might be old. A second term of comparison is the *Tale of Seasons and Years* (Повѣсть временъ и лѣтъ), a compilation of heterogeneous texts put together in early 12th-century Rus′. Deviations from these loose standards can be regarded as interference from Ruthenian habits, changes made either inadvertently or purposefully by successive scribes. If, however, one allows the premise that the translation was made after 1200 (or 1300) in Bulgaria or Serbia or some East Slavic realm, the evaluation of certain words, phrases, or syntactical constructions must be different. If, for example, the eye-catching *oxvota* 'gladness' (or *rastvoriti* 'destroy') is attributed to the translator, then the text must be assigned to the Belarusian-Ukrainian borderlands. But if it is taken as an intentional replacement for the ubiquitous *radostь* (or *razoriti*), then a maximal temporal and geographical range for the elusive translator is open.

The undeniably Ruthenian character of the available text can be discounted as secondary or taken as original. It is entirely plausible to assume that a Ruthenian Jew of Byzantine (not Ashkenazi) background made the translation in the 14th century, that it was copied and edited by East Slavs who introduced variegated changes—archaisms and exotic features as well as mistaken emendations—whose net effect was destructive to the sense. This scenario allows some justification for most of the difficulties we have described. It is not strong enough to rule out other alternatives, however.

Our inability to give categorical answers to these questions stems from the simple fact that the scope of Slavic cultural achievements before 1400 and particularly their social and political backgrounds remain—and, for lack of evidence, probably will remain—matter for speculation. We have tried to verify facts provided by our scholarly predecessors and to test their hypotheses and theoretical assumptions. The detailed information we have amassed over the years has allowed us to report some new items and to sift out many small points. It has made it possible to exclude certain proposals and to correct some misunderstandings. Yet it has also made us pose dozens of smaller questions—some, at least for the time being, unanswerable.

The unique place of Esther in the Slavic literary tradition led Evseev, and after him Meščerskij and others, to posit early Rus′ bookmen who translated a series of works directly from Hebrew. Closer analysis has shown that no translations from Hebrew into Slavic can be demonstrated before 1400. It is regrettable that some of our contemporaries are unwilling to scrutinize authoritative opinions that are hallowed by years of repetition; fair-minded examination often reveals that revisions are in order. Unfortunately, a scholarly myth (such as the hypothesis of a school of translators in Kiev in the eleventh century) too often becomes a sacrosanct dogma, zealously repeated as an act of faith and defended as a badge of national identity. We believe that scholars must admit when a question cannot be answered for lack of evidence. We regret that we cannot give definitive answers to basic questions about

Esther, but we believe that the data and the discussions we provide in this book illuminate the major problems (and, along the way, answer many smaller questions).

The question of *why* Esther was translated remains. Much of the extant literature about "Judaizers" among the East Slavs has been demonstrated to be off the mark, but not enough is yet known to offer more than hesitant suggestions. The earliest texts demonstrably translated from Hebrew come after 1400. Esther belongs rather with an earlier group with known Greek sources (*Testaments of the Patriarchs,* some apocrypha), treating Jews of the past who can be regarded as part of the Christian tradition. In the late 15th century these items may be adapted to include anti-Jewish polemics that show such intimate knowledge of Jewish tradition that they surely were produced by a converted Jew.

Perhaps a Judeo-Greek text of Esther was translated into Slavic in the Balkans and somehow made its way to Rus′ during the 14th century. Perhaps such a text made its way to Kiev or even Novgorod rather late in the century and was translated there. Delegations from Byzantium arrived in Novgorod about 1400. Might their translators include Byzantine Jews? Balkan Jews? These and related questions deserve to be explored.

Appendix I: **Meščerskij's 1978 Edition of Esther**

1 The only full printed text of the Slavonic Esther was edited by Nikita A. Meščerskij and appeared in the *Dissertationes Slavicae* of the *Acta* of the University of Szeged, Hungary. The text, NM tells us in his one-page introduction, (M78a 131), is based on RGB TSL 2, with variants from (a) RNB Q.I.2 ("П"), (b) BAN 45.13.4 ("А"), (c) RGB Volok. 9 ("В"), and (d) RGB Und 1 ("У").[1] Each page of the edition corresponds to a page of the manuscript. The manuscript lines are not indicated, however; the text is organized according to the chapter-verse divisions of the Hebrew tradition.[2] A set of lettered notes is intended to give "необходимые сведения о написаниях в издаваемой рукописи," and a second apparatus provides variant readings.

2.1 The text was photo-offset from a mediocre typescript produced on a Soviet typewriter, so that the letter "ѣ" was made by typing Ь and adding the horizontal upper stroke by hand. Titla also had to be added manually. Meščerskij specifies that titla are retained, but that "у" is used for *у* and ѫ, while "я" stands for ѧ and "ıѧ и др."[3] In fact, "у" is used for ѹ, and "я" for ѧ and ꙗ. In principle, Meščerskij puts superscript letters on the line with no special mark, although at times he makes the effort to reproduce the superscription.[4]

2.2 The typescript was inadequately checked; it is unsatisfactory. Unfortunately, few of the mistakes are self-correcting because T is such a faulty manuscript that one can expect almost any sort of blunder. Yet ж for х in Ажасъверосу 2:12 is not a scribal slip, but belongs to Meščerskij's typist, as does the opposite substitution in 2:15 доступихребии instead of the scribally correct жребии (and the space before ж we expect an editor to provide).

3 Scribes of the late 14th century were uncertain about the use of ъ and ь, and variation is often quite erratic. Yet the more than 50 examples where Meščerskij has incorrectly reproduced the readings of T with regard to these letters (and the morphemes in which they are expected to occur) will give readers a false impression of actual scribal usage, although these editorial flaws do not seriously affect the text. So, for example, it is textually insignificant that 6:1 has в ту нощь (not въ) . . . во снѣ (not в), 1:6 has оутриномь (not -мъ), 4:11 has вьси (not вси). Linguistically, it is somewhat more important that the aorist ꙗтъ has the correct final letter, and not the possible variant ять, as Meščerskij prints in 6:1.

4 However, Meščerskij has allowed over 130 errors of varying kinds that do affect the language and the text. There are omissions (цр҃цю 1:17, доже 1:20, бѧше 2:7, мѣсто 2:7, ѕ҃

[1] These are numbers 1, 2, 16 (our T, Q, U), 20, and 31 of our list. He presumably selected B as a representative of the Gennadian tradition, though he does not say so. He was unaware that U is a copy of T.

[2] The beginnings of verses 1:3, 6, 8, 13; 3:3, 11; 5:2, 8; 9:9 and 9:20 are incorrectly placed, while 9:10 is not marked at all.

[3] The graph ѫ does not occur in manuscripts T and Q; it would be interesting to see how it is used, if at all, in the other manuscripts. Does ıѧ actually occur in any of these texts? Surely Meščerskij meant to write ꙗ.

[4] The Ь for ѣ remains a half-dozen times, but titla are missing more than 80 times. These blemishes do not, on the whole, impede understanding, but they are symptomatic of Meščerskij's indifference to detail.

2:13, and at least 10 others) and many misprints (e.g., располону 3:13 for рос-, говѣиье 4:16 for -ѣите, останокъ 9:15 for -атокъ, живодяхуся 8:17 for жидовѧху сѧ, оумылиста 2:21 for -ысли-, вопемь 4:1 for воплемь, мышляше 9:24 for помышлѧшє, на 3:10 for дано). Some distort noun forms (e.g., Мардохаю 4:10 for -аꙗ, племени 6:13 for -не, имене 9:26 for -ни, на июдѣи 9:24 for -ѣꙗ). Innovating plurals are implied by болярамъ 1:3 and сн͠ами 9:25; such anachronisms are merely the product of Meščerskij's carelessness, for T has болѧромъ and сн͠ъми. Other typing errors misrepresent verbal forms (e.g., видѣху 1:14 for -ѧху, възвеличи 5:11 for -ҷа, събраше 9:16 for -ша, преступити 8:2 for -ати, оуслыша 9:1 for -шаша. Some adjectival desinences are inaccurate (e.g., июдѣискаго 6:13, 8:1, 9:9 for -ского). Even prepositions are misprinted (e.g., от Амона 8:2 for **оу** А-), and some other little words are wrong (e.g., в ц͠рь 3:15 for **а** ц͠рь, в д͠нь 9:19 for **и** д͠нь, всего 5:13 for все **то**, на 6:3 for нє, бы 7:4 for б**о**). Incorrect numerals are particularly misleading, и͞ '8' instead of н͞ '50' 7:9, є͞ '5' instead of ҂є '5000.'[5] Some mistakes are complex, e.g. 3:10 not растѣянии, but расѣꙗни и; 6:10 not сѣдяще, but иже сѣдѧше; 7:5 not иже такое помыслI, but ижє такы помыслы помыслї. We do not consider it worth the space to give a full listing.

5 Meščerskij's editorial practice is erratic.[6] In his *avtoreferat* (1956a), Meščerskij, like Roždestvenskij before him, minimized the number of omissions by comparison to the Hebrew text, but in the edition he had to face the problems more directly.[7] In principle, he points out omissions by means of his lettered notes (e.g. 1:3, 3:1, 4), but not always (e.g., 3:3, 14, 4:1).[8] Only in 8:8 is the lacuna indicated directly in the text as well as by a note.[9] In 9:24 Meščerskij correctly notes a lacuna but wrongly gives its sense as "И как Есфирь пришла к царю"; he has overlooked the fact that this clause is present, with quite different wording, as the beginning of verse 25. The missing clause concerns the casting of lots (*pur*) that is so important in the Jewish story and deserves to be noticed.[10]

6.1 Meščerskij's notes are sometimes ambiguous, and occasionally they seem wrong. Let us look closely at some examples. Note B to "яко волна" 1:8 reads "В рук. испр.: акы

5 In 3:13 Meščerskij prints the expected .гı. (Heb. '13th'), but T in fact has гı, a significant blunder.

6 Many inconsistencies suggest that the typescript was a working copy that never was fully edited. Thus 1:11 contains no note 13, although its location can be guessed at by the variants cited in the apparatus (so also note П in 2:6; 93, 94 in 3:7; 9, 13 in 6:13, and at least four others); in 2:14, n. 64 appears by mistake, though it is correct in the previous verse; n. 4 to 3:12 is not numbered in the apparatus. Note 61a to 5:6 is missing from the apparatus (where n. 64a is placed after 65), similarly 83a to 6:2. In 8:5 the notes go 53, 52, 51, and on the same page n. 59 fails to identify the manuscript from which the variant is cited. We have made no attempt to list all the slips of this kind.

7 Altogether, 21 omissions are mentioned by Roždestvenskij (195, n. 1; 197) and Meščerskij (1956a 207–8 and 1978a, passim). Of these, only two (1:3, 8:8) appear in all three sources; 7 are only in Roždestvenskij; one is shared by Roždestvenskij and 1956a (8:9); three are shared by Roždestvenskij and 1978a (1:16, 5:9, 9:24); four are only in 1956a and four only in 1978a. In our analysis, there are more than forty relatively straight-forward omissions in T, and at least a dozen more instances where omission is complicated by other kinds of textual corruption.

8 The unmentioned omission in 4:1 affects one of Meščerskij's arguments about the influence of Hebrew on the Slavonic, see C4:1.

9 The note states "должно быть восстановлено: и вы напишите июдѣям." M 56a 204 gave a correct translation (cf. Ro 197), "А вы напишите об июдеях." The dative of 1978a is inappropriate, and the letter ѣ indicates that Meščerskij is hypothesizing the old lost text; if so, the wording should be in the dual (вы [or ва] напишита [if imv]) because the king is addressing Mordecai and Esther.

10 For examples where Meščerskij falsely states that omissions occur, see below.

волна." What does Meščerskij consider original, and what is corrected? Even from the photos, we could see that аки represents original аки corrected to ѧко. The ѧ exceeds the normal boundaries of the space allotted for the original *a*, and the orthography of T does not allow ѧ in syllable-initial position. The second syllable has и (not "о"), despite the fact that T otherwise writes only кы, so that аки violates a rule.[11] Note Г (to такъ 1:8) reads, "В рук. испр.: тако." Here surely ъ is original, but again we are not certain what Meščerskij thought.[12] Note E, 1:10 "Емуума/нови/[E.]" reads, "Исп. по смыслу подлинника. Во всех списках порча." The implication is that "/нови/" is the dubious part of this proper name. Now, what we want is a dative of *Mehuman*, and we can easily posit *Муоуман-ови, with a modified first syllable. The mss actually have емуоуманови. The preceding word is рече, doubtless abbreviated in many copies. A scribe mistakenly prefixed е (surely because of the frequent occurrence of рече єму in many texts); it is this initial syllable that is awkward with regard to the Hebrew shape of the name.[13] Note Ж to 1:16 "ц^с^ря": "В рук. испр.: црци, как в П." This is an instance where the line-break may play a role. The word 'king' occurs at the end of a line earlier in the verse, ца|рю, 122.6–7, while the expected 'queen' comes directly at the end of 122.7 and is written ца|рѧ—surely because the scribe has shifted his attention to the immediately following accusatives. A later scribe has added ри in the margin, creating цари|рѧ. The text requires Nom. царица, or, in the current orthography, царицѧ. Meščerskij's "ц^с^ря" is misleading; the alleged "црци" of П is wrong: ms Q.I.2 has цр^с^цѧ.[14] Note З to 1:16 "въ всѣхъ[З.]" reads, "В рук. описка. Должно читать: въ вьсѣхъ." This apparently brands a normal spelling as incorrect; a reader will immediately ask why this stricture is not applied to всѣхъ in 1:8. Meščerskij obviously did not really mean *scribal lapse* (описка), but rather *corruption* (порча)—see C1:16—but his laconic note gives no hint of how he might have envisioned the problem and its solution.[15]

6.2 These examples illustrate, among other things, that Meščerskij did not decide just how to indicate places in the text which he wished to emend. Sometimes he emends in the text itself, sometimes he puts the emended portion between slashes, and sometimes he leaves the text untouched and comments only in the note.[16] Too often the reader is not given a clear distinction between the manuscript evidence and Meščerskij's opinions.

11 To our knowledge, акы is attested by E, while аки is in SGWV as well as Q. Meščerskij fails to cite other mss here. (Incidentally it is odd that the note is attached to волна, and not to аки/ѧко; ms T clearly has a supralinear mark we take to mean an apostrophe, вол'на.) Акы is an eastern OCS equivalent of older ꙗко, and the two coexist from the beginning of East Slavic literacy.

12 Here too, Meščerskij cites no supporting evidence. We find the appropriate такъ in QW, такь (!) in V, and тако in E.

13 Meščerskij in principle keeps "оу" as spelled in T; why did he change it to "у" here, in violation of T's spelling rules?

14 It is because Meščerskij's use of this manuscript is so misleading that we do not use the siglum П; in order to disassociate ourselves entirely from Meščerskij's work, we use the siglum Q.

15 In 8:12 Meščerskij gives во всѣ земля—a not impossible sequence—with n. 73 "въ всѣхъ земляхъ. П." Q in fact writes всѣ^х^, while T has во всѣ^х^ ꙁемля^х^; the reason for Meščerskij's note is unclear.

16 Comparable examples are handled inconsistently. In 2:4 Meščerskij's text has оулюбѣ, with note H, "В рукописи описка. Следует читать: И оулюбѣ. П; и оулюби. А." This fails to provide the dubious original spelling, оулобѣ. However, in 1:19 оулобѣе is retained in Meščerskij's text, with note K, "В рук. описка, вместо оулюбѣте, как в П." (It is strange that Meščerskij proposes the incongruous second person plural form, for the 3s is appropriate, 'if it please the king.')

7 Of the four manuscripts Meščerskij mentions, only П, А, and В are cited frequently. У appears only in notes 2 (unclear just what the reading is), 6, and 9 at the beginning, and then 42 (to 2:7). On the other hand, "К" is cited in notes 81, 82 (2:21), and "Г" in notes Л and О; we are not told what these manuscripts are, or why Meščerskij cites these particular instances. We may surmise that "Г" is our G (ms 25, the Gennadius copy of 1499).

7.1 Particularly disturbing are cases where Meščerskij appears to have confused the readings of T with those of other manuscripts. In 2:4 he prints /начнеть/ начнеть, with the note "в рукописи диттография"; in TQSGWV the word occurs a single time. Note Ц to 3:10 specifies an omission in all copies except T and П; the three words are in TQSGWV. Note Щ at the end of 3:15, "Здесь во всех списках рубрика, и начинается новая глава." This is false for the two oldest mss, T and Q (as well as WV). In G, *every* chapter starts on a new line with a large initial letter in the left margin (see C2:5). In 2:2, "доискали[35]" of the text is annotated, "да поискали. П.А.В."; T has да поискали (as do SGWV)—where did Meščerskij find the alleged доискали? In 4:5 T has оувѣдѧти but Meščerskij prints оувѣдати; note 26 says, correctly, that оувѣдати is a variant from П. In 4:16 T has the conjunction и; Meščerskij types "а," while note 50 says и is in ms A. Note 46 to 2:7, n. 53 to 5:3, n. 10 to 6:13, n. 98 to 9:3, and n. 31 to 9:30 attribute to П the variants which in fact are in T. His text of 6:10 differs from T in several significant details; he gives no notes. In 9:1, "постигняше[91]" is typed; note 91 gives precisely the same spelling as a variant from П.

7.2 Further confusion is created by lack of agreement between Meščerskij 1956a and Meščerskij 1978a. For example, 1956a 210 cites 8:7 "Иже поверглъ бяше руцѣ свои въ июдея." His edition reads: им же ввергль[56] бяше руцѣ свои[57] во июдѣи.[57] Note 56 cites повергль from П, and 57 says "в иудея. А. июдѣу. В."[17] The manuscripts we can verify all have имьже (V), им'же (W), имжє (Q), or иͫжє, and the implication of Meščerskij's lack of a note would indicate that AB agree with T: where did the Иже of 1956a come from? Meščerskij's 1976a note 56 attributes повергль (cited in 56a) to П; it is not there. All mss known to us have въвєрглъ.[18]

7.3 The most serious effect of all this confusion is that the two oldest manuscripts (T and Q) are made to appear to differ more significantly than in fact they do. Meščerskij cites "П" in his notes directly or indirectly ("all others") nearly 200 times. Of these, as many as 30% are false: the variants attributed to "П" are not in fact the readings of ms Q.I.2. Another 9% involve cases where in fact T = Q; examples have been given above. The chief class of differences between the two is a set of banal variations involving the use of the jer-letters ъ and ь; some 33% of Meščerskij's notes deal with such cases, but he is inconsistent and fails to mark them all. This leaves only about 28% of Meščerskij's references to "П" that are true and helpful. Unfortunately, readers of his edition have no way of singling out what is true from what is irrelevant or false.

17 M56a 210 believes that the въ constitutes proof of the influence of Hebrew idiomatic use of prepositions on the Slavonic text. On въ and H *b*-, see p. 166, fn 104.

18 Ro 201 cites "имъ жє въвєрглъ ... на Іѹдєю," while Meščerskij's note 57 seems to say that B has no preposition. The appropriateness of the preposition depends on the verb. First, на 'against' is generally applicable; then, surely, въ goes well with въ-вьрглъ, while по-вьрглъ—if it occurs at all—might well call for some other construction.

8 All in all, we are forced to conclude that Meščerskij's work in matters we can verify is unreliable on every level.[19] This means that it would be foolish to suppose that we can trust his judgement about materials we cannot check. Therefore we cite his observations very sparingly, and always with the proviso that such items should be utilized with utmost caution.

19 Meščerskij's initial article on Esther (1956a, cf. In7.31, pp. 9–10) is also without merit, as our detailed notes (*passim*) demonstrate. Further, his edition of Josephus (1958a), generally praised as a meritorious scholarly accomplishment (though Vaillant 1959 was reserved), turns out, according to Ernst Hansack, to have the same pervasive defects of imprecision, internal contradictions, and general lack of method (not to mention failure to mention major and minor debts to previous scholarship). Hansack was finally able to obtain a photocopy of the *Vilnius Chronograph,* the basis of Meščerskij's edition, and to check the edition against the manuscript text. He found so many flaws of so many kinds that he considered it necessary to write a review in 1992, thirty-four years after the book's publication, to caution scholars about the perils of trusting Meščerskij's opinions and decisions.

Appendix II: **The Gennadius Bible of 1499**

1.1 Two monuments in the history of the Slavonic Bible are the first complete manuscript, assembled at the behest of Archbishop Gennadij of Novgorod in 1499, and the first complete printed version, the Ostrih Bible of 1581. For most of the books, the Gennadian text underlies or is closely related to the OB text, whether the material has a long Slavonic history or was newly translated from the Vulgate. Esther is an outstanding exception. The Novgorodian editors joined the first nine chapters of the extant Slavonic text to a new translation of the additions from the Latin of the Vulgate.[20] The first nine chapters, derived ultimately from the faulty text of the ancestral *pervospisok,* had deteriorated to an almost incomprehensible state, and the new translation of the rest was very poor. The Ostrih editors, seeking where possible ("елико мощно") to conform to the Greek, based their Esther on a new translation from the LXX by Maxim the Greek (Maksim Grek); it told a connected and comprehensible story (see Taube-Olmsted).

1.2 For our purpose of establishing and analyzing the oldest attainable form of the Slavonic book of Esther, the Gennadian text has no independent value. As a component of the oldest surviving full Bible manuscript, however, these 164 verses deserve attention.

2 In the early stages of our investigation, it became clear that the two oldest mss, Q and T, from c1390–c1410, reflected an earlier text that was almost identical with the common ancestor of all of the younger copies. In fact, the later mss turned out to contribute remarkably little to the reconstruction of the *pervospisok,* but affirmed that this hypothetical original indeed underlies all of these copies.

2.1 The proliferation of variants from this single mid-14th century copy of Esther (already very faulty) shows two main lines, one rooted in the immediate ancestor of QT, to be dated c1370, and the other—of perhaps c1360—a somewhat vaguer ancestor of W and V, the two copies from close to 1500 that were first available to us. The common readings of QT differ from the common readings of WV in more than 180 cases. In only about 15 are the WV variants to be preferred. Most important are:

(1) 2:9 Q пристрою, T пр̓|строю vs. WV пристрои ю
(2) 2:9 QT стоꙗху vs. WV достоꙗшє
(3) 2:10 Q вѣда, T вѣдѧ vs. WV повѣда
(4) 2:14 QT ложницѧ vs. WV наложница [vs. TnX наложница[М]—best]
(5) 3:13 QT иꙁбавити vs. WV иꙁбивати [vs. Tn иꙁбити—best]
(6) 5:14 QT пришєд vs. W придєши, V приидєши
(7) 8:7 QT июдѣю vs. WV июдѣѧ

and (8) the presence of the phrase въ маслѣ маститѣ и [въ] 6 мц҃ь in 2:12.

[20] Jerome put his translation from the Hebrew first, appending the extra text he found in Gk mss as 10:4–13 and chapters 11–16 (cf. p. 3, n 4). In ms G the MT equivalents occupy nearly 11 pages (fol. 338–343r), the additions about 6 1/2 (f. 343v-346v)

2.2 W and V differ in something more than 30 instances, none clearly reflecting a good reading that could be ascribed to *1350, the *pervospisok*. They probably shared a common ancestor, dating perhaps from c1480.

3 An instructive example of the blending of textual traditions is provided by the important OT codex known as Undol′skij 1 (U, ms l6). Kloss dates it to 1482–83 (1971, n. 15), and asserts, on the basis of evidence from books other than Esther, that it was copied from ms T. Our analysis of Esther in U shows that while U disagrees with T in some minor details (thus in 3:8 ꙁаконы T, ꙁаконъ U; in 2:1 T inappropriately створєнєє but U сътворенїє; in 9:24 T has the Slavonic form мышлѧшє, but U has the Rusian мыслѧшє), there can be no doubt that U's text was copied from T. For example, the Ns плаѵє of 4:3, the erroneous пругъ of 4:11 (for прутъ), the възлюблєнѣкъ of 7:6, and the пооуѵиша of 9:17 (cf. Q поѵиша 'rested') have remained untouched. Far more often the inappropriate or mistaken forms of T were written in U and then corrected by Ivan Černyj (who died in 1490). For example, in 2:6 T's erroneous посломь (for полономь) was reproduced as посломъ but the "с" was erased and a marginal note gives с плѣномъ; in 2:9 стоꙗхꙋ is marked with dots and the margin provides достоꙗшє; in 2:10 любѧшє was copied from T, then бо added by Ivan; in 7:9 болѧшє was written, as in T, and the "ол" erased; in 7:10 the singular повѣси is made plural by an added superscript ша, in 9:22 the perfective послати is corrected to imperfective by an added superscript ы. In over 55 cases U agrees with T, while in 27 Ivan changed a T-variant to agree with the WV equivalent.

3.1 This means that a copyist using U as his model (and taking account of the corrections) would produce a new text that could not be fitted neatly to a genetic sort of family tree. Though we do not know of a copy of Esther that corresponds to the corrected text of U, we do have two other combinations of elements of QT with the WV tradition: the 1499 Gennadius book of Esther and the text of the approximately contemporaneous ms S (15 in our list). In terms of the eight contrasts listed above to illustrate superior, presumably inherited, readings in WV, G always shares the inferior variant with Q(T), agreeing with S only 3 times: GS=QT 1, 2, 4; G=Q, S=WV 3; G=QT, S= WV 5, 6, 7, 8.

4 G's clumsy blend of the QT tradition and the WV line is not unique; it surely existed in more than one copy by c1490. The editors who compiled G had no discernable criteria for selecting a copy of Esther. There is no hint that the translators of the additional chapters might have checked the sense of the Latin text and suggested modifications in the Slavonic, even to coordinate cognate phrases.[21] Rather, we must suppose, Gennadij's agents simply took a copy of Esther that happened to be available; they copied it unquestioningly and tacked on the newly-translated additional text. Gorskij and Nevostruev were aware that this "proto-Gennadian" text was reproduced in at least one ms that apparently did not use the actual Gennadian bible as its model. Ms 11 (GIM, Sinod. 462, 16th century, GorNev 180–81), keeps the old sequence of books (Joshua, Judges, Ruth, Tetrabasileion, Esther), but has the Gennadian text; a crucial detail, as GorNev point out, is that Esther 10:1–3 corresponds to the MT, not the Vulgate. This shows that it was the 1499 Bible that first replaced these verses with the new translation. Ms 7 (Volokalamsk 12, 16th century) agrees with 11, as we conclude from the selected variants Taube noted.[22] A somewhat different witness, to

[21] E.g., in Latin and Greek in 16:1 (E:1) as well as 1:1, the king ruled "from India to Ethiopia," but in G 16:1 has Артаѯесъ ruling ѿ Индєѧ до Еѳиωпїа, while 1:1 sticks with Ахазъверосъ and ѿ оудꙋ даже и до Хꙋсъ.

[22] In terms of contrasts between QT and WV, ms 7 agrees with G and QT some 29 times, and with G and WV in 26; 7 disagrees with G only 6 times.

judge from Meščerskij's citations, is Volokolamsk 9 (his ms 15 or B, our 31).[23] The ms offers a new collocation of OT books, Chronicles, Judith, Esther, Wisdom, and Jeremiah [part]: except for the first part of Esther, all this was newly translated from Latin. If Turilov 1986 is correct in including it in the 15th century, the ms may be regarded as a preliminary copy of texts prepared for the full 1499 copy. Meščerskij's skimpy data indicate that Vlk 9 is close to the Gennadian wording, and we infer from the lack of notes to 10:1–3 (plus the note reporting the variant shared by "ПАВ") that ms 31, like 11 and 7, reflects the 14th-century *pervospisok* in these verses. From the information at our disposal, we conclude that the Esther in the two Volokolamsk codexes is essentially the same.

5 Close to 50 readings in G differ from both QT and WV. Some of these recur in Vlk 12 and/or Vlk 9 (which we will label "B" here to signify that our information comes from M78a). 1:3 цр҇ства GS7, for QTWV цр҇ствиꙗ; 1:6 G ꙋтро^м^, 7 оутрьмь (SQT оутринъмь); 1:19 пр^о^рѵскаѧ GB (a bad replacement) for цр҇ьскаꙗ; 3:4 послуша GB, for послушаше, 5:6 проситвы G7,[24] for просьбы; 8:15 оушибъ GB7, for TQ оушьвъ, SWV оушивъ.[25] In every instance, G's singular readings are inferior; G contributes nothing at all to the reconstruction of the *pervospisok.*[26]

6 Of approximately 170 variants separating QT from WV, G agrees with QT in something over 55%, with WV in 44+%. The selection appears to be random, and the resulting text is inferior. Thus in 1:14 the names are Кар'рона and Софаръ with WV rather than the more correct Карсона, Сефаръ of QT, while in 2:6 иωхониємь reflects the superior spelling of WV and not the ωхониємь of QT. For QT 6:13, ꙁєреси (Haman's wife), G agrees with W on the garbled иꙁреѵєси (V иꙁре҇ѵси). G goes with QT in 5:14 on the mistaken прише҇д, not WV при(и)дєши. In 7:4, for correct прєпродана 'sold,' GWV have the senseless проповѣдана.[27]

7 G's orthography is conservative, but it usually employs "ї" before vowel-letter and often (but by no means systematically) "a" rather than "ѧ" or "ꙗ" in unblocked position, e.g., жєлѣнїа (9:22, Q жєланиꙗ). The jers are frequently written in prefixes and prepositions; the stem сътвори- is particularly likely to contain "ъ."[28] The king's name is Ахаꙁъвєрос- or Ахаꙁвєрос- except for 6:2, Ахасъвєросꙋ. The stem *Jew* is иудє- except for 6:10, иудѣю. *Mede* is always мєдѣиск-, rather than the мадѣиск- of QTWV. As in the other later texts, *Haman* tends to be Аммон- rather than Аман-.

[23] Mathiesen 1983a 27 (#88) mistakenly identifies Volokolamsk 12 with Meščerskij's #15, but M56a explicitly lists Volokolamsk 9, and M78a specifies Volokolamsk 9, relabelling it as B. He never mentions Volokolamsk 12, which, incidentally, is called "9 (12)" in Iosif 1881.

[24] M78a marks this word with superscript "61a" but provides no note.

[25] Taube's notes on ms 7 do not include most of the items where G does not agree with any of the four points of comparison, QTWV; the pervasive agreement of 7 and G in the data we do have leads us to suspect that 7 probably shares most of the readings that by our data seem peculiar to G.

[26] Ms S, on the other hand, has four minor contributions: it alone has распрашєници in 9:19 (the others have -щ-); събраша 2:19 (QTG -шє, WV -бирааше); и исповѣда 6:13 (others omit и); иже 1:11 (QT и єже, GWV и и^ж^). S's 11 singular readings are all inferior; e.g., 1:6 Добромь (for Бобръмь), 9:1 постигнєши (for постигнѧшє). Particularly misleading is the marginal gloss to ѿ ωдоу 'from India' in 1:1: ѿ Вавилона!

[27] S has Каррона and Иωхониємь, but Сєфаръ, Зєрєси, придєши, and прєпродана.

[28] In търт/тълт formulas, "є/о" is normal (пєрв-, молѵиши) in the old text of the first 9 chapters, but in the newly-translated materials from Latin, spellings of the SSl type are common (дръжа-).

Appendix III: **The Tixonravov Chronograph and the Xlebnikov Fragments of Esther**

1 A unique form of the Slavonic book of Esther has been incorporated into a historical work of a type called *chronograph* in Russian and Ukrainian scholarship, the Russian State Library's manuscript Tixonravov 704, (# 22 in our list, p. 12), hereafter Tn. Chronographs were put together by combining passages from the Bible with exegesis from the Church fathers, paraphrases from the Byzantine chronicle of George the Monk (the Sinner, Hamartolos), the chronicle of Malalas, and others, all apparently available in Slavonic translation of earlier date.[29] The 16th-century editor of Tn undertook to revise the presentation of stories of the Old Testament as he knew them from manuscripts he could consult, compilations very close to the *Full Chronographic Paleja* and the Trinity Chronograph (Троицкий хронограф). Oleg Tvorogov has meticulously analyzed the make-up of these manuscripts (1975), but in the absence of full publication of certain texts it is difficult to grapple with some of the basic questions.

2.1 The text of Esther in Tn has no marked beginning and end. It is preceeded by Daniel 6:16–28, which ends at folio 376.3,[30] plus a four-line bridge:

> (Dan 6:28) Данилъ^{ж} оуправи цр^{с}тво Дарьеви. Коура персѧнина (text not otherwise known) слоу^{ж} пре^{д} ц^{с}ремъ. бы^{с} же завѣ^{с}ть ѿтоле. Июдѣем^{м} соущи^{м} в Вавилони ѿ Халдѣи. хотѧщи^{х} и^{х} погꙋбити. па^{ч} же Амонъ милостникъ. цр̄ѧ Дарикѧ. и кнѧгини Иесфрь :х:

This ungrammatical patchwork may perhaps be interpreted, "And Daniel directed the kingdom for Darius and (directed) Cyrus the Persian, serving before the king. And from then on there was envy of the Jews who were in Babylon on the part of the Chaldeans who wanted to wipe them out, especially Amon, the favorite of king Darius, and Queen Esther."[31] The first two verses of Esther have been abridged and modified:

> В лѣ^{т} .г̄. цр^{с}тва Дарьева . наре^{ч}е^{н}наго Ахашвороша цр^{с}твующи в Сиганïи[32] граде. владѣющи емоу .р̄.мъ и .к̄.ма и .ӡ̄ю. князи. над ними же постави старешиноу Данила во всѣхъ.

Thereafter the text is comparable to QTWV.

2.2 The final verse (10:3, folio 395.8) is followed by an otherwise unknown sentence: и бы^{с} Июдѣем радо^{с}ть и велико веселие. живоущим в Вавилоне. Then (395.8–10) a statement known from the Trinity Chronograph: цр̄ь же Дарïи наре^{ч}е^{н}ныи

29 The ordering of topics (both non-biblical and biblical) is based on Ham, which was available no later than 1110; the date and place of translation remains controversial (cf. p 220, n 240). The origins of many other components are even less clear.

30 We have only folios 375v through 395 recto. To judge from the detailed lists of the component fragments of the Full Chronographic Paleja and the Trinity Chronograph (Tvorogov 1975, esp. 243–4, 263–4), it is likely that this passage starts with verse 15.

31 For Daniel we expect оуправи сѧ въ цр̄ствѣ Дарьевѣ и въ цр̄ствѣ Кvра Персѧнина, where the verb means 'prospered, κατηύθυνεν.'

32 Istrin 1912b 20 mistakenly printed Сидонïи.

Ахашворошь. приложи ко ѡц҃емъ своим. цр҃ьства лѣ^т^ .ѕ҃ı The word-order of the first sentence is odd, and the second lacks the expected reflexive particle сѧ, but the sense is appropriate to lead to the next topic. "And there was gladness and great joy for the Jews living in Babylon. And Darius, called Axašvoroš, joined his fathers, he ruled 17 years."[33] Then come two passages based on (but departing significantly from) Hamartolos, dealing with Cyrus and with the partial rebuilding of the temple in Jerusalem (395.10–16, 16–27; Istrin 1920 190.13–15, 191.6–13).[34] The story then turns to Scripture, Daniel 10:1; we may assume that the passage continues for several more verses.

2.3 The text of Esther is divided into two portions by a ten-page interpolation, 381v16–391v19. It is improbable that this was intended by an editor-compiler, for the insertion comes in the middle of 6:13, separating the verb рѣша from its indirect object ємоу. The рѣша of Est 6:13 is followed directly by и ѡбрѣтоша тоу of LXX Jeremiah 48:3 (MT [and OB] 41:3).[35] Surely the scribe who wrote Tn was copying from a codex where folia or gatherings were out of order; he unthinkingly reproduced the pages in the order he found them.

2.4 The interpolated pages show the usual cut-and-paste technique of chronograph compilers: reasonably coherent juxtaposition of items about a person or event with occasional digressions and abrupt changes of theme. Some twenty-one chunks or fragments may be discerned. The first five provide excerpts from Jeremiah and related non-biblical pieces, and correspond to items 70–75 in the Full Chronographic Paleja. The next four deal with Daniel (including Dan 3:31–4:34), as does the tenth, which corresponds to item 23 in the Trinity Chronograph. The rest correspond to items 24–33 of TrCh, except that Tn #20 is an editorial note signifying a return to the biblical text (391v16–17, Вы^ж^ паки на преднѧꙗ возврати^М^ сѧ—note that the initial capital letter should be М).[36]

3 The orthography of Tn is normal for a Ruthenian scribe of the 16th century—a rather careless scribe. The letter "ѣ" is not clearly distinct from "е" or "и" (e.g., гнева 1:18,

[33] The final sentence constitutes the end of item 38 in the Trinity Chronograph, cited by Tvorogov (1975 264): цесарь Дарии Артакъсърѣксъ нареченныи Ахасъ Веросъ...цесарьствовавъ лѣт 17. (Note that Tvorogov chooses to write the Hebrew name as two words.)

[34] Line 15 includes the phrase оуби Ахасвороша, but it involves a series of dubious rearrangements of text that need not concern us here. The significant point is that Darius is equated with Artaxerxes by Hamartolos (189.22–3), цр^с^твова Дарiи Мидѧнинъ иже Астигиꙗнъ и Артарексерексъ лѣт 17. то имаше женоу Мардахѣѡвоу Єстира нар^ч^ена. "Darius the Mede, also known as Astigian [Astyages] and Artaxerxes" is renamed *Axasveros* by East Slavic chroniclers who had access to the Slavonic Esther (cf. previous note). The compiler of Tn introduced *š* into the name from some source with a knowledge of Hebrew; see below. (Esther is Mordecai's wife in LXX and therefore in Greek historiography.)

[35] The wording should be иже сѧ обрѣтоша тоу, '(all the Chaldeans) that were found there' (as in OB). This sort of inaccuracy of detail is to be found throughout the pages of Tn that are available to us—in the biblical and non-biblical passages we are able to check.

[36] It is typical of East Slavic chronographs that the individual chunks are rearranged by different editors. Thus items 12–21 have almost identical texts in TrCh and FP, except that Tn 20 (the editorial note) is unique, as far as we know:

Tn 12–14 = Tr 25–27 = FP 47–9 : Tn 17–8 = Tr 30–1 = FP 87–8 :
Tn 19 = Tr 32 (FP lacks) : Tn 20 unique : Tn 21 = start of Tr 33 = FP 89

(#24 and #27 are based on Ham 188.1–2 and 7–11.) We will not speculate on the order of items before it was disturbed by this interpolation in Esther 6:13. (Istrin 1912b 21 saw item 20 as an *ad hoc* recognition by the editor-scribe that he was returning to the text of Esther; this is precluded by the presence of item 21.)

ѣз[Д]ѣть 6:8, венець 2:17, в' вѣнѣ 1:10 = въ винѣ, восхоти 4:4 = въсхотѣ, во свѣте 8:15 = въ свитѣ), and use of the jer-letters shows no archaisms.[37]

3.1 A striking characteristic is the presence of "ш" in the king's name, which is written Ахас(ъ)верос- in QT, often modified to Ахазверос- in later copies. The scribe is uncertain, however, and writes Аха**ш**воро**ш**- 4 times, Аха**с**воро**ш**- 7 times, but Ах**в**а**с**воро**ш**- twice, with both Ахасв**е**рошь and the clearly erroneous Аховрошa each once for the proper name,[38] along with 6 variants for 7 occurrences of the possessive adjective (Ах**в**асворо**шов**- twice, Аха**с**воро**шев**а, Аха**ш**воро**шев**ѣ, Аха**ш**воро**сов**ѣ, and the distorted Ахасворош**е**ров**а, Ахашво**рово**).

3.2 The name Haman also varies. Амон- appears 7 times in the noun, 6 times in the possessive, but оу Амана once. The dominant spelling is Гаман- (28x as noun, 6x as adj.), with Агаманъ twice, and з Гомано[М] and по Магана each once.

3.3 Queen Vashti is Астиръ twice, but Вастїи or a variant in the other 7 occurrences. However, long after Vashti has been deposed and Esther has been repeatedly mentioned, the possessive Єсфиринѹ is clumsily glossed: е[Ж] е[С] астир'ка толкоует' сѧ 'that is Astirka is interpreted' (cf. p 68, fn 24). Perhaps this is an early reflection of a popular Slavic and Jewish tradition that King Casimir the Great of Poland (1310–70) had a Jewish mistress named Esterke. The story is first told by the Polish historian Jan Długosz in his *Historia polonica*, 1455–80. Its credibility is enhanced by the fact that Długosz was tutor to the children of Casimir's great-grandnephew, Casimir IV (1447–92). (See Shmeruk 1985.)

3.4 All of these spellings clearly come from the idiosyncratic editor of the Tixonravov Chronicle (and/or the scribe of Tn). They are no help in establishing the names in the *pervospisok* *1350.

4 The value of Tn is the retention of text in more than 15 places where QTWVSG have omissions,[39] along with the absence of several words that are obvious additions common to the other copies.[40] Further, Tn sometimes supports an emendation that seems well justified by the sense of the Hebrew.[41]

5 However, Tn's Esther is a very poor text, often distant from the already faulty hypothetical *pervospisok*. The list of omissions, additions, and changes—in comparison with *1350—is well over 375 items. Many are routine, but but the sheer number means that in verse after verse errors combine to destroy grammar and sense.[42] Efforts to repair phrases and sentences have damaged the text further.

37 Within Esther the Rusisms generally correspond to those of QT, but examples in Daniel illustrate that East Slavic scribes could "nativize" words at will (e.g., жереломъ 'throat, voice' 375v10, Dan 6:20, for usual жрѣломь [cf. p. 106, n 2]; ѡзоро[ч] 'shape, look' 389.28, Dan 7:28, but озрачь [if not озрьчь] in all copies noted by Evseev, cf. A1.54).

38 To these we may add the Ахашворошь and Ахасвороша from the non-Esther interpolation, see §2.2 and fn. 5.

39 These range in size from the second syllable in домоу (6:8), through minor items like ємоу (6:6) to the 4 important words in 9:21 and more than half of the words of 9:4.

40 Along with trivialities like сѣмо (6:5) and puzzling redundancies like своихъ и власти (2:3), these include the disruptive бы[с] жє (1:5), Июдѣи (2:7), гл҃ть (3:14), and говѣху (9:17).

41 Thus цр҃ю in 7:9 is preferable to the majority на царѧ; ѿкрыто (8:13) is far better than ѿкрытомъ; Вихванъ (2:21) conforms to normal rules of transcription of Hebrew via Greek to Slavic (and Бихванъ, a troublesome exception, belongs to *1360); оумыслыша in 9:1 is precisely what might be predicted (while оуслышаша has nothing to do with the context).

42 About a dozen words are omitted in 2:19–20 (Мардоухаи же...заповѣдалъ еи Мардѹхаи) and in

5.1 Here are some of the simpler errors: на ны (= на ню 2:1), всегда (нъ єгда 2:14), столпъ (столъ 3:1), гоненїе (говѣние 4:3), распаленїе (расповѣдание 4:7), дивѧхоу сѧ (жидовѧху сѧ 8:17), просто (про что есть 4:5), простъ (простерыи 4:14), по^{д} градом своим (по г. с. 9:2), на^{д} домовъ гамановым (надъ домъмъ Амановомь 8:2), егда гл҃а емоу (да(сть) емоу 4:8), оуставиша на^{м} (оуставити имъ 9:21), оубо зрите по магана (оубързите по Амана 5:5). Some changes in grammatical form: придоша (придѧше 2:13), заповеда (заповѣдаше 8:9), приступиша (приступаше 9:27), ражьж^{д}еть^{с} (=pres, wrong, for correct aor ражьже сѧ, 1:12), поклонѧющих сѧ (покланѧху сѧ 3:2), наплнѧша^{с} (-ху сѧ 2:12), писахом и печѧтахом (= -хоу(ть) 3:12), поусти^{х} и^{х} (пустити ихъ 3:8); да аще погибноуть (да аще погыбноу да погыбноу 4:16).

5.2 Some additions are harmless (*ко* сосоу^{д} = съсоуду 1:7, и посла ї книги *црь* 1:22, соукно *его* 4:4, ѡбнесена бы^{с} *Єсфирь* 2:17), some are misleading (ѡтроци црви *и* слꙋги его 1:22, not two groups, but apposition—the young men *are* his servants; всѣх женъ *его* 2:17, his own wives), and some are disturbing (злоба *его* 7:7 complicates an already difficult sentence; Моурдоухаи, added before прѧмо in 4:6 and и приде, tacked onto the end of 4:2, are confusing). An expanded definition may cause only minor trouble (e.g., по всеи земли и во градѣх 8:11, for по всѣмъ градомъ), or it may wreck a verse (as when the мужь вражебныи of 7:6 reappears in 7:7 as жоуж вражебныи after ѿ Єсфири црци).

5.3 In 4:14 there is superfluous negation (аще не молчиши). In 1:17 an expected negation is missing twice (доньдеже возванъ боудеть; ıазъ въ^{з}вана бы^{х} приидe^{т}); in the latter example the 3pres verb, instead of infinitive, reduces the sentence to chaos. Expected а не прѣступи{т} 'and it (the decree) will not pass over' (? be revoked, see C1:19) is transformed to зане пристоупоу (? 'for I will draw near').[43]

5.4 More complex is the beginning of 1:8: питьба волна безмоужна. The first word is a reasonable formation, but is not attested elsewhere (L13.711). Волна might mean 'free; voluntary' (cf. C1:8). Безмоужьнъ used of a man is 'not a (real) husband, ἄνανδρος' (OCS, the Gk means also 'effeminate'), or (in *OCS hymns, see Koschmieder) 'not having known a man, virgin ἀπείρανδρος.' Can this phrase be assigned a meaning?

5.5 There are some fairly certain substitutions of lexemes: денничныи (sense unclear, 4x for дънѣшнии 'inner' C4:11); книги сонныꙗ (книги памѧтныꙗ C6:1); Амонъ злокозниvыи (Аманъ въꙁлюблєникъ 7:6); падаꙗ бо (аще падаꙗ 6:13); готовымъ (оуготованымъ 3:14), скоро (въскорѣ 3:15); любо (оулюбѣеть 8:8); ѡхаби сѧ 'neglect, cease' [inappropriate here] (оуѡхвоти сѧ 8:15); оутвержениꙗ (оувѣрениꙗ Н 'of truth'! 9:30); печѧленъ (желєнъ 6:12), жалость (желѧ 4:3) and ѿ жалости и^{х} (ѿ

9:14–15 (законъ в Соусане граде . . . [и] паки), 9 in 8:6 (видѣти /злобу . . . видѣти/ пагꙋбоу), 4 or 5 at the end of 8:8 and the beginning of 8:9. Elsewhere omissions are shorter and often combined with other textual disturbances, e.g., по три нощи 4:16, for по три дн҃и дн҃ь и нощь.

43 Instead of the faulty ıако нє пришла Вастиꙗ царицѧ of the other copies (cf. C1:19), Tn has ıако не пришли црци Васта, implying a change of subject, with Vashti the queen as indirect object (if the reader is able to identify "Vasta" at all), but still the wrong tense. Note that the form црци stands where Ns is required also in 1:16, 8:2, and 9:31. For ср^{д}ца instead of Ns queen, see C5:12, fn 10.

жєланиꙗ 9:22), cf. L14.1; доброзрачноу (добровӡорну 2:3) and и кр҇сна ѕело (добровӡорьна 2:7).[44]

Less clear are alternate derivational stems: Июдѣꙗнинъ (Июдѣи 3:4), работни^{М} свои^{М} (рабомъ своимъ 6:13); изыма (ꙗтъ she took/grasped [the end of the scepter] 5:2) is a poor choice, for иӡъимати is almost always specifically 'capture (an enemy)'—and imperfective. In 6:2 на^{Д}верники corresponds to Q's Accdu двьрника, but in Tn's changed context (see C6:2) this is probably to be read as preposition plus Ap noun. In 8:10, со приставни^{К} represents a distortion of со приставы коньникы.

5.6 Lexico-syntactic shifts can be seen in по ȣлицамъ гра^{Д}ски^{М} (оулицѧмъ града 6:11) and людии тоє земли (людии ꙁємныхъ 8:17); the first replaces a foreign noun adjunct by an adjective, overwhelmingly the norm for OCS and early Rusian, but the second substitutes the foreign construction for the native one. For 6:4 we may conjecture that it took a series of errors and/or emendations to produce the slightly odd къ дворȣ цр҇вȣ внȣтрь 'to (as far as) the king's court inside (?)' from the cumbersome къ двору дому царєва вънѣшнєго 'to the outer court' (cf. L1.22).

5.7 There are strings of letters that seem to be words but fail to make sense: иже бѣ и = и жрѣбии C3:17; збирати и стѧжати и ?'to gather and gain/acquire and' (сбирати и *стоꙗти на душахъ C8:11); оуже шелково во поут женѣ (оушивъ шєлковъ лєптужєнъ 8:15). In 8:15 Mordecai is dressed во червци (rather than ꙷьрви, cf. L5.41); we will not speculate how the scribe might have read the word or what it meant.

5.8 For a radical example of editing, here is verse 1:6 (see comm.):

Q etc.	бобръмь и оутринъмъ и ꙷьрвємь сниманънъ вьрвьми шьлковыми
Tn	со сребром полаты и шатры сниманы. верьв'ми шелковыми
	и лєптугъ на главахъ срєбрєныхъ и стълпи мрамордны
	и главы. лептоугомъ и шатромъ сребрѧным. и столпие мраморено. и полатах
	ложа ӡлата и срєбрєна на близку камєниꙗ драгаго стѣны и оустьꙗ
	и ложа сребрена позлащена. на блескȣ камени драгаго. и стѣны ѡкр^{С}тьныꙗ

We leave it to our readers to speculate about how these textual differences came about.

6 Apart from the lacuna-filling words and passages, what special items has Tn retained from *1350? Since we can confidently ascribe a long list of far-reaching changes to the scribes and editors in the history of Tn, we must be cautious in making conclusions on the basis of passages where the other available copies have readings that are questionable.

6.1 Above in 5.5 are three examples where the unusual root-shape *žel-* 'sorrow' of other witnesses is represented in Tn by more usual *žal-* or the ubiquitous *pečal-*. Q's participial оуготованымъ 'prepared' is opposed to Tn's simple готовымъ 'ready' in 3:14, but приготованом (for the same H) in 8:13 is also in Tn (with updated spelling). In these cases we have chosen to treat Tn's variants as secondary.

44 The spelling кр҇сна is surely to be read as the common adjective красна 'beautiful,' but the stem that is usually spelled with the abbreviating titlo is крестенъ (крьстьнъ) 'of the cross.'

6.2 The inappropriate particle(s) бы in 3:9 can be eliminated by Tn's probably superior reading, аще цр҃ви оубо доволно было. The awkward first person plural створимъ is paired in Tn with the appropriate singular сотворю in 5:6 but not in the other two examples (see C5:6). This could be an "unharmonized" remnant or an intelligent innovation.

6.2 Tn's phrase прѧмо двереи полатных 5:1 might be preferred to прѧмо дверемъ полаты because (1) all texts have genitive with прѧмо in 4:6, and (2) the adjectival modifier seems more natural than the noun adjunct, see 5.6 above. Since, however, the dative is far more usual with SSl прѣмо and ESl прѧмо, and the slightly artificial genitive noun adjunct is attested in Esther and elsewhere, there is no reliable basis for making a choice.

6.3 In 7:10 the metaphorical flame of the king's anger *died away,* was extinguished, потухну—a normal form of a productive type—in the majority, but Tn has потоуше—an obsolete form that is out of place in Rus′ and unexpected even in Macedonia or Croatia of 1350. It seems improbable that a Ruthenian bookman of 1350 (not to speak of 1450) could generate this form; see C7:10.

6.31 The word-order in QT on the whole agrees so closely with the Hebrew that it is plausible to assume that the Slavic translation was even more consistent. Therefore in 8:9 we presume that two nouns attested only in Tn, посадникѡм и тивоуном, have been reversed, so that the lexeme тиоунъ is associated ultimately with *'ḥšdrpnym* (as in 3:12 and 9:3, see L2.23). C8:10 notes that the postposed adjective in на коних бърздых (8:14) is a rare exception; as a rule, an adjective comes before the noun it modifies. Tn removes the exception by preposing the adjective, на борзых конех. But in view of the complex postposed definition in Hebrew (see C8:10), and the presence of the word *horses* in MT 8:10 but not 8:14, we are left with the suspicion that the hypothetical Greek intermediary may have had a phrase that caused difficulty to the Slavic translator. In 2:23 Tn miscopies a dual, повѣшена бы^с^ты ѡба на древе. Overlooking the confusion this might introduce (?'thou wast hanged'), we may see this as evidence that QT's повѣшєна быста на древє ѡба is secondary, for Tn's order agrees with H.

6.32 Against this are numerous examples of rearrangement that unquestionably belong to the history of Tn.[45] Somewhat more complex are: 6:3 ѡтроци слугы цр҃ви = ѡтроци царєви слугы єго; 9:28 поминающи д҃ни сии = и д҃нии сиꙗ поминающє суть.

7 A full study of the non-Esther texts in these folia of Tn is a task for the future, but they appear to be as bad as Esther. A look at the lines from Hamartolos and a sounding of passages from Daniel reveal the same sort of wretched sentences that imply a history of inept and indifferent scribes. In both the Hamartolos fragments rearrangement of words has totally confused individuals and distorted the over-all meaning. The Daniel passages clearly are derived from an *OCS version, but with such destructive modifications as to be barely recognizable. The extent of damage these bits of Hamartolos and Daniel have undergone is

45 Here are some relatively uncomplicated deviations in word-order; Tn's variant is first: 2:6 бѧше полоненъ = п. б.; 3:5 припадаꙗ ни приклѧкаꙗ = приклѧкаꙗ ни припадаꙗ; 6:1 во снѣ цр҃ь = царь въ снѣ; 6:2 и прочтены быша = и быша п.; 6:14 бѧше оустроила = оу. б.; 7:5 р^ч^е цр҃ь Ахасверошь = рєѵє Ахасверосъ цр҃ь; 7:9 единъ староста тых = єдин тѣх тивунъ; 8:11 и оуби^т^ и погоуби^т^ и растворити = и растворити и оубити и погубити; 9:2 чл҃вкъ никии = никыижє ѵл҃къ; 9:25 на древѣ со сы^н^ми = съ сынъми на дрєвѣ. We may therefore postulate that the order of words witnessed only by Tn is not reliable if it disagrees with H.

visible because we have much older copies that guarantee the existence of reasonably literate Slavic sentences in the 11th century. They lend credence to the hypothesis that Esther, in its retrievable *1350 form, may well go back to that early stage of burgeoning Slavic written culture.[46]

8 The Xlebnikov fragments of Esther

In the Xlebnikov chronicle, copied c1575 (cf. E4.3), two fragments of Esther, 2:1–21a and 9:2b-17 (+2:1) are tacked onto the end of the entry for 1291 without any indication of change of subject, cf. E4.3, p. 16. Short as it is, this material contains a dozen singular readings. One is definitely superior (повѣсѧ^т, see C9:13), and another is probably to be preferred (дары еѧ дати еи 2:9, vs. Q дары єи даꙗти єи). Three represent purposeful changes that eliminate variants (не поведоша, see L6.31, n 76). One shows an unsuccessful effort to clarify a passage (see p. 95, n 22).

The agreement of X with Tn includes—in addition to the text missing elsewhere in 9:4 and the preferred spellings of наложницам (2:14) and Пармаста (9:9)—a number of inferior readings, particularly the long omissions in 2:19–20 and 9:14–15 (cf. fn to §5 above) and the sense-distorting р^чеши (for речаше) of 2:15. Where Tn deviates from most texts, X goes with the majority in nearly 30 cases, including the presence of interpolated говѣахоу in 9:17. In 2:6 the majority has съ ѡхониємь царємь Июдинымь; X has an a-stem desinence on the name (ѡхонї^єю), as does Tn. Yet Tn has changed the order and distorted the final adjective (со цр҃мъ ѡхонїею июдеискимъ). The stemma on p. 15 does not attempt to deal with the fact that QXTn share the distorted врачюющи^с and познаваше (vs. TWV with the correct forms), but in the middle of the verse (2:14), between those two erroneous forms, XTn have the correct наложницам and QTV the dubious ложницѧ (and W a less satisfactory наложница).

[46] For Jeremiah we assume an OCS translation, but no old copies have survived; our only point of comparison is the 1581 Ostrih Bible, which is not much younger than Tn. The first few lines include: OB 41:5 (= LXX 48:5) ѿ сали^мма 'from Salem' but Tn ѿ єрл^сма 'from Jerusalem'; OB п҃ моужь, '80 men' but Tn .н҃ моу^ж, '50 men'; OB 41:9 сеи наполни Исмаилъ ꙗзвеныхъ '(even) this (pit) Ishmael filled with the wounded (*or* slain, τραυματιῶν)' but in Tn the last word is ꙗзыкъ 'with tongues (? with infidels?).' Perhaps the short Gp *ꙗзвьнъ confused an earlier scribe, but in any case Tn's text is hopeless.

References

A[bramovi]č, D[mitrij I.]

1917 [Review of Barac 1916] *Библиографическая летопись,* Общество любителей древней письменности, *Известия,* **III**, 54–58.

Abramovyč, Dmytro [I.]

1930 *Киево-Печерський Патерик.* Пам'ятки мови та письменства давньої України, том IV. Kyiv.

Adrianova-Peretc, Varvara Pavlovna et al.

1958 *История русской литературы в трех томах.* Moscow–Leningrad.

Afanas′eva, E. V., and Švarc, E. M.

1980 'Древнейший славянский перевод книги Иова (по пергаменным рукописям).' *Источниковедение литературы Древней Руси,* 7–32. Leningrad.

Aitzetmüller, Rudolf

1958–75 *Das Hexameron des Exarchen Johannes.* I–VII. Graz.

Alekseev, Anatolij Alekseevič

1980 *"Песнь песней" в древней славяно-русской письменности.* 2 vols. (=*Предварительные публикации,* 133–4, Проблемная группа по экспериментальной и прикладной лингвистике.) Инст. русского языка, АН СССР. Moscow.

1981 '"Песнь песней" по русскому списку XVI века в переводе с древнееврейского оригинала,' *Палестинский сборник* **27** 63–79.

1983 'К опредлению объема литературного наследия Мефодия (четий перевод Песни песней),' *Труды Отдела древнерусской литературы* **37** 229–55.

1984 *Переводческое наследие Кирилла и Мефодия и его исторические судьбы* (*Песнь песней в древней славянской письменности*), Афтореферат диссертации, ЛГУ, Leningrad.

1985 'Проект текстологического исследования кирилло-мефодиевского перевода Евангеля,' *Советское славяноведение* **1985/1**, 82–94.

1986 'Der Stellenwert der Textologie bei der Erforschung altkirchenslavischer Übersetzungstexte,' *Die Welt der Slaven* **31** 415–37.

1987a 'Переводы с древнееврейских оригиналов в древней Руси,' *Russian Linguistics* **XI** 1–20.

1987b 'Пути стабилизации языковой нормы в России XI–XII вв.,' *Вопросы языкознания* **1987/2**, 34–46.

1993 'Русско-еврейские литературные связи до 15 века,' *Jews and Slavs,* vol. I, ed. Wolf Moskovich, Shmuel Shvarzband, and Anatoly Alekseev, 44–75. Jerusalem–St. Petersburg.

1996 'Кое-что о переводах в Древней Руси (по поводу статьи Фр. Дж. Томсона «Made in Russia»,' *Труды Отдела древнерусской литературы* **49** 278–95.

Alekseev, Anatolij A., and Lixačeva, Ol′ga Petrovna

1978 'Супрасльский сборник 1502–1507 гг.' *Материалы и сообщения по фондам рукописной и редкой книги БАН СССР,* **54–88**. Leningrad.

Altbauer, Moshé
1960 [Review of Мещерский 1958a, in Hebrew], *Kirjat Sepher* (Bibliographic Quarterly of the Jewish National and University Library) **35**, no. 2, 203–209, Jerusalem.
1988 *The "Vilnius" Version of the Oldest Russian Translation of the Book of Esther (Vilnius Codex 52).* Jerusalem.
1992 *The Five Biblical Scrolls in a 16th Century Jewish Translation into Belorussian.* Jerusalem.

Altbauer, Moshé, and Horace G. Lunt, ed.
1978 *An Early Slavonic Psalter from Rus'.* Cambridge, MA.

Altbauer, Moshé and Moshé Taube
1984 'The Slavonic Book of Esther: When, Where, and from What Language was it Translated?' *Harvard Ukrainian Studies* **8** 304–320.

Andersen, F. I.
1983 '2 (Slavonic Apocalypse of) Enoch,' in Charlesworth 1983, pp. 91–221.

Arxangel'skij, A. S.
1888 *Очерки из истории западно-русской литературы XVI–XVII* вв. Moscow.

Arxipov, Andrej
1994 'К истории славянского перевода книги *Эсфирь*.' *Stanford Slavic Studies* **8** 105–24.
1995 'Славянская книга Эсфирь. К истории перевода,' in *По ту сторону Самбатиона: Этюды о русско-еврейских культурных, языковых и литературных контактах в X–XVI веках* (Monuments of Early Russian Literature, vol. 9), pp. 241–63. Oakland, CA.

Barac, German Markovič
1916 *Источники Слова о законе и благодати и Евангелистой песни. К вопросу о еврейском элементе в древне-русской литературе*, Kiev [reprinted in *Собрание трудов по вопросу о еврейском элементе в памятниках древне-русской письменности* (Paris, 1927), pp. 823–900].
1924 *О составителях «Повести временных лет» и ее источниках, преимущественно еврейских.* Berlin.

Beck, Hans-Georg
1971 *Geschichte der byzantinischen Volksliteratur* (=*Byzantinisches Handbuch*, 2–er Teil, 3–er Band). Munich.

Bickerman, Elias J.
1967 *Four Strange Books of the Bible: Jonah, Daniel, Koheleth, Esther.* New York.

Birnbaum, Henrik
1973 'On Some Evidence of Jewish Life and Anti-Jewish Sentiments in Medieval Russia,' *Viator* **4** 225–55. Los Angeles.

Blass, Friedrich (ed. Albert Debrunner)
1931 *Grammatik des neutestamentlichen Griechisch*[6]. Göttingen.

Blondheim, David Simon
1925 *Les parlers judeo-romans et la Vetus Latina: Étude sur les rapports entre les traductions bibliques en langue romane des Juifs au moyen âge et les anciennes versions.* Paris.

Bojkovsky, Georg, and Rudolf Aitzetmüller
1984–90 *Paraenesis: die altbulgarische Übersetzung von Werken Ephraims des Syrers.* 5 vol. Freiburg i. Br.

Briquet, Charles M.

1907 *Les filigranes. Dictionnaire historique des marques du papier dès leur apparition vers 1282 jusqu'en 1600.* Vol. 1–4. Geneva.

Bugoslavskij, Sergej

1924 [Review of Barac 1924] *Печать и революция*, Июль-сентябрь, книга 5–6, 400–401. Moscow.

Buslaev, Fedor Ivanovič

1861 *Историческая христоматия церковно-славянского и древне-русского языков*. Moscow.

Charlesworth, James H.

1983 *The Old Testament Pseudepigrapha, Vol. I, Apocalyptic Literature and Testaments.* Garden City, NY.

Complutensian Polyglot Bible.

(*Biblia polyglotta.* Alcalá de Henares. 6 vol. 1514–17.)

Čudov Ps[alter] = *Чудовская псалтырь XI века.* (Памятники старославянского языка, т. III, вып. 1.), ed. Valerii Pogorelov, St. Petersburg, 1910.

Daniel, Susan

1983 'Expressions with *head, mouth, heart* in the Septuagint Translation of the Bible,' [in Hebrew], *Hebrew Language Studies presented to Professor Zeev Ben Ḥayyim,* [in Hebrew] ed. M. Bar-Asher et alii, pp. 161–172. Jerusalem.

Dietze, Joachim

1977 *Frequenzwörterbuch zur Synodalhandschrift der Ersten Novgoroder Chronik.* Martin-Luther-Universität Halle-Wittenberg, *Wissensch. Beiträge,* **13** (F 11). Halle (Saale).

Dinekov, Petъr, ed.

1991–93 *Симеонов сборник* (*по Светославовия препис от* 1073 *г.*), 1. Изследвания и текст, 2. Речник-Индекс. Sofia.

Dobrev, Ivan

1983 'Из българската историческа лексикология,' *Български език* **33/2** 136–41.

Dubrovina, V. F.

1982 "К изучению лексики переводного памятника," *История русского языка, Исследования и тексты* (Инст. русского яз., АН СССР), 198–226. Moscow.

1987 'Следы греческих конструкций в сочинении древнерусского автора,' in *История русского языка и лингвистическое источниковедение*, ed. V. V. Ivanov, pp. 88–98.

Dumitrescu, Maria

1973–76 *Синайский патерик. Указатель слов и форм.* I–II. Bucharest.

Durnovo, Nikolaj N.

1969 *Введение в историю русского языка*^{2}. Moscow.

Eckert, Rainer and Kirill Kostov

1986 'Zur Figura Etymologica im Altbulgarischen,' *Palaeobulgarica* **10/3** 40–48.

Euch. = *Euchologium sinaiticum, Starocerkvenoslovanski glagolski spomenik,* II. del, *Text s komentarjem,* ed. Rajko Nahtigal. Ljubljana, 1942.

Evseev, Ivan E.

1898 'Заметки по древнеславянскому переводу св. писания,' *Известия Императорской Академии наук* **8**, ч. 2, 339–44.

1902 'Книга Пророка Даниила в переводе жидовствующих, по рукописи XVI в.,' *Чтения Общества истории и древностей российских* **202**, кн. 3, отд. 2, 127–64.

1905 *Книга Пророка Даниила в древне-славянском переводе.* Moscow.

1912 'Очерки по истории славянского перевода Библии,' вып. 2, *Христианское чтение* **92** 1343–1374.

Farrall, Melissa Lee

1981 *A Jewish Translator in Kievan Rus': a Critical Edition and Study of the Earliest Redaction of the Slavic "Life of Moses"* (Brown University Dissertation), University Microfilms, Ann Arbor MI.

Feldman, Louis H.

1984 *Josephus and Modern Scholarship, 1937–1980.* Berlin–New York.

Filin, Fedot Petrovič, ed.

1965– *Словарь русских народных говоров.* Moscow–Leningrad.

Flusser, David

1978–80 *The Josippon [Josephus Gorionides]*, edited with an Introduction, Commentary and Notes, 2 vols. [in Hebrew = *Sefer Yosippon*], Jerusalem.

Franklin, Simon

1982 'Some Apocryphal Sources of Kievan Historiography,' *Oxford Slavonic Papers* **15** 1–27.

Franko, Ivan

1896 *Апокріфи и легенди.* t. I. L′viv.

Freidhof, Gerd

1984 'Problems of Glossality in Newly Translated Parts of the Gennadius and Ostrog Bibles of 1499 and 1580–1.' In Henrik Birnbaum and Michael S. Flier (eds.), *Medieval Russian Culture* (=*California Slavic Studies* **12**), Los Angeles, 1984, pp. 343–64.

Garkavi, Abram Jakovlevič

1884 'Следы знакомства с еврейским языком в древней русской письменности,' *Еврейское обозрение*, янв. 1884, 57–64.

Gebhardt, Oskar

1875 *Graecus Venetus. Pentatuechi Proverbiorum, Ruth, Cantici, Ecclesiastae, Threnorum, Danielis versio graeca: ex unico Bibliothecae S. Marci Venetae codice.* Leipzig.

Gehman, Henry S.

1953 'Hebraisms of the Old Greek Version of Genesis,' *Vetus Testamentum* **3** 141–48.

Goetz, Leopold Karl

1905 *Kirchenrechtliche und kulturgeschichtliche Denkmäler Altrusslands nebst Geschichte des russischen Kirchenrechts* (=Kirchenrechtliche Abhandlungen, 18. u. 19. Heft), Stuttgart.

Golb, Norman and Omeljan Pritsak

1982 *Khazarian Hebrew Documents of the Tenth Century.* Ithaca NY and London.

1997 *Хазарско-еврейскые документы X века.* Ed. V. Ja. Petruxin. Jerusalem.

Gordis, Robert

1976 'Studies in the Esther Narrative,' *Journal of Biblical Literature* **95** 43–58. [Cited from reprint in Moore 1982, pp. 408–423.]

Gorskij, Aleksandr Vasil′evič and Kapiton Ivanovič Nevostruev

1855 *Описание славянских рукописей Московской синодальной библиотеки,* отд. 1. Moscow.

Gribble, Charles
1974 'Origins of the Slavic Short Version of the *Life of Nifont*,' *International Journal of Slavic Linguistics and Poetics* **17** 9–19.
Grossfeld, Bernard.
1983 *The First Targum to Esther According to the ms. Paris Hebrew 110 of the Bibliothèque nationale*. New York.
Gudzij, Nikolai Kallinikovič
1958 'Новейшие издание и исследование выдающегося переводного памятника древней Руси,' *Известия АН СССР, Отделение литературы и языка*, **17** 561–69.
1960 'Литература Киевской Руси и древнейшие инославянские литературы,' *Исследования по славянскому литературоведению и фольклористике*, 7–60. Moscow.
1962 *Хрестоматия по древнерусской литературе XI-XVII веков*[7]. Moscow.
Ham[artolos] = Istrin, 1920.
Hanhart, Robert, ed.
1966 *Esther* (=*Septuaginta: Vetus Testamentum Graecum, Auctoritate Academiae Litterarum Gottingensis editum,* vol. **VIII, 3**). Göttingen.
Hansack, Ernst
1978 'Zur Technik der Doppelübersetzung. Zwei Beiträge aus slavistischer Schrift.' *Anzeiger für slavische Philologie* **18** 79–127.
1979 "Zur Übersetzungsstil des Exarchen Iohannes" *Die Welt der Slaven* **24** 121–71.
1981 "Die theoretischen Grundlagen des Übersetzungsstil des Exarchen Iohannes" *Die Welt der Slaven* **26** 15–36.
1990–91 *Die Lexik des altrussischen Version des "Jüdischen Krieges" des Flavius Josephus,* vols 1–3. Regensburg.
1992 Review of Meščerskij 1958a, *Anzeiger für slavische Philologie* **21** 183–85.
Haupt, Paul
1908 'Critical Notes on Esther,' *American Journal of Semitic Languages and Literature* **24** (1907–08) 97–186. [Cited from reprint in Moore 1982, pp. 1–90.]
Hendler, Maximilian
1993 'Zamar'nyj, ein altrussisches hapax legomenon,' *Anzeiger für slavische Philologie* **22**/1 97–103.
Heppell, Muriel
1989 *The* Paterik *of the Kievan Caves Monastery*. Cambridge, MA.
Hesseling, Dirk C.
1901 'Le livre de Jonas,' *Byzantinische Zeitschrift* **10** 208–17.
Ilčev, St.
1974 *Речник на редки, остарели и диалектни думи в литература на XIX и XX век*. Sofia.
Istrin, Vasilij Mixailovič
1893 *Александрия русских хронографов*. Moscow.
1897a 'Первая книга Хроники Иоанна Малалы.' *Записки имп. АН,* ser. VIII, Историко-филологическое отделение, т. 1, кн. 3, 1–29.
1897b Откровение Мефодия Патарского; Апокрифические Видения Даниила в византийской и славяно-русской литературах. Moscow.
1898 *Замечания о составе толковой палеи,* (=*Сборник Отделения русского языка и словесности Императорской академии наук* **65** 6).

1902 'Хроника Иоанна Малалы в славянском переводе: книга вторая,' *Летопись Историко-филологического общества при имп. Новороссийском университете,* **7**, Византийско-славянское отдел. 437–86. Odessa.

1905 'Хронограф Академии наук № 45.13.4 (из Вологды),' *Летопись историко-филологического общества при Новороссийском университете,* **13** 314–41. Odessa.

1910 'Пятая книга Хроники Иоанна Малалы.' *Летопись Историко-филологического общества при имп. Новороссийском университете,* **16,** *Виз.-слав. отд.,* т. IX, ч. II, 1–51. Odessa.

1911 *Хроника Иоанна Малалы в славянском переводе, кн. шестая и седьмая.* (*Сборник Отделения русского языка и словесности Императорской академии наук* **89** kn. 3.

1912a *Хроника Иоанна Малалы в слав. переводе, кн. восьмая и девятая.* (*Сборник Отделения русского языка и словесности Императорской академии наук* **89**, kn. 7.)

1912b 'Особый вид Еллинского Летописца из собрания Тихонравова,' *Известия Отделения русского языка и словесности Императорской академии наук* **XVII**/3, 1–30.

1913 *Хроника Иоанна Малалы в славянском переводе, кн.* 11*ая*–14*ая.* (*Сборник Отделения русского языка и словесности Императорской академии наук* **90**, кн. 2.)

1914 *Хроника Иоанна Малалы в славянском переводе, кн.* 15*ая*–18*ая.* (=*Сборник Отделения русского языка и словесности Императорской академии наук* **91**, кн. 2.)

1920–30 *Хроника Георгия Амартола в древнем славянорусском переводе*, 3 vols. Petrograd–Leningrad. (Reprint, Slavische Propyläen, Bd. 135, 1–2. Munich, 1972.)

1934–38 *La prise de Jérusalem,* I–II, Paris.

Izbornik 1073 = Dinekov 1991.

Izbornik 1076 = Kotkov 1965.

Jagić, Vatroslav

1913 *Entstehungsgeschichte der kirchenslavischen Sprache*[3], Berlin.

Jobes, Karen H.

1996 *The Alpha-Text of Esther: Its Character and Relationship to the Masoretic Text.* Atlanta.

Karskij, Evfimij F.

1897 'Западно-русский сборник XV в. Имп. Публ. Библ. в С.-Петербурге Q.I.№ 391,' [reprinted in] *Труды по белорусскому и другим славянским языкам* Moscow. 1962.

Kazakova, Natalija Aleksandrovna, and Lur′e, Jakov Solomonovič

1955 *Антифеодальные еретические движения на Руси, XIV–начала XVI века*. Moscow–Leningrad.

Keenan, Edward L.

1978 Review of SRJaXI–XVII, vol. 1, *Russian Linguistics* **3** 63–80.

Kiparsky, Valentin

1967 *Russische historische Grammatik,* Bd. II. Heidelberg.

Klenin, Emily
1983 *Animacy in Russian: A New Interpretation.* Columbus, OH.
Kloss, Boris Mixailovič
1971 'Книги, редактированные и писанные Иваном Черным,' *Записки Отдела рукописей Государственна ордена Ленина Библиотеки СССР им. Ленина* **32** 61–72.
Kolesov, Vladimir Viktorovič
1991 'О руссизмах в составе древнерусских текстов,' *Древнерусский язык домонгольской поры*, pp. 121–55. Leningrad.
Kopanev, Aleksandr Il′ich, Margarita Vladimirovna Kukuškina, V. F. Pokrovskaja.
1965 *Исторические сборники XV-XVII вв.* (=*Описание Рукописного отдела Библиотеки Академии наук СССР*, т. 3, вып. 2).
Kopečný, František
1973–80 *Etymologický slovník slovanských jazyků, Slova gramatická a zájmena. svazek 1, Předložky, koncové partikule. sv. 2, Spojky, částice, zájmena a zájmenná adverbia.* Prague.
Koschmieder, Erwin
1955 *Die ältesten Novgoroder Hirmologien-Fragmente*, 2 (Abhandlungen d. Bayerischen Akademie der Wissenschaften, Phil-hist. Kl, NF, Heft 37). Munich.
Kotkov, Sergei I., ed.
1965 *Изборник* 1076 *года*. Moscow.
1971 *Успенский сборник XII–XIII.* Moscow.
Kovtun, Ljudmila S.
1975 *Лексикография в Московской Руси XVI–начала XVII в.* Leningrad.
Krys′ko, Vadim B.
1994 'Заметки о древненовгородском диалекте (I. Палатализации),' *Вопросы языкознания* **1994/5** 28–45.
Kudrjavceva, I. M., ed.
1957 *Артаксерксово действо: Первая пьеса русского театра XVII. в.* Moscow–Leningrad.
Kul′bakin, S. M.
1901 'Отчет Отделения русского языка и словесности Им. АН о занятиях в книгохранилищах Москвы и Петербурга с 25–го сентября по 23–е декабря 1898 г.,' *Сборник Отделения русского языка и словесности Императорской академии наук* **69/3** 1–54.
Kulik, Aleksander
1995 'О несохранившемся греческом переводе книги Эсфирь,' *Славяноведение* **1995/2** 76–80.
Kuz′min, Apollon G.
1977 *Начальные этапы древнерусского летописания.* Moscow.
Lampe, G. W. H., ed.
1961 *A Patristic Greek Lexicon.* Oxford.
de Lange, Nicholas
1993 'The Jews of Byzantium and the Greek Bible. Outline of the Problems and Suggestions for Future Research,' in Sed-Rajna, Gabrielle, ed., *Rashi 1040–1990. Hommage à Ephraïm E. Urbach* (Paris, 1993), pp. 203–10.
La Sor, William S.
1978–79 *Handbook of Biblical Hebrew: An Inductive Approach Based on the Hebrew Text of Esther*, 2 vol., Grand Rapids MI.

Lavrov, Petr A.

1933 'Библейские книги 1507 года,' *Slavia* **12** 85–112.

Lebedev, Vasilij

1890 *Славянский перевод кн. Иисуса Навина по сохранившимся рукописям и Острожской Библии*. St. Petersburg.

Leonid, Arximandrit

1883–85 'Сведения о славянских рукописях поступивших из книгохранилища Свято-Троицкой Сергиевой Лавры в библиотеку Троицкой Духовной Академии,' *Чтения Общества истории и древностей российских* 1883: 1, 2, 4; 1884: 3, 4; 1885:1.

1893 *Систематическое описание славяно-российских рукописей собрания графа А. С. Уварова*. ч. 1. Moscow.

Lépissier, Jacques

1968 *Les* Commentaires des Psaumes *de Théodoret (version slave)*. Paris.

Levenson, Jon D.

1997 *Esther. A Commentary*. Louisville, KY.

Lixačev, Dmitrij S.

1950 *Повесть временных лет*. Moscow.

1962 *Текстология: На материале русской литературы* X–XVII *vv.* Moscow– Leningrad.

Lixačev, Nikolaj Petrovič

1899 *Палеографическое значение бумажные водяных знаков*. T. 1–3. St. Petersburg.

Lunt, Horace G.

1950 *The Orthography of Eleventh-Century Russian Manuscripts*. Ann Arbor, MI.

1974 *Old Church Slavonic Grammar*[6]. The Hague.

1976 'The Byčkov Psalter,' *Slovo* **25–28** 255–61. Zagreb.

1979 'On *akanje* and Linguistic Theory,' *Harvard Ukrainian Studies* **2/3** 595–608.

1982 'On the Old Church Slavonic Codex Assemanianus,' *Makedonski jazik* **32–33** (1981–82) 405–416.

1983 'The transmission of the Apocalypse of Abraham' and 'Notes to Ryszard Rubinkiewicz's translation (of ApAb),' in Charlesworth 1983, pp. 686–705.

1985a 'On the Language of the Slavonic *Apocalypse of Abraham*,' *Slavica Hierosolymitana* **7** 55–62, Jerusalem.

1985b 'Slavs, Common Slavic, and Old Church Slavonic,' *Litterae Slavicae Medii Aevi*, ed. Johannes Reinhart (=Sagners Slavistische Sammlung, Bd. 8), pp. 185–204.

1985c 'On Common Slavic,' *Zbornik Matice srpske za filologiju i lingvistiku* **27–28** (1984–85) 417–22, Novi Sad.

1985d 'The OCS Song of Songs: One Translation or Two?' *Die Welt der Slaven* **30** 279–318.

1986 'Kurze Erwiderung [zu Alekseev, 1986]' *Die Welt der Slaven* **31** 437–8.

1987 'On the Relationship of Old Church Slavonic to the Written Language of Early Rus′,' *Russian Linguistics* **11** 133–62.

1988a 'On Interpreting the Russian Primary Chronicle: the Entry for 1037,' *Slavic and East European Journal* **32** 251–64.

1988b 'The Language of Rus′ in the Eleventh Century: Some Observations about Facts and Theories,' *Harvard Ukrainian Studies* **12/13** 276–313.

1988c 'Once Again the *Kiev Folia*,' *Slavic and East European Journal* **32** 341–83.

1990 'History, Nationalism, and the Written Language of Early Rus′,' *Slavic and East European Journal* **34** 1–29.

1994 'Lexical Variation in the Copies of the Rus′ *Primary Chronicle*: Some Methodological Problems,' *Harvard Ukrainian Studies* **18** 10–28.

1995 'What the Rus′ Primary Chronicle Tells Us About the Origin of the Slavs and of Slavic Writing,' *Harvard Ukrainian Studies* **19** 335–57.

1996 'Proto-Slavic or Common Slavic versus Pan-Slavic. Morpho-lexical puzzles of Early Slavic Written Dialects: I. *Slověnji,* II. *prosьba,* III (a) *vy-,* (b) *vyniti, vynide-*,' *International Journal of Slavic Linguistics and Poetics* **39–40** 279–98.

1997 'Common Slavic, Proto-Slavic, Pan-Slavic: What Are We talking About? I. About Phonology,' *International Journal of Slavic Linguistics and Poetics* **41** 7–67.

1998 'Еще раз о мнимых переводах в Древней Руси (По поводу статьи А. А. Алексеева),' *Труды Отдела древнерусской литературы* [to appear].

Lunt, Horace G., and Moshe Taube

1988 'Early East Slavic Translations from Hebrew?,' *Russian Linguistics* **12** 147–87.

1994 'The Slavonic Book of Esther: Translation from Hebrew or Evidence for a Lost Greek Text?,' *Harvard Theological Review* **87** 347–362.

Lur′e, Jakov S.

1960 *Идеологическая борьба в русской публицистике конца XV–начала XVI века*. Moscow–Leningrad.

L′vov, Andrej S.

1966 *Очерки по лексике памятников старославянской письменности*. Moscow.

Mathiesen, Robert

1983a 'Handlist of Manuscripts Containing Church Slavonic Translations from the Old Testament,' *Polata knigopisnaja* **7** 3–48. Nijmegen.

1983b 'The Typology of Cyrillic Manuscripts,' *American Contributions to the Ninth International Congress of Slavists, Kiev, Sept. 1983. Vol. I: Linguistics* (Columbus, OH), 193–202.

Meščerskij, Nikita A.

1956a 'К вопросу об изучении переводной письменности Киевского периода,' *Ученые записки Карело-Финского педагогического института*, том 2, вып. 1, 198–219, Петрозаводск [corrected reprint in 1995, 271–99].

1956b 'Отрывок из книги Иосиппон в Повести временных лет,' *Палестинский сборник* **2** 58–68.

1957 'К вопросу об источниках Повести временных лет,' *Труды Отдела древнерусской литературы* **13** 57–65 [1995, 46–57].

1958a *История Иудейской войны Иосифа Флавия в древнерусском переводе*. Moscow–Leningrad.

1958b 'К изучению лексики и фразеологии «Слова о полку Игореве»,' *Труды Отдела древнерусской литературы* **14** 43–48. [also in 1995, 148–55]

1958c 'Искусство перевода Киевской Руси,' *Труды Отдела древнерусской литературы* **15** 54–72.

1958d ‘Значение древнеславянских переводов для восстановления их архетипов,’ *IV международный съезд славистов. Доклады советской делегации*. Moscow.
1962 ‘О синтаксисе древних славяно-русских переводных произведениях,’ *Теория и критика перевода* (ред. Б. А. Ларин), 83–103. Leningrad [also in 1995, 317–37].
1964a ‘Проблемы изучения славяно-русской переводной литературы XI–XV вв.’ *Труды Отдела древнерусской литературы* **20** 180–231.
1964b ‘История текста славянской книги Еноха,’ *Византийский временник* **24** 91–108.
1965 Review of: ‘Л. С. Ковтун, *Русская лексикография эпохи средневековья*, 1963,’ *Известия АН СССР, Серия литературы и языка* **24** вып. 5 447–450.
1976 ‘Апокрифы в древней славяно-русской письменности (ветхозаветные апокрифы),’ *Методические рекомендации по описанию славяно-русских рукописей для Сводного каталога рукописей, хранящихся в СССР,* вып. 2, ч. 1, 101–209. Moscow.
1978a ‘Издание текста древнерусского перевода “Книги Есфирь*,” *Acta Universitatis Szegedensis, Dissertationes slavicae* **XIII**, 131–64.
1978b *Источники и состав древней славяно-русской переводной письменности IX-XV веков*. Leningrad.
1995 *Избранные статьи*. (ed. E. N. Meščerskaja). St. Petersburg.

Miklosich, Franz
1862–65 *Lexicon Palaeoslovenicum-graecum-latinum*. Vienna [reprint, 1977, Aalen: Scientia].

Minčeva, Angelina
1985 ‘Никодимово евангелие,’ *Palaeobulgarica / Старобългаристика* **9/4** 30–42.

Mixajlov, A. V.
1900–08 *Книга Бытия пророка Моисея в древне-славянском переводе*. Warsaw.
1907 ‘Древне-славянский перевод кн. Руфь,’ *Русский филологический вестник* **60** 1–30.
1912 *Опыт изучения текста книги Бытия в древне-славянском переводе, I: Паримейный текст*. Warsaw.

Moore, Carey A.
1971 *Esther*. (The Anchor Bible), Garden City, NY.
1982 (ed.) *Studies in the Book of Esther*. New York.

Mošin, Vladimir A., and Seid M. Traljić
1957 *Vodeni znakovi XII i XIV vijeka*. Zagreb.

Moulton, James Hope
1929 *A Grammar of New Testament Greek*[3], Edinburgh.

Mst[islav Gospel] = *Апракос Мстислава Великого,* ed. Lidija M. Žukovskaja. Moscow, 1983.

Nasonov, Arsenij Nikolaevič
1950 *Новгородская первая летопись старшего и младшего изводов*. Moscow–Leningrad.
1955 *Псковские летописи*, вып. 2-й. Moscow.

Nik = the apocryphal *Gospel of Nicodemus,* Vaillant 1968.

Nikolaev, S. L.
1988 'Следы особенностей восточнославянских племенных диалектов в современных великорусских говорах. I. Кривичи,' in *Балто-славянские исследования* 1986, ed. Vjač. Vs. Ivanov, pp. 115–54. Moscow.

Nikolova, Svetlina
1995 'К истории текста Книг Царств в славянской письменности,' in W. Moskovich et alii (eds.), *Jews and Slavs*, vol. 3, 54–68.

Niphon, Life of. = Rystenko, A. V., 1928. Матеріали з історії візантійсько-слов'янської литератури та мови, Odessa, 1928. [Reprint, Leipzig 1982.]

Ostrih Bible = *The Ostroh Bible of 1581: Острізька Біблія* (facsimile edition). Winnipeg, 1983

Peščak, Marija M.
1974 *Грамоти XIV ст.* Kiev.

Pičxadze (Pichkhadze), Anna Abramovna
1991 'К истории славянского паримейника,' in *Традиции древнейшей славянской письменности и языковая культура восточных славян*, ed. by V. P. Vomperskij, pp. 162–70.
1995 'К истории четьего текста славянского восмикнижия,' in W. Moskovich et alii (eds.), *Jews and Slavs*, vol. 3, 94–107.

Podskalsky, Gerhard
1982 *Christentum und theologische Literatur in der Kiever Rus' (988–1237),* Munich.

Pope, Marvin H.
1977 *Song of Songs.* (The Anchor Bible), Garden City, NY.

Popov, Andrej
1866 *Обзор хронографов русской редакции.* Moscow.

Porfir'ev, I. Ja., Vadkovskij, A. V., Krasnosel'cev, N. F., eds.
1881 *Описание рукописей Соловецкого монастыря находящихся в библиотеке Казанской Духовной академии.* Kazan'.

Предварительный список 1965 =
'Предварительный список славяно-русских рукописей XI-XIV вв., хранившихся в СССР,' *Археографический ежегодник за* 1965 *г.*, pp. 177–272.

Предварительный список 1986 =
Предварительый список славяно-русских рукописных книг XV в., хранящихся в СССР, составил А. А. Турилов. Moscow.

Pritsak, Omeljan
1990 "The Pre-Ashkenazic Jews of Eastern Europe in Relation to the Khazars, the Rus' and the Lithuanians" in *Ukrainian-Jewish Relations in Historical Perspective*[2], ed. Howard Aster, and Peter J. Potichnyj, 3–21. Edmonton, Alberta.
1998 *The Origins of the Old Rus' Weights and Measures: Two Studies in Western Eurasian Metrology and Numismatics in the 7th to 11th Centuries.* Cambridge, MA.

Proxorov, Gelian M.
1981 'Суды Соломона,' *Памятники литературы древней Руси: XIV–середина XV века*, 66–87. Moscow.

Pypin, Aleksandr N.
1862 *Памятники старинной русской литературы, вып.* з-й. St. Petersburg.

PVL = Повѣсть временъ и лѣтъ

Rječnik hrvatskoga ili srpskoga jezika Jugoslavenskoj akademii znanosti i umjetnosti. 23 vols. in 97 pts. Zagreb, 1880–1976.

Roždestvenskij, Ivan
1885 *Книга Есфирь, в текстах еврейском–масоретском, греческом, древне латинском и славянском.* St. Petersburg.

Růžička, Rudolf
1963 *Das syntaktische System der altslavischen Partizipien und sein Verhältnis zum Griechischen.* Berlin.

Sadnik, Linda
1967–83 *Des h. Johannes von Damaskus* Ἔκθεσις ἀκριβὴς τῆς ὀρθοδόξου πίστεως *in der Übersetzung des Exarchen Johannes.* 4 vol. (=Monumenta Linguae Slavicae Dialecti Veteris, Fontes et Dissertationes XIV (V,1–4). Freiburg i. Br.

SčS = *Staročeský slovník.* 1976–. Prague.

Seliščev, Afanasij M.
1925 'Des traits linguistiques communs aux langues balkaniques: un balkanisme ancien du bulgare,' *Revue des Études Slaves* **5** 50–57.
1951 Старославянский язык, vol. 1. Moscow.

Shinan, A.
1977 '"The Chronicle of Moses": the Genre, Time, Sources and Literary Nature of a Medieval Hebrew story' [in Hebrew], *Ha-Sifrut* No. 24 (VII) 100–116. Tel-Aviv.

Shmeruk, Chone
1985 *The Esterke Story in Yiddish and Polish Literature: A Case Study in the Mutual Relations of Two Cultural Traditions.* Jerusalem.

SJS = *Slovník jazyka staroslověnského.*

SK = Сводный каталог ...

Skaryna, Francysk
1519 *Книга Есьѳеръ.* Prague. (Reprinted in *Библия ўзнаўленне бібліі выдадзенай Францыскам Скарынаю ў 1517–1519 гадах у 3 тамах,* Minsk 1991, vol. 2, pp. 653–703.)

Słoński, Stanisław
1908 *Die Übertragung der griechischen Nebensatzkonstruktionen in den altbulgarischen Sprachdenkmälern.* Kirchhain N.-L.

Словарь русского языка XI–XVII вв. 1975–. Moscow.

Slovník jazyka staroslověnského. Lexicon linguae palaeoslovenicae. 4 vols. 1958–97. Prague.

Словник староукраїнської мови XIV–XV ст. 1–2. Kyiv, 1977–78.

Sobolevskij, Aleksej I.
1903 *Переводная литература Московской Руси XIV–XVII веков,* (=*Сборник Отделения русского языка и словесности Императорской академии наук* **74**).

Sollamo, Raija
1979 *Renderings of Hebrew Semiprepositions in the Septuagint* (=Annales Academiae Scientiarum Fennicae, *Dissertationes Humanarum Litterarum* 19), Helsinki.

Speranskij, Mixail N.
1908 *Из истории отреченных книг, IV: Аристотелевы Врата или Тайная Тайных* (=Памятники древней письменности и искусства, 171).

1960 *Из истории русско-славянских литературных связей*. Moscow.

SRJaXI = *Словарь русского языка XI–XVII вв.*

SSUM = *Словник староукраїнської мови XIV–XV ст.*

Stanojević, Ljubomir

1929 *Старе српске повеље и писма*, књ. I, први део. Belgrade.

Su, Supr = OCS codex Suprasliensis

Сводный каталог славяно-русских рукописных книг, хранящихся в СССР: XI-XIII вв. Ed. Lidija Petrovna Žukovskaja et al. Moscow, 1984.

Syrku, Konstantin

1898 *К истории исправления книг в Болгарии в XIV веке*, 1/1. St. Petersburg.

Ševčenko, Sergej

1917 Review of Barac 1916. *Русский филологический вестник* **77** 269–72.

Taube, Moshe

1985 'On Two Related Slavic Translations of The Song of Songs' *Slavica Hierosolymitana* **7** 203–210.

1986 'Old Russian блискъ – "pavement"?,' *Die Welt der Slaven* **33** 1–4.

1988 'An Early 12th-century Kievan Fragment of the Беседа трех святителей,' *Harvard Ukrainian Studies* **12–13** 346–59.

1989 'О генезисе одного рассказа в составе "Еллинского летописца второй редакции",' in W. Moskovich et al., eds., *Russian Literature and History: In Honour of Professor I. Serman,* 146–51. Jerusalem.

1991 'Une source inconnue de la chronographie russe: le "Dialogue de Timothée et Aquila",' *Revue des études slaves* **63** 113–22.

1992 'On Some Unidentified and Misidentified Sources of the Academy Chronograph,' in *Studies. . .in Honour of Professor Viktor D. Levin, on the Occasion of his 75th Birthday* (ed. Wolf Moskovich et al.), pp. 365–75, Jerusalem.

1993 'The Slavic *Life of Moses* and its Hebrew Sources,' *Jews and Slavs,* ed. Wolf Moskovich, Shmuel Shvarzband, and Anatoly Alekseev, pp. 84–119, Jerusalem–St. Petersburg.

1995 'The Kievan Jew Zacharia and the Astronomical Works of the Judaizers,' in W. Moskovich et al., eds. *Jews and Slavs,* vol. 3, 168–98, Jerusalem.

1997 'Послесловие к «Логическим Терминам» Маймонида и ересь жидовствующих,' in *IN MEMORIAM: Сборник памяти Я. С. Лурье* (ed. Natal′ja M. Botvinnik and E. I. Vaneeva), pp. 239–46, St. Petersburg.

Taube, Moshe, and Hugh Olmsted

1987 'Повѣсть о Есфири: The Ostroh Bible and Maksim Grek's Translation of the Book of Esther,' *Harvard Ukrainian Studies* **11** 100–117.

Thomson, Francis J.

1988 'The Bulgarian Contribution to the Reception of Byzantine Culture in Kievan Rus′: The Myths and the Enigma' *Harvard Ukrainian Studies* **12/13** (1988–89) 214–61.

1992 'On Translating Slavonic Texts into a Modern Language,' *Slavia Gandensia* **19** 205–219.

1993 ' "Made in Russia" A Survey of the Translations Allegedly made in Kievan Russia,' in *Millennium Russiae Christianae, Tausend Jahre Christliches Russland, 988–1988,* ed. Gerhard Birkfellner, pp. 295–354.

1994 'L'évolution de la manière de traduire chez les Slaves au moyen âge,' *Revue d'Histoire des Textes* **24** 313–36.

Tixonravov, Nikolaj Savvič
1863 *Памятники отреченной литературы*. I–II. St. Petersburg.
Torrey, Charles C.
1944 'The Older Book of Esther,' *Harvard Theological Review* **37** 1–40.
Tov, Emanuel
1982 'The "Lucianic" Text of the Canonical and Apocryphal Sections of Esther: A Rewritten Biblical Book,' *Textus*, Annual of the Hebrew University Bible Project, 1–25, Jerusalem.
Trubačev, Oleg N.
1974– *Этимологический словарь славянских языков; праславянский лексический фонд*. Moscow.
Tunickij, N. L.
1918 *Книги XII малых пророков с толкованиями в древне-славянском переводе*, вып. I, *Книги Осии, Иоиля, Амоса, Авдия и Ионы*, Sergiev Posad.
Turdeanu, Émile
1967 'La *Chronique de Moïse* en russe,' *Revue des études slaves* **46** 35–64.
1971 'Les Testaments des Douze Patriarches en slave,' *Journal for the Study of Judaism* **1** 148–84.
Turilov[, A. A. ed.] 1986 = Предварительный список 1986.
Tvorogov, Oleg Viktorovič
1975 *Древнерусские хронографы*. Leningrad.
Tvorogov, Oleg Viktorovič, and Vjačeslav Zagrebin, eds.
1988 *Рукописные книги собрания М. П. Погодина*: *Каталог*, Вып. 1. Leningrad.
Unbegaun, Boris
1935 *La langue russe au XVIe siècle (1500–1550)*. Paris.
Usp. (sb.) = Kotkov 1971.
Vaillant, André
1957 'Les citations des années 1110–1111 dans la Chronique de Kiev,' *Byzantinoslavica* **18** 18–38.
1959 'Une édition nouvelle du Josèphe slave,' *Semitica* **9** 89–93.
1964 *Manuel du vieux slave*[2]. Paris.
1966 *Grammaire comparée des langues slaves,* 3, *Le verbe.* Paris.
1968 *L'évangile de Nicodème: texte slave et texte latin.* Geneva–Paris.
Vajs, Josef
1926 *Kniha Rut v překladě staroslověnském.* Prague.
Van Schooneveld, Cornelis H.
1959 *A Semantic Analysis of the Old Russian Finite Preterite System.* The Hague.
Vasmer, Max (Фасмер, Макс)
1964–73 *Этимологический словарь русского языка*. (Transl. Oleg N. Trubačev.) Moscow.
Veder, William R.
1992 'The Merciful Nestor and Sozomen: Early Rusian Text Transmission in a Stratigraphic Perspective,' *Studies in Russian Linguistics* (=*Studies in Slavic and General Linguistics* vol. 17), pp. 321–82. Amsterdam.
Veselovskij, Aleksandr Nik.
1921 *Славянские сказания о Соломоне и Китоврасе* (=Соб. соч. А. Н. Веселовского, серия III, т. 1–й, вып. 1–й). Petrograd.

Vil. 262, Vilnius MCAD ms 10 (262) = Altbauer 1992
Vinogradov, Viktor V.
1958 *Основные проблемы изучения образования и развития древнерусского литературного языка*. Moscow.
Vladimirov, Petr V.
1888 *Доктор Франциск Скорина, его переводы, печатные издания и язык*. (=Общество любителей древней письменности, 90), St. Petersburg.
VMČ = *Великие минеи четии*. 1868–1912. Moscow.
Vostokov, A. X.
1842 *Описание русских и словенских рукописей Румянцевского музеума*. St. Petersburg.
1858–61 *Словарь церковно-славянского языка*, I–II. (=*Материалы для сравнительного и объяснительного словаря и грамматики*. vols. IV, VI, *Прибавления к Известии Императорской академии наук* CXXVII, CXCVI.
Vygoleksa Sbornik = *Выголексинский сборник*, ed. Sergei I. Kotkov. Moscow, 1977.
Vzdornov, Gerol'd I.
1978 *Киевская псалтирь 1397г*. Moscow.
Warsaw Jewish Chronograph = Warsaw ms. BOZ cim. 83.
Weingart, Miloš
1922–23 *Byzantské kroniky v literatuře církevněslovanské*. 2 vols. Bratislava.
Wutz, Franz
1914–15 *Onomastica Sacra: Untersuchungen zum Liber Interpretationis Nominum Hebraicorum des heiligen Hieronymus*, Hälfte 1–2 (=Texte und Untersuchungen zur Geschichte der altchristlichen Literatur, Bd. 411–12). Leipzig.
Xanthopoulos, T.
1902 'Traductions de l'Écriture Sainte en neo-grec avant le XIXe siècle,' *Échos d'Orient* **4** 321–32.
Yosippon = Flusser 1978–80.
Zaliznjak, Andrej A.
1986 *Коментарии и словоуказатель к берестяным грамотам (из раскопок* 1951–1983 *гг.)*, in Valerij P. Janin and A. A. Zaliznjak, *Новгородские грамоты на бересте*. Moscow.
1991 'Берестяные грамоты перед лицом традиционных постулатов славистики и vice versa,' *Russian Linguistics* **15** 217–45.
1995 *Древне-новгородский диалект*. Moscow.
Ziegler, Joseph
1957 *Ieremias, Baruch, Threni, Epistula Ieremiae*[2]. (=*Septuaginta: Vetus Testamentum Graecum, Auctoritate Academiae Litterarum Gottingensis editum*, vol. **XV**). Göttingen.
Zimmermann, Frank
1975 *Biblical Books Translated from the Aramaic*. New York.
Zlatanova, Rumjana
1992 'Zur slawischen Übersetzung des Zwölfprophetenbuchs,' *Anzeiger für slavische Philologie* **21** 158–81.

Dictionary

This listing is primarily to give the form and chapter-verse location of each word in ms Q or supplementary items we ascribe to the common ancestor of all the copies we were able to consult. Minimal glosses are in English, with references locating discussion of meaning (including, where pertinent, the relationship to a Hebrew equivalent), syntax, or grammatical aspects of a word.

Names of persons, peoples, places, and months—along with adjectives derived from names—are in a separate list at the end of the dictionary.

Entries cite attested words, alphabetized as though historical **ъ** and **ь** are present. Occasionally an infinitive or nominative singular is invented as heading; in such cases a left bracket separates this heading from the English definition.

Verbs with **сѧ** are not separated from non-сѧ forms, e.g., вратѧ сѧ is listed under вратити.

The letters **є** and **ѣ** are treated as alphabetical equivalents, ordered under **є** (as in Lunt 1969 and *SRJaXI-XVII*).

Thus вєльможа is between вєлми (for historical вєльми) and вѣньць. двєрємъ (for historical двьрьмъ) is between двоРъ and двьрьника.

A bold-face chapter-verse number signals that the word is discussed in the commentary to that verse. References to other chapters are given at the end of the entry.

.а҃.: 3:12 '1'; .а҃.го 3:7 '1st'
а and, but: 1:8, 1:14, 1:18 (2), 1:19, (2:16,) 3:8, 3:15 (2), 4:2, 4:11, 4:14, 5:1, 5:8, {8:8,} 8:14, 9:10
абиє at once, immediately: **1:12**, 7:6
абы (**A10.30**): 2:10 ꙁаповѣдалъ єи ~ нє повѣдала not to tell, 3:9 ~ написалъ may he write, let him write
  абыша 9:21 ~ творили that they should make (**A11.432–3**)
аꙁъ *1s pers. pron.*, I: 4:11, 4:16, 5:12, 5:13, 7:4, 8:5
  мєнє 4:16, 5:12, 6:6; [мѧ 5:12]; мнѣ 5:8, 5:13; мною 4:16, 7:8
аки like, as: **1:8** А питва аки вольна беꙁ нужа
ать *hortative conj*, let, may: ?1:19 Ащє царєвѣ оулюбѣє {ать} [ащє] иꙁидєть рѣчь царьскаꙗ ѡт нєго; 5:14 ать повѣсѧт Мардъхаꙗ
ащє (1) *conj*, if, whether: 1:19, 3:9, 4:14 (2), 4:16 (2) ~ си и нє по ꙁакону, да ~ погыбну да погыбну, 5:4, 5:8 ~ бы царєви тако оудобрѣло, 6:13 (2), 7:3 (2), 7:4 ~ бо быхом . . . прєпродани, 8:5, 9:13
  (2) *generalizing particle*: 2:13 всє єжє ~ whatever, **4:11** ꙗко ~ however, 9:1 идєжє ~ wherever;
  (3) ащє нє but: 1:16, 5:12 ащє нє мєнє
  [**1:19** ?{ать}] (**A10.4**)

беꙁ *prep w G* without: 1:8 А питва аки вольна ~ нужа
ближнии next, close: 1:14 а ижє ~ єму
блиску pavement: 1:6 на ~ камєниꙗ драгаго
блиꙁь near: 9:20 ~ и далєчє (**A8.43**)

бо *conj,* for: 7:4
бобръмь beaver (?), ?fine cloth: **1:6** Бобръмь и оутринъмь и ҹьрвємь (**L5.43**)
богатьство wealth: 1:4, богатьства *G* 5:11 (**L16.41**)
болє more: **6:6** болє мєнє
болꙗриноу nobleman: 6:9 на руцѣ мужу ~; болꙗры Ap 1:16 ащє нє на всꙗ боꙗры; болꙗръ 1:14 7 болꙗръ; 3:1 всѣхъ болꙗръ; болꙗромъ 1:3, 1:18, 3:12; болꙗры Ip 1:16, 1:21 (**L2.1**)
болꙗрынѣ noblewoman: Np 1:18 (**A3.2**)
боꙗры 1:16 *see* болꙗрин-
братьꙗ brothers: 10:3 вольникъ множьства ~ своєꙗ
бърꙁо swiftly: 6:10 ~ възми свиту; 8:14 А погонци . . . в{ы}нидоша ~ вънатъщь
бърꙁъ swift: **8:10, 8:14** на бърꙁдыхъ (Т борꙁых) кониxъ (**A1.51**)
быти to be: 3:14, (4:11}, 6:13, 8:13
єсмь 5:12 ꙁванъ єсмь; *aux1* 8:7 далъ єсмь
єси *aux1* 6:10 (2) гл͠алъ єси . . . єжє єси гл͠алъ; 6:13 ꙗко поҹалъ єси падати
єсть (є^{c}, є) 1:20, {3:7}, 3:7, 3:13, 4:5 (2), 5:3, 5:4, 5:6, 5:13,6:3, 6:4, 6:13, 7:5, 8:9, 8:12, 9:1
соуть *copula* 10:2 та ~ написана; 3:8 сє ~ людьє расѣꙗнии
aux2 9:27 ꙗкожє ~ творꙗщє 2 дн͠ии си; 9:28 И дн͠ии сиꙗ поминающє ~ и творꙗщє ꙗ; 3:8 и ꙁакона царєва ѡни нє ~ творꙗщє
сущи *Nsf* 2:7
буду 8:5 ащє . . . добра ~ аꙁъ прєд ѡҹима єго
будєть 1:20; 4:11; 5:3; 5:8
буди 3:11 срѣбро ~ дано тобѣ
будѣтє *aux2* 5:14 сдѣлающє ~ дрєво (**A11.441**)
будꙗшє 2:14 И нє прихожашє лапь къ царєви нъ єгда ~ волꙗ царєва на нєи
бѣ *copula* 2:3 ижє ~ тивоунъ; 2:18 и дасть дары ꙗкожє ~ сила царєва; 3:4 повѣда имъ ꙗко тъ ~ Июдѣи
aux1 5:12 на пиръ ижє створила ~; 7:9 дрѣво єжє створилъ ~ самъ Аманъ; 8:2 пьрстьнь свои ижє ~ ѡтꙗлъ оу Амана; 8:5 книгы . . . ижє ~ написалъ; 9:23 ꙗжє бѣ написалъ Мардъхаи
aux2 2:14 (2) И на вєҹєръ та ~ приходꙗщи, и ꙁаутра ~ {възвращающи} сꙗ; 4:1 Мардъхаи ~ вѣдаꙗ всє єжє творꙗшє царь; 6:11 и ~ клиҹа прєд нимь
бꙗшє *copula* 1:8; 2:5; 2:6 єжє полонєнъ ~; 2:7 (2) бꙗшє Єсфирь дщи стръꙗ єго, єижє нє ~ ѡт͠ца; 2:8; **2:21**; 3:2; 4:2; 4:3; **7:9**; 8:1; 8:11; 9:4
aux1 2:15 ижє поꙗлъ ю ~ собѣ; 2:20 (2) ꙗкожє ꙁаповѣдалъ єи бꙗшє Мардъхаи . . ., ꙗкожє ~ оутвєрдила сꙗ с нимь; 6:14 къ питвѣ ижє оустроила ~ Єсфирь; 7:7 ꙗко сконҹала сꙗ ~ ꙁлоба; 7:8 Аманъ припалъ ~ прєд постєлєю Єсфириною; 7:10 на дрєвє ижє створилъ ~; 8:3 мысль єго южє ~ помыслилъ на Июдѣꙗ; 8:7 имьжє въвьрглъ ~ руцѣ свои во Июдѣ{ꙗ}; 8:17 ꙗко оумножилъ сꙗ ~ страхъ Июдѣискыи на них; 9:3 ꙗко напалъ ~ страхъ Мардъхаєвъ на них; 9:25 мысль єго ꙁлаꙗ, ижє помыслилъ ~ на Июдѣꙗ
aux2 2:7 И бꙗшє пѣстуꙗ домаҹадицю сироту; 2:20 И нє ~ Єсфирь повѣдающи рода своєго,
бꙗху *aux1* 9:1 прєврати сꙗ то ижє поҹали ~ вра{гы} владѣти Июдѣи.
бѣша *aux2* 8:11 ижє ~ муҹили дѣти и жєны; 9:23 И подъꙗша Июдѣи ꙗжє ~ поҹали творити

быхъ (1) *pfv aor:* 4:11 азъ нє звана ~; 7:4 ижє прєпродана ~ азъ и людиє мои; (2) *condit.:* **5:4** на питву єже быхъ (?буду) створила єму; 7:4 мълчала быхъ
быстъ 1:1, [1:5], 1:21, 2:8 (2), 2:12, 2:15, 2:16, 2:17, 2:22, 2:23, 3:4, 3:6 (2), 3:15, 4:8, 5:1, 5:2 (2), 8:14, 8:16, 9:14, 9:25
aux2! 3:5
быхомъ *condit*: 2:2 да поискали ~ цареви 7:4 Аще бо ~ . . . прєпродани
быста *pfv aor*: 2:23 повѣшена ~ . . . ωба
бы 3:8 *condit*: ?а цареви бы нє право пустити ихъ;
3:9 (1+[1]); 5:4 (2) аще ~ сѧ цареви оудобрити, да ~ пришєлъ царь;
5:8 (2) аще ~ . . . оудобрѣло, да ~ пришєлъ царь;
6:6 кому хотѣлъ ~ царь створити чьсть
быша (1) *pfv aor*: 3:12 И призвани ~ писци; 6:1 (книгы) ~ проучєны прєд царємь; 8:9 И възвани быша писци
(2) *condit*: 2:3 да ~ събрали всѧкоу дѣвоую дѣвицю; 2:11 оувѣдѣти миръ Есфири и что ~ створили єи;
было 3:9
{быв'шаꙗ} 3:14

.в҃. '2': 6:2, 7:2, 9:27; .в҃і. '12' 2:12, 3:7 (2), 3:13, 8:12, 9:1
ваю *2du pers. pron., D* your: 8:8 (**A4.22**)
[**вѣда**] **2:10** {повѣда}?
вѣдають know: 4:11; вѣдаꙗ 4:1 Мардъхаи бѣ вѣдаꙗ все єже творѧше царь
вѣкъ age, eon: 9:28 въ всѧ {вѣ}кы вѣком
велии great: 9:4 Ибо бѧше велии Мардъхаи
великъ big, great: 2:18, 8:15, 9:4, 10:3; велика *Gs* 1:5, 1:20 ѿ ~ дажь и до мала; велика *Nsf* 4:3 желѧ велика; великъмь 4:1
величьа greatness, high status: *Gs* 6:3, 10:2
величьствиꙗ greatness, high status: *Gs* 1:4 ~
велми зѣло greatly, very much: 1:12, 4:4 (**A8.12, T3.121**)
вельможа *m* nobleman: 9:3 всѧ ~ земныꙗ; вельможамъ 1:3, 1:11, 2:18, 8:9; вельможами 5:11 (**L2.1**)
вѣньць wreath, crown: 8:15, -нець 2:17, 6:8; въ вѣнци 1:11 (**L5.2–21**)
веселъ joyful: 5:9, 5:14; веселыи 9:18 творѧху и тъ дн҃ь питвьныи; веселии **9:28** дн҃ье ~ си
веселье joy: 8:16 просвѣщениє и ~, 8:17 ~ и ωхвота, 9:19 ~ и питье; веселию 9:22 ѿ скърбии къ ~
веселиꙗ H *Purim* 9:29, 9:31, 9:32 ~ сего (**L13.2,** L13.72fn)
?веселии **9:28** *Gp?* or *Npm, see* веселъ
весельныи *adj* of rejoicing:› 9:17 твориша дн҃ь питвьныи и ~; веселныꙗ 9:22 створити ꙗ дн҃и питвьныꙗ и ~ (**L13.1**)
?**вѣсит**[**ы**] hang: 4:7 {н}авѣсит{и} (**L16.43**)
вѣсть: **2:22** И бысть вѣсть Мардохаеви 'it became known'
вѣсть knows: 4:14 да кто ~ (**A11.1, L21.54**)
вечеръ evening: 2:14 на ~
видѣти see: {3:4}, 8:6 (2); вижю 5:13; видѧху 1:14; видѣ 3:5; видѣша 9:26
вино wine: 1:7; винѣ 1:10
виньнѣмь *adj,* wine, of wine: 7:2 в питии ~; виньныꙗ 7:7 ѿ питвы ~; виньныхъ 5:6 въ прєпоихъ ~
владѣти rule: 9:1 (2) (**L9.4**)

власть dominion: **1:22** оутвьрдити всѧкому мужю ~ в дому своємь; province власти *Gs* 4:11 и людиє ~ царевы; *Ds* 1:22 (2) къ ~ и ~ ꙗко писаниє ихъ; *Ls* 8:5 по всеи ~ царевѣ; властии *Gp* **1:1**; властьхъ **1:16** въ всѣхъ {властєхъ} царѧ; 2:3 въ всѣхъ ~; властємъ 1:22 къ всѣмъ ~ царѧ; 9:2 по всѣм ~ царѧ; [власти 2:3] (**L9.3**)

власѧницю sackcloth: 4:1 въ ~ и сукно: власѧницѣ 4:3 ~ и сукна постилаху (**L5.3**)

вольникъ? {**иꙁ**}**вол**{**ю**}**никъ** favorite: 10:3 и ~ множьства братьꙗ своєꙗ (**L12.22**)

вольна free (?): **1:8** А питва аки ~ беꙁ нужа

волѧ wish, desire: 2:14 єгда будѧшє ~ царєва на неи, 3:6 ~ бы^с Амонова, 7:2 ѵто ~ твоꙗ и дамь дажь и до полу царьства моєго; волю (створити) ~ 1:8, 3:11, 7:2, 9:5; **6:6** ѵто створити мужю иже царѧ ~ ѵ҃тити єго; воли: {7:3 в' ~ моєи}, (**L12.15, 62**)

врагъ enemy: 9:24; врага Gs 8:1 домъ Амановъ, ~ Июдѣиского, 9:10 10 сн҃овъ Амановъ сн҃а Амъдафина ~ Июдѣиского; враꙁи **9:1** оуслышаша ~ Июдѣистии; врагъ Gp 8:13 ѡт ~ своих, {9:16}; вра{гы} Ip 9:1 поѵали бѧху вра[ꙁи] владѣти Июдѣи; враꙁѣх 9:2 мьсти творити на всѣх ~ своихъ, 9:5 створиша въ всѣх ~ своихъ волю свою; врагомъ 9:5 (**L1.1**)

вражду (? for **вражу**) lot: **3:7** въꙁвьржє ~ и жрєбии прєдъ Амонъмь (**A1.3**)

вражьбьныи hostile: 7:6 мужь ~ и нєприꙗꙁнивыи (**A3.4**)

врата] gate: *Gp* вратъ 2:21 иже стрѣжаста ~ єго, 4:2 И придє до ~ царѧ, 4:6 прѧмо ~ царєвъ; вратѣхъ 2:19: въ ~ царѧ 2:19, 2:21, 3:2, 3:3, 5:13, на ~ царѧ 6:10; вратомъ 4:2 къ ~ царєвъмь, 6:12 къ ~ царѧ

вратити turn, turn back: **8:5**, 8:8; врати сѧ 7:8 returned; вратѧ сѧ къ **4:13** turning to

[**враѵюющи**] сѧ 2:14: *see* въꙁвращающи

врєдно: **5:13** и всє то нє ~ [ли] єсть мнѣ (**L16.1**)

въ (**в**): *L* 1:2, 1:5 (2), 1:7, 1:9, 1:10, 1:11, 1:12, 1:14, 1:16, 1:19, 1:20, 1:22, 2:3, 2:5, 2:8, 2:9, 2:12 (2), 2:19, 2:21, 2:23, 3:2, 3:3, 3:6, 3:15, 4:2, 4:8, 4:13 (2), 4:16, 5:1, 5:2 (2), 5:6, 5:13, 6:1, 6:2, 6:6, 7:2, 7:3, {7:3}, 7:4, 7:8, 7:9, 8:12, 8:13, 8:14, 8:15 (3), {9:4}, 9:5, 9:6, 9:11, 9:12, 9:13, 9:14, 9:15 (2), 9:18, 9:32, 10:2, 10:3; въ томь 2:13
въ *A* (13) 1:17, 2:3, 2:8, 2:16, 4:1, 6:8, 6:12, 8:7 въ Июдѣ{ѧ}, 9:10, 9:15, 9:16; *A, time* 1:1, 1:2, 1:3, 1:10, 1:18, 2:12?, 2:16 (2), 2:21, 3:7, {3:12}, 3:13, 4:14 (2), 5:1, 5:9, 5:13, 6:1, 7:2, 8:1, 8:9 (2), 8:12, 9:1 (4), 9:11, 9:15, 9:17, 9:22, 9:28; въ другыꙗ for the second time 2:19; въ . . . мѣсто 2:4, 2:7, 2:15, 2:17; въ послухъ, *see* послухъ 1:17

въвьрглъ throw (?): 8:7 имьжє ~ бѧшє руцѣ свои въ Июдѣ{ѧ}. (**L6.311**)

въдасть give: 8:1 вдасть

въ другыꙗ, *see* другъ

въꙁвєлиѵа magnify, glorify: **5:11**, 10:2 (**L15.2**)

въꙁвєсєли сѧ be glad, celebrate: 8:15 оуохвоти сѧ и ~

въꙁврати сѧ return (up to): 6:12 ~ Мардохаи къ вратомъ царѧ

{**въꙁвращающи сѧ**} return (up to): **2:14** и ꙁаутра бѣ [враѵюющи] сѧ

въꙁвышє, -шѣє in height: 7:9 -шѣ; **5:14** -шѣє ~ 50 локотъ (**A8.42**)

въꙁвьржє throw, cast (lots): 3:7 ~ вражду и жрєбии прєдъ Амонъмь ѡт дн҃и къ дн҃и

въꙁдъхнувъ sigh: **5:10**

въꙁидє come up: 9:2 ~ гроꙁа H 'fear fell' (**L14.51**)

въꙁискаꙗ seek out, find, attain: 10:3 вꙁискаꙗ; въꙁискана, 2:23 И ~ бы^с рѣѵь

възложать put, impose: 1:20 ~ срамоту на мужь свои (**T9.23**); възложи 2:17, 10.1; възложенъ 6:8
възлюбленикъ loved one, beloved: **7:6** (**L3.2**)
възнесе exhalt: 2:9, 3:1 (2), 5:11 (**L12.91**)
възношаху 9:3 и ~ Июдѣꙗ (**L12.91**)
възоръ look, appearance: 1:11 показати . . . красоту еꙗ и еже добрыи ~ еꙗ
възва call: 4:5; възвани 8:9 ~ быша писци (**C3:12**)
възъпи cry out: 4:1 ~ въпльмь великъмь и горком (**L14.3**)
възѧ take, get: 6:11; възми 6:10 бързо ~ свиту и конь
вънатъщь in haste: 8:14 бързо ~ (**C3:15, A8.22**)
вънегда when: **1:10**, **2:15**; вънього 2:8
вънъгдаже when: **1:5**, **6:8**
вънѣшнего outer: 6:4 къ двору дому цареваа ~ (**L1.22**)
въображена (?**въобрѧжена**) H 'found to be correct': **2:23** И възискана бы[с] рѣчь и въображена
въпишеть write in, write down: 1:19 ~ въ книгахъ
въпль cry, outcry: въплѧ 9:31 рѣчи говѣньꙗ и ~ их; въпльмь: **4:1** възъпи ~ великъмь (**L14.3**)
въскорѣ quickly, swiftly: **3:15** (**A8.22**)
въсплака weep, burst into tears: **3:15** а градъ Сусанъ ~ сѧ; 8:3 ~ молѧщи его (**L14.3**)
въспомѧноу recall, remember: 2:1
въстанеть arise, be, take place: 4:14
вътрепета tremble: 7:6 (**L14.6**)
въсхожаше go up: **2:11**
въсхотѣ want: **1:12** не ~; 4:4 и не ~ приꙗти (**L12.3**)
{**вы**} you *Ndu*: 8:8 (**A4.23**)
выниде go out: 1:17 ꙗко вниде (?в{ы}ниде{ть}) глъ црицинъ; 4:1, 4:6 в{ы}ниде, 5:9, 7:8, 8:15; вынидоша 3:15 Погонци же ~ въскорѣ, 8:14 погонци . . . в{ы}нидоша бързо вънатъщь (**L19.1**)
вьрвьми rope, cord: 1:6 ~ шьлковыми
вьсь all: все **1:7** но ~ (?вси) разноличь, 2:13 и ~ еже аще речаше, 4:1 ~ еже, 5:13 и ~ то не вредно ли есть мнѣ, 10:2 ~ дѣло; всѧ 9:26 ~ рѣчь си; всего 6:10 не оуими рѣчи ~ еже еси глаголалъ; всю *Asf* 8:11, 9:29; всеи *Dsf* 3:8, 3:13, 8:5, 9:12; всемь 1:20, 3:6; вьси Np 3:2, 4:11, 5:14; всѧ 9:3 И ~ вельможа земныꙗ; вьсѧ *Apmf* 1:16 (2), 1:17, 1:20, 3:6, 3:13, 4:16, 9:27, 9:28; всѧ *Apn* 4:7, 6:13, 9:27; вьсѣхъ *G* 2:17 (2), 3:1, 3:8, 4:13, 9:24; L 1:8, **1:16**, 2:3, 3:1, 8:12, 8:13, 9:2, 9:5; вьсѣмъ 1:5, 1:18, 1:22, 2:18, 3:14 (2), 6:13, 8:11, 8:13 (2), 9:2, 9:5, 9:20 (2), {9:30}, 10:3; всѣми 1:13, 2:15, 5:11, 9:2
вьсѧкъ each, every: 2:11, 4:11, 8:17, 9:28; всѧка *Nsf* 4:3, 8:17; всѧку *Asf* 2:3, 5:13, 9:21; всѧкому 1:22
вѣ-: *see under* **ве-**

.{г҃} '3rd' 1:3;
г҃.и '3rd' 5:1, **.г҃.ии** 8:9
.гı. '13' 3:12, 3:13, 8:12, 9:1, 9:17, 9:18
главу head: 2:17, 6:8, 6:12, 9:25; главѣ 8:15; главахъ 1:6 на ~ сребреныхъ
гл҃ании speaking, act of speech: **3:1** по ~ тѣхъ всѣх (**L8.21**)

глати speak, say: 8:3; [глть **3:14**;] глющимъ 6:14; глющии сѧ 2:16, 3:7; глаше 7:9; глахуть 3:4; глалъ 6:10 (2)
глъ word: 1:17, 1:18, **1:22**?, 2:8, 7:8, {**8:5**}, 8:17, 9:1; глу 3:15; глы {3:4}, 9:32 (**L8.1, 21**)
гнѣвъ anger: 1:12, 2:1, 7:10; гнѣва 1:18, 5:9; гнѣвомь 7:7 (**L14.7**)
гнѣваꙗ being angry: 2:21 И ~ сѧ баше (**A12.1**)
гнѣвныꙗ angry: 3:5 (**L11.21**)
говѣниє fast: **4:3;** Np говѣньꙗ 9:31 (**L13.8**)
говѣти to fast: 4:16 ~ наѵнуть; говѣитє 4:16; [говѣху **9:17**] (**L13.8**)
година time, year: 9:27 и ꙗкоже ~ их по всѧ лѣта и лѣта; годину 4:14 въ ~ сию (2); 5:13 въ всѧку ~; 8:9 въ ~ ту; 9:21 абыша творили днии 14 всѧкоу ~ и ~; годины 1:13 мудрьцьм иже поꙁнаꙗху ~ (**L20**)
годы times, years: 9:31 (**L20**)
горкомь bitter: 4:1
градъ city: 3:15, 8:15, 8:17, 9:28 (2), 9:28, 8:17 ; града 4:1, 4:6, 6:9, 6:11; градѣ 1:2, 1:5, 2:5, 2:8, 3:15, 4:8, 4:16, 8:14, 9:6, 9:11, 9:12, 9:14, 9:15 (2), 9:18; граду 2:3; градомъ 8:11, 9:2, 9:19
грамотою document, letter: 9:25 съ ~
грамотнаꙗ referring to a document, letter: пеѵать ~ 3:14, 8:13; грамотных 10:2 въ книгах ~
гроꙁа ?threat: **9:2** (**L14.5**)
греѵьску (in the) Greek (language): 2:16 по ~

.дı. '14' 9:17, 18, 19, 20; 9:15 .д{ı}.
да *conj* that, in order to: 1:19 ꙗко да ... прєдастъ, (**4:7** да вѣсит{ь}), 2:2 да поискали быхомъ, 2:3 да быша събрали, 2:3 да бы приставилъ, 5:4, 5:8 да бы пришєлъ царь;
imperative: 4:16, 6:5, 6:8, 6:9, 8:5;
and: 2:7, 4:14, 4:16, 9:25 (**A10.31**)
дажє и (до) up to, as far as: 1:1, да{жє} да[м] 5:6
дожє и (до)1:20
дажь и (до)1:5, 2:13, 5:3, 7:2, 8:9 (**A8.121**)
далєѵє afar: 9:20 (**A8.43**)
даниє (?): see C8:13
дани taxes: 10:1
дары gifts: **2:9**, **2:18**,, 9:19, 9:22
дати to give: 2:9, 3:14, 5:8, 6:9; дамь 5:6 (2), 7:2; 9:12; дасть 2:18, 8:2, 8:11, да 3:10, 4:8, 5:7 да ѡтвѣтъ: дадимъ 7:2 ? и ~ тобѣ; дадѧше 2:13; далъ 8:7 ~ єсмь; данъ 3:15, 8:14, 9:14; дано 3:11 срѣбро буди ~ тобѣ; дана 4:8
даꙗти to give: 2:9; даꙗ **2:3**
дворѣ court: L 1:5, {?5:1}, 5:2, 6:4, 6:5; двору D 2:11, 4:11, 6:4 (L1.22)
двєрємъ door: 5:1 (**L1.221**)
двьрника doorkeeper: 6:2 (**L2.43**)
дѣва maiden, virgin: *Ns* 2:4 дв[у], 2:13 дваꙗ два, *Gs* дѣвы 2:12; *Np* 4:4, 4:16 двыꙗ ~ (**L2.46**)
дѣваꙗ *Ns* 2:13 дваꙗ два, *As* дѣвую 2:3, *Gs* дѣвыꙗ: дв[оу]ꙗ 2:12, *Ap* дѣвыꙗ: дв[ою] 2:19; двыꙗ *Np* 4:16: двыхъ *Ap* 2:2, *Gp* 2:17 (**L2.46**)
дѣвица maiden, virgin: 2:7; *Ap* 2:8 двца многы, 2:19 дв[ою] двиц[ю], 2:9 двица єꙗ; двицю 2:3, 2:9; двиць 2:2, 2:9, 2:17 (**L2.46**)

дѣло matter, affair: 9:3, 10:2; дѣла 3:9
десѧтьма ten: 1:1
дѣти children: 8:11 (**L4.1**)
дѣтѧтє child, baby: 3:13 ѡт дѣтѧтє и до старого
до *prep w G,* to (**A9.32**): 3:13; дажє (дажь) и ~ 1:1, 1:5, 2:13, 4:2, 5:3, 5:6, 7:2, 8:9; дожє и ~ 1:20,
добровзорна good-looking: 2:7; добровзорну 2:3; добровзорных 2:2 (**A5.21**)
добротварна shapely, well-built: 2:7 ~ и добровзорна (**A5.22**)
доброты goodness: 10:3
добръ good: 8:17, 9:19 дн҃ь ~; добрыи 1:11; добра 1:21, 8:5; доброє 7:9; доброму 9:22 къ дн҃и ~
добытокъ property (?), booty, **L18.11**: 3:13 ~ ихъ къ росполону; добыткы 8:11 ~ ихъ по росполону
довлѣєть (there is) enough, it suffices: 1:18
доволно sufficient: 3:9 (**T9.24, L12.61**)
дожє и до 1:20, *see* **дажє**
доидѧшє reached, arrived at: **4:3**, 8:17
домаѵадицю servant: **2:7** домаѵадицю сироту
домъ house: Ns 4:14; As 2:3, 2:8, 2:16, 6:12, 8:1 8:7; домъмь 8:2; дому Gs 1:8, 1:9, 1:22, 2:9, 2:13, 5:1 (2), 6:4; Ls 2:9, 2:14, 4.13, [5:1 {дворѣ}], 7:4, 7:8, 7:9, {9:4}; Ds 2:11, 2:13, 5:10, 7:8 (**L1.21**)
дондєжє **4:11** ~ нє 'until'
{**до**}**стоıа**{**шє**} it was proper: **2:9** стоıа[ху] дати
доступи reach, attain: 2:15; доступиши + G **4:14**
драготу? (1:20 var.; *see* **L15.3**)
драгаго dear, costly: 1:6
дрєво gallows: 5:14 (2), 7:9; дрєвє 2:23, 6:4, 7:10, 8:7, [9:12], 9:25
другъ 9:19 ~ къ другу to each other
другъ friend: **10:3** ~ царѧ Ахасъвєроса; другу Ds 9:19, 9:22
другому another, second: 2:14; другыıа Apf 9:29; **2:19** въ ~ 'for the second time'?
душа soul: **9:31;** души 7:7; душахъ **8:11** (**L6.4**)
два two: 2:21; двѣма 1:1
дънѣшнии inner: 7:8 ѡт ѡграда днѣшнєго, **5:1** дому днѣшнєго; **4:11** къ двору днѣшнєму, 7:7 къ ѡграду днѣшнєму (p. 140; **L1.22, 231**)
дьнь day: дн҃ь *Ns* 9:22; A 1:10, 1:18, 2:11 (2), 3:12, 3:13 (2), 3:14, 5:1, 5:9, 7:2, 8:1, 8:9, 8:12 (2), 9:1 (2), 9:10, 9:15, 9:17 (2), 9:18, 9:19; дн҃ь добръ **8:17**, 9:19; дн҃и *Gs* 3:7; дьнє **3:4** (2) И бы{сть} єгда гл҃ахуть єму дн҃є дн҃є; *Ds* 3:7, 8:13, 9:22 къ дн҃и доброму; дн҃ьє 2:12, 9:28; дн҃и *Ap* 1:1, 1:2, 1:5, 2:21, 4:16, 9:22, 9:26, 9:31; дн҃ии *Ap!* 9:28; дн҃ии *Gp* 1:4, 4:11, 9:21, дн҃овъ 1:5 (**A3.11**); дн҃ии [!] *Adu* 9:27; дн҃ьми 1:4
дн҃єсь today: 5:4
дн҃єшнии of today, today's; **1:18** а въ ~ дн҃ь (**L19.32**)
дщи daughter: 2:7, 9:29; дщєрє 2:15, въ ~ мѣсто 2:7, 2:15

.є҃. '5': .҂є҃. '5000' 3:9; .о҃. и ҂є҃ '75000' 9:16 (**A7.21**)
.єı. '15th' 9:18, {9:21}
є 2:9 є{и} *see* **онъ**
є **4:8** for Ap {ѣ} or {ѧ}: *see* **онъ**
є = **є**{**сть**} 4:5 (2), 6:3, 6:4, *see* **быти**
єдинъ one: 3:13, 4:11, 7:9, 8:12; only, sole єдиному 1:16, 3:6

єгда when: 1:2, 3:4; да ~ 2:7, 9:25; нъ ~ **2:14**
єгдажє when: **1:4**
ѣздит rides: **6:8**; ѣздѧху 8:14, ꙗздѧху 8:10 (**A1.2**)
є[жє] 5:6 є{сть} *see* **быти**
єжє, єижє *see* **ижє**
єлико as many as: **9:27** на всѧ ~ их приступаше къ ним
єликожє as many as: 1:5 ~ ихъ ѡбрѣтє (**T9.36**)
ємужє *see* **ижє**
єщє 6:14 ~ жє still, 9:12 still more

.ѕ҃. '6' 2:12 (2), 2:16

жє 1:17, 2:19, 3:2, 3:15, 6:14, 8:15
жєланиꙗ sorrow: 9:22 ѡт скърбии къ вєсєлию и ѡт ~ къ дн҃и доброму (**L14.1**)
жєлєнъ sad: 6:12 Амонъ идє в дом свои ~ и повѣсивъ главу свою (**L14.1**)
жєлѧ grief: 4:3 ~ вєлика Июдѣомъ (**L14.1**)
жєна woman, wife: 4:11, 5:14, 6:13; жєну 5:10; жєнѣ 6:13; жєны 1:17, 1:20, 3:13, 8:11; жєнъ 2:17
жєньскыи of woman, of women: 1:9 пиръ ~; 2:3 в домъ ~; 2:3, 2:8, 2:15 хранитєль ~; 2:12 законъ ~; жєньского 2:13 из дому ~; 2:11; жєньскому 2:14 дому ~; жєньстѣмь 2:9 в дому ~; жєньскыхъ 2:12 въ пристроꙗхъ ~
жидовѧху сѧ became Jews? acted like Jews? **8:17**
жидовьскому in the Jewish language: 2:16 по ~
жрєбии lot: **2:15** ~ Єсфиринъ; **3:7** възвьржє вражду и ~
жрєбиинѣмь of the lot: 9:26 прозваша дн҃и ты по имєни ~ (**A5.23**)

.з҃. '7': 1:5, 1:10, 1:14, 2:9, 8:9
за *prep. w A,* by, for: 5:2 (Єсфирь) ꙗтъ за конєць прута; 6:3 (2) за то in return for that
задѣти put, lay on: 2:21 ~ руцѣ цари Ахасъвєросѣ; 3:6 ~ руцѣ Мардъхаю; 6:2 ~ руцѣ царю Ахасъвєросу (**L6.311**)
законъ law: 1:13, 2:8, 2:12 ~ жєньскыи, **3:14**, 3:15, 4:3, 4:11, 8:14, 8:17, 9:1, 9:14; закона 3:8 ~ царєва ѡни нє суть творѧщє, 8:13; закону 1:15, 4:16; законы *Np*! 3:8 (**L8.5**)
законнымъ of the law: 4:8 пєчать {книгамъ} ~
занє{жє} because: 9:26
запєчатаху seal: **3:12**; запєчатано 8:8
запєчатлѣита seal: 8:8; запєчатлѣша 8:10
заповѣдати order, command: 4:8; заповѣдашє 3:12; 8:9; заповѣда 4:5, 10, 17; заповѣдалъ 2:10 бѧшє ~ єи; 2:20 ~ єи бѧшє (**L8.41**)
заповѣдь command: *Ns* 3:2, *As* 3:3 (**L8.41**)
заоутра: the next day 2:14; tomorrow 5:8, 5:14, 9:13 [cf. **наутриꙗ**] (**L20.51**)
зѣло very: 1:12, 4:4 (**A8.12, T3.121**)
зємлѧ H province 3:12 (2), 4:3 (2), 8:9 (2), 8:17 (2), 9:28 (2); зємлю 10:1; зємлѧ *Gs* 8:11; зємли *Ds* **3:8**, 3:12, зєм[н]и 3:12, 3:13, 9:12; зємль 8:9, 9:30; зємлѧх 8:12, 8:13 (2); зємлѧмъ 2:18, 3:14 (2), 9:16, 9:20 (**L9.321**)
зємныꙗ of the land, local: 9:3 *Npm!* всѧ вєльможа ~; зємнымъ 1:3, 8:9; зємных Gp 8:17 (**L9.321**)
златъ golden: 4:11, **8:4**, 8:15; злата 1:6; златыи 5:2; златыхъ 1:7 (**A5.31, 41**)

ꙁнаменіе 2:12 'signal' (H 'turn')
[**ꙁвати**] 2:4 *see* **царевати**
ꙁваше сѧ be called, be summoned: 2:18; ꙁванъ 4:11 дондеже не ~ будеть 5:12 аꙁъ ꙁванъ есмь; ꙁвана 4:11 а аꙁъ не ~ быхъ
ꙁлаꙗ bad, wicked 9:25 (**A5.31**)
ꙁлоба badness, evil: 7:7; ꙁлобу 8:3, 8:6

.і. '10' 2:16, 9:10, 9:12, 9:13, 9:14; .і. тысѧщь **3:9** (Tn)
и *Asm, see* **онъ**
и *conj* and; *emph. particle* also, even, indeed.
This ubiquitous item usually corresponds to the Hebrew connective, but it often has no equivalent, and often does not appear where we might expect it: see **A10.11**, p. 170. A full listing would serve no purpose. Here are references to specific comments: **1:1**, **1:3**, **1:4**, **1:11**, **6:2**, **7:7**, **9:2**, **9:4**, **9:18**, **9:31**
ибо for: 1:8, 9:4 (**A10.61**)
иди go: 4:16; иде 6:12
идеже where, in the place where: 4:3, 8:17, 9:1
иже *rel. pron.,* who: *Nsm* 1:1, 1:2, 1:9, 2:3 по руцѣ Егаевѣ, иже бѣ тивоунъ, 2:8, 2:15, **3:4** и{ж}е [и не] 3:4, 3:7, 4:5, 4:8?, 6:10, 7:5, 7:9, 9:22, 9:24; *Asm* 2:6 (2), 5:2, 5:5, 5:8, 5:12, 7:10, 8:2, 8:8, 9:1; *Asn* 9:1?; *Nsf* 1:15, 1:17?; *Asf* 1:12, 1:20 (2), 6:14, 9:25; *Is* 10:2; *Npm* **1:3** и иже ихъ ѡ немь; 1:10 седми старостъ иже служаху; 1:13 (2); 1:16; 1:14 (2); 1:14 а иже ближнии ему, 3:12, 8:9, 8:10, 8:11, 8:14, 9:15, 9:16, 9:18, 9:19, 9:20; *Npf* 2:9, 3:2; *Apf* 8:5; ꙗже *Nsf* 8:6; егоже *Asm* 6:9 (2), 6:11, 8:7; ньже 9:1 въ ньже, 9:22 въ нже; юже *Asf* 2:4, 8:3; емуже *Dsm* 4:11; еиже *Dsf* 2:7; нем'же 2:12 по ~; 6:8 конь на ~; ꙗже *Npf* 1:18; нѧже *Apm* 6:8; ꙗже *Apn* 8:11, 9:23 (2), 9:26
еже *Nsm* 2:6, {3:7}; *Nsn* 9:26?; *Asm* 1:11, 4:11?; *Asn* 2:1, 2:13 все ~ аще, 3:12, 4:1 все ~, 4:7, 6:4, 6:10 всего ~, 7:9; *Asf* 5:4, 5:13 (?въ нюже? егда?), 8:5; *Is* 5:11? (cf. 10:2); *Npm* 3:3, 8:11?, 9:12?; *Apm* 4:16
е[же] 5:6 ѵто е{сть} прошение твое
иже *conj* 1:13?, 1:15, 1:20?; 3:6, 7:4, и{же} **7:7**, 8:1 (**A10.62**)
иꙁ *prep w G,* from: 2:6, 2:9, 2:13, 7:8 (**A9.33**)
[**иꙁбавити**] 3:13 *see* иꙁб{и}ти
иꙁбавленіе salvation: 4:14
иꙁб{иа}ти kill: **3:13** (иꙁб[ави]ти); иꙁбиша 9:12
иꙁъбудуѵи сѧ avoiding, escaping: 4:13
{**иꙁ**}**вол**{**ю**}**никъ** *see* вольникъ
иꙁдрѧднѣе exceptional: **3:8**
иꙁидеть goes out: 1:19
иꙁобрѣте found: 6:2 (**A13.52**)
имѧ name: 2:5, ?2:22, ?3:12; по имени 9:26; именемь 2:14, 8:8 (2), ?[пис]меньмь 8:10
имѣꙗше had: 5:2
имуть are (not) to, must (not), will (not): **9:27** того не имуть преступати (**A11.2**)
имьже because: **8:7** им'же въврглъ бѧше руцѣ свои (**A10.61**)
иного other: 4:14
исповѣда told: 4:7, 6:13 (**L8.31**)
исполни сѧ was filled: 3:5; испълн{иша сѧ} испълн[ѧше] were filled **1:5**

.к҃. '20' 8:9
.кг. '23' 8:9
како 5:11, 8:6 (2)
каменига 1:6
кандилѣхъ ?perfumes: **2:12** въ кандилѣхъ
капии two talents: **3:9** 10000 капии сребра (**L16.42**)
кличa call, cry out: 6:11 и бѣ ~ пред нимь
конь horse: *As* 6:8, 6:9, 6:10, 6:11; *Ls* кони; {на кони} 6:9; коних 8:10 на бързых ~; 8:14 на ~ бързых (**A3.3, 3.5**)
коньникы horseman: 8:10 съ приставы ~ иже ꙗздѧху на бързых коних
конець end: 5:2
конучает end, finish: 9:28 памѧт не ~ сѧ ѡт чадъ их
красоту beauty: **1:11**; красоты 1:4
кромѣ except for: **4:11** кромѣ емуже простреть прутъ златъ (**T9.35**)
къ *prep w D,* to: 1:22 (3), 2:3, 2:12, 2:13, 2:14 (2), 2:15, 2:16, 3:7 (2), 3:8, 3:9, 3:9 (2), 3:12 (3), 3:13, 4:2, 4:6, 4:7, 4:8, 4:10, 4:11 (3), 4:13, 4:15, 4:16, 5:10, 5:12, 6:4, 6:5, 6:7, 6:12, 6:14, 7:1, 7:4 (2), 7:7, 7:8, 8:9 (3), {8:13}, 9:19, 9:22 (2), 9:23, 9:27, 9:30 (2) (**A9.21**)
къждо each: 1:22 ꙗкоже ꙗзыкъ людии къждо ихъ, **9:16** и оуби[тъ] къждо нелюбимого†; къмуждо 9:22 посылати дары ~ другу своему
книгы *pl. tant.,* book: 1:22, 6:1 ~ памѧтныꙗ, 8:5, 8:10, 9:20, 9:29, 9:30; книгахъ 1:19, **2:23** въ ~ памѧтьныхъ, 9:32, 10:2 в ~ грамотных; книгамъ {**4:8**}, **9:26**
кто who: 4:14, 6:4; кому 6:6

.л҃. '30': 4:11
лапь (*preceded by* не) not easily, with difficulty: 2:14 И не прихожаше ~ къ цареви (**A8.3**)
лептугъ ?purple cloth?: 1:6 и лептугъ на главахъ сребреныхъ (**L5.46, L21.21**)
лептужьнъ ?of purple cloth?: 8:15 и оушьвъ шьлковъ ~ (**A5.32, L5.46**)
лѣто year: 1:3, 2:16, 3:7; лѣта 9:27 (2) по всѧ ~ и ~ (**L20**)
ли whether: 4:14 да кто вѣсть аще въ годину сию доступиши ли ты царства; *introduces rhetorical question*: **5:12** [ли мѧ]; 5:13 [ли] (**A10.42, T9.38**)
лице face: 7:8 ~ Аманови спаде; 1:14 иже видѧху ~ царево; лица 8:15 ѡт ~ царева (**L6.1**)
ложа bed: 1:6 ложа злата (**L1.3**)
ложница? bedchamber: **2:14** хранитель ложницѧ ?{**на**}**ложниц**{**амъ**}
локотъ ell: 5:14, 7:9 възвышѣ 50 ~ (**A1**)
лучьши better: 1:19 предастъ подрузѣ еꙗ ~ еꙗ (**A5.37**)
любо for, because: 2:10, 8:8, 9:24 (**A10.61**)
любовью love: 2:17
людие people: 3:8, 3:11, 3:12, 4:11, 7:4, 8:9 (2); люди 3:6, 3:12, {7:3} 8:6 8:11; людии 1:22, 2:10, 2:20, 3:8, 3:12 (2), **8:17**; людьхъ 4:8; людьмъ 1:5, 3:14, 8:13, 1:11, 1:22, 8:13, 10:3; людьми 3:8, 9:2; людии ?*Ap* **3:6** (**L4.2**)
мала small: 1:5, 1:20 до мала
{**маслѣ**} oil: 2:12 {въ маслѣ маститѣ}
{**маститѣ**} fat: **2:12**
мати] mother: 2:7 мт҃и; мт҃ре *Gs* 2:7.
межю *prep w Inst.,* among: 3:8 ~ людьми (**A9.1**)
мене, [**мѧ**], **мнѣ**, **мною** *see* **азъ**

мѣсто place: 8:17; въ . . . мѣсто instead of 2:4, 2:7, 2:15, 2:17; ѿ мѣста 4:14
мѣсѧць] month: мц҃ь 2:12 (3), 2:16, 3:12, 8:9 (2), 9:1, 9:22; мц҃а 3:7 (2), 3:13, 8:12, 9:17, {9:16}, 9:19; мц҃ю 3:7
мєүєвою of (a) sword: 9:5 раною ~ (**A5.12**)
милость grace: 2:9, 5:8, 7:3, 8:5; милостью 2:17, милостию 2:15, 5:2 (**L12.9**)
минуша pass (away)?: **9:28** дньє веселии си нє минуша
миръ peace; welfare: 10:3; **2:11** ~ Есфири
младєнца Ap babies 3:13
мнѣ, мною *see* **азъ**
могоу be able: 8:6 (2); можєши **6:13**; [можєть] 8:8
мои my: 7:4 *Npm*; моꙗ *Nsf* 5:7 (2); *Ap* 4:16, {7:3}, 8:6; мою 5:8 (2), 7:3; моєго 5:3 (2), 5:3, 5:4, 5:6, 7:2, 8:6; моєи 7:3, {7:3}
молити ask, beg: 4:8 ~ єго; молѧщи 8:3 ~ єго
морьскыꙗ of the sea, marine: 10:1 на ѡстровы ~
мощи power, ability: 10:2 (**L9.1**) єго и ~ єго
мраморѧни of marble: 1:6 стълпи ~
мудрьци wise man: 6:13 рѣша єму ~ свои; мудрьцьмъ 1:13 рєүє царь ~ ижє поꙁнаꙗху годины
мужь man, husband: 2:5 (2), 4:11, 6:7, 7:6, *As* ?1:20 на ~ свои; мужа 6:9 да ѡблєүєт ~; мужєви 1:8, 6:9, 6:11; мужю 1:8, 1:22, 6:6, **6:9**; мужь Gp 1:17, 9:6, 9:12, 9:15
мука torture, pain: **7:8** ~ царицина
мүүили torture, torment: **8:11**
мүүитєлю tormenter: 3:10 Амонови . . . ~ Июдѣискому. (**L9.7**)
мълүати be silent: **4:14** Ащє мълүиши мълүаүи; мълүала 7:4 ~ быхъ
много much: 1:7 и вино царскоє ~; многы 2:8 ꙗкожє събра дв҃ца ~; многыми 1:4 дньми ~
множьство great quantity, multitude: 5:11 ~ сн҃овъ своихъ; 8:17 ~ людии ꙁємных жидовѧху сѧ; множьства 10:3 вольникъ ~ братьꙗ своєꙗ
мыслиши think: 5:3; мыслѧшє 9:24
мысль mind, spirit 1:10 вънєгда сѧ оудобрѧшє ~; thought, intention 8:3 ~ єго южє бѧшє помыслилъ, 8:5 вратити ~ Амонову . . . ижє бѣ написаль погубити Июдѣꙗ, 9:25 мысль єго ꙁлаꙗ, ижє помыслилъ бѧшє: 5:6 ~ просьбы твоєꙗ, 5:7 просьба моꙗ и ~ моꙗ, 5:8 {створити ~ мою}, 7:3 створиши ~ мою; мысли 3:5 исполни сѧ Амонъ ~ гнѣвныꙗ; 4:13, 6:6 въ ~ своєи (**L11.21**)
мьни consider, think: 4:13 Нє ~ си въ мысли своєи (**L11.2–24**)
мьсти vengeance: **9:2** ~ творити

.н҃. '50': 5:14, 7:9
на + *L* 1:2, 1:6 (2), 1:8, 2:14, 2:23, 5:1, 5:14, 6:4 (2), 6:5, {6:9}, 6:8, 6:10, 7:7, 7:9, 7:10, 8:7, 8:10, 8:14, 8:15, 8:17, 9:2, 9:3, 9:12, {**9:16**}; + *A* 1:16 (2), 1:17, 1:20, 2:1, 2:8, 2:11, 2:14, 2:17, 3:14, 4:6, 4:7, 5:4, 5:5, 5:8, 5:9, 5:12, 5:14, 6:9, 7:9, 8:3, {**8:8**}, 9:24, 9:25, 9:27 (3), 9:31, 10:1 (2) (**A9.21, A9.51**)
{н}авѣсит{и} ([д]а вѣсит[ы]) weigh out **4:7**; **навѣшю** I will weigh out 3:9 (**L16.43**)
надъ *prep w Inst,* above, over: И 5:11, 8:2, 9:2
наипьрвѣє first of all: 1:14 сѣдѧху ~ въ царьствѣ
{на}ложниц{а} concubine: **2:14** хранитєль ложницѧ (**L2.47**)
напалъ fall: 9:3 напалъ бѧшє страхъ (**L14.51**)
напишєть write: 8:5; написахуть 3:12; написа 2:23, 9:20, 9:29, 9:32; написаша 8:9, 8:10; написалъ 3:9 абы ~ погубити ꙗ; 8:5 мысль Амонову . . . ижє бѣ ~

погубити Июдѣꙗ, 9:23 бѣ ~; написана 10:2 и та соуть ~ в книгах; написано 3:12 ~ еже ꙁаповѣдаше; 6:2 И иꙁобрѣте в них ~ иже повѣда Мардъхаи
наполни сѧ be filled: 5:9
напълнѧху сѧ be filled: 2:12
нарѣканиє lamentation: **4:3** говѣнье и плаꙋь и нарѣканиє (**L14.2**)
наоутриꙗ in the morning: 5:12 (**L20.51**)
наꙋнєть begin: 2:4 [царь ꙁвати] {царевати} ~; наꙋьнуть 4:16 говѣти ~; †наꙋа **8:3** (**A11.2**)
нє 1:12, 1:15, 1:16 (2), 1:17 (3), 1:19 (2), 2:7, 2:10 (2), 2:14, 2:15, 2:20, 3:2 (2), **3:4** (also [нє]), 3:5, 3:8 (2), 4:2, 4:4, 4:11, 4:13, 4:16 (2), 5:9, 5:12 (2), 5:13, 6:3, 6:10, 6:13, 7:9, 8:8, 9:2, 9:9, 9:15, 9:16, 9:27, 9:28 (2), 9:28
{нѣ} 7:4 небо {нѣ} (н[є])
нєбо for: 7:4 небо н{ѣ} тѣсноты, 8:6 небо како могоу видѣти ꙁлобу (**A10.61 n**)
нєбонъ for: **2:12** небон[є] тако напълнѧху сѧ днье пристроꙗ єꙗ (**A10.61 n**)
нєврѣдъ 3:6 И въ неврѣдъ ѡꙋима его бысть (**L16.1**)
нєлюбимого unloved one: **9:16** къждо ~
нєприꙗꙁнивыи unfriendly, hostile; 7:6 мужь вражьбьныи и ~
нєуподоблєнъ dissimilar, ?incomparable: **1:7** (**A5.23**)
ни nor: 2:7, 2:10, 2:20, 3:5 (2), 4:16, 5:9, 6:4
николижє never: 9:28
никтожє no one: 8:8
никыижє no, none: **9:2** ~ ꙋл҃вкъ не ѡстоꙗше пред ними
ниꙋтожє nothing: **6:3** не створено єму ниꙋтоже ꙁа то
но, *see* **нъ**
ногама leg, foot: 8:3
нощь night: **4:16**, 6:1
нужа force, need: **1:8** беꙁ нужа
нъ but: 1:7 но, 2:14 нъ егда, 2:15 нъ ꙗкоже (see also C1:6, ms сниманъ·нъ)
нынѣ now: **9:27**

.ѻ҃. '70': .ѻ҃. и ҂є҃ '75000' 9:15 (**A7.21**)
о *prep w L,* around, about: **1:3** и иже ихъ ѡ немь, 4:8
оба both: 2:23
облаꙋить сѧ dress self, get dressed: 6:8
облєщи dress, clothe: 4:4; ѡблеꙋе{т}? **6:9** облеꙋемъ; ѡблеꙋе 6:11; ѡблеꙋе сѧ 4:1, 5:1
облюби love, ?fall in love: 2:17 И ѡбълюби царь Есфирь паꙋе всѣхъ женъ (**L12.72, L21.21**)
обнєсєна borne, raised up: 2:15 бы^с . . . ѡбнесена мл҃стью, 2:17, 5:2 (**L12.91**)
обрати сѧ ?be turned back: **9:25**
обрѣтє find: 1:5 людьмъ елико же ихъ ~ въ Сусанѣ; ѡбрѧку 7:3 (**A1.4**), 8:5 ѡбрѧщеши 4:16 събери всѧ Июдѣꙗ еже ихъ ~
оградъ] garden: Gs ѡграда 1:5, 7:8; къ ѡграду 7:7 (**L1.231**)
одєжи clothing, clothes: 4:2 въ ~ сукнѧнѣ (**L5.1**)
онъ he, she, it, they: **она** *Nsf* 1:17;
  и *Asm* 5:11 възнесе и; 8:2 дасть и; *Asm* 1:17 предъ **нь**;
  єго *Asm* 3:1 възнесе его, 4:8 молити ~, 8:3 молѧшти ~, 5:11 вьꙁвелиꙋа ~, 10:2; 6:6 ꙋьстити ~, 6:7, 6:11 (**L12.15**);
  ю *Asf*: 2:7, 2:14, 2:15, **2:17**;

ню: 2:1 на ~;
нєго *Gsm* 1:19 ѡт ~; 4:4 с ~ ;
єго (*poss*) 1:12, 1:20, 1:22, 2:2, 2:7, 2:8, 2:16, 2:21, 3:6, 4:3, 4:4, 4:11, 5:2, 5:14, 6:3, 6:8, 6:13, 8:3 (2), 8:5, 8:15, 8:17, 9:1, {9:2}, 9:25, 10:2 (2);
єꙗ *Gsf* 1:19 лучьши ~;
єꙗ *Gsf* (*poss*) 1:11 (2), 1:19 (2), 2:1, 2:9, 2:12, 3:12, 4:4;
нємь *Lsm* 1:3 и иже ихъ ѡ нємь; 1:12 в ~, 5:14 на ~;
нєи *Lsf* 2:14 на ~;
єму 2:5 (*poss.*) имѧ єму Мардахаи; 3:4, 3:5, 3:6, 4:5, 4:7, 4:8, 4:10, 4:17, 5:4, 5:14, 6:3, 6:4, 6:11, 6:13 (2), 8:1, {8:6};
нєму *Dsm* 6:5 к нєму;
єи *Dsf* 2:9 (4), 2:10, 2:11, 2:12, 2:13, 2:20, 4:4, 4:8 (2), 5:3, 8:1;
нєи *Dsf* 5:12 к ~;
єи *Dsf, poss* 2:7 (2) ѿц҃ь ~ и мт҃и ~, 2:17 на главу ~, 8:9 писаниє ~;
нимь: *Ism* пред ~ 2:9 [нєю], 2:17, 2:20, 4:8, 5:9, 6:11, 6:13 (2); с ~ 2:20, {8:5} 6:14 *'prevail against'*;
н[єю] *Ism* 2:9 прєдъ {нимь}, 2:13; 4:5 с ~;
има *Ddu*: 5:8, **5:11**;
ѡни *Npm* 3:8;
ꙗ *Ap*: 3:9, 4:7, {8:11}, 9:22, 9:24, 9:28;
є *Ap* {ѣ}: **4:8**;
ихъ *Gp* 3:4, 3:8, 1:3 и иже ~ ѡ нємь, 1:5 єлико жє ~ ѡбрѣтє, 1:22 къждо их, 4:16 Июдѣꙗ єже ~ ѡбрѧщеши, 8:11 Июдѣомъ єже ~ бѧшє, 9:27 всѧ єлико их приступаше къ ним;
ихъ *Gp, poss* 1:22, 2:3, 3:8, 3:12, 3:13, 8:9 (3), 8:11, 9:2, 9:27 (2), 9:28, 9:31
нихъ *Lp*: 6:2 в ~, 8:17, 9:3 на ~;
имъ *Dpm*: 2:3, 3:2, 3:4, 6:14, 9:21, 9:22, 9:26;
нимь: къ ~ 9:23, 9:27;
ими *Ip*: 9:1 владѣти ~;
ними: *Ip* прєд ~1:17, 9:2

{ѡноє} **7:9**
оправи сѧ set self right?, sit up?: **8:4** и ~ Есфирь и ста прєд царьмь (**L21.21**)
остатокъ the rest, remnant: 9:16 ~ Июдѣи
остоꙗшє withstand: **9:2** нє ~ прєд ними
островы island: 10:1 на ~ морьскыꙗ
осуди judge, pass sentence: 2:1 єже ~ на ню
отвѣща answer: 4:15 ~ Есфирь къ Мардъхаєви, 7:3 ~ . . . и рєчє
отвѣтъ answer: **5:7** да{сть} ~ и рєчє
отроци servants: 2:2, 6:3, 6:5 young men, servants (**L2.45**)
от *prep w G,* from: 1:1, 1:5, 1:19, 1:20, 3:7 (2), 3:13, 4:5, 4:14, 5:8, 7:7 (3), 7:8, 8:9, 8:13, 8:15, {9:16}, 9:22 (3), 9:28 (2) (**A9.1**)
открыти open: 3:14 и ~ всѣмъ людємъ; открыто[мъ] 8:13 ~ всѣм людємъ
откуду from where: 7:5 кто то, и ѡткуду єс{ть}
отьць] father: 2:7 ѡц҃ь; ѡц҃ѧ 2:7, 4:14
отѧлъ take off: 8:2 и снѧ царь пьрстєнь свои иже бѣ ѡтѧлъ оу Амана
охвота eagerness?, gladness: 8:16, 8:17 (**A1.52, L13.4**)
охвотьнъмь eager?, glad: 5:9 вєсєлъ и ѡхвотьнъмь ср҃дцьмь (**A1.52, A5.51, L13.4**)
очью eye: 3:11; ѡчима 2:9, 3:6, 5:2, 7:3, 8:5, 8:8 (**L5.2**)

.п҃. '80' 1:4
пагубу destruction, ruin: 8:6
падати fall: 6:13 ꙗко поꙋалъ еси ~ прѣд нимь; падаꙗ 6:13 и аще ~ падеши прѣд ним (**L19.8**)
падеши fall: 6:13; паде 8:3
пакы again: 1:9, 4:16, 5:8, **5:12** (2), 7:2, 9:15 (**L20.53**)
памѧть memory: 9:28
памѧтныꙗ of memory: 6:1 книгы ~; памѧтьныхъ **2:23** въ книгахъ ~ 6:1
паꙋе than, more than: 2:17 (2), 3:8 than, 4:13
пѣстуꙗ nourish, bring up: **2:7** И бѧше ~ домаꙋадицю сироту
пеꙋать seal, ?copy: 3:14 ~ грамотнаꙗ,
4:8 ~ {книгамъ}, 8:13 Пеꙋать грамотнаꙗ, пеꙋатью 8:8 ~ царевою, 8:10
пеꙋать[никомъ] 4:8: *see* **пеꙋать**
пиръ banquet: 1:3, 1:5, 1:9, 2:18 (3), 5:5, 5:8, 5:12, 5:14, 8:17 (**L13.7**)
писано written: 8:8 ~ есть
писание writing: 1:22, 8:9 (**C3:12**)
писци scribe: 3:12, 8:9 (**L2.42**)
писмѧ letter (of alphabet); writing system: **3:12**, 8:9, 9:27, писм[енемь]? 8:8; писменьмь 8:10 ~ царевъмь Ахасъвероса for именемь
питва drink, drinking; party: 1:8; питву 5:4; питвы 7:7 ѿ ~ винныꙗ; къ питвѣ 6:14 (**L13.7**)
питвьныи *adj to* питва: 9:17 твориша днь ~ и веселныи, 9:18; питвьному 7:8 къ дому ~; питвьныꙗ 9:22 дни ~ и весельныꙗ
пити drink: 3:15 а царь и Аманъ сѣдоста ~; питъ *supine* 7:1 И приде царь и Аманъ питъ къ Есфирии; пиите 4:16 не ꙗдите ни ~; пьꙗху 1:7
питье drinking: 9:19; питии 7:2 в ~ виньнѣмь
плаꙋь weeping: 4:3 (**L14.2**)
племѧ tribe: 9:27; племене 6:13 ~ Июдѣиского (**L4.2**)
по *w L* 1:12 (2), 1:15, 2:1, 2:3, **2:8**, 2:12, 2:14, 3:1, 4:16, 9:26; по нем'же; *w A* **5:5** оубързите по Амана; 1:5, 4:16 по 3 дни, 9:27 по вся лѣта и лѣта; *w D* 1:15, 2:16 (2), 3:8, 3:12 (2) 3:13, 3:14, 3:15, 4:16, 6:9, 6:11, 8:5, 8:11 (2), 8:14, 9:2 (2), {9:4, 9:12, 9:16, 9:19, 9:20, 9:20 (?ко) (**A9.36, L20.41**)
повелѣ command: 6:1 (**L8.41**)
повелѣнье command, order: 2:20; повелѣниꙗ 1:15 (**L8.41**)
повѣдати tell, recount: 4:8; повѣдающи 2:20 И не бѧше Есфирь ~ рода своего; повѣда 2:10 [вѣда], 2:22 (2), 3:4, 4:9, 6:2, 8:1; повѣдаша 3:4, 3:6, 4:4, 4:12; повѣдала 2:10 абы не ~ (**L8.3**)
повѣсити hang: 6:4; повѣсѧт 5:14 ать ~ Мардъхаꙗ; повѣсите 7:9; повѣсиша 7:10, 8:7, 9:13, 9:14; повѣсивъ 6:12 ~ главу свою; повѣшенъ 9:25 ~ быс{ть}; повѣшена **2:23** ~ быста
погоньци courier: **c3:15**, 8:14; Ip **3:13** погоньц[ѣ] (**L2.44**)
погубити destroy, cause to perish: 3:6, 3:9,
{3:13}, 4:7, 7:4, 8:5, 8:11, 9:24; погубиша 9:6, 9:12 (**L17.1**)
погублениемь destruction, annihilation: 9:5 раною меꙋевою и оубьениемь и ~
погыбну perish: 4:16 (2) да аще ~ да ~; погыбнеть 4:14
подвигнуща сѧ move, budge: **5:9**
подѣша put, place: 9:15, 9:16 не ~ рукъ (**L6.311**)
подруга friend: подрузѣ 1:19 (**L3.1**)
подъстави minor official: **9:3** Np

подъıаша undertake: 9:23 И ~ Июдѣи ıакоже бѣша поѵали творити; 9:27 и ~ Июдѣи на сѧ и на племѧ своє

поʒнаıаху know: 1:13 (2) мудрьцьмь иже ~ годины . . . прѣдъ всѣми иже ~ ʒаконъ и судъ

поʒвашє call, summon: 2:14 ~ ю именемъ

поиду go: 4:16

поискали seek out, find: 2:2 да ~ быхомъ цареви двѹхъ двѹць добровʒорных

показати show: 1:11, 4:8; показа 1:4

покланѧху сѧ bow, make obeisance: 3:2 (**L10.1**)

поклони сѧ bow: 3:2 (**L10.1**)

покоихъ rest (?): **9:16**

полаты palace: 5:1 Gs; полатѣ 5:1 Ls palace; полатѣ D 4:7; полатам 3:9 treasury (**L1.2**, p. 260 §5.8)

полонъ booty, captives: 9:10 а въ ~ не простроша рукъ своих, 9:15, 9:16 и въ ~ не подѣша рукъ своих; {полонъмь} 2:6 съ [пол^н^ъмь] иже поло{не}ни съ Охониемь (**A1.54, L18.212**)

полони take prisoner: 2:6; полоненъ 2:6; поло{не}ни 2:6 (**L18.212**)

полу half: до ~ црства 5:3, 5:6, 7:2

помилованиє mercy; ?alms: **9:22** ~ сиротамъ

поминающє remember, recall: 9:28 И днии сиıа ~ суть

помысли think: *imv* 9:12 ~ ты; *aor* 6:6 И ~ Аманъ в мысли своеи; 7:5 иже такы помыслы ~; помыслилъ 8:3 мысль его юже бѧше ~ на Июдѣıа; 9:25 мысль его ʒлаıа, иже ~ бѧше на Июдѣıа (**L11.23**)

помыслы plan, intention: **7:5** иже такы ~ помысли

{**посадником**} governor, administrative official: 8:9 (**L2.23, 262 §6.31**)

послушашє obey: 3:4; послушан{а} 1:20 и будеть послушан[ие] рѣѵь царева

послухъ 1:17 и не въ послухъ пред ними

посредѣ amid, in the center of: 4:1 ~ града

постави put, place 3:1, 8:2

постелею bed: 7:8 пред ~ (**L1.3**)

постигнѧшє reach, attain: 9:1 (**C4:3**)

постилахоу spread: 4:3

послати send: 9:22; посла 1:22, 4:4, 9:20, 9:30; послаша 8:10; пославъ 5:10

посылающє send: 9:19; посылаху 3:13

потухну (or **потушє**) be quenched, cease burning: **7:10** гнѣвъ царевъ ~ (**A1.311, L14.71**)

поѵалъ begin: 6:13 ıако ~ еси падати; поѵали **9:1** то иже ~ бѧху вра{гы} владѣти Июдѣи; 9:23 ıаже бѣша ~ творити (**A11.2 n**)

поѵиваху rest: 9:18

поѵиша rest: 9:17, 9:22

поıаʒдити ride: 6:11 и сътвори ~ ему по оулицѧмъ града (**A1.2, T9.31**)

поıалъ take: 2:15 иже ~ ю бѧше; поıата 2:8, 2:16

право (1) right: 3:8 а цареви бы не ~ пустити ихъ; 4:2 а то бѧше не ~ прити; (2) indeed: 7:8 ~ мука царицина; **7:9** ~ [бѧше] древо

превратити turn: **8:3**; преврати сѧ **9:1**, 9:22

превышии very high, highest: **3:1**

предъ *w A* 1:11, 1:17, 1:19, 8:1, 9:10, 9:25; *w Inst.* 1:10, 1:13, 1:16, 1:17, 1:21, 2:23, 2:9, 2:15, 2:17, 3:7, 4:5, 4:8, 5:2, 5:9, 5:14, 6:1, 6:11, 6:13 (2), 7:3, 7:6, 7:8, 7:9, 7:10, 8:1, 8:3 (2), 8:4, 8:5 (2), {8:5}, 9:2 (**A9.34**)

прєдасть give, give over (to): 1:19
(?**пр{ѣ}идє** cross: 4:17)
{**прєпишє**[т]} *2du? pres* write: **8:8**
прєпоихъ drinking (?): **5:6** въ ~ виньныхъ (**L13.7**)
прєпродана sell: 7:4 ижє ~ быхъ азъ и людиє мои; прєпродани 7:4 Аще бо быхом къ рабом и къ рабынꙗмъ ~, мълчала быхъ
прѣстрои reestablish, set up again: **2:9** пр{ѣ}стро{и} ю {и} дв҃ица єꙗ (**A1.53**)
прєступати transgress: **9:27** и нн҃ѣ того нє имуть ~; прєступаєши 3:3
прєступи transgress: **1:19** а нє прєступи ?*pres.*
приближи сꙗ approach, come near: 5:2
привєсти bring: 1:11, 1:17, 6:14; привєдє 5:10, 5:12
приготованом prepared, ready: 8:13 (**C3:14**)
призвани invited, summoned: **3:12**
приклꙗкаꙗ kneel: 3:5 нє бы[с] Мардъхаи ни ~ ни припадаꙗ єму (**L10.2**)
приклꙗкну kneel: 3:2 нє приклꙗкну; приклꙗкноуща 5:9 оузрѣ Аманъ Мардъхаꙗ нє подвигнуща сꙗ ни ~ прєд нимь (**L10.2**)
(**приклꙗну** 3:2 T; *see* **приклꙗкну**)
принєсти bring: 3:9, 6:1; принєсоут 6:8 да ~ пърты царєвы
приобрѣтє find, obtain: **8:6** злобу ꙗжє ~ люди моꙗ
припадаꙗ fall down, prostrate self: 3:5 ни приклꙗкаꙗ ни ~; припадающ{є} 3:2 И вси раби царєви . . . припадающ[а] покланꙗху сꙗ Амонови (L10.1)
припалъ fall (near?): **7:8** и Аманъ ~ бꙗшє прєд постєлєю Єсфириною
приставилъ appoint: 2:3 да бы ~ царь приставникы
приставникы minor official, commissioner: *pqd* 2:3 (**L2.24**)
приставъ: minor official: пристав{ом} 3:12 къ ~ по зємли; приставы 8:10 и послаша книгы съ ~ коньникы (**L2.21**)
[**пристрою**] *see* прѣстрои
пристроꙗ ?ointments: 2:12 тако напълнꙗху сꙗ днье ~; пристрою **2:3** даꙗ имъ ~ ихъ, 2:9 и оубързи ~ єи; пристроꙗхъ 2:12 въ ~ жєньскыхъ
приступашє approach: 9:27
приступиша approach: 6:14
прити come: 1:12, 1:17, 2:12, 2:13, 2:15, 4:2, 4:8, 4:11; при{дєши} 5:14 (при[шєд]); придєть 4:11, 6:5; придꙗшє 2:12, 2:13; придє 4:2, 4:9, **4:17** (пр{ѣ}идє?), 5:10, 6:4, 6:6, 7:1, 8:1, 9:10; придоша 4:4; придоста 5:5; пришєлъ 5:4, 5:8 да бы ~ царь; пришла 1:19 ꙗко нє ~ Вастиꙗ; [пришєд] 5:14
приходꙗщи come: 2:14 И на вєчєръ та бѣ ~, и заутра бѣ възвращающи сꙗ; прихожашє 2:14, 9:25
приꙗти take, receive: 4:4 нє въсхотѣ ~; приꙗтъ 2:7 ~ ю Мардъхаи
приꙗзнь friend: 5:10 привєдє ~ свою; приꙗзни Np 5:14
про *prep. w A,* concerning: **4:5** и оувѣдати чєму то є и ~ что є (**A9.1**)
провєсти lead, escort: 6:9 ~ по оулицамъ града
{**провозвѣщю**} ?: **8.5**
прозваша proclaim: 9:26 И того ради ~ дни ты по имєни жрєбиинѣмь
проповѣдаꙗ announce, proclaim: 10:3
прост{оръ} *see* **простєрыи**
просвѣщєниє (**8:16**)
простръть **4:11** кромѣ ємужє ~ проутъ златъ; простръ 5:2, 8:4; простроша 9:10
просити ask, request: 5:3 и что мыслиши ~ цар҃ства моєго; проси imv 9:12 ~ ты и дам ти; *aor* 2:15 нє ~ рѣчи (**L12.11, 13**)

?**простєрыи 4:14** простєрыи иꙁбавлєниє: ?прост{оръ и}
просьба request, petition: 5:7; просьбу 5:8; просьбы 5:6 ѵто єсть мысль ~ твоєꙗ, 7:2 ѵто ~ твоєꙗ, Есфирии царицє?; просьбѣ 7:3 створиши мысль мою в ~ моєи (**L12.13**)
противу *w D,* against: 2:11, 5:1 (**A9.35**)
прошєниє request, petition: 5:6 ѵто ѣєжє ~ твоє (**L12.11, 13**)
проѵьтєны read: 6:1
прутъ wand: **4:11**, 5:2, 8:4; прута 5:2 и ꙗтъ ꙁа конєць ~ (**L21.21**)
прѧмо *w G, D,* opposite: 4:6 ~ вратъ царевъ; 5:1 ~ двєрємъ полаты (**A9.35**)
пустити let, permit: 3:8 а цареви бы нє право ~ ихъ
пърты garments, clothing: **6:8**, 6:9 (**L5.1**)
пьрстьнь ring: 3:10, 8:2; пьрстньмь 3:12

.р҃. '100': .р҃.мь власти 1:1, 1:4, 8:9: .ркꙁ. '127' 9:30
раби slave: 3:2, 3:3, 4:11; рабомъ 1:3, 2:18, 6:13, 7:4; Ip рабы 5:11 (**L2.451**)
рабынѧмъ slave woman: 7:4 къ рабом и къ ~
ради for the sake of: 3:3 ѵьто ~; 4:16 мєнє ~; 9:19 того ~, 9:26 (2)
ражьжє сѧ be enkindled, start to burn: 1:12
раꙁвѣ except for: **9:12**
раꙁгнѣва сѧ become angry: 1:12 (**L14.7**)
раꙁдѣлєни separate: : 3:8 раꙁдѣлєни[є]
раꙁдра tear, rip: 4:1 и ~ Мардъхаи риꙁы своꙗ
раꙁноличь different, varied: 1:7 (**A5.11, L21.4**)
раною blow, wound: 9:5 ~ мєѵєвою и оубьєниємь
расѣꙗни scattered: 3:8
расповѣда recount: 5:11 (**L8.31**)
расповѣданиє account, ?amount: **4:7** ~ срєбра єжє рєѵє Аманъ да вѣситы къ полатѣ царѧ; 10:2 и ~ вєлиѵьа Мардъхаєва
распра{ш}єници those who are scattered, dispersed: **9:19** Июдѣи распра[щ]єници ижє сѣдѧху по градом распрашєным
распрашєным scattered, dispersed: 9:19
растворити ?annihilate: **3:13** ~ и иꙁб{ива}ти вса Июдѣꙗ; 4:8 И пєѵатьникомъ ꙁаконнымъ ижє бы{сть} в Сусанѣ градѣ дана ~ є; 7:4 ижє прєпродана быхъ аꙁъ и людиє мои ~ и оубити и погубити; 8:11 ꙗжє дасть царь Июдѣомъ єжє ихъ бѧшє по всѣмъ градомъ сбирати и дш҃ахъ своих ~ и оубити и погубити (**L17.21–63**)
раѵи wish, deign: **1:17** ѡна жє нє ~ прити (**L12.3, L21.51**)
рєщи say: 6:4; рєѵєши 5:14; рєѵашє 2:13, 2:15; рєкуѵє 6:9; рєкомыи 3:7, 3:13, 8:9, 8:12, 9:1; рєкомаго 9:15, 9:17, 9:19; рєѵє 1:10, 1:13, 1:16, 1:17, 1:21, 3:8, 3:11, 4:7, 4:10, 4:13, 5:3, 5:4, 5:5, 5:6, 5:7, 5:12, 5:14, 6:3, 6:4, 6:5, 6:6, 6:7, 6:10, 7:2, 7:3, 7:5, 7:6, 7:8, 7:9 (2), 8:5, 8:7, 9:12, 9:14; рєкоша 1:17, 1:18, 6:3, 6:5; рѣша 2:2, 3:3, 6:13 (**A11.31**)
рєѵєниє 9:32 И ~ Есфирино оустави гл҃ъ вєсєлиа сєго написа въ книгах (**L8.23, 41**)
рѣѵь word, thing, affair: 1:13, 1:20, 1:21, 2:4, 2:23, 4:3, 5:8, 5:14, 9:26; *A* 5:5, 9:20; рѣѵи *Gs* 9:31; *Ds* 1:12 рѣѵи, 8:14; *Ap* 4:9, 4:12, 9:30; рѣѵи *thing Gs* 2:15, 6:10; рѣѵьхъ 2:1 (**L8.1**)
риꙁы outer garment: 4:1, 4:4, **5:1**, 6.11 (**L5.1**)
родъ kin, relatives: **9:28** (2); *Gs* рода 2:20 ~ моєго; роду 2:10 ни ~ своєго (**L6.3**)

росполону booty, plunder: **3:13** добытокъ ихъ къ ~; 8:11 добыткы ихъ по ~ (**A1.54, L18.12**)
рукы hand: 3:10 с ~ своєꙗ; руцѣ: 8:7 въвьрглъ бѧше ~ свои въ Июдѣ{ѧ}, 2:21 ꙁадѣти ~ цари Ахасъверосѣ, 3:6 ꙁадѣти ~ Мардъхаю єдиному, 6:2 ꙁадѣти ~ царю Ахасъверосу, 2:3, 2:8 по ~ Егаєвѣ; 2:14 по ~ Сааꙁъгаꙁовѣ; 2:8 на ~ Егаєвѣ; 6:9 дати . . . на ~ мужю; рукъ 9:9 в полонъ нє простроша ~ своих; 9:15, 9:16 в полонъ нє подѣша ~ своих; рукахъ 1:15, 1:12 по ~ старостъ; руку 5:2 въ ~ своєю (**L6.3**)

самъ self: 7:9; сама 4:16
{**сатрапомъ**} satrap: 1:3 [странамъ] (**L2.3–34**)
свиту garment: 6:10; свитѣ 8:15 (**L5.1–11**)
своꙗ own: **5:14** жєна ~; свои Asm 1:20 ?на мужь ~; 3:10, 6:12, 8:2; свою 5:10 (2), 6:12, 9:5, 9:25; своє 9:27; своєго 1:2, 1:3, 1:4 (2), 1:8, 2:3, 2:10, 2:16, 2:20, 5:1, 5:11; своєꙗ 3:10, 10:3; своєму 5:10, 9:22, 1:22; своєи 4:13, 5:1, 6:6, 6:13, 7:7; свои *Npm* 6:13; своꙗ *Ap* 4:1, 9:31 (3), ?1:20 *Ap* свои{х}; своимъ 1:3 (2), 2:18 (2), 6:13, 9:2, 9:5, 10:3 (2); своими 2:15, 5:11; своихъ 1:17, [2:3,] 2:20, 3:1, 4:8, 5:11, 9:2, 9:5, 2:10, 8:11, 8:13, 9:9, 9:15, 9:16 (2), {9:16}; свои *Adu* 8:2; своєю 5:2; своима 2:9
сє see! lo!: **3:8**, 4:11, 6:5, **6:14**, 8:7
сєдми seven: 1:10; сєдмью 1:1
сѣдѧща sit, be sitting: 5:13; сѣдѧшє 2:19, 2:21, 5:1, 6:10; сѣдѧху 1:14, 9:19
сѣдє sit down: **1:2**; сѣдоста 3:15
сѣмо hither, to here: 6:5
си *see* **сь, собѣ**
сила power; capability: **1:7** ꙗкожє ~ царєва ; 2:18 ꙗкожє бѣ ~ царєва; силу 8:11 вьсю ~; силѣ 1:3 ~ Фарисѣистѣи и Мадѣистѣи (**6.34, L9.1**)
силна strong, powerful: **1:20**
сир{**у**} *see* C2:7
сироту orphan: ?**2:7** бѧшє пѣстуꙗ домаѵѧдицю ~; сиротам ?paupers 9:22
скорѣ *see* въскорѣ
скърбии sorrow, affliction: 9:22 ѿ ~
слугы servants: 2:2, 6:3; слугами **2:15** (H *r'yh* 'who look on her')
служаху serve: 1:10
{**слухъ**} fame: 9:4
собѣ self: 2:7, 2:15; **сѧ** *pronoun, As* 9:27; **си** 4:13 Нє мни си въ мысли своєи (**A4.2**)
срамоту shame:**1:20** ??; срамоты 1:18
срѣбро silver: 3:11; срѣбра 3:9, срєбра 4:7
срєбрєна of silver: 1:6; срєбрєныхъ 1:6
срєдѣ, *see* посрєдѣ
ста stop, stand: 5:1, 8:4; **7:7** ~ на д҃ши своєи
старѣишинамъ elder, leader, official: **4:3**; старѣишинахъ дому 1:8 (**T6.3**)
старого old: 3:13
староста] elder: *Gp* старостъ 1:10, 1:12, 1:15 (**L2.2–22, L21.2**)
стѣны wall: 1:6 (**L1.23**)
стоить stand, be standing: 6:5, 7:9; стоꙗшє 4:5; стоꙗху 9:16
[**стоꙗху**] **2:9** *see* {до}стоꙗ{шє}
столъ chair: 3:1; столѣ 1:2, 5:1 (**L1.3**)
странамъ? 1:3 {сатрапомъ}: see L2.3
страхъ fear: 8:17 ~ Июдѣискыи, 9:3 ~ Мардъхаєвъ (**L14.52**)

стрѣжаста guard: 2:21
строю: **3:9** къ ~ дѣла (perhaps стро{ѧщ}ю or стро{ител}ю) manager (**L2.41**)
стръи] uncle, father's brother: *Gs* стръꙗ 2:7, строꙗ 2:15
стълпи pillar, column: 1:6 ~ мраморѧни
судъ judgement: 1:13
судии 6:9 'a high official' (**L2.3**)
†**сукно** ?ashes: **4:1** въ власѧницю и ~, 4:4; †сукна 4:3 власѧницѣ и ~
сукнѧнѣ made of rough cloth: 4:2 въ ѡдежи ~
съ *w Inst,* 'with' 2:6 (2), 2:13, 3:10, 2:13, 4:4, 4:16, 5:4 , 5:12 (2), 5:14, 6:13, 6:14, 7:7, 7:8, 8:10; 9:25 (2); съ *w G,* '(down) from' 3:10, 4:4
сбирати collect, gather: 8:11; сбираху сѧ 9:2, 9:18
събєри collect, gather: 4:16; събраше 2:19; събра 2:8; събраша сѧ 9:15, 9:16; събрали 2:3 да быша събрали
събысть сѧ take place: 9:26
сдѣлающє make: 5:14 ~ будѣтє (L11.44)
сключьшаꙗ сѧ happen, take place: 4:7, 6:13
сконѵала finish, end: 7:7 ~ сѧ бѧшє ʒлоба
съкривила ?wrong: **1:16** нє царю єдиному ~ Вастии ца҃рицѧ, ащє нє на всѧ боꙗры и на всѧ ꙗʒыкы
смѧтє сѧ become confused: **6:1**
сниманънъ 1:6, see comm.
сънъ sleep: : 6:1 въ снѣ
снѧти take off: 4:4; сънѧ 3:10, 8:2
спадє fall: **7:8** лицє Амонови спадє
съсудъ vessel: 1:7 (3) пьꙗху въ съсудѣхъ ʒлатыхъ и съсоудъ съсоуду нєоуподоблєнъ
створєниє doing, what one does 2:1
створити do: 1:8, 3:11, 5:8 ~ мысль; 1:15, 6:6, 6:9; 6:6 ~ ѵ{ьс}ть; 9:1, 9:22; створю 5:8 а ʒаутра створю ꙗкожє будєть рѣѵь царєва, 5:8 на пиръ ижє ~; створимъ *1s*? 5:6, 9:12 ~ тобѣ; 7:2 ~ ти волю твою; створиши 7:3 ~ мысль мою; створи *imv*: 9:14; створитє *imv* 5:5 ~ рѣѵь Єсфирину; створи *aor*: 1:3, 1:5, 1:9, 1:15, 1:20, 1:21, 2:4, 2:17 ~ ю царицу; 2:18, 2:18, 4:17, 5:5, 5:14, 6:4, 6:10, 6:11, 6:11 ~ поꙗʒдити єму по оулицѧмъ града, 7:5; створиша 9:5 ~ волю свою; 9:12 ѵто ~; створилъ 7:9 дрєво єжє ~ бѣ; 7:10 на дрєвє ижє ~ бѧшє; створила 5:4 на питву єжє быхъ ~ єму; 5:12 на пиръ ижє ~ бѣ; створили 2:11 оувѣдѣти . . . ѵто быша ~ єи; створєно 6:3 (2) (**L7.1**)
с[ы] ?being: **7:6** с{ьи}? с{ъи}?
сынъ son: 2:5, 9:24; сына 2:5 (2), 3:1, 8:5, 9:9; сыну 3:10; сыновъ 5:11, 9:9, 9:12, 9:14
сь] this: *Nsm* с[ы]? **7:6**; си *Nsf* 9:26; сии 3:14 *Asm*; сию 4:14 (2), 9:20; сє 6:9 *Asn*; сєго 9:31, 9:32 вєсєлиꙗ ~; си 9:27 *Adn*; си **9:28** *Npm?*; си *Npn?* 4:16; сиꙗ *Apm* 9:28; симъ *Dp* 9:26
сьрдцє] heart: **5:9** вєсєлъ и ѡхвотьнъмь ср҃дцмь
сѣ- *see under* **сє**-
сѧ particle, *preposed* 1:10, 5:4; *postposed* 1:12 (2), 2:1, 2:12, 2:14, 2:16, 2:18, 2:20, 2:21, 3:2 (2), 3:5, 3:7, 3:15, 4:1, 4:4, 4:7, 4:8, 4:13 (2), 5:1, 5:2, 5:9 (2), 5:14, 6:1, 6:8, 6:12, 6:13, 7:7, 7:8, 8:4, 8:13, 8:15 (2), 8:17 (2), 9:1, 9:2, 9:15, 9:16, 9:18, 9:22, 9:25, 9:26; ?сє 6:9

.т҃. '300' 9:15
такъ this kind of: 1:8 ибо бѧше ~ оуставъ; такы 7:5
тако thus, in this way: 2:4, 2:12, 3:2, 5:8, 6:9, 6:10, 6:11, 7:5, 9:14
твоє your (2s): 5:6; твоєго 3:8, 3:9, 4:14; твоєꙗ 5:6, 7:2; твоєю 3:11; твоима 7:3; твоꙗ 7:2; твою 7:2
творити do, make: 9:2 мьсти ~, 9:23 И подъꙗша Июдѣи ꙗже бѣша поꙋали ~; творѧщє 3:8 и ꙁакона царева ѡни нє суть ~, 9:19 сѣдѧху. . . ~, 9:27 ꙗкожє суть ~ 2 д҃нии си; 9:28 И д҃нии сиꙗ поминающє суть и ~ ꙗ; творѧшє 2:20 и повєлѣньє Мардахаєво Есфирь ~, 4:1 Мардъхаи бѣ вѣдаꙗ всє єжє ~ {сѧ} [царь]; творѧху 9:18 и ~ и тъ д҃нь питвьныи; твориша 9:17 ~ д҃нь питвьныи; творили 9:21 оуставити имъ абыша ~
твьрдь ?affirmation, authority: **9:29** И написа Есфирь . . . всю ~; твєрди 10:2 И всє дѣло ~ єго и мощи єго
тѣсноты crowdedness, lack of space: **7:4** нєбо н{ѣ} тѣсноты в дому
ти(в)унъ steward: 2:3; 2:15, 4:5; тивуна 2:14; тивунъ Gp 7:9; тивоуни 4:4,; тивуни 6:14, 9:3; тивуномъ 3:12, {8:9}; тивоуна Nd 2:21; Ad 6:2 (**L2.22, 23, L21.2, 262 §6.1**)
три three: 4:16 по три д҃ни
тъ that: 2:18 тъ пиръ, 3:4, 7:5 кто т[о]; 8:1, 9:10 въ д҃нь тъ, 9:1 въ тъ д҃нь, 9:1 въ 12 м҃ць т[о] є Адаръ, 9:18 и творѧху и тъ д҃нь питвьныи; то [3:4], 3:13, [7:5], 8:9, 8:12, 4:2 придє до вратъ царѧ а то бѧшє нє право прити къ вратом, 4:5 оувѣдати ꙋєму то є и про ꙋто є, 5:8 И ащє бы царєви тако оудобрѣло, [то] дати мнѣ просьбу мою, 5:13 и всє то нє врєдно ли єсть мнѣ, 6:3 (2) ꙁа то, 9:1 прєврати сѧ то ижє поꙋали бѧху вра{гы} владѣти Июдѣи ??; та 2:14 та бѣ приходѧщи; ту 6:1 в ту нощь, 8:9 в годину ту; того 8:8; тому 8:13; томь 2:13 в ~; 4:16 по ~; та *Npn* 10:2 та соуть написана; ты *Ap* 1:2, 1:5, 2:21, 9:26; тѣхъ 2:1, 3:1, 7:9, 7:10
тъгда then: [2:14,] 6:4
тъкмо only: **4:11**
тъщь *see* **вънатъщь** 8:14
ты you (*2s*), thou: 3:3, 4:14 (2), 9:12 (2); *D* ти 5:3 (2), 5:6 (2), 7:2, 9:12; тобѣ 3:11, 5:6, 7:2, 9:12
{**тысѧщь**} thousand: **3:9** (**A7.22**)

оу *w G,* near, at, at the place of: 8:2 ~ Амана; 5:1 [у дому царєва]
оубииць killer?: **9:11** оуби{єнъ}
оубити kill: 7:4, 8:11; оуби[тъ] *3s aor* **9:16**; оубиша 9:10, 9:15; оуби{єнъ} **9:11** {оубьєну быты} **4:11** [къ оубою]
оубо therefore: 3:9 И ащє царєви бы оубо доволно [бы] было
?**оубою** ?killing: **4:11** єжє къ ~ {оубьєноу быти} *see* оубити
оубърꙁи hasten, speed up: 2:9 и ~ пристрою єи; оубърꙁиша 6:14 приступиша и ~ привєсти Амана; оубърꙁитє 5:5 И рєꙋє царь, ~ по Амана
оубьєниємь killing: 9:5 раною мєꙋєвою и ~ и погублєниємь
оувѣдати find out, learn: 4:5
оувѣдѣти find out, learn: 2.11 (**A11.1, L21.54**)
оувѣрєныꙗ convinced (?): **9:30** рѣꙋи оумирєныꙗ и ~
оувидѣ see, catch sight of: **7:7**
оуврєдити value, esteem: **1:17** ꙗко нє ~ мужь своихъ (**L16.1**)
оуготованымъ prepared, ready: 3:14 быти ~ на д҃нь сии

оудобрѣло?: **2:9** и пр{ѣ}стро{и} ю {и} дв҃ица єꙗ ~ в дому женьстѣмь.
оудобрю approve, ?improve: 7:3, 8:5 аще цареви ~; оудобрѣло 5:8 И аще бы цареви тако ~, то дати мнѣ просьбу мою (**L12.6, .711**)
оудобрити сѧ approve: 5:4 аще бы сѧ цареви оудобрити; оудобрѧше сѧ 1:10 въньгда сѧ оудобрѧше мысль царева въ винѣ; оудобри сѧ 5:14 и оудобри сѧ рѣчь пред Аманъмь (**L12.712, L21.21**)
оудолѣша vanquish: 9:5 И ~ Июдѣи всѣмъ врагомъ своимъ
оужасє сѧ be amazed: 4:4
оуӡрѣ see: 5:2, 5:9
оужє already: 4:11, 6:13
оуими take away, omit: 6:10 и нє оуими рѣчи
оулицю street: 4:6; оулицамъ 6:9, 6:11 (**L1.1**)
оулоб- *see* **улюб**- and L12.5
оулюби please, like: 2:9 И ~ дв҃цю †царь ѡчима своима, 6:11 тако створити мужеви єгожє царь ~ чьстити єго; оулюблѧшє 2:4 И дв҃у юже царь и [царь ӡвати] {царєвати} начнєть (**L12.51**)
оулюбѣєть be pleasing: 8:8 ꙗкоже ~ ѡчима ваю, оулюбѣ 2:4 и ~ рѣчь цареви; оулюбѣє 1:19 Аще цареви ~ (**L12.5–6**)
оумилосьрдити сѧ 4:8 (**L12.141**)
оумирєныꙗ at peace, reconciled (?): **9:30** Посла книгы . . . рѣчи ~ и оувѣрєныꙗ
оумножилъ сѧ increase, multiply: 8:17 ꙗко ~ сѧ бѧшє страхъ Июдѣискыи на них
оумрє die: 2:7
оумыслиста plotted, intended: 2:21; 6:2; оу{мысли}ша **9:1** оу[слыша]ша
оумьсти{ти} сѧ avenge self, take vengeance: 8:13 оумьсти сѧ ѡт врагъ своих
оунє *w G*, about, regarding: 4:5, 4:10 и ӡаповѣда єму ~ Мардъхаꙗ (**A9.4**)
оуѡхвоти сѧ be glad?: 8:15 Градъ жє Сусанъ ~ и въӡвєсєли сѧ
оуподоблєнъ *see* **нєоуподоблєнъ**
оупочиша} rested: **9:16**
оуслышаша hear: 1:18, [9:1 оу[слыша]ша (оу{мысли}ша); оуслышанъ 2:8
оуставити decree, establish: 9:21 ~ им абыша творили дн҃и 14 ЗвсѧкУ годину и годину; 9:29 ~ книгы вєсєлиꙗ сєго другыꙗ; 9:31 ~ дн҃и вєсєлиꙗ сєго; оустави 9:31 ꙗкоже ~ Мардъхаи, 9:32 И рєчєниє Есфирино ~ гл҃ы вєсєлїа сєго написа в книгах; оуставиша 9:27 И ~ и подъꙗша Июдѣи на сѧ и на племѧ своє 9:31 ꙗко ~ дш҃а своꙗ на чада своꙗ
оустави сѧ abate, subside: 2:1 И ꙗко ~ гнѣвъ царєвъ Ахасъверосовъ
оуставъ regulation: 1:8 ибо бѧшє такъ ~ царєвъ
{**оуставны**} ?valid: **3:4**
оустроила arrange, set up: 6:14 къ питвѣ ижє ~ бѧшє Есфирь (**L13.74**)
оустыꙗ ?openings: **1:6** на близку камєниꙗ драгаго стѣны и [ѡ]стыꙗ
оустъ mouth: 7:8 И вынидє гл҃ъ иӡ ~ царєвых
оутвьрдити affirm: **1:22** ~ . . . власть . . . и гл҃ъ; оутвєрдила **2:20** ꙗкоже бѧшє ~ сѧ с нимь
оутѣху consolation, comfort: 2:18 створи ~ ӡємлѧмъ
(**оутра, оутриꙗ** *see* ӡаоутра, наоутриꙗ)
оутринѣ fine cloth: 8:15 въ свитѣ царьстѣи и въ чєрви и в ~; оутринъмь 1:6 Бобръмь и ~ и чьрвємь (**L5.44**)
оутрьнєго inner: 1:5 въ дворѣ ѡграда оутрьнєго царєва
оушьвъ ?head-band: 8:15 и ~ шьлковъ лєптужьнъ (**L5.2, .45–6**)

.ф. '500' **9:6**, 9:12

хожаше go: {9:4}, **9:4**
хощеть want, wish: 6:7, 6:9 (2); хотѣлъ 6:6 кому ~ бы царь створити ꙋ^с^ть (**L21.51**)
хранитель keeper, guard, guardian: ~ женьскыи, 2:3, 2:8, 2:15; 2:14: ~ ложницѧ (?)

{**царевати**} rule as king: **2:4** [царь ꙁвати] наꙋнеть
царевъ (?**цьсаревъ**)] king's; kingly, royal: царево 1:14, 9:3; царева *Nsf* 1:7, 1:10, 1:13, 1:20, 2:14, 2:18, 3:2, 4:3, 5:8; *Gs* 1:15, 2:9, 2:13, 2:14, 3:8, 5:1, 6:4, 8:15; *Nd* 2:21; *Ad* 6:12; цареву *Asf* 3:3; царевы *Gsf* 4:11; царевѣ *Ls* 1:9, 1:11, 7:4, {9:4}; *Dsf* 3:13, 8:5, 8:14, 9:12; царевою 8:8 (2), 8:10; царевъмь *Is* 3:12, 8:8 (2), 8:10; цареву *Dsm* 5:1, 6:9; царевы *Apm* 6:8; *Apm* 5:11; царевых *Gp* 7:8; царевъмъ *Dp* 1:18, 3:12, 4:2;
царица (?**цьсарица**) queen: 1:9, 1:12, 1:16, 1:19, 4:4, 5:12, 7:3, 7:6, **8:2**, 8:3, 9:29, 9:31; царице *V* 5:3, 7:2; царицю 1:11, 1:17, 2:17; царици *Gs* 7:7; *Ls* 7:1, царицѣ 7:7; *Ds* 1:15, 2:22, 7:1, 7:5, 8:1, 8:7, 9:12; царицею 7:6
царицинъ queen's: 1:17, 1:18; царицина 7:8 (**A5.14**)
царь (?**цьсарь**) king:1:2, 1:5, 1:12, 1:13, 1:17, 1:19, 1:21, 2:3, 2:4, 2:6, 2:9, 2:17, 2:18, 3:1, 3:10, 3:11, 3:15, (4:1 {сѧ},) 4:11, 5:1, 5:2 (2), 5:2, 5:3, 5:4, 5:5 (2), 5:6, 5:8, 5:11, 6:1, 6:3, 6:4, 6:5, 6:6 (2), 6:7, 6:8 (2), 6:9 (2), 6:10, 6:11, 7:1, 7:2, 7:5, 7:7, 7:8 (2), 7:9, 8:1, 8:2, 8:4, 8:11, 9:12, 9:14, 10:1, 10:2 царѧ *As* 1:11, 7:9, 8:1, 9:10, 9:25; *Gposs* 1:22, 2:19, 2:21, 3:2, 3:3, 3:9, 3:15, 4:2, 4:7, 4:13, 5:13, 6:6, 6:10, 6:12, 7:9, 8:12, 9:2, 9:16, 9:20, ~ Ахасъвероса 1:16, 3:12, 10:3; ѡт ~ 5:7; цари *Ls* 2:21; царю *V* 7:3; *D* 1:16, 2:12, 2:16, 3:7, 3:8, 4:8, 6:2; цареви *Ds* 1:19, 2:4, 2:13, 2:14, 2:15, 2:22, 3:8, 3:9, 4:11 (2), 4:16, 5:4, 5:14, 6:4, 6:7, 7:3, 8:5; царьмь (12) 1:10, 1:16, 2:6, 2:23, 5:12 (2), 5:14, 6:1, 7:9, 8:3, 8:4, 8:5; цареви *Np* 2:2, 3:2, 3:3, 3:12, 4:11, 6:3, 6:5, 6:14, 8:9; царевъ *Gp* 10:1 (**E11.61**)
царьскыи royal: 2:17; царьскаꙗ 1:19; царьское 1:7; царьскыꙗ 5:1; царьстѣи 8:15
царьство kingdom: 1:19; царьства 1:2, [1:5,] 2:3, 2:16 (2), 3:8, 4:14, 5:1, 5:3 (2), 5:4, 5:6, 7:2, 9:30; царьствѣ 1:14, 3:6
царствоваше rule: 1:1 (**L9.5**)
царьствье] kingdom: *Gs* 1:3 царствиꙗ; *Ls* 1:20 царьстви

ꙋада children: Gp 9:31; ꙋадъ 9:28; ꙋадом 10:3 (**L4.1**)
ꙋасть *see* ꙋьсть
ꙋинѧще do: 9:3 ~ дѣло manager (**L2.41**)
ꙋисло number: 9:10
ꙋловѣкъ man, human being: 9:2
ꙋерви fine crimson cloth: *Ls* 8:15; ꙋьрвемь 1:6
ꙋьстити honor: 6:6, 6:7, 6:9 (2), 6:11 (**L12.15**)
ꙋьсть honor: *N* 8:16, A 1:4, 6:6; ꙋ[а]сть 5:11; ꙋьсти 1:4, 6:3 (**L15.1**)
ꙋьто what: 1:15, 2:11, 4:5, 5:3 (2), 5:6 (2), 6:3, 6:6, 7:2 (2), 8:1, 9:12; ꙋто ради 3:3; **ꙋему** 4:5 оувѣдати ꙋему то е и про ꙋто е

шьлковъ silken: 8:15 оушьвъ ~ лептужьнъ; шьлковыми 1:6 вървьми ~ (**L5.46**)

ꙗдите eat: 4:16 (**A1.2**)
ꙗко 'as, according to' 1:22, 3:12 (2), 8:9 (3), 9:31 (2); 'that' 3:4, 3:5, 4:11, 6:13, 7:7; introducing quote 1:15, 1:17 (2); 'when' 2:1, 5:2; ꙗко аще **4:11**; 'since, because' 3:2, 8:17, 9:2, 9:3, 10:3; 'so that' 1:19 (2) (**A10.7**)

ıакожє 'as' 1:21, 2:20 (2), 4:17, 5:8, 6:10, 8:8; нъ ~ 2:15; 'according to' 1:7, 1:22 (2), 2:12, 2:18, 8:9 (2), 9:27 (3); 'that' 9:22; 'when' 2:8, 2:12, 2:19, 5:9 (**A10.71**)
ıатъ take hold of: 5:2 И приближи сѧ Есфирь, и ~ ʒа конєць прута
ıаʒдѧху ride: 8:10 (see also ѣʒд-; **A1.2**)
ıаʒыкъ 'language' 1:22 (2), 3:12, 8:9 (2), 8:9; ıаʒыкы 'tribes' 1:16

Dictionary of Names

The Slavic name is followed by the usual English transcription of the Hebrew name, then the Hebrew consonantal spelling in italics, then known Greek equivalents.

The Greek spellings are from Hanhart's edition of LXX and L Esther (cf. A2.31, with note), with reference also to Josephus (*Jewish Antiquities,* book XI) and the printed *Complutensian Polyglot Bible* (1514–17), which often reflects Hebrew forms closer to the expected reflexes of MT. For discussion of the relationships, see pp. 146–52.

Авихаиловъ *poss. adj.,* Abihail's, *'byḥyl* αβιχαιλ *Compl.,* 9:29 дщи Авихаилова; Авихаиловы 2:15
Адамафана Admatha, *'dmt'* αδμαθα *Compl.* 1:14
Адалиıа (Т Ада[р]иıа) Adalia, *'dly'* αδαλια, *Compl.,* 93, 9:8
Адаръ Adar (month) 3:7, 3:13, 8:12, 9:1; Адара 9:15, {9:16}, 9:17, 9:19
Агаги Agagite, *'ggy* αγαγι 3:1, 3:10, 8:3, 8:5; 9:24 the Agagite, *h'ggy,* *Ααγαγι, Аагаги
Аировъ *poss. adj.,* of Jair, Иаиръ, *y'yr* ιαϊρ 2:5
***Амдаѳинъ** *poss. adj.,* of Hammedatha (*Амадаѳа), *hmdt'* αμαδαθου (*Gs*): Амдавина *Gsm* 8:5 вратити мысль Амановоу с҃на ~ Агаги
Амдафинъ 9:24 Амонъ с҃нъ ~ Аагаги; Амъдафиина *Asm* 3:1 с҃на ~ Агаги; Амъдафина *Gsm* 9:10 с҃на Амъдафина врага Июдѣиского; Амъдафину *Dsm* 3:10 Амонови с҃му ~ Агаги
Амановъ *poss. adj.,* Haman's: Asm 8:1, 8:7; Амановѣ *Lsm* 7:9; Амановомь *Ism* 8:2; Амановъ *Gpm* 9:10, 9:12, 9:13; Амоновъ 'Haman's' *Gpm* 9:14; Амонова Nsf 3:6; Амановоу *Asf* 8:3, 8:5
Аманъ Haman, *hmn* Αμαν: 3:5 (2), 3:8, 3:12, 3:15, 4:7, 5:5, 5:8,5:9 (3), 5:10, 5:11, 5:12, 6:4, 6:5, 6:6 (2), 6:7, 6:11, 6:12, 6:13, 7:1, 7:6 (2), 7:7, 7:8, 7:9, 9:24; Амана A 5:5, 6:14 *G* 8:2: Аманъмь 5:4, 5:14;
Амонъ 3:5 (2), 3:12; Амона A 6:14, 7:9, 7:10; Амонови 3:2, 3:4, 3:10, 3:11, 6:10 7:8; Амонъмь 3:7
Априль April: 3:7 {Н}исанъ гл҃ющии сѧ Априль
Аридаи Aridai, *'rydy* αριδαι, *Compl.* 9:9
Аридаса Aridatha, *'rydt'* αριδαθα, 93 *Compl.* 9:8
Арисаи Arisai, *'rysy* αρισαι, O *Compl.* 9:9
Аспасъ Aspatha, *'spt'* ασφαθα, *Compl.* 9:7
***Аѳахъ** Hatak, *htk* αθαχ, *Compl.*:
Афанъ N 4:6; A 4:5; Афану D 4:7
Афахъ 4:9, Афахови D 4:10 (**A2.351**)
Ахасъвєросъ Ahashwerosh, *'ḥšwrwš* αχασβερωσου (Gs), *Grec. Ven.,* Gebhardt: N 1:2, 1:9, 1:17, 3:1, 7:5, 8:1, 10:1; As 1:19 ıако нє пришла Вастиıа царицѧ прєдъ царь Ахасъвєросъ; Ахасъвєроса 1:15 нє створи повєлѣниıа царєва ~, 1:16 въ всѣхъ {властьхъ} царѧ ~, 3:12 имѧ царѧ ~, 8:10 писмєнємь царєвъмь ~, 8:12 въ всѣх ʒємлѧх царѧ ~, 9:2 по всѣмъ властьмъ ц҃рѧ ~, 9:20 по всѣмъ

ꙁемлѧмъ царѧ ~ близь и далєче, 10:3 другъ царѧ ~; L Ахасъверосѣ 2:21 и оумыслиста ꙁадѣти руцѣ цари ~; Inst Ахасъверосъмь 1:10

Ахасъвєросовъ *poss. adj.,* of Ahashwerosh: 2:1 гнѣвъ царєвъ ~; Nsf Ахасъвєросова 9:30 127 ꙁемль царства ~; Dsm Ахасъвєросоу 3:7 въ лѣ[т] 12 цр҃ю ~, 6:2 иже оумыслиста ꙁадѣти руцѣ царю ~, 2:12 къ царю ~ 2:12, 2:16, 3:8; *Lsn* Ахасъвєросовѣ 3:6 иже въ всем царствѣ ~; *Apm* Ахасъвєросовы 1:1 въ дн҃и ~ иже царствоваше

Бихванъ *see* **Вихванъ**

Ваавахфану *Ваавагѳану and Abagtha: *w'bgt'* *βααβαγθαν 1:10, αβαγαθα 93 (**A2.36**)

Вавєроса *Ваѳєрєса and Theresh, *wtrš* *βαθερες 6:2 на Вигъхвана Вавєроса 2 тиоуна царєва двьрника

вавулоньскыи Babylonian: 2:6 Навходъносоръ царь Вавулоньскыи (**A2.2**)

Ваиꙁаса *Ваиꙁаѳа Vaizatha, *wyzt'* βαιζαθα, *Compl.,* ουαιζαθα O 9:9

Варкохасу *D* *Вахаркасу and Charkas, *wkrks* *βαχαρκας 1:10

Васти Washti, *wšty* ουασθι/ουαστι: *Nom* 1:12, *also N* Вастиꙗ 1:9, 1:19, *and* Вастии 1:16; *A* Вастию 1:11, 1:17, Васти 2:1; *G* Вастии 2:4, [Мастиѣ] 2:17, *D* 1:15

Вафєсъ *Ваѳєресъ 'and Teresh', *wtrš* *βαθερες (θαρας O) 2:21 Бихванъ и ~, два тиоуна царєва

Вєниаминовъ *poss. adj.,* of Benjamin: 2:5 мужь ~

Вигъфаноу *Вигѳану Bigtha, *bgt'* *βιγθα(ν) 1:10

Вигъхвана *Вигѳана Bigthana, *bgtn'* *βιγθα(ν) 6:2 на Вигъхвана Вавєроса 2 тиоуна царєва двьрника

{**В**}**ихванъ** *Вигѳанъ, Bigthan, *bgtn* βαγαθαν 2:21 (*see* **A2.33**)

Виꙁъсану *Виꙁѳану Viztha, *bzt'* *βιζθα(ν) 1:10 (**A2.351**)

(**грєчьску**: *see main listing above*)

Далфанъ Dalphon, *dlpwn* *δαλφον 9:7

Дєкѧбрь December: 2:16

Єгаєвъ *poss. adj., Hegai's:* Єгаєвѣ 2:3 по руцѣ ~, иже бѣ тивоунъ, 2:8 (2) по руцѣ ~ . . . на руцѣ ~, иже бѧше хранитель женьскыи

Єгаи Hegai, *hgy* *εγαι (αγαι, *Compl.*) 2:15

Ємуоуманови *Меуманови Mechuman, *mhwmn* *μεουμαν 1:10 (**A2.35**)

Єрусалима Jerusalem 2:6 (**A2.2**)

Єсфирь (**Єсѳирь**), Esther, *'str* Ἐσθηρ 2:7, 2:8, 2:10, 2:15, 2:16, 2:17, 2:20 (2) 2:22, 4:5, 4:10, 4:15, 4:17, 5:1, 5:2 (2), 5:4, 5:5, 5:7, 5:12, 6:14, 7:3, 7:6, 8:2, 8:3, 8:4, 9:29 Єсфир[и], 9:31; A 5:2; D Єсфири 2:11, 2:22, 4:8, 4:9, 5:6, 7:5, 7:7, 8:1, 8:7; Єсфирии 4:13, 5:2, 7:1, 7:2, 8:4, 8:7, 9:12; Voc Єсфири 5:3, Єсфирии 7:2

Єсфиринъ *poss. adj.* Esther's: 2:15 жрєбии ~; 2:18 пиръ ~; Єсфирину 5:5 створитє рѣчь ~; Єсфириною 7:8 пред постєлєю Єсфириною; Єсфирины 4:4 придоша дв҃ы ~; 4:12 Повѣдаша Мардъхаєви рѣчи ~

Єсфириино 9:32 рєчєниє ~

(**жидовьскому**: *see main listing above*)

Зъвихфару *Зиѳару Zethar, *ztr* ζηθαρ, *Compl.* 1:10

Зєрєсъ Zeresh, *zrš* ζαρας O, ζαρασαν *As,* Josephus: 5:14 рє[ч] єму ~ жєна своꙗ, 6:13 ~ жєна єго, 5:10 ~ жєну свою; Зєрєси 6:13 Исповѣда Амонъ ~ жєнѣ своєи

Иєхонии, *see* **Охонии**

Июдѣи Jew: *Ns* 3:4, 9:29, 9:31 10:3; (?[Июдѣи] 2:7); Июдѣꙗ *Asg* 5:13 Июдѣю 6:10, 8:7; Июдѣи *Np* 9:1 9:2 9:5 9:6, 9:12, 9:15, 9:18, 9:19, 9:22, 9:23, 9:27; Июдѣꙗ *Ap* 3:6, 3:13, 4:16, 8:3, 8:5, 8:7, 9:3, 9:24, 9:25; Июдєи *Gp* 4:13, 9:16, 9:24, 9:28;

Июдѣихъ 4:7 на ~, 10:3 въ ~; Июдѣомъ 4:3, 4:14, 8:9 (2), 8:11, 8:13, 8:16, 8:17, 9:20, 9:30 (**A2.2**)

Июдѣискыи Jewish: 2:5, 8:17 страхъ Июдѣискыи; Июдѣистии 9:1 врази Июдѣистии; Июдѣиского 6:13 плєменє ~, 8:1 домъ Амановъ, врага Июдѣиского, 9:10 10 сн҃овъ Амановъ сн҃а Амъдафина врага Июдѣиского; Июдѣискому 3:10 Амонови сн҃у Амъдафину Агаги, мучителю Июдѣискому. (**A2.22**)

Июдинъмь *poss. adj.,* of Judah: *yhwdh* Ιουδα 2:6 съ Охониємь царємь Июдинъмь

Июнь June 8:9 мц҃ь Сиванъ, рєкомыи Июнь

Карсона Karshena, *kršn'* καρσενα, *Compl.* 1:14

Кисова *poss. adj.,* of Kish: *qyš* κις, Gs adj κισαιου LXX 2:5 Мардахаи, сн҃ъ Аировъ, сн҃а Симаина, сн҃а Кисова, мужь Вениаминовъ,

Мадѣискъ of the Medes: *mdy* μαδαι, LXX Gen. 10:2: *Lsf* Мадѣистѣи 1:3; Npf Мадѣискыѣ 1:18; Мадѣискыхъ Gp 1:14, 10:2; Мадѣискахъ 1:19 въ книгахъ Фарисѣискахъ и ~

Мардаха- *see* **Мардоха-**

Мардохаєва *poss. adj.,* of Mordecai: 2:15; Мардохаєвъ 3:6 людии ~, *Gp for A, or Np* Мардохаєв{и} ; Мардохаєвы 3:6 люди ~;

Мардъхаєвъ 9:3 страхъ ~; Мардъхаєва, 10:2 расповѣданиє вєличиꙗ ~; Мардъхаєво 2:22 имѧ ~; Мардъхаєвы {3:4 гл҃ы ~, 4:9 рѣчи ~

Мардахаєво 2:20 повѣлєньє ~

Мардохаи Mordechai, *mrdky* Μαρδοχαῖος 2:10, 2:11, 6:12; *D* Мардохаю 3:6, Мардохаєви 2:22, 4:12, 4:15, 6:3, 7:9, 7:10, 8:2;

Мард**а**хаи 2:5, 2:19; Мардахаєви 4:6;

Мардъхаи 2:7, 2:20, 2:21, 3:2, 3:5, 4:1 (2), 4:7, 4:13, 4:17, 6:2, 6:13, 8:1, 8:9, 8:15, 9:4, 9:20, 9:23, 9:29, 9:31, 10:3; Мардъхаꙗ *A* 4:4, 5:9 (2), 5:14, 6:4, 6:11, 8:2; G 4:10 оунє Мардъхаꙗ (**A2.311**)

Марсона Marsena, *mrsn'* μαρσενα, *Compl.* 1:14

Мартъ March 3:7, 3:13, 8:12, 9:1; Марта 9:15, 9:17, 9:19

[**Мастиѣ**] 2:17 {**Вастии**}

Мєрєсъ Meres, *mrs* μερες, *Compl.* 1:14

*__Мєоуманови__ *see* **A2.35**

Мумуханъ Memuchan, *mmwkn* μεμουχαν, *Compl.* 1:14, 1:16, 1:21 (**A2.35**)

Навходъносоръ Nebuchadnezzar: 2:6 ~ царь Вавулоньскыи (**A2.2**)

Нисанъ Nisan 3:7 ~ гл҃ющии сѧ Априль (Q Писанъ)

Оду Hodu, India, *hdw* Οδου 1:1 ωт Оду даже и до Хусъ, 8:9 О[до]ду

*__Охонии Иєхонии__, *yknyh* Ιεχονιος LXX 2:6 иже полони съ Охониємь царємь Июдинъмь

Пармa{с}та *Пармаста Parmashta, *prmšt'* φαρμασθα, *Compl.* 9:9

Парсанъда[c] *Парсандаѳа? Parshandatha, *staršndt'* φαρσανδαθα, *Compl.* 9:7

Порафа *Пораѳа, Poratha, *pwrt'* φουραθα O 9:8

Саазъгазовѣ *poss. adj.,* Lsf] *__Саасгазъ__, Shaashgaz, *š'šgz* *Σαασγαζος: 2:14 по руцѣ ~ тивуна царєва

Сєфаръ *Сєѳаръ Shethar, *štr* σηθαρ, *Compl.* 1:14

Сиванъ Sivan: 8:9 мц҃ь ~, рєкомыи Июнь

Симаина (var. Симеина, ms 16 [Und. 1]) *poss. adj., Gs* Shimei's, *šm'y* *σιμει, LXX Σεμεϊου, *Compl.* σεμει 2:5 сн҃ъ Аировъ, сн҃а ~

Сусанъ Shushan, *šwšn* σουσαν 3:15, 8:15; Сусанѣ 1:2, 1:5, 2:5, 2:8, 3:15, 4:8, 4:16, 8:14, 9:6, 9:11, 9:12, 9:13, 9:14, 9:15 (2), 9:18; Сусану 2:3

Тарсисъ/Θарсисъ, Tarshish, *tršyš* *ταρσις, θαρσις, *Compl.* 1:14

Тєвєфъ *Тєвєѳъ, Tebeth, *ṭbt* *τεβεθ, τηβηθ *Compl.* : 2:16 въ мцҍь 10 глющи сѧ ~ по жидовьскому, а по грєѵьску Дєкѧбрь

Тирисъ 1:14 *see* **Тирисъ**

Фарисѣискыи (Фарсиискыи/Фарсѣискыи, **A2.34**) of the Persians, *prs* *Φαρσων/ *Φαρσειων/*Φαρσαιων *Gp* 1:3 силѣ Фарисѣистѣи и Мадѣистѣи; Фарисѣискыѣ 1:18 рєкоша болѧрынѣ ~ и Мадѣискыѣ; Фарисѣискых 1:14 7 болѧръ ~ и Мадѣискыхъ; *Lp* 10:2; Фарисѣискахъ 1:19 въ книгахъ ~ и Мадѣисках

Харвуна Harbona, *ḥrbwnh* χαρβωνα, *Compl.* 7:9

***Харвунанъ** Harbona, *ḥrbwn'* χαρβωνα *Compl.* or *χαρβουνα(ν), *Ds* Харву{н}анови 1:10 (cf. Харвуна)

Хусъ Cush, Ethiopia, *kwš* Χους LXX Gen. 10:6, 1:1 иже царствоваше ωт Оду даже и до Хусъ; 8:9

Index of Slavic Words from Sources Other than Esther

є = ѣ; ѫ = оу = у; ω = о; ѕ = ʒ = з

Letter-prefixes (A, C, E, In, L, T) indicate chapters; numbers without prefix indicate pages.

HARVARD UKRAINIAN RESEARCH INSTITUTE
Publications Office
Selected Publications

An Early Slavonic Psalter from Rus'. Ed. Moshé Altbauer and Horace G. Lunt. Harvard Series in Ukrainian Studies. Clothbound, ISBN 0-674-22310-1.

The Old Rus' Kievan and Galician-Volhynian Chronicles: The Ostroz'kyj (Xlebnikov) and Četvertyns'kyj (Pogodin) Codices. Intro. Omeljan Pritsak. Harvard Library of Early Ukrainian Literature, Texts, 8. Clothbound, ISBN 0-916458-37-7.

The Hagiography of Kievan Rus'. Translated into English with an introduction by Paul Hollingsworth. Harvard Library of Early Ukrainian Literature, English Translations, 2. Clothbound, ISBN 0-916458-28-8; softcover, ISBN 0-916458-52-0.

Testament to Ruthenian: A Linguistic Analysis of the Smotryc'kyj Variant. Stefan Pugh. Harvard Series in Ukrainian Studies. Clothbound, ISBN 0-916458-75-X.

A Lexical Atlas of the Hutsul Dialects of the Ukrainian Language. Comp. and ed. Janusz A. Rieger. HURI Publications. Clothbound, ISBN 83-86619-90-2.

The Lords' Jews: Magnate-Jewish Relations in the Polish-Lithuanian Commonwealth during the 18th Century. M. J. Rosman. Harvard Series in Ukrainian Studies. Clothbound, ISBN 0-916458-18-0. Softcover, 0-916458-47-4.

The Origins of the Old Rus' Weights and Monetary Systems: Two Studies in Western Eurasian Metrology and Numismatics in the Seventh to Eleventh Centuries. Omeljan Pritsak. Harvard Series in Ukrainian Studies. Clothbound, ISBN 0-916458-48-2.

Crisis and Reform: The Kyivan Metropolitanate, the Patriarchate of Constantinople, and the Genesis of the Union of Brest. Borys Gudziak. Harvard Series in Ukrainian Studies. Clothbound, ISBN 0-916458-74-1.

A Description of Ukraine. Guillaume Le Vasser, sieur de Beauplan. Translated into English, with an introduction by Andrew B. Pernal and Dennis F. Essar. Harvard Series in Ukrainian Studies. Clothbound with illustrations and 28 reproductions of 17th-century maps of Ukraine and 1 guide map and separate mapcase, ISBN 0-916458-44-X.

Byzantium and the Slavs. Ihor Ševčenko. Renovatio, 1. Clothbound, ISBN 0-916458-12-1.

To receive a free catalog of all Ukrainian Research Institute publications (including the journal *Harvard Ukrainian Studies*) please write, fax, or call to:

HURI Publications
1583 Massachusetts Avenue
Cambridge, MA 02138
USA
tel. 617-495-3692 *fax.* 617-495-8097

e-mail:
huri@fas.harvard.edu
on-line catalog:
http://www.sabre.org/huri/publications/index.html